PRAISE FOR

The Great Experiment

"With the sweep of a historian and the sure hand of a man who has been in the arena, Strobe Talbott has given us a brilliant, provocative, and thoughtful book about the most important questions of our time—questions that are, in St. Augustine's phrase, ever ancient, ever new."

—Jon Meacham, author of *Franklin and Winston* and *American Gospel*

"Strobe Talbott has spent his career as both a witness to history and a shaper of it. In *The Great Experiment* he displays his unique range of gifts—combining the stylistic verve of the former columnist, the geographic and cultural breadth of a life-long historian, and the heretofore untold insights of a key U.S. policy-maker. *The Great Experiment* is a vivid and vital reckoning with the tools we have tried—and those we urgently need—to manage and contain global threats."

—Samantha Power, author of *A Problem from Hell:
America and the Age of Genocide*

"Few people understand the logic of community either locally or internationally. Strobe Talbott not only understands the logic but explains in an extraordinary historic overview of why communities have evolved and how they actually can lead to the larger public good. But he offers much more: a remarkably clear explanation of the views of different philosophers and their perspectives on the role of governments, including possible international governing regimes. By bringing this discussion into the current debates on how international regimes can deal with challenges ranging from climate change to terrorism to pandemics, Talbott offers a crucially important book for our times."

—Dennis Ross, author of *Statecraft: And How to Restore
America's Standing in the World*

"*The Great Experiment* ends, as it must, with the Bush years, ones that are about as far from Talbott's dream of global cooperation as it is possible to imagine. But that is why this book is so important. There will be a new president not so long from now, and even if he or she tries to ignore the world, the world will not be ignored. One way or another, we are going to have to find our way to back international cooperation, and when we do, the life, times, and ideas of a person as thoughtful and patriotic as Strobe Talbott will once again come into fashion."

—Alan Wolfe, *The Boston Globe*

"A riveting narrative that puts the swaggering, go-it-alone policies of the George W. Bush administrations and the challenges facing the next U.S. president in a sweeping historical context. . . . Popular history at its best, a compelling account of the development of one of the central ideas of our civilization, how our current foreign policy has tragically failed and what's on the urgent to-do list for our next president."

—Larry Cox, *Tucson Citizen*

"Strobe Talbott's credentials speak directly to his task in this articulately dense, perceptively thoughtful, and ultimately fascinating book on history's long march toward the formation of the United Nations and other future global organizations."

—Sam Coale, *The Providence Journal (Rhode Island)*

"A professional diplomat's riff on human history. . . . Alive because of its hopeful, can-do spirit and good ideas."

—Michael D. Langan, *Buffalo News*

"Talbott is a fluent, smart observer of the international scene. . . . A withering assessment of current U.S. foreign policy. . . . This book makes for lucid dissent."

—*Kirkus Reviews*

"In this engrossing and highly readable book, Strobe Talbott combines his own high-level government experience, reportorial flare, and his historical research to produce an important work on the most basic question facing the world today: does humanity have the will-power and the capacity to respond to the overwhelming issues we face, from nuclear proliferation to climate change?"

—Kati Marton, author of *The Great Escape: Nine Jews Who Fled Hitler and Changed the World*

"A book of stunning breadth, analyzing past efforts at transcending isolation and conflict and explaining the next stage of human development, the inescapable need for global cooperation. A fast-moving survey, steeped in an account of the relevant past and ending with admirable prescriptions of what this country needs to do—and what not. A complex subject of imperative immediacy, elegantly accessible, and made still more credible by illuminating autobiographical touches. A rare feat for a large public."

—Fritz Stern, author of *Five Germanys I Have Known*

"Strobe Talbott's career has been unique, and so is his new book. Path-breaking *Time* correspondent and columnist, author of authoritative books on foreign policy and arms control, former U.S. Deputy Secretary of State, founder of the Yale Center for the Study of Globalization, now president of the Brookings Institution, Talbott draws on his rare blend of talents and experiences to produce a wise, trenchant, immensely readable book that combines philosophical reflection, diplomatic history, policy prescription, and personal memoir."

—William Taubman, Pulitzer Prize–winning author of
Khrushchev: The Man and His Era

"Drawing on history, social science, philosophy, and his own formidable experience as journalist, scholar, diplomat, and public servant, Strobe Talbott has brought us an absorbing, original, wide-ranging, and thoughtful meditation on the ways human beings have striven for lasting order. At a time when that striving has never been more necessary, this important book should be a vital part of the debate."

—Michael Beschloss, author of *Presidential Courage: Brave Leaders and
How They Changed America, 1789–1989*

"Strobe Talbott—a talented linguist, scholar, and diplomat—is the most sophisticated and articulate representative of a dwindling company: the American foreign policy elite. In *The Great Experiment*, he offers an account—part history, part memoir—of the possibility (and urgent necessity) of international collaboration and collective governance; he concludes with a thoughtful, cogent, and devastating summary of the damage America has done to itself and the world under the aberrant presidency of George W. Bush. Americans should read this book—and hope for a day when its author will once again be in a position to help restore his country's fortunes."

—Tony Judt, author of *Postwar: A History of Europe Since 1945*

"This book by one of our best foreign policy minds and statesman practitioners is for the legions of Americans and others who know we can't escape or solve our vast international problems without something larger in place—a system for global order and governance. Talbott takes on all the big issues others run away from, and the next president needs to hear about."

—Leslie H. Gelb, former *New York Times* columnist and
president emeritus of the Council on Foreign Relations

ALSO BY STROBE TALBOTT

Engaging India
The Russia Hand
At the Highest Levels
  (with Michael Beschloss)
The Master of the Game
Reagan and Gorbachev
  (with Michael Mandelbaum)
Deadly Gambits
The Russians and Reagan
Endgame

EDITED AND TRANSLATED
Khrushchev Remembers: The Last Testament
Khrushchev Remembers

THE GREAT

STROBE TALBOTT

EXPERIMENT

The Story of Ancient Empires,
Modern States, and the Quest
for a Global Nation

Simon & Schuster Paperbacks

New York   London   Toronto   Sydney

Simon & Schuster Paperbacks
A Division of Simon & Schuster, Inc.
1230 Avenue of the Americas
New York, NY 10020

First Simon & Schuster trade paperback edition March 2009

*SIMON & SCHUSTER PAPERBACKS and colophon are
registered trademarks of Simon & Schuster, Inc.*

*For information about special discounts for bulk purchases,
please contact Simon & Schuster Special Sales at
1-800-456-6798 or business@simonandschuster.com*

Designed by Karolina Harris

Manufactured in the United States of America

10   9   8   7   6   5   4   3   2   1

The Library of Congress has cataloged the hardcover edition as follows:

*Talbott, Strobe.
    The great experiment : the story of ancient empires, modern states,
and the quest for a global nation / Strobe Talbott.
—1st Simon & Schuster hardcover ed.
        p.   cm.
    Includes bibliographical references and index.
    1. International organization—History.   2. State, The—History.
3. Empire—History.   4. Geopolitics—History.   I. Title.
JZ1318.T35   2008
320.1—dc22   2007037539
ISBN-13: 978-0-7432-9408-9 (hardcover)
ISBN-10:   0-7432-9408-4 (hardcover)
ISBN-13: 978-0-7432-9409-6 (pbk)
ISBN-10:   0-7432-9409-2 (pbk)*

To my parents, Jo and Bud;
my wife, Brooke;
our sons, Devin and Adrian;
our daughter-in-law, Lauren;
and our granddaughter, Loretta Josephine

Contents

Introduction

A GATHERING OF TRIBES   1

One: THE IMPERIAL MILLENNIA

1. CARAVANS AT REST   15

2. A LIGHT UNTO THE NATIONS   26

3. THE ECUMENICAL STATE   41

4. THE POET AND "THE PRINCE"   66

5. PERPETUAL WAR AND "PERPETUAL PEACE"   86

6. BLOOD AND LEATHER   104

Two: THE AMERICAN CENTURIES

7. MONSTERS TO DESTROY   125

8. EMPTY CHAIRS   148

9. THE MASTER BUILDER   174

10. A TRUSTEESHIP OF THE POWERFUL   203

11. AN END AND A BEGINNING   237

Three: THE UNIPOLAR DECADES

12. THE NEW WORLD ORDER   255

13. SEIZING THE DAY   280

14. HARD POWER   299

15. A THEORY OF THE CASE   324

16. GOING IT ALONE   347

17. A CONSEQUENTIAL ABERRATION   370

Conclusion

YES, WE MUST   393

ACKNOWLEDGMENTS   411

ILLUSTRATION CREDITS   414

NOTES   415

INDEX   463

Of the increase of his government and peace
there shall be no end.

Isaiah 9:7

In my father's house
are many mansions.

John 14:2

Reason and experiment
have been indulged,
and error has fled before them.

Thomas Jefferson

THE GREAT EXPERIMENT

Introduction

A GATHERING OF TRIBES

Some peoples wax and others wane
And, in a short space, the order of living things is changed
And, like runners, hand on the torch of life.
—*LUCRETIUS*[1]

If I had a world to govern
of kingdoms so contentious,
by far would I prefer
never to have a realm at all.
—*GOTTFRIED VON STRASSBURG*[2]

"MULTILAT is hell." It was a jarring way for Victoria Nuland to begin our morning staff meeting, but she knew what she was doing. She was a professional diplomat used to dealing with the influx of political appointees that comes with a change in administrations. As my executive assistant, she had the job that day, in September 1993, of preparing me for my first United Nations General Assembly, or UNGA. Veterans of the annual gathering pronounce the acronym "un-guh," making it sound like a groan of weariness at the prospect of yet again having to see if representatives of nearly two hundred nations can accomplish anything cooperatively—or, in the language of diplomacy, multilaterally.

The member states of the UN range alphabetically from Afghanistan, one of the most ungovernable nations on earth, to Zimbabwe, one of the worst governed. They vary in size from tiny relics of history, such as the Principality of Liechtenstein, a sixty-two-square-mile constitutional monarchy in the Alpine foothills, and newborn microstates, such as Kiribati and Vanuatu in the South Pacific, to the Asian giants, India and China.

In the autumn of 1993, virtually all the presidents, prime ministers, and monarchs who were about to descend on New York City hoped to meet Bill

Clinton, a newcomer to their ranks. Many would get face time with him. Some would have formal "bilats" at the American mission across the street from the UN, or at the Waldorf-Astoria, where the White House and State Department staffs set up camp. Others would be granted "pull-asides" at one of the numerous receptions every evening, or on the margins of the General Assembly itself.

From his first UNGA in 1993 to his last in 2000, Clinton looked forward to the several days he spent each fall in New York as a jamboree of networking that brought together some of the world's most ambitious, accomplished, and self-confident extroverts. In other words, people like him. He was more at home there than any other American president, with the possible exception of his immediate predecessor, George H. W. Bush, who had thrived in the post of "permrep," or permanent representative (as ambassadors to the UN are formally known), twenty years before. Every year, as the requests for appointments poured in, protecting Clinton from his own gregariousness often meant telling him no when he wanted the answer to be yes. That part of my job was never easy or pleasant, nor did I always succeed.

I also had my immediate boss to worry about. For much of the 1990s, I was deputy secretary of state. In no other setting was the first word in that title more operative than at the UNGA. I frequently had to substitute—first for Warren Christopher, then for Madeleine Albright—in tasks for which the secretary had neither time nor interest nor obligation of protocol. Such assignments ranged from ones that I found genuinely interesting to others that were tedious but necessary, to a few that were downright embarrassing. The worst was being designated to sit in as head of the American delegation in the General Assembly for no purpose other than to wait for Fidel Castro to come to the podium so that I could stage the Americans' annual solo walkout. It was a protest not over anything the Cuban leader said, since I left before he opened his mouth, but over the impertinence of his still being in power despite more than forty years of American antagonism. How this ritual was supposed to make *him* feel isolated, I never quite understood. My exit up the center aisle, with what seemed like the whole world watching, none too sympathetically, seemed to take forever. I remember thinking to myself: multilat may sometimes be too much of a good thing, but unilat is often too little. The trick is to find the right combination of the two.

The United Nations faces the same challenge. Its purpose is to take action against hunger, poverty, disease, aggression, and, in more recent years, outrages perpetrated by governments against their own citizens. But agreeing on exactly what action to take requires seemingly endless talk—everyone from everywhere talking to everyone from everywhere else about everything under the sun.

Hence Victoria Nuland's rueful quip. But we both knew Winston Churchill's riposte, when he and Dwight Eisenhower were sharing their hope for a UN-negotiated settlement in Indochina after the French defeat at Dien Bien Phu in 1954: "To jaw-jaw is better than to war-war."

Churchill made the line rhyme; the UN's job is to make it meaningful. On another occasion, Eisenhower made the same point, though more prosaically: "With all the defects, with all the failures that we can chalk up against it, the UN still represents man's best organized hope to substitute the conference table for the battlefield."[3]

SOMETIMES, AFTER GIVING JAW-JAW every possible chance, the UN must resort to force. On those occasions, the organization yields to the power of a few countries that are able to act. That often means yielding to the United States. More than any other country, it is able to get its way on its own terms. That is largely because it has the strongest military on earth and is the leader of several alliances. The oldest and largest of those is the North Atlantic Treaty Organization (NATO), the world's only permanent international mechanism capable of exerting the muscle that is sometimes necessary to back up exhortations, condemnations, and threats.

The most dramatic example of robust multilateralism that I experienced during my stint in government in the nineties was in the Balkans. The worst outbreak of violence in Europe since World War II required a division of labor among the UN, NATO, the European Union (EU), the Organization for Security and Cooperation in Europe (OSCE), and an ad hoc arrangement to enlist the diplomatic assistance of the Russians. Each of these bodies was, in its own way, important for reaching an outcome the world could live with: NATO provided the crucial ingredient of air power in Bosnia and Kosovo; the UN Security Council gave the operation in Bosnia a useful degree of international legitimacy; in the more difficult case of Kosovo, the secretary-general, Kofi Annan, took it upon himself to speak out on the need for a U.S.-led intervention to stop mass murder and ethnic cleansing.

Despite the UN's imperfections and uncertainty about its future, it sometimes resolves the paradox reflected in its name and lives up to its lofty but elusive goals. It did that in large, conspicuous ways in the Balkans, and it does it in small, little-noticed ones every day: providing food, shelter, and care to refugees; deploying border observers, police trainers, election monitors, and weapons inspectors; coaching governments on economic reform; and slogging away against corruption and illicit traffic in drugs, women, and children, and in dangerous technology and weaponry. During the summer of 2007, there were eighteen UN peacekeeping missions deployed on four continents, involving 100,000 personnel, many of them soldiers, from about a hundred countries.

In all these cases, the UN is exercising, on behalf of all nations, responsibilities and powers that used to be largely if not exclusively in the domain of sovereign national governments. On a highly selective and circumscribed basis, the member states of the UN pool their authority and resources to achieve common purposes, often in concert with other international bodies. Some, such as the World Bank and the World Health Organization, are considered part of the UN system, but they operate separately, with variable and in some cases tenuous ties to the UN itself. Others, such as NATO, the EU, and the OSCE, are separate from the UN except that their members belong to the UN as well, and their interests often coincide with, and their capacities serve, the UN's objectives.

When the nations of the world take joint action, they are, in both senses of the verb, *practicing* global governance: they are doing something necessary and difficult; and with experience, they are learning to do it better.

THE PHRASE "GLOBAL GOVERNANCE" appears frequently in the course offerings of universities and on the agendas of public-policy conferences in many countries. That is less the case in the United States.* In the nation that is host to the UN's headquarters, the very term "global governance" tends to be used with nervous caution, as though with tweezers, especially in my hometown, Washington, D.C. I noticed early in my time at the State Department that foreign service officers used euphemisms, of which *multilateralism* was one. They had learned, sometimes to the jeopardy of their careers, that public mention of global governance can be politically radioactive. Either it has the ring of woolly-mindedness, or, far worse, it is taken as code for a belief in a world government that turns nations into provinces of a global superstate. To those inclined to see it that way—and there are many—the UN is a stalking horse for a conspiracy to deprive the United States of its independence and its citizens of their freedoms.

* The London School of Economics has a Centre for the Study of Global Governance; the University of Warwick and the University of Victoria jointly publish a journal on global

It is not surprising that talk of global governance should elicit more skepticism, suspicion, and sometimes bilious opposition in the United States than elsewhere. The more powerful a state is, the more likely its people are to regard the pooling of national authority as an unnatural act. What is surprising is that, in the second half of the twentieth century, precisely during the period when the United States was asserting itself as the most powerful state ever, eleven presidents—six Democrats and five Republicans, from Franklin Roosevelt to Bill Clinton—recognized global governance as a natural element in world politics and as a useful, even indispensable instrument of American foreign policy. While they too called it by other names that emphasized U.S. interests and U.S. leadership, they made global governance an American project.

GEORGE W. BUSH did not so much abandon that project as change the way in which it was conducted and perceived. He accentuated what he saw— and wanted the world to accept—as America's right to make and enforce the rules by which other nations must abide. In so doing, Bush broke with the tactics, tone, doctrine, and worldview that had guided more than half a century of U.S. foreign policy. Especially striking was the contrast with the two previous occupants of the Oval Office. "Bush 41" and Clinton had been archmultilateralists. "Bush 43," particularly during his first term, was a radical unilateralist. More than any of his predecessors, he adhered to an uncompromising and extreme variant of American exceptionalism—a form of nationalism that ascribes to the United States superior qualities, universal values, global interests, unique responsibilities, and a divine dispensation to use its might on behalf of what its leaders deem to be right.

The test case was in Iraq, and the result was a failure and a backlash. Many around the world, including allies and traditional friends, had already come to see the United States less as a leader to be followed and more as a highhanded, often arbitrary boss, to be resented, resisted, counterbalanced, and "contained"—a word I began to hear in my travels abroad as early as 2001.

---

governance; the Bucerius Summer School on Global Governance is an annual seminar run by several German foundations; the Centre for International Governance Innovation is Canada's largest think tank devoted exclusively to the study of international affairs; and the World Economic Forum has a commission on the subject, with which Clinton and I, along with many others, have been associated. By contrast, "global governance" is relatively rare in American curricula and in the names of academic institutes. The State Department includes as topics covered on its Web site "global affairs" (a cluster of bureaus created in the Clinton administration) and "global corruption," but not "global governance."

In part because effective global governance and successful American foreign policy are closely linked, both enterprises fell on hard times, and they will have to be resuscitated together. Among the most urgent pieces of business Bush will leave his successor will be that of restoring American standing in the world. Many who had worked in previous administrations, and some who worked for Bush himself, hoped that presidents coming after him would not have to learn the hard way that multilat, while sometimes hellishly hard, is indispensable to the mutually reinforcing goals of pursuing American national interests and strengthening international institutions.

DURING THE BUSH 43 PRESIDENCY, Victoria Nuland served as ambassador to an expanded NATO and found herself immersed in multilateralism; the status of Kosovo was a subject of UN-brokered negotiations that the Americans and West Europeans hoped would lead to independence; and Clinton whirled around the globe on a variety of good-works projects, including two with the UN: the battle against HIV/AIDS and, in a partnership that burgeoned into a genuine friendship with the elder President Bush, a campaign to provide relief to victims of the 2004 tsunami. I spent the academic year 2001–2002 in New Haven, where my wife, Brooke, and I helped Yale University set up two new international programs, then returned to Washington when I joined the Brookings Institution.

In 2003, I started writing this book on a subject that I had been thinking about for several decades: how the origin of individual nations and the formation of the international system have been similarly motivated. Both occur when disparate people unite for the sake of safety and prosperity. Just as a nation is a gathering of tribes, so the international community is a gathering of nations—an incipient global nation, in the sense that humanity is learning to govern itself as a whole on those issues where it can do so to the benefit of all, and especially on those where it must do so to avert planetary disaster.

There has always been, and always will be, a tension—sometimes creative, sometimes destructive—between, on the one hand, the concept of an international community that recognizes interdependence as a fact and collective governance as a necessity and, on the other, the appeal of a national community that thinks of itself as independent and sovereign. The forces that unify individual states—a sense of shared identity and destiny, a desire for collective order and defense—have often led to war between and among states. On other occasions, however, comparable forces have led states to come together for purposes of advancing common goals and defending themselves against common threats. Over the ages, there has been progress in the form of what development economists call the "scaling up" of governance from the national to the international level.

That story is just one of the many subplots of history, but it is one that has fascinated me all my life. My parents were active in the internationalist wing of the Republican Party in the late forties and early fifties. They nudged me, at an early age, toward an awareness of how far the world had to go in learning to govern itself sensibly. Under their influence, I gravitated, early in my schooling, toward the study of foreign cultures and world history. Whatever my profession, I have never stopped thinking of myself as a student of those subjects. This book is a reflection on some of what I have learned and an attempt to relate it to some of what I have seen, and done, in international politics.

I HAVE TRACED THE GREAT EXPERIMENT of global governance from the origins of the concept in ancient religion and philosophy through its evolution in the minds of political thinkers and in the strivings of political leaders. A big idea becomes a good idea—not just logically sound and ethically noble but practical as well—through thousands of years of struggle and testing, incremental progress, and catastrophic setbacks.

I look back to our once-nomadic ancestors who settled long enough to think of themselves as having their own homelands, protected by their own gods. I focus on the people who called, first themselves and then the land they believed their God had given them, "Israel," which I see as a prototype of nationhood, not least because it experienced both absorption by and liberation from empire.

The imperial system, which held sway for millennia, is the subject of Part One of this book. From the earliest recorded history, leaders have sought to impose authority from above while fostering acceptance of that authority from below in a way that made it possible to rule multiple nations. Alexander the Great conceived of an ecumenical realm embracing what, for him, was the known world. The expansion of his domain and those of other conquerors—the Romans, Genghis Khan, the Qin Emperor in China, Ashoka and Akbar in India, the Ottomans, the Hapsburgs, the Spanish, the Dutch, and the British—established the basis for governance on a vast scale in two ways: first by connecting remote regions and cultures, and in the process establishing networks of economic interdependence and cultural cross-fertilization; second, by developing organizational practices and technologies that were capable of projecting force, and therefore authority, and providing security for diverse nationalities spread out over great distances.

The more successful empires incorporated some degree of institutionalized tolerance and administrative decentralization. Those diversified polities were more likely to prosper and endure if they allowed communities within their borders to follow their own customs and manage their own affairs, even though the emperor, great khan, or sultan retained responsibility for order within the realm and its protection from external enemies.

But the degree to which any single imperial system could succeed was always limited. Many empires failed because they were inherently hierarchical and therefore unjust: the concentration of power in the hands of the emperor often translated into institutionalized *in*tolerance, which in turn provoked among subject peoples alienation, sullen resistance, or outright rebellion. Yet too much decentralization meant that the center could not hold, and things would fall apart.

For one of these reasons or the other, and sometimes because of a combination of the two, the ability of the metropole to rule its colonies could not last forever. Nor could the imperial system as such.

As nation-states broke free from empires, they found that being small—or at least smaller—required collective security. They entered into alliances and treaties to deter predatory behemoths and also to keep from going to war against one another. Peace was conducive to trade, which, in turn, was regulated by commercial agreements. Beyond its economic benefit, the movement of goods and services, along with people, ideas, and technology, drew states into a web of associations, common practices, and mutual dependency—the components of what today we call globalization.

In following this pattern, I concentrate on Western civilization, since that was the source of so much of the experience and intellectual raw material on which modern international structures came to be based. For centuries, Europe was a busy, bloody, yet productive laboratory for experimentation with ideas and institutions that would eventually replace empire. As nation-states came into their own, they shared a growing sense that they formed a single continental community. The dialectic between these two developments established the premise for various methods of keeping the peace that extended governance horizontally rather than imposing it from above. One result was the concept of balance of power among states as a replacement for imperial predominance.

Another European invention was federalism, which became an export to the American colonies in the eighteenth century and, in the late twentieth and early twenty-first centuries, the basis for supranational governance under the flag of the European Union. Despite its current doldrums, the EU is an undertaking of great boldness and promise, a model for what is possible in other parts of the world.

But before Europe could become the zone of peace that it is today, it spent centuries at war, primarily with itself though also with the forces of Islam that either pushed into Europe or repelled European incursions into the Holy Land. Then, having spread their commerce and culture to the far corners of the earth through their empires, the Europeans unleashed, within a twenty-year period, two world wars. The first of those conflagrations made Europe ripe for a pair of totalitarian ideologies, German fascism and Soviet communism, each with proponents who believed their movement would take over the world. The United States was indispensable in rescuing Europe and the world from those monstrosities, in ending the age of empire, and in giving Europe the sense of security it needed to form the EU.

Part Two of the book deals with America's rise to unparalleled and unprecedented power. The Founding Fathers set about governing themselves and building a constitutional democracy—a postimperial multinational state—out of a wide continental wilderness that was shielded from the outside world by two even wider oceans. Yet even as they looked westward and inland, Americans also looked over their shoulders, across the Atlantic and back to the Old World from which they had broken free. They believed they were creating not just a new nation or even just a new kind of nation, but a new and better way for all nations to govern themselves. They were convinced that what they were doing mattered to all humanity and deserved universal approval.

But they knew they would have to earn that approval in the way they made the case for their own great experiment as an object of admiration and emulation. The Founders promised, in the first sentence of the Declaration of Independence, to show "a decent respect to the opinions of mankind." That line can be read as a caveat about the danger of rubbing other countries' noses in American exceptionalism.

Europe continued to loom large in Americans' thinking because it was not just where most of them or their forebears came from—it was where their founding *ideas* came from. American leaders acknowledged a debt to ancient Greece and Rome and to European civilization. Separation of church and state, the sanctity of civil and human rights, and other principles of the U.S.

Constitution grew out of the humanist movement that started in Italy in the fifteenth century and that nurtured the Renaissance and the Enlightenment.

Today's disputes over American foreign policy echo those of Europe centuries ago. Dante Alighieri's vision of a universal kingdom and Immanuel Kant's concept of a democratic (or as he put it, "republican") peace anticipated today's liberal internationalism, whose adherents imagine and seek to build a better world. For its part, the realist school, which prides itself on dealing with the hazards and opportunities of the world as it is, pays homage to Niccolò Machiavelli and Thomas Hobbes.

While individual Americans have staked out opposing sides in this debate, their country as a whole has tried to have it both ways—and has often succeeded. In imbuing idealism with pragmatism (and vice versa), America has developed and sustained a sense of a global mission to advance values as well as interests, and to do so as much as possible by example and consent rather than by conquest.

The most violent of centuries, the twentieth, opened just as the United States was coming into its own as a world power. America set about to champion abroad the liberal principles of pluralistic democracy, rule of law, and protection of the rights of the individual citizen. In Woodrow Wilson, America had a leader who believed that if those tenets of national governance could be institutionalized internationally, the world would be safer, more prosperous, and more humane.

At the Paris Peace Conference after World War I, which produced the Treaty of Versailles, Wilson briefly took charge of the on-again/off-again European venture in multilateral diplomacy that had begun with the Peace of Westphalia in 1648 and continued with the Congress of Vienna in 1814–15. The result, in 1919, was the League of Nations. It ended in ruins, partly because of the U.S. Senate's repudiation of Wilson and America's refusal to participate in the League.

A quarter of a century after Versailles, and after a second global calamity and the defeat of the original axis of evil—which ran from Tokyo through Berlin to Rome—the world and the United States had a second chance. This time, working off a blueprint left to them by Franklin Roosevelt, Harry Truman and his successors came closer to getting it right. In the final days of World War II, Truman presided at yet another of those postwar gatherings of tribes exhausted by war—a conference, held in San Francisco in the spring and early summer of 1945, that founded the United Nations. The U.S. Senate overwhelmingly approved the UN charter at the end of July. A little more than a week later, the detonations of atomic bombs over Hiroshima and Nagasaki gave impetus to the one-world movement, an international effort to apply the ideas of Dante and Kant to ending the era of total war.

I WAS BORN THE FOLLOWING YEAR. More pertinently, so were George W. Bush and Bill Clinton, classmates of mine at Yale and Oxford respectively. Our generation grew up with the UN. The baby boom was the result of a burst in American optimism, confidence, and energy. But to be a baby boomer was also to be a child of the cold war. That competition was a cause of constant anxiety and occasional terror. For just that reason, the world required a new, highly specialized form of governance. The joint regulation of the U.S. and Soviet nuclear arsenals averted Armageddon and established the basis for a compact whereby most other nations agreed to forgo having such weapons. Living under what George F. Kennan called "the cloud of danger" had a lot to do with my fascination with U.S.-Soviet and, later, U.S.-Russian relations and with nuclear diplomacy. What has been justifiably called "the American system" of global governance was a three-way synthesis of the hegemonic aspect of empire (America as unchallenged leader of the free world), the reliance on the balance-of-power system of the nineteenth century (updated as the balance of terror between the superpowers in the twentieth), and the all-important, distinctively American element of constitutionalism: universally applicable and equitably enforced rules, checks and balances, and the consent of the governed.[4]

Part Three deals with American preeminence since the end of the cold war, a distinction that the country used largely to its advantage and the world's until the misadventures of Bush 43 foreign policy and, in particular, the war in Iraq. In those chapters, I have drawn on experiences and observations from three stages of my career: twenty-one years at *Time,* which coincided with the decrepitude of the world's last empire and the beginning of the post–cold war era and, in the triumphalist rhetoric of the right, America's "unipolar" moment; eight years at the State Department, which gave me a carpenter's perspective on what Kant called "the crooked timber of humanity"; and eight years at Yale and Brookings, where I have worked with scholars deeply knowledgeable about many of the subjects that I have delved into here.

I bring the story up to the election of Barack Obama, then look ahead, in a conclusion, to what I believe should happen during his administration if the planet is to be spared the ravages of climate change and a new wave of nuclear proliferation. These and other perils that cloud our future come with the modern condition. But the dilemma they pose—how to reconcile our tribal instincts with our common fate—is much older: it is part of the human condition, a theme in human history, and rooted in human nature.

One

The
Imperial
Millennia

1

CARAVANS AT REST

The scattered Bektashi and the Rufayan, the Mevlevi dervishes of the Tower of the Winds, the Liaps of Souli, the Pomaks of the Rhodope, the Kizilbashi near Kechro, the Fire-Walkers of the Mavrolevki, the Lazi from the Pontic shores, the Linovamvaki—crypto-Christian Moslems of Cyprus—the Donmehs—crypto-Jewish Moslems of Salonika and Smyrna—the Slavophones of Northern Macedonia, the Koutzo-Vlachs of Samarina and Metzovo, the Chams of Thesprotia, the scattered Souliots of Roumeli and the Heptanese, the Albanians of Argolis and Attica, the Kravarite mendicants of Aetolia, the wandering quacks of Eurytania, the phallus-wielding Bounariots of Tyrnavos, the Shqip-speaking Atticans of Sfax . . . to name a few.
—*PATRICK LEIGH FERMOR,*
   Mani: Travels in the Southern Peloponnese[1]

"What do you mean 'we,' paleface?"
—*BILL COSBY,*
   Punch line in a joke about Tonto's final exchange with the Lone Ranger

NATIONS answer a primal human need to belong, to embed individual identity in a collective one, thereby making the most of our similarities and the best of our differences. That much about the character and purpose of nations we understand intuitively, even as children. But there is much about nationhood that is mystifying, even irrational. I remember from my own childhood that the more I looked at a map, the less sense it made, especially as I began to learn how particular nations came into being, why they assumed the size and shape they did, and who lived there. The Rand McNally globe that my parents gave me when I was in my early teens, before I went off to the Hotchkiss School in the Berkshires, was a spherical jigsaw puzzle, perverse in its ingenuity. Somehow the pieces fit together, but why they were cut the way they were seemed utterly random. Sometimes a mountain range or river would form an international boundary (the Pyrenees between France and Spain; the Rhine between parts of Germany and France; the Himalayas between India and China). But the correlation of natural borders to political ones was usually arbitrary. Why should the Rio Grande divide the United States from Mexico while a surveyor's abstraction—the 49th parallel—separates much of the United States from Canada?

There were answers to these questions in books I read and courses I took at Hotchkiss and Yale; but they often hinged on quirks of fortune, and they raised other questions, including counterfactual ones. What if the clash of ideas, faiths, armies, and colonial ambitions of the European powers had gone differently in the sixteenth, seventeenth, and eighteenth centuries? Would I be writing this book in French, Dutch, Spanish, or German? What if Abraham Lincoln had not gotten around to replacing the sober General McClellan with the heavy-drinking General Grant? Would the Union have lost to the Confederacy, and would some distant cousins of mine in Texas be living in a separate country? And what if the artillery shell that wounded Corporal Hitler during the Battle of the Somme in 1916 had killed him? Would my father's generation have been spared their own battles at Cassino, Normandy, and the Bulge nearly three decades later?[2]

Lincoln and Hitler are reminders of the crucial role that individuals have played in determining the fate of nations. The Scottish essayist, Thomas Carlyle, made "the Great Man"—with a big ego, big ideas, big plans, and huge luck—the protagonist of a theory of history.[3] It was one of many propounded in the nineteenth and early twentieth centuries. When I studied at Oxford in the late sixties and early seventies, I attended several lectures by Patrick Gardiner, a philosophy don at Magdalen College who compiled an anthology of conjectures by the heavyweights, from Vico and Hegel to Spengler and Toynbee, about the "laws" of nature that supposedly predetermine progress and decline.[4] Gardiner explicated these theories but never, as far as I recall, endorsed any of them. He offered them for what they were: earnest and intellectually impressive attempts to impose some order on the capriciousness of the human story. But none, in the end, was convincing to me or, more to the point, to Gardiner. I took comfort from his decision to include, amid all the systems and certitudes of the philosophers, Leo Tolstoy's warning about "the difficulty of defining the forces that move nations." Tolstoy had little use for theoretical debates over how the world came to be organized the way it is, but he shared the conviction of many of the theorists that *there has to be a better way* to organize it in the future. That was a theme of Tolstoy's own life, especially in his later years, when he increasingly devoted himself to utopian causes.

THE GYPSIES OF OXFORDSHIRE

Attending Oxford gave me my first chance to live outside the United States. The experience exposed me to fresh and instructive curiosities about the complexity of national identity. For example, the United Kingdom of Great Britain and Northern Ireland, as such, did not have a team competing in the 1968 World Cup. Instead, England, Northern Ireland, Scotland, and Wales each had a team of its own. Only the English one qualified to go to Mexico City, where its fans waved the Cross of Saint George, a throwback to the Crusades and the banner of the Church of England, rather than the Union Jack. So the Kingdom was only in a sense and up to a point United.

And then there were the Gypsies who still roamed the English countryside. Previously, I had known about them only from their cameo appearances in books I read, or had read to me, as a child. In *The Wind in the Willows*, Gypsies are among the few human characters. I assumed they, along with Badger and Mr. Toad, had long since disappeared from the scene. I discovered otherwise when I took weekend bicycle trips into the Cotswolds. On fields outside villages, near fairgrounds, along waterways, I would slow down just long enough to exchange curious stares with grimy but colorfully dressed children playing by the highway.

During my second year at the university, I moved from a room in an annex of Magdalen to North Oxford in order to be closer to St. Antony's College, where I was studying twentieth-century Russian literature. On Leckford Road I shared a house and solidified a friendship with Bill Clinton that led to my serving in his administration a quarter of a century later. At the bottom of the road was a rustic wooden gate opening to a rutted footpath that crossed Port Meadow, an expanse of common land set aside since Roman times for local farmers. A canal ran through the fields of uncut grass. The Isis, as the Thames is known in those parts, meandered along the far side, ensuring mist in the morning and often at dusk as well. An alluring destination by itself, the meadow was also a shortcut to a riverbank pub called the Trout that served my favorite meal, steak-and-kidney pie and Mackeson's stout.

Just near enough to the Trout for its owners and customers occasionally to complain, but just far enough for the authorities to avoid taking action, a band of Gypsies had parked a caravan of dilapidated cars, trucks, and trailers. On my way to or from the pub, I would sometimes take a detour for a closer look at these exotic folk. I never felt inclined, much less invited, to make small talk with them. The few conversations I had were brief and strained and left me feeling like a trespasser.

The Gypsies in the area worked as tinkers, auto mechanics, and basket-weavers, or at seasonal agriculture, road repair, the building trades, and other jobs compatible with their itinerant lives. The *Oxford Mail* some-times carried stories about the county government's uneasy accommodation and occasional trouble with these most numerous and conspicuous of migrants, whom the English called Travellers—a euphemism that was capitalized as though to indicate a separate people and a permanent condition. Around that time, Parliament was debating whether to change the law from one that made Gypsies legal residents of Britain only as long as they were on the move—in effect, forbidding them from having established residences—to one that barred them from living in many areas of the country.

On trips to the continent, especially a tour of the Balkans during a spring vacation in 1970, I found myself in a Gypsy heartland: the Vojvodina in northern Serbia and parts of Hungary, Bulgaria, and Romania. In markets and along country roads, they were often in the picture, though always, it seemed, off to the side and slightly out of focus.

I read up on the Gypsies' story. They came from northern India, and their language is based on Sanskrit. They refer to themselves as *Rom*, meaning sim-ply "man." They call all others *gadje*, which has the connotation of "bump-kin" or "barbarian." They began moving westward in the first millennium CE and never stopped. They passed through Persia on their way to Anatolia and the Middle East (but not Egypt, even though that's the basis for the word *Gypsy*). They lingered long enough in central Europe to be enslaved, perse-cuted, stigmatized, and slaughtered. During the Holocaust, the Nazis sent Gypsies to the gas chambers.[5] Like Jews at the time, Gypsies were a people without a homeland, and as such subject to a special hatred on the part of the most murderous nationalists.

The Gypsies reached Britain in the sixteenth century but did not get to America until the early twentieth and to Australia in the second half. I dis-covered that English Gypsies had communal leaders they called kings and queens who presided over clusters of encampments they called nations. I was intrigued by the idiosyncratic use of these words, especially the last one. I had always thought of a nation as having a fixed address, a blotch of color on globes like the one that accompanied me from one school to the next. Yet here were people who called themselves a nation even though they were always on the road, with no place to plant a flag.

Most of the peoples on earth have states they can call their own—including, as of 1948, the Jews. Or at least they have states they share with others. Basques live on both sides of the border between Spain and France. The Palestinians, even though many of them live under Israeli occupation, have established the principle that they will, someday, have a state of their own. Thirty million Kurds are spread out in the borderlands of four states: Turkey, Iraq, Iran, and Syria. "The Basque Country," "Palestine," and, in northern Iraq, "Kurdistan" represent geographically defined, though politically contested, homelands.

The Gypsies have no such thing. Their language, Romani, abounds with proverbs that celebrate rootlessness: "May my favorite horse break a leg and my wagon burn to ashes if I do not keep my word," and "We are all wanderers on this earth; our hearts are full of wonder, and our souls deep with dreams." Other sayings lament the way they have been treated during their endless travels: "Bury me standing, for I have spent my life on my knees."[6] When borrowing such words as *king, queen,* and *nation,* they seem to be mocking the sedentary *gadje,* who have abandoned their wagons for houses, whose hearts are barren, whose souls are shallow, whose caravans have come to rest, and who lie down in their graves.

During my excursions to New York for the UN General Assembly in the 1990s, I caught a glimpse, among the sidewalk merchants doing brisk commerce in tchotchkes on Dag Hammarskjöld Plaza, of a woman selling garish costumes who, I learned, was one of the more flamboyant regulars. Her name was Luminitsa Kwiek, and she was a Polish-Gypsy "princess." The International Romani Union has "consultative status" in several UN agencies, which is probably as close as the Gypsies will come to being treated like a conventional nation.

Gypsies are said to have lived all these centuries "outside history," a phrase that suggests they are a mysterious exception to the human proclivity for settling down. I came to think of them differently, as a living connection with our forebears, for whom mobility was necessary for self-preservation. The Gypsies would pause in their wanderings and rest for a while, or perhaps longer, but not forever. They comprise a real though restless nation. Because they have nowhere to call home, they make themselves at home everywhere. Their presence in our midst is both an affirmation of the need of all people for national identity and, at the same time, a reminder of how elusive, mutable, and expansive the concept of nationality is.

DEFINITIONS

The word *nation* entered English in the fourteenth century by way of Anglo-Norman and Middle French. It comes from the Latin *natio*, a noun based on the verb *nasci*, "to be born." Corresponding words in other languages have similar connotations: nature confers nationality on the native. In some languages, words associated with patriotism shift genders, often depending on whether the context is war or peace. The common Russian word for homeland is *rodina*, usually translated as "motherland," since it is a feminine noun from a root associated with child-bearing. But when the Russian nation defends itself against its enemies, the word most often used is *otetchestvo*, from "father" (World War II is known as "the Great Fatherland War").

Yet a nation is not a natural phenomenon. Rather, it is an artifact, a product of happenstance, human ingenuity, and improvisation, with all the resulting possibilities for successful trial and ruinous error.

The same is true of a state. That word, like *static* and *stability,* comes from the Latin *stare*, "to stand," "to abide," or "to endure," which reinforces the illusion of permanence and immutability. Yet history is a story of nations and states appearing and disappearing, expanding and contracting, in a kaleidoscope of fission and fusion. The state that some twenty million Soviet citizens died for during the Great Fatherland War barely made it past the lifespan of "threescore years and ten" that the 90th Psalm allots to mortals. A septuagenarian today has seen the death of fifteen countries—and the birth of some 130.*

The *Oxford English Dictionary* (OED) defines *nation* as meaning a "large aggregate" of people "united by factors such as common descent, language, culture, history, or occupation of the same territory, so as to form a distinct people. Now also: such a people forming a political state."[7] The near useless-

---

* In the 1960s alone, nearly fifty nations achieved independence, many of them in Africa as a result of decolonization. Nearly thirty new nations arose in the 1990s with the breakup of the U.S.S.R. and Yugoslavia, as well as Eritrea splitting from Ethiopia.

ness of that definition is not the fault of the lexicographers, any more than the messiness of the map is the fault of geographers. Words can only be precisely and uniformly defined if the concepts for which they stand are precisely and uniformly established. Such is not the case with a nation. Virtually each of the words that the OED uses invites confusion or argument over its own meaning and its application to historical and contemporary reality. The first word and the last in the OED's definition of *nation* suggest that it is a "large state." If so, why are Liechtenstein, Vanuatu, and East Timor considered, in the eyes of the world, independent states? The answer is that their people want to be considered that way and the UN, the closest thing that the world has to a governing body, agreed to let them in as members.

The OED is equally misleading in the other attributes that are supposed to distinguish nations. One is language. Yet no language is truly distinct and therefore truly distinguishing; each is derivative and syncretic—and few are more so than English. The words in this paragraph, for example, are a tangle of Sanskrit, Latin, ancient Greek, Anglo-Saxon, Teutonic, Norse, and other Indo-European roots that can be traced back to long-dead, widely dispersed, yet intricately interwoven civilizations.

As for *culture,* that is a particularly elastic word standing for a particularly elusive concept. It can be defined as either what makes us the same or what makes us different; it has been both a rallying cry and a fighting word. History has often come down to a dispute over who is different (or "distinct") from whom; who decides the operative distinctions and their implications for others; how much distinctiveness entitles a people to "occupy the same territory," and what that territory's boundaries are—in other words, what "same" means.

Central Asia, where I traveled as a journalist for *Time* in the eighties and as a diplomat in the nineties, is made up of various *stan*s, a Persian word that connotes a homeland for a people: Tajikistan for Tajiks, Kazakhstan for the Kazakhs, Turkmenistan for the Turkmens, Uzbekistan for the Uzbeks. But because history has been more a blender than a separator, many of the eponymous peoples ended up in someone else's *stan*. There are no better examples than Pakistan and Afghanistan. *Pakistan* means "land of the pure" in Urdu, but it is also an acronym for the various parts of British India that were divided by partition (*P* for Punjab, *K* for Kashmir) or that ended up entirely in Pakistan (*S* for Sind). Afghanistan, too, is an artificial construct: the country is populated by Pashtuns in the south, Tajiks and Uzbeks in the north, Kirghiz in the east, Hazara (descendants of the Mongols) in the middle, whose common history is not so much the experience of living in a single state as banding together against the incursions of czarist Russia and the British Raj. In 2005, nearly a century after the last czar and nearly sixty years after the last viceroy, Hamid Karzai, who bore the title but not the power of president, had the impossible task of governing Afghanistan through a traditional gathering of tribes known as the *loya jirga*. His authority was constantly undermined by warlords. After receiving a delegation from a remote province and hearing that jobs in the province were being allocated on the basis of tribal affiliation, Karzai exclaimed, "What are these people thinking? I prefer an orphan, a child without a father, or even better, someone who doesn't know what nationality he is than such people."[8]

Similar combinations of ethnic stranding and scrambling have occurred practically everywhere on the planet, leaving a legacy of conflict among self-conscious, aggrieved minorities, or between a minority and a majority, over identity and loyalty, borders and flags.

"National pride," wrote John Adams when his own nation was only nine years old, "is as natural as self-love."[9] In fact, national pride is a form of self-love. In extremis, it can carry intimations of the immortality that many believe comes with self-sacrifice in defense of one's own nation against its enemies. Recalling his service as an infantryman in the Civil War in a Memorial Day address to the Harvard Class of 1895, Oliver Wendell Holmes, Jr., rhapsodized, "Now, at least, and perhaps as long as man dwells upon the globe, his destiny is battle, and he has to take the chances of war . . . Who is there who would not like to be thought a gentleman? Yet what has that name been built on but the soldier's choice of honor rather than life? . . . [T]he faith is true and adorable which leads a soldier to throw away his life in obedience to a blindly accepted duty, in a cause which he little understands, in a plan of campaign of which he has little notion, under tactics of which he does not see the use . . . War, when you are at it, is horrible and dull. It is only when time has passed that you see that its message was divine."[10] And so on— an ecstatic ode to patriotic gore by a figure revered as a great civilian.

For most of us, nationality may be, just as the word suggests, something we acquire at birth, keep for life, and, if necessary, defend to the death. But that is not, by any means, true for all of us. Many, in the course of their lives, change their nationality, and often their names as well. Both nationality and name are, after all, designations assigned to us not *by* birth but *at* birth; they are bestowed on us by other people: in the case of our names, by our parents; in that of our nationality, by the authorities who have jurisdiction where we are born. Upheaval, famine, economic depression, and political repression often conspire to drive people out of their native countries, or they come upon an opportunity to live a better life somewhere else, or they are seized by an urge or a sense of obligation to follow their families.

Others, while never migrating, salute some flag other than that of the country where they live. William Butler Yeats, who was no less a gentleman than Justice Holmes, carried a British passport much of his life but identified with "the nationality of Ireland [that] is in her songs and in her stories, and in her chronicles and in her traditions," and he found nothing noble or glorious in the Great War of his age ("I think it better that in times like these / A poet's mouth be silent, for in truth / We have no gift to set a statesman right").[11] Bedřich Smetana's *My Country* is an ode to his native Bohemia, not to the Austro-Hungarian Empire of which he was a subject. Jean Sibelius's best-known patriotic composition was written in the 1890s, when Finlandia was still a grand duchy under the Romanovs.

Not only does nationality mean different things to different people—it can mean different things to the same people in different contexts. A colleague of mine, Vishakha Desai, has said that when she is asked what is happening in her country, she usually answers as a naturalized American who has all the rights of a native-born citizen (*almost* all, that is: she can be president of the Asia Society but under the Constitution, not of the United States). Sometimes, however, depending on who is asking the question, who else is listening to her answer, and where the conversation is taking place, she thinks of herself as an Indian-American, an American of Indian origin, or, simply, an Indian. Occasionally she even thinks of herself as a Gujarati—a native of the state in northwestern India where she was born—while in other settings she thinks of herself as an Asian.[12]

AMONG SCHOLARS, THE DEBATE over how people come to identify with a nation breaks down into at least four camps. The so-called "primordialists," who are out of fashion in academe today, see nations as ancient, necessary, and, indeed, "natural" parts of social organization from the dawn of human history. The "perennialists" do not go that far, but they acknowledge important continuities between ancient and modern concepts of nationhood: modern nations, as they see it, are formed around "ethnic cores" developed from premodern communities that share a collective proper name ("Greeks," "Turks," "English")—a myth, in other words, of common ancestry, elements of common culture, historical memories, an association with a specific homeland, and a sense of solidarity. For two other camps, the "modernists" and the "constructivists," nations and nationalism are modern phenomena, without premodern roots, often deliberately constructed for functionalist purposes, such as raising taxes and armies, uniting disparate tribes, or manipulating mass support for other elite goals. According to this view, nationalism was impossible in agrarian societies since it took industrialization to generate the social and economic need for cultural and political homogeneity.[13]

Scholars have also engaged in intellectual combat over the origin of nation-states and the question of which comes first, the nation or the state. In a lecture, famous in the annals of social science, the nineteenth-century French philosopher Ernest Renan argued that nations are formed by the experience of common suffering (a "grand solidarity constituted by the sentiment of sacrifices") and the willingness of individuals to pledge allegiance to the group in an "everyday plebiscite."[14] Max Weber believed that nations exist prior to states, while other leading theorists, such as Ernest Gellner and Charles Tilly, have argued that states play an essential role in creating nations out of racial, linguistic, or tribal connections.

Rather than joining this chicken-and-egg argument, some scholars, including some of the most eminent, have in effect thrown up their hands over the difficulty in defining a nation. The British historian Hugh Seton-Watson, writing in the late 1970s, was reduced to tautology: "All that I can find to say is that a nation exists when a significant number of people in a community consider themselves to form a nation or behave as if they formed one."[15] Others have come up with mordant aphorisms. My favorites are Julian Huxley's dictum that "a nation is a society united by a common error as to its origins and a common aversion to its neighbors," Charles Glass's definition of nations as "tribes with flags," and Yuri Slezkine's variant, "book-reading tribes," which he intends to be especially applicable to the Jews, since so many of them do not have a flag of their own.[16]

Benedict Anderson, a political scientist at Cornell, has pondered the question, "What is a nation?" He sums up his answer in the title of his best-known book, *Imagined Communities.* The size of the largest imaginable nation, he believes, is limited to about a billion people, about a sixth of humanity. He has to let his own imagination reach that far since India and China each has a population of a bit more than a billion. Drawing the line there, Anderson asserts, "No nation imagines itself coterminous with mankind."[17]

That is self-evidently true, since nations, by the OED's definition and any other (including the UN's), exist in the plural; they imagine themselves into existence precisely in order to distinguish—and, if necessary, defend themselves—from others.

YET SINCE ANCIENT TIMES, some individuals have been able to imagine themselves belonging to a community that *is* coterminous with mankind. For them, communal identity is more than just a matter of sharing language, culture, history, and territory; they believe people can identify with others who are unlike themselves and who live far away, and they will accept increasingly expansive political structures as long as they are convinced that doing so will make them safer and better off.

Socrates

According to Plutarch, among the unorthodox views that got Socrates into fatal trouble was his declaration that he was not an Athenian or a Greek but "a citizen of the world." [18] Twenty-two centuries later that phrase would echo in the rhetoric of the American Founding Fathers, and nearly two hundred years after that, it would be part of the ethos of the UN, which acknowledges in its name the multiplicity of nations but in its goals and accomplishments posits a community of all nations.

In Socrates' day, the assertion of global citizenship smacked of sedition—as it sometimes does today. Finding him guilty, Socrates' judges gave him the choice of death or banishment, which was the civic equivalent of death.

2

A LIGHT UNTO THE NATIONS

[He] hath made of one blood all nations of men for to dwell on all
the face of the earth . . .
—*Acts 17:26*

The Lord shall go forth as a mighty man, he shall stir up jealousy
like a man of war: he shall cry, yea, roar; he shall prevail against his
enemies.
—*Isaiah 42:13*

TREASON—the crime for which Socrates was condemned—was formally known as "refusal to accept the gods of the state."[1] The notion that a state has its own gods is a telling conceit. The Athenians were indulging in the presumption that their earthly domain had divine sanction. Socrates' stubbornness was in keeping with the more theologically reasonable view that the supreme authority of the universe feels proprietary toward all humanity and therefore individual human beings should indeed think of themselves as citizens of the world.

In theory, religion—a primordial component of culture and therefore of politics as well—should be the ultimate unifier. The idea of a single human community is inherent in the concept, common to most belief systems, of a universal order. In practice, however, since people—and peoples—have such different beliefs about divinity, religion has been a great divider. It is often what sets people apart, sometimes violently, not just from their neighbors but from those in their own midst who, as the OED would have it, occupy the same territory but are of different descent, culture, and language—and who worship, if not different gods, then the same god in different ways.

Israel is a case study of the interaction between religion and politics. It gave the world the first of the three great monotheistic religions. Israel's history, from its ancient origins to its rebirth as an independent country in modern times, dramatizes the evanescence of a nation, the durability of national identity, and the crucial role that religion plays in shaping and maintaining that identity, even when a people is scattered across the face of the earth.

The word *Israel* has referred both to a place on the map and to the people who have lived there, or have wanted to live there. But they are a people who, like Gypsies, have, in multitudes over many millennia, lived everywhere, under myriad flags, yet often felt that they fully belonged nowhere, and who therefore have kept the idea of their homeland alive in their remarkably portable culture.

Israel's story is both an inspirational tale and a cautionary one. Because of the Jews' determination to maintain themselves as a distinct community, they have been subject to persecution, absorption, dispersal, and, in our own era, genocide. In the precepts ancient Israel developed for ensuring its welfare and survival, it established a concept of statehood and precedents for many of the institutions of governance that would take hold in later eras, especially in Europe, and eventually in European colonies around the world that would, like Israel itself, eventually attain—or regain—independence.

Much of that story is told in the Bible. According to Genesis, Adam himself was a great but flawed experiment—one that kept going awry, demanding his maker's constant intervention and correction. God's first improvement in the first member of the human race was compassionate and practical. "It is not good," said the Lord, "that the man should be alone" (Genesis 2:18). So he added a woman to the Garden of Eden. Absolute self-reliance and solitude gave way to companionship; the individual became part of a community of two—the original first-person plural.

The family is the basis for the institutions and norms of society and the state. Human beings enter the world as helpless infants who, as they grow up, learn to follow rules and accept obligations; they must obey their parents who, in their prime, provide sustenance, care, and protection, and who then, in their old age, expect the same in return. This arrangement ensures that the community, unlike its individual members, lives on. The idea of the parental state resonates in words like *motherland, fatherland,* and *patriotism,* with their connotations of a strong, fair, nurturing, protective, but often stern earthly power that demands and rewards loyalty. If citizens disregard or defy authority, they, like delinquent children, are punished.

That is a lesson of the opening chapters of Genesis. God's only stricture to

Adam and Eve while they were still in the Garden was that they not eat the fruit growing on "the tree of the knowledge of good and evil," or, as some biblical scholars have interpreted the passage, "the tree of knowing all things." On its face, it was a puzzling rule. What was wrong with Adam's acquiring knowledge, particularly the knowledge of good and evil—and, presumably, the difference between them? The Bible seems to say that it is all right for man and woman to think and to acquire knowledge. But if they think they know too much—if they show excessive pride, certitude, self-confidence, and ambition in the way they use the cognitive and creative faculties that God has given them and that distinguish them from other animals—they will come to believe that they are masters of their own fate. The plans and rules they make for themselves will supplant those of God, and they will become less obedient to him.

When Adam and Eve committed the sin of disobedience, God cast them out of Eden. According to early interpreters of the Hebrew Scriptures, Adam and Eve, once in exile, became mortal. Death was not just a fate they and their progeny had to suffer—it was one they could inflict on others, as humankind wasted no time in demonstrating. In a fit of jealousy, Cain slew Abel. So the first death, committed by the first couple's first son, was not merely murder, it was fratricide, a metaphor for all the wars that would follow. Under God's interrogation, Cain replied, "Am I my brother's keeper?" God's answer, in effect, was, "Yes, you are." That has been a basic principle as ties extended from kinship to community, from community to nationality, from nationality to statehood, and from statehood to "the brotherhood of man," a phrase that has permeated UN rhetoric from the organization's earliest days.

Just as God had earlier evicted Adam and Eve from Eden, he now banished Cain from his parents' fold—his mother-and-fatherland. The bad seed propagated along with the good. From its first chapter, the story of the human family is about how disobeying authority and fomenting discord will lead not just to war but to dispersion of an originally homogenous and harmonious people—or in Greek, *diaspora*.[2]

THE SCIENTIFIC VERSION OF GENESIS is a story of fitful progress, from primates to human beings and from cave to civilization. The first hominids started to walk upright about four million years ago. Some two and a half million years later, the more advanced, adventuresome, and desperate of them trekked out of the savannahs of Africa across the Sinai peninsula. By 100,000 BCE, in the Late Paleolithic age, the genus *Homo* had yielded the species of anatomically modern humans called *Homo sapiens*: "man who knows"—which sounds like a nod to Adam and Eve's insistence on tasting the fruit of the tree of knowledge. They fashioned tools, developed methods of vocal communication, and organized themselves into groups that could defend and provide for themselves.

Over time, they worked out codes of conduct, legends about their ancestors, and religious beliefs. They were as curious, as needy, as prone to hope, love, despair, and imagination as we are. In moments of private distress or contemplative solitude, they would ponder, just as we do, mystery and mortality. Who made this world? Who put us in it—and why? Where, if anywhere, will we go when we leave it? To whom do we appeal for comfort in the face of all that is painful in life and all that is frightening about death?

For many, asking these questions and having no answers only added to their sense of loneliness and helplessness. Huddling with others around a fire and staring together into the darkness beyond helped, but it was not enough. Misery may love company, but it wants more than that. The vexations of life and the certainty of death, the loss of loved ones who precede us to the grave, and all the other pains and perils of the natural world inclined both the individual and the group to supernatural answers.

Communities tended to be sturdier if they offered their members an established faith that included a system of rules to guide them in answering down-to-earth questions as well as cosmic and spiritual ones: How should we go about our daily lives? How should we behave toward others? How can we rightfully expect others to behave toward us? Whom can we trust? Who is on our side, and who are our enemies? Whom should we follow? What rules should guide us on the path of life and in our hope for an afterlife? It was the beginning not just of religion but of society.

Shamans served as mediums between the visible and the supernatural worlds. Their claim to be able to commune with the sun, the stars, or the spirits of the forest entitled them to tell the tribe what to hunt, where to camp, what (and whom) to sacrifice for the common good. Elemental systems for establishing leadership and dividing labor emerged. It was the beginning of politics and economics.

Then something happened again and again that constituted the beginning of geopolitics. Motivated by some combination of hunger, fear, and wanderlust, a band would hold council around a fire in a valley and decide to set off over a mountain. Off the warriors would go, chanting phrases that anticipated doctrines of manifest destiny, the need for living space, or preemptive defense. When they reached the next valley, they would massacre, enslave, and eventually absorb some weaker band that was clustered around some smaller fire.

ABOUT TEN THOUSAND YEARS AGO, the nomadic life of hunter-gatherers began to give way to a more settled one. Anthropologists believe that "sedentism"—the transition from life on the move to staying put—was the most important *ism* of all. The Neolithic Revolution, when agriculture replaced hunting and gathering, ushering in complex social organizations, is often said to be the single most significant development in human history. Early societies began to congeal around great rivers or by the sea. As these peoples became more productive economically and more efficient politi-cally—capable of protecting themselves from external enemies and preserv-ing internal order—their populations grew. Over the ages the saddle, the wheel, and the sail increased the speed and distance they could travel; the spear, the shield, and the bow enabled them to overpower those in their way. As these capacities increased, strong political units grew stronger and more expansive and brought smaller, weaker ones under their sway.

In the Late Bronze Age (from the sixteenth until the twelfth century BCE), the Minoans established trade links, backed by military power, which spread their civilization from Crete through the Aegean islands and up the Greek peninsula; the early Canaanites built the city of Ugarit on the Mediterranean; the Sumerians, Akkadians, Babylonians, and Assyrians were concentrated be-tween the Tigris and Euphrates; and the Egyptians spread out from the Nile, establishing the longest-lived of the ancient kingdoms. Their pharaohs were believed to be incarnations of Ra, the sun god and the creator of the universe, who was often depicted as a man with the head of a hawk. Because they were god-kings, the pharaohs laid claim to the entire earth. They extended their rule from central Africa into Mesopotamia until they collided with other civ-ilizations, led by other god-kings. These were the world wars of that era.

WANDERING WITHIN AND AMONG those sprawling, often contest-ing kingdoms was a hardy Semitic people whose story is the main plot of the Hebrew Scriptures.* The first book is largely a genealogical narrative that si-

---

* "Semitic" is a designation for those groups that spoke related languages in the Levant, Mesopotamia, and the Arabian peninsula, including Hebrew, Arabic, Akkadian, Canaanite, Phoenician, Aramaic, and many others (but not Egyptian, which was a separate branch of the Afro-Asiatic language family).

multaneously reinforces the idea of "the family of man" yet also recognizes the reality of humanity's political and cultural fragmentation. As Adam and Eve's original family becomes increasingly extended, it loses its sense of common origin and common identity. All those "begats" in Genesis produce different tribes that often take the names of their patriarchs. As they go their own ways, many stray further and further from the path that God intended. In several generations, humankind becomes so wicked that God comes close to giving up entirely on the experiment he began with Adam. He wipes out the whole species except for one virtuous man, Noah, and his immediate family.

Once the flood waters start to recede, Noah sends a dove out of the ark to see if there is any dry land. On the second try, the dove returns bearing the olive branch, thereby providing the modern world with a symbol of peace and the UN with an image to accompany the globe on its flag. The incorporation of the story of Noah into official imagery of the UN can be seen as a giveaway of its founders' bias toward Western civilization as the progenitor of modern institutions. But according to the Bible's own chronology, the flood predates the division of humanity into separate civilizations and separate nations; it goes back to a time when—as in Eden—the family of man was just that, a single family.

THE STORY OF NOAH may be the earliest point in the Bible where the scribes were applying their imagination to an actual event in the distant past.* They put their own interpretation on a dim memory that they inherited, in mythologized form, from earlier civilizations.

Gilgamesh, the hero of a Babylonian epic originating in the second millennium BCE, meets the survivor of a great flood that had been brought about by Marduk, originally the god of thunderstorms who defeated the dragons of chaos and became the god of light and the creator of humanity. The Babylonians built cities around temple complexes that featured terraced pyramids known as ziggurats. These original skyscrapers, it is conjectured, were religiously motivated: they may have been man-made mountains intended to allow mortals to get closer to their gods so that they could appeal for sufficient rain for their crops. The Babylonians believed that the mythical

---

* Some geologists, relying on traces of dwellings on the floor of the Black Sea, have theorized that the melting of glaciers at the end of the Ice Age, some seven thousand years ago, caused the Mediterranean to swell and a wall of seawater to surge across much of Anatolia and the Middle East.

warrior-king Nimrod decided, in case the gods could not be propitiated, to build the first ziggurat too high for the waters to reach.

In the eyes of his own people, Nimrod was the ruler of the whole earth. The responsibility of a Mesopotamian king was to mediate between his realm and all creation. As the anthropologist Henri Frankfort writes in *Kingship and the Gods*, "The ancients experienced human life as part of a widely spreading network of connections which reached beyond the local and the national communities into the hidden depths of nature and the powers that rule nature . . . Whatever was significant was imbedded in the life of the cosmos, and it was precisely the king's function to maintain the harmony of that integration."[3]

Here was a royal corollary of the Socratic concept of global citizenship: the divine right of kings, which carried with it a universal writ. For a king's power to be challenged by any other ruler, not to mention any mere citizen, was an abomination not just against the royal personage himself, on his earthly throne, but against the divine authority in whose name he ruled.

Hence the title "king of kings," which remained in use until late in the twentieth century. I was among the last reporters to hear it used by a sitting monarch. In late 1978, I conducted an interview with Mohammad Reza Pahlavi shortly before he was driven from Iran's Peacock Throne by masses loyal to the Ayatollah Khomeini. As I listened to the shah tell me about how the CIA was behind the revolution—we talked in his besieged palace in downtown Tehran, with tanks guarding the compound and the chants of protestors in the distance—he insisted that I identify him in print not just as the Shah but as the *Shah-an-Shah*. He would carry that title with him as he wandered for a year and a half, from one barely hospitable country to another until he died in Cairo, and it would be inscribed on his tomb in the al-Rifai Mosque in Egypt.

In the sixth and fifth centuries BCE, a series of Persian emperors took the same title literally and acted on it aggressively. Just to emphasize that its implications were unlimited and uncompromising, they added reinforcing epithets. Cyrus was "king of the world, great king, legitimate king, king of Babylon, king of Sumer and Akkad, king of the four rims of the earth." The Hebrew Scriptures have him declare, "The Lord God of Heaven hath given me all the kingdoms of the earth." Darius the Great was "king of all the people of all origins, king of the great earth and beyond." Xerxes was "king over all this distant and vast world."[4]

The determination of ancient conqueror-kings to act out their ambition to rule over the whole world was the beginning of imperialism, an institution that would last for some six thousand years.

ACCORDING TO GENESIS, one of Noah's grandsons, named Egypt, ends up in North Africa as a precursor of the pharaohs. Nimrod, a great-grandson of Noah, settles in Mesopotamia and is identified with a biblical phrase sometimes translated as "the first potentate on earth."[5] Chapter 10 of Genesis concludes with Noah's descendants being "divided in the earth after the flood" and differentiated according to "their families . . . their tongues . . . [and] their nations."

Then comes one of the more abrupt and incongruous transitions in the Bible. Chapter 11 begins, "And the whole earth was of one language, and of one speech. And it came to pass, as they journeyed from the east, that they found a plain in the land of Shinar," in the Tigris-Euphrates valley, where Nimrod established his kingdom. The city at its center Genesis calls Babel.[6] "They," it would seem, constitute all humanity, which is on the verge of forging itself into a universal race. They set about building a capital of the world, with a tower that will reach into heaven: "Let us make us a name, lest we be scattered abroad upon the face of the whole earth." The Lord is mightily displeased and puts a stop to the venture.

I remember being perplexed in Sunday school over why God was so angry about Babel. Unlike Adam and Eve, the builders of the Tower were not directly violating one of God's injunctions. Unlike Cain, they had not committed murder, nor were the denizens of Babel guilty of the depravity that provoked the flood or the destruction of Sodom and Gomorrah. Rather, the city fathers had simply gone on a building spree that was motivated by an impulse to keep all humanity together in a single political, linguistic, and cultural entity.

What, exactly, was wrong with that? Insofar as the story provides its own answer, it seems to be that the offense is hubris: in God's eyes, the builders of the Tower are trying to make themselves masters of his creation. If they succeed, "Nothing will be restrained from them, which they have imagined to do." Men would, more than ever, follow their own laws rather than those that the Lord had promulgated.[7]

This time God's intervention is, in its ramifications, highly political and explains how the first phase of the great experiment, which had started with a single man and a single family, ends up in the fractionation of humanity and a multiplicity of nations.

The Lord decides to "go down, and there confound their language . . . [so] that they may not understand one another's speech." In the Babylonians' language, *Bab-ilu* meant "Gate of God," a designation suggesting divine approval. However, in Hebrew, *Babel* is a play on the verb *balal*, which means "to confuse, or mix up." God's intervention leaves the officials and citizens of the city reduced to babbling over their plans for the Tower and, by implication, over their plans for world domination. It is a linguistic form of mass banishment. By turning one language into many, God makes it impossible for the citizens of Babel to continue to dwell and govern themselves together within a single state.

The story of the Tower concludes with a repetition of the phrase "scattered abroad upon the face of all the earth." The leaders of Babel have brought down on themselves exactly the fate that they sought to avoid by building the Tower in the first place.[8]

A CHOSEN PEOPLE

If the story of Babel had ended with the destruction of the city, the world would simply have returned to the condition in which it found itself before the ill-fated project to unify humanity. But as Genesis continues, a bad empire yields a good nation—a recurring theme in the narrative of history. God singles out for his favor and protection a group of migrants who settle, on his instructions and with his blessing, in a land some six hundred miles west of Babel. They have separated themselves geographically, linguistically, and religiously from the Babylonians. Their scribes put their own spin on what happened to Babel: they look back on the citizens of that city as pagans, who provoked God's wrath by trying to climb closer to a false heaven, inhabited by false gods.

Some of these wanderers were called *Habiru,* the root of *Hebrew.* Their chieftain was Abraham, whose name means "Father of a Multitude" and who is believed to have lived around the late twentieth and early nineteenth centuries BCE.[9] God's first commandment to Abraham is to tell him where to go—to Canaan, between the Jordan River and the Mediterranean—and God promises him that once he gets there, his family and his followers and those who came after them will, with God's help, be able to govern and defend themselves: "Now the Lord had said unto Abraham, Get thee out of thy country, and from thy kindred, and from thy father's house, unto a land that I will shew thee; And I will make of thee a great nation, and I will bless thee, and make thy name great; and thou shalt be a blessing: And I will bless them that bless thee, and curse him that curseth thee: and in thee shall all families of the earth be blessed." [10]

Gowy, Hebrew for "nation," implies not just what we would call a nationality group but also an independent political entity—a state. In "making thy name great," God is using the phrase that the Bible later applies to kingdoms. [11] Yet while Abraham is the progenitor of what would see itself and be seen by the world as a new race and a new nation, he also personifies the element of self-invention that attends racial and national identity. Try as they might to assert their uniqueness, all races and nations are derivative of others. The Hebrews and the Babylonians were distant relatives, just as Cain and Abel were close ones.

Genesis identifies Abraham as coming originally from Ur, site of one of the largest of the ziggurats, and having lived for a while in Haran, another Mesopotamian city that had been under Babylonian rule. Since the forebears of Israel had lived in the shadow of the Tower and presumably worshipped the multiple gods to which it was dedicated, it follows that the first great monotheistic religion gradually grew out of polytheism. As further evidence of this tie, one of the names that the ancient Hebrews used for their God was *El,* who figured in the Canaanite pantheon as the sky god. Psalm 82 opens with the line: "God standeth in the congregation of the mighty; he judgeth among the gods." [12] The Psalm concludes with the God of Abraham in effect putting an end to this collective heavenly power by sentencing to death any gods worshipped by other peoples: "I have said, Ye are gods; and all of you are children of the most High. But ye shall die like men, and fall like one of the princes." In other biblical references, subordinate deities are demoted to the status of angels—messengers of God, but also ghosts of earlier, long-dead religions from which Judaism, Christianity, and Islam are derived.

The Bible depicts God contending not only with his competitors for supremacy in heaven but with a mortal for the loyalty of a nation on earth that God can call his own. One of the more enigmatic passages in the Hebrew Scriptures is about Jacob, the son of Isaac and the grandson of Abraham, wrestling with a stranger through the night at a ford on the West Bank of the Jordan River. At the break of day, the stranger says he must leave. Jacob refuses to let his opponent go until he reveals, obliquely, that he is God and gives Jacob a new name: *Israel,* which is sometimes interpreted as "the one who struggles with God," sometimes as "May God show his strength." Either way, the words flicker with the extraordinary image of the riverside wrestling match. I have asked but never quite gotten a satisfactory answer to the question of why God settles for a draw.[13] In any event, once the Lord reveals himself, he commands Jacob to return to "the land of your ancestors and to your kindred." Jacob's offspring are called the children of Israel, a name that comes to apply to a whole tribe and, eventually, to a homeland where the Hebrews can speak their own language and practice their own religion—which means worshipping their own god, who in turn protects them as his own people. Their holy book constantly reminds them that, since they owe the existence and independence of their state to that god, they must forsake deities of the older, larger civilizations from which Israel has emerged.

Just as Jacob struggles with God, so the early Hebrews struggle with one another over which deity will be their divine patron. They finally come together around the "God of Abraham, Isaac, and Jacob," or "the God of our fathers." Genesis concludes with the story of how the covenant—the sacred pact between God and his chosen people—passes from one generation to the next and thus to an extended family, a tribe that has a piece of real estate it can rule and defend as its own.[14]

EXODUS TELLS ANOTHER STORY in a different setting, with a different cast of characters, but with the same implication that Israel was a nation born of empire. Another of Noah's wayward grandsons, Egypt, founds a civilization that conquers the Hebrews. Much like Genesis, Exodus depicts the Hebrews as distant relatives of their captors and tormentors.[15] Just as Abraham, Isaac, and Jacob separate themselves from Babel, so Moses—the leader of another wave of settlers, sometime around 1200 BCE—breaks whatever ties he and his followers have with Egyptian civilization. The scribes say these newcomers are descendants of Abraham who had been enslaved by Pharaoh and are liberated by Moses with divine guidance and assistance.

The Jews have their own God, who sends plagues to punish their oppressors and, as they make their way to their destined homeland, uses the Red Sea to drown their pursuers. When God speaks to Moses on Mount Sinai, it is in the same highly personal tone he used with Abraham, Isaac, and Jacob; God makes clear that his relationship with Israel is exclusive and transactional. "I am the Lord thy God, which have brought thee out of the land of Egypt, out of the house of bondage," he says, before giving Moses the tablets with the rules—or laws—by which the Jews must live. Significantly, the first of the Ten Commandments is "Thou shalt have no other gods before me." That is the deal: obedience to this God and no other, and to his laws and no others, will make the Jews his people.[16]

Thus, in Exodus as in Genesis, a universal, inclusive, polytheistic divine order has become a national, exclusive, monotheistic one. The maker of the cosmos, the earth, and all its creatures is trying something new; it is as though, having seen the human aspect of his grand scheme of creation go wrong so often and in so many ways, he decides to concentrate on a pilot project; he will make of one nation a Promised Land for his chosen people.

Sometimes God denies ethnocentricity and favoritism. "I'm not just *yours*," he says in the book of Amos, "I'm everyone's": "To me, O Israelites, you are just like the Ethiopians . . . True, I brought Israel up from the land of Egypt, but also the Philistines from Caphtor and the Arameans from Kir." In that passage and others, writes Jaroslav Pelikan, a biblical scholar whose lectures I attended at Yale in the sixties, the Lord "was not a tribal deity but the God of all the nations." [17]

Nonetheless, the Almighty makes rarer appearances in that guise than as the God of Israel. As a compromise between the tribal or national dimension of religion and the universal one, the idea emerges of Israel as an exemplar to all humanity, "a light unto the nations." That phrase, which in modern times has been a motto for Zionism, is, in the Hebrew Scriptures, attributed by Isaiah to God himself: "I have called you [Israel] in righteousness; I have taken you by the hand and kept you; I have given you a covenant to the people, a light unto the nations, to open the eyes that are blind, to bring out the prisoners from the dungeon, from the prison those who sit in darkness." [18]

This is the small-is-beautiful alternative to imperialism: Israel will liberate other peoples not by the sword but by example—by the power of its God-given ideas and ideals about how to live and how to govern.

BUT ISRAEL ALSO HAD THE NEED, the power, and the divine blessing to resist and defeat its enemies. Just a few verses after quoting God as an all-embracing deity, Isaiah invokes him in a very different guise, as *Yahweh Sabaoth*, the God of Armies—*Israel's* armies. The Canaanites and Philistines are depicted as morally corrupt, therefore deserving slaughter. When push comes to shove among the peoples of the region, as it so often did in those days and so often would in the centuries that followed, God is on his people's side against other nations who are, in the Israelites' eyes, illicitly occupying the land God intends for them. He commands his people to show their foes no mercy:

[T]hou shalt smite them, and utterly destroy them; thou shalt make no covenant with them, nor show mercy unto them: neither shalt thou make marriages with them; thy daughter thou shalt not give unto his son, nor his daughter shalt thou take unto thy son . . . [Y]e shall destroy their altars, and break down their images, and cut down their groves, and burn their graven images with fire.[19]

The scripture continues with a pragmatic justification of the ferocity of this exhortation:

For thou art an holy people unto the Lord thy God: the Lord thy God hath chosen thee to be a special people unto himself, above all people that are upon the face of the earth. The Lord did not set his love upon you, nor choose you, because ye were more in number than any people; for ye were the fewest of all people.

As for how the leaders of Israel should rule their subjects, biblical law recognizes the nation's eclectic origins and the diversity of its population. It seeks to reconcile Israel's identity as a Jewish kingdom with tolerance for religious minorities within its borders, such as Moabites, Philistines, and Canaanites: "The stranger that dwelleth with you shall be unto you as one born among you, and thou shalt love him as thyself."[20]

But pluralism has its limits: "One ordinance shall be both for you of the congregation, and also for the stranger that sojourneth with you, an ordinance for ever in your generations: as ye are, so shall the stranger be before the Lord."[21] That means the God of Israel. If "the stranger" worships other gods, then his sojourn in Israel will be that of an outsider, and his graven images will, presumably, suffer the same fate as those of Israel's enemies.

As the story of Babel, Egypt, and Israel shows, each system of governance—empire and nation—had the vulnerability of its virtue. An empire's inclusiveness, its pretensions of universality, made it prone to eventual breakdown and breakup. The Minoans went into decline, perhaps initially because of a volcanic eruption on a nearby island, but also because of invasion by other civilizations. The Hittites eventually succumbed to constant raids from mountain tribes and "the Sea Peoples," who came from the northern Mediterranean coast and its offshore islands. The Egyptian empire was whittled away by the encroachments of Ethiopians, Assyrians, Persians, and, finally, Greeks. Each of these empires and all those that would follow came into being through a process in three stages: conquest, absorption, and integration. Then sooner or later, that sequence would go into reverse: conquest provoked rebellion; absorption proved incomplete and inequitable; integration gave way to disintegration. Within restive communities, often on the edge of the empire, a sense of common grievance abetted the growth of a sense of common identity and common purpose. And that purpose was to achieve independence.

But then the virtues of national identity would show themselves to be vulnerabilities in disguise: the exclusivity and distinctiveness that made a nation cohesive also predisposed it to conflict with its neighbors and made it a target for ascendant and covetous empires.

So it was with Israel. It came into existence as what today would be called a sovereign state under King Saul in the eleventh century BCE and attained its height under his successors, David and Solomon. Israel remained unified for only three generations—about a century—then split into a northern kingdom, which retained the name, and a southern one that called itself Judah, which survived until the sixth century BCE. By then, the Hittites had given way to the Assyrians, who in turn were supplanted by the resurgent Babylonians, who, in effect, rebuilt the Babel of Genesis. Jeremiah had predicted Judah's destruction: it would be wiped off the map by a predatory and neighboring state—which is geopolitics in its most basic, brutal, and rapacious form.

Early in the sixth century BCE, King Nebuchadnezzar II sent his armies westward into Syria, Egypt, and Palestine, took captive many of the nobles, warriors, and artisans from the Jewish kingdom of Judah, and brought them to Babylon. Eleven years later, Nebuchadnezzar's armies returned, sacked Jerusalem, destroyed the Temple of Solomon, and deported many of the remaining Israelites. That period of exile, known as the Babylonian Captivity, continued until Babylon itself fell to Cyrus and the Persians. Cyrus allowed the Jews still exiled in Babylon to return to their homeland. Many Jews living in Babylon—perhaps a majority—did not take up the offer. Instead, they became part of the oldest continuous diaspora of them all, the body of Jews who would remain dispersed among nations outside Palestine, including in Babylon itself, until the rule of Saddam Hussein. (By the time American troops reached Baghdad in spring of 2003, there were perhaps two dozen old Iraqi Jews left in the country, the last remnant of a continuous 2,600-year diaspora in the region. Most were airlifted to Israel.)

After the Babylonian Captivity, waves of empire washed over the Promised Land. After the Babylonians came the Persians, then various Greek dynasties. A successful revolt by the Maccabees, in 168 BCE—which Jews celebrate with Hanukkah—recreated an independent Jewish state, called Judea, which lasted for about a century, until the Romans conquered it and classified the Jews as a *natio* within the empire. Then came the Byzantines, several Arab regimes, the Crusaders, the Egyptian Mamluks, the Ottomans, and finally the British.

Not until the mid-twentieth century did Israel once again become an independent state, recognized by the United Nations shortly after the organization itself was born. By then imperialism was in terminal decline. The following two decades—the nineteen-fifties and sixties—would be the heyday of decolonization. Dying empires begat new nations. But those new nations would have troubles of their own. Israel is a chronically vexing example. In modern times as in ancient ones, that nation has represented both the strength and the weakness of nationhood itself. Israel grew out of a gathering of tribes that had come to think of themselves as constituting a single tribe, with their own divine mandate, a single defining culture, and a homeland to be defended against the hostile tribes on its borders. The fate of Israel and its Arab neighbors over the next sixty years would be a nagging reminder that the post–World War II international system, symbolized and—in episodic and partial fashion—governed by the UN, was an improvement on the old imperial one in many ways. But not in all ways. While imperialism had its fatal flaws, it also had its not-quite-saving graces as a means of bringing together many nations spread over huge distances and sometimes on different continents.

3

THE ECUMENICAL STATE

A state is not a mere society, having a common place, established for the prevention of mutual crime and for the sake of exchange. . . . Political society exists for the sake of noble actions, and not of mere companionship. . . .
—*ARISTOTLE*[1]

I am proud not of imperialism itself but of some things it left in its wake.
—*CHRIS PATTEN*[2]

O
N a grim, chilly day in November 1971, shortly after my wife, Brooke, and I arrived in Belgrade to take up a two-year assignment covering Eastern Europe, we hailed a taxi in front of our apartment building on Ulica Lole Ribara and asked to go somewhere across town—the train station, perhaps, or a government ministry for an interview, or to a friend's home for a meal. What made for a lasting memory was not the destination but the explanation for why we were late in getting there. The cab made it about three blocks from where it had picked us up when the engine coughed and died. The driver shook his head wearily, sighed, and looked at us over his shoulder. "What can you expect?" he said. "We were under the Turks for five hundred years."

Over the next two years, we heard essentially the same thing from many of our Serbian hosts, sometimes as they sipped what most of the rest of the world knows as Turkish coffee but they called *srpska kafa*. The pollution of the Danube, the uncertainty of Yugoslav railroad timetables and airline schedules, the largely unwelcome presence on the streets of Albanian Muslims, in their white skullcaps, doing menial jobs—these and other inconveniences and embarrassments were, it seemed, all the fault of the Ottomans, whose empire had passed into history more than fifty years before, in the aftermath of World War I.

When Brooke and I traveled around Bosnia, then still a republic of Yugoslavia, the legacy of empire looked quite different. Bosnia had fallen under the Ottomans almost a century before Serbia, and much of its population had abandoned the cross for the crescent and taken Islamic names not under threat of death but for reasons of conviction or convenience. The descendants of these converts whom we met in the 1970s therefore had, as far as we could sense, little residual bitterness toward "the Turks." Moreover, they lived and worked alongside their fellow Bosnians who happened to be Catholic Croats or Orthodox Serbs. As we drove through the countryside, often the first signs we would see of a village were a pair of church spires and a minaret. Bosnia, in short, seemed to be a harmoniously multicommunal vestige of a harmoniously multinational empire.

The same could be said of other corners of other empires. The people who lived there were not masters of their own fate. Their ultimate masters were far away, and were of a different stock, often of a different religion. Yet these subjects of empire often lived more peacefully than they did when, eventually, they acquired independence. When that happened, they frequently turned not only against their overlords but against one another as well.

Despite the inequities, cruelties, and structural weaknesses that ultimately brought all empires to an end, the more robust of them practiced—if not constantly, then for long periods of time, and if not with all their subjects, then with many of them—an administrative broad-mindedness that made political, strategic, and economic sense, and that made for a durable form of governance rooted in the rulers' enlightened self-interest. If military power did not have to be constantly deployed for the suppression of internal dissent and the forcible conversion of nonbelievers, it could be used instead for territorial defense and expansion (which itself was a form of defense).

The internal peace that came with accommodation of the differences among the constituent communities of the empire stimulated trade and therefore prosperity. Coercion and punishment were always part of the reality with which the subjects of empire had to reckon. But so were cooperation, commerce, and cultural cross-fertilization that helped bind scattered, often antagonistic nationalities together.

Imperialism at its best established the precedent for the post–World War II international system that would attempt to replace empires with sovereign nations while avoiding nationalism at its worst. That system would fail spectacularly in the Balkans in the 1990s, but by then it would have succeeded in much of the rest of Europe.

MASTERS OF THE UNIVERSE

One reason imperialism is so discredited in postimperial times is that, contrary to the old saw, history has often been written not by the victors but by the vanquished—or at least by those who tell the story from the vantage of their aggrieved, often enslaved forebears. There is no better example than the stories told in the Hebrew Scriptures. They often serve to settle old scores. The scribes believed they had every reason to vilify the Babylonian kings and Egyptian pharaohs who had persecuted the Jews and kept them in bondage, depriving them of their God-given birthright to a nation of their own. But some of the historical figures on whom those biblical tyrants were based were also, in important respects, just and tolerant rulers and pioneers of the novel idea that peace was preferable to war in relations among god-kings.

If there was a real Tower of Babel, it could well have been the ziggurat known as Etemenanki ("House of the Foundation of Heaven on Earth") on the site of the Marduk temple in Babylon. If so, it would have been the work of Hammurabi, the greatest king of the first Babylonian dynasty, who ruled in the eighteenth century BCE. That was about five hundred years before the Hebrews began to emerge as a separate tribe and twelve hundred years before the Babylonian Captivity. Insofar as anything like facts can be deduced from fragmentary evidence—much of it in his own words or promulgated in his name—Hammurabi, during his approximately forty-year reign, codified a set of rules to govern social and political life. "Hammurabi's Law," engraved in cuneiform characters on a seven-foot-high monolith of black basalt, propounds the principles of peace, justice, "stable government and benevolent rule," and the admonition that "the strong may not oppress the weak." While little is known about the extent to which these humane and modern-sounding precepts were observed in practice, Hammurabi is celebrated as a founder of international law, and a replica of the tablet with his code (the original is in the Louvre) is mounted at the UN just outside the entrance to the General Assembly Hall.

AN EXAMPLE OF AN EMPEROR who may have been better than his reputation is Ramses II. He appears in the Bible as the Egyptian monarch who ordered the slaying of the Jews' firstborn and, as divine retribution for this and other outrages against God's chosen people, brought the ten plagues down on his own people. Yet that same ruler may well have been a warrior who turned statesman by negotiating one of the earliest known peace treaties. In the thirteenth century BCE, sweeping north from the Nile Valley, Ramses' armies clashed with the Hittites, who had surged south from Asia Minor. After the long and debilitating Battle of Kadesh, in what today is Syria, Ramses and his Hittite adversary Hattušili agreed to fix the borders between the two realms, provide for the exchange of maps on the location of harbors and land routes that would be open to travelers and merchants, establish an extradition agreement, and commit each side to come to the other's aid in the event of attack by an outside power. There is no hint of that early statesmanship in the Bible, not to mention in Cecil B. DeMille's *Ten Commandments,* which casts a brooding Yul Brynner as the villain Ramses to Charlton Heston's Moses.

HISTORY (NOT TO MENTION HOLLYWOOD) has been kinder to Alexander III of Macedon, whose father, Philip, had turned a pastoral moun-

Alexander the Great

tain kingdom into the most powerful of the Greek states. Building on that accomplishment, Alexander, in the course of a life that lasted only thirty-three years, managed to vanquish Darius the Great and the Persian dynasty that had produced all those "kings of kings." Alexander became the master of most of the world known to him and his busy legions. In pulling off that prodigy of ambition, will, and discipline, Alexander showed himself capable of the vanity, brutality, and treachery typical of conquering nonheroes of that age and later ones as well. In destroying Thebes, he slaughtered thousands and carried off many more in chains. Given to fits of paranoia and drunken rage, he killed his most trusted general and a historian who accompanied him on his campaigns.[3]

Yet Alexander also left in his wake new cities that would come to bear his name, an economic and trading system based on silver and gold coinage, Greek as the language commonly in use from Gibraltar to the Punjab, and a culture that is still called Hellenic. The geographical reach of his conquest and, even more impressive, his lasting mark on those lands were the result not just of military genius but of a new idea about how to rule the territory he brought under his sway and the people who lived there. His predecessors believed that Greeks were, by nature, free, while non-Greeks were properly enslaved. Alexander, by contrast, experimented with *koinonia*, an expansive form of fellowship that included not only the Greeks' allies but those who willingly submitted to their rule.

In this respect, Alexander was a pupil who improved on what he had learned from the ultimate teacher. From the age of thirteen until he became king five years later, Alexander had been tutored by Aristotle. The great philosopher instilled in Alexander a desire to learn about—and learn from—the peoples he conquered. Aristotle believed in the city-state as the ultimate organized society and in the Greeks' superiority over all others. Alexander had a bigger and better idea. He imagined a political community that was geographically far more expansive and culturally more inclusive than the city-state. He set as his goal the establishment of *oikumene*, sometimes translated as "a sense of communion with all the peoples of the world" (a concept Alexander had learned from Aristotle, and the root of *ecumenical*) to be ruled from a *cosmopolis*, or world city.[4] He is believed to have influenced Zeno of Citium, the founder of the Stoic school of philosophy.*

Two decades after Alexander's death, Zeno predicted that the model of the Greek city-state would be supplanted by ever-larger forms of governance; he argued that the world as a whole should be seen as one great city and that every individual should see himself as a citizen of that city. Or, as Plutarch quotes Zeno, "We should all live not in cities and tribes, each distinguished by separate rules of justice, but should regard all men as members of the same tribe and fellow citizens; and that there should be one life and order as of a single flock feeding together on a common pasture."[5]

To realize this radical departure from the hierarchical and discriminatory Greek view of subject peoples, Alexander promoted, often forcibly, intermarriage among his officers and local leaders. He set an example by marrying Roxana, a princess of Bactria, in what is now northern Afghanistan. "This is the way that wise kings join Asia with Europe," wrote Plutarch of Alexander in the first century CE. "It is not by beams or rafts, nor by lifeless and unfeeling bonds, but by the ties of lawful love and chaste nuptials and mutual joy in

---

* Not to be confused with the Zeno of Elea, the mathematician who left his name to a series of paradoxes.

children that they join the nations together."[6] It is worth noting the contrast to Isaiah's injunction, cited in Chapter 2, that the Hebrews should not intermarry with those they conquered.

The Roman philosopher Apuleius, looking back four hundred years later, proclaimed Alexander "the sole conqueror in the memory of mankind to have founded a universal empire," while the early-twentieth-century Scottish historian W. W. Tarn credited Alexander as the first person known to have enunciated the idea of a single global political community.[7]

ALEXANDER HAS BECOME A PRIME EXAMPLE of the force that a singular personality can exert on the course of history. But it was the Romans who institutionalized the concept of the ecumenical state.

The Latin word *imperator* referred not only to a civilian ruler who interpreted and carried out the law but also to a victorious commander of one or more Roman legions. Political power derived from military strength and organization. It was the Romans' superior prowess in battle that enabled them to replace the Greeks in the Mediterranean, but it was their concept of citizenship that allowed them, as imperialists, to achieve a reach and duration that far exceeded the Greeks. The Romans allowed conquered elites who paid taxes and obeyed imperial authority to become citizens.

With that status came mobility. The Romans built an infrastructure of communications and transportation suitable to a domain that, at its height, stretched from the Atlas Mountains in northwest Africa to Mesopotamia and to what is now Scotland—in all, about five million square miles with a population of some fifty-five million, as much as 30 percent of humanity at that time. The construction of fifty-three thousand miles of paved road was intended primarily to permit rapid deployment of troops and tax collectors, but it also improved trade and communications between distant regions.

Citizens throughout the empire felt they belonged to a single entity. In order to regulate commerce and undergird their ability to govern, the Romans had a legal system that allowed them to maintain the rough stability known as the Pax Romana for three centuries. Virgil, the principal poetic ideologue of the empire, wrote that while "others" (he had in mind the Greeks) might have been more refined and accomplished in the arts, the Romans had the advantage of law, not just for the benefit of the rulers but for the protection of those they ruled as well.[8]

Even more than their language and architecture, the Romans' system of law is their most enduring and pervasive bequest. It has contributed to the governance of every modern nation where the Romans ruled, and also of a host of countries in areas of the world where they never set foot, such as South Africa, Sri Lanka, Guyana, Indonesia, Haiti, and, prominently, the United States.*

While at many times and in many ways arbitrary and repressive, Roman law was highly deferential to communal authorities, on the theory that one way to keep peace in the provinces was to empower the provincials to enforce their own rules. It operated on a simple principle—that people are more likely to accept a far-off authority that allows them to run their own lives as much as possible—which would be the essence of what, centuries later, became known as federalism.

In the first century BCE, Cicero proclaimed a vision of *respublica totius orbis*—the republic of the whole world. He chafed against the implication of coercion in the word *imperator:* "We could more truly have been titled a protectorate than an empire of the world."[9] For such a thing to be possible, its leaders must rule by consent from below as well as by force from above. A generation after Cicero, the historian Livy put it this way: "An empire remains powerful so long as its subjects rejoice in it."[10] In the second century CE, during the reign of the Emperor Antoninus Pius, one subject who so rejoiced was Aelius Aristides, a renowned Greek orator. Traveling to Rome to deliver a paean to his rulers, he proclaimed that all previous empires had failed because the conquerors "passed their lives in giving and receiving hatred," while the Romans "rule over men who are free . . . [and] conduct public business in the whole civilized world exactly as if it were one city state."[11]

Anthony Pagden, a professor of intellectual history at the University of California, Los Angeles, believes that it was largely because of this feature of governance that the Roman state was more accommodating of diversity than any other empire in the ancient world. As a result, Rome was "more than an empire. It was always for those who were drawn into it what the Romans called a *civitas*, the word from which, much later, the far more ambiguous modern term 'civilization' would be derived. It was a society which, although it had always looked to Rome, the 'mother' and the 'prince' of cities, had no fixed place, and indeed would one day gather all humanity into what Cicero called a single community 'of gods and men.' "[12]

IN PRACTICE, CICERO'S CONCEPT meant that different men could have different gods—that is, the inhabitants of far-flung nations within the

---

* Roman law became the basis for European civil law and had a direct effect on English common law, which colonists imported to America; Roman law also heavily influenced U.S. mercantile and maritime law, and American legal scholarship.

empire could have different religions. The Romans insisted on obedience to Caesar, but not on worship of Jupiter and Juno, Mars and Venus, Janus and Minerva. As Edward Gibbon wrote, "The various modes of worship, which prevailed in the Roman world, were all considered by the people, as equally true; by the philosopher, as equally false; and by the magistrate, as equally useful."[13]

Fifteen hundred miles from Rome, the Jews in the Roman province of Judea could worship the God of Abraham, Isaac, Jacob, and Moses, their deliverer from an earlier empire that had held them in bondage. Therefore there was no need for another exodus. They had a homeland, even though it was incorporated into an immense state. Some of the imperial agents sent from Rome to govern Judea not only recognized the Jews' freedom to practice their religion but also their right to manage religious disputes among themselves, largely so that local squabbles would not get out of hand and require the intervention of imperial forces.

That was when Rome was practicing a benevolent and permissive form of imperial administration. When such was not the case, the results were bad for the stability of the empire itself. Caligula (who reigned 37–41 CE) ordered that the Jews venerate statues of him in the Temple in Jerusalem. It was only his death that prevented a rebellion. Thirty years later, the high-handedness of an imperial administrator set off the Great (or First) Jewish Revolt, which provoked the sack of Jerusalem and the destruction of the Temple by the Roman army. (It was at the end of this war that the Zealots committed mass suicide at Masada.) The next few decades saw a restoration of Roman control, punctuated by occasional Jewish-Roman violence. In 132 CE, the Second Jewish Revolt began—largely as a result of Hadrian's restrictions on religious freedoms. Only when Antoninus Pius rescinded Hadrian's orders did peace return, after great cost in Jewish blood.

CONVERSION AND ABSORPTION

During a period of relatively enlightened Roman rule, the devolution of power together with respect for the autonomy of the provinces gave birth to a new religion that was, like Judaism, monotheistic. Unlike Judaism—and like Cicero's idea of Rome itself—it was universalistic. This new faith would replace the belief system of the Romans, outlast their empire, dominate its successors, and spread throughout the world. It began with a minor intracommunal disturbance during the reign of Tiberius Caesar (14–37 CE). The Jewish high priests found the teaching of a young reformist preacher and faith healer disruptive to the peace of the community and a challenge to their standing within it.

According to the Christian Scriptures, it was trouble that Jesus of Nazareth did not ask for. Other than occasionally attacking corruption (such as priests permitting merchants and moneylenders to do business in the Temple), he tried to stay out of politics. The Pharisees, members of a Jewish sect that promoted strict interpretation of Mosaic Law, tried to trick Jesus into crossing the line by asking whether it was right for Jews, whose nation was, against its will, being ruled from Rome, to pay tribute to Tiberius. Showing them a coin, Jesus asked whose likeness was imprinted on it. "Caesar's," was their reply. "Render unto Caesar what is Caesar's," said Jesus, "and to God what is God's." [14]

Jesus' insistence on the separation of temple and state would have sat well with the far-off emperor, but it did not mollify the leaders of the local establishment, for whom religious and political authorities were intertwined. When Jesus chastised them for hypocrisy and corruption, they formed a tribunal of their chief priests, charged him with blasphemy, and condemned him to death.

The case went to Pontius Pilate, the Roman military governor of Judea, and became a test of his ability to preserve peace in the community, which he believed required upholding the prerogatives of its leaders. Pilate asked the prisoner if he believed himself to be the king of the Jews, which would have made him a political threat. According to the Gospel of John, Jesus denied any such claim: "My kingdom is not of this world: if my kingdom were of this world, then would my servants [i.e., followers] fight, that I should not be delivered to the Jews: but now is my kingdom not from hence." According to Matthew, Mark, and Luke, he refused to answer directly. [15] In either case, Jesus was adhering to a tradition in Judaism: prophets stick to prophesying, while Jewish secular leaders, no matter how powerful, must not claim to speak for God.

Pilate was impressed: the man before him was not a rebel. But while Jesus' disclaimer solved Rome's problem, it did not solve Pilate's local one. He was fearful that unless he affirmed the tribunal's sentence, there might be an uprising instigated by the Jewish establishment, and Rome would get reports of trouble in Judea. Therefore he let the crucifixion go forward.

After Christ's death, there was a debate among his disciples about whether they should convert only Jews or whether they should reach out to gentiles as

well. The later view, advocated by the Apostle Paul, prevailed, not least because the new creed needed numbers to survive. Paul was from Tarsus, lo-
cated on a trade route between East and West, and he inherited from his
father Roman citizenship, which had been granted to members of the local
elite.[16] That status allowed him to take advantage of the mobility within the
empire and travel freely, preaching the gospel and proselytizing for two decades through Syria, Cyprus, Anatolia, and the Greek islands and mainland.
Among Paul's rights as a citizen was that of being sentenced by a Roman
court and decapitated by a Roman executioner under the authority of a
Roman emperor—Nero, a strong contender for the worst of the lot. (Paul's
fellow apostle Peter, who was not a citizen, also met his death in Rome, but by
crucifixion.) It is a testament to Saint Paul's success in converting gentiles
that my family worshipped at an Episcopal church bearing his name nineteen hundred years later and 4,600 miles away, on Fairmount Boulevard in
Cleveland Heights, Ohio.

FOR THREE CENTURIES, the powers of Rome did their best to stamp
out this offshoot of Judaism that had broken out of a mononational mold
and was spreading far and wide. They failed in part because Christianity defended itself by going on the offensive, albeit peacefully, taking full advantage
of religion as a unifying, consolidating, and expansive force.

Jesus' followers presented his teachings as an invitation to members of
other communities and adherents of other faiths to embrace theirs. In pursuit of converts, Christianity encouraged tolerance for their customs. A passage in Matthew—"Not that which goeth into the mouth defileth a man; but
that which cometh out of the mouth, this defileth a man" (15:11)—was helpful in converting gentiles who wanted to continue observing their own dietary laws, and so helped make Christianity seem all-welcoming and
egalitarian.

The second line of what became known as the Lord's Prayer, "Thy kingdom come. Thy will be done in earth, as it is in heaven," suggested to Jesus'
disciples and their pupils through the ages that belief in him and his teachings would unify those who were otherwise divided. As Paul put it in his epis-
tle to the churches he founded in the Roman province of Galatia, in central
Anatolia, "There is neither Jew nor Greek, there is neither bond nor free . . .
for ye are all one in Christ Jesus."[17]

Paul was offering those who chose to join the new religion the ultimate re-
ward in heaven. But many of those who were drawn to Christianity naturally

hoped for a secure, peaceful life on earth as well. They wanted to be part not just of a spiritual union but also of a temporal one. Protection for the community required power for its leaders and obedience from its members. Over time, the proactive inclusiveness of the Mother Church led to a firmly enforced proviso: open-mindedness about who might join the church did not mean brooking heterodoxy about what they were to believe once they had joined. Secular harmony depended on doctrinal unity. The Nicene Creed was intended to commit all who uttered it to unquestioning acceptance of Christ's divine inception, resurrection, and, in the fullness of time, the limitlessness of his kingdom, not just in heaven but on earth as well.*

When I learned to recite this basic part of the Christian liturgy in Sunday school in the 1950s, I remember thinking that it sounded like the pledge of allegiance that began each day in the elementary school I attended during the week.

THE NICENE CREED WAS PROMULGATED in 325 CE by a political figure who saw Christianity as a rallying force that would enable him to defeat his enemies and secure power on earth.

Like many Roman rulers of his era, Constantine the Great was an *imperator* in the original sense of a warrior-emperor. Born an army brat at a Roman outpost in the Balkans, Constantine followed his father, Constantius I, from one embattled frontier to another, including to the rugged fortresses of Britain, which was under constant threat from Saxon pirates operating in the English Channel and Scottish invaders from the north.

Just as the empire itself was under attack along its periphery, so the belief system of the ancients was giving way to outside influences. By Constantine's time, the worship of the panoply of gods around Jupiter had already moved toward monotheism, worshipping one supreme deity while accepting the existence of others. Sol, the sun god, was believed to be the visible manifestation of an invisible *summus deus* ("Highest God") who ruled the universe and, not incidentally, provided advice on grand strategy to the Roman emperor.

By the third century CE, the incumbent, whoever he was, needed all the

---

* The key passage of the Nicene Creed: "For us and for our salvation he came down from heaven: by the power of the Holy Spirit he became incarnate from the Virgin Mary, and was made man. For our sake he was crucified under Pontius Pilate; he suffered death and was buried. On the third day he rose again in accordance with the Scriptures; he ascended into heaven and is seated at the right hand of the Father. He will come again in glory to judge the living and the dead, and his kingdom will have no end."

help he could get. His office had fallen into disrepute and his realm into disarray, largely because of chronic misrule by a string of incompetent, sadistic, and insane predecessors, of whom Caligula was the most notorious.

One line of speculation would, if proved, underscore the warning that technological progress of the sort that helps civilizations advance comes with its own risks. Centuries later, the prime examples would be the internal combustion engine, electricity, and nuclear energy, but in the beginning of the third century CE it was the efficient delivery of water to city dwellers. Eleven aqueducts around Rome delivered to the city 250,000 gallons per day; it was then distributed by a system of lead pipes. Anthropologists have discovered ten times the normal amount of lead in bones they have found in excavations, leading them to conjecture that steady poisoning may have had something to do with the epidemic of madness among the emperors of the period.[18]

If that theory is true, Constantine had the advantage of growing up far from Rome. He was born in a city in what today is Serbia, when his father was a military official there, and raised in what is now Turkey at the court of the Eastern Roman Emperor Diocletian.

Constantine's incentive to convert to Christianity was almost surely as much military and political as spiritual. Christianity had long since emerged as one of the most important religions of the empire. Moreover, it was a useful force for promoting stability, allegiance, and efficient organization.[19] According to legend, on the eve of a battle in Italy against one of his rivals, Constantine dreamed that Christ appeared to him and told him to put the Greek *XP*, the first two letters of Christ's name, on the shields of his troops. During the battle, a cross appeared in front of the sun—the symbol of the new religion partially eclipsing that of the old—along with the inscription "in this sign you will be the victor." Constantine won and gave credit to "the God of the Christians." The Roman Senate hailed him as a savior and made him co-emperor with a peasant-born general, Licinius. Constantine immediately mandated the end of persecution of the Christians throughout the Empire. Thirteen years later, he presided, in Nicaea, over an assembly of bishops that produced the Nicene Creed—the first of many councils to be given the Alexandrian designation "ecumenical."

The power-sharing arrangement between Constantine and Licinius was a formula for rivalry, conflict, and treachery. When it led to a series of civil wars, Constantine prevailed and soon decamped from the banks of the Tiber and moved about 850 miles east, to the ancient Greek site of Byzantium on the shores of the Bosporus. He named the city after himself, devoted the last decade of his life to expanding and beautifying it, and was baptized shortly before his death. It is believed that one factor motivating Constantine to move was a desire to be closer to the Holy Land. His mother, Helena, also converted to Christianity and, at the age of eighty, set off on a pilgrimage to Jerusalem, where she is said to have found the True Cross.

The Community of the Faithful

A momentous consequence of Constantine's decision to move the seat of the Roman Empire eastward was an eerie case of history repeating itself. The "first" Rome—its capital on a peninsula jutting into the middle of the Mediterranean—had, in its Levantine hinterland, unintentionally nurtured Christianity, which was working its way west, gaining in political potency as it acquired converts. "The second Rome," as Constantinople was called, exerted a cultural influence on the disparate peoples to its east that was strong enough to give them a sense of common identity but not strong enough to bring them into the Byzantine Empire. This dynamic helped create the conditions for the rise, early in the seventh century CE, of Islam.

Most Arabs of the early sixth century, while observing pagan traditions, recognized a supreme deity whom they called "al-Lah" ("the God"). The more sophisticated of them believed him to be the same god worshipped by Jews and Christians. The Jews, however, had their own prophets, and the Christians had their own redeemer. Believers in those religions also had their own scriptures, allowing God to speak to them in their language, thereby making them feel that he was truly guiding and protecting *them*. The Arabs, in this respect, were left out: they too wanted a god of their own. Since Arabs were largely a nomadic people, their society was fragmented and prone to feuds. As Karen Armstrong, a scholar of religion, writes, "It seemed to many of the more thoughtful people in Arabia that the Arabs were a lost people, exiled forever from the civilized world and ignored by God himself." [20] They had just enough exposure to the more cohesive and advanced civilizations around them to know what they were missing: they were in need of a leader who could give them their own sense of spiritual and political identity.

Sometime around 570 CE, Mohammed ibn Abdullah was born in Mecca, an important Arabian trading settlement and destination for pilgrims since the time of Abraham. Mohammed was part of that tradition himself. In his youth, he had contact with Christians and Jews, among travelers to Mecca, and on his own trips as a spice merchant with caravans to Syria. In middle age, Mohammed believed he was visited in his sleep by Gabriel, the archangel who appears several times in the Hebrew Scriptures to reveal God's will and who, in the Christian Scriptures, informs Mary that the child in her womb is the son of God. Mohammed, who was frightened and perplexed by this experience, consulted a Christian monk who helped persuade him that with this divine vision came a divine mission. Mohammed's followers believe that Gabriel later transported him to Jerusalem to meet Abraham, Moses, and Jesus. Mohammed called his followers Muslims ("those who have submitted"—*Islam* itself means submission, or obedience), established himself in their view as the last of the prophets, and led them from Mecca, where they were a persecuted minority, to Medina, where they established a city-state.

There is a marked difference between the revelations that Mohammed received over a thirteen-year period in Mecca and recorded in the Koran (*Koran* means the "recitation" of the word of God as revealed to his Prophet) and those that later came to him in Medina. The so-called Meccan verses are, much like the teachings of Jesus, addressed to humanity as a whole and infused with a spirit of what a prominent Muslim scholar calls "peaceful persuasion," in contrast to the compulsion by the sword.[21] It was in Medina that Mohammed heard God command the faithful to "fight and slay the pagans wherever you find them, and seize them, beleaguer them, and lie in wait for them in every stratagem [of war]."[22] This and other militant exhortations—which came to Mohammed as the leader of the city-state of Medina, when war was an essential part of statecraft—would be adopted by jihadists in the late twentieth and early twenty-first centuries. In the seventh century, however, their context, while militant, was more conventionally political and, indeed, geopolitical. They were part of the ideological ammunition of a community that was itself beleaguered by enemies and that, like Israel fourteen centuries before, had to fight for survival.

But there were also important distinctions in the political manifestation of Islam. In the community that Mohammed and his followers established, there was no divide between secular and religious authority. Nor, in theory at least, was the community defined by national identity or confined by any borders on the map. Unlike the Hebrew Scriptures, which speak of the "God of Abraham, Isaac, and Jacob," "the God of our fathers," and "the God of Israel," the Koran suggests no such familial, tribal, linguistic, or geographical limitations.

Christianity was comparably expansive and inclined to merge spiritual authority with political power, but it was three hundred years after the birth of Christ that the religion founded in his name became, with Constantine, the firm basis of earthly rule. It took Islam only a dozen years, and it happened not just during the Prophet's lifetime but as a result of his own ambition and skill. Unlike Jesus, for whom God's kingdom was "not of this world," Mohammed proclaimed, "I am the Messenger to you all of Him to whom belongs the kingdom of the heavens and the earth." [23] Mohammed was chieftain and priest, lawgiver and judge. In order to protect and extend the community of the faithful, or *umma*, he was also supreme commander, and his martial prowess turned out to be as impressive as his political skill and spiritual authority. [24]

This new monotheistic, universalistic religion spread with dizzying speed. With its claim on all aspects of life and its ability to impose discipline on scattered, warring bands, it quickly filled a theological and political void across a huge area. Mohammed's followers were not building a nation, a state, or an empire in the sense that we use those words today. Rather, they were establishing a domain where the reigning and uniting principle was submission to God, the one and only, making it a domain that should, in its ideal form, have no boundaries. By the time of his death, in 632, Mohammed had gathered under his authority most of the tribes of the Arabian peninsula.

Over the course of a century, Muslim warriors reached the Himalayas in the East and the Pyrenees in the West. A Berber chieftain who defeated the king of Castile dispatched cartloads of Christian heads to other cities in Spain. The mass decapitations were intended more to make clear who was now in charge than to punish adherents of other faiths or force their conversion to Islam. Far from abominating other religions, the Koran says that God sent messengers to all the peoples on earth, and it treats the multitude of faiths as building toward the perfection of Islam. Mohammed himself had set a precedent for relative tolerance when he captured the oasis town of Khaybar in northern Arabia in 629 and allowed the Jewish and Christian communities to live in peace and safety as long as they paid a religious tax. He wrote letters inviting the leaders of Egypt, Abyssinia, Byzantium, and Persia to accept Islam while emphasizing that Muslims' fellow "People of the Book"—Christians, Jews, and Zoroastrians—would not be forced to convert. [25]

THIS PRINCIPLE, HOWEVER, was often honored more in the breach than in the observance. Moses Maimonides, a towering figure in Jewish history, lived his exemplary life entirely under Muslim rule and experienced both the best and the worst of that world. At the time of his birth in the Spanish city of Cordoba in 1135, the Moors had, for the most part, sheathed their scimitars and were governing, rather than repressing or terrorizing, the locals. Christians and Jews were allowed to keep their heads as long as they bowed them to the emir. Philosophical inquiry was not subject to religious dogma. The great works of Greek thought, which had been largely lost to Europe in the chaos that accompanied the fall of the Roman Empire, were reintroduced to the continent under the Moors.[26] Science, too, thrived, in part because the Koran exhorted the faithful to indulge curiosity and reason.[27] The civil and religious rights of Jews were protected by Koranic law, and they had access to universities, libraries, hospitals, and public facilities. The notion that Islam is inherently obscurantist or intolerant is nonsense.

But in the hands of fanatics, Islam could, with its insistence on the unity between the secular and spiritual realms, serve as a basis for militant dogmatism, just as it has in our own time. When Maimonides was a teenager, a Berber sect, the Almohads ("those who proclaim the unity of God"), seized power in Iberia and North Africa and forced Jews and Christians to convert on pain of death. Maimonides' family was among the many who fled the Almohad repression. For five years, when the family lived in Fez, Maimonides feigned conversion and took the name Abu Imran Musa ibn Maymun. In one of his early interpretations of Jewish law, he determined it was permissible for Jews to pretend they had become Muslims and thereby stay alive, as long as they continued to adhere to their true faith in private.

Thus, under the Almohads, the Jews, already in what seemed permanent exile from their promised land, could only secretly worship their God and imagine their community. Yet despite the horrors perpetrated by the Almohads and others, Maimonides still considered the divide between Judaism and Islam narrower than the one between Judaism and Christianity. His reasoning was that Jews and Muslims both eschewed what they considered the idolatrous worship of icons like the cross and images like those of the Virgin Mary and the saints. Also, Muslims believed Mohammed to be only a prophet, a status that Jews could understand even if they did not accept it, while the Christians saw Jesus as the messiah, a belief that was unacceptable to the Jews.[28]

Once again, Maimonides and his family moved, finally coming to rest in Alexandria, where Alexander himself had encouraged Jews to settle.[29] Under the caliphs of the Fatimid dynasty and then under the suzerainty of the great

Kurdish warrior-chief Saladin, Egypt enjoyed a sustained period of prosperity, flourishing culture, and communal harmony—the third being a condition for the first two. (Saladin was equally protective of the Jews during the Crusades. When he reconquered Jerusalem from a French knight in 1187, he allowed those indigenous Jews lucky enough to have been merely expelled by the Crusaders to return and practice their religion in peace.)

Alexandria was the site of some twenty institutions of higher learning. It was there—in a land where the children of Israel had been persecuted by the pharaohs, but in a city named for the Greek conqueror who believed in an inclusive empire—that Maimonides attained lasting prominence as a sage and a position of leadership in the diaspora ("Our brethren of the House of Israel, scattered to the remote regions of the globe, it is your duty to strengthen one another, the older the younger, the few the many"), even as he made a decent living as personal physician to Saladin and his son.[30]

THE ABODES OF WAR AND PEACE

The Ottomans, who figured so oppressively in the resentments and insecurities of Brooke's and my Serbian neighbors in the 1970s, also often made tolerance of cultural diversity a principle of governance. They were descended from the Seljuk Turks, nomads from Central Asia who had migrated westward, converted to Islam in the tenth century, and taken control of much of the Byzantine Empire, leaving Constantine's successors with only western Anatolia and the Balkan peninsula. A Seljuk chieftain, Osman (1258–1324), founded a dynasty that bore his name and that is rendered in English as *Ottoman*. That word, however, came to connote neither a family, a place, a race, a nation, nor a language. For long periods, Greek was as much an Ottoman lingua franca as Turkish. "An Ottoman," writes Jason Goodwin in *Lords of the Horizons*, was "not born, but made."[31] The royal ministers (or viziers), bureaucrats, magistrates, courtiers, janissaries, and soldiers came from all over and traveled all over. The *Devlet-i Aliye-i Osmaniye*, or "Ottoman Sublime State," was a sturdy, expansive, and aggressively inclusive political construct.

For centuries the sultan was not just an absolute monarch—he was also the caliph, the supreme religious leader.[32] Like almost all overlords, the Ottomans were capable of great cruelty, especially when subduing new subjects and repressing uprisings. But in practice, much like the Romans, and for much the same reason, the Ottomans by and large granted their provinces a degree of political autonomy and cultural license commensurate with the variety of languages, races, and religions to be found in a realm that, at its height in the sixteenth century, encompassed about eight million square miles. The Ottomans believed in what they called the Circle of Justice, a concept they had inherited from the Seljuks: rulers depended on the army; raising an army depended on raising taxes; plentiful tax revenue depended on a contented populace; and the contentment of the populace depended on the effective—and equitable—dispensation of justice.[33]

Lands beyond the martial reach, and therefore the administrative control, of the Sublime Porte (as the sultan's court was known) were known as *Dar ul-Harb*, "The Abode of War." The Arabic term—which derived not from the Koran but from the politics of empire—suggested not just hostility on the part of those who lived there but their ripeness for conquest. Those who were already Ottoman inhabited what was called the *Dar ul-Islam*, a phrase usually translated as "The Abode of Peace," although *Islam* means "submission" as well. Even the linguistic ambiguity is instructive: to submit to the sultan— who wanted to be seen as ruling by the will of Allah—was to enjoy his protection, and the right to live in peace extended to the multitudinous and distinctive tribes and communities that made up the state. Many of those were Christians and Jews. Christians had to be careful not to build their churches with spires higher than the minarets of the nearby mosques, but they could worship freely. On a reporting trip to Syria in the late 1970s, I visited what had been the Ottoman province of Şam and saw the remains of the church of Saint Nicholas. "Under the Turks" (as the Serbs would say), it was used by Christians and Muslims alike. In that region and many others, there were long periods when Muslims recognized Christian saints.[34] As Goodwin notes, Ottoman Jews were "so free of ghetto pallor as to be practically unrecognizable" to visitors from western Europe.[35]

I have borne these snippets of history in mind when I have heard commentators blame political turmoil in the modern Middle East and Balkans on "ancient ethnic and religious hatreds." This cliché does an injustice to long periods when those regions were often an abode of peace for the ancestors of people who have been at one another's throats in recent decades. It also provides an alibi for the failure of contemporary leaders to create a postimperial version of the ecumenical state.

THE TWIN GIANTS

The legacies of Mohammed and Alexander had profound influence in Asia, although for different reasons. Mohammed's followers succeeded in spreading the universalistic faith he founded as far as Indonesia, while Alexander's attempt to extend his imperial reach into South Asia provided an incentive for those in his path to stop fighting among themselves and join forces against a common enemy.

According to legend, on reaching the Hyphasis River (today known as the Beas, in Pakistani Punjab), Alexander shed tears of frustration because there were no lands left for him to conquer. But historians (including Plutarch) believe that Alexander's exhausted and homesick Macedonian troops mutinied when they heard rumors that if they proceeded they would face a massive Indian army with cavalries mounted on elephants.[36] Alexander retreated through Persia and died soon afterward in Babylon.

If Alexander was an irresistible force, Chandragupta, a myth-shrouded hero of Indian history, was an immovable object. Believed to have been born poor into the warrior caste and brought up by peacock tamers, Chandragupta exploited the lingering threat of another invasion by the Greeks to assemble a war machine that he later used to unite India. After driving back the remnants of Alexander's army, Chandragupta recovered the Punjab and went on to found the Mauryan dynasty. Within two generations, its domain encompassed most of the subcontinent.

When I first visited India in 1974 as a reporter covering Secretary of State Henry Kissinger, I was struck by almost worshipful references to Chandragupta's grandson, Ashoka. He seemed to be one of those shining figures whose reputation is too good to be true, or at least entirely true. That may be because, as in the case of Hammurabi, most of what we know about Ashoka is deduced from edicts inscribed on pillars that he erected throughout his realm. A successful warrior who battled his brothers for his father's throne and added the modern state of Orissa to his domain, he is believed to have been seized with remorse over the bloodshed and suffering that came with imperial expansion. He renounced armed force, converted from Hinduism to Buddhism, and applied its spiritual precepts of moderation, tolerance, and nonviolence to statecraft.

Ashoka adopted a policy he called "conquest by *dharma*," a word that refers to Buddha's teachings about the virtuous life as the path to enlightenment. In governing his people, he sought to codify and institutionalize civility of public discourse, requiring "restraint in regard to speech, so that there should be no extolment of one's own sect or disparagement of other sects on inappropriate occasions, and it should be moderate even on appropriate occasions." Forceful argument on behalf of one's own position was fine, as long as "other sects should be duly honored in every way on all occasions." He also believed that logic and rationality rather than tradition should guide public administration.

If Ashoka practiced anything like what he preached, he was the closest thing in history to a philosopher king: he promulgated his commands

Emperor Ashoka

through powers of persuasion rather than coercion, showed mercy to his enemies, gave succor to the weak and the poor, celebrated the religious and ethnic differences among his subjects, protected animal rights, planted trees and established rest houses by roadsides, and dispatched diplomats and missionaries (including his own children) to neighboring kingdoms. After Ashoka's death, invasions, defections, and quarrels over succession took their toll on the territory over which he had ruled so benevolently.

Modern scholars, such as the Nobel Prize–winning economist and essayist Amartya Sen, see Ashoka's forty-one-year rule as a variant of Alexander's concept of *koinonia*, a wellspring of what is best in Indian society and democracy today, and a model for the rest of the world.[37]

NO HALO ADORNS the image of Ashoka's Chinese contemporary, Qin (pronounced "chin") Shihuangdi (meaning First Emperor). He was in many ways a central-casting despot—ruthless, paranoid, and self-aggrandizing. He traveled widely in search of the secret of eternal life. As a second-best option, he ordered that when he died he would be buried along with dozens of his concubines and retainers and thousands of life-size terra cotta soldiers and horses to protect his spirit in a massive tomb complex near the modern city of Xian. He united remnants of an earlier feudal regime, made up of independent and warring kingdoms, by scorched-earth conquest and wholesale repression. In order to preempt their protests against his policies, he buried alive hundreds of scholars. As part of a campaign to fortify China's northern frontier against rampaging nomads and other invaders, he is believed to have linked several fortifications into the beginnings of the Great Wall.

During one of my first visits to China—again, as a reporter covering Kissinger in the 1970s—the press corps was bused out from Beijing to see the wall while Kissinger met Mao Zedong. One of our group's barbarian-handlers, as we called our exceedingly cautious English-speaking guides, told me, in muted tones, that Mao, who was responsible for the deaths of as many as forty million of his own citizens and was still keeping China largely walled off from the world, regarded the Qin Emperor as "one of the great heroes in our history."

Qin Shihuangdi

But just as there may have been less to Ashoka's beneficence than his stone tablets would suggest, there was more to the Qin Emperor than tyranny, vanity, and xenophobia. He instituted a combination of bureaucratic governance and military rule based on merit rather than noble birth. Slaves who worked as farmers were liberated and allowed to own land. A system of standardized weights and measures, along with a uniform written language, was extended throughout the realm. So was a legal code, although it was enforced with great brutality.

The Qin Emperor's domain, like Alexander's and Ashoka's, fell into civil war upon his death. But within a decade the Han dynasty reunited China and retained many of the Qin Emperor's innovations: the system of forts and roads, the administrative division of the country into prefectures, and the standardization of writing, laws, and measurements—the hardware and software necessary for governing diverse and widely scattered peoples.

ANOTHER FIGURE WHOSE LEGACY shaped both India and China was Genghis Khan, founder of the largest contiguous empire of all time—at its height, nearly six times larger than the Roman Empire. During his life (ca. 1162–1227), Genghis united nomadic confederations called hordes into the Great Mongol Nation (or, more literally and evocatively, "the Great Mongol Tribal Commonwealth"), which stretched across the Gobi Desert and Siberian tundra, from Manchuria to the Altai Mountains in Central Asia. Genghis and his successors went on to extend a single regime, for the only time in history, over the entire length of the trade routes that linked the Far East, Persia, the Indian subcontinent, and Europe. That expanse of the earth's surface is now home to the majority of humanity, well over three billion people, including about thirty countries on today's map: in addition to India and China, the two Koreas, Iran, Iraq, Russia, most of the other former Soviet republics, and, briefly, Poland, Hungary, and eastern Germany—and, of course, Mongolia itself, which remained the core of the empire, the place to which chieftains would return when it was time to choose a new khan.[38]

The Mongols considered all other nations ripe for absorption within their seemingly ever-expanding borders.[39] Once the Mongols subdued all in their path, they settled down to an activity that did not come naturally: civil administration. "The empire," one of their noblemen said, "was created on horseback, but it cannot be governed on horseback."[40] Like the Romans and Ottomans, the Mongols tended to let obedient subjects maintain their cultural identity. Genghis Khan was a believer in meritocracy and a master of co-option. He would fold defeated armies into his own, quickly promoting the ablest of his former enemies and employing captured artisans to develop catapults and "ballistas" (huge crossbows that shot giant arrows, often tipped with flame) so that each siege could be more effective than the previous one. The Mongols left little of physical permanence in their wake (except, significantly, bridges), but they encouraged the invention of new technologies (such as combining European bell-casting with Chinese gunpowder-making to produce the cannon), innovations in commerce (the introduction of paper currency), and new ways of traveling and communicating over great distances (improvements in mapmaking and timekeeping and the introduction of a pony-express-like network of couriers).

Genghis Khan

The Mongols' protection of the Silk Road and other Eurasian trade routes ushered in more than a century known as the Great Mongol Peace. Jack Weatherford, an anthropologist and biographer of Genghis, writes that at the height of their power, the Mongols "displayed a devoutly and persistently in-ternationalist zeal in their political, economic, and intellectual endeavors. They sought not merely to conquer the world but to institute a global order based on free trade, a single international law, and a universal alphabet with which to write all languages." [41] They were, in short, agents of what eight hundred years later would be called globalization, in both its positive and nega-tive aspects (traffic along the Silk Road is believed to have introduced the bubonic plague, or "Black Death," to Europe, wiping out as much as a third of its population in the fourteenth century).

Genghis Khan asserted his right to reign in the name of the sky god Ten-giri, who "has given me the empire of the earth from east to west." [42] But he granted freedom of worship to his subjects. The principal incentive for a local Christian lord to capitulate to the Mongols was the certain knowledge that he and all his followers would be put to the sword if he refused. But he also had some confidence that if he submitted, he and his community would be allowed to practice their own faith. A Russian prince, in relinquishing the keys of Novgorod to one of Genghis's grandsons, Batu, said, "To thee, Czar, I bow, since God hath granted thee the sovereignty of this world." There was considerable irony packed into this pledge of fealty: a Christian, in recogniz-ing the suzerainty of a pagan khan, was addressing him by a title derived from the name of Julius Caesar.*

According to Weatherford, the Mongol capital of Karakorum—which today is a pastureland scattered with a few archeological remains on the bank of the Orhon River in central Mongolia—was, in the thirteenth century, "probably the most religiously open and tolerant city in the world at the time. Nowhere else could followers of so many different religions worship side by side in peace." [43]

GENGHIS KHAN WAS AS PHENOMENAL in procreation as he was in territorial aggrandizement. DNA evidence suggests that there may be more than sixteen million of his direct descendants living today in about thirty countries—a statistic that could serve as an advertisement for the benefits of compound interest as well as a spectacular refutation of the idea of ethnic and national purity. [44]

* Weatherford believes that the Mongol sympathy for Christianity can be explained, at least in part, by the coincidence of a similarity between the name *Jesus* and the Mongolian word for nine, a sacred number, as well as Yesugai (also spelled Yesügei), the name of Genghis Khan's father and the founder of the dynasty.

However, another consequence of Genghis's multiple offspring—dynastic rivalry—contributed to the dissolution, within three generations, of the empire he founded. The Mongols' penchant for adopting the techniques, customs, and institutions of those they conquered made them prone to becoming part of the sophisticated civilizations that they ruled. The two principal examples were the giant kingdoms forged by Ashoka and the Qin Emperor in the third century BCE.

About half a century after Genghis's death, another of his many grandsons, Kublai Khan, moved the Mongol court from Karakorum to the Chinese city of Shangdu (sometimes transliterated as Xanadu). Once he had conquered most of China, Kublai built a permanent capital two hundred miles south, on the site of present-day Beijing. From there, his lineage ruled as the Yuan dynasty. While Mao Zedong dismissed Genghis as a nomad "who only knew how to draw his bow at the eagles," by 2006 the Chinese were officially celebrating the Mongol conqueror as one of their own national heroes.[45]

ANOTHER DESCENDANT of Genghis Khan, Akbar, was the greatest of the emperors of India known as the Moguls. The word *Mogul* comes from the Persian for Mongol, since the Moguls' roots were traceable to Timur (often called Tamerlane), a Turkic warlord of Mongol ancestry whose hordes poured from Central Asia westward into Anatolia, southward into Persia, and eastward across northern India.

Akbar

Akbar's reputation in India for combining conquest with conciliation is not quite as rosy as Ashoka's. That is partly because he was from a line of alien conquerors, a Muslim autocrat presiding over a Hindu majority, while Ashoka is commonly regarded as a native son and a practitioner of two homegrown religions, Hinduism and Buddhism. Also, Akbar lived nineteen hundred years after Ashoka, so we know much more about the often merciless methods he used to bring Gujarat, Kashmir, Sind, and Bengal into his domain.[46]

Still, Akbar was a visionary who initiated an array of reforms to institutionalize tolerance and communal harmony. These included a high degree of autonomy for provinces; direct imperial appointment of governors who were punished if they abused power or mistreated the poor and the weak; a bureaucracy open to members of all faiths; freedom of worship and respect for dietary and other laws of various religious communities; and the repeal of a tax on non-Muslims.

Like Alexander the Great and Genghis Khan, Akbar believed in the blending of gene pools. Many of his hundreds of concubines were Hindu princesses, and the first of his four official wives was a Rajput, from the zealously independent and martial Hindu elites of Rajasthan.

While believed to be illiterate, Akbar displayed a capacious curiosity about the wisdom available from other religions. Like Kublai Khan, Akbar welcomed Jesuit priests in his courts, and he established what amounted to multifaith discussion groups in a special facility called the *Ibadat Khana* (literally, "place of worship"). Under the influence of a Sufi mystic, Akbar experimented with a fusion of Hinduism and Islam called *Din-i-Ilahi* ("Divine Faith"). By building his capital near Delhi, he sought to interweave Hindu and Muslim architectural styles, commissioned the translation of Sanskrit classics into Persian, and loosened Muslim strictures on music and the visual arts so that his people, whatever their faith, could appreciate the influence of the Renaissance that was then at its height in Europe.[47]

THUS, A PAIR OF HISTORICALLY, culturally, and genetically connected Asiatic regimes fostered practices and institutions that held together over the centuries. The people living north of the Himalayas came to call themselves Chinese and now number well over a billion. An almost equal number of people on the southern side of that mountain range have long since come to think of themselves as Indians. India and China each qualify as a civilizational state, a polity that has proved more durable than the empires that have risen and fallen within their boundaries. At the beginning of the twenty-first century, more than a third of the 6.5 billion people on earth are governed from two capitals, Beijing and New Delhi. That fact weighs in favor of the argument that a single system of governance can encompass vast and diverse populations. Moreover, given the economic dynamism that marks India's and China's emergence as major powers, "the East" is poised to break the near monopoly that "the West"—Europe and North America—have had in setting the rules and running the institutions of global governance for the past several hundred years.

THE POET AND "THE PRINCE"

Europe wasted her time for thousands of years; that is where her inexhaustibility and fertility comes from. . . . The Creator of Europe made her small and even split her up into little parts, so that our hearts could find joy not in size but in plurality.
—*KAREL ČAPEK*[1]

Purity of race does not exist. Europe is a continent of energetic mongrels.
—*HERBERT ALBERT LAURENS FISHER*[2]

EUROPE, too, is a civilization, but not until the middle of the twentieth century did its leaders buckle down to the task of making it into their own version of a civilizational state. Their successors still have a long way to go in that project. But, then, the Europeans started late. When the pharaoh Khufu was building the largest of the pyramids at Giza in the twenty-sixth century BCE, the region bounded by the North Sea, the Atlantic, the Mediterranean, and the Black Sea was populated by pastoral nomads. When Hammurabi was promulgating his code in the eighteenth century BCE, the inland tribes north of the Alps were just making the transition from stone to bronze tools. And when Ashoka was applying Buddhist principles to the governance of the Indian subcontinent and the Qin Emperor was starting work on the Great Wall in the third century BCE, Nordic sun-worshippers were working their way south and making contact with Celtic tribes that would teach them how to make implements of iron.

In 1981, I attended a lecture by the renowned French historian Fernand Braudel when he came to Yale to receive an honorary degree. He used a phrase that stuck in my mind and that I later found in his *History of Civilizations:* Europe, he said, was "a peninsula of Asia."[3] Even when its inhabitants finally came to think of themselves as occupying a continent of their own, they tacitly acknowledged their Asiatic origins. In Greek mythology, Zeus swooped down from Olympus, found a Phoenician princess, Europa, and carried her off to Crete. Aeneas, the founder of Rome, was a refugee from the ruins of Troy, on the coast of Asia Minor. Christianity was an import from even farther to the east and south. As Anthony Pagden neatly summarizes it: "An abducted Asian woman gave Europe her name; a vagrant Asian exile gave Europe its political and finally its cultural identity; and an Asian prophet gave Europe its religion."[4]

AND, PAGDEN MIGHT HAVE ADDED, Asian invaders gave Europe a sense of a common danger, which accelerated the pace at which that Asian-born religion, Christianity, came to be at the core of European culture and politics.

When Samuel Huntington popularized the catchphrase "clash of civilizations" in the 1990s, he was using it in a global context.[5] But the term could just as well have pertained to the consolidation of modern Europe in the Middle Ages. Civilizations define themselves not just in the way they evolve internally but also in the way they clash with others, even if the result entails as much absorption as conquest. So it was with Europe.

The first major threat was from the Huns in the fourth and fifth centuries CE. Their thunderous arrival along the northern frontier of the Roman Empire accelerated its decline. Like *Rom*, the Gypsies' Sanskrit name for themselves, *Hun* (and the related Chinese word *Han*) simply meant "man" or "human being." The Western history course I took at Hotchkiss depicted the Huns as "barbarians," with that word's implication of violent, pagan, bloodthirsty marauders, usually from the dark lands to the east. Yet that word, too, was originally neutral. *Barbarian* meant simply a foreigner whose language and customs differ from those of the speaker—i.e., someone not from around here. It comes from *bar-bar*, which is how the Greeks, mimicking the sound of sheep, parodied stuttering.[6] In their day, however, the Huns were seen as a terrifying combination of subhuman and superhuman. Attila, the most notorious of their chieftains, was called "the Scourge of God." As the Huns swept from the steppes of Central Asia into southeastern, then central Europe, they displaced the Franks, the Germanic people along the Rhine from whom the modern French took their name (itself an irony, given that Franco-German hostility would very nearly be the undoing of modern Europe). The Huns conquered Gaul and swept southward, followed by Visigoths, Vandals, Ostrogoths, and Lombards.

In the fifth century, Romulus Augustulus—his second name was a diminutive because he was a teenager whose father ruled in his name for the year of his reign—was the last Roman emperor in the West. A hundred years later the Eastern Emperor Flavius Phocas Augustus, his own realm crumbling, elevated Boniface III, the patriarch of Rome, to a position of primacy over the other major bishops of the Christian world—those in Antioch, Alexandria, and Constantinople—and bestowed on him the title Vicar of Christ, or Pope. By then, Rome's population—which at its peak, three hundred years earlier, had been nearly a million—had been reduced to around a twentieth of that.

While the barbarians did plenty of the sacking and pillaging that indelibly defined them for posterity, many of them settled peacefully in lands that had been abandoned by the Romans. "Invasion" was often what today we would call migration, the search for a better life. Norse raiders would surge all the way to the Mediterranean and to the Slavic heartland in what is now Ukraine. Like earlier waves from the east, these northern tribes set down roots that became entwined with those of the indigenous peoples and earlier invaders. Their warrior-kings converted to Christianity and made alliances with Boniface's successors.

Here was a perfect example of how religion came to be inextricably bound up with identity, community, and security. One God, represented on earth by one church, would protect those who worshipped him. But to deserve that protection, they had to obey God's bishops and those who ruled in his name. It was medieval Europe's equivalent of the compact between Adam and Eve and their creator, and of the one between the Israelites and their God. But there was a difference. The covenant of Eden was personal; the covenant of Israel was familial and, by extension, tribal; the covenant of Europe extended to various tribes, or protonations, speaking different languages, occupying and defending different homelands, but also defending a common faith.

Nations' flags often derive from those that their ancestors carried into battle. That explains why, at the beginning of the twenty-first century, no less than ten of the nations that make up today's highly secularized and pluralistic Europe fly flags that feature the cross (Britain's Union Jack and those of all five Nordic countries, and of Greece, Switzerland, Malta, and Slovakia). In 2004, Georgia provided another example: knocking on the door of NATO and European Union, Georgia's impatiently pro-Western new government reinstated a flag that incorporates in its design *five* crosses.

· · ·

CHARLEMAGNE'S FLAG was another symbol from Christian iconography: the fleur-de-lis, a lily associated with baptism and the Virgin Mary. Charlemagne came from a line of Frankish warrior-kings. His grandfather, Charles Martel, had stopped the Moors' advance from Spain into France at the Battle of Tours in 732 and, seven years later, driven the Muslims out of the Rhône valley. The realm that Charlemagne founded on Christmas Day in 800 would come to be known as the Holy Roman Empire, a massive but rickety polity that Voltaire and future historians would disparage as a triple misnomer. Yet it would endure until the early nineteenth century and extend over most of central and western Europe.*

Charlemagne himself lived long enough to hear himself hailed as *pater Europae* (father of Europe) and *caput orbis* (head of the world), titles that were, in the minds of his subjects, nearly synonymous.[7] Today, the *Economist* runs a regular column on European affairs under the pseudonymous byline Charlemagne, and the German city of Aachen, once the great man's capital, awards an annual prize in his memory for service to the cause of European unity.

Yet what Charlemagne built began to crack within decades of his death. One cause was the usual bickering and bloodletting over succession. Another was an absence of sturdy institutions of national governance. Charlemagne had been able to tame dissension and forge tribal alliances through ambition, vision, and luck. His successors could not maintain what he built. Imperialism of the kind perfected by the Romans—with its sophisticated, effective administrative structures, its elaborate system of laws, and its mobile, disciplined military—had long since gone the way of the caesars. Europe was now so beset with disasters, plagues, and impoverishment that, in Braudel's words, it "could not bear the weight of very large States. They were no sooner formed than they collapsed or crumbled."[8]

The turmoil and decay of that period had the unintended consequence of clearing the ground of old forms of social and political organization and preparing the way for new ones. Local lords provided their peasants with protection, including from faraway popes and emperors, in exchange for labor. In addition to ordering the economic ties between those who owned the land and those who worked it, the feudal system provided a degree of security and stability.

---

* The term *Sacrum Romanum Imperium* dated from 1157, when the emperor Frederick I ("Barbarossa") sought to challenge the authority of the pope by adding the first word to the other two, which his predecessors had used to invoke for themselves the glory that was Rome.

The German invaders who had conquered the Western Roman Empire in the fifth century substituted their own armies for the Roman legions they destroyed. Warriors served their chieftains for honor and booty. A variant of this web of political and military loyalties among the nobility helped keep medieval Europe from disintegrating with the fall of Charlemagne's empire.

Braudel and other historians saw in these bargains an early version of the social contract at the national level. Over time, rigid, exploitative, and hierarchical arrangements would give way to more egalitarian and meritocratic forms of communal organization, and the newly wealthy and empowered burgher class would challenge the aristocracy and the clergy, often in alliance with the peasantry.[9]

But this process was marked by lapses into tyranny and chaos. The establishment of a judiciary, the rule of law, equitable taxation, parliamentary representation, and the other necessities for democracy all came slowly and painfully.

This was a lesson of history that I tried, not always as vividly as I should have, to keep in mind when I was involved at the State Department during the 1990s in ventures known, simplistically, as "nation-building" and "democracy-promotion." These terms, bursting with can-do Yankee optimism, are deceptive since they refer to tasks that have, in Western history, taken decades to begin and centuries to accomplish.

FIENDS FROM HELL

As the Dark Ages gave way to the Middle Ages, once again a galvanizing factor in the consolidation of Europe was the looming presence on the edge of Europe of rapacious outsiders. Before it had been the Huns; this time it was the forces of expansionist Islam. Even though in its origins Islam was intimately related to Christianity, it was seen in the heart of Europe as alien and evil, "the Great Other." In the face of this threat, Europeans felt that whatever their national and other differences, they all belonged to "Christendom." That word shares a suffix with *kingdom* and thus conjures up the image of a well-armed and sternly governed community of the faithful—much like the Islamic *umma*. Defending the faith meant not just protecting the lands where the faithful lived but recapturing those that had been, with the withering away of the Byzantine Empire, absorbed into an expanding Islamic civilization.

The Crusades were the most dramatic and sustained case in history of an expeditionary war waged on religious grounds. They drew to the cause of liberating the Holy Land tens of thousands of soldiers and camp followers from kingdoms and principalities all over Europe during the course of three centuries. The venture repeatedly failed in its objective. But it enriched and empowered whoever sat on the throne of Saint Peter, and it made the Vatican the capital of what amounted to a theocratic supermonarchy.

The papal blessing for a crusade against the foreign infidel stoked the determination of the church and its allies to eradicate apostasy and resistance to the church's authority within Europe itself. Of all the atrocities committed in the name of God—and they were legion—one of the most prolonged and brutal was a twenty-year campaign, in the late twelfth and early thirteenth centuries, to exterminate a sect of ascetics called Cathars or Albigensians (after their principal city, Albi, in southern France). The Cathars rejected a number of church doctrines and criticized clerical corruption. That made them the enemy within, a perceived threat to the internal security of Christendom, hence all the more a target for extermination. When infantry troops raised by the barons of northern France approached the Cathar town of Béziers in 1209, their commanders asked the papal representative accompanying them how they should distinguish heretics from true believers. "Kill them all," he replied, "God will know his own."[10] In Béziers alone, about twenty thousand died, including more than a thousand women and children who had taken refuge in the Church of Saint Mary Magdalene.

DURING THAT BENIGHTED PERIOD, while the warriors of the Third and Fourth Crusades were trying and by and large failing to liberate the Holy Land, Europe sustained a wave of Mongol incursions that reached all the way to the Adriatic. Like their Hunnish ancestors, the Mongols were seen as fiends from hell, sent, many believed, by God to punish impious Crusaders for having plundered sacred relics. If a walled town or castle resisted the khans' demand for surrender, everyone inside was slaughtered. One of the few words to find its way from the Mongols' language into English is *hurrah*, the cheer with which they celebrated the fall of yet another besieged city. The hordes killed tens of thousands of European knights, a depletion of the medieval elite that further devastated the feudal aristocracy.

The Golden Horde reached its point of deepest penetration into the West in 1241. Just as the Mongols were finding pasturage for their horses scarce in the plains of Hungary, word came that Genghis Khan's son and heir, Ögödei, had died; so, taking his army with him, the leader of the invading horde returned to Karakorum for a council to elect a new great khan.[11]

WHAT TURNED OUT TO BE A LUCKY YEAR for Europe was anything but that for its Jews. Descendants of that ancient tribe that had formed one of the earliest of nations were too far removed, in time and place, from their original homeland to have the protection that comes with nationhood. The year 1241 happened to be the year 5000 in the Jewish calendar, which begins with the creation of Adam. Since European pseudoscience of the age tended to give millennial round numbers apocalyptic significance, church scholars concocted a theory to explain the ravages inflicted by the Golden Horde: the Mongols, it was suggested, were a lost tribe of Israel, bent on revenge for the Babylonian Captivity, and they were about to take over the world. The Jews, therefore, must have been a fifth column of a militant conspiracy, "the alien in our midst," a scapegoat for whatever went wrong, including Mongol invasions. Massacring small, peaceful communities of Jews on the edge of European towns was infinitely easier and safer than trekking to the edge of Europe itself and taking on the real invaders.

The Mongol retreat did little to diminish the frenzy of European anti-Semitism. The pretext for persecuting Jews was variable, but persecution itself was a constant. If fantasies failed, facts came in handy. Christ, after all, had been sentenced to death by his fellow Jews, so that made them Christ-killers. Since the Jews were determined to maintain their own culture, with their own religion at its core—and since that meant they did not follow the forms and rules of the One True Church—how could they be counted on for allegiance to the state? From the late thirteenth to the mid-fourteenth centuries, England, France, and the various German kingdoms and principalities forcibly expelled their Jews. At the end of the fifteenth century, when King Ferdinand II and Queen Isabella drove the Moors out of Spain and back into North Africa, many Jews accompanied the Muslims into exile. In yet another instance of Ottoman pragmatic multiculturalism, the sultans of the time invited Jews expelled from Spain to settle in Izmir, Thessalonica, Edirne, and Istanbul. Those who accepted the hospitality of the Abode of Peace were spared having to submit to a royal edict that gave Spanish Jews a choice between converting to Christianity or subjecting themselves as heretics to the Spanish Inquisition.

HUMANISM IN LIMBO

During the life of Dante Alighieri—in the second half of the thirteenth century and the first two decades of the fourteenth—the forces of European religion and politics combined in ways that seemed almost designed to stoke the flames of intolerance, cruelty, corruption, and conflict. The popes and monarchs of the Holy Roman Empire had settled into a symbiosis that made it easy for them, along with those who enjoyed their favor, to accumulate wealth, settle scores, eliminate rivals, and exploit the lower classes. Abuse of power was a recurring incitement to rebellion, which in turn provoked repression and reprisal. Thus, Christendom was not only a fortress against external enemies, particularly those who worshipped Allah—it was, within its walls, the scene of nonstop brawls among Christian sects and savage treatment of non-Christian minorities.

Repelled by this aspect of his own time, Dante was a paragon of the early Renaissance in both his selective nostalgia for the past and his vision of the

Dante

future. He admired the original Roman Empire and, in particular, the reign of Caesar Augustus (63 BCE–14 CE), which restored unity and orderly government after a century of civil wars, and he believed that there had to be a better set of ideas on which to base the way we live on earth, even as we prepare ourselves for the kingdom to come. Dante earned his place in world literature in part because of his ability to imagine communities. In *The Divine Comedy,* he accompanies Virgil on a tour through a hierarchy of communities—the Inferno, Purgatory, and Paradise—inhabited by the souls of those who lived in the past. In his political writings, he imagines a future where the living might inhabit a community of nations united in peace by a single system of governance.

From the scattered shards of information we have about Dante's life, we know that he was caught up in outbreaks of civil war over the rights of the nobility and the degree of self-rule granted to the Italian city-states. As a twenty-four-year-old in 1289, he fought in the battle of Campaldino and the siege of Carpona, in which armed rabble, loosely organized infantrymen, knights, and mounted lancers hacked away at one another while crossbow-men contributed to the carnage from the flanks. Later, Dante participated vigorously in Florentine politics, serving as an elected prior of the city and an ambassador to the Papal See.

Paying the price for choosing the losing side in one of the factional strug-gles of the time, he was banished from Florence and threatened with being burned alive if he returned. His writings make clear that he was revolted by the propensity of politicians to let their ambitions and jealousies erupt into violence. He developed a conviction that war could be eradicated only if there were a system of governance that held rivalries in check and provided an incentive for cooperation among factions, city-states, and nations. In exile, he remained intermittently active in politics and diplomacy. During a mission as Ravenna's ambassador to Venice, in 1321, he contracted malaria and died at the age of fifty-six.[12]

DANTE SAW EUROPE as an ecumenical civilization, a light unto the world. "European Union" was not just a concept Dante might have imag-ined—it was a reality that he believed already existed in culture and lan-guage, one that could, with wise leadership, be extended to civic life and political institutions.

In a treatise he wrote in 1305, he used the story of Babel to support his op-timism. By destroying the Tower, God punishes the Babylonians for their ar-rogance, but that does not mean he is condemning humankind to be forever divided into small, polyglot, and warring units. Quite the contrary: since the story begins with the premise that humanity once spoke a single language, it stands to reason that Europeans, whose ancestors lived in Babel, speak what are really dialects of "the same idiom."[13]

Six years later, Dante wrote a political tract titled *On Monarchy*. It is osten-sibly a tribute to Henry VII, the latest in a line of Germanic kings who had taken the title of Holy Roman Emperor from Charlemagne's Frankish heirs. In the document, Dante laments the natural belligerence of mortals and ap-peals for supernatural help: "O humanity, in how many storms must you be tossed, how many shipwrecks must you endure, so long as you turn yourself into a many-headed beast lusting after a multiplicity of things! . . . 'Behold how good and pleasant it is for brethren to dwell together in unity.' "

That unity, Dante believed, need not be confined to Europe. Dante imag-ined all the kingdoms of the world under a global emperor who would pre-side over a "universal peace [that] is the most excellent means of securing our happiness."[14] As the title of the work suggested and the times demanded, Dante accepted monarchy as the natural and necessary form of governance at the highest level—a "model for rulership of the world."[15] But at lower levels, he suggested, leaders might be "raised to office by the consent of others." In other words, they could be elected.

Dante's decision to write *The Divine Comedy* not in Latin but in the *volgare* (also called Tuscan), an early version of modern Italian then spoken by the common people, reflected his desire to democratize literature. A similar impulse shaped his view of a self-governing world: "When we say 'humankind can be ruled by one supreme prince,' we do not mean to say that minute decisions concerning every township can proceed directly from him. . . . For nations, kingdoms and cities have different characteristics which demand different laws for their government, laws being intended as a concrete rule of life."

Administrative power would thus pass to regional and subregional units. Dante was advocating federalism four hundred years before the term was invented.

For someone of his era, Dante also took a distinctively tolerant and inclusive view of both life on earth and the afterlife. He did not explicitly challenge the Catholic insistence on assigning all non-Christians to hell, although in the *Inferno* the great pagan philosophers suffer the lightest possible sentence: they are consigned to Limbo. It is there that Dante encounters, in addition to Aristotle, Socrates, and Plato, such Hebrew patriarchs as Abraham, Noah, and King David, as well as shining examples of the Islamic Renaissance in the eleventh and twelfth centuries: the Arabian philosopher-physician Avicenna and the astronomer-jurist Averroës. Dante pretends to be surprised—and intends his readers to be genuinely so—when he comes across "fierce" Saladin in Limbo.[16] By putting the nemesis of Richard the Lion Heart and the protector of the Jews of Jerusalem in the company of great figures from the history and legends of the West, Dante may be telling us what he thought of the popes' habit of waging holy war in the Holy Land.*

DANTE WAS ONE OF THE FIRST and most illustrious figures identified with humanism, a term that suggests expansive values and affinities that

---

* Dante's dispensation for Muslims had its limits. In canto 28 of the *Inferno*, Dante sees the Prophet Mohammed in the Eighth Circle of Hell, where schismatics undergo eternal disembowelment ("rent from the chin to where one breaketh wind," in Henry Wadsworth Longfellow's translation).

trump those of tribe or nation. More narrowly defined, humanism was an intellectual and cultural movement that sought to revive classical learning and speculative inquiry. Beginning in Italy during the early Renaissance and working its way north, it was a reaction to the dominant philosophical school of the Middle Ages, known as scholasticism, which reinforced the absolute and universal authority of the Catholic Church. According to their humanist critics, the scholastics ignored large and meaningful questions while squabbling over trivial ones. The best-known, much-ridiculed though semi-apocryphal example is the debate over how many angels can dance on the head of a pin.*

Seen more broadly, humanism was an antidote to the dangers, so apparent in medieval and modern European history, of giving religious dogma the upper hand in civic and political life. Even at its best, dogma is an obstacle to common sense and inclusive, deliberative, and consultative governance; at its worst, it legitimates inquisitions and royal orders to slaughter innocents and infidels. Humanism is the friend of rationality, learning, individuality, and tolerance. That makes it the enemy of dogma. Therefore, during the Renaissance and afterward, humanists were vulnerable to punishment and extirpation at the hands of church and state.

On matters of faith, at least initially, humanists tended to accept religious doctrine; but, in the realm of visible phenomena, they trusted their powers of observation and reason. When Galileo peered through a telescope in the first decade of the seventeenth century and saw evidence in support of the Copernican theory that the earth and other planets revolved around the sun, he believed he was learning about the laws of the natural universe, not violating the laws of the church. But the Inquisition rejected the distinction between astronomy and theology and pronounced Galileo "suspect of heresy," in effect allowing him to plea-bargain: by renouncing Copernicus, Galileo escaped a death sentence and spent the rest of his life confined to a villa in the hills above Florence.

LIKE GALILEO, most of those historical figures who today are associated with the flowering of humanism were by no means irreligious, nor, in many cases, were they anti-Catholic. Desiderius Erasmus—the widely traveled

---

* Semi-, but not entirely apocryphal. In his *Summa Theologiae*, Thomas Aquinas poses the question, "Whether several angels can be at the same time in the same place?" and goes on to ruminate at great length on the answer.

Dutch scholar who helped enrich the intellectual life of northern Europe with his knowledge of the Italian Renaissance—was educated in monastic schools, studied scholastic philosophy, and was an ordained priest. Yet he was his era's quintessential citizen of the world, so reverent toward the ancients that he rhetorically beatified a pagan: "Saint Socrates, pray for us!" he exclaimed in an essay making the case that Christians had much to learn from pre-Christian sages.[17]

Another of the great humanists, Thomas More, achieved literal sainthood, but he did so in the realm of politics: he was martyred on a charge of treason rather than heresy. As a young man, More abandoned the contemplative life of a monastery and entered Parliament. For much of his career, he managed, by force of intellect, competence, and charm, to gain and, until near the end of his life, retain the favor of Henry VIII. Largely for that reason, he won a knighthood, membership on the Privy Council, and, ultimately, the post of lord chancellor. While holding increasingly high public office and enjoying friendship with the king, More criticized the way society was organized— and, by extension, the way the state was governed.

More undertook a long diplomatic assignment in Antwerp to help negotiate commercial and diplomatic treaties for England as it took early steps toward integrating its commercial and political interests with those of the continent. In Flanders he solidified a friendship with Erasmus, who called him a "man for all seasons."[18] While on that mission, More started writing a description of life on a fictitious island that, unlike his native England, encouraged communal property, universal education, civic peace, and religious tolerance. He titled the work *Utopia*, from the Greek for "No-Place." In the following centuries, that word would be used to sneer at idealism and, eventually, at the dream of world peace and world government. But in More's use of the word there was an implication that idealism and realism could be reconciled in the minds and actions of wise and successful leaders—and that, in a world they led, while evil could not be eliminated, it could at least be mitigated.

More's downfall came when he refused to support King Henry's insistence that the pope annul his marriage to Catherine of Aragon so that he could take the second of his six wives, Anne Boleyn. Excommunicated, Henry repudiated papal jurisdiction over the religious institutions of England. Henry had More beheaded for his refusal to recognize the supremacy of his monarch over his pope.

The very name of what became the Church of England underscored the extent to which the idea of the universal church was giving way to the reality of religion in the service of the will of a national sovereign. The instruction I received as a child in Episcopalian Sunday school downplayed the unedifying origin of our mother church in a randy king's partiality for multiple divorces and decapitations.

It took the passage of four hundred years and the succession of forty popes for the church finally to canonize More. That happened in 1935, when the beginning of Hitler's crackdown on the Catholic clergy in Germany led the Vatican to reevaluate the significance of More's having stood up to another political authority, in Hampton Court. When I read Peter Ackroyd's biography of More, it occurred to me that if Sir/Saint Thomas had lived in Rome rather than in London, he probably would have ended up in as much trouble with the pope of the time, Clement VII, as he did with King Henry VIII—and with the same fatal result. He was, after all, by temperament a contrarian, by political bent a liberal, and by profession a lawyer, for whom rigorous argument was a noble and necessary exercise of the God-given capacity of reason.[19]

A HOUSE DIVIDED

Humanists tended to view the persecutions swirling around them either as sincere but misguided attempts to defend the faith from heresy or as cynical exploitations of religious doctrine to attain political power. Whatever the motivation of the Inquisition and other enforcements of church teachings and rulings, the consequences were, in the humanist view, an offense against the values inherited from the ancients and reinforced by Christ's teachings.

Humanism was an assertion of the right and the ability of the individual to think for himself, including on the question of where rationality ends and faith begins. It was, at least by extension, an affirmation of the sovereignty of the citizen as opposed to that of the ruler. That made it a source of ideas that eventually found a home in the institutions of liberal democracy within states and that would inform the effort to imagine, then to build a peaceful international system.

Precisely because humanists believed open-minded questions should elicit rational answers, keepers of the faith and their secular allies were not imagining—or for that matter, exaggerating—the threat humanism posed to the established order. By the sixteenth century, humanists were all the more inclined to challenge the intellectual authority of an institution whose moral authority was in decline. With the church's power had come corruption, and with corruption on high came demands for reform from below. The canonical answers cruelly enforced by popes and cardinals began to elicit not obedience but skeptical questions posed by turbulent priests.

In the sixteenth century, much as in the first century, the might of Rome, now personified by a pope rather than a caesar, was shaken by a young preacher in the far reaches of the empire. In 1517, in the German city of Wittenberg on the Elbe, Martin Luther, a district vicar and professor of theology, promulgated his Ninety-Five Theses attacking papal and clerical abuses, such as the selling of church offices and get-out-of-Purgatory-free passes known as indulgences.

What Luther intended as a religious protest played into the economic and political resentments of the German commercial classes and the peasantry against the princes and higher clergy. Without intending to do so—and to his subsequent dismay and fury—Luther became an inspiration to a popular revolution that erupted into widespread violence. In 1525, he published a pamphlet with a title that let his feelings be known: *Against the Murdering, Thieving Hordes of Peasants*. Beyond denouncing the uprisings, he called for harsh reprisals, but he had little restraining influence. The Reformation, aside from the many beneficial results that justified its name, also contributed to a frenzy of bloodletting in the sixteenth and seventeenth centuries. The revolt against German power, wealth, and privilege quickly spread southward, much as German nobility itself had done in the seven centuries since Charlemagne.

OF ALL THE CONNECTED, inbred, yet contending royal families, the one that occupied the most thrones over the longest period was the Hapsburgs. Their characteristically jut-jawed visages adorn the walls of museums, palaces, castles, and manor houses across Europe and represent thirty-three generations, from a Germanic nobleman called Guntram the Rich, who ruled near the Aar River in what today is northern Switzerland in the tenth century, to the grandchildren of the family's patriarch as of 2007, Otto von Hapsburg, the son of the dynasty's last monarch, Emperor Karl I of Austria, who died in 1922.*

The power of the Hapsburgs reached its apogee, then began its decline in

---

* Otto von Hapsburg, who was ninety-four in 2007, served from 1979 until 1999 in the European Parliament. He also headed the International Pan-European Union, which promotes European integration.

the first half of the sixteenth century under Charles V, a neurasthenic and feckless grandson of Ferdinand and Isabella. For much of his life, he was king of Spain, king of the Netherlands, and Holy Roman Emperor. That made him the ostensible master of about three-quarters of Western Europe.[20]

According to the globes of the day, Charles was much more than that. Explorers and adventurers, with merchants and missionaries in their wake, had, for a century, been setting off from Florence, Venice, Milan, Genoa, and Barcelona, planting the Hapsburg flag throughout much of the world. Charles was also, therefore, proclaimed "Ruler of Africa and Asia and Sovereign of the Indies and the Mainland of the Ocean Sea." The last part of that mouthful was a reference to a cluster of islands and a continent that a German cartographer suggested naming after the Florentine navigator Amerigo Vespucci, who had recently accompanied an expedition across the Atlantic.

For all his titular grandeur, Charles was an unhappy potentate whose reign ended in abdication. He was defeated not so much by his enemies on the battlefield or intriguers in his various courts (although he had plenty of both) as by the burden that came with royal birth. He was exhausted by rivalry with France, which frequently flared into war, and by uprisings in Germany. Meanwhile, as the Reformation gathered momentum, the "holiness" of the empire—the legitimacy conferred on the emperor by the pope—steadily eroded. Protestantism became an increasingly potent challenge to Catholicism's claim to being what the historian Antony Black has called "an international, indeed universal society [that] nobody questioned."[21]

Worn down by conflict and defiance within Europe, Charles failed to form an effective alliance against the Ottomans, who were pounding on the door of Europe with battering rams. In 1521—less than three decades after the expulsion of the Moors from Spain by Charles's grandparents, Ferdinand and Isabella—the armies of Suleiman (known to his own people as the Magnificent) wrested Belgrade from Hungarian rule. That was one of the last steps in the imposition of the "Turkish yoke" on southeastern Europe that Brooke and I would hear so much about when we lived in Serbia in 1971–72.

In the baleful decade of the 1550s Charles gave up his various crowns. He relinquished the Netherlands and Spain to his son Philip II, then announced his intention to abdicate the imperial throne in favor of his brother, Ferdinand I. At fifty-six, Charles retired to a monastery and died soon after, gluttonous and batty, playing with elaborate clockwork devices. If the careers of Alexander, Mohammed, Charlemagne, and Luther support Carlyle's Great Man theory of history, the hapless Charles V illustrates the far more common phenomenon of rulers who are vested with immense power yet are overwhelmed by forces they neither understand nor control.

IN PROVIDING IMAGES of what it was like to live during Charles's reign, art helps bring history to life. The dilapidation of the House of Hapsburg and the savagery perpetrated in its name are depicted in the work of Pieter Bruegel the Elder, who lived in Antwerp and Brussels in the decade when the Duke of Alva, a tyrannical Spanish nobleman and general, viciously crushed local revolts. The duke set up a kangaroo court called the Council of Troubles that sentenced thousands to death or imprisonment. Bruegel had friends and patrons who were arrested and tortured for their religious beliefs and political activism, and he witnessed the execution of several. During Bruegel's last illness, he instructed his wife to destroy many of his works lest they endanger her after his death. Among the surviving drawings and paintings are *The Triumph of Death,* a landscape filled with corpses and wheels on which bodies have been broken, and *The Massacre of the Innocents,* which sets King Herod's killing of the firstborn Jewish males in the Dutch countryside, with Roman soldiers in Hapsburg uniforms.

Bruegel also used his talent to appeal for rationalism, religious tolerance, and civil discourse. The most notable example is a drawing called *Temperance,* which shows, on one side of a busy scene, three figures clearly intended to be recognized as a Jew, a Catholic, and a Protestant. They are surrounded by accoutrements of science and culture, and they are engaged in vigorous debate of the kind that humanists were advocating as an alternative to the more common practice of resolving interfaith disputes with the sword, the ax, the rack, and the stake.

In addition to being a patriot of Flanders, Bruegel—like Erasmus and Thomas More—was a modern European. He spent much of his life crossing borders and incorporating into his own thinking and sensibility the best of what he found in other lands. He lived in several of the major cities of the Low Countries and traveled as far as Italy, where he studied the works of his contemporary Michelangelo. Wandering around the ruins of the once-mighty Roman Empire gave him an historical perspective on the weakness of its "Holy" successor.

Like Dante two hundred and fifty years earlier, Bruegel found, in the tale of Babel, a coded way of commenting on the politics of his own time. In 1563, six years before his death, he painted an oil-on-oak panel of the Tower that came eventually to hang in the Kunsthistorisches Museum, on Maria-Theresien-Platz in the heart of Vienna. In the early 1970s, that city, the gracious if musty capital of neutral Austria, was a regular stop for Brooke and me as we traveled around central Europe. Nearly every time I was there, I revisited Bruegel's Tower. It fascinated me that a piece of painted wood could be so eloquent and contemporary in its insights and message. The artist, who thoroughly understood the principles of sound architecture, surely meant the viewer to see that this grandiose project is certain to fail, largely because of its grandiosity. Despite its outlandish buttresses, the massive spiral is crooked—it is the Leaning Tower of Babel. The base, modeled on the Roman Coliseum, is appropriate to a stadium but not to a skyscraper. The unfinished façade reveals a honeycomb of passages that have no rational connection with one another or with the helical ramps outside. The exposed barrel-vaulted galleries are as ugly as they are pointless.[22]

The Tower, reaching into the clouds, sits solidly on a promontory of massive rock. It could withstand earthquakes but not the foolishness of its builders, who are shown, in the foreground, paying obeisance to their foolish king. In the shadow of the Tower we see the source of the kingdom's wealth: ships offloading their cargoes with the help of Rube Goldberg–like hoisting devices. Those vessels are presumably laden with goods and building materials from far-off lands, of which Bruegel gives us a glimpse: in the distance,

Bruegel's Tower of Babel

near the top right-hand corner of the frame and on the edge of the horizon, is an island—or perhaps an outcropping of a continent. (When I first saw it, the painting reminded me of the most famous and imitated of Saul Steinberg's *New Yorker* covers, which pokes fun at a Manhattanite's parochial perspective on what it means to live in a globalized world, with California a sliver at the other end of a foreshortened continent and Japan just barely visible on the far side of a pond-like Pacific.)

Bruegel's Tower is surely the House of Hapsburg, and the crowned figure in the foreground is Charles V. Like the original in Genesis, it stands not for the dream of a unified world but for the reality of an imperial edifice that looms oppressively over the political landscape of the era and that is—again, like the one in Babel—destined for destruction.

THE SPREAD OF THE PROTESTANT MOVEMENT was both a cause and a consequence of the long, fitful decline of the Holy Roman Empire. The Hapsburgs found that they could keep their reign intact only by accommodating the diverse religious affiliations of the nobility. In 1555, the Peace of Augsburg, in Germany, recognized what would become known as Lutheranism in that part of the empire.

New centers of power looked for ways to manage competition and ensure enough political stability for commerce to prosper. In Bruegel's corner of the continent, an early form of national self-determination was on the rise. So was an early form of regional integration: a loose political and military alliance among autonomous countries, duchies, and principalities, each seeking independence but recognizing that they had to make common cause against their imperial oppressors. In 1579, a number of the Low Countries and the separate cities and provinces of the Netherlands joined forces against Spain as the Union of Utrecht.

The harder it was for the emperor and pope to claim divine sanction for their earthly rule, the more the sovereignty of territorial states came to reside with their own rulers. Britain, which had never been part of the Holy Roman Empire, and France, which had been outside it for more than six centuries, were among the first of these modern monarchies. The ruler had the right to sign a treaty, marry off a child for purposes of a dynastic alliance, behead a rival or a suspect courtier, or start a war. As Fernand Braudel puts it, "The modern state arose from the new and imperious needs of war: artillery, battle fleets and larger armies, made combat ever more costly."[23] In order to raise those forces, the sovereign needed—and obtained—the authority to do so.

•   •   •

THE WRITER AND THINKER best known for advocating and rationalizing the linkage between authority and force was Niccolò Machiavelli

Niccolò Machiavelli

(1469–1527). Like Dante, Machiavelli espoused, in *The Prince,* what was implicitly a secular alternative to the long-standing view that authority was derived from God and the church. Machiavelli considered himself a humanist and a democrat who sided with the common people in their desire not to be dominated by the aristocracy.[24]

But there was a basic difference between these two most famous sons of Florence. In *On Monarchy,* Dante stressed the principles of good governance—tolerance, pluralism, and consent of the governed. He believed that with the emergence of organized means to promote and safeguard those virtues, there was no limit to the geographical scope of a benevolent kingdom. Humanism, if institutionalized, might even lead to a political order that would encompass all humanity.

Machiavelli, by contrast, was not so much interested in imagining a better world as in understanding the real world and setting forth precepts for how to get ahead in it. And the real world did not mean the *whole* world: it meant the Florentine Republic. For him, the "territorial state" could be a very small piece of territory. Indeed the smaller the state, the more clever and ruthless the custodian of its fortunes must be in using force to protect its sovereignty: "The chief foundations of all states, new as well as old or composite, are good laws and good arms; and as there cannot be good laws where the state is not well armed, it follows that where they are well armed they have good laws. . . . A prince being thus obliged to know well how to act as a beast must imitate the fox and the lion, for the lion cannot protect himself from traps, and the fox cannot defend himself from wolves. One must therefore be a fox to recognize traps, and a lion to frighten wolves."[25]

That message resonated in the sixteenth century and continues to do so today. Machiavelli rose to prominence and influence because his patrons saw the utility of his ideas to the fulfillment of their ambitions. He is remembered now as one of the original "realists"—a secular saint for that school of political practice and theory that has, in recent decades, contended, often successfully, against liberal internationalists in the debate over American foreign policy. I remember from my years in the 1970s covering Henry Kissinger—the archdruid of contemporary realism—that, during stopovers in Rome, he would sometimes soften up the Italian press corps by referring, with at least as much reverence as irony, to "the land that gave us Machiavelli."

Three decades later, in 2006, when I participated in a high-brow international conference in Venice, I found that my Italian hosts could quote whole passages from *The Divine Comedy* and were well versed in medieval Catholic cosmology. But few had even heard of Dante's *On Monarchy*, with its dream of a "universal peace" that would come to this world when "humankind can be ruled by one supreme prince." That was because they—like Machiavelli and Kissinger—believe statecraft requires not the imagination of poets but the cunning of foxes in the service of lions in an age of wolves—and never more than when all these beasts are, as is their habit, at one another's throats.

5

PERPETUAL WAR AND "PERPETUAL PEACE"

Bellum omnium mater (War is the mother of all things).
—HERACLITUS[1]

Dulce bellum inexpertis (War is sweet to those who do not know it).
—ERASMUS[2]

PEOPLE have been butchering one another in the name of God for millennia, but it is when historians write about Europe in the sixteenth and seventeenth centuries that they capitalize "Wars of Religion." In addition to the savagery and turmoil of the antagonism between Catholics and Protestants, rival Protestant sects went at each other with pikes, maces, muskets, and ropes. A series of conflicts between 1618 and 1648 was among the most destructive episodes in European history. What began as a religious struggle became increasingly political as various European powers, notably Sweden and France, asserted themselves against the Holy Roman Empire. By the end of the Thirty Years War, combat, along with disease, famine, and migration caused by marauding armies and the resulting devastation of economies, had reduced the population of central Europe by about a third.

By 1644, the combatants were looking for a way to end the fighting. Representatives of nearly two hundred Catholic and Protestant rulers gathered in the northeastern German region of Westphalia. Even when seeking peace, leaders of the two religious camps refused to meet face-to-face. The Catholics set up their base in Münster, while the Protestants gathered thirty miles away, in Osnabrück. Intermediaries, shuttling between the two towns, haggled over process, protocol, and a complex system for the distribution of dispatches and memoranda. There was intrigue, spying, and wrangling within and between delegations. As the talks dragged on, armies remained in the field and frequently clashed. ("In winter we negotiate, in summer we fight," as one participant put it.)[3]

The Peace of Westphalia—as the pact finally signed in 1648, along with several auxiliary treaties that followed, came to be known—established a pattern that would continue for the next three hundred years: increasingly destructive wars led to increasingly ambitious treaties; having exhausted their populations and treasuries in battle, leaders would hold marathons of multilateral diplomacy intended to reorder the political landscape. Like those that came later, the Westphalia agreements were intended to do more than weaken and punish the losers; they were also meant to stifle the forces that had ignited the fighting in the first place. As Anthony Pagden observes, "Europeans may have been one of the most consistently belligerent groups of peoples anywhere in the world. But . . . the opposite was true as well: [they were also engaged in] a perennial quest for an idea of eternal universal peace."[4]

Since the casus belli of the Thirty Years War had been religious disputes within as well as between the various German states, the peacemakers resolved that the religion of each state would be determined by its king or prince—Catholic, Lutheran, or Calvinist; if a ruler changed his religion, he would forfeit his lands.

The Catholic proponents of this feature of the treaty intended it to discourage rulers from converting to Protestantism and accelerating the spread of the Reformation. They hoped in that fashion to preserve the European status quo and the Holy Roman Empire as its bulwark. The effect was the opposite. Westphalia enhanced the power of political leaders within their own domains and thereby further weakened the empire by creating a mélange of about three hundred largely autonomous polities. They included numerous monarchies as well as free states such as Saxony and Bavaria and republics such as the Swiss Confederation and the United Provinces of the Netherlands. They ranged in size from statelets such as the Landgraviate of Hesse-Darmstadt, which was controlled by an independent nobleman, to tiny church holdings subsequently incorporated into Germany, to large entities, roughly unified by language and culture, that are fixtures on the map today.

LOOKING BACK ON WESTPHALIA and seeking to explain its result, nineteenth-century scholars came up with the term "nation-state." The hyphen meant that nationality and statehood were closely aligned. It was a designation for a supposedly new, *non*-ecumenical political construct, since most nations in pre-Westphalian Europe had been embedded within much larger states or empires.

The cobbling together of "nation" and "state" into a single term lent credence to national distinctiveness as the basis of statehood. Yet the idea of a culturally homogenous community remained as much a myth as ever.* France and Sweden are still cited as the archetypal Westphalian nation-states: France for the French, Sweden for the Swedes. But those countries can also be seen as monuments to the artificiality of the concept of the nation-state. People who speak various dialects of French and who occupy a territory that they and their neighbors identify as France are a linguistic, ethnic, and cultural amalgamation. Centuries of conquest and accretion fused Normandy, Brittany, and Gascony, each of which had been, until suppressed, a distinctive and combative nation. To take one example that would provide tinder for the conflagrations of the nineteenth and twentieth centuries, the Westphalian settlement granted to France the regions of Alsace and Lorraine, on the west bank of the Rhine, but the common people there continued to speak German even after the elites learned French.

Similarly, the Swedes are a conglomeration of different and often hostile Nordic tribes. The repeated, tumultuous clashes that preceded their unification are reflected in the sanguinary plot of *Beowulf*, with its dragons and monsters, heroics and perfidy, alliances and blood feuds, loyalty to clansmen and vengeance against enemies. When the Treaty of Westphalia was signed, the state that emerged, while ruled by a Swedish king, included large numbers of Finns and Balts, who would thereafter nurture—and, given a chance, act upon—their national grievances and aspirations.

Even the phrase "Peace of Westphalia" was, for many of the peoples affected by it, a cruel deceit. It certainly meant little peace for the Poles and Lithuanians, who were soon subjected to what they still remember as "the Deluge," an invasion by Swedes combined with incursions by Russians and Cossacks. In the ensuing chaos, as much as a third of the Polish population died from war or disease. The economy was devastated, and a formerly moderate, tolerant elite became increasingly radicalized and vindictive against

---

* The OED's definition of *nation-state* is revealingly contorted: "an independent political state formed from a people who share a common national identity (historically, culturally, or ethnically); (more generally) any independent political state. A nation-state may be distinguished from states which comprise two or more historically distinct peoples, or which comprise only part of a historical people." The editors of the OED feel compelled to add, "However, such distinctions are frequently problematic."

non-Catholics—with the Jews, as usual, taking the brunt of persecution. Moreover, Poland's weakness facilitated the emergence of its neighbor Prussia as an independent state, a development of considerable consequence since Prussia's martial tradition, going back to the Teutonic Knights four centuries earlier, would serve Frederick the Great well when he set about to build a militarized and expansionist state a hundred years later.

LIKE MANY OF HIS CONTEMPORARIES, Thomas Hobbes never had any illusion that the new European order was going to be all that orderly. The English philosopher and political theorist had been repelled by the carnage of the Thirty Years War and by the tumult and bloodshed of Britain's own Civil War, a constitutional struggle that pitted the Puritan Roundheads in Parliament, led by Oliver Cromwell, against the forces of Charles I, whom Cromwell beheaded as a tyrant. For Hobbes, both episodes—one on the continent, the other in Britain—showed the tendency of politics to degenerate into anarchy, a "state of nature," in which the only law was that of the jungle (or "war of all against all").

In Hobbes's view, the decentralization and iconoclasm of the Reformation had gone too far. The life of man was likely to be all the more "solitary, poor, nasty, brutish, and short" without a powerful sovereign ruling through the authorities and institutions of a strong, well-governed state, which he compared to the huge aquatic beast that had swallowed Jonah: "The multitude so united in one person, is called a Commonwealth. . . . This is the generation of that great Leviathan, or rather, to speak more reverently, of that mortal god, to which we owe under the immortal God, our peace and defense."

Thomas Hobbes

Since there would be a multitude of such beasts, and since Hobbes could not imagine there ever being "one Man or Assembly . . . to compel" peace among them, there was the ever-present danger that states would take up arms against each other. "[I]n all times," Hobbes wrote, "Kings and Persons of Sovereign authority, because of their Independency, are in continual jealousies, and in the state and posture of Gladiators; having their weapons pointing, and their eyes fixed on one another . . . which is a posture of War. . . . And if a weaker Prince make a disadvantageous peace with a stronger, for fear, he is bound to keep it."[5]

In 1683, four years after Hobbes's death, a trauma on the edge of Europe concentrated the minds of princes, strong and weak, on the need to keep peace among themselves. Christendom's common enemy, the "Turks"—who had been pressing against the central European kingdoms for three hundred years—were back with a vengeance. An army under the command of the Grand Vizier Kara Mustafa Pasha laid siege to Vienna for two months before being defeated by the combined forces of the Hapsburgs and their Polish-Lithuanian allies. While the Ottoman Empire never again posed such a serious military threat, there is still in Europe today, and not just in its German-speaking countries, *Türkenangst*. It has come to mean fear of what an influx of Muslims would mean for European culture and jobs. But subliminally, the word suggests a shiver that runs up many Europeans' spines when they imagine what "their" continent would be like if Kara Mustafa Pasha had succeeded.

THE LAW OF NATIONS

Once the Ottomans had been beaten back from the gates of Vienna, it was easier for Europeans to think expansively about how to make the wider world safe for commerce and colonization—activities that went hand in hand and had been under way for hundreds of years. In the first half of the sixteenth century, a Dominican theologian, Francisco de Vitoria, had argued that the establishment of a global "commonwealth" of nations, embracing Christendom and all other civilizations, should override the justification for any war waged for the "profit and advantage" of a single state or alliance of states.[6] Two generations later, the Duc de Sully, a Protestant in the court of Henry IV of France, proposed a "Grand Design" that would bring all the branches of Christianity together in a "Consistory of the Church" with a "Court of Peace" that "will see to it that nowhere does one nation rise against another." Another Frenchman, the Catholic monk and schoolmaster Emeric Crucé, proposed a plan for a world union that would be fostered and led by a united Europe. A Dutch philosopher and classicist, Franco Petri Burgersdijk, borrowed from the terminology of Alexander the Great in proposing an *Imperium Oecumenicum*. But that goal could only be achieved through "the conversion of the infidels, whereby paganism, Judaism and Mohammedanism will come to an end."[7]

Given how spectacularly the Europeans had failed in the Crusades and how far the Ottomans had penetrated into Europe itself, the formula of conquest-plus-conversion had little plausibility in the Islamic lands to the east of Europe. But it seemed to be working better in other parts of the world that were now accessible to the Europeans. Starting in the late fifteenth century, with the advent of large, sturdy ships and improvements in navigation, the Portuguese had found a sea route to India and Asia around Africa's Cape of Good Hope, and the Spanish had stumbled on the Americas. By the seventeenth century, the Dutch had achieved a commercial foothold in North America, parts of Africa, and the East Indies. Within fifty years, the British and French were in the game as well.

Competition among the European colonial powers led them to establish a virtual condominium over much of the planet. Channeling competition into commerce required rules among states. The Spanish Jesuit Francisco Suárez and the Dutch jurist and statesman Hugo Grotius, who wrote in the early seventeenth century, are widely considered to be among the founders of the modern concept of international law. Suárez tended toward abstraction (he extrapolated from the commonalities of human nature the rationale for a "universal society" governed by a single system of law).[8]

Grotius was, quite literally, more down-to-earth. He wrote his *Freedom of the Seas* when Britain, Portugal, and other naval powers were trying to claim not just exotic shores but large swaths of the high seas as well. Grotius argued that the ocean was not property subject to national sovereignty but an international space—or, in modern parlance, a "global common." He expanded on this theme in *On the Law of War and Peace*, which held that all nations are bound by "natural law" that necessitated a theory of "just war" based on such modern liberal principles as proportionality of force, the legitimacy of preemptive force only in the case of imminent threat, and protection of civilians. Grotius also stipulated that a just peace, while obviously preferable to a just war, required a system of adjudication and enforcement.[9]

EVEN THE MOST TENTATIVE PROGRESS toward establishing international law would have been far more difficult if the Europeans had been consumed with wars among themselves on the continent. In that sense, the aftermath of Westphalia facilitated not only peace in Europe, but also, partly as a consequence, the spread and consolidation of European global power as

well. If any state seemed to be aggrandizing itself on the continent, its neighbors closed ranks to reinforce the Westphalian norm of respect for the sovereignty and territorial integrity of nation-states. For example, after the death
of the last of the Spanish Hapsburgs (the childless Charles II), France's Bourbon monarchy claimed the throne and asserted the Hapsburg right to rule
Spain. A "Grand Alliance" of English, Dutch, Danish, Austrian, Portuguese,
and German forces—led by John Churchill, First Duke of Marlborough—
inflicted a series of defeats on the French.

The so-called War of the Spanish Succession embroiled not only the nations of Europe but their colonies in America as well. It came to an end in
1713 with the Treaty of Utrecht, a trio of agreements that strengthened
Britain, blocked French ambitions, and still managed to ease, for a while, tensions between Britain and France.

Thus, a little more than half a century after Westphalia, a growing number
of European leaders were beginning to see a common interest in keeping
their territorially ambitious neighbors from achieving continental dominance. In 1715, Alexander Pope summarized this inclination toward collective restraint in a couplet:

> Now Europe balanced, neither side prevails;
> For nothing's left in either of the scales.

A principle associated with the international politics of the nineteenth
and twentieth centuries—balance of power—was already emerging at the
beginning of the eighteenth.

BUT WHILE EQUILIBRIUM may be a natural condition in the physical
world, it was nothing of the kind in the political realm. People and nations
were competitive, often combative. Taming that aspect of human nature required rules, both within states and among them. There had to be limits to
what nations, in pursuit of their interests, were *allowed* to do; national sovereignty itself had to be in balance with the principle and enforcement of international law. A French delegate at the peace conference that produced the
Treaty of Utrecht, the Abbé de Saint-Pierre, put forward, as part of what he
called a "Project for the Perpetual Peace," a proposal for "the establishment of
permanent arbitration among sovereigns, in order to settle their future differences without recourse to war." [10]

However, if "sovereigns" were to accept a system of rules, arbitration, and enforcement in order to realize Dante's dream of a universal peace, they would, whether they admitted it or not, be giving up some measure of sovereignty itself. Keeping that measure to a tolerable minimum led logically to another idea that the Florentine poet had foreshadowed in *On Monarchy*: a united Europe would have to grant a high degree of autonomy to its member states—in a word, federalism. That concept had, among its proponents, four of the leading polymaths of the eighteenth century: the German mathematician, scientist, theologian, diplomat, and councilor to monarchs Baron Gottfried Wilhelm von Leibniz; the Scottish historian and philosopher David Hume; and two Frenchmen, the essayist and jurist Montesquieu, and the philosopher, political theorist, botanist, and musician Jean-Jacques Rousseau. They believed Europe was entering an Age of Enlightenment, to be distinguished by a prevailing belief in the perfectibility of the human condition through the power of reason.

Reason had long argued for federalism, but it was Leibniz who gave it that name. Derived from the Latin verb *fidere*, "to trust" and related to *foedus* ("treaty"), the word *federal* had previously been used most commonly as a theological term that referred to the divine devolution of responsibility to human beings (i.e., the covenants whereby God made Abraham and Moses responsible for ensuring that Israel worshiped the one and only God, and Christ responsible for redeeming humankind).[11] In its secular context, a federal system was one in which the highest authority devolved power to subsidiary ones.[12]

Hume refined the concept. He sought to combine the advantages of local accountability with those of the large state. While he had in mind his native Scotland's perennially fraught relationship with England, he was also taking account of what he saw as a basic trait of human nature: a citizen wants his welfare to be provided for as much as possible at a local level, by authorities he knows and trusts, but he recognizes that there are other benefits that can come only from a powerful state.[13] What was required, Hume concluded, was a system that left as much power as possible at the lower levels while investing as much as necessary at the higher ones.[14]

Similarly, Montesquieu urged the rulers of his day to think in terms not of conquest but of what in the twentieth century would be called interdependence, integration, collective security, and the politically salutary effects of international commerce: "A prince believes that he will become greater through the ruin of a neighboring state. The opposite is true. The condition in Europe is such that all states depend on one another. France needs the opulence of Poland and of Muscovy, just as Guyenne [in the southwest of France] needs Brittany [in the northwest]." Europe should be thought of as "a state composed of several provinces," and peace among them would be "the natural effect of trade."[15]

In the same vein, Rousseau—even though he is often depicted as a progenitor of the realist school of political theory—saw Europe to be "not only, as is the case with Asia or Africa, a collectivity of nations with only a [continental] name in common, but also a real society, which has its own religion, its own morality, its own way of life, and even its own laws. . . . Today there are no more French, Germans, Spaniards, or even English, no matter what you may be told: there are only Europeans." While critical of Saint-Pierre's "Project for Perpetual Peace," Rousseau could see that it stood to reason that Europe should someday come together under a single, though federalized, political authority: "Almost all small states, whether republics or monarchies, thrive solely because they are small, because all their citizens know and respect one another, because the leaders can see for themselves the evil that is done and the good that needs to be done, and because their orders are carried out before their very eyes. All big nations, crushed by their very mass, groan either in anarchy . . . or under a hierarchy of subaltern oppressors whom the rulers need to keep them in order." To avoid the fatal cumbersomeness of giant states, a united Europe had to permit local and regional authorities to exercise as much power as possible.[16]

However, the major figures of the Enlightenment, like their descendants three centuries later, were by no means unanimous about the practicality of European political unity. Voltaire, for example, could see the virtue of institutions that brought different nationalities together, particularly for mutual economic benefit. He hailed the London Stock Exchange as "a place more respectable than many a court. You will see assembled representatives of every nation for the benefit of mankind. Here the Jew, the Mohammedan and the Christian deal with one another as if they were of the same religion, and reserve the name 'infidel' for those who go bankrupt. Here the Presbyterian puts his trust in the Anabaptist, and the Anglican accepts the Quaker's promissory note. Upon leaving these peaceful and free assemblies, one goes to the synagogue, the other for a drink; yet another goes to have himself baptized in a large tub in the name of the Father through the Son to the Holy Ghost; another has his son's foreskin cut off, and over the infant he has muttered some Hebrew words that he doesn't understand at all: Some others go to their church to await divine inspiration with their hat on their head. And all are content."[17]

But Voltaire was skeptical about whether it was possible to quell, once and forever, the forces of war. "The only possible perpetual peace among men," he said, "is tolerance"—a matter of attitude and behavior, not of political structures or negotiated agreements. Voltaire mocked Saint-Pierre as "Dr. Goodheart," whose perpetual peace "will no more be realized than among elephants, rhinoceroses, wolves, or dogs. Carnivorous animals will always tear one another to pieces at the first opportunity."[18]

THE PROFESSOR OF KÖNIGSBERG

While Leibniz, Montesquieu, and Rousseau were champions of the freedom and rights of the individual, it was another figure of the Enlightenment, Immanuel Kant, who most fully and systematically developed those principles. He did so in the course of a long life devoid of adventures, war stories, sojourns in the courts of emperors, or romance (he never married or even, as far as his biographers can tell, had any love affairs). Courteous but aloof, he was a relentlessly disciplined scholar who rose at 5 A.M., had a cup of tea, smoked a pipe, then sat down at his writing table and, depending on his teaching schedule, worked on his essays and lectures until 1 P.M., when he would have the principal meal of the day, often with a few guests for lively, wide-ranging conversation. He would take an hour-long stroll in the afternoon with such regularity that his neighbors joked that they could set their clocks by his passing. In the evening, he usually read. If he went out for dinner, he excused himself by nine so that he had time at home to make a few notes on the ideas he would write up in the morning.[19]

Kant, who lived from 1724 to 1804, spent almost all those eighty years in Königsberg, where he held a chair in logic and metaphysics at Albertina University. He left the city only once, and then to a country estate only sixty miles away to serve as a private tutor for the sons of a Prussian knight.[20] Yet even though he was a stay-at-home bookworm, Kant kept himself immensely knowledgeable about the affairs of the day largely by circulating in a busy port filled with merchants and seamen from Poland, Lithuania, England, Denmark, Sweden, and Russia, as well as religious refugees, particularly Mennonites from Holland and Huguenots from France.

Königsberg was more than a home to Kant; its history and spirit nurtured his ideas. Since the fourteenth century, the city had been part of the Hanseatic League, which was the shining example of the European "confraternity of trade." The League stitched together a community concentrated along the littoral of the Baltic and North seas that also included market towns as far away as Novgorod, which was a source of timber, fur, tar, honey,

Immanuel Kant

and flax from the depths of Russia. Free-trade agreements with merchants in England and in Flanders made Königsberg bankers and merchants rich enough to become benefactors of universities and the arts.

The League had come into being in the twelfth century as an essentially protectionist effort. Its original purpose was to defend the trading interests of north German towns and merchants against robbers, pirates, and other hostile forces. *Hansa* derives from a medieval German word for guild; that word, in turn, is from a Gothic one meaning a military unit. Members of the League sent armed vessels to escort merchant convoys and soldiers to guard caravans. They also cooperated to increase the chances of survival against the dangerous forces of nature by building lighthouses and by training pilots and navigators.

Thus, ingrained in the way members of the League thought about their enterprise, there was a connection among disparate but compatible concepts and objectives: the central importance of commerce to economic development, the need for armed alliances to protect independent political entities, and the requirement of a peaceful environment for trade. The League sometimes bribed foreign leaders who refused to play by Hanseatic rules. If that failed, the League might resort to embargoes and blockades, but it seldom went to war. One of the rare exceptions was a military campaign against a Danish king (Valdemar IV) who was trying to break Hanseatic domination of trade in the Baltic area in the fourteenth century. The League won that war but was not eager for another. The preservation of peace as a condition for trade created an incentive for maritime and international commercial law. The League was also conducive to diplomacy, since it reflected its members' growing self-confidence and recognition that their interests would be served by reaching out to new markets through negotiated trade agreements that in turn were reinforced by political arrangements. To be a Hanseatic city-state was, by definition, to be open to the world.

In Kant's day, Königsberg was a hub in the network of interdependent polities whose commercial and political cooperation would, nearly two hundred years later, serve as a model first for the European Common Market, then for the European Union. The city represented, just as Kant personified, the revival of the classical Greek ideal of *cosmopolitanism*, a manner of living and thinking that incorporates an appreciation of the perspectives and interests of people from other parts of the world. No wonder, then, that a thinker whose view of the world was formed in Königsberg during its glory days would anticipate the rationale for the European Project of the second half of the twentieth century. It was largely because he was a denizen of that city at that time that Kant, in the words of his biographer Manfred Kuehn, "considered himself first and foremost not a Prussian but a citizen of the world. Kant was glad to be alive while momentous changes were taking place in the history of mankind, and he saw himself as rising to the challenge, addressing the important issues resulting from the changes, and trying to nurture what was good in them."[21]

Kant is one of those celebrities of intellectual history whose work is more often evoked than read. Much of his writing, particularly the cornerstone of his philosophy, *The Critique of Pure Reason*, is, for many who have made a stab at it, somewhere between exceedingly difficult and absolutely impenetrable. If you can follow Kant's explanation of everything going on in these two statements—"The house is black," and "Two plus two equals four"—you will fully understand the difference between empirical and *a priori* propositions. You would also have passed with flying colors a course that I audited for a while in my sophomore year at Yale but gave up on after several weeks, transferring to H. Bradford Westerfield's Origins of Communism, which seemed more relevant to my interest in the Soviet Union. Three years later, when I was at Oxford and reading more about the formation of nations and international systems, several of my teachers urged me to skip the metaphysics and give Kant another try, this time as a political visionary. The effort it required to take that advice paid off. I came to understand why Kant occupies such an esteemed place in the pantheon of great thinkers. Moreover, he became a guide to me in my own attempts to understand the past, assess what is happening in the present, and refine my hopes for the future.

Like many of the humanists, Kant's starting point was a desire to reconcile religion with reason. He had entered university to study theology but quickly developed a passionate interest in physics and mathematics, then in logic and moral philosophy. Some of Kant's contemporaries who understood the fine points of his writings, or thought they did, could be stimulated not just to intellectual passion but, being Prussians, to acts of ritualistic violence. Two students of metaphysics fought a duel over their conflicting interpretations of *The Critique of Pure Reason.* The uninitiated, with whom I sympathized during my false start with Kant at Yale, found his writings heavy going. Near the end of Kant's life, a visitor described him as "the most cheerful and most entertaining old man, the best companion, a true bon-vivant in the most honorable sense. He digests the heaviest foods as well, while his readers get indigestion over his philosophy." [22]

However, when Kant turned from epistemology to political theory, his prose style became simpler and his message more accessible. He had plumbed virtually all the writings touched on earlier in this chapter, including Saint-Pierre's "Project for Perpetual Peace." He saw himself making his own contribution to a collective effort to imagine a bigger, better, more equitable, more peaceful community than the Europe of his day. Like a number of those to whom he owed an intellectual debt, his hope was for a united, federative Europe that might serve as the precursor and eventual leader of a united, federative world. The form of governance of its member states must be, in his view, "republican," although the term that many of his interpreters have used is "democratic." [23]

Kant based this conviction on his view of sovereignty. In the hands of an absolute monarch, sovereignty is a license for tyranny; it is, as one political scientist has put it, "authority without accountability," since the sovereign answers to no one. [24] Over time, sovereignty had come to apply to the state as a whole, thereby diluting the power of the monarch—but not that of the state, since its leadership had the right to use force as it saw fit, with responsibility to no higher authority nor to the people whom the state was supposed to protect and serve. By the Enlightenment, it was fashionable to speak of sovereignty being extended downward. Rousseau, for example, asserted that, as part of the social contract, men should qualify as "citizens, insofar as they participate in the sovereign authority." However, Rousseau went on to say that citizens enjoy sovereignty only when they act *collectively.* [25] It was Kant who introduced an explicit version of an idea implicit in humanism—and which was part of the intellectual bedrock of the American Revolution: that the individual himself was sovereign. In Kant's view, the legitimacy of a governing authority flowed *upward,* not just from the citizenry as a whole but from each citizen. It followed that the government must not only reflect the consent of the governed but must respect the rights of those who dissent from the majority and therefore from the decisions of the government.

Starting from that premise, Kant addressed the question of what form of government was most likely to ensure peace among nations. The answer was definitely not monarchy, since it was an extension of the ambitions, whims, jealousies, and rivalries of the monarchs themselves. Their behavior was self-ish and "anti-social," in that it led to the pursuit of their interests, disguised as national ones, at the expense of other nations'.

Europe in Kant's day was awash in evidence to support his diagnosis. The Seven Years War, which raged when he was in his thirties, pitted Britain, Prussia, and Hanover against France, Russia, Austria, Sweden, and Saxony. Since the conflict sparked clashes in colonies from North America and the Caribbean to Africa, India, and the Philippines, historians have seen the Seven Years War as a precursor to the global conflagrations of the twentieth century. For five years, Königsberg itself was under Russian occupation. The city's leaders had to swear allegiance to Catherine the Great. Trade in the markets and shops where Kant went every day had to be conducted in rubles. At the other end of Europe, Russia and Turkey were waging a war of their own. And on the far side of the Atlantic, Redcoats dispatched by King George III were trying to suppress a rebellion fueled by what were no longer just republican ideals but instead had become a republican program.

Kant believed that the only way to attain a peaceful future was to transfer sovereignty within countries from monarchs to citizens under a system that today we would call a constitutional democracy, with a representative legislature, independent judiciary, and separation of powers. He called it a *Volkerbund*, or "federation of the people."

In 1784, when he was sixty, Kant took the federal concept from the national to the international level. He published an essay entitled "An Idea for a Universal History with a Cosmopolitan Purpose," in which he predicted, "The political constitution of our continent . . . will probably legislate eventually for all the other continents." For that to happen, however, Europe would have to abandon not only monarchy at home but also imperialism abroad.[26]

IN 1795, AT THE AGE OF SEVENTY-ONE, Kant brought the various strands of his thinking together in a "philosophical project" that he called *Zum ewigen Frieden*, or "Toward Perpetual Peace," a forty-page work that became the basis for what Kuehn, in his biography of Kant, has called a "civil religion" and stands to this day as a testament to the ability of intellectuals, even those who spend most of their lives in studies, libraries, and lecture halls, to produce ideas of profound and lasting effect on the world of politics and policy.

"Perpetual Peace" begins with a disclaimer that can be construed as a preemptive defense by a philosopher who wanted no trouble from the authorities. The cogitations of a mere "theoretical politician" and "academic," Kant wrote, posed no danger to the state and were probably not worth the attention of a "worldly-wise statesman" or a "practical politician." The treatise then takes the form of a charter for a "league of peace . . . to make an end of all wars forever," modeled, he suggested, on the ancient Greeks' Amphictyonic (or Neighbors') League of Delphi, which was formed by adjacent states on the basis of a common religious shrine.

Kant's concept anticipates some of the major, if still unfulfilled, features of the United Nations system: international (or what Kant called "cosmopolitan") law, open covenants openly arrived at, nonintervention and nonagression, the international regulation of national defenses (i.e., disarmament and arms control), decolonization, self-determination, democratization, the punishment of war crimes, and a universal code of civil and human rights.[27]

Kant constructs a grand syllogism in support of liberal principles as the basis for global governance: if individual states could govern themselves according to an "ideal civil constitution," they would naturally incline toward a "universal cosmopolitan existence . . . as the matrix within which all the original capacities of the human race may develop." The ultimate result he envisaged would not be a single world state (a *civitas gentium*) created by a single treaty (*pactum pacis*), but a peaceful union or federation (*foedus pacificum*) that "maintains itself, prevents wars, and steadily expands."[28]

Yet when imagining a world federation of republican states, Kant was neither blind to reality nor deaf to the cautions of realists. He knew there was an obvious tension between, on the one hand, the dictates of rationality and morality, and on the other the inconvenient fact that human nature is often irrational and that the demands of politics are often amoral or immoral. Kant knew, too, that these tensions would be intense and disruptive not just in his time but in the future. He captured this truth in what would become, with help from Isaiah Berlin nearly two centuries later, perhaps his most famous sentence: "Out of the crooked timber of humanity, nothing entirely straight can be made." The full context makes these few words all the more germane: building a just and peaceful international system, Kant wrote, is "the most difficult of all tasks, and a perfect solution is impossible. . . . Nature only requires of us that we should approximate to this idea. A further reason why this task must be the last to be accomplished is that man needs for it a correct conception of the nature of a possible constitution, great experience tested in many affairs of the world, and above all else a good will prepared to accept the findings of this experience. But three factors such as these will not easily be found in conjunction, and if they are, it will happen only at a late stage and after many unsuccessful attempts." [29]

In short, the task of bringing forth "a harmony from the very disharmony of man" would require decades, perhaps centuries, of trial, error, and compromise. The sacrifice of certain aspects of independence for the benefits of interdependence ran counter to what Kant called the "attachment of savages to their lawless freedom" and their preference for "ceaseless combat" rather than "subjection to a lawful constraint which they might establish." It would take humankind a long time to get over its "brutish degradation" and the "perverseness of human nature which is nakedly revealed in the uncontrolled relations between nations."

Kant understood the strength and resilience of what Rousseau termed "carnivorous" nationalism; what Dante had called "the many-headed beast lusting after a multiplicity of things"; and what Hobbes had made the centerpiece of his own grim view of man, with its implications for the authoritarian nature of the state. Kant knew that, for a long time and perhaps forever, noble abstractions would not stand much of a chance against *raison d'État*. He recognized that there was "no instant on record when a state has ever been moved to desist from its purpose because of arguments backed up by the testimony of such great men" as Grotius.

All this he saw as a deplorable but inescapable part of the human condition. The happy outcome summed up in the phrase "perpetual peace" and the global system that would make it possible were, as he would acknowledge a decade after he wrote his treatise on the subject, a "sweet dream." Perpetual peace should be seen—and strived for—as "the ultimate end of all international right," but it was also "an idea incapable of realization," at least in the foreseeable future. Separate, sovereign nations would probably not be able to form a world state or a strong and "indissoluble" federation "like that of the American states," which by then had been independent for nine years and were four years away from adopting a federal constitution. Therefore, ever the Enlightenment rationalist and believing in practical as well as pure reason, Kant reiterated, as forcefully and clearly as possible, the case for the best option:

> For states in their relation to each other, there cannot be any reasonable way out of the lawless condition which entails only war except that they, like individual men, should give up their savage (lawless) freedom, adjust themselves to the constraints of public law, and thus establish a continuously growing state consisting of various nations (*civitas gentium*) which will ultimately include all the nations of the world.

However, while leaders of the future must not lose sight of the ideal goal of perpetual peace, they might have to settle for something less universal, less perpetual, and less peaceful—but still better than the world the way it was:

> [If], under the idea of the law of nations, the [separate states of the world] do not wish [to unite], rejecting in practice what is correct in theory, if all is not to be lost, there can be, in place of the positive idea of a world republic, only the negative surrogate of an alliance which averts war, endures, spreads, and holds back the stream of those hostile inclinations which fear the law, though under constant peril of their breaking loose again.[30]

Kant concludes this passage with the words *Furor impius . . . intus fremit horridus ore cruento*—a fragment from a passage in Virgil's *Aeneid* that the English poet John Dryden translated as:

> Imprison'd Fury, bound in brazen chains;
> High on a trophy rais'd, of useless arms,
> He sits, and threats the world with vain alarms.

By this Kant meant that until the democratic nations of the world, starting with those of Europe, could unite, they should at least form an alliance to deter tyrannical and menacing states from aggression. This was close to being a prophecy of the solution that Europe would adopt, with crucial American support, some hundred and fifty years later.

As for the democratization of tyrannies, Kant counted on that process to come about internally rather than through intervention. In this respect, the seminal figure in the history of modern internationalism was what today would be called a "sovereignty hawk." As Kant put it in *Perpetual Peace*, "No state shall by force interfere with the constitution or government of another state. . . . Rather [than being a pretext for intervention] the example of the evil into which a state has fallen because of its lawlessness should serve as a warning [to others]."

He made an exception, however, for those cases where sovereignty itself lost meaning in the context of civil war or anarchy in one country, thereby threatening the stability of its neighbors and the peace of the region. In that situation, he believed, other powers had a responsibility to intervene. Thus to the list of late-twentieth- and early twenty-first-century issues that Kant foresaw we can add that of failed states, like those of the Balkans and Africa.[31]

NEAR THE END OF HIS LIFE, the professor of Königsberg had the satisfaction of knowing that the adjective *Kantian* had come into wide use, and it remains so to this day. Its approximate antonym is *Hobbesian.* Kant, ever the gentleman, even with regard to long-deceased philosophical adversaries, tended to be oblique in intellectual combat. Hobbes was one of the few whom Kant took on by name: he found Hobbes's view of humanity unjustifiably bleak and, if adopted as the basis for governing, likely to be self-fulfilling: the state would indeed be a monster and gobble up the individual.[32]

In the late twentieth and early twenty-first centuries, Kant and Hobbes would be regarded as intellectual heroes by the opposing camps in the great debate over American foreign policy. For self-avowed realists, Hobbes applied to his prescription for national and international governance an acceptance of the human propensity for conflict, the frequent need for authoritarianism as an antidote to anarchy, and the indispensability of force as the arbiter of disputes, while Kant's writings provided a touchstone for liberal internationalists and their hopes for the democratic peace.

Kant lived long enough to see what he and many others thought was reason for hope that his view would triumph over Hobbes's in Europe, and he was just barely spared by death from seeing that hope dashed.

6

BLOOD AND LEATHER

In the world of art, as in the whole of our great creation, freedom
and progress are the main objectives . . . We moderns are not quite
as far advanced in solidity as our ancestors, yet the refinement of our
customs has enlarged many of our conceptions as well.
—*LUDWIG VAN BEETHOVEN*[1]

There is no such thing as *natural law* . . . Before law comes into
being, there is nothing *natural,* except a lion's strength, or the needs
of the creature who suffers from hunger, from cold . . .
—*STENDHAL, Scarlet and Black*[2]

WHEN Immanuel Kant learned of the French Revolution in the
summer of 1789, he was so elated about what he believed it portended for Europe that he changed the route of his daily constitutional, setting out southwestward, in the general direction of Paris, which
was suddenly the capital of "the West" in its modern ideological connotation.
It was there that the ideas of the Enlightenment had been converted into
principles of governance applicable to everyone everywhere. Each month
brought more good news: the gathering of the Estates-General in May, the
formation of the National Assembly in June, the fall of the Bastille in July, and
the Declaration of the Rights of Man and of the Citizen in August.

The people of France were overthrowing a monarchy—the kind of government Kant detested—and proclaiming in its place a republic, the one he
advocated for all humanity. It further heartened him that the Jacobins saw
what they were doing as not just a national enterprise but as an international
one. During the revolution, Robespierre had said, "The men of all countries
are brothers and the different peoples should help one another, according to
their means, as if they were citizens of the same state." It was, said Robes-

pierre in a speech before the National Assembly in May 1790, "in the interest of all nations to protect the French nation because it is from France that the freedom and happiness of the world must stem."[3]

"Now let your servant go in peace to his grave," Kant exclaimed, "for I have seen the glory of the world."[4]

BUT WHILE THE RALLYING CRY *Liberté, Egalité, Fraternité* was intended to have an international ring, the first of these watchwords took on a bellicose tone and the third a nationalistic one: France would liberate *others*, whether they liked it or not, and bring them under the protection of France itself. In 1791, *Patriote français*, the organ of a relatively moderate Jacobin faction, issued a call to arms: "War! War! This is the cry of every patriot, the wish of every friend of freedom from one end of Europe to the other. This is all they are waiting for, a pretext for attacking and overthrowing the tyrants." The execution of Louis XVI in 1793 was just the beginning of the busy work of Dr. Guillotin's invention on the Place de la Concorde. Soon the flow of blood was so copious that it was feared to be contaminating the water supply of Paris.

The euphoria among many leading figures of the Enlightenment turned to disillusionment—then to despair. Kant remained favorably disposed toward the ideals of the revolution but condemned its violent methods. The British statesman Edmund Burke, who had been willing to give the Jacobins time to translate liberal rhetoric into liberal policies, became one of the fiercest critics of the French Revolution. He saw in the Reign of Terror a warning to beware of a revolutionary regime that spouts idealistic and universalistic slogans while ruthlessly dispatching its enemies, real and imagined. Such an ideology was likely to be contagious, and such a state was likely to be aggressive. Burke believed that other states should join forces against the new common threat: "Such is the law of civil vicinity. Now where there is no constituted judge, as between independent states there is not, the vicinage [neighborhood] itself is the natural judge. It is, preventively, the assertor of its own rights; or remedially, their avenger. Neighbours are presumed to take cognizance of each other's acts. . . . This principle, which, like the rest, is as true of nations as of individual men, has bestowed on the grand vicinage of Europe a duty to know, and a right to prevent, any capital innovation which may amount to the erection of a dangerous nuisance."[5]

In that one paragraph, written in 1793, Burke articulated an essentially Kantian idea that would be tested—and, to a degree, vindicated—in the second half of the twentieth century, when the United Nations would begin to take on the responsibility of thwarting or punishing dangerous behavior on the part of member states.

But before that would happen, history followed a Hobbesian plot. Those who shared Kant's dream of perpetual peace and Burke's idea of Europe as a "vicinage," where benevolent international norms could be enforced against national malefactors, were about to be reminded of the difference between thinkers and doers. They were what would today be called public intellectuals, ahead of their contemporaries but, in part for that reason, on the sidelines of the political action.

In championing reason, science, and humanism against ignorance, dogma, and despotism, the great figures of the Enlightenment were waging, with their minds and their pens, what was often a losing battle against forces armed with blunter instruments. They were still sources of big ideas, but they did not yet have the means of translating those ideas into action, policy, or facts. In a world where disputes between individuals and states were so often resolved not by reason or merit or virtue but by force, the power of ideas alone did not stand much of a chance against the power of violence.

HISTORY ON HORSEBACK

Napoleon Bonaparte understood the power of ideas and violence when they were combined. As he accelerated the surge in territorial aggrandizement that began under the Jacobins, he proclaimed his commitment to supporting, in many of the lands he conquered, reforms similar to those that the Revolution had promised would transform France itself: modern forms of administration along with a new legal code that still bears Napoleon's name and that guaranteed the rights and liberties of the individual. When, on campaigns in Italy, he found Jews confined to ghettos (an Italian word), he set them free. Where he found serfdom, he abolished it—as long as the beneficiaries were white and European. (In France's Caribbean colonies, Napolean sought to re-impose slavery, which had been abolished in the wake of the Revolution. As a result, a simmering revolt in Haiti boiled over, leading to a defeat for France and independence for Haiti—although that second of the Western Hemisphere's republics would know little civic peace for the next two hundred years.)

Napoleon saw himself as a new kind of ruler who would, in his own words, create "a great European federal system . . . in conformity with the spirit of the century and favorable to the advance of civilization." That ambition was culturally and geographically boundless. "Europe is too small for me," he said. "I must go East." He promised that however far he might extend his rule, it would be "wise and liberal." It would replicate the confederacies of ancient Greece, incorporating the values of the Enlightenment and the ecumenical ideal of Alexander the Great, with whom he identified.

Like Alexander, Napoleon portrayed conquest as liberation. In the spirit of the French Revolution, Napoleon was militantly secular. Recognizing religion as a vital component of national identity and intent on bringing many nations into his domain, he claimed to embrace all their faiths: "It was by making myself a Muslim that I established myself in Egypt. In making myself a [devotee of the papacy] I won men's hearts in Italy. If I were to govern a Jewish people, I would re-establish Solomon's temple."[6] Looking back on his life near its end, Napoleon said, "In Egypt . . . I created a religion. I saw myself on the highroad of Asia, mounted on an elephant, a turban on my head, and in my hand a new Koran which I would have written as I pleased. I would have united in my undertakings, the experience of two worlds, searching for my ends through all the histories of the world."[7] This audacious nonsense led Victor Hugo later to call Napoleon, approvingly, "a Mohammed of the West."[8]

Napoleon

Giants of culture and humanism elsewhere in Europe swooned over Napoleon in his prime as a figure, both promethean and protean, who was capable of imagining and leading a community of many nations and cultures. Ludwig van Beethoven, who had been inspired by the French and American revolutions to write his First Symphony, dedicated his Third (*Eroica*) to Napoleon. Catching a glimpse of Napoleon riding by in the German city of Jena on the eve of his victory over the Prussians there, Georg Wilhelm Friedrich Hegel said it was like seeing the world-spirit on horseback.[9]

BUT IT SOON BECAME APPARENT to many of his early admirers that Napoleon's forced march was an ego trip of epic proportions. In 1804, the

First Consul of the French Republic crowned himself emperor. Bitterly disillusioned, Beethoven erased Napoleon's name from the title page of the Third Symphony.[10] Kant had died three months earlier, just missing this last stage of France's makeover from a republic into an autocracy.

Having embraced monarchy, the principal institution of the *ancien régime*, Napoleon tried to perpetuate his power and fame by founding a dynasty. Coming from a family of eight children, he made one brother (and later a brother-in-law) the king of Naples, another the king of Westphalia, yet another the king of Spain. He converted the Dutch Republic into the kingdom of Holland in order to exert tighter control over the region. After divorcing the Empress Josephine, he sought to bind his clan to the oldest ruling house of Europe by marrying a Hapsburg, Marie Louise of Austria.

Napoleon's military triumphs resulted in the formal dissolution of the Holy Roman Empire after more than a millennium. Though many of its possessions had enjoyed de facto independence since the Peace of Westphalia, the patina of imperial authority remained until July 1806, when Napoleon sent an ultimatum to the Holy Roman Emperor Francis II: give up the title within three weeks or be crushed. Francis assented, although he was allowed to remain king of Hungary and Bohemia and emperor of Austria.

Napoleon added to his own growing list of titles that of Protector of the Confederation of the Rhine, which consisted of most of the German states.

Goya's "They will still be helpful," from the Disasters of War

For the next six years, he was master of the European mainland. Under the rubric of "the Continental System," Napoleon mounted a commercial boycott against his only remaining major enemy, Britain. When Portugal refused to bend to his will, Napoleon launched an invasion through Spain in 1808 in order to bring all of Iberia under his control. The Spanish uprising that ensued triggered the French repressions that Francisco Goya captured in his series of etchings on "the Disasters of War."

Provoked by Napoleon's Peninsular Campaign, the British launched an expeditionary force in defense of the Portuguese. The other great imperial power that would be his undoing had a foothold on the continent. Many in Europe now saw Napoleon's internationalism for what it was—chauvinism mixed with expansionism. Napoleon operated on the principle that what was good for the French was good for everyone, but everyone did not agree. He had given those he had humbled or threatened an incentive to put aside their differences long enough to join forces against him.

Seeing that danger, Napoleon deployed his diplomats to buy time for La Grande Armée to accomplish his goals. In 1807, he had signed a treaty with Czar Alexander I that would have divided the continent into spheres of French and Russian influence, largely so that he could focus on his rivalry with Britain. Then, in 1812, he invaded Russia and sacked Moscow, only to be beaten by "General Winter" and forced into a long, debilitating retreat.

Even then, Napoleon continued to enjoy considerable loyalty and adulation in France. The Marquis de Laplace, a mathematician and astronomer who served briefly as France's minister of the interior, exulted, "Napoleon the Great has brought half of Europe under his sway, his shining example exercises the most fortunate influence on the other half. Thanks to his Genius, all Europe will soon be one immense family, with one religion, one code of laws, and one system of weights and measures."[11]

What the pan-European religion would be, given the sectarian diversity of the continent and the emperor's own zany pronouncements on the subject, is anybody's guess. It did not matter, for in October 1813, shortly after de Laplace's giddy testament, a coalition of armies from Britain, Russia, Spain, Portugal, Prussia, Austria, Sweden, and some of the smaller German states met Napoleon near Leipzig. It would be the largest battle in Europe before World War I, with approximately half a million soldiers engaged. Outnumbered nearly two to one, Napoleon suffered a massive defeat that led to his abdication and exile to Elba off the coast of Italy.

Thinking they had disposed of the French menace once and for all, much of the royalty and nobility of the continent accepted the invitation of Prince Klemens von Metternich, the foreign minister of the Hapsburg state, to a conference in Vienna, only to have the proceedings interrupted by the news that the prisoner had escaped from Elba.

Back in power, Napoleon instructed the liberal philosopher Benjamin Constant to write a document setting forth a plan for a European federation, and he offered peace to the countries arrayed against him.[12] The allies, who now had Prussia on their side, were sure enough of their superiority to refuse compromise and resume their work in Vienna on the rules and maps for post-Napoleonic Europe. While these deliberations were under way, a member of the British delegation, the Duke of Wellington, packed up and left for Flanders to intercept Napoleon's armies as they marched toward Belgium to attack the Prussian army stationed there.

AFTER NAPOLEON'S EPIC DEFEAT at Waterloo, he was stripped of all his titles and taken prisoner by the British. They kept him under heavy guard at sea in the English Channel, then transferred him to the HMS *Northumberland* for a two-month voyage to Saint Helena, a British possession in the South Atlantic that had been named after the mother of Constantine the Great. That volcanic outcropping was chosen for Napoleon's second and terminal exile because it was the point of land farthest from any other on earth.[13]

As he suffered through the various ailments that would kill him within six years, Napoleon obsessed not just about his defeat at Waterloo but about his failure in Russia. Had he succeeded there, he believed, he might have fulfilled what he wanted posterity to recognize as his own version of Dante's and Kant's dream of a united and republican Europe:

Peace concluded in Moscow would have been the consummation and the end of my military campaigns. It would have been, as far as the great cause is concerned, the end of risks and the beginning of security. New horizons, new tasks to be accomplished were opening up, calculated to bring well-being and prosperity to all. The European system would have been founded, and my only remaining task would have been to organize it. . . . Satisfied on these major points and secure everywhere, I too should have had my Congress and my Holy Alliance. These ideas were stolen from me. In that assembly of all sovereigns, we should have negotiated our interests *en famille*, and settled our accounts with the peoples, as a clerk does with his master.

The "European confederacy," he said, in his attempt to justify his hubris, "would soon have formed actually a single nation, and every traveler would have everywhere found himself in one common homeland. . . . One of my greatest ideas was bringing together the concentration of the same geographical peoples that had been dissolved, fragmented, by revolution and by politics. . . . To have achieved this would have been to go down to posterity gloriously and to be blessed by all the centuries to come. I felt equal to it!" [14]

Whether Napoleon had this vision in mind while he was riding high before Leipzig and Waterloo is doubtful. As the historian Denis de Rougemont notes, "[T]he deposed tyrant was able to form a coherent view of the motives which inspired his political action only thanks to his compulsory idleness on Saint Helena." [15] Nevertheless, Napoleon's adoption of this explanation of his career was significant: the idea of a federated Europe had seized the collective imagination of the continent's actors, thinkers, and poets; Napoleon wanted to be remembered as a champion of that cause. In 1829, eight years after Napoleon's death, Johann Wolfgang von Goethe imagined a Europe in which French, English, and German ideas would form a cosmopolitan culture, "capable of fusing the countless individual differences into a more or less harmonious whole." But for that to happen, the world needed more than a great man on horseback; it would need, wrote Goethe, an international system of "moral laws and firm principles such as obtain in private relations." [16]

THE GREAT POWER PEACE

The outcome of the Congress of Vienna hinged almost entirely on private relations between public men. The assembled statesmen transacted much of their business in small groups, often in tête-à-têtes. Acrimony and distrust abounded but was not allowed to thwart diplomacy. When Metternich sought an audience with Alexander I of Russia to present a proposal on the partition of Poland, the czar threw the Austrian minister out and, for good measure, followed up with a challenge to a duel, which Metternich simply ignored. (The crisis was defused through a negotiated compromise: Russia would eventually cede parts of Poland to Austria and Prussia and incorporate the remaining territory as the Kingdom of Poland under Russian control.)

The participants at the Congress often did their deals in hushed tones over lavish dinners or in the corner of a ballroom during grand soirées. As one participant noted, "*Le congrès ne marche pas—il danse.*" The most celebrated cultural figure on hand was Beethoven, whose biographer, Edmund Morris, sees him as "the ideal bard of the moment, a sort of composer laureate with a gift for resolving discord into concord"—the musical equivalent of the diplomatic result, which came to be known as the Concert of Europe.[17]

The Congress ended with a hastily arranged signing ceremony nine days before Waterloo. Once Napoleon was truly and finally out of the way, the Final Act—inscribed in a bound volume, and ratified with the signatures and red seals of the attending plenipotentiaries—created a mechanism, known as the Congress System, which would be convened some thirty times over a period of decades, thereby institutionalizing diplomacy-by-conference and prefiguring some of the forms, purposes, benefits, and limitations of twentieth-century multilateralism.

Even though thirty-nine other parties were involved, the Congress, like the United Nations, was dominated by five countries. Four were the principal victors in the Napoleonic wars—Austria, Britain, Prussia, and Russia; the fifth was the French regime that had replaced that of Napoleon. The monarchy-turned-republic-turned-empire now had a Bourbon king, Louis XVIII, back on its throne. The new map of Europe was a slightly amended version of the one that had existed before Napoleon redrew it. Thanks largely to the skillful and highly adaptive Charles-Maurice de Talleyrand—who had served as foreign minister in both the French republic and Napoleon's empire—France would have a say in any changes.

In the wake of the Congress, these five states came to be known as the Great Powers. They saw themselves—and were seen by others, with varying degrees of relief, acceptance, and resentment—as the self-constituted board of directors of Europe. Much like Napoleon on Saint Helena, the officials assembled in Vienna claimed that they were inspired by a vision of continental harmony and union. They were, according to various pronouncements, "negotiating peace with France in the name of Europe, the latter forming a single whole. . . . The allied Courts feel the full strength of the European league. . . . The peace will be a European peace, any other is inadmissible." The host of the grand affair, Prince Metternich, proclaimed piously, "Europe has long been a fatherland to me."[18] This professed commitment to good governance and cross-border collaboration based on common values and cultural kinship coexisted with a reaffirmation of balance of power as the basis for international order.

That feature of the Congress of Vienna and its aftermath earned the approval of at least two twentieth-century American secretaries of state. Dean

Acheson credited the Concert of Europe with "permit[ting] a century of international peace and of greater technologic and economic development than in the whole period since the invention of the sail and the wheel."[19] Henry Kissinger's doctoral dissertation at Harvard, first published in 1957, was an admiring analysis of the Congress. When Kissinger graduated from the study to the practice of statecraft, he paid tribute to Metternich and his fellow statesmen for having ushered in "the longest period of peace Europe had ever known. . . . There was not only a physical equilibrium, but a moral one . . . [wherein] continental countries were knit together by a sense of shared values."[20]

In practice, however, the "moral" questions of the nineteenth century—that is, how to define, interpret, apply, and enforce within individual states the norms that supposedly distinguished European political culture—were left to the governing authorities of those states to answer for themselves, without external interference or accountability. The Congress System gave maximum weight to the obligation of rulers to stay within agreed borders—no small thing, after all that Europe had suffered as a result of Napoleon's expansionism. However, the system gave minimum weight to how rulers governed within their borders. In the eyes of his most powerful contemporaries and their successors, Napoleon deserved a lonely death on the far side of the world not because he had betrayed the ideals of republicanism or the hopes of Dante, Leibniz, Rousseau, Kant, and Burke, nor because he had committed the repressions that so horrified Goya and Beethoven; rather, he earned his fate because he had upset the balance of power.

With that balance restored, Europe did indeed enjoy a long period of relative tranquility. The Industrial Revolution, which had already been under way in Britain for more than half a century, became a European phenomenon. James Watt's steam engine increased the efficiency with which goods could be manufactured and the speed with which they could reach their markets. Commerce in ideas thrived as well. What Paul Kennedy has called "the Great Power peace," a relief to society and a boon to the economy, brought dividends in intellectual ferment.[21]

OF ALL THE THINKERS WHOSE IDEAS caught fire, none was more influential than Charles Darwin. His name, like those of Kant and Hobbes, would become an adjective, although unlike theirs, his would become a shibboleth in realms where he had never ventured and where promiscuous and often nutty applications of his theory would have appalled him.

Darwin was as meticulous as he was imaginative—as methodologically conservative as he was conceptually radical. After his five-year voyage aboard the HMS *Beagle*, he spent two decades refining his theory that species differentiate themselves slowly, through a process whereby certain advantageous variations in the makeup and capacity of an organism are passed on by heredity, so that each generation is slightly better able to adapt to its environment. *On the Origin of Species*, which took the world by storm in 1859, was a study of plants and animals. It was not until 1871 that Darwin applied his theory to human beings. Notwithstanding its title, *The Descent of Man* is about an ascending journey. Still, it is a journey that has proceeded at a snail's

Charles Darwin

pace and been guided not by providence or the innate nobility of man but by the relentless logic of natural selection, to which human beings are subject as much as earthworms or finches.

Darwin very rarely—and then, very cautiously—ventured into the implications of his ideas for the politics of his day or of the future. In the midst of a long discourse in *The Descent* comparing the mental powers of human beings with those of the lower animals, Darwin speculates on how human attitudes and, accordingly, human behavior might be undergoing slow but steady progress, with potentially salutary implications for international relations:

> As man advances in civilization, and small tribes are united into larger communities, the simplest reason would tell each individual that he ought to extend his social instincts and sympathies to all the members of the same nation, though personally unknown to him. This point being once reached, there is only an artificial barrier to prevent his sympathies extending to the men of all nations.[22]

Darwin left it at that and got back to biology, probably not attaching more importance to his digression than its brevity suggested. Individual sympathy for all mankind is a long way from the desire, not to mention the ability, of the entire species to organize itself into a single political unit. Darwin was too good a scientist to dwell on a notion that seemed to have popped into his mind and offer it as a theory worthy of further development.

Nonetheless, what for Darwin was little more than a throwaway line was for others, some of whom had scientific pretensions of their own, a big idea that could be the basis of world peace: much as *Homo sapiens* had evolved from less intelligent and capable primates, *Homo politicus* might evolve— through the lessons of experience and willful behavior modification, not through natural selection—into a citizen of a single state embracing all humanity. That dream, not unlike Dante's five hundred years before, raised a question: what system of governance would a world state require? And would that system evolve slowly, like a new species, from the system prevalent among the myriad states of the nineteenth century, or could evolution be short-circuited through revolution, collective action that would destroy the old atomized system to make way for a new unified one?

In 1891, a radical French writer, Paul Lafargue, predicted that "the political unity of humankind . . . will be founded on the ruins of the existing national unities."[23] Lafargue was deeply influenced by his father-in-law, a ne'er-do-well German economist and philosopher who lived much of his life in poverty and relative obscurity in London. Karl Marx intended to call his intellectual invention "scientific socialism," a phrase that would

surely have struck Darwin as very dangerous indeed, especially since Marx explicitly intended his theory not just as a means of making sense of the past and the present but as a plan for engineering the future.[24]

Karl Marx

Marx owed a debt to the French philosopher Auguste Comte, who believed that human progress was governed by laws similar to those of nature. History had already passed through two stages; one featured the divine right of kings and the other was characterized by liberal notions such as the social contract, the rights of the individual, and the sovereignty of the people. Humanity, Comte believed, was now on the threshold of the third and ultimate stage: democracy would give way to government by an elite that would apply scientific solutions to human problems and thereby make possible a stable, peaceful, and prosperous society on a global scale.

Comte and Marx were believers in determinism, a doctrine that discerns—or imagines—in the apparent chaos of facts as they have unfolded over time not just *a* pattern but *the* pattern in history and current events, the one and only explanation for what has been and the one and only basis for what must be. Unlike Darwinism, determinism denies the element of chance; unlike the Great Man theory, it sees human events as driven not by individual will but by ineluctable historical forces.

Many religious believers held to their own version of determinism, believing that human fate is subject to the will of God. Marx, however, was an atheist. He and his collaborator Friedrich Engels believed that a great struggle between economic classes was the central plot line in the deterministic narrative of history. They saw the combined forces of trade and technology making of the world a single community, dominated by those who profited from the burgeoning of commerce: "The need of a constantly expanding market for its products chases the bourgeoisie over the whole surface of the globe. It must nestle everywhere, settle everywhere, establish connections everywhere. The bourgeoisie has, through its exploitation of the world-market, given a cosmopolitan character to production and consumption in every country." [25]

Those whose labors the bourgeoisie exploited would have to fight back, also on a global scale. The solidarity of the proletariat would supersede national identity and bring about the "withering away" of the traditional state. Marx and Engels's hopes were concentrated on western and central Europe, where the tensions between the working class and the bourgeoisie were most acute and therefore, they believed, where the prospects for a purgative upheaval seemed most auspicious. In deciding to live in Paris, London, and Manchester, they were positioning themselves at what they saw as the epicenter of a social and political movement that would someday sweep the world.

THE *COMMUNIST MANIFESTO*, WHICH CLOSED with the exhortation "Workers of the world unite!" appeared in 1848. That was the year when a loose coalition of workers, students, and liberal intellectuals set up barricades in the streets of Paris, overthrew the corrupt and lethargic Bourbon monarchy, and proclaimed a new republic based on universal suffrage, a minimum wage, and a maximum ten-hour workday. Similar uprisings broke out in Austria (where Metternich was driven from power), Prussia, Bohemia,

Hungary, and Italy. Britain, where Engels already lived and where Marx would settle the following year, was one of the few countries spared the turmoil, largely because its government had used the preceding decades to introduce gradual reforms that empowered the middle classes. Marx and Engels believed that "their" revolution had already begun.

In fact, however, the upheavals of 1848 gave rise to a phenomenon that was almost exactly the opposite of what Marx and Engels predicted and advocated: a burst of "bourgeois" liberalism, with a strong religious impetus. Vincenzo Gioberti, a theologian and politician who was among the foremost proponents of republicanism and federalism in Italy, ventured that "Christ, who set civilization the ultimate earthly goal of unifying the great human family, suggested the dialectical idea of the nation which is, so to speak, the city-state enlarged, humanity in miniature." He foresaw "a united Europe, a kind of Amphictyonic federation of the Christian states that would lead to the process of unification which is tending to encompass the entire human race."[26]

Gioberti's muddle of religious faith, federalism, and belief in the universality of republican values was as delusional as Marx and Engel's conviction that proletarian solidarity would prove stronger than nationalism. The Greeks, with British and Russian help, had waged a successful war of independence against the Ottomans in the 1820s. By 1848, Slavs, Hungarians, and Gioberti's fellow Italians were pressing for independence from the Hapsburgs. The struggles in Italy would eventually lead to the introduction of a new word, *irredentism*, for the attempt to regain parts of a nation that had been lost to another state.

In Germany, too, elites and popular movements were pressing for the amalgamation of various post-Westphalian kingdoms, duchies, and bishoprics. A customs union sponsored by Prussia after the Congress of Vienna gradually expanded to provide an early form of economic integration for most of the German states during the 1830s and '40s. German nationalism took multiple forms, some moderate, liberal, and peaceful, but others violent, expansionist (i.e., irredentist), and anti-Semitic. The poet Heinrich Heine observed the uglier side of what was happening in his homeland from Paris, where he spent the last two decades of his life. He predicted a continental contagion that would take a long time to burn itself out: "All the peoples of Europe and the world will have to go through this agony so that life may arise from death, and pagan nationality may be succeeded by Christian brotherhood. . . . Dark ferocious times are approaching; we can hear them rumble.

The future has a strong smell of leather, blood, impiety, and the sound of flesh on flesh. I advise our grandchildren to come into the world with very thick skin." [27]

HEINE WAS RIGHT ABOUT THE FATE awaiting Europe two generations in the future. But the children of his contemporaries (he had none of his own) would enjoy forty years of relative stability, prosperity, and comity. The second half of the nineteenth century saw the emergence of a new crop of pragmatic, moderately conservative leaders who permitted just enough reform to prevent popular discontent from getting out of hand. In France, Bonaparte's nephew, Louis Napoleon, won the presidency in a landslide election in the tumultuous year of 1848. Three years later, faced with a Bourbon royalist challenge, he staged a coup, changed the name of the Second Republic to the Second Empire, and took the title Napoleon III. He had broad popular support for dictatorial methods (although over time, he accepted limitations on his powers) and soon found himself in a feud with Russia (largely because the land of the czars had had enough of Frenchmen named Napoleon) and a rivalry with Prussia. The Franco-Prussian war of 1870–71 was the first major breakdown in the Concert of Europe and ended in another humiliation for France. It led to the loss of the provinces of Alsace and Lorraine that France had controlled since Westphalia. Napoleon III's fate bore an eerie resemblance to that of his uncle: defeat, capture, and death in exile.

While in the past, peace had tended to be a brief interlude in long periods of war, this time it was the other way around, and the strongest of the Great Powers that oversaw and benefited from the ensuing peace was Germany.

WILHELM I—THE LATEST IN THE LINE of the Hohenzollerns, who had ruled first Brandenburg, then all of Prussia for several centuries— was crowned emperor of Germany in the Hall of Mirrors at Versailles after German troops captured Paris in January 1871. The Prussian victory bestowed on Wilhelm sufficient strength and prestige among the kings of Bavaria, Saxony, and the other rulers of the German Confederation for them to declare him emperor of a united Germany. But it was Prince Otto von Bismarck, the architect of an integrated Germany and its first chancellor, who became the most prominent figure on the continent.

A German word of then-recent coinage described not just Bismarck's own approach to foreign policy but the prevailing one of the times: *Realpolitik*. It was a virtual synonym for the sixteenth-century term *raison d'État* and an updating of that tenet of international relations that had been ratified by the Peace of Westphalia and reaffirmed by the Congress of Vienna: what happened inside any state—the repression, say, of a national minority—was no business of any other state. *Realpolitik* was intended to serve as a guiding principle for diplomacy or, if political means failed, as a justification for the pursuit of political ends by other means—the definition of war put forth earlier in the century by another Prussian, the soldier and military theorist Carl von Clausewitz. However, those ends should not justify, and those means should not include, interference in the internal affairs of another state. Bismarck exceeded Metternich as an object of Henry Kissinger's admiration and, to some extent, emulation.[28]

The term *Realpolitik* was then, and is today, often used approvingly to support the policies of the Iron Chancellor and to refute a variety of other schools, ranging from romantic nationalists to liberal internationalists, not to mention radical socialists.[29]

Marx and Engels lived long enough—until 1883 and 1895 respectively—to die frustrated and discouraged. Neither set foot in Russia, nor did they give that country much thought in developing their theories and predictions. It was in the West that they saw fertile ground for communism. They believed that Russia, having had practically no experience of the Industrial Revolution, lacked the necessary conditions for the triumph of a proletarian one.[30]

THE TWILIGHT OF EMPIRE

The boom in commerce during the Great Power peace prompted the establishment of a wide range of international agencies and commissions to expedite economic activity. Mechanisms to regulate maritime trade, river traffic, and postal services, along with improvements in the steam engine and such new technologies as the telegraph, spread quickly to the rest of the world, largely because much of it was being run from European capitals.

In retrospect, it is clear that the nineteenth century was the twilight of imperialism, but at the time it seemed like high noon. In 1814, just before Napoleon's downfall, European empires ruled a little more than a third of the land on the planet. By 1878, when Bismarck was at the peak of his career, that proportion had doubled. The European powers spent the last two decades of the century in a frenzy of colonial expansion. The motivation was largely economic—a race for new markets and new sources of raw materials. But planting European flags in far-off lands also provided an outlet for swelling national pride and ambition back in Europe. The balance-of-power system kept competition in Europe largely in the diplomatic realm, redirecting strategic rivalry outward, as a scramble for colonies.

Western empires capitalized on the decline of far more ancient ones in the East. At midcentury, the ostensible rulers of China and India held their thrones at the sufferance of European powers. The weak and xenophobic Qing dynasty, in its attempt to keep Western merchants out, provided the Europeans with a pretext to press their mercantile ambitions by force of arms. Rather than impose the kind of direct control they would exercise elsewhere, the Europeans insisted that the Chinese accept enclaves and other privileged zones within which European citizens would be beyond the reach of local laws. The main beneficiaries of this arrangement were Britain, Germany, Russia, and France.

In India, the enfeebled Moguls and the maharajahs who ruled the princely states had come increasingly under the sway of the British East India Company. After a series of uprisings that culminated in the "Mutiny" of 1857, the British government assumed direct administrative control over much of India. In 1876, Queen Victoria, a diminutive widow often pictured wearing a lace headdress, assumed the additional title Empress of India. In the years that followed, the Raj expanded into Burma and beyond, while the Portuguese clung to their outposts, including Goa on the coast of India, Macau near Hong Kong, and Malacca on the Malay peninsula. The Netherlands secured holdings in the East Indies.

Queen Victoria

In Africa, some ten thousand indigenous polities were amalgamated into forty European colonies and protectorates.[31] The British and Portuguese had long held territories on the African coast, but once France entered the fray, other European powers joined in a land rush for the continent as a whole. Germany seized much of modern Tanzania, Cameroon, and Namibia; Spain took parts of Morocco and Western Sahara; Italy tried and failed in the 1880s and '90s to conquer Ethiopia, which for decades remained one of the few uncolonized African states.

Belgium—homeland of Bruegel and other leading lights of European culture and humanism; a country that had been in the forefront of European political reform and cultural achievement in the sixteenth century; a masterpiece of bicommunalism that would twice be the victim of aggression in the first half of the twentieth century; host to the headquarters of the European Union into the twenty-first century—earned special opprobrium for its record as a colonizer in the nineteenth. Under King Leopold II, who ruled from 1865 until 1909, Belgian authorities perpetrated more than their share of the brutality that attended the institution of colonialism. For twenty years starting in 1884, Congo was Leopold's personal property, although he never went there. In his name and largely for his profit, a territory of nearly eight hundred thousand square miles—about seventy-five times larger than Belgium itself—was plundered for its rubber and ivory. By some accounts, as many as ten million Congolese were killed or maimed. The phrase "crime against humanity" was first used when the world finally learned the extent of the systematic savagery.

Yet Leopold was applauded by many of his European contemporaries. In 1884, the *Daily Telegraph* of London congratulated him for having "knit adventurers, traders and missionaries of many races into one band of men, under the most illustrious of modern travelers [H. M. Stanley] to carry into the interior of Africa new ideas of law, order, humanity, and the protection of the natives." Not until early in the twentieth century did reformers (along with novelists, such as Joseph Conrad, who published *The Heart of Darkness* in 1902) have much success in exposing the nature of imperialism at its worst. A commission established by King Leopold himself held him responsible for the atrocities in Congo.[32]

THE MIDDLE EAST, TOO, was increasingly subject to European encroachments in the nineteenth century. The Ottoman Empire, which had been in decline since the Battle of Vienna in 1683, was regarded in the West two centuries later as the "Sick Man of Europe." That perceived condition opened much of the Mediterranean littoral to the European powers.[33] The British and French jostled for the allegiance of the beys who ostensibly ruled North Africa on behalf of the Sublime Porte. France ended up with control over Algeria and Tunisia, Britain over Egypt, Italy over Libya, while Spain and Germany vied with France for Morocco.

As the Ottoman Empire shrank, it lost its ecumenical character. The Sublime Porte, its viziers, and its governors became increasingly less tolerant and more repressive toward non-Turkish—and in particular, toward non-

Muslim—nationality groups. The principal victims of forced migration and slaughter were Christians and vast numbers of Armenians in western urban areas around Istanbul and Izmir, as well as in the provinces of central and eastern Anatolia.[34]

IN 1914, ON THE EVE OF WORLD WAR I, 85 percent of the earth's territory consisted of countries that were either imperial powers, colonies, or independent states ruled by peoples of European descent.[35] Joseph Chamberlain, a prominent British politician and former colonial secretary, confidently proclaimed in 1904: "The day of small nations has long passed away. The day of Empires has come."[36]

Chamberlain's smug view was highly selective with regard to the Western Hemisphere, where the British had bested the French and brought under Victoria's rule a three-thousand-mile-wide expanse, from Newfoundland on the Atlantic to British Columbia on the Pacific.

However, south of the Canadian border, stretching nearly seven thousand miles to Tierra del Fuego, the picture and the prospects were quite different. Those lands were among the earliest that the Europeans had colonized. But it was also there that the process of decolonization was most advanced. The political transformations that began in the late eighteenth century, most spectacularly and consequentially in North America, played a key role not just in bringing European empires to an end but in putting imperialism itself out of business and replacing it with a quite different, better set of ideas and institutions for governing the nations of the world and the international system as a whole.

Two

The American Centuries

7

MONSTERS TO DESTROY

Establishing the liberties of America will not only make that people happy, but will have some effect in diminishing the misery of those, who, in other parts of the world, groan under despotism.
—*BENJAMIN FRANKLIN*[1]

We are the heirs of the ages, and yet we have had to pay few of the penalties which in old countries are exacted by the dead hand of a bygone civilization.
—*THEODORE ROOSEVELT*[2]

I LOOK back on the years I spent at *Time*, from 1971 to 1992, as an extension of my liberal arts education, with a concentration in history and international relations. Lengthy flights and train rides, along with downtime in hotels and layovers in airport departure lounges, gave me plenty of chance to read about the countries I visited. Since I was in the question-asking business, it came naturally, once I had what I needed to write the story of the week, to use interviews to test what I had learned from books and what I had heard back in Washington against the attitudes and perceptions I encountered. I took a special interest in the extent to which the world is a laboratory for the great experiment that is the subject of this book. I often circled back to the idea that, while there was nothing predetermined about a dramatic breakthrough that would ensure a peaceful twenty-first century, there had been real if unsteady progress toward effective global governance in the past, and there was a powerful case to be made that humanity had every reason to step up its efforts to move further and faster in that direction. In July 1992, I devoted the biweekly column I wrote for *Time* to making that case. It appeared under the headline "The Birth of the Global Nation" and included a sentence that would be played back to me after I entered government about six months later: "I'll bet that within the next hundred years (I'm giving the world time for setbacks and myself time to be out of the betting game, just in case I lose this one), nationhood as we know it will be obsolete; all states will recognize a single, global authority."

The piece made me briefly popular with foreign policy liberals and, not so briefly, a target of brickbats from the right.

My subsequent experience in the State Department gave me a fresh perspective on the power of nationalism in many varieties, notably including the American one, as well as on the shortcomings of internationalism. As a result, I have qualified my forecast somewhat, but not in essence. Of course nations in the traditional sense of that word will exist far into the future, with their own territories and borders, their own flags and armies, and their own seats in the UN or, perhaps, in some successor organization. But as the problems requiring multilateral solutions grow in magnitude and complexity, there is reason to hope—and also to predict—that individual states will increasingly see it in their interest to form an international system that is far more cohesive, far more empowered by its members, and therefore far more effective than the one we have today.

"GLOBAL NATION" IN THE SENSE I used it in 1992 never caught on, but the phrase, with a very different meaning, did become part of the rhetoric of American exceptionalism several years later. I believe the first person I heard refer publicly to the United States as a global nation was a soldier: John Shalikashvili, who was the chairman of the Joint Chiefs of Staff from 1993 to 1997, and one of the most admirable, astute, and farsighted figures I worked with in government. With trouble brewing in the Balkans, in the Middle East, and on the Korean Peninsula, "Shali"—as he was known to virtually everyone except those who called him "General," "Sir," or "the Chairman"—gave a television interview in September 1997 explaining why it was in the American national interest to quell outbreaks of instability in far corners of the world. The United States, said Shali, was a "global nation with global interests."

Two years later, Governor George W. Bush of Texas, early in his campaign for the White House, spoke of his desire to lead "a global nation." Once Bush was president, his secretary of defense, Donald Rumsfeld, picked up the phrase and used it to press Congress for increases in defense spending. In recent years it has been part of the rhetorical arsenal of my friend and colleague Richard Holbrooke in his sparring with the Bush administration and its defenders; Holbrooke used it in essentially the same way Shali had, although with implications for the United States' role in the fight against pandemics like HIV/AIDS as well as in the more traditional context of international security.[3]

Needless to say, none of them came anywhere near the meaning of "global nation" I had in mind. The connotation of America as a country with a unique mission in the world resonated with a catchphrase that Henry Luce, the founder of the media empire in which I worked for over two decades, had coined on the eve of America's entry into World War II. In February 1941, ten months before Pearl Harbor, Luce wrote an editorial in *Life* that looked back at his country's achievements: "Throughout the seventeenth century and the eighteenth century and the nineteenth century, this continent teemed with manifold projects and magnificent purposes. Above them all and weaving them all together into the most exciting flag of all the world and of all history was the triumphal purpose of freedom." He exhorted his countrymen to accept as their "manifest duty" a sustained effort "to be the Good Samaritan of the entire world" and thereby "create the first great American Century."

An updated version of that slogan remains fashionable more than sixty-five years later, particularly among those commonly known as neoconservatives, such as the leaders of the Project for a New American Century, which has offices three blocks from Brookings: their stated goal is to "strengthen our ties to democratic allies and to challenge regimes hostile to our interests and values . . . to promote the cause of political and economic freedom abroad . . . and accept responsibility for America's unique role in preserving and extending an international order friendly to our security, our prosperity, and our principles."

These principles are neither the monopoly of conservatives, nor are they "neo," since they reflect a vision for the United States that harks back to the War of Independence.

EMPIRE OF LIBERTY

In recent decades, there has been much talk of a "transatlantic divide." Disputes have flared over the deployment of American missiles on European soil, agricultural subsidies, the price of bananas, aircraft sales and landing rights, genetically modified foods, policy toward Israel (not to mention Iraq), the hegemony of Hollywood, the ubiquity of McDonald's, Coca-Cola, and Starbucks, even the astrological difference between the two geopolitical cultures ("Europeans are from Venus, Americans are from Mars"). Yet aggravation over specifics has been diluted by a general sense of common values. Even what has been, for many years, the chronically strained relationship between the United States and France has been salved by reminders that these two republics were born around the same time and that they were of the same philosophical parentage.

The American and French revolutions were both repudiations of monarchy, a common and often dominant form of government since the dawn of civilization. Both propounded theories of governance that were supposed to be applicable to all humankind. Largely for that reason, their borders did not limit their ambition to expand. So expand they did.

But the ways in which the United States and France expanded, and the systems of government they developed in the wake of their revolutions, were very different. The French Revolution started as a burst of populist and internationalist energy that gave way to despotism and wars of conquest. Peace in Europe was restored through the balance-of-power system, which gave priority to national interests over the Enlightenment ideals. America, by contrast, was able to maintain the slow, fitful, often painful process of becoming a unitary but federalized state and a pluralistic democracy.

FOR OVER A HUNDRED AND THIRTY YEARS, America kept its political distance from Europe. Not until the end of the nineteenth century did the leaders of this new nation feel prepared and provoked to begin acting globally. But when that happened, they could draw from impulses that had been there from the beginning.

Thomas Paine proclaimed, in *Common Sense*—published in 1776—"The Cause of America is in a great measure the cause of all mankind," and, in *The Rights of Man*, "My country is the world, and my religion is to do good."[4] Benjamin Franklin, in a conversation with Paine, said, "Where liberty is, there is my country."[5] Paine and Franklin were echoing Socrates, and like Socrates, they were prepared to die for the sentiment, insofar as it made them traitors who would have been hanged if the revolution had been crushed.

Moreover, there was, among the first Americans, a widespread conviction that God—or at least destiny—was on their side. James Madison saw the "great struggle of the Epoch . . . between liberty and despotism," and Alexander Hamilton believed that victory was assured because the American story was being written "by the hand of the divinity itself."[6]

The Founders had considerable writing of their own to do, and they drew liberally from European sources: Rousseau and the English philosopher John Locke on the social contract; Montesquieu on the separation of powers; and Burke on the virtues of representative government. When Thomas Jefferson and his colleagues drafted the Declaration of Independence, they had, in Locke's *Two Treatises on Government*, philosophical ammunition to make the case that the people could rescind the power of a king or a parliament that failed to protect their lives, liberties, and property. Madison sometimes had, next to him in his study, David Hume's *Essays* open to the pages predicting that "a Perfect Commonwealth" might be realized "either by a dissolution of some old government, or by the combination of men to form a new one, in some distant part of the world."[7]

What Europeans read as critiques of the status quo, the Americans read as recipes for an alternative polity. They believed they were creating something new—although they sometimes used an old word to describe it. Hamilton called America "Hercules in the cradle . . . the embryo of a great empire."[8] Since America had just broken free of an empire, that term might seem out of place, but it usually carried a connotation of something quite different from and better than the European system. George Washington, in a letter to governors on June 8, 1783, wrote: "The foundation of our Empire was not laid in the gloomy age of Ignorance and Superstition, but at an Epoch when the rights of mankind were better understood and more clearly defined, than at any former period."[9]

Thomas Jefferson referred to America as an "empire of liberty," a combination of words that sounds like an ironic refutation of the way Europeans expanded and enforced their rule. Jefferson used the phrase in the context of westward settlement of a wilderness, not the acquisition of colonies. In settling that wilderness, the Americans had to contend not only with indigenous inhabitants but also with the French, Spanish, and British. During his own presidency and then cheering on his friend and successor, James Madison, Jefferson saw expansion as a matter of liberating from European empires as much of the American continent as possible. (Plaques in the House of Commons in Ottawa commemorate battles in which the Canadians turned back invasions from the south.) Looking into the future and at the wider world, Jefferson believed in "conquest without war." Liberal governance of the kind that his country was pioneering, he believed, would eventually replace monarchies, not through force of arms but through the appeal of democracy itself, supported by American diplomacy.[10]

Thus, whatever other debts the Americans owed to the continent from which most of their forebears had come, they did not owe one to Westphalia:

the country they were building was not a nation-state so much as an *idea*-state—a new light unto the other nations of the world. Its self-invention required a distinctive myth of nationhood, based not on purity of blood but

Thomas Jefferson

on purity of ideals. It was a myth in the sense that it oversimplified and glorified a complex and often inglorious story. The American mythmakers had to downplay or rewrite two chapters in particular: the campaign of decimation, subjugation, and deportation of millions of members of over five hundred tribes—or "nations"—of indigenous people who had populated North America for some ten thousand years; and the continuing ownership of slaves for eighty-five years after America gained its independence and for three decades after Britain itself abolished slavery.

E pluribus unum—a line from a minor poem by Virgil that the Founders chose as a motto on the Great Seal of their new country—neatly reconciles diversity and unity.* But a tension between those two virtues was there from the beginning. The Americans conducted a roiling and suspenseful debate over whether they would be citizens of thirteen highly autonomous, even sovereign states or a single one. It took thirteen years to move from loose confederation to federal union and to define what that meant. The opening words of the Constitution coupled a plural pronoun with a singular noun: "We the people." In laying the intellectual foundations for the Constitution, several of its authors recalled the "Grand Design" that the Duc de Sully had proposed to Henry IV. Franklin suggested to a European friend, "I do not see why you might not in Europe carry the Project of good Henry IV into execution, by forming a Federal Union and One Grand Republic of all its different States and Kingdoms, by means of a like convention, for we had many different Interests to reconcile." Madison and other Americans of the period expressed the conviction that by putting into action the ideas of European thinkers, they were creating a model of federal union in the New World that others, including in the Old World, would adopt in the future.[11]

---

* "Moretum," the Virgil poem, is a celebration of the rustic life, and the American motto is taken from a reference to a mixed salad favored by Roman peasants.

In 1789, Immanuel Kant, who was sixty-five at the time, was following news of the Constitutional Convention in Philadelphia from his study in Königsberg. He was relieved and admiring when he saw the Americans adopt the principle of federalism and separation of powers that he had championed in his writings, especially at a time when republicanism was giving way to terror in France.[12]

WITHIN A FEW YEARS, the Founders were further encouraged when their big idea seemed to take hold elsewhere in the hemisphere. In 1807, a twenty-four-year-old Creole from Caracas, Simón Bolívar, who had been studying the works of Montesquieu, Rousseau, and Voltaire in France, was on his way home bent on liberating his native Venezuela and welding it with its fellow Andean colonies into a single independent republic. En route, Bolívar stopped briefly in Philadelphia, Charleston, and several other cities on the East Coast. What he saw there increased his confidence that he could succeed when he got to Venezuela.

Spain, having largely neglected its holdings in Latin America during the Napoleonic Wars, tried to reassert its control in 1808. But one by one, Argentina, Chile, Colombia, Venezuela, Ecuador, Peru, and Bolivia achieved independence. Bolívar became president of Gran Colombia—an area that today subsumes Venezuela, Colombia, Ecuador, and Panama—which Bolívar hoped would one day form the core of a U.S.-like federation. However, once the multiple revolutions had succeeded, the sense of common purpose evaporated. Local aristocrats protected their own gains rather than give up authority to Bolívar.

The difference in political culture between North and South America was not lost on Bolívar himself: he compared the relative liberty that North Americans had enjoyed for centuries, even under the British, to the "three hundred years of servitude" to which the Spanish colonies had been subjected. Feuds among local aristocrats led to civil war in Gran Colombia in 1827 and the secession of its various parts, starting with Venezuela itself in 1829. After trying to hold the federation together with dictatorial powers for two years, Bolívar resigned and Gran Colombia was dissolved in 1830.

EVEN IN NORTH AMERICA, while the effort to create a federal unitary state eventually succeeded, it was no easy task, nor was the outcome certain in the early decades of the republic. The colonies-turned-states were nearly bankrupt. The weak central government established under the Articles of Confederation did not have the authority to raise revenues to deal with national debts without unanimous consent of the states. Protectionism impeded interstate trade. Pennsylvania and Connecticut nearly went to war with each other over conflicting land claims.

No wonder, then, that this newest, most idealistic and international of nations was disinclined, as George Washington put it in his farewell address of 1796, to "interweav[e] our destiny with that of any part of Europe, entangle our peace and prosperity in the toils of European ambition, rivalship, interest, humor, or caprice." Instead, America should "steer clear of permanent alliances with any portion of the foreign world." [13] Or as John Quincy Adams enjoined his countrymen while he was serving as secretary of state in the Monroe administration, the nation should avoid the temptation of going "abroad, in search of monsters to destroy." [14]

Yet even during those first fifty years, far from looking inward, the United States was constantly pushing outward toward the Pacific and, in the process, taking on Europeans whenever they were in the way. The United States engaged France in a series of naval skirmishes in 1798–1800, Britain in the War of 1812, and the "Barbary pirates" in the first fifteen years of the nineteenth century. (In "Perpetual Peace," Kant cited these rulers of small North African states, technically subjects of the Sublime Porte, as international outlaws: "The inhospitable ways of coast regions, such as the Barbary Coast, where they rob ships in the adjoining seas or make stranded seamen into slaves, is contrary to natural law.")

In all three cases, America took military action against threats to its access to the sea lanes on which its economic survival depended. With the Monroe Doctrine in 1823, the United States drew the line against European encroachments in the Western Hemisphere. It was a defensive posture, but it implied a willingness to go on the offensive if necessary.

THEN, IN 1861, AMERICA WAS PLUNGED into the bloodiest conflict it would ever experience. The Civil War was also, at the most basic level, about the nature of democratic governance, since victory meant the eradication of slavery as an institutionalized abomination against the very idea of the rights of man.* William Henry Seward, who served both Lincoln and Andrew Johnson as secretary of state, had confidence that once the United

---

* Robert Kagan argues in *Dangerous Nation* (New York: Knopf, 2006) that the Civil War was actually an international conflict that pitted the Union, as the champion of individual liberty, against a separate state, the Confederacy, as the defender of slavery. Kagan notes that Abraham Lincoln came to the presidency believing that "American nationalism [was]

States cleansed itself of the shameful stain of slavery, the path lay open to global hegemony: "Control of this continent [will become] in a very few years the controlling influence of the world." [15]

Many Europeans feared exactly that eventuality. As Prince Metternich watched the wave of what he called—half fearfully, half disdainfully—the "liberal" revolutions against Spain that swept through Latin America, he fretted that the "flood of evil doctrines and pernicious examples" threatened "the moral force of our governments, and of the conservative system that has saved Europe from complete dissolution." [16]

Had Metternich lived to see the outbreak of the Civil War, he would surely have been one of those who hoped the conflict would consume the energies of the upstart across the Atlantic, since a weakened—better yet, a fractured—America would be less of a challenge to Europe. In the spring of 1863, after the Union had suffered several serious defeats, a member of Parliament, J. A. Roebuck, rose in the House of Commons to observe, gloatingly using the past tense, that "America, while she was united, ran a race of prosperity unparalleled in the world." He expressed the hope of many on his side of the Atlantic in wishing that the Confederacy would prevail, thereby preventing the United States from becoming "the great bully of the world." [17]

WHILE MANY IN EUROPE looked west with alarm, a few, since early in the nineteenth century, sensed that there was a real threat on the rise in the East, in the depths of the Eurasian landmass. Between 1550 and 1700, Russia had been gobbling up an area equivalent in size to the modern Netherlands every year. Prominent among Russia's motives was aggressive self-protection. Catherine the Great is supposed to have explained, "I have no way to defend my borders except to extend them." [18]

Soon after the American Revolution, the Swiss-born historian Johannes von Müller pondered the huge territory within which these two transconti-

---

inherently infused with international moral responsibility." The Union's defeat of the Confederacy—and the ideas about governance for which it stood—was, in Kagan's view, "America's first experiment in ideological conquest," and the Reconstruction of the South was "America's first experiment in 'nation-building.' " Kagan acknowledges that this view differs profoundly from that of Lincoln himself, who saw the conflict very much as a civil war that obligated him, under his oath to defend the Constitution, to put down an insurrection. (Kagan is a scholar at the Carnegie Endowment for International Peace, next door to Brookings, and the husband of Victoria Nuland, for several years my executive assistant at the State Department, and, as of 2007, ambassador to NATO. It was Kagan who injected the Venus/Mars dichotomy into the transatlantic debate.)

nental nations could expand and the unimaginable natural wealth they would have access to as a result. "The future," he predicted, "will belong either to Russia or America." Some twenty years later, Napoleon, wasting away on Saint Helena, had a similar foreboding: the whole world, he feared, would be either an American republic or a Russian monarchy. For Heinrich Heine, neither outcome was one to wish for. He regarded France and Germany as "the two noblest civilized peoples," and therefore pronounced himself "discouraged" at the prospect of Europe being caught in a vice between two backward behemoths, America and Russia.[19]

Alexis de Tocqueville was more discriminating. He spent nine months traveling around the United States in the early 1830s. Although he never visited Russia, he paid close attention to what was going on there through his reading and his connections to his fellow French nobles, some of whom undertook diplomatic assignments to Moscow and Saint Petersburg. Unlike Heine, Tocqueville saw American and Russian power as polar opposites:

> The American struggles against the obstacles that nature opposes to him, [while] the adversaries of the Russian are men. The former combats the wilderness and savage life, the latter, civilization with all its arms. The conquests of the American are therefore gained by the plowshare; those of the Russian by the sword. The Anglo-American relies upon personal interest to accomplish his ends and gives free scope to the unguided strength and common sense of the people; the Russian centers all the authority of society in a single arm. The principal instrument of the former is freedom; of the latter, servitude. Their starting point is different and their courses are not the same; yet each of them seems marked out by the will of Heaven to sway the destinies of half the globe.[20]

In the latter decades of the nineteenth century, many Americans disliked what they knew of Russia. Their antipathy was based not so much on geopolitical rivalry, since "Seward's folly," the American purchase of Alaska for $7.2 million in 1867, had pushed Russia out of the Western Hemisphere. Rather, it reflected abhorrence of czarist autocracy and racism in Russian society, particularly as manifest in the treatment of Jews. Under Czar Alexander III, two hundred thousand Russian Jews immigrated to America, doubling its Jewish population. Concentrated in northeastern cities, they worked with other religious and civic advocacy groups to make sure that the U.S. government knew—and reacted—when repressions occurred.[21]

In response to one wave of officially inspired anti-Jewish violence in Russia, James Blaine, who served as secretary of state in the 1880s and again in the '90s, called on the United States not to feel bound by the long-standing premise that what rulers did within their own borders was their responsibility and no one else's. Instead, the United States should be guided by its "moral duty . . . to the doctrines of religious freedom we so strongly uphold, to seek proper protection for those citizens and tolerance for their creed, in foreign lands." [22] When Alexander III imposed additional anti-Semitic regulations and unleashed more pogroms, President Benjamin Harrison proclaimed that the "banishment" of Russia's Jews was "not a local question."

George Kennan (1845–1924), an Ohio-born surveyor and explorer, wrote and lectured extensively about his travels through the Caucasus and Siberia. His vivid descriptions of Russia's sprawling network of penal colonies and mistreatment of its national minorities, especially Jews, stoked revulsion against the Romanov regime. Mark Twain earned approving laughs on the speaking circuit with a stock anti-Russian crack, "If such a government cannot be overthrown otherwise than by dynamite, then, thank God for dynamite!" [23]

Another American who saw Russia in much the same light was Theodore Roosevelt. In 1897, as the thirty-nine-year-old assistant secretary of the navy in the administration of William McKinley, Roosevelt concluded that Americans would never be able to get along with a country that despised "our political institutions." The nature of Russia's own institutions made it a threat to countries on its borders: "While he can keep absolutism," the Russian would "possess infinite possibilities of menace to his neighbors." Moreover, "If Russia chooses to develop purely on her own line and resist the growth of liberalism, she will sometime experience a red terror that will make the French Revolution pale." [24]

THE ROUGH RIDER AS PEACEMAKER

Theodore Roosevelt's most famous slogan was "Speak softly and carry a big stick; you will go far," supposedly a West African proverb. [25] For him and many others, "going far" meant literally reaching out beyond their country's shores, with a big stick in hand to mete out justice to the villains of the world.

But insofar as America was spoiling for a righteous fight against old-fashioned imperialism, it was highly selective in its choice of targets. The one close at hand was the Spanish colony of Cuba. Roosevelt, soon after arriving at the Navy Department, wrote to Captain Alfred Thayer Mahan, the premier naval strategist of his day, "Until we turn Spain out of the island [of Cuba] (and if I had my way that would be done tomorrow) we will always be menaced by trouble there." The trouble was not just European encroachment on America's hemispheric interests but humanitarian outrages that offended American values. U.S. newspapers carried stories that the Spaniards were torturing and killing Cuban *insurrectos* in concentration camps all over the island, including in the eastern city of Guantánamo.[26]

In January 1898, the battleship USS *Maine* steamed into Havana Harbor to protect Americans there. An explosion—possibly touched off by a malfunction in the engine room but immediately attributed to the Spaniards—sent the *Maine* to the bottom. American newspapers brayed for revenge and popularized the slogan "Remember the Maine, to hell with Spain!" It had long been a principle of international law that a ship on the high seas enjoyed an extension of its homeland's sovereignty. The United States was, at the very least, stretching the point, since the *Maine* was in Cuban waters uninvited, and the cause of the explosion was never proved.

In the ensuing war, the United States demanded the end of Spanish rule of Cuba. Roosevelt, who left his desk job in the Navy Department and signed up as a lieutenant colonel in the army, had a chance to make a name for himself as second in command of a volunteer cavalry unit, the Rough Riders, that stormed a Spanish outpost on Kettle Hill and helped win the decisive Battle of Santiago. In December 1898, Spain abandoned Cuba and ceded Guam, Puerto Rico, and the Philippines to the United States. Roosevelt saw in this development a way to demonstrate that Americans had assumed "our place among the great world powers." Besides, the new Pacific possessions would provide coaling stations for a two-ocean navy.

Still, the idea of replacing Spaniards as colonial overlords caused many Americans to recoil. An immediate consequence of the war was the founding of the American Anti-Imperialist League. Its rolls would include former president Grover Cleveland, the industrialist Andrew Carnegie, the labor leader Samuel Gompers, the Harvard psychologist and philosopher William James, the Yale economist and sociologist William Graham Sumner, and such writers as Ambrose Bierce, Edgar Lee Masters, and Mark Twain. "I have read carefully the treaty [ending the Spanish-American War]," wrote Twain in 1900, "and I have seen that we do not intend to

Theodore Roosevelt

free, but to subjugate the people of the Philippines. We have gone there to conquer, not to redeem. . . . And so I am an anti-imperialist. I am opposed to having the eagle put its talons on any other land." [27]

Even President McKinley and his secretary of state, John Hay, had some ambivalence about America's new holdings in the Pacific and the Caribbean.[28] They, like much of the political establishment, were more comfortable with the idea of what Henry Adams, who was among the most influential political commentators of his day, called "a combine of intelligent equilibrium based on an intelligent allotment of activities." The United States should "pool interests" with Britain, France, and Germany and go on a diplomatic offensive in Asia in order to open markets there, especially in China. The result, Adams believed, would be, "for the first time in fifteen hundred years, a true Roman pax." [29]

Roosevelt, too, was drawn to the idea of combining the force of arms with those of diplomacy and international law. He supported the founding principle of the Hague Conventions: war should be subject to its own version of the Marquess of Queensberry rules. At the first convention, in 1899, twenty-six nations agreed to prohibit the use of several new lethal technologies—asphyxiating gases, dumdum bullets, and balloons to drop bombs. They also established a Permanent Court of Arbitration for solving conflicts peacefully. The following year, as Roosevelt was about to vault from the governorship of New York to the vice presidency of the nation, he wrote: "In the long run civilized man finds he can keep the peace only by subduing his barbarian neighbor. . . . The rule of law and of order has succeeded to the rule of barbarous and bloody violence. Until the great civilized nations stepped in there was no chance for anything but such bloody violence." [30]

Roosevelt saw America—by virtue of its youthful vigor, its ascendancy when the European "great powers" were showing their age, its growing military capacity, and the international appeal of its national idea—to be on its way to establishing itself as the greatest of those civilized nations.

WHEN AN ANARCHIST ASSASSINATED MCKINLEY in 1901, Roosevelt rose to the presidency at the age of forty-two. He had, until then, made the most of his status as a war hero. Once in the White House, however, he threw himself into the task of speaking, if not softly (he had a boisterous manner, and it was he who called the presidency "the bully pulpit"), then *very* diplomatically, and with conspicuous restraint about wielding the big stick of military force. He quickly made international adjudication and peacemaking one of the hallmarks of his leadership.

An early crisis that Roosevelt faced was a dispute between an order of Franciscan friars in California and the Mexican government over land rights. After some sharp diplomatic exchanges, Roosevelt agreed to submit the dispute to the recently established Permanent Court of Arbitration in The Hague, where it was resolved. In his second State of the Union message, Roosevelt asserted:

> It is earnestly to be hoped that this first case will serve as a precedent for others, in which not only the United States but foreign nations may take advantage of the machinery already in existence at The Hague. . . . As civilization grows, warfare becomes less and less the normal condition of foreign relations. . . . Wherever possible, arbitration or some similar method should be employed in lieu of war to settle difficulties between civilized nations, although as yet the world has not progressed sufficiently to render it possible, or necessarily desirable, to invoke arbitration in every case. The formation of the international tribunal which sits at The Hague is an event of good omen from which great consequences for the welfare of all mankind may flow. . . . More and more the increasing interdependence and complexity of international political and economic relations render it incumbent on all civilized and orderly powers to insist on the proper policing of the world.

In 1905, Roosevelt's desire to be peacemaker led him to intervene diplomatically in a conflict on the far side of the Pacific, where the Russo-Japanese War was raging. At issue was control over Korea and Manchuria. In August and September, Roosevelt invited representatives of the combatant countries to Portsmouth, New Hampshire, for intense negotiations. He was at pains to strike the necessary pose of evenhandedness in dealing with the two. That was not easy, since Roosevelt had brought with him to the White House his "loathing of the Czarist form of government." In his first days as president, Roosevelt had made clear to his associates and in his diary that he still brooded about the menace posed by "the Russian."[31]

Roosevelt drew a distinction between Czar Nicholas II, the feeble figurehead of the Romanov empire, and the German ruler Wilhelm II—who bore the title *Kaiser* (which, like *czar*, comes from *caesar*). Of the two, the Kaiser posed by far the greater objective threat to world peace. Germany was building up its navy to challenge Britain on the high seas and strengthening an army that was already viewed as the most powerful on earth. That made Germany, in Roosevelt's view, America's most likely enemy in the next major war.

Nonetheless, Germany still figured in his thinking as "civilized" and therefore as an eventual, if not immediate, member of "the Atlantic system." Russia, however, did not so qualify, primarily because of the way its leaders treated its own people.

The challenge of Germany, as a major European land power with growing maritime capacity and therefore global ambitions, was geopolitical. The problem with Russia, a backward autocracy with little exposure to the Enlightenment, was cultural and ideological. Roosevelt believed that there would be—and, indeed, *should* be—trouble between the United States and Russia for essentially that reason. He had come to that view fully twenty years before Russia succumbed to a small clique of revolutionaries armed with a new ideology that they believed entitled and empowered them to rule the world.

Yet despite his anti-Russian feelings, Roosevelt was determined to bring the Russo-Japanese War to an end. During fifteen months of fighting, Russia had lost every land battle and sent its entire Baltic Fleet all the way around the world to the Tsushima Strait, between the East China Sea and the Sea of Japan, only to see it destroyed in the largest sea battle since Trafalgar. During the two-month negotiation in Portsmouth, Roosevelt brought the full force of his personality and office to bear in extracting from both sides concessions that many believed unlikely. At one point during the talks, Roosevelt found the Russian negotiating tactics so frustrating that he fantasized lining up Czar Nicholas II along with all his ministers and envoys on the edge of a cliff and "run[ning] them violently down a steep place into the sea." [32] But he suppressed such thoughts when he invited the negotiators to come meet with him on Long Island. In those talks, he played up his "deep sympathy for ordinary Russians and their culture."

Roosevelt was able to soothe Japanese pride and sensitivities as well. When the Japanese delegation complained of "talk about the Yellow Terror" in the West, Roosevelt replied that he could sympathize with their resentment, as the custodians of a great civilization, at being regarded as barbarians. His own ancestors in the tenth century, he said, had been part of a "White Terror" of Norsemen that "represented everything hideous and abhorrent and unspeakably dreadful to the people of Ireland, England, and France." [33]

ROOSEVELT, WHO BECAME THE FIRST U.S. PRESIDENT to win the Nobel Peace Prize, for his success in ending the Russo-Japanese War, had three motives for undertaking the project. One of those—to prevent the rise of Japan from upsetting a regional balance of power—was right out of nineteenth-century Europe, but the other two established what would be recurring themes in twentieth- and early twenty-first-century American foreign policy. He felt a humanitarian desire to end the bloodshed, since the Russian blood being shed was mostly from common soldiers and sailors, not aristocrats and other perpetuators of the czarist system. And he wanted to demonstrate his own country's rise as a force for good in the world, notably as a peacemaker.[34]

OVER THERE

As the first decade of the new century came to an end, another early Nobel Prize winner, the British economist Norman Angell, wrote a bestseller, *The Great Illusion*. The title referred to what Angell believed was the false equation of political and military power. Angell was a booster of globalization before the word existed. He believed the myriad connections among modern societies and economies were so beneficial that rationality required the major nations of the world, especially those of Europe, to cooperate rather than compete. War, particularly aggressive war, was widely believed to be quite simply a thing of the past.[35] It was taken as a good sign that the latest innovations in military technology and tactics—the machine gun, barbed wire, and trench warfare—were better suited to defense than offense.[36]

What Angell and many others at the time overlooked was the irrationality of human behavior, including at the highest levels, and a defect in all those salutary international connections: they were primarily among companies, private sources of capital, and agencies to facilitate commerce, such as the International Telegraph Union, the Universal Postal Union, and the International Conference for Promoting Technical Uniformity in Railways. Governments, however, were going their own ways, with little collaboration and much mutual suspicion. Diplomacy, which had been decisively important for the Concert of Europe and its aftermath, was by now largely moribund. What remained of the nineteenth-century balance-of-power theory as practiced in the early twentieth century was its military component: a web of alliances and agreements—Serbia with Russia; Russia with France; Britain with France, Russia, Japan, and Belgium; Germany with Austria-Hungary—that had been assembled to discourage countries from going to war. As the historian John Keegan has noted, "Nineteenth-century Europe had produced no solid instruments of inter-state co-operation or of diplomatic mediation. . . . [As a result, Europe] was a continent of naked nationalism." [37]

Nationalist rivalry was especially potent among the three most powerful and competitive countries in Europe: France, Germany, and Britain. For over forty years, the French had been nurturing grievances over the territory that their country had lost to Germany in the Franco-Prussian War. The Germans, meanwhile, envious of British naval supremacy and of the French and British colonial empires, had begun to acquire maritime power.

In 1912, Georges Sorel, a radical French theoretician who saw nationalism as a curse and violence as a catharsis necessary for political change, taunted the continent's complacent elite: "Europe is a graveyard, inhabited by peoples who burst into song as they go off to kill each other. The French and the Germans are going to be singing pretty soon." [38]

A COROLLARY TO THE GREAT MAN THEORY of history might acknowledge the importance of the little guy at the right (or wrong) place at the right (or wrong) moment. On the Sunday morning of June 28, 1914, a nineteen-year-old student with a grudge and a pistol was the most influential person on earth.

Gavrilo Princip, who may have read about the Peace of Westphalia before he was expelled from high school, was a champion of the aggrieved would-be nation-state. Poor, sickly, and bookish, he fell in with radical Serbian irredentists who wanted an independent Greater Serbia for all Serbs, including ones, like themselves, who were stranded in the Austro-Hungarian province of Bosnia. Through a combination of luck and recklessness, Princip was able to carry out an assignment from his comrades to assassinate Archduke Francis Ferdinand, the heir to the Hapsburg throne of Austria-Hungary, who was on an inspection tour in Sarajevo (Princip accidentally killed the archduke's wife as well).

Suddenly the elaborate system of European alliances went into action—but with catastrophic results. Encouraged by Germany, Austria confronted Serbia with an ultimatum designed to be unacceptable. When Russia mobilized, so did Germany; France joined Russia; Germany declared war on Russia and France and overran Belgium, an ally of Britain; Britain declared war on Germany. In the course of a week, "the shot heard 'round the world" started a grab for territory in a backwater of Europe that escalated to a war involving all the major powers.

Romanticizing their cause, the Allies demonized the enemy as "the Hun," never mind that the Germans' ancestors had been among Attila's victims. Just as Sorel had predicted, soldiers sang as they marched off to battle. So did their families and friends and fellow townspeople cheering them on their way. Everyone expected a quick and glorious affair.

"THE GREAT WAR" LASTED four years. Thirty-two countries were directly involved. Most of the battlefields were in Europe, but other parts of the world—Africa, Latin America, India, China, and Indochina—were changed forever. The major players in Europe turned to their colonies for cannon fodder and labor: foot soldiers and porters from West Africa, Egypt, India, Algeria, Tunisia, Morocco, South Africa, Nigeria, and Indochina; the British recruited one hundred thousand Chinese laborers for logistical work and cranked up their demands for manufactured goods from India, which brought to a boil long-simmering resentments and aspirations on the subcontinent. Mohandas Karamchand Gandhi, a young lawyer from Gujarat who had been organizing the oppressed Indian minority in South Africa, returned home to lead the anticolonial movement. He and others pressed harder their demands for home rule.

Even though the Romanovs had entered the war on what ultimately was the winning side, they and their country were among the biggest losers. The decimation of the czar's troops at Tannenberg in East Prussia and Gorlice in Poland, along with the depletion of Russia's resources and the huge internal migrations of refugees fleeing the war zones, enflamed popular unrest that had been building for decades.

Throughout Europe, the devastation was worse by far than anything the world had ever known or imagined. New technologies—machine guns that could fire six hundred bullets per minute and hit targets a thousand yards away; huge, mechanized artillery pieces; the first tanks, fighters, bombers, and submarines—magnified lethality. Other innovations—chemical weapons such as mustard gas, a "blistering agent" that attacks the eyes and skin, and phosgene, a "choking agent" that destroys the respiratory system—were violations of the 1899 Hague Convention.* Ostensibly defensive tactics, such as trench warfare and the use of barbed wire, contributed to prolonged stalemates and unprecedented slaughter.

---

* The Hague Convention lacked enforcement provisions but still carried just enough weight for neither side to want to be the first to break the rules. Before the Germans used chemical agents at Ypres, they released documents purporting to show that the French had already used gas in an earlier battle.

On the battlefield in World War I

Of the 65 million soldiers mobilized, more than 8.5 million were killed and more than 21 million others wounded. Casualties among the 9 million British soldiers were 35 percent; of 8 million French, 73 percent were killed or wounded; of 12 million Russians, 76 percent; of 8 million Austro-Hungarians, 90 percent. Of the 11 million German casualties (65 percent of those who served), one was an infantryman named Karl Julius Maria van Beethoven. A journalist born in Munich, he was the composer's great-great-nephew and the last male to bear the Beethoven name. He died in a Viennese military hospital in 1917.[39]

In addition to those killed in battle, as many as 13 million civilians died of starvation, disease, massacres, and other consequences of "total war": the mobilization—and the victimization—of entire societies.

WILSON BECOMES A WILSONIAN

The person most responsible for ending the conflagration that Gavrilo Princip had sparked was the president of the United States. More than eighty years after Woodrow Wilson's death, he remains a figure both revered and polarizing. Prominent members of the administration I worked in, including President Clinton himself, considered themselves Wilsonians, although they sometimes used modifiers like *neo* and *pragmatic*. That was because we were often on the defensive against critics who used *Wilsonian* pejoratively, as a synonym for naïve.[40]

Wilson still lends himself to caricature, especially by those who identify

Woodrow Wilson

with his predecessor and rival, Theodore Roosevelt. They often simplistically depict U.S. foreign policy in the twentieth and early twenty-first centuries as a see-saw contest between idealism and realism; between high principle and raw power; between two images of Uncle Sam, one big-hearted but starry-eyed, the other two-fisted and hardheaded. In this supposed dualism, Wilson's severe visage, professorial hauteur, long coat, and top hat are an unflattering contrast to the image of Theodore Roosevelt in his Rough Rider gear.

In *Diplomacy*, published in 1994, Henry Kissinger devotes an entire chapter to the contrast ("The Hinge: Theodore Roosevelt or Woodrow Wilson").[41] Yet, as Kissinger acknowledges, American foreign policy going back to the birth of the country has not been an either/or competition between the approaches embodied by Roosevelt and Wilson. Rather, it has been a yin-and-yang coexistence of the two. U.S. leaders, with broad backing from their constituents, have almost always sought to combine realism and idealism in the role they try to play in the world. There is, in the American mainstream as well as in the foreign policy elite, a hankering after something nobler and more altruistic than *raison d'État* or *Realpolitik*. The United States has explicitly and persistently, though by no means always successfully, sought to defend and advance its national interests while promoting universal values—and treating the two pursuits as complementary.

Roosevelt often made that point, both in office and afterward, when he was stumping around the country as America's most famous private citizen. He would have been offended to hear himself depicted as a Yankee Talleyrand or Metternich. He preached the gospel of muscular idealism before Wilson did, although he had no tolerance for what he regarded as woolly-headed internationalists who believed that the "brotherhood of man" superseded loyalty to the United States of America, or who, like Samuel Johnson, scorned patriotism as "the last refuge of scoundrels."[42]

As for Wilson, with very few exceptions, he had not devoted much attention to foreign policy, although one of those exceptions was noteworthy. In
an essay he wrote as a junior professor of history at Bryn Mawr College and
published in 1887, Wilson predicted a U.S.-led world federation:

Our duty [as Americans] is, to supply the best possible life to a federal organization, to systems within systems; to make town, city, county, state, and federal
governments live with a like strength and an equally assured healthfulness, keeping each unquestionably its own master and yet making all interdependent and co-operative, combining independence with mutual helpfulness. . . .
If we solve this problem [at home] we shall again pilot the world. There is a tendency . . . as yet dim, but already steadily impulsive and clearly destined to prevail, towards, first the confederation of parts of empires like the British, and
finally of great states themselves. Instead of centralization of power, there is to be
wide union with tolerated divisions of prerogative. This is a tendency towards
the American type—of governments joined with governments for the pursuit of
common purposes, in honorary equality and honorable subordination.[43]

This paragraph—like Charles Darwin's glimpse, in *The Descent of Man*, of
a future when "small tribes are united into larger communities . . . extending
to the men of all nations"—is tangential to the author's principal concern,
which in Wilson's case was American governance. Nonetheless, it is a tanta-
lizing intimation on the young Wilson's part of a big idea that would have its
day in the sun sixty years later, in the middle of the twentieth century. It was
all the more remarkable for its assertion that the trend toward world federalism was, in Wilson's entirely un-Darwinian phrase, "clearly destined to prevail." But it was also a theme on which he did not dwell and to which he did
not return, at least not in those explicit and deterministic terms.

The remainder of Wilson's twenty-five-year academic career was American in focus, not international, as was his prepresidential political experience, which consisted of two years as governor of New Jersey. He rarely
traveled abroad and never beyond the English-speaking world (he visited
only Britain and Bermuda). He ran for the White House in 1912 on a mostly
domestic platform. When seeking reelection in 1916, with Europe in flames
and the Kaiser's army fighting for mastery of Europe, Wilson campaigned
under the slogan that he had kept America out of the war. He was already
thinking about the need for intervention, but he believed the public was not
yet ready to hear that case. In that electoral season, it was Roosevelt who de-

nounced Germany for its "breach of international morality" and called for "a great world agreement among all the civilized military powers to back righteousness by force," with the United States leading the way. "We ought not," wrote Roosevelt, "solely to consider our own interests."[44]

ROOSEVELT WAS CHOOSING his words carefully. The American national interest may not have been the *sole* consideration, but it was then, and would continue to be, the primary one when the United States went to war. Germany's decision to wage unrestricted submarine warfare roused America to self-defense; secondarily, the threat of German hegemony in Europe offended America's own concept of *Realpolitik*. It was that combination of factors that brought the United States into the conflict, with calamitous consequences for Germany.

In May 1915, a German U-boat sank the British liner *Lusitania*, killing 1,198 people, including 128 Americans. But unlike the sinking of the *Maine* in Havana, this time while there was an outcry in the United States there was not yet a surge of support for American intervention. Only in 1917, after Wilson had been returned to office, did he finally send doughboys (as American infantrymen were known) across the Atlantic; only then did he invoke *Moralpolitik* as the motive. He mobilized domestic support by saying that Americans must wage "the war to end all wars"—one that would "make the world safe for democracy."[45]

Wilson had come to that position reluctantly after the revelation, four days before he was to give his second Inaugural Address, of the "Zimmermann Telegram," a document revealing a bizarre plan hatched by the Kaiser's foreign minister: if Mexico would ally itself with Germany against America, Germany would return to Mexico three American states that had been annexed in the Mexican-American War of 1846–48—Texas, Arizona, and New Mexico. Once decoded by British cryptographers and made public, the telegram shocked and infuriated Americans as the diplomatic equivalent of an attack on their homeland. Seventeen days after that news broke, U-boats sank three U.S. merchant ships. Two weeks later, Wilson went before Congress to seek a declaration of war.*

By then, the Allies' economies were at the breaking point; their factories could not produce enough armaments to sustain the war effort much longer.

---

* Wilson asked Congress for permission to go to war against Germany on April 2, 1917. The Senate gave its approval two days later, the House six days after that. However, the United States did not formally declare war against Austria-Hungary until, coincidentally, December 7.

American entry provided an emergency infusion of cash and industrial capacity. A million fresh soldiers crossed the Atlantic to help rescue the Allies from the quagmire of the second battles of the Somme and the Marne and turn back a fierce German offensive in the spring of 1918. (Only later would another consequence be known: the so-called Spanish flu of 1918–20— which killed tens of millions worldwide, far more than all the soldiers and civilians who died in the war itself—first broke out at a U.S. Army camp in Kansas and was carried to Europe by the U.S. Expeditionary Force.)[46]

More than 100,000 Americans died in combat and about 200,000 were wounded, a grievously high number in the absolute, but not relative to what the Europeans suffered. (The British alone suffered 60,000 casualties on the first day of the Battle of the Somme in July 1916 and more deaths at the Battle of Passchendaele in 1917 than the number of Americans killed in both world wars.)[47]

My paternal grandfather was twenty-four in April 1917, when the United States declared war on Germany. The next morning he signed up at the post office in his hometown, Dayton, Ohio. He was sent to France to serve as a general's aide-de-camp. His letters home expressed impatience tinged with shame at "drinking tea" in the safety of headquarters while his fellow soldiers were fighting and dying in the trenches. Therefore, he told his mother, he was requesting reassignment to the front. She had sent him off to war with expressions of pride that he was doing his duty to God and country. Now she was appalled. "Why should you select to be an active part of all this murder and carnage?" she wrote back. "Why not thank Dear God every waking moment that you are spared the horror of it all? You brace up, and if you have to drink tea as your share of the war, drink it—and thank God it isn't arsenic!"

Touched but undeterred, her son got the transfer he wanted and ended up as an artillery officer. In a field hospital, he met a Red Cross nurse from Chicago who became my grandmother. The courtship of two Americans from the Midwest, in the midst of the epochal conflict in which the United States played a decisive role, became part of our family lore. Hearing the story told and retold during my early childhood had some effect in shaping my sense of history and the world even before I began to read books or study maps. As a small boy I knew my grandfather, so I felt I had an intimate connection with that generation of Americans who, like their European contemporaries, sang as they went off to war. One jaunty song that echoed down the years was "Over There," by George M. Cohan. It conjured up a place far away, across an ocean, where there were monsters for us to destroy.

8

EMPTY CHAIRS

In the end, [the League of Nations] is what it is; above all else it is the work of human beings and, as a result, it is not perfect. We all did what we could to work fast and well.
—*GEORGES CLEMENCEAU*[1]

Universalism without toleration, it's clear, turns easily to murder.
—*K. ANTHONY APPIAH*[2]

As Woodrow Wilson looked ahead to peace, he based his hopes and his policies on two big ideas: self-determination for individual nations and a league to bind them together in the cause of a peace. He had come to them gradually and, once he made them his own, he subjected neither to much public explanation or testing. Both goals had been advocated by Theodore Roosevelt since the first weeks of the Great War, when he chided Wilson over American neutrality. "[S]urely the time ought to be ripe," Roosevelt wrote in September 1914, "for the nations to consider a great world agreement among all the civilized military powers to back righteousness by force. Such an agreement would establish an efficient World League for the Peace of Righteousness. Such an agreement could limit the amount to be spent on armaments and, after defining carefully the inalienable rights of each nation which were not to be transgressed by any other, could also provide that any cause of difference among them, or between one of them and one of a certain number of designated outside nonmilitary nations, should be submitted to an international court, including citizens of all these nations, chosen not as representatives of the nations but as judges—and perhaps in any given case the particular judges could be chosen by lot from the total number. To supplement and make this effectual it should be solemnly covenanted that if any nation refused to abide by the decision of such a court the others would draw the sword on behalf of peace and justice and would unitedly coerce the recalcitrant nation."[3]

Another of Wilson's predecessors in the White House, William Howard Taft, was among the worthies who had gathered at the Century Association in New York in early 1915 to sketch out a plan for what they called a League to Enforce Peace. "The signatory powers," said one of the documents they produced, "shall jointly use forthwith both their economic and military forces against any one of their number that goes to war, or commits acts of hostility, against another of the signatories." In short, they were promoting collective security—the principle that the security of each state depends on the security of all—and the creation of a mechanism to punish those who violated that principle. These were ideas that Dante had envisioned for a universal kingdom and Kant for a perpetual peace.[4]

By the time Wilson asked Congress to support the war in April 1917, he too sounded as though he was speaking from a script ghostwritten by Kant. "Our objective," he said, "is to vindicate the principles of peace and justice in the life of the world as against selfish and autocratic power and to set up among the really free and self-governing peoples of the world such a concert of purpose and of action as will henceforth ensure the observance of those principles." He foresaw "a universal dominion of right by such a concert of free peoples as shall bring peace and safety to all nations and make the world itself at last free."

NINE MONTHS LATER, on January 8, 1918, Wilson appeared before the joint houses of Congress to set forth his Fourteen Points on the conditions for peace. He was responding not just to the continuing war in Europe but to the separate peace that Vladimir Lenin, the leader of the Russian Revolution, had made with Germany.

The United States had not only lost an ally, it had gained a new kind of potential enemy. Russia had been offensive to many Americans when it was an anachronism; now it had become a futuristic experiment in absolutism, with power concentrated in the hands of a few men who claimed to represent all the workers of the world. At first the Bolsheviks hoped to spread their revolution everywhere by means of what Leon Trotsky called the "permanent revolution," which was to be coordinated by the Communist International.

Wilson intended his Fourteen Points to help counter the appeal of communism in war-torn Europe. He couched that purpose in the softest possible terms, emphasizing engagement of Russia rather than its isolation. Wilson's Point 6 promised the Bolshevik leadership a "sincere welcome, . . . assistance also of every kind [and] intelligent and unselfish sympathy" if it would join "the society of free nations." Rather than throwing down the gauntlet to what would soon become the Soviet state, Wilson was holding out the incentive of its integration into the international community—on the condition that postczarist Russia adopt that community's defining norms, including democratic governance.[5] (Herbert Hoover, who was then one of Wilson's advisers, privately warned the president that this would never happen. "The Bolsheviki," wrote Hoover, constituted a "tyranny that is the negation of democracy" and that posed the threat of world domination.[6])

Setting forth what he hoped would be the rules of a postwar world, Wilson called for a readjustment of frontiers by means of "friendly counsel along historically established lines of allegiance and nationality." He knew that delicate negotiations would be required, since the defeat of the Central Powers—Germany, Austria-Hungary, Turkey, and Bulgaria—would reopen old disputes about whether "the established lines" were indeed just, and persuading all the parties to see them as such would be difficult.

Wilson already had fixed in his mind the idea that the principles of a democratic society could be made to work internationally. "What we seek," he said in a Fourth of July speech four months before the armistice, "is the reign of law, based upon the consent of the governed and sustained by the organized opinion of mankind." But there too he saw a risk: "[i]ntroducing new or perpetuating old elements of discord and antagonism . . . would be likely in time to break the peace of Europe, and consequently of the world."[7] As late as September 1918, with peace now only two months away, he was still wrestling with the dilemma of how to fulfill the "well-defined" national aspirations of the peoples of the Austro-Hungarian Empire without totally dismantling the imperial structure.[8]

Three months later, accompanied by a squadron of destroyers and battleships, Wilson set off across the Atlantic aboard the *George Washington*, a former German passenger liner that had sought refuge in New York at the beginning of the war and been commandeered by the U.S. Navy. During the voyage, Wilson's advisers pored over maps of Europe and tried to align new international boundaries as much as possible with existing ethnographic ones.

When I first read of this scene, it made me think of my own attempts to make sense of the helter-skelter of political geography. Left to their Hobbesian instincts and Machiavellian devices, the Europeans had spent the previous centuries drawing and redrawing those borders in blood, reflecting the relative strength, ambition, and luck of kings and emperors. Here, as Wilson saw it, was a chance, born of the failure of *Realpolitik*, to redraw the map yet again, this time peacefully and based on the principles of rationality, equity, and the republican form of governance.

WHEN WILSON ARRIVED in the French port of Brest, he became the first incumbent American president to set foot on European soil. He embodied the transformation of the United States from a hemispheric power into a transatlantic one. The United States was now a major military, political, economic, and ideological presence on the Eurasian landmass, and its leader was welcomed accordingly. The European media hailed him as the most powerful and honored man on the earth. Placards in Brest and at every stop along Wilson's way through France, Britain, and Italy proclaimed him "the Champion of the Rights of Man," "the Founder of the Society of Nations," "the God of Peace," "the Savior of Humanity," and "the Moses from Across the Atlantic." [9] Crowds cheered and threw flowers as he passed. Streets and squares were renamed after him.

On January 18, 1919, he arrived in the Hall of Mirrors at Versailles for the opening of the Paris Peace Conference. The French prime minister, Georges Clemenceau, had chosen the venue and date because it was there, exactly forty-eight years before, that Wilhelm I had been crowned emperor of Germany. For many present, the American guest was, far more than the French host, the hero of the occasion, not least because Wilson, alone among the assembled leaders, seemed more interested in the future than in settling scores from the previous century. [10]

Once the conference settled down to work, Wilson served as chairman of a steering committee of five great powers: Britain, France, Italy, Japan, and the United States. The European members of the steering committee all had long-standing imperial histories, as did Belgium, the Netherlands, and Portugal. Yet none of those nations would recover the material wealth, military strength, or political backing they needed from their citizens to hang on to their colonies. The Romanovs had been swept away by revolution. Two major imperial dynasties on the losing side—the Hapsburgs and the Hohenzollerns—were forced to abdicate in favor of republics. The capitulation of the Ottoman sultan, Mehmed VI, to the Allies triggered a military uprising led by Mustafa Kemal, whose forces managed to expel the Greek, British, French, and Italian troops that had occupied parts of Turkey's remaining territory, as well as overcome resistance from Ottoman units still loyal to the sultan. In 1922, a Turkish Grand National Assembly, organized by Kemal, voted to abolish the sultanate, and the following year, Turkey was declared a republic with Kemal as its first president. The caliphate, which the Ottomans had held since the sixteenth century, was abolished in 1924. (Ten years later, the assembly would confer upon Kemal the name Ataturk, or "Father of Turks.")

IMPERIALISM AS A SYSTEM of globe-spanning governance was fatally wounded, a fact Wilson recognized and welcomed. Communications within his entourage and exchanges with his administration back in Washington were full of references to "autonomous development," "the rights and liberties of small nations," and the application, to peoples who had been subjects of empire, of "the American principle"—a commitment to independence, unity, constitutional democracy, and, of course, self-determination. In an address to a joint session of Congress on February 11, 1918, Wilson said, "National aspirations must be respected; peoples may now be dominated and governed only by their own consent. 'Self-determination' is not a mere phrase. It is an imperative principle of action, which statesmen will henceforth ignore at their peril."

But there was still little clarity about how all this rhetoric would be translated into new lines on the map.[11] The extent to which Wilson was making it up as he went along dismayed his secretary of state, Robert Lansing. "When the President talks of 'self-determination' what unit has he in mind?" Lansing wondered in his diary. "Does he mean a race, a territorial area, or a community?" Lansing wished his chief had never stumbled—and for Lansing, that was the right verb—upon the idea of self-determination, since, in his view, "It will raise hopes which can never be realized. It will, I fear, cost thousands of lives. In the end it is bound to be scorned as the dream of an idealist who failed to realize that danger until it was too late to check those who attempt to put the principle into force."[12]

LANSING'S APPREHENSION looks valid in light of what happened later. Many historians and political scientists have depicted Wilson's attachment to the idea of self-determination as an inexcusable folly that contributed to the catastrophes of the thirties and forties—and, for that matter, to those of the 1990s in the Balkans.

However, just because World War II broke out twenty years after Versailles does not mean that Wilson's ideas, which so dominated the peace conference, led ineluctably to subsequent disasters. It is legitimate to criticize Wilson's ideas for being defective, his decisions for being made on a wing and a prayer, and his management of the domestic politics of foreign policy for being high-handed and therefore likely to backfire. But it is not analytically sound to conclude that what happened in the thirties and forties was rendered inevitable by Versailles.

Wilson had a plan that might have worked if it had been better implemented. All those books and charts he reviewed on his voyage to Europe reminded him that there were far more self-conceived nationalities in the world than there could possibly be candidates for self-determination. Instead of simply a return to the Westphalian nation-state as the replacement for empire, which could lead to the atomization of Europe, he proposed the creation of *multi*national states for kindred ethnic groups. Westphalia had yielded France for the French and Sweden for the Swedes; Versailles would create Czechoslovakia for the Czechs and Slovaks and a Kingdom of the Serbs, Croats, and Slovenes, which later changed its name to Yugoslavia, "the Land of the Southern Slavs."

Wilson and the architects of Versailles also knew perfectly well that these two new countries contained several non-Slav communities. For example, there were Hungarians in the north and ethnic Albanians in the south of Serbia, which was now part of Yugoslavia. Similarly, the German-speaking population of Bohemia found itself living on territory that various treaties and commissions granted to Czechoslovakia.

There was nothing necessarily wrong with the idea of states that included ethnic and other minorities. Indeed, there was no way to avoid that outcome. Czechoslovakia and Yugoslavia were artificial states, born out of the wreckage of a war. But so were many, indeed most, states on earth. The question was not just how to construct a viable, liberal state, whether made up of one nationality group or several or many, but also how to build an international structure around it that would support its viability.

To that question, Wilson's answer was collective security of the sort envisioned by Roosevelt, Taft, and the others during the war. A one-for-all-and-all-for-one principle would be written into the Treaty of Versailles as Article 10. It committed all signatories "to respect and preserve as against external aggression the territorial integrity and existing independence" of all states. This obligation was unprecedented. The nineteenth-century alliances intended to maintain the balance of power were for the protection of their own members. Article 10 was far more expansive—it was, in theory at least, universal. Moreover, it was intended to be binding and permanent. Wilson believed that "the great game . . . of balance of power" would be "now forever discredited." [13]

Collective security was to be reinforced by disarmament. Wilson's Fourteen Points included a requirement that "national armaments be reduced to the lowest point consistent with national safety"—a measure, included virtually verbatim in Article 8 of the treaty, that Wilson hoped would limit the means of waging wars of aggression.

BY FAR THE MOST CONSEQUENTIAL of the Fourteen Points was the last: the assertion that "a general association of nations must be formed under specific covenants for the purpose of affording mutual guarantees of political independence and territorial integrity to great and small states alike." That arrangement, like others, would be achieved through "open covenants of peace, openly arrived at." As Wilson elaborated the concept, no longer could "peoples and provinces" be treated as "mere chattels and pawns": the small powers would know what the great powers were up to—and they would have the greatest of those powers to look out for them.[14]

What Wilson called an "association," various peace groups active in the United States and Britain during the war wanted to call a "league," in part because of the word's association with the Amphictyonic League that had so appealed to Kant. A leading contemporary advocate of making that regional arrangement of the ancient Greeks a model for a global one in the twentieth century was Lord Robert Cecil, a British Conservative who served briefly in the Red Cross at the beginning of World War I before holding a number of government posts.

Not until the fall of 1918 did Wilson start using the word *league* himself. For him the most important word associated with the postwar order was *covenant*. Its religious connotations reflected the devout Presbyterian in him and his determination to establish what the historian Zara Steiner calls a "spiritual base of the new social contract that was to replace the old system that had failed so spectacularly."[15]

The Wilsonian concept of a covenant had much in common with the concept of federalism that Leibniz, Hume, and Kant had derived from ecclesiastical doctrine during the Enlightenment and that figured so centrally in the Constitution of America itself. The Covenant of the League—which comprised the first twenty-six articles of the Versailles treaty—made member states responsible for governing themselves while entrusting to the League the authority to preserve peace and maintain collective prosperity. One passage in the Covenant even suggested, though it did not quite assert, that the authority to make war resided with the League rather than with national governments.*

That still left the question of how to protect the rights of the German-speaking population of Czechoslovakia, the Hungarians and ethnic Albanians of Yugoslavia, and numerous other communities that had been stranded on what, from their standpoint, was the wrong side of the postwar boundaries. The League was supposed to hold its members to certain norms regulating not only their international conduct but also the manner in which they treated their own populations, especially minorities.

For Wilson, a degree of self-determination at the sub-state level was as important as the creation of post-Versailles states such as Yugoslavia and Czechoslovakia. He believed that the rights of minorities within a state, like those of the individual citizen, were integral to democracy. It had been to make the world safe for that form of government that Wilson had brought his country into the Great War, so it followed, in his mind, that only democracies would qualify for the benefits of the postwar order. He pounded away on this theme: "Only the free peoples of the world can join the League of Nations. . . . No nation is admitted to the League of Nations that cannot show that it has the institutions we call free. No autocratic government can come into its membership, no government that is not controlled by the will and vote of its people . . . [O]nly a nation whose government [is] its servant and not its master could be trusted to preserve the peace of the world." [16]

DEFEAT ON THE HOME FRONT

Woodrow Wilson was in Versailles on June 28, 1919—five years to the day after Gavrilo Princip opened fire on the archduke and duchess in Sarajevo—to sign the treaty that formally ended the war. In the months that followed, Wilson was unable to convince the United States Senate to ratify it. As a result, America would not be a member of the League that its president, more than anyone else, had brought into existence.

There had been plenty of warning signs that this might happen. Even while Wilson was being lionized in Europe, critics back home questioned whether he should even have made a trip that symbolized America's assump-

* The final sentence of Article 10 read: "In case of any such aggression or in case of any threat or danger of such aggression the Council [of the League] shall *advise* upon the means by which this obligation shall be fulfilled" (italics added).

tion of responsibility for sorting out the mess that Europe had made of itself and the world.

Opposition was concentrated among Republicans. They had won control of both houses of Congress in the midterm elections of 1918. That setback for Wilson's party was ominous for him personally and for the project on which he had staked his presidency, since it elevated one of his most determined foes, Henry Cabot Lodge of Massachusetts, to the chairmanship of the Senate Foreign Relations Committee.

In August 1919, Lodge explained his determination to defeat the Versailles treaty in terms that deliberately echoed George Washington's farewell address: "The United States is the world's best hope, but if you fetter her in the interests and quarrels of other nations, if you tangle her in the intrigues of Europe, you will destroy her power for good and endanger her very existence. Leave her to march freely through the centuries to come as in the years that have gone. Strong, generous, and confident, she has nobly served humankind. Beware how you trifle with your marvelous inheritance, this great land of ordered liberty, for if we stumble and fall, freedom and civilization everywhere will go down in ruin." Washington, he added a month later, "did not say that we should keep clear from 'entangling alliances' in the Farewell Address. He said that we should keep clear of *permanent alliances*, and that temporary alliances would be sufficient to meet an emergency—as they were in the war just closed." [17]

As the prospects for American participation in the League grew bleaker, Wilson denounced his enemies for wanting America to retreat into "sullen and selfish isolation." But as Lodge's statement suggested, *isolationism*—a term that would be used to describe the national mood and policy that prevailed for most of the next two decades—was something of a misnomer. It conjured up the image, favored then and since by political cartoonists, of an ostrich with its head in the sand. In fact, Lodge and his political allies were not urging the United States to isolate itself from the world. Rather, they were challenging Wilson's inclination, as they saw it, to compromise American sovereignty and to overextend American power and responsibility; binding covenants and the institutions they created were not the proper means of engagement; the United States should lead by glorious example and through the free exercise of its political will, backed by its military and economic strength. Precisely because America had a unique role to play in the world, it also had a right and indeed an obligation to reject the "fetters" of treaties like Versailles and organizations like the League.

• • •

THE MOST CONTENTIOUS ISSUE between Wilson and Lodge was Article 10, which dealt with collective security. Wilson regarded it as his principal contribution to the covenant. No leader of the great powers other than Wilson himself was enthusiastic about it. Even Lord Cecil, one of the founders of the League, tried to water down the controversial language. He saw Article 10 as Wilson's attempt to conjure up a deus ex machina to solve all the problems of the postwar world, while in fact the League was "only another piece of machinery. After it has been created, the fundamental difficulty will remain. No machinery can do more than facilitate the action of the peoples. Unless they and their Governments really put the enforcement of the law and the maintenance of peace as the first and greatest of national interests, no Confederation or Federation can compel them to do so."[18]

Wilson was no more prepared to compromise on Article 10 with the Allies in Paris than he was with the Senate in Washington. In the end, his obduracy and sense of embattlement, combined with the partial incapacity he suffered as a result of a stroke in October 1919, hindered his ability to save the treaty. In November it failed in the Senate by a vote of 53 to 34. The following March, a modified version, with fifteen reservations to its original text, fell short of getting the necessary two-thirds majority. Among the more consequential setbacks—which Wilson saw as a betrayal—was that Taft, Harvard University president Lawrence Lowell, and their colleagues in the League to Enforce Peace reversed their earlier support for the League of Nations and sided with Lodge.[19]

In Paris, where the League had held its opening session on January 16, 1920, Prime Minister Clemenceau directed that an empty chair be put at the table for the missing American representative.

In December of that year, after the Democrats were crushed in the presidential and congressional elections, Wilson and Léon Bourgeois, who had represented France on the League of Nations Commission at Versailles, were invited to appear together for a single ceremony in Oslo at which they would be awarded the Nobel Peace Prizes for 1919 and 1920 respectively. Wilson disliked Bourgeois and resented being asked to share the stage. In the end, Wilson's illness prevented him from making the trip, and the American minister to Norway, Albert Schmedeman, read a brief statement on the president's behalf: "Mankind has not yet been rid of the unspeakable horror of war. I am convinced that our generation has, despite its wounds, made notable progress. But it is the better part of wisdom to consider our work as one begun. It will be a continuing labor."

WITH THE UNITED STATES on the sidelines, the remaining great powers found it easier to protect their national prerogatives in Geneva than if an American official had been there to champion Wilson's vision of the League. They established a small council, made up of Britain, France, Italy, and Japan as permanent members (the same four that, along with the United States, had served as the steering committee at Versailles). Several nonpermanent members were elected by a larger assembly. The council was to meet at least three times a year to consider political disputes, including charges of aggression. Since council decisions had to be unanimous to take effect, each member had a veto. Thus, the major European powers and Japan were every bit as able to protect their sovereignty as members of the League as the United States was by staying out of it.

THE LULL BETWEEN THE STORMS

Just as generals tend to fight the last war, statesmen tend to base their prescriptions for keeping the peace on a diagnosis of the last breakdown in diplomacy. There was, at Versailles and in the years afterward, a widespread belief that the Great War had come about because of a giant blunder. Edward Grey, a member of the House of Lords and special envoy with the assignment of trying to get the United States to join the League, reflected shortly after the armistice that "the war came into being largely by default, because the forces of negotiation and peaceful settlement marshaled against it suddenly collapsed."*

Here was a participant in and a spokesman for the victors, with every reason to blame the Kaiser and "the Hun" for starting the war. Yet he chose instead to depict the whole thing as a colossal accident—what Inis Claude, a leading historian of international institutions, has termed a "predicament war, unplanned and unwanted by any of the parties involved," as opposed to a "policy war, deliberately launched by a state or group of states in the effort to execute a plan of aggression and conquest."[20]

---

* It was Grey, as British foreign secretary in 1914, who had famously intoned, "The lamps are going out all over Europe; we shall not see them lit again in our lifetime." Barbara Tuchman made the stumbling-into-war argument in her 1962 bestseller *The Guns of August*, which influenced John F. Kennedy's analysis and handling of the Cuban missile crisis.

It followed that the purpose of the peace should be, first and foremost, to prevent such catastrophic miscalculations from happening again. That aspiration was less ambitious—and, those who were so motivated would have said, more realistic—than Wilson's hope that the Great War would be the last war.[21] The conflict just concluded had been sufficiently devastating to convince its European and Japanese victors that they could not afford another one *any time soon*. In their view it was still a Hobbesian, Clausewitzian world, not a Kantian or a Wilsonian one. War as such, if it were properly prepared for and based on sound geopolitical calculation, was not out of the question. Therefore those in positions of power in London, Paris, and Tokyo had no more enthusiasm for the disarmament provisions of the Versailles treaty than they did for Article 10. The British and French in particular sought to combine a focus on economic recovery with a long-term strategy to preserve and, over time, enhance their own military power as the ultimate means of deterring future enemies and ensuring the security of their states.

With this strategy in mind, the British government in 1919 adopted the so-called "Ten-Year Rule," based on a guess that it would be at least a decade before there would be another European war.

DURING THAT RESPITE, the League attained some modest achievements and established some useful precedents that, given the magnitude of its overall failure, have tended to be forgotten or undervalued. It headed off armed confrontations in seventeen disputes and successfully mediated an end to hostilities in at least seven. As early as 1920, the League brokered a compromise between Sweden and Finland over the Åland (pronounced "oh-lund") Islands, whose overwhelmingly Swedish-speaking residents remained citizens of Finland but enjoyed a high degree of autonomy. That outcome stands to this day as a model for how to protect the rights and accommodate the interests of a minority while maintaining a unitary state. Other measures were intended to guard the cultural, political, religious, and linguistic rights of minority communities living in Albania, Austria, Bulgaria, Czechoslovakia, Estonia, Greece, Hungary, Latvia, Lithuania, Poland, Romania, Turkey, and Yugoslavia. In these cases, too, the League's record, while mixed, was marked by some successes in compensating for expropriated property; providing assurances that Jews would not be penalized for observing the Sabbath; ending some restrictions on educational and cultural activities; and imposing penalties on public officials who abused the rights of minorities.[22]

The Permanent Court of International Justice, the League's judicial arm, labored under a number of constraints (it had jurisdiction to settle cases only if the contending parties agreed to submit to its judgment, and its opinions were nonbinding), but its very existence made it easier for countries with grievances to accept mediation and the proposed compromises and other rulings that the court handed down.

The League also put in place a reasonably effective system for dealing with the multitudes of refugees created by the war. As the twenties unfolded, most European states were able, with the League's help, to stabilize their currencies and find peaceful means of defusing national tensions. Finally, the Wilsonian concept of self-determination showed some promise of working in that more people lived under governments of their own choosing than ever before.[23]

THE BEST THAT CAN BE SAID OF THE LEAGUE'S handling of colonialism is that it reflected established Western attitudes of the time—and the best that can be said of those attitudes is that they were Euro-centric; a harsher verdict would be that they were racist. While the victors at Versailles were all for respecting ethnic and other minorities in Europe, the Western leaders there (including Wilson) blocked a Japanese attempt to include a clause on racial equality in the treaty. When the ink was dry, the overwhelming majorities living under imperial rule in Africa, the Middle East, and Asia had only the dimmest glimpse of self-determination in a distant future.

The mechanism whereby the League disposed of German and Ottoman colonies was to award them as "mandates" to imperial powers on the winning side in the war.* The mandates were to be administered with a degree of control that reflected their stage of social, political, and economic development and their geopolitical importance. In theory, this arrangement was intended to be a step away from colonialism and toward eventual independence. The role that the mandatory powers were assuming was supposed to be more custodial than imperial. In practice, however, that distinction had little meaning for most of the people subject to the system.

Among the numerous transfers in Africa was Belgium's assumption of control over Rwanda and Burundi, which meant inheriting from the Ger-

---

*Japan, while rebuffed on its racial-equality proposal, was given control over Germany's island holdings in the Pacific north of the equator.

mans responsibility for managing two principal tribes with a history of conflict. Long before Europeans arrived on the continent—since at least the fifteenth century—people who called themselves Tutsis had ruled the kingdom of Rwanda, while the majority in the area called themselves Hutus. When, in the nineteenth century, Rwanda and Burundi were ceded to Germany as a joint colonial territory, the Germans supported the primacy of the Tutsi. Once the Belgians assumed control of Rwanda and Burundi as a mandate from the League of Nations, they, too, exploited the distinction between Hutus and Tutsis for administrative purposes. Sometimes a Tutsi was deemed to be anyone associated with the ruling class of Rwanda, or someone with more than ten cows, or who was tall and had a long nose. In any event, Tutsis were a privileged minority—often, throughout history and around the world, a dangerous category.

It would be another seventy years before the consequences of German-Belgian policy in Africa played out in their full horror.

THE BRITISH, TOO, INADVERTENTLY lit some long-burning fuses. They took on the postwar administration of Palestine—the former Ottoman lands between the Mediterranean and the Jordan River. Counting on a commitment that David Lloyd George's government had made in the Balfour Declaration during the war, members of the worldwide Zionist movement hoped that Britain would establish a "national home" for the Jews in the Holy Land as part of the partition of the Ottoman empire. But the Balfour Declaration also stipulated that "nothing shall be done which may prejudice the civil and religious rights of existing non-Jewish communities in Palestine." How to square that circle was a challenge left for another day.

A further task that fell to the British was patching together a new country called Iraq out of three Ottoman provinces in Mesopotamia. Arnold Wilson, the British commissioner in charge, put his home office on notice that this project would be arduous, costly, protracted, and dangerous, not least for a reason that had its analogue in Rwanda: the Shiite Muslim majority in Iraq would chafe at a perpetuation of the Sunni minority's political dominance. An American missionary who knew the tribal culture well warned another British administrator, Gertrude Bell, "You are flying in the face of four millenniums of history if you try to draw a line around Iraq and call it a political entity." The more immediate problem was that a broad-based insurgency united Shias, Sunnis, and Kurds against the foreign occupiers. The brutality of the military response shocked the British public. London in effect threw up its hands and installed an Arabian prince on a hastily created Iraqi throne. In 1932, Iraq graduated from being a mandate to a sovereign member of the League.[24]

The League had never taken the criterion of a self-governing state to mean what Wilson intended—a state governed by its own citizens. Rather, by the League's lights, self-governing meant independent, not democratic. Yet even with its flaws, the mandate system represented a potential breakthrough in world politics. Under the rules of the League, the mandatory authorities did not have sovereign power over the former colonies and imperial holdings they were charged with administering; they were accountable to the League itself; the League was, in that respect, *above* their own governments—that is, *supranational*. That word had come into use early in the century, and Lord Cecil helped put it into common usage. In October 1921, the Glasgow *Herald* proclaimed, "It [is] only a developed sense of supranationalism that would in the future make war unthinkable."

THERE WERE SIGNS DURING THE TWENTIES that the United States, even though it was boycotting the League, was still looking for a way to play a leadership role on the world stage. In 1921–22, the administration of Wilson's successor, Warren Harding, convened the International Conference on Naval Limitation in Washington. The American hosts brought together representatives of eight other countries. Four were major naval powers: the United States, Britain, France, and Japan. In addition, Belgium, China, Italy, the Netherlands, and Portugal participated. The purpose was to regulate sea power, especially battleships, and to defuse tension in the Pacific and East Asia. The conference produced what amounted to a gentlemen's agreement that would, if enforced, have limited total tonnage of capital ships, restricted the use of submarines in war, and banned poison gas.

In 1928, the administration of Calvin Coolidge took the lead in negotiating a pact simply and stirringly known as the Treaty for the Renunciation of War. It committed fifteen major powers to swear off war as an instrument of national policy. Like the Washington naval treaties, this agreement was developed outside the framework of the League.

The Senate ratified the pact by a near-unanimous vote—but with a proviso that rendered it all but meaningless. The State Department had to distribute diplomatic notes to the other signatories stating that the United States did not view the treaty as curtailing the right of self-defense of any nation, nor did the United States feel obligated to take action against countries that violated the treaty. In short, there was no commitment to collective security. The treaty was invoked in 1929, when China and the Soviet Union broke off diplomatic contact and engaged in military skirmishes over railroad rights in Manchuria. But, once again, there was no provision or means for enforcement, so, not surprisingly, the U.S.S.R. and China paid no attention.

However, in the minds of many, it was the thought that counted. Secretary of State Frank B. Kellogg, one of the treaty's co-sponsors and drafters, was awarded the 1929 Nobel Peace Prize. His colleague, French Foreign Minister Aristide Briand, proposed that "among peoples constituting geographical groups, like the peoples of Europe, there should be some kind of federal bond . . . primarily economic [which] might also do useful work politically and socially, and without affecting [national] sovereignty." That same year, a 128-nation conference in Geneva promulgated another in a set of rules—the so-called Geneva Conventions—on the humane treatment of prisoners of war.*

Here were sovereign states contemplating the ultimate breakdown in civility and cooperation, yet they were committing themselves to rules and restraints in the way they would make war against each other. It was all very noble and innovative—an odd amalgam of national interest, *Realpolitik*, and humanitarianism. Only a few skeptics pointed out that this diplomatic advance conceded that there were indeed going to be more wars in which prisoners would be taken.

THE RED AND THE BROWN

The twenties ended with a lesson about the extent to which international peace was a hostage to the fortunes of the international economy, which in turn was highly dependent on the American economy.

In late October of 1929—three months after the entry-into-force of the Kellogg-Briand Pact—prices on the New York Stock Exchange, which had been falling since Labor Day, collapsed. The crash happened in a single week, beginning on October 24 ("Black Thursday"), worsening on October 28 ("Black Monday"), and culminating in the panic sell-off of October 29

---

* This was the third Geneva Convention. The first, adopted in 1864, related to the protection of soldiers who were wounded or fell sick "in the field." A second dealt with those members of the armed forces at sea who were wounded, sick, or shipwrecked. A fourth would be adopted in 1949 to protect civilians in time of war.

("Black Tuesday"). The U.S. Federal Reserve, paralyzed by indecision, allowed banks to fail and credit to evaporate.

The United States was the largest creditor nation in the world. Britain and France owed America war debts, and Germany had borrowed heavily from the United States to pay reparations. The U.S. Federal Reserve and Treasury held much of the world's gold reserves. Rather than making it easier for debtor countries to service their loans, or recycling America's vast gold reserves, thereby preventing a national catastrophe from becoming a global one, the United States did the opposite: it halted foreign lending, and it set up new obstacles to imports. In 1930, Congress passed the Smoot-Hawley Tariff Act, which raised already-high American tariffs.

More than a thousand leading economists wrote President Hoover a letter warning that American protectionism would contribute to a worldwide depression, but he signed the bill into law anyway. Cut out of the U.S. market, debtor countries defaulted on their loans. A wave of bank failures swept through Europe and around the world. A scramble for gold exacerbated both the downward economic spiral and the rise of nationalism.

INSOFAR AS THERE WAS STILL TALK of supranationalism, the liberal ideal suggested by that word gave way to an ugly mutation. On the eve of the Great Crash, Count Hermann von Keyserling, a German social philosopher of mystical bent, argued for a form of "supranationality" in keeping with the resurgent spirit of xenophobia: he believed that the nations of the West had to band together against those of the East. "Europe is emerging as a unity because, faced at closer range by an overwhelming non-European humanity, the things which Europeans have in common are becoming more significant than those which divide them, and thus new factors are beginning to predominate over the old ones. . . . A living 'Europe' is therefore arising today as a branch of the all-human ecumene. . . . Hitherto the difference between the French and the German being could be regarded as a primary significance. Today it is outweighed by the consciousness of that difference from the Russian being, and above all from the Asiatic."[25]

Keyserling and other self-identified "real" Europeans associated Russians and other Slavs with the sinister East partly because of cultural prejudice, but also for reasons of politics. By the late 1920s, Joseph Stalin was already consolidating his unique form of dictatorship and perfecting something new under the sun: the "communist party-state."[26] Stalin converted the internationalist ideology of Marx and Engels to his own goal of perfecting what he called "socialism in one country," thereby breaking with Trotsky and others who believed in a worldwide revolution. In order to gain, wield, and expand power, Stalin had to have a secure national territory from which to operate, and he had to command the national loyalties of those who lived there. For him, that meant creating a new nationalism that would pretend to be pan-Soviet but would in fact be Russocentric.

Stalin personified the contradiction of that strategy. He had been born in Georgia and christened Joseph Vissarionovich Dzhugashvili. In 1913, a year after Lenin brought him into the Bolshevik leadership, Dzhugashvili, then thirty-four, gave himself a Russian name that meant "Man of Steel." All his life he enjoyed the company of fellow Georgians (including those he murdered) and spoke heavily accented Russian. Yet some of his most vicious purges were against the ethnic groups of the Caucasus. He used his post as the Bolsheviks' first People's Commissar of Nationalities to divide and subjugate the national minorities of the U.S.S.R. so that they would never be able to defy the Kremlin, a fortress in which Stalin intended to take

Joseph Stalin

up residence and from which he would rule with absolute power as the successor to those earlier autocrats who had borne the title "Czar of All the Russias."

PARTLY BECAUSE OF THE RED MENACE now on the eastern edge of Europe, there was, in the West, a forgiving, even supportive, attitude toward the appearance of a movement whose members called themselves *Fascisti*. The *fasces* was an ancient Roman emblem of authority. It consisted of a bundle of rods (for beating unruly plebeians) bound together around an ax (for beheading traitors and other enemies of the state). Benito Mussolini adopted it as a symbol of his determination, through the monopoly of violence as an instrument of state power, to make Italy a worthy heir of the Roman Empire. He was fond of saying that "only blood . . . makes the wheels of history turn," and he was bent on creating a system of government that subordinated all institutions to one political party and demanded complete subservience to "the corporate state." [27]

Mussolini had contempt for the ideas of international law and a peaceful world order. In his harangues, he sometimes lumped the League, Immanuel Kant, and Woodrow Wilson together as objects of sarcasm. But since fascists were virulently anticommunist, many Western contemporaries saw Mussolini's movement as the lesser of two evils and even rooted for its success. Well into the 1930s, Winston Churchill—who vilified the Bolsheviks as "wicked men, this vile group of cosmopolitan fanatics" and called for "the overthrow and destruction of that criminal regime [in Moscow]"—hailed Mussolini as a "great man" and "wise ruler," who in addition to "revivify[ing] the Italian nation," was standing up against the "bestial appetite and passions of Leninism." [28]

THE WEIMAR REPUBLIC—named for the town in Thuringia, once home to Goethe and Friedrich von Schiller, where the postwar German constitution was written and a government formed—had replaced the Hohenzollern monarchy in Germany. It was an object lesson in how a weak democracy, hated by remnants of the old order and with a tenuous claim to the public trust, can be a breeding ground for tyranny. Adolf Hitler spent the twenties organizing the National Socialist, or Nazi, Party. His tirades, delivered in a harsh, often quivering, raspy voice—a result of his having been gassed during the war—enchanted ever-larger crowds. His followers marched through the streets, first in Munich, later throughout Germany, in ski caps, knee breeches, thick woolen socks, combat boots, and, most distinctively, brown khaki shirts purchased from the shrunken and impoverished German army.

In its first decade, Nazism was viewed widely as a manifestation of economic discontent. Weimar Germany suffered from disastrous inflation and massive unemployment, in large measure the consequence of the deposed Kaiser's irresponsibility in the way he had financed the war. Legless veterans navigating the sidewalks on wheeled planks were reminders of the national humiliation and human toll of the defeat. There was—and still is—a widespread belief that the victors, and the vengeful French in particular, had used the Treaty of Versailles to subject Germany to a Carthaginian peace. In fact, the sturdy structure that Bismarck had built, while diminished by the war and the punitive peace that followed, was by no means dismantled. Germany had to give up some territory under the terms of Versailles, but it remained, after Russia, the second most populous country in Europe, still possessed a stout industrial base, and was poised to regain great-power status. [29]

However, what mattered at the time was not the facts but rather the belief of many Germans that Versailles had been unfair. As a result, they were receptive to Hitler's revanchist exhortations. Therefore he had broad support when he assumed the chancellorship after the Nazis won a plurality in parliamentary elections in 1933. Within six months, political parties, a free press, and an independent judiciary had all been destroyed.

MY EDUCATION, BOTH AT SCHOOL and in my travels as a journalist, gave me considerable opportunity to learn about the origins of Soviet totalitarianism, but I was less familiar with the German variety, since it had passed into history before I was born and did not cast a shadow over the world I grew up in the way Stalinism did. In the mid-eighties, I was able to fill in my education when I got to know Fritz Stern, first through his writings, then through personal acquaintanceship. Stern, who immigrated from Germany to the United States in 1938 and went on to a distinguished career at Columbia, has written extensively on the history of his native land. He served in the early nineties as an adviser to Richard Holbrooke, then U.S. ambassador to Germany.

During after-dinner discussions in the second-floor study of Holbrooke's residence in Bonn and on walks along the Rhine, I listened to Stern explain how Nazism had roots in the anti-Western, illiberal components of Germany's political culture. In that sense, it was a perversion of some strains in the German romantic nationalism of the nineteenth century that had often expressed itself in music, philosophy, and literature.[30]

The subject fascinated and puzzled me. Nationalism, by definition, is geographically bounded, even if the boundaries are elastic and contested (as in the case of the Palestinians, Basques, and Kurds). The only exception is the national identity of people whom history has deprived of a state of their own, such as the Gypsies (whom to this day European racists sometimes scorn as the descendants of Cain and bearers of the curse the Lord had put on him: "a fugitive and a vagabond shalt thou be"[31]). Yet even though Nazism was assertively nationalistic, it managed to vie with Soviet communism—which was just as assertively internationalistic—in the struggle for world domination. Both in his writings and in our talks in Bonn, Stern helped me understand how Hitler pulled off the considerable feat of bestowing on German hypernationalism and totalitarianism a deterministic mandate to expand boundlessly.

It was a particular irony that Hitler seized on the Jews, a people without a land of their own, to say nothing of an army, as a foil in stirring up German paranoia and xenophobia. He convinced himself and most of the German military establishment that Germany, Europe, and Western civilization faced a mortal threat from "international Jewry," "Jewish Bolshevism," and the American and British "plutocrats," also supposedly in league with, if not under the control of, the Jews in a worldwide conspiracy against the German people. Germany, therefore, had to strike first, using military conquest as a means of subduing weaker states (all states were weaker, in Hitler's view) and as a cover for enslaving or exterminating inferior races (all races were inferior) in order to create *Lebensraum*, or "living space," for German "Aryans."

Rather than confining themselves to a plausibly German adjective for the Master Race—say, *Teutonic*—Hitler, Alfred Rosenberg, Josef Goebbels, and Heinrich Himmler (who would bear, among his titles, that of Commissioner for the Strengthening of Germandom) wanted a more expansive category that would better fit the geographical reach of their ambitions. They were prepared to extend to Scandinavians, Dutch, Flemish, Luxembourgers, and German-speaking Swiss the status of Aryans. How Anglo-Saxons would fare when Germany ruled the world was an open question. Hitler, Rosenberg, Goebbels, and Himmler distinguished among Aryans and considered the British to be the "most Jewish." As evidence, they noted accusingly that Anglicans and Jews both evoked Hebrew prophets and both had a proclivity for commerce, banking, and other forms of "money-grubbing."

The Nazi choice of the word *Aryan* was farcical. Among the many tongues that linguists classify under that broad rubric are the Slavic languages spoken by people Hitler regarded as among the lowest of the *untermenschen*. Moreover, *Aryan* itself comes from Sanskrit, in which it refers to a nation "comprising the worshippers of the gods of the Brahmans"—hardly a Wagnerian or Nietzschean archetype. *Swastika*, too, is from the Sanskrit *svasti*, for well-being, although the Nazis reversed the direction of the bent cross to obscure its iconographic connection to religions of the East. So Hitler's ideologues were borrowing from an ancient culture that had produced, among many other peoples, the Gypsies, whom Hitler's social engineers sought to obliterate.

Nazism was encrusted with layer upon layer of this sort of illogic. Within Germany, despite the Nazis' supposed dedication to preserving "racial hygiene," they kidnapped thousands of children of other races who "looked German," proclaimed them orphans, and gave them to certifiably German couples to raise. This practice, known as "harvesting" or *Heuaktion* ("hay action"), was an implicit concession that race is, literally, in the eye of the beholder and that distinctive ethnicity is a sham. Further compounding the absurdity, the Nazis began to make good on their plans to euthanize the handicapped—including not just the congenitally disabled, the chronically infirm, the mentally ill, and the elderly, but also veterans who had been invalided in World War I.[32]

While the Nazis gave priority to their conquest of the European "East," their plan on its broadest scale would have allowed the Master Race to rule a *Weltherrschaft*, a "World Order," which would restore German colonies in Africa and take over the other European ones as well. Eventually a racially purified Germany would dominate the globe.

Hitler and his generals intended to implement this plan first by winning a series of short blitzkriegs against divided opponents, then by toppling Stalin's supposedly rickety Soviet Union and using the resources conquered in the East to defeat on the high seas the only remaining credible opponent, the United States. The Nazis would temporarily subcontract other regions to their Axis allies, Italy and Japan, but Britain would remain under the direct control of Germany. Berlin, renamed

Adolf Hitler

"Germania," would be the capital of the world. All this was supposed to be achieved by 1950 and to last for a thousand years.[33]

BACK IN THE EARLY TWENTIES, when Hitler was still on the fringes of German politics and refining the program and instruments of Nazism, he looked to Mussolini as a natural ally, given their shared antipathy to communism, which matched their shared contempt for liberal democracy. Mussolini had banned political parties and trade unions, shut down socialist and communist newspapers, and murdered leftist politicians. Hitler would do the same when he had the chance. Yet many of Hitler's methods for seizing power and destroying real, perceived, and potential enemies were in fact modeled on those of Stalin.[34]

Even though fascism and communism were, for nearly two decades, locked in what appeared to be a mortal struggle—Nazi brownshirts and red-flag-waving communists assassinated one another in the back alleys of Berlin—both ideologies invested the state with maximum responsibility for, and authority over, society (hence both called themselves socialist); both concentrated power in one political party; and both combined the most extreme aspects of nationalism and internationalism.

John Keegan, the British military historian, sees these two movements, the red and the brown, as a direct result of World War I, which had

> damaged civilization, the rational and liberal civilization of the European enlightenment, permanently for the worse and, through the damage done, world civilization also. Pre-war Europe, imperial though it was in its relations with most of the world beyond the continent, offered respect to the principles of constitutionalism, the rule of law and representative government. Post-war Europe rapidly relinquished confidence in such principles. . . . Within fifteen years of the war's end, totalitarianism, a new word for a system that rejected the liberalism and constitutionalism which had inspired European politics since the eclipse of monarchy in 1789, was almost everywhere on the rise.[35]

It was primarily the emergence of the twin evils of Soviet communism and German fascism—initially inimical to each other, then briefly in alliance—that clinched the failure of the League of Nations and destroyed what was left of the peace it was meant to keep.

THE BEGINNING OF THE END

Britain's Ten-Year Rule proved uncannily prescient. A little more than a decade after Versailles, the League foundered and the Kellogg-Briand treaty came unraveled, first in the Far East.

Japanese aggression against China had been a long time coming. Toward the end of the Great War, with the Kaiser's armies bogged down on the western front, the Japanese, who had annexed Korea in 1910, saw an opportunity to expand their empire. They threw in their lot with the Allies, declared war on the Central Powers, and seized the German-held Shantung peninsula of China. The loose collection of warlords who had filled the vacuum left by the fall of the Qing dynasty in 1912 made humiliating concessions to the Japanese. Thousands rallied in Beijing's Tiananmen Square to denounce the failure—or, as they saw it, the refusal—of the Versailles peacemakers to protect China's own right to self-determination against Japanese expansionism. The demonstrators were also protesting their own government's weakness.

That incident and other outpourings of public anger around the country emboldened communists and other radicals, who were further inspired to action by the speed with which the Bolsheviks had come to power in Russia. The ground was laid for Mao Zedong and his comrades to found the Communist Party in 1921 and, six years later, begin a civil war against the ruling Nationalist Party, or Kuomintang, led by Chiang Kai-shek, thereby making China all the more vulnerable to the Japanese.

In 1931, Japan, which had troops stationed in Manchuria to protect its business interests there, poured forces into the region, renamed it Manchukuo, and installed the last Qing emperor, who had been deposed in China twenty years earlier as the ceremonial head of state.

It took the League of Nations two years to muster a consensus to condemn the aggression. That action, such as it was, had little consequence except to prompt Japan to quit the League. Germany had joined the League in 1926 when it was still the Weimar Republic. By 1933, Hitler was chancellor, and Germany had a new name: the Third Reich. The second word has long since entered English, although it is worth underscoring that it can be translated as "empire." Nazi Germany was intended to be a successor to the Holy Roman Empire and the forty-seven-year-reign of the Kaisers, which had ended with the abdication of Wilhelm II at the end of World War I.

Hitler pulled Germany out of the League nine months after assuming power. The raison d'être of that organization was, quite simply, incompatible with his plans. A month later, a referendum showed that 95 percent of the Germans polled supported the decision. As Inis Claude has noted, "The League, established to prevent [another] accidental war [like World War I], was unable to cope with Hitler's deliberately plotted campaign of conquest." *

In 1935, Mussolini invaded Ethiopia and proclaimed Italy's figurehead King Victor Emmanuel III as Ethiopian emperor in place of Haile Selassie, who fled the country. Paul Kennedy makes a strong argument that Italy was so weak economically and so overstretched militarily that a show of force by the British and French on behalf of the League would have caused Mussolini to reverse course.[36] Instead, the League did little more than wring its hands,

* Claude, now a professor emeritus of government and foreign affairs at the University of Virginia, is an authority to whose work I have often turned over the years. As a GI in 1944, he sailed to France on the *George Washington*, the by-then-ancient vessel that had taken Wilson to Europe for the Paris Peace Conference after World War I. He spent much time on the voyage reflecting on Wilson's failed hopes for the League. The citation is from his *Swords into Plowshares*, p. 41.

and when Ethiopian delegates were allowed into the League in September 1936, Italy stopped attending meetings.

No doubt emboldened by the ease with which his Italian ally had seized Ethiopia, Hitler began his carefully planned, efficiently executed campaign to dominate Europe. In 1938, he annexed Austria (to the approval of many Austrians), then went after the Sudetenland, the section of Bohemia that the peacemakers at Versailles had awarded to Czechoslovakia. Ethnic Germans who lived there greeted the Nazis as liberators. The seizure of the rest of Czechoslovakia came next, followed by the invasion of Poland in 1939 and Norway and Denmark in April 1940; then came the lunge into France, Holland, Belgium, and Luxembourg in May 1940. Every bit as important as the League's failure—indeed, integral to that failure—was the British and French policy of appeasement; the institution, after all, could not have more foresight and backbone than its principal members.

The "Nonaggression" Pact, which the German and Soviet foreign ministers signed in August 1939, was actually a co-aggression pact. Hitler attacked Poland from the west, precipitating the formal start of World War II, and Stalin did so from the east, occupying the Baltic states of Estonia, Latvia, and Lithuania as well. The Soviet Union was ejected from the League on December 14, 1939, when it tried, unsuccessfully, to conquer Finland. Stalin did not even bother to respond to the expulsion—the only one in the League's history.[37]

THE NUMBER OF EMPTY CHAIRS was growing in Le Palais des Nations, the League's headquarters in a park inhabited by peacocks, overlooking Lake Geneva with a panoramic view of the Alps. Other than the United States, the principal countries that were unrepresented—Germany, Italy, Japan, and the U.S.S.R.—were precisely those governed by ideologies that put a premium on aggression as a means of conducting foreign policy. During the war, the League moved several small service units to Princeton, New Jersey, and Montreal, Canada, where skeleton staffs whiled away their time organizing archives and waiting to be replaced by a new organization once the war came to an end.

Zara Steiner offers this epitaph for the League:

> The "Geneva system" was not a substitute for great-power politics, as [Wilson] had intended, but rather an adjunct to it. It was only a mechanism for conducting multinational diplomacy whose success or failure depended on the willingness of states, and particularly the most powerful states, to use it. The

growth of the new institution was fostered by the increasing internationalization of so many questions previously considered solely of national concern, but it always operated within prescribed limits. The sovereign state was the only source of the League's power. There could be no authority above that of the state, and no state could be legally bound without its own consent [i.e., not real supranationalism]. The League of Nations was never intended to be a superstate. It was an experiment in internationalism at a time when the currents of nationalism were running powerfully in the opposite direction.[38]

In addition to being a fair assessment of the subject at hand, Steiner's judgment could, with the alteration of a few words, apply to the new system that would replace the Geneva one on April 8, 1946, when the forty-three remaining members of the League unanimously voted for its abolition and the transfer of its functions, archives, and properties to the UN. "The League is dead," remarked Lord Cecil. "Long live the United Nations!"

The new organization would have many of the same characteristics as the League, including some of its limitations and disabilities. But the UN would be different in a key respect: this time, not only would an American president be the founding force, but ten of his successors would ensure that even if it did not fully succeed, at least it would not catastrophically fail.

9

THE MASTER BUILDER

Son, it's going to be a long war.
—*GEORGE MARSHALL, in early 1942, answering an aide who asked
why the Army chief of staff went home at 5 P.M. every day.*[1]

If Man does find the solution for world peace, it will be the most
revolutionary reversal of his record we have ever known.
—*MARSHALL, September 1945, two weeks after V-J Day*[2]

I T took the Imperial Japanese Navy's attack on Pearl Harbor and a declaration of war by Japan and Germany—not the Wehrmacht's rampage
across Europe—to bring America into World War II. Yet even though the
Japanese raid caught the United States by surprise, Franklin Roosevelt was
entirely ready to be a wartime president. Moreover, he was also already thinking about how he would succeed where Woodrow Wilson had failed when it
came time to set the terms of a postwar peace.

During World War I, Roosevelt had given up a seat in the New York state
senate to serve as assistant secretary of the navy—the same post his distant
cousin Theodore had held in the McKinley administration. In 1926, when
FDR was spending most of his time in Warm Springs, Georgia, at a spa that
specialized in polio treatment, he traveled to Milton Academy outside Boston
to deliver a speech expressing his hopes for the League of Nations. He professed his staunch belief in progress as destiny: "I remember that my old
schoolmaster, Dr. Peabody, said, in days that seemed to us then to be secure
and untroubled [that is, before the Great War], 'Things in life will not always
run smoothly. Sometimes we will be rising toward the heights—then all will
seem to reverse itself and start downward. The great fact to remember is that
the trend of civilization itself is forever upward; that a line drawn through the
middle of the peaks and the valleys of the centuries always has an upward
trend.' "Then Roosevelt added a point reminiscent of Wilson's youthful mus-

ings about world federalism and Darwin's brief speculation about the evolution of a global human society: "First [there was] the self-sufficient small community, then the grouping of several communities, then the small state, then the nation, then alliances between [nations] and now a congress of nations."[3]

ROOSEVELT ASSUMED THE PRESIDENCY in 1933, the year Hitler became chancellor of Germany. From the White House he watched the League go from disappointment to debacle. While not given to brooding, Roosevelt would sometimes sit alone in the Cabinet Room, stare at Edmund Tarbell's portrait of Wilson, and ponder the tragedy of the League of Nations' failure to live up to Wilson's hopes.[4]

As early as 1939, FDR ordered that work begin on a plan for a postwar world. The leader of the project was Leo Pasvolsky, a Russian-born Jew whose family had fled the pogroms. In 1924, Pasvolsky, an economist, joined a public-policy research institution recently founded by Robert S. Brookings, a Saint Louis businessman and philanthropist who had moved to Washington to help Woodrow Wilson in the war effort. Pasvolsky spent several years as Secretary of State Cordell Hull's personal assistant, making himself, in the words of one historian of the period, a "one-man think tank for Hull, [but] also a doughty infighter." Pasvolsky worked out of the limelight to push the postwar strategy forward, drawing on his scholarly and bureaucratic experience, as well as his firsthand view of the Paris Peace Conference in 1919, which he had covered as a young journalist.[5]

In his January 1941 State of the Union message to Congress, Roosevelt's proclamation of the Four Freedoms (of speech and religion, from want and fear) was explicitly intended as a guide for American foreign policy based on universal principles: "That is no vision of a distant millennium. It is a definite basis for a kind of world attainable in our own time and generation. . . . The world order which we seek is the cooperation of free countries, working together in a friendly, civilized society."

Roosevelt first referred publicly to "the United Nations" on New Year's Day, 1942, three weeks after Pearl Harbor.[6] He intended the term to do double duty: in its immediate context, it pertained to the twenty-six nations pledged to defeat the Axis; but Roosevelt was also looking ahead to a structure that would undergird the eventual peace, and that would be based on an American blueprint, with the United States as its master builder—its chief architect, general contractor, and principal funder.

• • •

IN ROOSEVELT'S EFFORT TO CULTIVATE domestic and international support for the UN, he had, in Wendell Willkie, an invaluable ally. Willkie had been a dark-horse candidate for the Republican nomination in 1940, when true isolationists, such as those who formed the America First Committee, were at the height of their influence. Willkie was one of the few prominent internationalists pitted against those in his party who were determined to keep the United States as far as possible from the calamity in Europe, not least because the Axis seemed to be winning. Hitler completed his capture of France two days before the Republican convention. Newsreels showed German troops goose-stepping down the Champs-Elysées. Against that backdrop, Willkie, who had long warned of the dangers of Nazism, stormed from the back of the pack to win the nomination. Throughout the campaign, he advocated intervention to an extent that cost him votes but made it easier for Roosevelt to manage divisions within the country. Willkie supported Roosevelt's call for a draft and let it be known that he would not oppose sending mothballed American destroyers to the British Navy in return for naval basing rights.

After the election, Willkie returned to private life as a lawyer. Roosevelt sent him to London and, on his return to Washington, enlisted his help in securing passage of the Lend-Lease Act. Once the United States joined the war, Roosevelt dispatched Willkie on a round-the-world trip to China, the Middle East, and the Soviet Union, which had become an American ally only when Hitler launched Operation Barbarossa in the summer of 1941 and pushed his Panzer divisions to the outskirts of Moscow. In 1943, moved by the goodwill he encountered on his travels, Willkie published *One World*, which passionately argued for postwar international cooperation and helped lure many of his fellow Republicans to his side in supporting the UN.[7]

Roosevelt was mindful that Wilson's hopes for the League of Nations had come a cropper, both in the U.S. Senate and in Europe, largely because Article 10 in the Covenant committed member states to collective security without creating a realistic mechanism for enforcement or ensuring that individual nations would contribute troops to such a mechanism even if it existed. Roosevelt carefully avoided depicting the UN as a supranational body. "We are not thinking of a superstate with its own police forces and other paraphernalia of coercive power," said Roosevelt in June 1944. "We are seeking effective agreements and arrangements through which the nations would maintain, according to their capacities, adequate forces to meet the needs of preventing war and of making impossible deliberate preparations for war and to have such forces available for joint action when necessary."[8]

He was vague about what those arrangements would be, but he left no doubt that the United States would retain control over whether, when, and how to deploy its own forces.

THE PHRASE "ACCORDING TO THEIR CAPACITIES" signaled another key feature of the UN that Roosevelt had in mind. Those countries with the greatest capacity to ensure peace in the postwar world would constitute the powerful inner circle of what would become the Security Council. In addition to the United States, Roosevelt looked initially to Great Britain, the Soviet Union, and China to serve as "the Four Policemen." The Soviet Union was the United States' single most important ally. At horrendous cost to his own people, Stalin was keeping the major part of the German military machine tied down on the eastern front. That made the Soviet generalissimo, in American eyes, "Uncle Joe." Roosevelt, caught up in the good feeling of being on the same side in the war, could even imagine Stalin as a worthy partner in building what came next—never mind the irreconcilable ideological differences between Stalin and the West, and never mind Stalin's treachery in making common cause with Hitler in their 1939 pact.

Roosevelt was eager to avoid the mistake Wilson had made in not giving sufficient thought to backing the League of Nations with force. But Roosevelt's concept of the Four Policemen set a trap for his successors: it conceded to Stalin a sphere of Soviet influence in which self-determination would not stand a chance, at least not for a long time to come. The historian Robert Skidelsky has condemned this concession as "the most spectacular misjudgment in American history."[9] Yet even now, it is not clear what Roosevelt should have done instead: he had a war to win and a postwar peace to prepare, and one way or another, the Soviet Union was essential to achieving victory and would therefore have to be given a major part in whatever arrangements the Allies put in place in peacetime.

IF ROOSEVELT HAD HAD A CRYSTAL BALL, he might have paused before giving China—the most populous country on earth—a policeman's badge and a place at the table of the Big Four. But in the early forties, China looked like a potential counterweight to the Soviet Union in Asia. Mao Zedong's communists were still a ragtag band of rebels in the remote hills of Shaanxi Province hiding from Chiang Kai-shek's nationalist army.

Roosevelt's view on China put him at odds with Winston Churchill, who routinely referred to the Chinese as "Chinks" and "Chinamen." Roosevelt gently (and generously) remonstrated with his friend that this prejudice was forty years behind the times and that, in another forty or fifty years, China was likely to be a major military power, and the UN would need its support.[10]

In October 1943, Secretary of State Hull met in Moscow with the British and Soviet foreign ministers and issued a declaration in the name of their three governments. It contained a pledge to establish "at the earliest practicable date a general international organization, based on the principle of the sovereign equality of all peace-loving states, and open to membership by all such states, large and small, for the maintenance of international peace and security."

The phrase "sovereign equality" instantly acquired a canonical sanctity. It referred to equal status before international law, not to equal political power in the UN. Here were the representatives of three governments—invoking the name of a fourth, China, that was partially under Japanese occupation and mired in a civil war—promising to reorganize the world on behalf of all states that would prove themselves "peace-loving." That phrase, too, had a dubious quality, given the nature of the government that was hosting the conference. The U.S.S.R. had been willing to ally itself with Hitler only four years earlier, and Stalin, looking to the postwar world, was already planning to make colonies out of as many of his neighbors as possible.[11]

Stalin, Roosevelt, and Churchill

The crucial feature of a veto for each of the permanent members of the Security Council was something on which Stalin insisted; Roosevelt wanted it, too, primarily because it would help him get the Senate to agree to American membership in the UN. Churchill joined Stalin and Roosevelt on the need for a veto at their summit in Yalta in February 1945. France, which was not represented at Yalta, also wanted to be part of the emerging inner circle of veto-bearing permanent members. It was pushing on an open door, since the United States and Britain recognized that France was going to be a major economic and political power in Europe, and the Soviets expected the French to be easier to deal with than the Americans and British.

Thus, out of a meeting of the Big Three emerged the prospect of a Big Five—the same seemingly magic number that had figured in the Congress of Vienna and the Treaty of Versailles. The postwar world might be peaceful, at least by comparison with the past, but it would be kept that way by a large, even universal, organization in which privilege and responsibility commensurate with power would reside with a small directorate. Skeptics at the time could be forgiven for suspecting that the principles of sovereignty and equality, to say nothing of democracy, would characterize the new international system no more than they had the old one.

IN FACT, HOWEVER, the consequences for empire after World War II would be quite different from those after World War I. The victors in 1919 had dismantled only enemy empires, while the postwar system Roosevelt had in mind would get rid of not just the imperial holdings of the Axis—the Thousand-Year Reich, Mussolini's "New Rome," and the Empire of the Sun—but also, eventually (and from FDR's standpoint, the sooner the better) those of the Allies as well: Belgium, Britain, France, and the Netherlands.

Roosevelt had long been an anti-imperialist.[12] It was with relish in 1935 that he had signed legislation granting independence to the Philippines. His insistence on adding decolonization to the postwar agenda was another source of tension between him and Churchill. Their argument went on for years, in tones that ranged from polite disagreement to mutual irritation, sometimes turning to rage. Churchill was a committed imperialist who saw himself as the custodian of a great enterprise that had come into its own and must prosper after the war. In the words of Brian Urquhart, a British statesman who helped found the UN and who has been, in recent decades, a leading chronicler of its work, "During the twenty years between the two world wars the entire British imperial system functioned—for the first and last time—as a worldwide political and economic institution."[13]

Yet Churchill's long life would require him to watch the empire shrink from ruling around 20 percent of the world's landmass at the time of his birth to only about 1 percent at the time of his death, in 1965. One of Churchill's consignments to the political wilderness, in the early 1930s, had been a result of his refusal to support the Conservative Party's consideration of dominion status for India, which would have meant autonomy and local legislative authority within the empire, much as Canada and Australia already enjoyed. He scorned Indian pretensions to independent statehood, calling India "merely a geographical expression . . . no more a single country than the equator." [14]

The dispute over the fate of the British Empire caused tension between Roosevelt and Churchill as early as August 1941—four months before Pearl Harbor—when they met on British and American warships in Placentia Bay off Newfoundland to negotiate the Atlantic Charter. When Roosevelt insisted on a self-determination clause, Churchill tried to exempt colonies. Roosevelt was adamant that the charter affirm "the right of all peoples to choose the form of government under which they will live," and that respect for "inherent dignity" and "equal and inalienable rights" apply to humanity as a whole, not just to those who had fallen under Axis rule. Churchill returned to the subject frequently in his correspondence and meetings with Roosevelt during the war. The two basically fought to a standoff. Roosevelt held all the high cards, but Churchill held India—and was not about to let go. [15]

Roosevelt had a similar experience with Charles de Gaulle, whom he detested. On his way to meet Churchill in Casablanca in 1943, Roosevelt stopped in Gambia and found the British colony a "hell-hole"—a judgment he conveyed to Churchill on arrival in Casablanca. While there, Roosevelt promised the Sultan of Morocco, whose country had been a French protectorate since 1912 and was under the wartime control of the Allies, that the United States was fighting for self-determination for all the peoples of the world. This statement got back to de Gaulle, who was determined that France would get Morocco back. After the war, Paris regained its hold on Morocco and kept it for another eleven years. [16]

IN ROOSEVELT'S VIEW, after the American-led destruction of the Axis as a system based on aggressive tyranny would come the construction, also American-led, of a network of organizations, treaties, alliances, regulations, and financial arrangements that would operate by consent achieved through American diplomacy, backed but not imposed by American force of arms. For Roosevelt, the American motive was enlightened self-interest. He was given to quoting Ralph Waldo Emerson's adage, "The only way to have a friend is to be one." The United Nations would legitimize the United States' interests in the eyes of other states, allowing America to leverage its resources and more efficaciously achieve its goals; other nations would accept the predominance of U.S. power if they saw themselves as willing participants in, and beneficiaries of, the structures through which that power was to be exercised. Roosevelt's fourth and final Inaugural Address on January 20, 1945, called for building a new structure out of the ruins of war: "We have learned that we cannot live alone, at peace; that our own well-being is dependent on the well-being of other nations, far away. We have learned to be citizens of the world, members of the human community."

Roosevelt believed the UN would be the principal manifestation of his most important legacy, but he did not delude himself that the UN could fulfill that legacy by itself. There was, in his vision, an important difference from what Wilson and Lord Cecil had tried to create after World War I. They were relying almost exclusively on the League of Nations as the means of keeping the peace and regulating international relations. Roosevelt, by contrast, saw the weakness in counting on one structure. He had in mind a multilayered, multifaceted complex of institutions—some global, others regional; some political, others economic or military. Together, they would make up the superstructure of global governance.

ROOSEVELT LEFT ANOTHER LEGACY that would not be revealed to the world until after his death. In 1939, Alexander Sachs, a Wall Street economist and old friend of the president's, brought him a letter from Albert Einstein about the military potential of nuclear fission: "A single bomb of this type, carried by boat and exploded in a port, might very well destroy the whole port together with some of the surrounding territory." Einstein alluded obliquely to the danger that Germany might already be working on such a weapon and recommended that the United States undertake a crash program: "Certain aspects of this situation which has arisen seem to call for watchfulness and, if necessary, quick action on the part of the Administration."

"Alex," said Roosevelt, "what you are after is to see that the Nazis don't blow us up."

Albert Einstein

"Precisely," Sachs replied.

"This requires action," said Roosevelt, and ordered work to begin.[17]

Einstein would have been a natural member of the scientific team to lead the effort. But he had been, by his own description, a "militant pacifist" in the 1920s, when he belonged to an organization called War Resisters' International, and an advocate of universal disarmament. As he watched the rise of Hitler, Einstein modified his pacifism but believed all the more fervently that the only antidote to nationalism was supranationalism. Einstein's latest biographer, Walter Isaacson—a colleague of mine at *Time* and a close friend—believes that the great physicist's view of how the world should be organized was of a piece with his theory about how the universe worked: "Just as he sought a unified theory in science that could govern the cosmos, so he sought one in politics that could govern the planet, one that would overcome the anarchy of unfettered nationalism through a world federalism based on universal principles." In 1932 Einstein wrote to Sigmund Freud, "The quest of international security involves the unconditional surrender by every nation, in a certain measure, of its liberty of action—its sovereignty that is to say—and it is clear beyond all doubt that no other road can lead to such security."[18]

After reviewing the record that the Federal Bureau of Investigation had been keeping on Einstein, J. Edgar Hoover denied him a security clearance because of his "radical background," in particular his outspoken pacifism and participation in conferences that Hoover considered "pro-Soviet."[19]

COINCIDENCE LINKED SEVERAL OF MY RELATIVES to what happened next. In the 1930s, my father attended the Los Alamos Ranch School near the town of Alamogordo, New Mexico. In 1943, an elite group of American scientists and military officers took up residence in the dormitories on what had been the campus of the school to build an atomic bomb. Shortly afterward, in a converted indoor tennis court on my great-grandparents' property outside Dayton, Ohio, one of my father's uncles, Charles A. Thomas, a chemist and later chairman of the Monsanto Chemical Company, assembled a team of scientists to produce an isotope of a radioactive element known as polonium that would be used in the trigger for the bomb.* While my father served in the navy, conducting rescue operations in the North Atlantic and supporting preparations for D-Day, my mother was a high-tech

---

* Polonium 210 would make headlines more than sixty years later in an international murder mystery, when a former Russian secret agent in London died of radioactive poisoning.

version of Rosie the Riveter, laboring away in Philadelphia at an IBM plant that produced tabulator punch cards for a project that she would, only later, discover had been code-named the Manhattan Engineering District.

Roosevelt died in Warm Springs on April 12, 1945. Two and a half hours later, back in Washington, Harry Truman was sworn in as president. Secretary of War Henry Stimson told him that he would need to be briefed about "a new explosive of unbelievable power." In the trauma of the moment, neither man dwelt on the matter. The new president of the United States was still largely in the dark about what was going on at Los Alamos. Joseph Stalin, however, was not. As early as 1942, Soviet spies had penetrated the Manhattan Project and were, by 1945, hard at work on an A-bomb of their own.

TRUMAN WAS BOTH AN OLD-FASHIONED CONSERVATIVE and an idealist ahead of his time. The former aspect was evident, the latter well disguised. He had been an army captain who was gassed in World War I, a haberdasher turned operative of Missouri machine politics during the Depression, and a lackluster backup choice as FDR's running mate in 1944. (Henry Wallace of Iowa, the sitting vice president, was regarded as too liberal for the ticket because of his strong support for civil rights and his sympathy for the Soviet Union.) Few thought Truman was either destined or equipped for national, not to mention international, leadership.

Yet Truman had been, from his youth, consistently and passionately an internationalist. After World War I, he considered the Senate's refusal to ratify American participation in the League of Nations as disastrously shortsighted. After being elected to the Senate himself in 1934, Truman often spoke in favor of international engagement. Looking back to American rejection of the League, he said, "We did not accept our responsibility as a world power." [20]

In the earliest days of World War II, Truman was one of the Senate's staunchest supporters of Roosevelt's effort to create the UN. In that area more than any other, Truman was prepared to pick up where Roosevelt left off. If anything, he wanted to push the plan further—indeed, much further. From the

Harry Truman

time he graduated from high school in his hometown of Independence, Missouri, in 1901, Truman kept tucked in his wallet a scrap of paper with a twelve-line fragment of Alfred, Lord Tennyson's sprawling, sentimental poem, "Locksley Hall." Tennyson had begun the work as a meditation on a rundown country house in Staffordshire in 1830, when he was twenty-one and coming to terms with a failed engagement. By the time the poem was finally published, twelve years later, it had grown to include a long passage in which the poet lifts himself out of his melancholy by imagining what awaits the human race in the century ahead. The prophecy opens with an ecstatic glimpse of the marvels that technology might bring:

> For I dipt into the future, far as human eye could see,
> Saw the Vision of the world, and all the wonders that would be;
> Saw the heavens fill with commerce, argosies of magic sails,
> Pilots of the purple twilight, dropping down with costly bails . . .

A couplet later, the blessing turns to a curse. Tennyson foresees a conflict eerily like the Battle of Britain:

> Heard the heavens fill with shouting, and there rained a ghastly dew
> From the nations' airy navies grappling in the central blue;
> Far along the world-wide whisper of the south-wind rushing warm,
> With the standards of the people plunging thro the thunderstorm . . .

Then, just as suddenly, the dark vision gives way to a reverie of political redemption:

> Till the war-drum throbbed no longer, and the battle-flags were furl'd
> In the Parliament of Man, the Federation of the World.
> There the common sense of most shall hold a fretful realm in awe,
> And the kindly earth shall slumber, lapt in universal law.[21]

Truman recopied this text by hand as many as forty times during his life. The poem was a summation of his own hopes for what the UN might become.

ON APRIL 25, 1945, two weeks before V-E Day, the Allies' formal victory in Europe, Truman was preparing for his radio address to the representatives of the forty-six founding member states of the United Nations Organization (UNO) who had gathered in San Francisco that day to begin negotiating its charter (another four would join over the next two months). Stimson wrote the president a memo giving him a fuller picture of the work under way at the Los Alamos Laboratory—"Within four months, we shall in all probability have completed the most terrible weapon ever known in human history"—and advising Truman to postpone the San Francisco conference. Stimson believed that the United States government needed some time to consider the transforming effect that atomic weaponry would have on international politics:

> To approach any world peace organization of any pattern now likely to be considered, without an appreciation by the leaders of our country of the power of this new weapon, would seem to be unrealistic. No systems of control heretofore considered would be adequate to control this menace. Both inside any particular country and between the nations of the world, the control of this weapon will undoubtedly be a matter of greatest difficulty and would involve such thorough-going rights of inspection and internal controls as we have never heretofore contemplated. . . . [I]t is extremely probable that the future will make [a nuclear bomb] possible to be constructed by smaller nations or even groups, or at least by a large nation in a much shorter time. . . . The world in its present state of moral advancement compared with its technical development would be eventually at the mercy of such a weapon. In other words, modern civilization might be completely destroyed. . . . On the other hand, if the problem of the proper use of this weapon can be solved, we would have the opportunity to bring the world into a pattern in which the peace of the world and our civilization can be saved.[22]

Truman saw Stimson's point but decided to let the conference proceed. The delegates had already assembled; an unexplained cancellation would call into question either the new president's commitment to the venture or his confidence about being able to bring Roosevelt's dream to fruition. In either case, if the United States seemed to be backing away, the UN—much like the League of Nations—would have been orphaned at birth. Moreover, Truman saw the successful conclusion of the San Francisco Conference—while much of the world was still at war in the Pacific and therefore hungering for peace—as an opportunity to be seized or perhaps forever lost.

•   •   •

ARCHIBALD MACLEISH, THE AMERICAN POET, novelist, and playwright, was one of the wordsmiths of the UN Charter, a job that fell to him because of his wartime service as an assistant secretary of state for cultural affairs. He had been a classmate of Dean Acheson's at Yale, and of my grandfather's there and at Hotchkiss as well. I came to know MacLeish toward the end of his long life (he died in 1982 just shy of his ninetieth birthday). Over a dinner in New Haven in October 1976, he took pride in having helped make sure that the preamble of the Charter echoed, and thus paid homage to, the language the American Founding Fathers had used in Philadelphia to unify the thirteen states 156 years before the creation of the UN.[23]

The American Constitution begins with the words, "We, the People of the United States, in Order to form a more perfect Union . . ."; the Charter begins, "We, the peoples of the United Nations, determined to save succeeding generations from the scourge of war, which twice in our lifetime has brought untold sorrow to humankind, and to reaffirm faith in fundamental human rights, in the dignity and worth of the human person, in the equal rights of men and women and of nations large and small, and to establish conditions under which justice and respect for the obligations arising from treaties and other sources of international law can be maintained, and to promote social progress and better standards of life in larger freedom."

After that stirring opening, the Charter comes down to earth in nineteen chapters containing 111 articles. Chapter I, Article 1 reiterates the bedrock principle of "sovereign equality" for all member states; but the structure and procedures laid out in the rest of the document, especially those relating to the authorities of the Security Council, bolster in numerous mutually reinforcing ways the *un*equal sovereignty of the United States that Roosevelt and Truman regarded as essential if the UN was to have the support of the Senate.

Chapter I, Article 2, Paragraph 7 states that "[n]othing contained in the present Charter shall authorize the United Nations to intervene in matters which are essentially within the domestic jurisdiction of any state." Part of the subtext here was a desire on the U.S. administration's part to make sure that segregationists in the Senate (and there were plenty) had no grounds for fearing that the UN might someday have something to say—or even do—about the United States' treatment of its black citizens. It was one thing for the UN to advance the cause of human, civil, and minority rights elsewhere in the world, but if the Charter was going to pass the Senate, the United States would have to be exempt—an extreme form of exceptionalism that John Ruggie, a professor of international relations at Harvard and a former official of the UN, has dubbed "exemptionalism."[24] Chapter VII, Article 51, asserts that "[n]othing in the present Charter shall impair the inherent right of individual or collective self-defence if an armed attack occurs against a Member of the United Nations."

Along with American permanent membership on the Security Council and the veto, these provisions ensured that Chapter VII, Article 42, which empowers the Security Council to authorize "such action by air, sea, or land forces as may be necessary to maintain or restore international peace and security," would never be used against the United States, nor would the United States ever have to rely on the UN for its own defense. The use of the verb *may* rather than *shall* in Article 42 is also significant: the United States would never have to deploy forces in an operation that it judged unwise or in any way counter to its own interests.

As a result of these features, Republican support for the Charter was virtually assured. Senator Arthur Vandenberg, who had been an ardent isolationist up until Pearl Harbor, was, in 1945, the ranking Republican on the Foreign Relations Committee. In that capacity, he could have played the spoiler much as Henry Cabot Lodge had done in the debate over the League. But Roosevelt had co-opted Vandenberg by making him a core member of the U.S. delegation in San Francisco, where he was one of the most vocal and visible Americans. He called the Charter "a new emancipation proclamation for the world." Even John Foster Dulles, a Republican mandarin not given to hyperbole, called it "a greater Magna Carta."[25]

THE SHATTERER OF WORLDS

In a speech at the close of the signing ceremony for the Charter in San Francisco on June 26, President Truman was sufficiently confident of Senate approval that he could safely deliver to the world, on behalf of the mightiest nation on earth, a message of self-restraint and willingness to let American policies and behavior be guided by international opinion and international law: "No matter how great our strength, we must deny ourselves the license to do always as we please." Two days later, in another speech, at the University of Kansas City, he elaborated: "Now, if Kansas and Colorado have a quarrel over a watershed, they don't call out the National Guard of each state and go to war over it. They bring suit in the Supreme Court and abide by its decision. There isn't a reason in the world why we can't do that internationally." [26]

Truman was proclaiming a view that Socrates had paid with his life to defend: one can—and indeed, should—be a patriot and internationalist at the same time. But it further inclined Truman to take this magnanimous, even self-abnegating position to know that the United States was about to demonstrate its willingness and ability to do exactly what it felt necessary, without the knowledge, to say nothing of the consent, of the rest of humanity. Truman knew of the work that was proceeding apace at a site for a test, code-named "Trinity," about 1,200 miles to the southeast.

Three weeks later, on July 16, a metal sphere, about six feet in diameter, atop a hundred-foot-high steel tower, exploded. Watching from a bunker about six miles away, his eyes shielded by a makeshift facemask of aluminum sheets and welders' goggles, was my great-uncle Charlie Thomas. As he later wrote, "All of a sudden there was an intense speck of light. It grew to a giant ball which rose rapidly in the air—it was awful! It was literally a sun coming up too close." [27] Next to him, the director of Los Alamos, J. Robert Oppenheimer, recalled a passage from the Bhagavad-Gita, an ancient Hindu text, in which the warrior Arjuna has a vision of Lord Krishna as a charioteer guiding him into battle:

> If the radiance of a thousand suns
> Were to burst at once into the sky
> That would be like the splendor of the Mighty one . . .
> I am become Death,
> The Shatterer of Worlds.

The news reached Truman in Potsdam, Germany, where he had just arrived for a conference with Churchill and Stalin. Stimson showed the president a top-secret telegram that had just come in from his special assistant, George Harrison: "Operated this morning. Diagnosis not yet complete but results seem satisfactory and already exceed expectations." Late the following night, a second cable arrived: "Doctor has just returned most enthusiastic and confident that the little boy is as husky as his big brother. The light in his eyes discernible from here to Highhold and I could have heard his screams from here to my farm." The clerks decoding the message thought the seventy-eight-year-old Stimson had just become a father. The "light in his eyes" and "screams" referred to the flash at Alamogordo, which had been visible for 250 miles, the distance from Washington to Highhold, Stimson's estate on Long Island, and to the thunderous report, which carried fifty miles, the distance to Harrison's farm in Virginia. The references to the little boy and his big brother meant that the experts believed the smaller, more efficient uranium bomb would be as powerful as the plutonium one that had just been tested.[28]

As Truman confided to his diary, "We have discovered the most terrible bomb in the history of the world. It may be the fire destruction prophesied in the Euphrates Valley Era, after Noah and his fabulous Ark. . . . I have told [Stimson] to use it so that military objectives and soldiers and sailors are the target and not women and children. Even if the Japs are savages, ruthless, merciless and fanatic, we as the leader of the world for the common welfare cannot drop this terrible bomb on the old Capital [Kyoto] or the new [Tokyo]. He & I are in accord. The target will be a purely military one and we will issue a warning statement asking the Japs to surrender and save lives. I'm sure they will not do that, but we will have given them the chance. It is certainly a good thing for the world that Hitler's crowd or Stalin's did not discover this atomic bomb. It seems to be the most terrible thing ever discovered, but it can be made the most useful." [29]

When Truman shared the news with Churchill in Potsdam, they decided to tell Stalin. On the afternoon of July 24, Truman walked over to the Soviet leader and "casually mentioned . . . that we had a new weapon of unusual destructive force." Stalin, just as casually, said he was "glad to hear it" and moved on to other subjects. The offhand reaction baffled some of Truman's aides, who thought perhaps the president was too vague or perhaps Stalin was obtuse. In fact, Stalin had learned from his own intelligence service about the successful test at about the same time as Truman had been informed by Stimson.[30]

ON JULY 28, THE U.S. SENATE approved the UN Charter. The vote, 89–2, reflected opinion polls showing about 80 percent support.* Twelve days had passed since the Trinity test. By then, "Little Boy," a uranium-based weapon, and "Fat Man," which had a plutonium core and used the trigger my father's Uncle Charlie had helped develop, were arriving at a U.S. air base on Tinian Island in the Northern Marianas.

---

* The two "nays" were from Republicans William Langer of North Dakota and Henrik Shipstead of Minnesota, the most hardened of the isolationists in the Senate.

Later in the year, Vandenberg would be among those members of Congress who sponsored a resolution, unanimously adopted, to invite the United Nations to establish its permanent home on American territory. The midterm congressional elections of 1946 would give the Republicans a majority in the Senate and elevate Vandenberg to the chairmanship of the Foreign Relations Committee. He remained a staunch supporter of a bipartisan foreign policy until his death in 1951. He noted in his diary that he supported the UN precisely because it was not "a wild-eyed internationalist dream of a world state." [31]

Dean Acheson, who in 1945 became undersecretary of state (the number two person in the department), sometimes saw himself as Jiminy Cricket on Truman's shoulder, a voice of sobriety and caution, offsetting others' excessive enthusiasm for the new organization. The UN, as Acheson saw it, was a gathering of separate states, no less sovereign for gathering under one roof: "They are still nations, and no more can be expected of this forum for political adjustment than the sum total of the contributions. In the Arab proverb, the ass that went to Mecca remained an ass, and a policy has little added to it by its place of utterance." [32]

Acheson believed that at the end of the day American power, wisely employed, was the ultimate guarantor of peace and security in the world. The UN, as he put it in a 1951 speech to the National War College, was "not something apart from its members. Its strength has no sources independent of the strength supplied by those who belong to it and are willing to back it up." That was true (and remains so today). But Acheson went further: he did not see the UN as having much value as a means of legitimizing and leveraging American power. Hence his comment that the UN was "certainly an American contribution to a troubled world, [but] I personally am free of the slightest suspicion of paternity." Toward the end of his life he turned vitriolic toward the UN and its progenitors. In a letter he wrote in 1967, four years before his death, he railed against his country's propensity for "damned moralism, beginning with Woodrow Wilson's self-determination and ending with that little rat Leo Pasvolsky's United Nations." [33]

It was a harsh but telling outburst from an old realist, one of many who believed that the balance of power was as suitable a basis for world peace in the second half of the twentieth century as it had been in the nineteenth.

IF JOSEPH STALIN HAD HAD HIS WAY, "security"—i.e., prevention of war—would have been virtually the sole function of the UN, and therefore the Security Council would have been the only body that mattered. But first Roosevelt, then Truman insisted on giving the UN a much broader mission that would deal with health, finance, economic development, culture, and social issues. The Mexican secretary of foreign relations, Ezequiel Padilla, articulated the widespread support this concept enjoyed among most of the delegates in San Francisco, particularly those from poorer parts of the world. "The Charter," said Padilla near the end of the conference, "is not only an instrument of security against the horrors of war. It is also, for the people who have been fighting to uphold the principles of human dignity, an instrument of well-being and happiness against the horrors of a peace without hope, in which men would be subjected to humiliating privations and injustices. 'Blood, sweat, and tears'* comprised the glorious but provisional rule of war. It must not become the rule of peace." [34]

A key member of the staff of the American delegation had been making that same point for three years. "The real objective . . . of schemes of future international organization," said Ralph Bunche, "must always be the good life for all of the people. International machinery will mean something to the common man in the Orient, as indeed to the common man throughout the world, only when it is translated into terms that he can understand: peace, bread, housing, clothing, education, good health, and above all, the right to walk with dignity on the world's great boulevards." [35]

Bunche, whose grandmother had been born a slave and whose father was a barber in Detroit, had written a doctoral thesis at Harvard on the mandate system of the League of Nations. During World War II, he was the premier analyst of Africa and colonial issues for the Office of Strategic Services (the forerunner of the CIA). After that, he served as the chief expert on these issues for the State Department.

Bunche was deeply involved in the drafting of those chapters of the Charter that would enable the UN to deal with colonies and, he and others hoped, manage and hasten the process of decolonization. The result, however, was not much of an improvement on the old mandate system of the League of Nations. The League had made it easy for imperial powers to procrastinate in giving up the colonies they had taken over from the Germans and the Ottomans. The UN established a Trusteeship Council to deal with leftover League mandates and a separate system for all colonies—known as "Non-

---

* This was one of Churchill's most famous wartime phrases, although here, as so commonly elsewhere, it is misquoted. He actually said, in his maiden speech to the House of Commons as prime minister, on May 13, 1940, "blood, toil, tears, and sweat."

Self-Governing Territories"—not covered by the trusteeship system. The Charter did not empower the UN as such to drive or supervise the progress of the "NSGs" toward self-government, and it imposed on the countries controlling those territories only the vaguest obligation to keep the UN secretary-general informed about what they were doing to prepare their charges for graduation to statehood. It was, as Inis Claude puts it, "an imperfect universalization of the principle of international trusteeship" that "ratified [through the Trusteeship Council] the doctrine that all colonies [were] minor wards of the human family to be brought to self-respecting and self-reliant adulthood, rather than chattels to be ruled and used at the pleasure of their owners."[36] Claude's judgment, written in 1956, captured, with deliberate irony, the paternalism of the European powers. They were in no hurry to realize Roosevelt's dream that the UN would hasten the process whereby all colonies would eventually attain independence on their own or join neighboring independent states.

EVEN IN EUROPE, however—and most dramatically in Britain—there was a growing awareness that imperialism was doomed. In July 1945, Churchill was turned out of office by voters who wanted to focus on the home front after the long war. As Lord Wavell, the viceroy of India, prepared to return to Delhi a month after the election, Churchill pleaded with him, "Keep a bit of India!"[37] The new government of Clement Attlee moved quickly to accede to Mahatma Gandhi's long-standing demand that Britain "quit India." Two years later, in August 1947, the Raj came to an end after two centuries of British influence and eighty-nine years of direct crown rule.

At almost the same time, Britain, having already spun off Transjordan from the mandate, pulled out of Palestine as well. British forces had come increasingly under fire from Arabs and Jews. On November 29, 1947, in response to London's request for a solution to "the Palestine Question," the UN General Assembly voted 33–13 for a resolution that would establish two states, side by side, one for Jews, one for Palestinian Arabs. The Jewish state was to consist of three regions, one along the Mediterranean coast, another on the Syrian border, and a third in the southeast, mostly consisting of the Negev Desert. The Arab state was to include the Gaza Strip and most of central Palestine on the West Bank of the Jordan River. Jerusalem was to be administered as an international territory.

Jewish leaders accepted the resolution, while Arab leaders did not. Three days after the vote in the General Assembly, Arabs in Jerusalem rampaged through the city, burning buildings and attacking Jews. Jewish militias retaliated. On May 14, 1948, the day before the British Mandate expired, Israel proclaimed its existence as a state. The next day, all of its neighbors—Egypt, Lebanon, Syria, and what was then called Transjordan, with troops from Iraq, Saudi Arabia, and Yemen as well—began an attack against Israeli forces.

Bunche was called away from his post in the secretariat dealing with the Trusteeship Council to be deputy to Count Folke Bernadotte, a Swedish diplomat who was charged by the UN to mediate a cease-fire. When Bernadotte was assassinated by an extremist Jewish group, Bunche took over.* After eleven months of negotiations on the island of Rhodes, Bunche persuaded the Arab combatant states to sign armistices that left Israel with 20 percent more territory than when it was created. On his return to New York, Bunche was the guest of honor at a banquet at the Waldorf-Astoria, and he would be awarded the 1950 Nobel Peace Prize.

Relief and self-congratulation were in order, but so was a sense of foreboding. The new world was going to be treacherous in new ways. The immediate consequence of the United Nations' first major action, the creation of the state of Israel, had been the first in a series of regional wars. Two prominent Jewish intellectuals, Hannah Arendt and Isaiah Berlin, speculated that the first Arab-Israel war and those that followed might have been avoided if a well-established international entity, the British Commonwealth, had in 1947 taken formal responsibility for keeping the peace between the Arabs and the Palestinians. Berlin, an ardent Zionist, believed that the Arabs might have been deterred from attacking Israel if doing so had constituted an attack on Britain itself.[38] It is a what-might-have-been worth considering, if only because of a lesson that the world would have to learn over the decades that followed: nation-building and conflict prevention are more likely to succeed if multiple international organizations are involved in a coordinated and mutually reinforcing fashion. A reborn Israel had only a new-born UN on its side.

BY 1949, BRITAIN had pulled out of Burma, Sri Lanka, and all of Egypt except the area around the Suez Canal. The sun was setting on other empires as well. When the UN was founded in 1945, about 750 million people—a

---

* The so-called Lehi Group—an acronym standing for *Lohamei Herut Yisrael* ("Fighters for the Freedom of Israel")—was better known as the Stern Gang, after its first leader. Yitzhak Shamir, a member of the group, would serve as prime minister in the late 1980s and early '90s.

third of the earth's population at that time—lived under colonialism. By the late 1980s, that number had shrunk to less than two million. Eleven territories in Africa and the Pacific, with populations totaling fourteen million people, were originally under the authority of the Trusteeship Council. All eventually achieved independence. Some, such as Ghana and Cameroon, did so quite quickly, others more slowly.[39] It would take nearly fifty years before the last trust territory—the Palau Islands, which had been occupied by the Japanese before and during World War II and administered by the United States afterward—joined the UN as the 185th member. The Trusteeship Council in effect went out of business without much fanfare. It continued to exist on paper for years and had its own designated chamber next to the Security Council chamber, although that space was used as just another meeting room.

THE WAKE-UP CALL

While the Charter and the organization it brought into being were marked—and in many ways marred—by compromise, ambiguities, contradictions, and unintended consequences, they nonetheless amounted to an improvement over the League. "The phenomenal feature of 1945," observes Inis Claude, "was not so much that the great powers extracted concessions to their strength as that they accepted far-reaching treaty obligations for the responsible use of their strength . . . [I]n essence, the Charter scheme represented acceptance by the great powers of a framework of constitutional limitations within which their de facto power was to be exercised. The most celebrated of the special privileges granted to the Big Five, the right of veto in the Security Council, was not so much an instrument of great power dictatorship over small states as a factor injected into the relationships of the great powers among themselves."[40]

Those relationships were now codified in what Wilson had sought and failed to achieve a quarter of a century earlier: an "open covenant of peace, openly arrived at." But it was not the United Nations as such that kept the peace over the decades that followed. The very public American project that produced the Charter in San Francisco—helpful as it would prove to be in many ways—could not, by itself, restrain the age-old penchant of nations to go to war. The transformative development in 1945 was the secret American project that produced an explosion in the New Mexico desert, and then, shortly afterward, two more explosions on the far side of the Pacific.

Atomic bomb blast at Nagasaki

· · ·

A MUSHROOM CLOUD ROSE over Hiroshima on August 6, and three days later another billowed over Nagasaki. The attacks incinerated or crushed more than 120,000 Japanese, mostly civilians, and consigned another 230,000 to slow death from radiation and other injuries.

The American scientists and engineers who had made "Fat Man" and "Little Boy" knew how puny those bombs were compared to what was to come. On hearing the news about Hiroshima, Einstein's immediate reaction was "*Vey iz mir*" (Yiddish for "*Woe is me*").[41]

In keeping with his initial desire to hit "purely" military targets, Truman and his advisers had weighed the possibilities of demonstrating the bomb on a deserted island in the Pacific or on a military installation in Japan far away from any population centers. Those options were discarded because an explosion on an isolated military target or a test in the middle of nowhere might not have broken Japan's will to continue the war. Hiroshima and Nagasaki were selected in part because they were important naval ports and sites of major armaments plants. Even after approving the decision, Truman stressed his desire "to avoid, *insofar as possible*, the killing of civilians" (italics added).[42] He went to his grave twenty-six years later, convinced that the attacks ended the war in the Pacific and saved tens of thousands of American lives that might have been lost if the United States had been forced to subdue Japan with a D-Day-like invasion.*

Still, Truman left no doubt, as he put it publicly in October 1945, that "the release of atomic energy constitutes a new force too revolutionary to consider in the framework of old ideas." [43] He understood that with perfection and proliferation, this new form of weaponry could exterminate life on the planet. Total war had acquired a whole new meaning. Woodrow Wilson and others after World War I had unsuccessfully challenged the legitimacy of war. Now its very sanity was in question, and so was the survival of the human race. "You have got to understand that this isn't a military weapon," Truman later remarked to his aides. "It is used to wipe out women and children and unarmed people, and not for military uses. So we have got to treat this differently from rifles and cannon and ordinary things like that. . . . The human animal and his emotions change not much from age to age. He must change now or he faces absolute and complete destruction and maybe the insect age or an atmosphereless planet will succeed him." [44]

SUPPORT FOR THE UNITED NATIONS briefly soared, but so did concern that the UN would not be up to the task of coping with this new phenomenon. Even before the A-bomb attacks on Japan, the essayist E. B. White had been worrying in the pages of the *New Yorker* that the UN was insufficiently ambitious: "The name 'United Nations' will presumably have to be dropped, since the organization is to be an association, not a union, and it is unwise to lead people into believing that they are getting something they aren't. One of the San Francisco papers made an unconscious suggestion for a title the other day when its proofreader was dozing. The paper came out with a reference to 'the Untied Nations,' a far more accurate name than the one intended." Later, White suggested that "United Notions" was an equally apposite typo.

Immediately after Hiroshima, White returned with fresh vigor and no humor to his complaint: "The political plans for the new world, as shaped by statesmen, are not fantastic enough. . . . The only conceivable way to catch up with atomic energy is with political energy directed to a universal structure. The preparations made at San Francisco for a security league of sovereign nations to prevent aggression now seem like the preparations some little

---

* Historians continue to debate how decisive a factor the A-bombs were in forcing the Japanese surrender. Another was the Soviet Union's declaration of war against Japan on August 8 and the Soviet drive across Manchuria into Korea.

girls might make for a lawn party as a thunderhead gathers just beyond the garden gate. The lemonade will be spiked by lightning. The little girls will be dispersed. Nuclear energy and foreign policy cannot coexist on the planet. The more deep the secret, the greater the determination of every nation to discover and exploit it. Nuclear energy insists on global government." [45]

Article 51 of the Charter acknowledged what had always been the single most fiercely guarded right of the individual nation: self-defense. But many considered it neither utopian nor unpatriotic—nor, for that matter, inconsistent with self-defense—to advocate an overarching authority that would diminish the chances that, in exercising their right of self-defense with this fearsome new weapon, individual states would destroy one another and perhaps much of the rest of the world.

Albert Einstein was just one of the distinguished American physicists who advocated collective stewardship of nuclear weaponry. They felt responsibility for the discovery of the physical principles that made possible the invention of this new technology. In September 1945, Einstein wrote his friend and colleague J. Robert Oppenheimer: "The wretched attempts to achieve international security, as it is understood today by our governments, do not alter at all the political structure of the world, do not recognize at all the competing sovereign nation-states as the real cause of conflicts. Our governments and the people do not seem to have drawn anything from past experience and are unable or unwilling to think the problem through. The conditions existing today force the individual states, for the sake of their own security based on fear, to do all those things which inevitably produce war. At the present stage of industrialism, with the existing complete integration of the world, it is unthinkable that we can have peace without a real governmental organization to create and enforce law on individuals in their international relations. Without such an over-all solution to give up-to-date expression to the democratic sovereignty of the peoples, all attempts to avoid specific dangers in the international field seem to me illusory."

Oppenheimer replied, "I am in complete agreement." [46]

That same month, Einstein went public with his plea: "The only salvation for civilization and the human race lies in the creation of world government," he said in an interview. "As long as sovereign states continue to have armaments and armaments secrets, new world wars will be inevitable." [47] The following year he elaborated the argument in his contribution to a pamphlet, published by the Federation of American Scientists and titled *One World or None*—an echo of the title Wendell Willkie had chosen for his own book three years before. "It is necessary," Einstein wrote, "that conditions be established that guarantee the individual state the right to solve its conflicts with other states on a legal basis and under international jurisdiction. It is necessary that the individual state be prevented from making war by a supranational organization supported by a military power that is exclusively under its control." [48]

Einstein had the support of a nonscientist who contributed to *One World or None*. Walter Lippmann was the dean of American foreign affairs columnists. As a young man, he had been part of Woodrow Wilson's team of advisers in designing the League of Nations. That experience had been chastening. Lippmann's chapter in *One World or None*, "International Control of Atomic Energy," argued that "not another League of Nations but a world state, in the exact meaning of the term, is inherent and potential in the embryonic organism of the United Nations . . . as an oak tree is in an acorn."

Even Edward Teller, who would later earn fame as the father of the hydrogen bomb and as a hawk much revered on the right, wrote in 1946, "Nothing that we can plan as a defense for the next generation is likely to be satisfactory; that is, nothing but world-union." [49]

Robert Maynard Hutchins, the chancellor of the University of Chicago, saw the atomic bomb as heralding "the good news of damnation"—the ultimate wake-up call—that would frighten the leaders of the world into taking "those positive steps necessary to the creation of a world society." [50]

Some leaders of the realist school—advocates of national interest and balance of power as the ordering principles of American foreign policy and the international system—acknowledged the logic of the case for world government even if they did not fully embrace the movement. The most prominent was Hans Morgenthau, then at the University of Chicago, whose disciples, decades later, would include Condoleezza Rice. [51] In 1948, the first edition of Morgenthau's classic *Politics Among Nations* concluded that "the argument of the advocates of the world state is unanswerable. There can be no permanent international peace without a state coextensive with the confines of the political world [and] a radical transformation of the existing international society of sovereign nations into a supranational community of individuals." He cautioned, however, that he could imagine such an outcome only in the long term. [52]

From the far side of the Atlantic came the voice, in a distinctly Kantian key, of another hardheaded political thinker. The eminent French thinker Raymond Aron, who was no apologist for the left, believed that while the latest advance in military technology threatened humanity, the spread of Western industrial technology to the rest of the world was an irresistibly homogenizing force: "We have reached a phase where we are discovering both the limited validity of civilization [as a distinguishing feature of different cultures] and the need to transcend that concept. . . . The phase of civilizations is coming to an end, and for good or ill, humanity is embarking on a new phase"—one, he believed, that would be marked by a political integration and a merging of economic systems.[53]

The prophets of doom now had allies among the optimists of social science.[54] Starting in the mid-forties, there was a revival of pseudo-Darwinian wishful thinking, fashionable a hundred years earlier, that humankind might be evolving toward a single, global polity.*

SOME INTELLECTUALS in the immediate postwar period, even as they advocated world government, warned that political integration, welcome though it might be as a way of avoiding nuclear cataclysm, must be accompanied by measures to respect and preserve cultural pluralism. Like Dante in the thirteenth century and Alexander Pope in the eighteenth, poets joined the debate. In a series of lectures that were broadcast over the radio in occupied Germany in March 1946, T. S. Eliot said,

> An error of the Germany of Hitler was to assume that every culture other than
> that of Germany was either decadent or barbaric. Let us have an end of such
> assumptions. The other direction in which the confusion of culture and poli-
> tics may lead is towards the idea of a world state in which there will, in the end,
> be only one uniform world culture. I am not here criticizing any schemes for
> world organization. Such schemes belong to the plane of engineering, or de-
> vising machinery. Machinery is necessary, and the more perfect the machine
> the better. But culture is something that must grow; you cannot build a tree,

---

* Purveyors of this idea have often seized on the work of Franz Boas, who died in 1942. One of the pioneers of American anthropology, Boas was known for his rigorous analysis of cultural and linguistic structures. A paper of his, published posthumously in 1945, argued, in the jargon of his profession, that "societal augmentation through successful competition" would bring about "supra-communal aggregation": "[T]he history of mankind shows us the grand spectacle of the grouping of man in units of ever increasing size. . . . Not withstanding all temporary revolutions and the shattering of larger units for the time being, the progress in the direction of unification has been so regular and so marked that we must needs conclude that the tendencies which have swayed this development in the past will govern our history in the future. . . . The practical difficulties that seem to stand in the way of the formation of still larger units count for naught before the inexorable laws of history."

you can only plant it, and care for it, and wait for it to mature in its due time; and when it is grown you must not complain if you find that from an acorn has come an oak, and not an elm-tree. And a political structure is partly construction, and partly growth, partly machinery and the same machinery, if good, is equally good for all peoples, and partly growing with and from the nation's culture, and in that respect different from that of other nations. . . . This unity of culture, in contrast to the unity of political organization, does not require us all to have only one loyalty: it means that there will be a variety of loyalties. It is wrong that the only duty of the individual should be held to be towards the State; it is fantastic to hold that the supreme duty of every individual should be towards a Super-State.[55]

LOOKING FOR A WAY to achieve the salvation of world government without infringing on individual, communal, and national freedoms, many—again like Dante and Kant—saw federalism as the answer. The Campaign for World Government, which had been formed on the eve of World War II, reconstituted itself after the war as the World Federalist Movement. One of its most active branches was in the United States. In February 1947, representatives of numerous grassroots world-federalist organizations met in Asheville, North Carolina, to create the United World Federalists. Its roster read like a Who's Who of academe, science, politics, the media, the legal community, business, and labor.* Surveys showed that the movement had widespread support in the general public, especially among those with college educations, and also among freshman members of Congress elected in 1946, including a young Republican from California, Richard Nixon, and a young Democrat from Massachusetts, John F. Kennedy. Also drawn to the cause of world government was a politically inclined young actor named Ronald Reagan.[56]

---

* Among the notables associated then or later with world federalism were, from the literary world, John Hersey, Lewis Mumford, Robert Sherwood, Edna Ferber, Sinclair Lewis, Clifford Odets, Edna St. Vincent Millay, Upton Sinclair, James Thurber, and E. B. White; from government, politics, and the military: Supreme Court Justices Owen Roberts and William O. Douglas, Thomas K. Finletter (who would serve as Truman's secretary of the air force), Chester Bowles (governor of Connecticut), John Winant (the Republican governor of New Hampshire), Senator J. William Fulbright, and two future senators (Alan Cranston and Harris Wofford); from business and finance, W. T. Holliday (president of Standard Oil of Ohio), Beardsley Ruml (chairman of the Federal Reserve Bank of New York), Harry Bullis (president of General Mills), Grenville Clark (a prominent former Wall Street lawyer), and Robert Gaylord (chairman of the executive committee of the National Association of Manufacturers); from the media, numerous magazine and newspaper editors, most prominently Norman Cousins, the editor of *Saturday Review*.

Some of the delegates in Asheville were known as the maximalists. They advocated a supranational body that would be empowered to control nuclear weapons, end colonialism, eradicate poverty, put tyrants on trial before a much-strengthened World Court, and have its own armed forces to intercede in conflicts and compel compliance with international law. The "minimalists" held a position that was hardly modest: their version of world government would have as its "only" purpose the prevention of war. All other functions of governance would remain with national states. In the end, the minimalists prevailed, and the Asheville conference supported the UN and a willingness to accommodate the multistate system rather than try to replace it with a global state.[57]

ONE OF THE BRIGHT LIGHTS of the World Federalist movement was Kingman Brewster, who went on to be president of Yale and a mentor of mine when I was an undergraduate. Another was Cord Meyer. His was a name and a story I heard as I was growing up. He had been at Yale with my father, in the wartime class of 1943. Meyer was a natural leader, editor of the campus literary magazine, star of the hockey team, and winner of the award given to the outstanding member of the class. He entered the Marine Corps, fought valiantly in the Pacific, lost an eye on Guam and his twin brother, also a Marine, on Okinawa. Meyer's slightly fictionalized account of his combat experience, "Waves of Darkness," won the 1946 O. Henry Prize for the best short story by a previously unpublished author.

After the war, Meyer went to work for Harold Stassen, the former governor of Minnesota and a leader of the liberal wing of the Republican Party as well as a member of the U.S. delegation to the San Francisco Conference. Meyer felt that the UN, because it perpetuated the sanctity of national sovereignty, was at best a makeshift that would have to suffice until it could be given law-making and law-enforcing powers.

In May 1947, Meyer, at the age of twenty-six, became the first president of the United World Federalists. He took to the road, speaking and raising money for the cause. That year my parents, who were moderate Republicans, joined some friends from both parties in founding a Dayton chapter of the organization.

World federalism had been a subject of the Einstein-Oppenheimer correspondence since at least October 1945. While seeing the virtues in the idea, Oppenheimer believed that the American experience with federalism was cause for caution rather than enthusiasm: "The history of this nation up through the Civil War shows how difficult the establishment of a federal authority can be when there are profound differences in the structure and values of the societies it attempts to integrate." Einstein took the point but still felt that the human race had no choice but to make the effort. In a letter to Meyer, he wrote, "Without the world state [there can be] no world security, and without security no effective solution concerning the singular problem of protection against the atomic bomb . . . [T]he world government project should be worked out by the best minds." [58]

However, some of the best minds, including Oppenheimer's, were already turning to a more immediate issue. In one of his 1945 letters to Einstein, Oppenheimer warned about the paramount challenge of managing "the dangers of competitive armament between two all-powerful nations."

The United States still had the bomb to itself, but as Truman himself publicly acknowledged, such would not be the case forever, or even for very long: atomic energy constituted a "means of destruction hitherto unknown, against which there can be no adequate military defense, and in the employment of which no single nation can in fact have a monopoly." [59]

However, in that bleak and unprecedented fact lay the basis for something equally unprecedented: peace between the two most powerful antagonists the world had ever known.

10

A TRUSTEESHIP OF THE POWERFUL

Whether you like it or not, history is on our side. We will bury you!
—*NIKITA KHRUSHCHEV*[1]

[P]ower without wisdom is deadly.
—*DWIGHT EISENHOWER*[2]

THERE was no doubt which country Americans—and many others—worried would get the bomb next. Even before World War II was over, Joseph Stalin was expanding his empire at a rate that Catherine the Great would have envied. By the beginning of 1946, twelve states of central and Eastern Europe were already under Moscow's influence. In February, George F. Kennan sat down at his desk in Moscow and wrote a five-thousand-word report on the challenge that the Soviet Union posed for the United States. He was Ambassador Averell Harriman's deputy and a first cousin twice removed of the explorer and writer of the same name who had alerted Americans in the late nineteenth century to the evils of czarism. Sent as a cable back to the State Department, Kennan's "Long Telegram" concluded that the U.S.S.R. was "highly sensitive to the logic of force. For this reason it can easily withdraw—and usually does—when strong resistance is encountered at any point. Thus, if the adversary has sufficient force and makes clear his readiness to use it, he rarely has to do so."

Eleven days later, Winston Churchill, whose Conservative Party had been defeated in the election of July 1945 and who was therefore now the leader of the opposition, sounded the alarm in a speech at Westminster College in Fulton, Missouri: "From Stettin in the Baltic to Trieste in the Adriatic, an iron curtain has descended across the Continent." In a passage far less frequently cited—and with Harry Truman nodding in approval beside the lectern—Churchill went on to say: "A world organization has already been erected for the prime purpose of preventing war. The UNO, the successor of the League of Nations, with the decisive addition of the United States and all that that means, is already at work. We must make sure that its work is fruitful, that it is a reality and not a sham, that it is a force for action and not merely a frothing of words, that it is a true temple of peace in which the shields of many nations can some day be hung up, and not merely a cockpit in a Tower of Babel."

Walter Lippmann popularized the phrase "the Cold War" as the title of a collection of his columns in which he argued that the United Nations was the best hope of averting World War III.[3]

But the UN could not be the only hope. As the failure of the League of Nations had demonstrated, keeping the peace was sure to require the use, or at least the plausible threat, of force. The UN, like the League, did not have an army of its own. It could call on member states to contribute troops, but the rivalry between the United States and the Soviet Union threatened to deadlock the Security Council on any issue where their interests clashed. Kennan had this obstacle to the UN's effectiveness in mind when he called publicly (though anonymously, in an article in the July 1947 issue of *Foreign Affairs* under the byline "X") for an American policy of "patient but firm and vigilant containment of Russian expansive tendencies."

By then, the U.S.S.R. had installed puppet regimes in Poland, Romania, Bulgaria, and Hungary. Under the terms of the Potsdam agreement, the Soviets annexed part of East Prussia, including Immanuel Kant's hometown, Königsberg. The Kremlin renamed the city Kaliningrad, after the titular head of state of the U.S.S.R. In 1948, Soviet-backed communists in Czechoslovakia staged a coup that brought them to power.

It was widely feared in the West that, after only the briefest of respites, the recent great war had made the world no safer for democracy or peace than the first one. In George Orwell's dystopian novel *1984* (the title inverted the last two digits of 1948, the year when it was published), he imagined a world divided into three despotic superstates—Oceania, Eurasia, and Eastasia—permanently at war with one another. Big Brother, an amalgam of Stalin and Hitler, was the omniscient, omnipotent ruler of Oceania, which included Britain.

In a lecture to the National War College in 1947, Kennan warned that American society was not "immune" to the ugliest forms of nationalism. "The fact of the matter is that there is a little bit of the totalitarian buried somewhere, way down deep, in each and every one of us. It is only the cheerful light of confidence and security which keeps this evil genius down. . . . If confidence and security were to disappear, don't think that he would not be waiting to take their place." [4]

The sense of confidence and security that had come with the defeat of the Axis was already beginning to wane, creating the conditions for the emergence of the demon Kennan worried about. As early as 1946 a growing right-wing movement began to depict the United Nations as atheistic and un-American. That year a Marine veteran and former circuit-court judge named Joseph McCarthy was elected the junior senator from Wisconsin; he would later identify the UN as being an agency of communist influence. U.S. officials and foreign diplomats who were assigned the task of scouting sites for the UN were subjected to insults as they drove around New York state in specially tagged cars. [5] The Truman administration became the target of potshots from conservative members of Congress who believed that civil servants "with strong Soviet leanings" were being given refuge in the State Department, where they were shifting "the center of gravity in the process of United States foreign policy formulation from a national to an international organization via the supranational United Nations Organization. . . . The [goal] of this ideology may be fairly described as a socialized America in a world commonwealth of Communist and Socialist states dedicated to peace through collective security, political, economic, and social reform, and the redistribution of national wealth on a global basis." [6]

JOSEPH PANUCH, A STATE DEPARTMENT OFFICIAL who had provided congressional critics with ammunition to make this charge, was fired, and for several years the conspiracy theory he and others tried to spread was confined to the fringe of American politics. Public opinion polls showed that support for the UN and even world government remained a mainstream sentiment. [7]

The Soviets inadvertently helped insulate the United World Federalists from accusations within the U.S. that they were part of a leftist plot. On instructions from Moscow, the American Communist Party's journal, *New Masses*, attacked "the reactionary utopianism of the world state project" on the grounds that it promoted "solutions in abstract reason and justice rather than in the actual class forces in society." In 1947, Andrei Zhdanov, the Soviet Central Committee secretary in charge of ideology and propaganda, complained that "the idea of a 'world government' has been taken up by bourgeois intellectual cranks and pacifists." [8]

If they had dispensed with the modifier "bourgeois," the Kremlin propagandists would have sounded as though they were in agreement with American right-wingers. The vituperations from the two ends of the spectrum tended to cancel each other out and encouraged the view among moderates in the United States that, if anything, the UN did not go far enough toward world government. As late as June 1949, sixty-four Democrats and twenty-seven Republicans in the House of Representatives—including John F. Kennedy, then in his second term, and a freshman, Gerald Ford of Michigan—sponsored a resolution declaring that "it should be a fundamental objective of the foreign policy of the U.S. to support and strengthen the UN and to seek its development into a world federation open to all nations with defined and limited powers adequate to preserve peace and prevent aggression through the enactment, interpretation and enforcement of world law."

Lobbying on behalf of the measure, Cord Meyer and several other World Federalists met with Truman. As Meyer recalled later, the president "listened attentively, with his head cocked to one side, and then asked a few questions that showed considerable skepticism." Secretary of State George Marshall later testified before the House Committee on Foreign Affairs that the administration would not oppose an amendment along the lines of the resolution, but he believed it premature since there was insufficient support for it in the Congress, the country, and the UN itself.[9]

AS THE COLD WAR BECAME an increasingly oppressive reality, Truman took some consolation from his advisers' confidence that at least the United States would have a monopoly on the bomb well into the fifties. It would need the superweapon to hold back what *Time* magazine called, in June 1949, "the red tide that threatens to engulf the world."[10]

Three months later, a U.S. Air Force reconnaissance plane, flying over the North Pacific, picked up traces of radioactivity in the atmosphere east of the Kamchatka Peninsula at the eastern end of Siberia. Analysts quickly concluded that the Soviets had tested a device in the Ustyurt desert of Central Asia some weeks before. What Moscow dubbed "Stalin's Reactor-Engine No. 1" the Americans nicknamed "Joe One." It was modeled on Fat Man and made full use of the secrets that Soviet spies had stolen from the Manhattan Project.

On October 1, a week after Truman announced to the world the news of the test, Mao Zedong formally established the People's Republic of China. From its new island redoubt of Taiwan, the Nationalist government of Chiang Kai-shek would continue to represent China in the United Nations and hold a permanent seat in the Security Council for another twenty-three years. The population of Taiwan was about eight million, while at least half a billion Chinese—more than a fifth of humanity at the time—were under communist control. So much for Franklin Roosevelt's hope that Russia and China would join the United States and Britain in policing the world.

These shocks strengthened Truman's determination to make the most of having the United Nations headquartered in an American city and therefore better able to fortify the United States' leadership of "the Free World."[11] On October 24, 1949—"UN Day," the fourth anniversary of the Charter's entry into force—Truman traveled to New York to join the first secretary-general, the Norwegian Trygve Lie, in laying the cornerstone. As Truman spoke, he knew that urgent and secret meetings were under way back in Washington on whether to step up the effort to build an American hydrogen bomb ("the Super") now that the Soviets had the A-bomb. Still, he used the occasion to reiterate his belief in the mission and potential of the UN in high-flown language devoid of reference to the cold war:

> These are the most important buildings in the world, for they are the center of man's hope for peace and a better life. This is the place where the nations of the world will work together to make that hope a reality. . . . We who are close to the United Nations sometimes forget that it is more than the procedures, the councils, and the debates, through which it operates. We tend to overlook the fact that the organization is the living embodiment of the principles of the Charter—the renunciation of aggression and the joint determination to build a better life for the whole world. But if we overlook this fact, we will fail to realize the strength and power of this great organization. We will fail to understand the true nature of this new force that has been created in the affairs of our time. The United Nations is essentially an expression of the moral nature of man's aspirations. The charter clearly shows our determination that international problems must be settled on a basis acceptable to the conscience of mankind. Because the United Nations is the dynamic expression of what all the peoples of the world desire, because it sets up a standard of right and justice for all nations, it is greater than any of its members. The compact that underlies the United Nations cannot be ignored—and it cannot be infringed or dissolved.

THE BUILDINGS IN WHICH THE PRESIDENT of the United States invested such hope were designed by a committee of architects from eleven countries: the five permanent members of the Security Council; two of their allies in World War II, both English-speaking (Canada and Australia); a small Western European state that had been liberated from German occupation twice in twenty-seven years (Belgium); and a token neutral (Sweden). A pair of South American noncombatants (Brazil and Uruguay) was picked, in effect, to represent the rest of the world, much of which, back in the 1940s, was still under colonial rule.

The most celebrated member of the design committee was Le Corbusier, the Swiss-born master of functionalism who had long advocated an architectural form suitable for all nations and climates.[12] The post of chief architect, however, went to Wallace K. Harrison, a patrician New Yorker who specialized in museums and skyscrapers. It was his country that provided the bulk of the funding and the real estate for the new organization on an inlet of the East River known as Turtle Bay.

That name has its own piquant, if esoteric, relevance to the UN. Its origin has nothing to do with turtles. Rather, it was a corruption of an archaic Dutch word, *deutal*, for a bent, scimitar-like sword, similar in shape to the sheltered cove that early-nineteenth-century shipbuilders found well suited for the practice of their trade. When the cove was filled in, it came to be known as Deutal Bay Farms. So etymologically, *Turtle Bay* suggests both swords and plowshares. During the Civil War, those farmlands were soaked in the blood of immigrants who worked in the nearby train yards and slaughterhouses and rioted against the draft laws.

The construction materials and furnishings for the UN were selected from as many lands as possible: English limestone for the facings of the General Assembly Building, Italian marble for the windowless façades on the north and south sides of the Secretariat; Scottish carpets, fabrics from Czechoslovakia and Greece, furniture and shelving from Cuba, Congo, Guatemala, France, Norway, the Philippines—and Switzerland, even though, out of fealty to its long tradition of neutrality, that country was the only one that refused to join the organization.*

The complex, when completed in 1950, was considered a showpiece of the International Style, which had grown out of the Bauhaus movement in Weimar Germany and bore the influence of Russian constructivists and Dutch abstractionists mixed with a heavy dose of Yankee practicality. The

---

* The Swiss believed, correctly, that the UN would have to use force to deal with aggression and felt that prospect would compromise their neutrality. They finally joined in 2002 as the 190th member.

motto of the International school was "form follows function," and its goal, according to one of its advocates, was "to achieve the triumph of absolute harmony over an imperfect and chaotic world, a Utopian ideal"—a formulation that could stand just as well for the hopes invested in the UN itself.[13]

The iron-fenced, eighteen-acre compound's landscaped plaza was cantilevered over FDR Drive, creating the illusion that the whole thing might at any moment break off and slide into the East River.

Even seen from street level, the main structures have always been more incongruous than imposing. The UN Secretariat Building, a thirty-nine-story slab of aluminum, glass, and marble, and the General Assembly's domed auditorium, with its white concrete sloping roof and concave walls, were meant to make a modernist statement that consciously avoided reference to any era or culture—and therefore seemed to be just as consciously mocked by a gargantuan fifties-vintage neon Pepsi-Cola sign on the far side of the river.

Everything about the UN, starting with the aesthetics of its buildings, was anomalous. For decades to come, the message to those who wanted to read it that way would be: *not from around here.* Harry Truman, however, never yielded in his defiance of widespread skepticism about whether the UN belonged in New York and whether it could live up to its lofty goals. He saw the UN as the best that humanity could hope for in the real—and, it was now apparent, divided—world. He knew that the cold war made world government impossible. The very phrase "one world," which had been fashionable only a few years before, suddenly sounded naïve if not seditious. Truman recognized that his dream of a "parliament of man" and a "federation of the world" would have to be deferred to the next generation or beyond.

In a nationally broadcast commencement address at the University of Missouri, on June 9, 1950, the president concluded on an elegiac note: "Oh, I wish it could be my privilege to be graduated here today with you. How I wish I could see the next fifty years. We are facing the greatest age in history. Some of you will see a world of untold and unimagined wonders. I read Alfred Tennyson's 'Locksley Hall.' He saw the future about a hundred years ago. How much greater a future you face, only the greatest imagination can foresee."

SIXTEEN DAYS LATER, in the early morning hours of June 25, the North Korean army attacked South Korea along the length of the 38th Parallel that Americans and Soviets had set in Potsdam as a cease-fire line. The North Koreans overran UN observation posts, leading Trygve Lie to utter one of the few memorable statements of his otherwise undistinguished tenure: "That's war against the United Nations!"

It could also have been the end of the UN. Stalin had given the North Koreans a green light for the invasion. He would surely have used the Soviet veto in the Security Council to stop the UN from taking action if his ambassador, Jacob Malik, had been present when the council met in emergency session. Fortunately, however, Stalin had withdrawn Malik in protest over the UN's refusal to give the Chinese permanent seat to Mao Zedong's communist regime, which had, nine months earlier, driven Chiang Kai-shek's Nationalists from the mainland.

As a result of the Soviets' leaving their chair empty in New York, Truman was able to send an international force to Korea under American military command—yet also under the blue flag of the world body. "In the final analysis," Truman told an aide, "I did this for the United Nations. I believed in the League of Nations. It failed. Lots of people thought it failed because we weren't in it to back it up. Okay, now we started the United Nations. It was our idea, and in this first big test we just couldn't let them down."

Even in the midst of the Korean War, Truman was still thinking wistfully about "Locksley Hall." Riding in his limousine after an early morning walk with the author John Hersey in 1951, Truman took the folded piece of paper out of his wallet and let Hersey read it. "Notice that part about universal law," said the president. "We're going to have that someday. I guess that's what I've really been working for ever since I first put that poetry in my pocket."[14]

IN THE EARLY STAGES OF THE WAR, the North Koreans, capitalizing on surprise, drove back the forces of the United States and its allies. Douglas MacArthur, the American general in command of the UN operation, staged an end run that trapped much of the North Korean force in the South and allowed the allies to push close to the North Korean border with China. That provoked a Chinese intervention that sent the UN army reeling. MacArthur wanted to expand the war into China itself—and said so. Truman fired him for insubordination.

The war continued through Truman's term. During the 1952 presidential campaign, Dwight Eisenhower vowed, "I shall go to Korea!" He never said what he would do when he got there. He did not need to: visiting Korea to assess the situation as president-elect in late November 1952 allowed him to present himself to the American people and the world as a soldier-statesman who was willing to end the war-war and start the jaw-jaw.

In July 1953, a UN-sponsored armistice stopped the fighting where it had started three years before. The 38th parallel was the perfect example of a man-made boundary, dividing a single "nation," in the dictionary sense, into two states. Negotiations at Panmunjong in the Demilitarized Zone continue to this day.

THE COLD WAR, having barely been so named, had already turned hot. Keeping that from happening again and on a larger scale was going to be a challenge for military officers and diplomats. But competing with—and containing—the Soviet Union created the need for spies and covert operators as well. A number of young veterans of World War II who had been liberal internationalists in the 1940s joined the CIA in the fifties. One of those was Cord Meyer. He had personified the idealism—or, as he and others saw it at the time, the new realism in the face of the bomb—that had led many establishment figures to become one-worlders. But once the Soviet Union had its own

Dwight D. Eisenhower

bomb, Meyer felt the United States was confronted with yet another new reality and a new kind of war, requiring a new kind of warrior. Now there were two worlds, irreconcilable in their differences and locked in a titanic struggle that would last generations. Meyer had already come to feel that his was a voice in the wilderness and resigned as president of the United World Federalists when he went into the agency in 1951. He worked at its headquarters in Langley, Virginia, and in the field until his retirement in 1977.[15]

In the spring of 1968, shortly before I graduated from Yale, my father returned to the campus to visit me and attend his twenty-fifth reunion. He ran into Meyer in a college courtyard at a bar set up for the alumni in their blazers and bow ties and big blue lapel buttons announcing their name and class. "The world is in a fight to the death between us and the other side," growled Meyer, "and I am the Lord High Executioner." The lesson he had learned from the carnage and stalemate in Korea was that the devil of communism had to be ruthlessly exorcised before the better angels of humanity would have a chance. In 1969, the United World Federalists dropped the word *united* from its name and added "U.S.A. branch"; in 2004, they retreated further, changing their name to Citizens for Global Solutions, although they continue to run an in-house think tank called the World Federalist Institute.*

The Kremlin learned its own lesson from the Korean War: never again would it leave its chair empty at an important meeting of the Security Council. Soviet permanent representatives would use the veto 119 times between 1945 and 1991, including all but three of the 83 vetoes cast during the UN's first decade.†

STATIC CHESS

John Lewis Gaddis, a historian at Yale who is widely acknowledged as the dean of cold war studies and whose course I audited when I returned to New Haven for the academic year 2001–02, is a connoisseur of counterfactuals. He finds it useful to speculate on what might have happened at various points in the cold war, if only to remind us how close the world came to going over the brink. Gaddis imagines Truman authorizing MacArthur to vaporize the advancing Chinese columns. If that had happened, Mao might have invoked the Treaty of Friendship and Alliance that he had signed with Stalin in

---

* In 1980, after his retirement from the CIA, Cord Meyer wrote in his autobiography, *Facing Reality*, that he never gave up on the possibility that the Soviet Union would someday be transformed into a country that might work together with the United States in putting the world back on the path toward world federalism: "[B]y confining the Soviet empire within the boundaries that emerged from World War II, we had our best chance of assisting developments that might eventually lead to basic internal changes in the Soviet system itself. . . . I believed then, as I do now, that the talented and long-suffering Russian people would eventually demand a greater voice in the management of their own affairs and a wider scope for the expression of individual talent and opinion. When that day came, I believed we would have a new opportunity to build together a supranational structure of enforceable law."

† In that same ten-year period, France used the veto twice (once, to block a resolution condemning the Franco regime in Spain; the other regarding hostilities between Indonesia and the Netherlands that had broken out after the end of World War II). The third non-Soviet veto in that first decade was cast by Taiwan, which then held the Chinese seat on the Council, in denying UN membership for Mongolia (which would not join until 1960). The United States never used the veto during that first decade, although starting in the mid-fifties it made up for lost time, casting 69 vetoes by 1991.

1950. Stalin could have ordered the obliteration of several South Korean cities that were serving as headquarters for the UN forces. The United States might then have retaliated by A-bombing Vladivostok. In return, Stalin might have struck Frankfurt and Hamburg. Gaddis's scenario fades out at that point, leaving to our imaginations what the United States would have done with the 350 atomic bombs then in its arsenal.[16]

One reason the Korean War was fought to a standstill with conventional weapons was that the leaders who had the power to escalate the conflict to the nuclear level had internalized a paradox that the scientists who conceived the bomb, notably Einstein, had understood for years: once the Americans and Soviets both had it, the ultimate weapon was actually the ultimate non-weapon; it was good for only one thing—deterrence.

The Soviets recognized that fact too. Shortly after the test of Joe One in 1949, Stalin remarked to an aide, "Atomic weapons can hardly be used without spelling the end of the world." In 1953, one of Stalin's immediate successors, Georgi Malenkov, said publicly that a war waged with "modern weapons" would be "the end of world civilization."

THE UNITED STATES TESTED its first deliverable hydrogen bomb in March 1954. It was 750 times more powerful than the Hiroshima weapon. The Soviets set off an H-bomb of their own only a year and a half later. In the late fifties—around the time that the Soviets donated to the UN a bronze, socialist-realism sculpture of a brawny blacksmith beating a sword into a plowshare—they were already working on a "Czar Bomb" with an explosive potential equivalent to a hundred million tons of TNT, more than 6,500 times the one used on Hiroshima. The bomb weighed twenty-seven tons, about two and a half times the normal carrying capacity of a Tupolev-95 bomber, the workhorse of the Soviet air force. The plane's bomb bay doors had to be removed and parts of its fuselage cut away to accommodate the monster. Only a specially designed and aerodynamically dubious test version of the plane could get off the ground with the bomb aboard. Most analysts believe that the weapon was a political statement rather than a deployable device.[17] For many years, it sat on display at a nuclear weapons design facility in the Nizhny Novgorod region, which was off limits to foreigners. While intended as a symbol of Soviet power, the Czar Bomb was actually a monument to the truth acknowledged in a secret report to the Kremlin: the detonation of a hundred H-bombs could "create over the whole globe conditions impossible for life."[18]

• • •

ANY ERA KNOWN AS A "WAR," even if only a cold one, would not seem to be propitious for global governance. Yet the period between the rise of the Iron Curtain and the fall of the Berlin Wall was precisely that. The fact that the United States and the Soviet Union, each the leader of an armed camp, remained at a standoff for nearly half a century is not just a mercy but a wonder. It is not, however, a mystery: the new reality of the bomb had rendered obsolete war of the kind that had been a staple of human history.

The seven presidents who followed Truman—from Dwight Eisenhower to Ronald Reagan—refined, each in his own way, the policy of containment while at the same time using diplomacy to avoid a cataclysm. It is difficult, I suspect, for anyone under the age of about fifty to appreciate how real and constant the threat of thermonuclear catastrophe seemed in the cold war. One of my indelible memories from early childhood is seeing, in *Life* magazine, pictures of children who had, for a while at least, survived Hiroshima with disfiguring burns. I incorporated those images into nightmares about mushroom clouds rising over Cleveland.

An important subplot of the cold war was the attempt by public officials and those who advised them to answer the nuclear riddle: if custodians of the bomb admitted that it was so dangerous as to be useless as an instrument of war, then what leverage did it give them in maintaining the peace? Furthermore, regardless of what Soviet archives and memoirs have since revealed about Stalin and Malenkov's recognition of how insane it would be to fight a nuclear war, their American contemporaries could not assume common sense or even sanity (to say nothing of human decency) in the Kremlin. Nor could they let Soviet leaders assume that the United States would shrink from pulling the trigger in a showdown, since any sign that an American president might flinch would embolden the Soviets to use their own bomb to intimidate their enemies and conquer more of their neighbors. Doctrine—what officials in Washington *said* about their willingness to use nuclear weapons in certain contingencies—became a crucial aspect of policy. As a result, in the name of realism, the United States staked out a macabre piece of moral low ground: having already, at the end of World War II, been the only country to use the A-bomb, the American government asserted its willingness to be the first to use the H-bomb in World War III.

In January 1954, John Foster Dulles, Eisenhower's secretary of state, warned that the United States would respond to Soviet aggression or provocation "at places and with means of our own choosing" and that "local defense [i.e., conventional forces] must be reinforced by the further deterrent of massive retaliatory power." Eisenhower adopted "massive retaliation" as the cornerstone of United States strategic doctrine—not because he believed a nuclear war was winnable but because he thought it would make deterrence of Soviet aggression more credible. Also, he saw the bomb as a cost-effective alternative to vast armies equipped with conventional weaponry.

In the minds of some defense specialists, the Eisenhower-Dulles threat failed to meet the credibility test precisely because the retaliation would be massive. Instead of brandishing a blunt instrument, they believed, the United States should develop a doctrine of "flexible response" that would combine the use of tactical nuclear weapons with conventional ones. One proponent of this view was Henry Kissinger, a thirty-four-year-old lecturer at Harvard whose 1957 book, *Nuclear Weapons and Foreign Policy*, brought him to the attention of the policymaking elite. Another theoretician who got the attention of policymakers was Herman Kahn, a researcher at the RAND Corporation. He made a profession out of what he called "thinking about the unthinkable." The irony was deliberate: it was meant to underscore the logic, such as it was, of deterrence. Kahn and his fellow "megadeath intellectuals" believed the United States needed to have a large number of bombs and plans for their use in multiple contingencies.

Neither Kissinger nor Kahn, however, could be confident, or at least inspire confidence in others, that a conflict would follow the intended script. What started as a "limited" nuclear "exchange" had the potential for mimicking a chain reaction. Kissinger recognized that danger but felt that it was unwise to let that recognition dictate American doctrine. Otherwise, as he once put it to me when I was following him around the world for *Time*, the United States would be "the cobra's victim, paralyzed by its own fear."

Having spent hundreds of hours in the seventies and eighties with Soviet defense specialists, I heard variations on this theme from the other side of the table. The superpowers ended up playing a weird, static form of chess: the two players sat staring at the board and, occasionally, at each other. They racked their brains figuring out how the pieces should line up defensively, each moving his pieces with great care so as *not* to threaten the other's king.

The result was arms control, a game with the objective of minimizing the chance of disastrous miscalculation.

That enterprise got under way because of a near-death experience. John F. Kennedy had run to the right of Richard Nixon for the presidency in 1960, ef-

John F. Kennedy

fectively but falsely accusing the Eisenhower administration of having put the United States on the wrong side of a "missile gap" from the Soviet Union. After his razor-thin victory, Kennedy authorized an invasion of Cuba by anti-Castro exiles that ended in fiasco for the United States and emboldened Khrushchev to put missiles into Cuba. The result, nearly a year and a half later, was, for my generation, among the more frightening experiences of our lives. By then I was at Hotchkiss, where chapel service was, for most students, a boring though mercifully brief requirement at the beginning of the day. That was not the case on a sunny October morning in 1962, when the U.S. Navy had encircled Cuba, and Khrushchev's missiles were on alert, aimed at American cities. Every boy and teacher in the school was on his knees as the headmaster, Bill Olsen, led us in prayer.

Looking back on the episode forty years later, Nikolai Leonov, who had been chief of the KGB's Department of Cuban Affairs, remarked, "One mistake at the wrong time in October 1962, and all could have been lost. I can hardly believe we are here today, talking about this. It is almost as if some divine intervention occurred to help us save ourselves, but with this proviso: we must never get that close again. Next time, we would not be so lucky." [19]

DWIGHT EISENHOWER HAD PROPOSED in 1957 that the United States and the U.S.S.R. stop testing of nuclear weapons, but the Kremlin had not been interested. In the wake of the Cuban crisis, Khrushchev sent Kennedy a message agreeing to serious negotiations. Kennedy replied publicly. In order to attain "not merely peace in our time but peace in all time," mankind must take small, gradual steps. "Let us focus," he said in a commencement speech at American University in June 1963, "on a more practical, more attainable peace, based not on a sudden revolution in human nature but on a gradual evolution in human institutions—on a series of concrete actions and effective agreements which are in the interest of all concerned."

Four months later, a treaty banning nuclear tests in the atmosphere, in outer space, and under water—i.e., permitting them only underground—was signed; it went into force within a year. The so-called Limited, or Partial, Test Ban was envisioned as a first step toward one that would ban testing entirely. It had wide political support for environmental as well as arms control reasons: not only must the world avoid blowing itself up—it also had to find a way of saving the planet from the slower death of radiation poisoning.

KENNEDY'S SUCCESSOR, LYNDON JOHNSON, had some significant accomplishments, especially in civil rights, but his record in foreign policy ended as an instructive tragedy. In trying to defeat what he saw as Soviet and Chinese communist proxies in Vietnam, Johnson made three fatal errors: he misread the nature of the enemy, underestimated their tenacity, and did not have sufficient support from the American people and the international community for a sustained prosecution of the war. Richard Nixon tried and failed to achieve "peace with honor" in Vietnam. Driven from office by Watergate, Nixon turned over to Gerald Ford the task of managing what was, up to that point, America's only major military defeat. Among the lessons of Vietnam was, or should have been, an enduring recognition that the United States must galvanize and sustain an international as well as a domestic consensus in support of its foreign policy, especially when it came to containing—or destroying—monsters in far-off lands.

In the field of arms control, however, the Johnson, Nixon, and Ford administrations were marked by a high degree of continuity and success. In 1967, Johnson held a summit with one of Khrushchev's successors, Aleksei Kosygin, in Glassboro, New Jersey—a site chosen because it allowed the two leaders to meet halfway between the neutral ground of the UN and Washington, D.C. That meeting began a process that would become known as the Strategic Arms Limitation Talks, or SALT. Secretary of State Dean Rusk predicted that the negotiations would become "history's longest permanent floating crap game." Rusk intended the remark to be less sardonic than it sounded. In fact, it was an optimistic and accurate prophecy. The game was designed to be one in which each side would have neither the illusion that it could win a nuclear war, nor the fear that it would lose unless it struck preemptively against the other. The common goal of the players was a deliberate and permanent draw in their competition to develop and deploy nuclear weapons.

Robert McNamara, secretary of defense in the Kennedy and Johnson administrations, was the intellectual godfather of a key objective in SALT—the Anti-Ballistic Missile, or ABM, Treaty. McNamara will long be remembered as the stubborn rationalist whose faith in logic and numbers led him to persist in Vietnam long after he should have seen that the administration was losing, both in the field and on the home front. But the same qualities that caused McNamara to miscalculate the winnability of that conventional war also led him to see, with admirable clarity, the unwinnability of nuclear war. His wry nickname for the only sane doctrine to guide the development and deployment, as well as the limitation and reduction, of nuclear weaponry was "MAD," which stood for mutual assured destruction. The balance of terror became the nuclear-age successor to the balance of power. It followed that, in addition to regulating offensive weaponry, arms control should ban strategic defensive systems. Making this deal with the Kremlin was part of the unfinished business that Richard Nixon inherited from Johnson.

I conducted a series of interviews with Nixon toward the end of his life, as he was staging his final comeback as an elder statesman and foreign policy sage.[20] He was the strangest person in American public life I ever met. To spend time with him was to witness the triumph of discipline and determination over affect. It was a marvel, though not a pretty sight. Nixon was physically awkward, deeply insecure, misanthropic, cynical, and given to flashes of breathtaking nastiness. Yet listening to his carefully rehearsed, cogent, often insightful assessments, prognoses, and prescriptions, I began to understand how he had risen to the top of a profession that rewards charisma, charm, and a capacity for empathy. He compensated for his conspicuous lack of those qualities with willpower and cunning. He believed that if he could outwit his many real and perceived enemies, so could the nation he led.

Nixon was not given to quoting Machiavelli, Talleyrand, Metternich, and Bismarck, but Henry Kissinger was. Kissinger was Nixon's uneasy, sometimes disdainful, but indispensable partner in a form of statesmanship that applied nineteenth-century *Realpolitik* to the realities of the nuclear age. Nixon and Kissinger's two great diplomatic accomplishments—détente with the Soviet Union and rapprochement with China—were part of a single game, the object of which was to play the two communist giants off each other to the advantage of the United States. I never heard Nixon or Kissinger use the phrase "global governance"—it sounds too soft to have come naturally to either of them. Nonetheless, they advanced that cause by stabilizing relations among the three nations that could, in one combination or another, plunge the world into nuclear war.

At the heart of détente was a set of agreements that codified mutual deterrence. In 1972, Nixon and Leonid Brezhnev, by then the supreme leader of the U.S.S.R., completed and signed SALT I, which translated the principle of "parity," or rough equivalence, in offensive strategic weapons into obligations and limitations on both sides; it did the same with the principle of mutual vulnerability as a prerequisite for mutual deterrence. Because nuclear weapons would probably be with us forever, the ABM component of SALT I was a treaty intended to last in perpetuity.

WITH HENRY KISSINGER AT HIS SIDE, Gerald Ford nursed the arms control process further, toward a SALT II treaty. By 1977, when Jimmy Carter had replaced Ford, the talks were no longer floating among capitals; they settled down in Geneva and would eventually migrate to Helsinki. "SALT has become part of the fabric of international relationships," said Carter's secretary of defense, Harold Brown. The process not only produced treaties, it provided a forum for managing the U.S.-Soviet relationship in good times (of which there were few) and bad ones (of which there were many). Delegations of diplomats and military officers sat across from each other at long tables and haggled over the composition and capabilities of each side's arsenals—technical details of the most sensitive kind, which spies were paid, and could be executed, for trying to ferret out. In both governments, arms control became a prestigious career track. Personal and institutional networks between Soviet and American SALT specialists proved useful not just for conducting nuclear diplomacy, but as channels for dealing with other potentially dangerous issues. The institutionalization of arms control turned out to be durable enough to withstand the intrinsic animosity of the U.S.-Soviet relationship and the vacillations of American policy as presidents' popularity rose and fell and administrations came and went.

During the Nixon, Ford, and Carter presidencies, two rounds of SALT succeeded in freezing the number of strategic ballistic missile launchers at existing levels and imposing a complex set of additional limits that helped slow down and stabilize the arms race. Carter and Brezhnev signed the SALT II treaty in 1979. It was never ratified by the U.S. Senate, largely because of American anger over the Soviet invasion of Afghanistan later that year, but its terms were observed by the superpowers even after Ronald Reagan moved into the White House in early 1981.

Reagan changed the name of the negotiations from SALT to START (for Strategic Arms *Reduction* Talks), in keeping with his intent, which was ultimately fulfilled, to lower levels of missiles on both sides. In another area of arms control—managing the competition in intermediate-range nuclear forces, often known as "Euromissiles"—Reagan was able to get the Soviets to agree on a "zero option" that banned the deployment of all weapons of that category.

But Reagan wanted to go further than reducing numbers of intercontinental weapons and eliminating intermediate-range ones: he was a nuclear abolitionist. In pursuit of that goal, he was wedded to a fanciful scheme—known officially as the Strategic Defense Initiative, or SDI, and lampooned as "Star Wars"—to defend the United States with an impregnable shield against enemy warheads. He offered to share the system with the U.S.S.R. if the Kremlin would join in a commitment to eliminate the arsenals of the two countries. The Soviets refused. They had come to accept mutual deterrence as a stabilizing factor in the relationship and feared that SDI would touch off another round in the arms race and put them at a technological and economic disadvantage.*

ATOMS FOR PEACE

For all the twists and turns of this saga as it unfolded, the central plot was the same: by its very nature, the nuclear age required a series of political and diplomatic innovations, in almost all cases originated by the United States, to stabilize a polarized international system and rule out war as an option for settling an ideological and geopolitical contest that played out over decades on a global scale.

The superpowers' bilateral effort to regulate and eventually reduce their nuclear arsenals formed the basis for an arrangement that embraced most of the rest of the world. SALT and START were accompanied by a set of multilateral agreements meant to discourage other countries from concluding that they too needed nuclear weapons to deter their own enemies.

The first attempt to stop the spread of nuclear weapons had been in 1946,

* START produced a treaty after Reagan left office. It was signed by his successor, George H. W. Bush, and Mikhail Gorbachev in 1991. I have chronicled these negotiations in three books—*Endgame: The Inside Story of SALT II* (1979), *Deadly Gambits: The Reagan Administration and the Stalemate in Nuclear Arms Control* (1984), and *The Master of the Game: Paul Nitze and the Nuclear Peace* (1988)—and in a fourth one that Michael Beschloss and I coauthored, *At the Highest Levels: The Inside Story of the End of the Cold War* (1993).

when the United States proposed to give up its own bomb if it could be assured that no other country would ever have one. A committee chaired by David Lilienthal, the chairman of the Tennessee Valley Authority, and reporting to Dean Acheson, then undersecretary of state, recommended that the UN Atomic Energy Commission be given responsibility for every potential source of uranium or plutonium in the world. Once all the fissile material was under international control, the United States would share with other countries the know-how to develop peaceful nuclear energy, and would abandon its atomic arsenal. This was a step in the direction that Truman himself had suggested in 1945, when he called for "effective, reciprocal, and enforceable safeguards [on nuclear energy] acceptable to all nations."[21] The president designated the financier and elder statesman Bernard Baruch to present a plan to the UN with the proviso that the UN Atomic Energy Commission should be immune from anyone—i.e., the Soviets—using a Security Council veto to limit its powers. But since the Soviets already had the veto, they were able to keep the Baruch Plan from going anywhere.

In 1953, about four years after the Soviets set off Joe One and fourteen months after the British tested their first atomic device, Dwight Eisenhower took an important practical step to nip the danger of nuclear proliferation in the bud: he went before the UN to propose a plan whereby states that did not possess nuclear weapons would be eligible for international assistance in acquiring the means to use nuclear energy for medicine, agriculture, water management, and the generation of electricity.

Eisenhower is not often remembered for uplifting rhetoric, but one passage from the "Atoms for Peace" speech is, even half a century later, notable, for it managed to combine the warning of massive retaliation with an appeal for an end to the arms race, both on the U.S.-Soviet track and in the increasingly populous field of would-be nuclear powers:

> Should . . . an atomic attack be launched against the United States, our reactions would be swift and resolute. But for me to say that the defense capabilities of the United States are such that they could inflict terrible losses upon an aggressor—for me to say that the retaliation capabilities of the United States are so great that such an aggressor's land would be laid waste—all this, while fact, is not the true expression of the purpose and the hope of the United States. To pause there would be to confirm the hopeless finality of a belief that two atomic colossi are doomed malevolently to eye each other indefinitely across a trembling world. To stop there would be to accept helplessly the prob-

ability of civilization destroyed—the annihilation of the irreplaceable heritage of mankind handed down to us generation from generation—and the condemnation of mankind to begin all over again the age-old struggle upward from savagery toward decency, and right, and justice. . . . Surely no sane member of the human race could discover victory in such desolation. Could anyone wish his name to be coupled by history with such human degradation and destruction? Occasional pages of history do record the faces of the "Great Destroyers" but the whole book of history reveals mankind's never-ending quest for peace, and mankind's God-given capacity to build. It is with the book of history, and not with isolated pages, that the United States will ever wish to be identified. My country wants to be constructive, not destructive. It wants agreement, not wars, among nations. It wants itself to live in freedom, and in the confidence that the people of every other nation enjoy equally the right of choosing their own way of life. So my country's purpose is to help us move out of the dark chamber of horrors into the light. . . . My recital of atomic danger and power is necessarily stated in United States terms, for these are the only incontrovertible facts that I know. I need hardly point out to this assembly, however, that this subject is global, not merely national in character.

In 1957, the UN established the International Atomic Energy Agency, a body empowered to inspect nuclear reactors and plants to ensure that they were being run for peaceful purposes. Eisenhower's "Atoms for Peace" deal looked good, or at least acceptable, to many countries around the world that were still a long way from having the technological and other resources needed to build their own bombs. But it had less appeal for those that wanted to be in the nuclear club. In 1960, the French blasted their way into membership with a test in the Algerian desert. In a debate with Richard Nixon during the 1960 campaign, John F. Kennedy predicted that "ten, fifteen, or twenty nations, including Red China" would have the bomb by 1964. Nearly three years later, in March 1963, Kennedy told reporters that he was no less pessimistic, although he was now looking ahead a decade: "I see the possibility in the 1970s of the president of the United States having to face a world in which fifteen, twenty, or twenty-five nations may have these weapons."[22] Kennedy did not live to see the Chinese set off a nuclear explosion the following year.

WITH THE UNITED STATES driving the process, negotiations intensified on a Non-Proliferation Treaty (NPT) that would be as comprehensive as possible. The NPT sought to freeze the number of nuclear weapons states at five—Britain, China, France, the Soviet Union, and the United States—which had already tested weapons when the treaty went into force in 1970. Under the treaty's terms, the nuclear haves promised "to pursue negotiations in good faith on effective measures relating to cessation of the nuclear arms race at an early date and to nuclear disarmament, and on a treaty on general and complete disarmament under strict and effective international control"; the nuclear have-nots were to be rewarded for their willingness to forgo having the bomb with financial and technical assistance in developing nuclear technology for peaceful purposes.

The deal was patently lopsided; it reinforced the special status of the five countries whose nuclear capabilities were grandfathered. In 1970, four of the five were already part of the "P-5," the permanent members of the UN Security Council. The following year, the Beijing government replaced Taiwan on the Council, so the P-5 were now the N-5 as well. No one believed that those privileged few would take seriously the stated goal of "general and complete disarmament"—that was a sop to the have-nots. Still, by 1971, ninety-five of the UN's 132 member states, plus Switzerland, had signed the NPT. They did so for essentially the same reason that the delegates gathered in San Francisco in 1945 had accepted the inequity of the Security Council: the system that the most powerful states insisted on was one the rest of the world could live with, since it was better than any feasible alternative—a necessary accommodation to the unequal distribution of power in the world.

To a significant extent and for a long time, the NPT worked. Many advanced industrial states could have gone nuclear but decided it was in their best interests not to. Several countries that set out to develop nuclear weapons in the 1970s and 1980s—Argentina, Brazil, South Korea, and Taiwan—canceled their programs; South Africa dismantled the capability it had developed. Even Iran, Iraq, Libya, and North Korea joined the NPT as "non-nuclear-weapon states," although they had covert programs to develop the bomb. The only countries that refused to join were Israel, which kept silent and allowed everyone to assume it had a nuclear weapons capability, and India and Pakistan, which started secretly to build their own bombs. As long as Israel, India, and Pakistan refrained from testing the weapons they were presumed to have developed, the world was prepared to look the other way.

For all their differences, the United States and the Soviet Union both wanted an effective NPT. They enabled the UN to establish a network of agencies and committees to solidify and expand a global nonproliferation regime. The UN was, in a phrase Franklin Roosevelt had used during World War II, "a trusteeship of the powerful," and at its core was a modus vivendi between the superpowerful, the United States and the Soviet Union.[23]

At the old League of Nations headquarters in Geneva, where the peacocks still squawked and strutted on the manicured lawns, the UN's permanent Conference on Disarmament served as a forum for negotiating a variety of agreements, including, in 1974, a U.S.-Soviet Threshold Test Ban Treaty, which prohibited testing devices with a yield exceeding 150 kilotons (equivalent to 150,000 tons of TNT)—another step toward a comprehensive ban, on tests of any size anywhere.

Despite all the imperfections, inequalities, and loopholes, these and other arms control, test ban, and nonproliferation efforts helped prevent Kennedy's dire prediction from coming true.

THE WORK OF NATIONS

Arms control and nonproliferation also created an international environment in which the UN's extended family of associated agencies, committees, funds, institutes, and commissions was able to develop and go to work. That work is done, day in and day out, by a massive, complex network of bureaucracies. Every one of the people who make up the UN system personifies, each in his or her own way, the difficulty that the institution has in doing its job. They are citizens of more than 140 countries. Many are diplomats, military officers, and others whose job is to represent their own governments. For them, the UN is a teeming bazaar in which they hunt for bargains and cut deals on behalf of their home offices. Whatever the issue of the moment, no matter how petty or momentous, their objective is to trade away as little of their own country's authority as possible for maximum advantage in security and political or economic benefit.

The more than sixty-three thousand staffers who work in the UN system worldwide—in New York, Geneva, Vienna, The Hague, Rome, and Nairobi—also work for it. They include legions of economists, demographers, statisticians, accountants, engineers, doctors, communication specialists, security guards, protocol officers, weapons experts, interpreters, back-office clerks, and front-office secretaries. Some sixteen thousand of those UN employees are at the headquarters in Turtle Bay, which, by treaty, enjoys "extraterritoriality." They technically leave the jurisdiction of the United States when they report for duty each day. The UN has its own fire-fighting and security units, and its own post office with the right to issue its own stamps. Foreign embassies and consulates, which also have extraterritorial status, are, in effect, transplanted patches of the countries whose flags they fly, while the UN represents all its member states and flies a flag of its own. At its center is a circular map of the earth, enwreathed by olive branches on a blue field. The globe is depicted in what geographers call the azimuthal equidistant projection, which serves the politically correct purpose of taking in all six inhabited continents.

UN employees are surrounded by reminders of the ideals that are supposed to guide them. Just outside the Meditation Room off the visitors' lobby in the General Assembly building, a twelve-foot-high stained-glass window designed by Marc Chagall portrays symbols of peace, amity, and beauty—a child being kissed by an angelic face emerging from a cluster of flowers, and notes from the score of the choral finale of Beethoven's Ninth Symphony. The lyrics were drawn from Friedrich von Schiller's "Ode to Joy." The Westerners who dominated the UN in its formative years considered that work an anthem of the human race.*

Yet however sincere their commitment to what the organization stands for, regardless of who signs their paychecks, and regardless of their obligation under the Charter to take instructions only from the UN itself, some members of the staff feel conflicting and even overriding loyalties to their own nations and governments.[24] A few—perhaps more than a few—are spies. When exposed, they serve as a reminder of how far the UN still is from realizing the high hopes that attended its birth.

BY THE 1970S, AROUND THE TIME I started covering the UN as part of my job as a foreign affairs reporter for *Time*, lamenting if not gloating over the organization's deficiencies had become something of a cottage industry. The Tower of Babel, especially as depicted in Bruegel's famous painting, be-

---

*Beethoven had taken liberties with the original lyrics, especially in the climactic refrain: Schiller's "Bettler werden Fürstenbrüder" ("Beggars become princes' brothers") is, in Beethoven's version, "Alle Menschen werden Brüder" ("All men become brothers"). Schiller, it can safely be speculated, would have approved. Harassed and persecuted by the authorities in his native Stuttgart in 1783, he fled to Weimar, proclaiming himself "a citizen of the world who serves no prince. I lost my fatherland, to exchange it for the great world. What is the greatest of nations but a fragment?"

came a useful cliché for anti-UN cartoonists and writers who scorned what one called "The Tower of Babble." *

Some attacks came from those who had once had high hopes for the enterprise and, in many cases, dedicated years of their lives to realizing those hopes. One such cri de coeur that made a powerful impression on me was *Defeat of an Ideal,* by Shirley Hazzard, an Australian-born novelist and essayist who spent a decade working at the UN. After despairing over the institution's many defects, she called for "a revitalized and radically different United Nations" that "must come about through the insistence of the peoples of the world" in order to "honor the confidence originally invested in it by humanity."

I remember wondering, What in God's name does she mean by *that?* The UN had come into existence not because "humanity" made it happen but because a handful of leaders, principally two American presidents, Franklin Roosevelt and Harry Truman, invested heavily in an idea that ran counter to much of human habit and experience. As for remedying the UN's flaws or replacing it with something better, "the peoples of the world" could not "insist" on anything beyond what their governments were prepared to do in concert. Those governments, in turn, were represented by individuals who went about their difficult, thankless, sometimes impossible jobs as best they could, fighting off the disillusionment that finally overcame Hazzard. I found the most convincing and pertinent sentence in her book to be the one with which she begins her introduction: "The United Nations concept is often said to be new: rather, it is as ancient as human reason, and as primitive as the instincts of conciliation and self-preservation." [25] While she meant that statement as an epitaph for a failure, I read it as a fitting epigraph for a story that was neither over nor destined to end badly. The very fact that the UN system could accomplish *anything* during the cold war seemed reason for hope. In fact, it had already accomplished a lot, and would accomplish more during the decades to come.

FRANKLIN ROOSEVELT HAD FORESEEN THE DANGER that the UN would run into trouble if too much was expected of it. He felt the rational division of the work of nations required a dense network of other organizations, some of which would be directly associated with or subordinate to the UN, while others would be independent. The UN system has provided

---

* Dore Gold (a former Israeli ambassador to the UN), *The Tower of Babble: How the United Nations has Fueled Global Chaos* (New York: Crown Forum, 1994), which has a color print of Bruegel's painting on its cover.

plenty of ammunition to those who are inclined to ridicule its proliferation of acronyms and initials: IAEA, IBRD, IMF, GATT, WTO, ILO, ICJ, UNESCO, UNDP, UNICEF, WFP, UNHCR, WHO. Each stands for a bureaucracy, but it also stands for a sustained international effort to deal with problems that are far beyond the capacity of individual nations, even the most powerful ones, to handle by themselves.

The International Atomic Energy Agency (IAEA) provides a forum for co-ordinating peaceful nuclear energy programs as well as experts to monitor compliance with arms control and nonproliferation agreements. A cluster of smaller institutions with eye-glazing names—the Bank for International Settlements, the Basel Committee on Banking Supervision, the International Organization of Securities Commissions, the International Association of Insurance Supervisors, the International Accounting Standards Board, the UN Commission on International Trade Law—indicates the extent to which functions traditionally associated with national governments have begun to take on a transnational, often global dimension.[26]

The International Labor Organization (ILO) promotes and protects standards and rights in the workplace; the International Court of Justice (ICJ) settles legal disputes submitted by individual states and provides advisory rulings on questions referred to it by international organizations; the UN's Universal Declaration of Human Rights is an internationally agreed-upon set of standards for judging when those rights are violated; and the UN Educational, Scientific and Cultural Organization (UNESCO) conducts research, exchanges, conferences, and projects ranging from literacy campaigns to the designation of World Heritage Sites, such as the Great Wall, the Great Barrier Reef, the Acropolis, Vatican City, and the Taj Mahal.*

A number of UN agencies and programs are responsive to the exhortations of Ezequiel Padilla, Ralph Bunche, and other founders of the UN more than sixty years ago that the organization devote considerable resources and energies to helping parts of the world that are neither powerful, privileged, nor prosperous. UN Volunteers, partially modeled on the American Peace Corps, has sent nearly ten thousand people to work on development projects

---

* American far-right organizations have attacked the World Heritage Sites program as a covert attempt to deprive countries of their sovereignty over the designated places, especially those in the United States (the Grand Canyon, the Statue of Liberty, Monticello, and the University of Virginia). This delusion, combined with legitimate criticisms of mismanagement of the agency, led the United States to boycott UNESCO for nearly two decades, from 1984 to 2003.

around the world. The Human Settlements Program helps build or repair urban infrastructure in war-ravaged countries, and the UN Population Fund has provided reproductive health assistance to mothers.* The UN Children's Fund (UNICEF) puts professionals on the front lines of emergency situations to educate, immunize, feed, and shelter children, especially girls; the Food and Agriculture Organization (FAO) has the lead in trying to alleviate hunger; the World Food Program (WFP) feeds tens of millions of starving people a year; and the High Commissioner for Refugees (UNHCR) provides legal protection, shelter, and care for millions displaced by political persecution, war, and other catastrophes. The world body also has, in the UN Development Program (UNDP), its own mechanism for providing grants, building democratic institutions, and extending other forms of what Americans think of as "foreign aid."

But the principal means of reducing global poverty resides with three other autonomous parts of the UN system: the World Bank (formally known as the International Bank for Reconstruction and Development, or IBRD), which distributes development loans and grants to poor and middle-income nations; the International Monetary Fund (IMF), which works with national governments to stabilize exchange rates and provides loans, advice, and technical assistance to countries recovering from financial crises; and what was for decades called the General Agreement on Tariffs and Trade (GATT) and became the World Trade Organization in the midnineties. The WTO has the potential to be the driving force in opening markets in developed countries to exports from poorer ones.

In many cases, the best that the UN system can do, at least in the near term, is turn dreadful and acute problems into merely serious and chronic ones. But the World Health Organization's campaign against smallpox is one example of a UN body that has succeeded not just in ameliorating a scourge but in defeating it. When the British scientist Edward Jenner developed the first smallpox vaccine at the end of the eighteenth century, Thomas Jefferson congratulated him for having "erased from the calendar of human afflictions one of its greatest. Yours is the comfortable reflection that mankind can never

---

* The UN Population Fund has been a target of opposition from American anti-abortion activists. All three of the most recent Republican presidents—Ronald Reagan, George H. W. Bush, and George W. Bush—have prevented funds from going to the organization on the grounds that it provides family-planning services in countries, such as China, whose governments perform forced abortions—even though the UN Population Fund itself does not provide support for abortion services.

forget that you have lived. Future nations will know by history only that the loathsome smallpox has existed." But the disease continued to rage for nearly another two centuries. In the first three quarters of the twentieth century, it killed some 300 million people—about twice as many people as both world wars, the Holocaust, and the Stalinist and Maoist purges combined.[27] By the 1950s, endemic smallpox had been nearly wiped out in Western Europe, as well as in North America, the U.S.S.R., and Japan. In poorer nations, the epidemic was largely unabated. It was fatal for every fourth victim, and the disease scarred or blinded many survivors. In 1967, the World Health Organization set, and subsequently met, the goal of eradicating smallpox in ten years. The organization's director at the time, Halfdan Mahler of Denmark, called the program a "triumph of management, not of medicine."[28]

Management, in the context of multinational efforts to cope with global challenges, is another word for *governance.* Even with all its inadequacies, the UN system has been able to foster habits of cooperation on issues where competition had previously been the norm and conflict often the result; it has created the basis for what Paul Kennedy calls an "international civil society." That phrase too connotes governance.[29]

SO DOES *peacekeeping,* which became an early, crucial and enduring part of the UN's vocabulary even though the word is not even mentioned in the Charter.

Roosevelt's idea of the Security Council as a global police force quickly fell victim to the cold war. The dream of one world had dissolved into the reality of three: the First World, led by the United States; the Second World, led by the U.S.S.R.; and the largely postcolonial, nonaligned Third World, which was the scene of turmoil and jockeying for advantage between the superpowers. As a result, peacekeeping is a function that the UN has had to make up as it goes along, with meager resources and shaky support.

In theory, peacekeepers are soldiers who don't fight and police who don't crack heads; they are usually volunteered by neutral states at the request, or at least with the consent, of adversaries when there is a risk of conflict; they are supposed to remain impartial and help the opposing sides reach a negotiated settlement; they refrain from using force except in self-defense and from coercing the parties into accepting a settlement. In short, "peacekeeping" presumes that there is a peace to keep, and that international troops, wearing blue helmets or blue berets, interposed between armies of contending nations, or hostile factions within a nation, can buy time for diplomats to broker a compromise that will keep war from breaking out. Brian Urquhart, the British diplomat who helped create the UN and was instrumental in making it work for four decades, describes peacekeeping as "the projection of the principle of non-violence onto the military plane."[30]

But as in everything else about the UN, the ideal constantly comes up against messy, often bloody reality; theory collides with practice, and the principle of non-violence encounters violence. Peacekeeping usually means the combined deployment of mediators and troops to stop a war that has already begun and prevent it from resuming. That is a difficult and dangerous mission, since the blue-helmeted troops are at risk of becoming hostages or victims if the fighting continues or a ceasefire breaks down.

IT WAS IN THE TREACHEROUS TERRAIN of the Middle East that the UN was first put to twin tests of war-ending and peacekeeping. Three years after Ralph Bunche mediated an armistice after the first Arab-Israeli war, the pan-Arab leader Gamal Abdel Nasser overthrew a corrupt and incompetent Egyptian monarchy of Albanian descent. In 1956, Nasser nationalized the Suez Canal Company, in which the British and French held a majority of the stock. Britain, France, and Israel launched a military operation to topple Nasser. They did not inform their ally and protector, the United States. Dwight Eisenhower was incensed. In a televised address on October 31, the president said that the British-French-Israeli action could "scarcely be reconciled with the principles and purposes of the United Nations to which we have all subscribed."

The American war hero turned president worked in tandem with Dag Hammarskjöld, the cerebral, spiritual secretary-general of the United Nations. Hammarskjöld's effectiveness derived largely from his personal qualities, not from his office.

Nowhere in the Charter is the secretary-general invested with the authority to tell states what they must and must not do. He may occupy the loftiest suite of offices in Turtle Bay, on the thirty-eighth floor of the Secretariat Building, but he has no vote in the General Assembly or the Security Council. He is the organization's chief administrative officer, not its CEO or even its COO ("more secretary than general," according to a well-worn line about the office, often used by those who have held it). The "SG" is empowered only to "bring to the attention of the Security Council any matter which in his opinion may threaten the maintenance of international peace and security."

Yet from this circumscribed job description, from his claim to being the only official on earth who had been chosen by the international community as a whole, and from what he called "the philosophy" of the Charter, Hammarskjöld inferred and asserted an obligation to serve as the world's peacemaker in chief. He understood that, unlike his native Sweden, he did not have to be neutral; he had only to be independent. That meant he could be active.

Dag Hammarskjöld

Eisenhower and Hammarskjöld joined in calling a rare emergency session of the General Assembly, which voted 64–5— with the U.S.S.R. voting "yes"—to establish, with Egyptian consent, the first standing UN peacekeeping operation.* The six-thousand-troop "Emergency Force" in the Sinai, made up of units from Scandinavia, India, Indonesia, Colombia, Canada, Yugoslavia, and other countries, formed a buffer between Israel and Egypt. "UNEF," as it was known, provided a model for subsequent peacekeeping operations and permitted the resumption of commercial traffic through the canal for the next eleven years (although the Egyptians continued to ban Israeli and Israel-bound ships from the canal).

The lesson of the episode was clear: even in the darkest days of the cold war, and even in the face of discord among the Western allies, the UN could be much more than a "tower of babble." But it could fulfill the hopes of its founders if and only if the president of the United States wanted it to do so. And it helped if, as was then the case, the secretary-general was willing to rise above his limited mandate, stand up to powerful forces—including in the Security Council—and exert moral and political leadership.

The episode was encouraging to those who hoped to see the UN grow in authority and strength, and, conversely, a bit worrying to those who did not want to see the UN become too strong. The U.S. permanent representative in Turtle Bay at the time, Henry Cabot Lodge, Jr., the grandson of Woodrow Wilson's principal opponent in the fight over the League, arched his brow at one of Hammarskjöld's statements during the crisis: "The principles of the

* The armistice agreement Ralph Bunche had mediated between the Arabs and Israelis was monitored by a small observer group known as the UN Truce Supervision Organization, and another monitoring group was interposed between India and Pakistan in 1949—and is still there today. Neither of these was designated a peacekeeping operation.

Charter, are, by far, greater than the organization in which they are embodied, and the aims which they are to safeguard are holier than the policies of any single nation or people."[31] Lodge felt it necessary to respond that the UN was still a long way from becoming a world government. He wanted no one to miss the point that the two had made common cause over Suez only because Eisenhower's judgment of where American interests lay coincided with Hammarskjöld's interpretation of UN principles. It was one thing for the Charter to trump the policies of Britain, France, and Israel; it would be quite another for anyone, at the UN or anywhere else, to suggest that the United States itself was subject to another authority.[32]

HAMMARSKJÖLD'S OTHER HEROIC EXERTION on behalf of UN peacekeeping was in Africa, a continent that was, in the 1950s, demonstrating how much easier it is to dismantle an empire than it is to build a nation. The formation of a viable state is a gradual, iterative process, whereas African decolonization was rapid and slapdash. Africans were understandably in a hurry to get out from under imperial rule. History suddenly seemed to be on their side. With the end of World War II, democratic representation seemed to have gained universal acceptance as the ideal of national governance, to the point that even the most despotic of the new states that had just appeared on the map called themselves democracies (the most grotesque example was the Democratic People's Republic of Korea). The anticolonial movement in Africa was inspired by the slogan "Freedom Now!" which resonated in the General Assembly. Accordingly, members of that movement were impatient with the Trusteeship Council and the other UN efforts to prepare colonies for eventual self-government.

When colonialists and imperial administrators realized it was time to go, many of them simply boarded planes and flew home to Europe. Most who stayed behind were resigned to making do under new, local management. Left to their own devices, Africans tried to govern themselves with institutions that their European masters had imposed on them.

An emblematic case was Congo. As the drive toward independence grew stronger throughout Africa, the Belgians, like other European colonialists, did little to lay the ground for democratic governance of a tribally diverse society. Ralph Bunche was among those who warned that various forces would fight to fill the vacuum created by the abrupt withdrawal of Belgium.[33] It was what one expert would later call "an experiment in instant decolonization."[34]

Within five days of independence, Congo went to war against itself: fighting broke out among units of the mutinous and largely leaderless army. Belgian troops returned to try to quell the civil war. The greatest threat to the survival of the newborn state was a secessionist movement in Katanga, a southern province distinguished by an abundance of copper, coal, iron, gold, silver, diamonds, tin, cobalt, and uranium—and, not coincidentally, by a high proportion of Belgians and other European expatriates. Prime Minister Patrice Lumumba appealed for help to Eisenhower, who urged Lumumba to take the matter to the UN. Hammarskjöld persuaded the Security Council to approve a peacekeeping force that would replace the Belgians.

This in itself was a pathbreaking development. For the first time, the UN assigned itself a peacekeeping operation within the boundaries of a single turbulent state. The Soviets went along with the plan because they, like the Americans, wanted the Belgians out. A UN force of three thousand international troops was in place within three days, reinforced by another seven thousand in less than a week.

Faced with the specter of Katangese secession, Lumumba turned to the Soviet Union for military equipment. That move put Congo, in American eyes, on the front line of the cold war—and Lumumba in the enemy camp. Dissident government forces loyal to Lieutenant-General Joseph Mobutu, the army chief of staff, captured Lumumba, probably with help from the Belgians as well as with the connivance of the CIA. Mobutu delivered Lumumba to the Katangese, who beat him nearly to death before putting him before a firing squad.

Hammarskjöld was determined to prevent the breakup of Congo, since that outcome would set the worst example for the rest of the continent. Through the force of his own will and eloquence, combined with strong support from the United States, Hammarskjöld persuaded the Security Council to authorize, for the first time, the use of force to keep intact a country that was dissolving in civil war.

It was both a pragmatic and a visionary response to a dilemma that would repeatedly confront the UN in the years to come: under-armed blue helmets arrive after the killing has begun, or the slaughter begins after they are in place. In either case, the peacekeepers are at risk of becoming casualties, caught in the crossfire, or hostages captured by one party or the other. In those circumstances, either peacekeeping fails or the UN must suspend the principle of nonviolence and accept a necessary paradox: the use of force in the name of making peace. That was the choice Hammarskjöld made in Congo. In an important respect, he was vindicated. The UN operation, under the command of an Indian general and with forces from his country as well as Sweden, Ireland, and Ghana, eventually defeated the mercenary-led Katangese army.

That result was possible only because the UN had American help in airlifting necessary arms to its forces.

NOW IT WAS NIKITA KHRUSHCHEV'S TURN to look at Congo through the prism of the cold war. In Soviet eyes, Lumumba was the hero of a "war of national liberation" and a victim of American imperialism, while Hammarskjöld was a stooge of the West. The Soviets did everything they could to stymie the secretary-general and, while they were at it, to cripple the UN itself, lest it become an extension of American power. They vetoed a resolution that would have given Hammarskjöld broader powers to deal with Congo. In a speech to the General Assembly in October 1960, Khrushchev demanded Hammarskjöld's resignation. When rebuffed by the General Assembly, the Soviet leader called for Hammarskjöld's replacement by a "troika" representing Soviet, Western, and third-world interests. That attempt, too, was rejected.

Hammarskjöld took it upon himself to mediate an end to the conflict before the Soviets had a chance to use the UNGA in the fall of 1961 to stir up more trouble among the delegates and in Congo. On a mission to meet with the Katangese leadership in Northern Rhodesia (today Zambia), Hammarskjöld's DC-6 crashed in the jungle. That December, he was posthumously awarded the Nobel Peace Prize.

In 1962, the Katangese leader, Moise Tshombe, realizing that military victory was impossible, was persuaded to send his representatives to participate in the parliament in Leopoldville, the central capital. The UN operation was withdrawn in mid-1964 in an atmosphere of cautious optimism. After the war ended, the Congolese president, Joseph Kasavubu, appointed Tshombe premier in an effort to co-opt the Katangese. That tactic worked for about a year. Then tensions between Kasavubu and Tshombe provided a pretext for Mobutu to take over the government. His thirty-two-year kleptocratic dictatorship turned Congo from one of the naturally richest countries on earth into one of the most impoverished, violent, corrupt, and unstable.

That fate, which continued even after Mobutu's death in exile in 1997, tends to obscure the UN's accomplishment in Congo: the world body prevented what could have been a continent-wide outbreak of states disintegrating along tribal lines.

Yet in the eyes of American conservatives, the UN was all the more suspect, since the Soviets had demanded and been given a powerful say in what action the UN could take in Congo. For years afterward, especially when UN peacekeeping operations were in the news, talk-radio commentators conjured up the image of "black helicopters" swooping down on the town squares and schoolyards of Middle America and running up the UN flag in place of the Stars and Stripes. Such nativist fantasies were by and large confined to noisy, well-financed, and politically potent groups on the far right, but occasionally they slipped into the mainstream. In 1987 an ABC television miniseries, *Amerika,* looked ten years into the future and imagined the United States living under a Soviet occupation enforced by UN peacekeepers.

WHATEVER ENTERTAINMENT THE SHOW PROVIDED, it was a spectacularly bad piece of prophecy. By 1987, the Soviet Union had already begun to reform itself out of existence and the cold war was winding down. Those developments made it possible for the Security Council finally to make sustained progress in performing the police function that Franklin Roosevelt and the UN's other founders had intended. In 1988 and 1989, the Council established missions on the border between Iran and Iraq after their ten-year war, in Afghanistan as the Soviets were pulling out of what had become a quagmire, and in Nicaragua to monitor and implement a peace agreement between the Soviet-backed Sandinistas and the U.S.-backed Contras.

The UN also helped in the transformation of South Africa. Going back to the early 1960s, the Security Council and the General Assembly had passed a series of resolutions calling for an end to apartheid and the release of Nelson Mandela from prison. The UN imposed an arms embargo on the Pretoria regime and organized a series of conferences that kept attention focused on the issue and generated support for trade sanctions, disinvestment campaigns, and other measures to isolate South Africa, such as banning its athletes from participating in international sporting events.

During the late eighties, Africa became far more amenable to UN peacekeeping. When the Soviets withdrew from the continent and their Cuban allies pulled out of Angola, the UN was able to move in and help bring the long Angolan civil war to an end. As the white supremacist regime in South Africa crumbled, Pretoria loosened its grip on Namibia, a former German colony that South Africa had acquired after World War I as a mandate under the League of Nations.

In 1989, the UN did something unprecedented: it took over the administration of a trust territory from a member state and administered Namibia while organizing a free, fair, and extraordinarily high-turnout election. In November of that year, 97 percent of the eligible Namibians turned out to vote for a government of their own.

This good-news story starring the UN would have received more attention around the world had it not coincided with the collapse of the Berlin Wall. The decade that followed would see another thirty-six peacekeeping missions, twice as many as during the previous forty years.[35] A major reason why this happened was that there was no longer a Soviet veto in the Security Council—for the simple reason that there was no longer a Soviet Union.

11

AN END AND A BEGINNING

If Spain is the problem, Europe is the solution.
—*JOSÉ ORTEGA Y GASSET*[1]

Have I said clearly enough that the community we have created is
not an end in itself? The community itself is only a stage on the way
to the organized world of tomorrow.
—*JEAN MONNET*[2]

THE dissolution of the Union of Soviet Socialist Republics on December 25, 1991, preceded by about six weeks the signing of a treaty that created the European Union. These events consummated processes that had unfolded in parallel, but they occurred for obverse reasons. Both political entities called themselves unions, but what unified them could hardly have been more different. The European states came together because they shared interests and values. The U.S.S.R. and the Warsaw Pact came apart because they had been held together forcibly; once that force weakened and their relationship became consensual, the Soviet republics and satellites stampeded for the exits.

Both developments were connected with the end of imperialism. In the wake of World War II, a number of Western European states—Britain, France, Belgium, the Netherlands, and Portugal—lost the economic benefits of their overseas colonies. That gave them an additional incentive to make the most of integration within Europe. For its part, the Soviet camp, as the world's sole remaining empire, gave up on a supposedly self-sufficient command economy that was in fact exceedingly inefficient and ultimately unsustainable.

The coming together of war-weary nations in the West and the falling apart of the bellicose, backward, and self-isolated empire in the East enhanced the prospects for global governance. The EU was a promising experiment in supranationalism, potentially applicable to other regions of the world, while the U.S.S.R. and its satellites were a failed experiment in socialist internationalism. With the rise of Europe, the demise of the Soviet system, and the end of the cold war, the idea of one world regained some of the plausibility it had briefly enjoyed in the immediate aftermath of World War II.

Neither the beginning of the European Union nor the end of the Soviet Union would have happened had it not been for the policies of the United States.

"A Sort of Second America"

Before Europe reached the midway point of the twentieth century, it had already given birth to two forms of totalitarianism, two world wars, and a holocaust. Many Europeans believed that their continent, after so many centuries of ever-more-destructive warfare, had to become a zone of peace.

Policymakers in Washington not only wished the Europeans well in making good on this resolve—they insisted on it. The defense and reconstruction of that region would depend on infusions of American wealth and the deployment of American armed forces. There was no point in the United States investing in a better future for Western Europe unless the Western Europeans themselves, particularly the French and the Germans, laid to rest their long-standing and deadly rivalries. Progress in that direction was a precondition for American assistance.[3]

Visionary proposals and cynical pieties out of the past—Dante's federative union that would allow "brethren to dwell together in unity," Edmund Burke's "grand vicinage of Europe," Kant's cosmopolitan "federation of the people," Napoleon's professed belief in the idea of a "European confederacy," and Metternich's invocation of a pan-European "fatherland"—now seemed like premonitions of Europe's only way of saving itself from another, even more destructive war.

A NUMBER OF EUROPEANS, including the most prominent of them all, had for some time been advocating political unification as an antidote to Europe's propensity for conflict. In June 1940, as the Wehrmacht bore down on the scattered, demoralized remnants of the forces defending France, Winston Churchill was desperate to keep the French government from surrendering. Perhaps, as he put it, by offering the French "some new fact of a vivid and stimulating nature" he could motivate them to keep up the fight. What emerged, after a frenzy of negotiations between London and Paris, was a plan for a single "Franco-British nation," a vaguely conceived association with joint citizenship; consolidated ministries of defense, foreign affairs, and finance; and shared responsibilities between the two parliaments. The proposal was transmitted in mid-June to the French War Cabinet. After a lengthy debate, its members rejected the plan. A number of the leaders involved, including Marshal Pétain, the hero of World War I who would later lead the government in Vichy that collaborated with the Germans, believed that their country was already beaten and that Britain, too, would fall within a few weeks. Besides, said one of the participants, Jean Ybarnegaray, the minister of health, who joined Pétain in Vichy, "Better to be a Nazi province. At least we know what that means."[4]

After the war, when British voters consigned Churchill to the opposition benches in Parliament, he gave a lecture at the University of Zurich that would, he hoped, help maintain his reputation as a source of big ideas for the future. "If the European countries succeeded in uniting," he said, "their three hundred to four hundred million inhabitants would know, by the fruit of their common heritage, a prosperity, a glory, a happiness that no boundary, no border could contain. . . . We must construct such a thing as the United States of Europe." Back in Britain, he continued to promote "the idea of a United Europe in which our country will play a decisive part" and claimed that many Conservatives like himself were prepared to surrender national sovereignty for the sake of European unity.[5]

While Churchill's rhetoric was stirring, the few specifics he had in mind— an intergovernmental coordinating mechanism and a consultative assembly with no decision-making powers—were less ambitious and coherent than those of Jean Monnet, a French economist and pragmatic internationalist who had served, in his early thirties, as deputy secretary-general of the League of Nations. After World War II, Monnet worked quietly and effectively toward the goal of a politically united Europe, or what he called, "a sort of second America."

IN JUNE 1947, IN A COMMENCEMENT ADDRESS at Harvard, Secretary of State George Marshall announced the plan that would come to bear his name, and Truman signed it into law the following spring as the European Recovery Program. Marshall believed that the plan would succeed only if the Europeans went beyond economic cooperation and started the process of political integration as well.[6]

That, in turn, would happen only if the Europeans felt protected from the threat looming in the East. In 1948, Britain, France, and the Low Countries (Belgium, the Netherlands, and Luxembourg) signed the Brussels Treaty committing them to mutual defense as well as cooperation in other areas. The following year, the Truman administration crafted a pact that created the North Atlantic Treaty Organization made up of twelve members: ten in Europe plus the United States and Canada. Article 5 asserted that "an armed attack against one or more of them in Europe or North America shall be considered an attack against them all." It was the largest, strongest, and longest-lasting component of what would be, at the height of the cold war, a globe-girdling system of alliances.*

At first, a protective and supportive American presence was far from universally welcome in Europe. *Le Monde* editorialized in favor of a militarily self-sufficient and neutral France that would be able to stand up to both Uncle Sam and Uncle Joe. In 1952, many French who had poured into the streets to welcome the Yanks as liberators eight years before were back again, this time to protest over the arrival of General Matthew Ridgway who replaced Dwight Eisenhower as Supreme Allied Commander in Europe. On the other side of the Channel, Harold Nicolson, a journalist and politician who had been close to Churchill during the war, wrote in his diary that Europeans were justifiably "frightened that the destinies of the world should be in the hands of a giant with the limbs of an undergraduate, the emotions of a spinster, and the brain of a peahen."[7]

Such grumbling subsided as the governments of Western Europe came to see the American "defense umbrella" as necessary to their own attempt to translate the idea of a single Europe into functioning transnational institu-

---

* The original twelve members of NATO were Belgium, Britain, Canada, Denmark, France, Iceland, Italy, Luxembourg, the Netherlands, Norway, Portugal, and the United States. To counter communism in Southeast Asia, a 1954 agreement bound Australia, France, New Zealand, Pakistan, the Philippines, Thailand, Britain, and the United States into the Southeast Asia Treaty Organization (SEATO). In the Middle East, Britain, Iran, Iraq, Pakistan, Turkey, and the United States formed in 1955 the Central Treaty Organization (CENTO). In addition to these multilateral arrangements, the United States signed bilateral security alliances with Japan, South Korea, the Philippines, Thailand, Australia, and New Zealand. Iraq quit CENTO in 1959 after the Ba'ath Party swept to power and aligned the country with the Soviet Union, and Iran quit in 1979 after the revolution against the Shah brought Ayatollah Khomeini to power.

tions. The first such effort, in 1951, was the European Coal and Steel Community. Conceived by Monnet, formally proposed by the French foreign minister, Robert Schuman, and signed by six nations (Belgium, France, Italy, Luxembourg, the Netherlands, and West Germany), it was more than an economic arrangement. Since coal and steel were indispensable for an armaments industry, this particular form of cooperation between France and Germany sent a powerful signal that they would never again go to war. The success of the Coal and Steel Community led, in 1957, to the Treaty of Rome, which established the European Economic Community and eliminated a range of trade barriers and monopolistic practices. Another treaty set up the European Atomic Energy Community to facilitate cooperation in developing peaceful uses of nuclear power. These organizations were staffed by their own civil service overseen by a council of ministers representing their home countries, an assembly of elected or appointed representatives, and a court to settle disputes. In the 1960s, the various pan-European communities were consolidated into a single structure wih common institutions. The seventies saw the addition of Britain, Ireland, and Denmark and the first direct elections for a European parliament.

In the eighties, the European Community (EC) brought its membership to twelve when Greece, Spain, and Portugal joined. All three countries had been through prolonged periods of dictatorship: Greece under a junta of colonels between 1967 and 1974, Spain's forty years under Francisco Franco, and Portugal's domination by António de Oliveira Salazar. The EC had been conceived as a community of democracies, and that criterion for admission was prominent among the factors that led Greece, Spain, and Portugal to replace military regimes with democratic ones.

The Kantian principle of "republican peace" had been applied to postwar Europe.

The Prison House of Nations

The Soviet bloc operated on the opposite principle: Stalin and his successors imposed on the nations of the Warsaw Pact the same top-down, center-outward methods by which they ruled the peoples of the U.S.S.R. Autarky and totalitarianism cut those countries off from a world in which the free movement of people, goods, services, money, and ideas was increasingly the norm. For decades, Soviet leaders were in denial about the consequences of that choice. They not only fooled themselves, they fooled many in the West, who looked east and saw a mortal and permanent threat. One of the few who saw the U.S.S.R. as mortal in another sense was George F. Kennan. In the copious and impressive literature that he produced during his long life, one sentence, from an article he wrote in 1947, stands out more than any other: Kennan discerned in the U.S.S.R. "tendencies [that] might eventually find their outlet in either the break-up or the gradual mellowing of Soviet power."* Two years later, he imagined the "possibility that Russian Communism may someday be destroyed by its own children in the form of the rebellious Communist parties of other countries. I can think of no development in which there would be greater logic and justice."[8] Returning to the pages of *Foreign Affairs* in 1951, he advised the West on how to increase the chances that the Soviets would eventually abandon their pretensions to commanding an armed camp in a divided world and, instead, join the larger community of nations: "Give them time; let them be Russians; let them work out their internal problems in their own manner. The ways by which people advance toward dignity and enlightenment in government are things that constitute the deepest and most intimate processes of national life."[9]

DURING THE 1952 PRESIDENTIAL CAMPAIGN, John Foster Dulles briefly floated the notion of "rolling back" Soviet power, but soon after Dwight Eisenhower moved into the Oval Office, he made containment rather than rollback the basis of U.S. policy. By then, Kennan regretted what he felt was the way his brainchild had been overmilitarized, particularly through the creation of NATO, which he vehemently opposed.

I met Kennan nearly twenty years later, shortly after I arrived at Oxford in the autumn of 1968. Leonid Brezhnev was in the Kremlin, and Soviet power was aggressively defending its turf: Warsaw Pact tanks had just invaded Czechoslovakia and crushed Alexander Dubček's efforts to give communism "a human face."

At Oxford, I was writing a thesis on Vladimir Mayakovsky, a poet who had wasted much of his considerable talent producing agitprop in verse for the Russian Revolution, only to be driven to suicide by the onset of Stalinism. My supervisor for that project was Max Hayward, a renowned translator of Russian literature and an old friend of Kennan's. Hayward invited me to join the

---

* This was the "X" article on "The Sources of Soviet Conduct" in *Foreign Affairs,* in which he first proposed "containment" as the main element of American policy toward the U.S.S.R.

two of them for dinner at La Luna Caprese on North Parade Street, not far from St. Antony's College, where Hayward had his lodgings. I listened while they continued a long-running debate over whether Russia might ever "join the modern world." Hayward doubted it, while Kennan could still see the Russian people rejecting the Soviet system "like an alien skin graft."

I had been studying Russian language, culture, and history for six years, at Hotchkiss and Yale, but had yet to see the Soviet Union. Once I began traveling there regularly, I accumulated experiences and observations that I came to realize, with the benefit of hindsight, amounted to a confirmation of how right Kennan was. Even though the Soviet Union was, by several measures, the second most powerful nation on earth, it failed, in a basic sense, to meet the *Oxford English Dictionary* definition of a cohesive and sustainable nation. Covering more territory than any other state, the U.S.S.R. certainly qualified as a "large aggregate," but it had failed to become, as the OED puts it, "united by factors such as common descent, language, culture, history, or occupation of the same territory, so as to form a distinct people." That failing was due to the repressive and divisive policies of its government. On my trips starting in 1968, I saw those policies in action and occasionally had intimations of their eventual consequences.

During the Christmas–New Year's holiday of my first year at Oxford, I set off by rail from London, took a ferry across the English Channel, and boarded a Soviet sleeping car on a train in the Belgian port of Ostend for the two-day journey to Moscow. I had a compartment to myself until Warsaw, where I was joined by a pair of young Soviet men returning home. For all I knew, they had been assigned to figure out who I was and what I was up to. Each had two passports, one "external," emblazoned with the hammer-and-sickle, and the other "internal," an identity card that specified his nationality. In their cases, that meant Russian; for others, the entry said Ukrainian, Uzbek, Kazakh, Estonian, Georgian, or Jew. This curious trapping of Soviet citizenship exposed one of the many failures of the U.S.S.R.: it pretended to be the incubator of "Soviet man," yet the administrative use of ethnic distinctions was a reminder of the divide-and-conquer strategy Stalin had relied on when he was People's Commissar of Nationalities.

Six months later, I returned to Moscow, this time as an intern in *Time* magazine's bureau there. During that summer, I traveled, again by rail, to Uzhgorod, near the U.S.S.R.'s frontier with Czechoslovakia, Poland, and Romania. A large contingent of border troops was garrisoned nearby. Those soldiers had little to keep themselves occupied, since all three neighboring states had communist regimes and belonged to the Warsaw Pact. In order to earn hard currency from the West, the Soviet authorities let the Italian producer, Dino de Laurentiis, and one of the U.S.S.R.'s leading directors, Sergei Bondarchuk, turn the fields outside Uzhgorod into a sprawling movie set where they refought the Battle of Waterloo. Rod Steiger played Napoleon Bonaparte, Christopher Plummer played the Duke of Wellington, and two divisions (nearly twenty thousand strong) of the Soviet Army played the cavalry, infantry, and artillery units that had met on the gently rolling farmlands of central Belgium 154 years before.[10]

Shortly after arriving, I badgered my way into Steiger's presence. An intense, cerebral actor, Steiger had just finished a long day on location. He received me in his room at the town's sole hotel for foreigners, a drab establishment called the Druzhba (Friendship), which Steiger had nicknamed "The Elba," implying, as he told me, that he had every intention of escaping as soon as possible. Meanwhile, however, he was fully in character. He was unshaven and wearing breeches and a tunic that were soaked with real sweat and stained with fake blood. A black velvet three-cornered hat with red marabou trim and a campaign jacket with metallic epaulets lay on a narrow bed, and muddy knee-length riding boots were propped against the wall. He invited me onto his balcony and, over a bottle of Chianti (compliments of the Italian film crew), launched into an impressive display of how much homework he had done for his part in the movie. He had pored over military histories, biographies of the Corsican corporal who crowned himself emperor, and the results of an autopsy performed on Saint Helena, six years after Waterloo.

Steiger had gained weight so that he could portray Napoleon in his last battle as fat, aging, and sick. During the great battle, the French leader was suffering possibly from cancer, probably from ulcers, and certainly from venereal disease and hemorrhoids. This last affliction was so agonizing that he had slept little for several days and was unable to command his forces from horseback. Steiger believed that Napoleon's immobility and the impairment of his judgment may have explained a series of tactical mistakes that contributed to his defeat, which had epic consequences for the remainder of the nineteenth century in Europe—and, perhaps, beyond. Steiger speculated at entertaining length about how different the world might be if Napoleon had made better use of Marshal de Grouchy's cavalry against Field Marshal Blücher's retreating Prussians. "Maybe," said Steiger with a chuckle, "if that poor bastard had gotten a decent night's sleep, everyone around here would be speaking French today." I had neither the knowledge nor the gumption to argue with Steiger. Besides, it made for good copy.[11]

The better story in Uzhgorod was one I didn't write. It featured the locals and the extras in the movie and the glimpse they gave me of the future.

My stay in the town was prolonged when the Italians staged a strike to protest the Soviet customs authorities' holding up the weekly shipment of pasta at the railway border crossing at Chop, just south of Uzhgorod. With all quiet on the set, I had the leisure to wander around and, to the obvious displeasure of my official minders, talk to the people I met on the streets. On one of these excursions I fell into conversation with a friendly and loquacious woman in her late sixties or early seventies. She invited me to sit with her on a park bench while she supervised her grandchildren and reminisced about her life.

Her story was rich in evidence of the transitory nature of states, the disconnection between nationality and statehood, and the fickleness of history. She had been born in Uzhgorod and never left, yet she had lived in four countries. As a child, until 1914, she had been a subject of the Austro-Hungarian Empire; between 1919 and 1938, Uzhgorod was the capital of Ruthenia, an autonomous province of Czechoslovakia; during World War II, the region was occupied by the Nazis, who gave it to their satrapy Hungary; after the war, the U.S.S.R. annexed the area, and Uzhgorod became the administrative center of Transcarpathia, the southwesternmost province of the Ukrainian Soviet Socialist Republic.

A day or so later, the Italians got their pasta and went back to filming the battle scenes. From a hilltop, I watched through binoculars as Soviet troops, many on horseback, charged, clashed, and retreated, all in nineteenth-century uniforms, armed with sabers, muskets, and cannons. They were supposed to be French, Prussian, Saxon, English, and Dutch, but it was obvious from their Asiatic physiognomies that most of them were conscripts from the Caucasus and Central Asia. The moviemakers dealt with this awkwardness by mustering a special battalion of troops with European-looking faces to appear in carefully staged close-ups.

That evening, during a stilted reception at which the foreign moviemakers mingled with the Soviet officers in command of the border troops, I buttonholed a major who was obviously pained at having his men dressed up in period costumes like toy soldiers. Perhaps for that reason, he was more willing than he might otherwise have been to talk about the serious business of guarding the U.S.S.R. from its real enemies rather than about redefeating Napoleon. I asked him why so many of the troops on the western border were brought from the other end of the country. He paused and furrowed his brow, trying to remember the officially approved answer. It was something about how Soviet soldiers were given a chance to serve far from their own homes so that they might "see more of the country" and show off to the world the "unified character of our multinational state."

I suspected at the time that, in fact, the major's masters in Moscow were uneasy about relying on large units of national minorities to defend their own regions. That was especially true in Transcarpathian Ukraine, where the local population included ethnic Hungarians, Romanians, and Slovaks, who had strong ties to nations—and states—just over the horizon, on the far side of the fortified Soviet border.

Only later did I fully appreciate the significance of what I saw and heard in Uzhgorod. But even at the time, I sensed the weakness of a state that the entire world then considered fearsome. Walled off from the world, the "Soviet camp" was very much like the concentration camps on which it had relied for both punishment and labor. Vladimir Lenin, who made the rise of Stalin possible, had called czarist Russia a "prison house of nations," but the Soviet Union far outdid its predecessor in that regard. I could understand Kennan's intuition that, sooner or later, the inmates would overpower the wardens. I made some notes for an article along those lines, but I did not have the confidence to commit these ideas to print until the eighties.[12] If I had published them in 1969, I would have had a scoop, but I might as well have used the byline "Cassandra."

FOR A DECADE, starting in the mid-seventies, a cluster of developments further—and as it turned out, fatally—weakened the Soviet Union. Under Brezhnev, the Soviet economy by any measure—GDP, industry, agriculture, and investment—was in sharp decline. Virtually the only commodities enjoying robust production and sale were oil and vodka. The revolution in communications technology confronted the party and the police with a dilemma. They knew that once data could be transmitted digitally, it would be much harder to control the distribution of information and opinion. Yet without a computer-literate society, the U.S.S.R. would fall even further behind the rest of the world in its industrial and military sectors. Soviet citizens began to speak of living in "the era of stagnation."[13]

While slowly rotting on the inside, the U.S.S.R. came under pressure from the outside. The West's principal means of exerting that pressure was the thirty-five-nation Conference on Security and Cooperation in Europe (CSCE). This gathering was a Kremlin initiative. Its intent, in the Soviets' mind, was similar to that of the Congress of Vienna of 1814–15: to stabilize the status quo. The effect, however, was the opposite: by opening up the Soviet empire to Western influences, the CSCE hastened the end of Soviet rule and, accordingly, the end of the cold war.

The long-running CSCE negotiation brought together members of the Warsaw Pact and NATO, along with other European states. The agenda covered disarmament, trade and cultural issues, and human rights. The West turned the CSCE into a platform for criticizing communist regimes for violating the human rights of their citizens. President Gerald Ford inherited from Richard Nixon a U.S. position in the CSCE that led (as did the Congress of Vienna a hundred and sixty years before) to a document called the Final Act. It was signed in Helsinki, in 1975, by all the participating states, including the U.S.S.R. and its satellites. The document was divided into three "baskets." Basket 1 ratified the boundaries established at the Yalta and Potsdam conferences for post–World War II Europe, including the division of Germany. Basket 2 provided for increased economic cooperation between East and West. Basket 3 committed all signatories to respect human rights, including freedom of expression, religion, and travel.

The Kremlin leaders agreed to the concessions they were making in Basket 3 because they thought they were getting, in Baskets 1 and 2, the better end of the bargain. That was a massive miscalculation. "The Helsinki Process," as it came to be called, took on an institutional character, providing a permanent forum for Western countries to criticize communist regimes for violating the rights of their citizens. Those criticisms heartened liberal reformers and dissident intellectuals within the Soviet sphere, accelerating the self-questioning and "mellowing" that Kennan had predicted.

DURING THE SAME PERIOD, the U.S.S.R. found itself on the receiving end of American counter-pressure of a rougher sort, although it was applied indirectly—through guerrilla groups who served as local American proxies in the global struggle. In the mid-seventies, the Soviets had seen what looked like geopolitical opportunities in the Third World, especially Africa and Central America (Ethiopia, Somalia, Angola, and Nicaragua). In 1979, they occupied Afghanistan. With Soviet power overextended, the United States selectively revived the concept of rollback.

In 1977, shortly after Jimmy Carter became president, his national security adviser, Zbigniew Brzezinski, publicly advocated undermining Soviet-dominated regimes rather than accepting them as extensions of Moscow's influence.[14] Even though this assertive, competitive policy was established during the Carter administration, it came to be known as "the Reagan Doctrine." That was because it was not until after Ronald Reagan replaced Carter as president in 1981 that the United States went all out, on four continents, to support resistance movements against pro-Soviet regimes. The principal beneficiaries of this policy were the Solidarity trade union movement in Poland, anticommunist guerrillas in Angola, the militant Muslim mujahideen in Afghanistan, and the Contras in Nicaragua.[15]

I WAS NEVER A WAR CORRESPONDENT, but I had two memorable exposures to the Reagan Doctrine at ground level in the most literal sense.

The first was in Soviet-occupied Afghanistan, where I went in 1981 to interview Babrak Karmal, one of a series of Kremlin quislings. I pressed him on reports that he was losing ground to "the muj," who already controlled the outskirts of Kabul. Karmal laughed heartily at this foolish rumor and instructed his underlings to take me to the edge of the city so that I could see for myself how quiet everything was. We stopped at a sorry excuse for a golf course and immediately came under withering sniper fire from a clump of brush next to the fairway. After taking cover in a sand trap, my escorts and I crawled to our vehicles and hightailed it back into the city.

The other close call was in May 1983 in northern Nicaragua. I went there with several colleagues from *Time* and the *Washington Post* to cover an inspection tour by the Sandinista comandante Daniel Ortega.* He and several other high-ranking officials from Managua flew by helicopter into the provincial village of Jalapa near the Honduran border, leaving us to get in and out by means of a convoy of jeeps. A band of about a hundred Contras had set up an ambush just outside the town. As we drove past them, mortars suddenly exploded around us, forcing us to dive out of the jeeps into a ditch on the side of the road. Steady fire from machine guns kept us pinned down for nearly two hours. Two of the teenage Sandinista soldiers assigned to protect us were killed outright. Another boy lay writhing in the road, screaming in pain and calling out for his mother. That night, attended by an American nun, he died, noisily, in the tiny clinic next to the ramshackle hostel where my colleagues and I were billeted.

---

* Ortega was a leading member of the leftist junta that overthrew the right-wing dictator Anastasio Somoza in 1979. Ortega served as president from 1984 to 1990, when the Sandinistas were defeated in an election, and he won back the presidency in 2006.

On both occasions, as I lay as flat as I could thinking mostly about matters other than international relations, it occurred to me that the bullets whizzing over my head were paid for by the U.S. taxpayer. I also appreciated as never before the old adage, *the map is not the territory.* A piece of paper cannot warn a platoon leader about the minefield or the blown-out bridge up ahead or the snipers' nest around the next bend. Nor does it show who is really in charge of an area, or how the locals feel about the national government in the capital. Maps, with their color coding and clearly defined borders, create a false sense of the stability of states and the cohesiveness of their citizenries.

DURING MY NUMEROUS VISITS TO the U.S.S.R. and Eastern Europe in the 1980s, I began to notice more signs of the corrosive effect that the information revolution was having on the monolith of Soviet power. I think it was on a visit to Berlin that I first heard about "terrestrial overspill," which allowed East Germans to watch West German television. On a reporting tour of the Soviet-occupied Baltic States, a young Estonian who served as my interpreter told me she had learned her idiomatic American English, complete with Southern accent, from reruns of *Dallas* shown in neighboring Finland that could be picked up by TV antennas in Estonia.

I remember thinking that maybe George Orwell had been wrong to fear that technological advances would increase the ability of despots to keep citizens under surveillance and pry into their private lives. In *1984*, the Thought Police rely on a ubiquitous "oblong metal plaque like a dulled mirror" to keep the citizens of Oceania brainwashed and obedient: "The instrument (the television, it was called) could be dimmed, but there was no way of shutting it off completely." [16] In fact, the transformation of society by high technology and mass communications made it possible to infiltrate images of a competing reality across borders, causing trouble for Big Brother and undermining the credibility of the Big Lie.

STILL, IT TOOK THE RIGHT LEADER at the right time to realize that totalitarianism simply didn't work. In the early eighties, the Kremlin was a geriatric ward. Leonid Brezhnev, Yuri Andropov, and Konstantin Chernenko expired in rapid succession, each after a period of on-the-job incapacity. The state-controlled radio stations had to be careful not to play classical music in a minor key unless they intended to signal that Red Square was, yet again, about to become an al fresco funeral parlor.

In March 1985, the Politburo, clearly with actuarial tables in mind, selected as Chernenko's replacement Mikhail Gorbachev, a vigorous, charismatic fifty-four-year-old with a law degree and prodigious self-confidence. What he allowed to happen amounts to the best imaginable evidence in support of the Great Man theory of history. Anyone with John Gaddis's (or Rod Steiger's) taste for counterfactuals has to wonder how different the world would be today if, when Chernenko died, the Politburo had picked as the next general secretary of the Communist Party one of the other candidates: Andrei Gromyko, the old warhorse of Soviet foreign policy, or Viktor Grishin or Grigory Romanov, the party bosses of Moscow and Leningrad respectively. The Soviet empire and the cold war would surely have lasted longer; perhaps we would still be waiting for them to end.

One of the many ways Gorbachev differed from his predecessors was his outgoingness. He was eager to interact with Western journalists, and when he did, he was confident and loquacious. With a reporter's notebook and often a tape recorder in hand, I saw quite a bit of him in the eighties and early nineties.[17]

But far more important than anything I heard him say was what the world saw him do. As he prepared to assume the leadership of the country, he brushed aside the briefing papers prepared by the sycophants of the party bureaucracy and convened a group of relatively sophisticated academicians from several economic and scientific institutes. He asked for a candid assessment of the Soviet economy and a projection of how well the U.S.S.R. would be able to hold its own in the global economy over the coming decades. The answers he got were grim, and the advice was urgent: unless he quickly imposed radical reforms, the Russian bear would enter the twenty-first century lagging behind Asian tigers such as South Korea and Thailand.

Through *perestroika* (restructuring), Gorbachev sought to demilitarize Soviet foreign policy so that he could divert resources to the Augean task of fixing a hopelessly inefficient economy and reduce the extent to which the Soviet system relied on force, both at home and abroad. Through *glasnost* (openness), he went a long way toward substituting facts and rationality for lies and dogma as the basis for governance.

In order to concentrate on modernizing the society and economy, and on integrating the Soviet Union into the outside world, Gorbachev, in effect, sued for peace in the cold war. He and his advisers promulgated what they called "new political thinking," which meant giving up on the winner-take-all concept of history that Lenin had captured in the slogan "who-whom" ("who will prevail over whom?").

As an indication of Gorbachev's xenophilia, he started borrowing words from English. He took the title *prezident* and started using *partnyorstvo*, or partnership, to describe his vision of relations with the United States. To him and his advisers, that term meant moving from "negative peace"—the avoidance of a cataclysmic conflict—to joint efforts between the superpowers, based on the recognition that they had more compatible interests than competing ones.

Reagan, who had denounced the U.S.S.R. and its satellites as an "evil empire," initially assumed that Gorbachev would be "totally dedicated to traditional Soviet goals." In that assessment the American president was not alone. But more quickly than many experts and most of his own aides, Reagan came to recognize that Gorbachev's goals, far from being traditional, were downright revolutionary. Without much fuss and without many of his supporters noticing, Reagan started, through intense, sustained personal engagement, to adopt Gorbachev's idea of partnership and thereby convince the Soviet leader that the United States would not make him sorry for the course he had chosen.

When Ronald Reagan died in 2004, Margaret Thatcher, Joseph Lieberman, John McCain, and other notables eulogized him with variations of the headline that the *Economist* ran on its own cover story obituary: "The Man Who Beat Communism." It remains an article of faith among many American conservatives that Reagan's commitment to the Strategic Defense Initiative—the effort to build a leak-proof antimissile shield—caused the Soviets to throw in the towel in the arms race and therefore, by extension, in the cold war. That is an exceedingly dubious contention, since by the last year of Reagan's presidency, SDI was already widely considered to be a pipe dream, including by Andrei Sakharov, the U.S.S.R.'s most eminent physicist and leading critic of the regime.[18]

The applause line that Reagan used at the Brandenburg Gate in 1987—"Mr. Gorbachev, tear down this wall!"—is often cited as though the thought had never occurred to Gorbachev until the Great Communicator suggested it. In fact, Gorbachev was already tearing down walls inside the

Ronald Reagan and Mikhail Gorbachev

Soviet system as well as creating conditions that would, within a little more than two years, empower the East German people to go to work with pick-axes on the concrete, steel, and barbed-wire barrier that separated them from the West.

Reagan gave himself second billing in the most dramatic development of the second half of the twentieth century. Asked at a press conference in Moscow in 1988, his last year in office, about his role in ending the cold war, Reagan replied, "Mr. Gorbachev deserves most of the credit, as the leader of this country." [19]

What neither man knew was that the country in question—the Soviet Union—would survive for only three more years, and *superpower* would soon be a noun that could only be used in the singular.

Three

THE
UNIPOLAR
DECADES

THE NEW WORLD ORDER

For the first time in this century, for the first time in perhaps all history, man does not have to invent a system by which to live. We don't have to talk late into the night about which form of government is better.
—GEORGE H. W. BUSH, *Inaugural Address, January 20, 1989*

What is at stake is more than one small country; it is big ideas, a new world order, where diverse nations are drawn together in common cause to achieve the universal aspirations of mankind—peace and security, freedom, and the rule of law.
—BUSH, *State of the Union address, during the Gulf War, January 29, 1991*

T H E period from the late 1970s through the beginning of the nineties seemed momentous at the time and, if anything, looks more so in hindsight. Communist reformers killed communism. Deng Xiaoping lifted China out of the madness of the Great Proletarian Cultural Revolution and set it on a course toward becoming a dynamic market economy, open to the world and vested in a peaceful international system. Starting in the second half of the eighties, Mikhail Gorbachev's *perestroika* and *glasnost* rapidly led to the collapse of the Berlin Wall, the Iron Curtain, and the Soviet Union. For the first time in history, there were no great-power antagonisms comparable to those that pitted the ancient Egyptians against the Hittites, the Greeks against the Persians, Athens against Sparta, England against Spain, Napoleon against the rest of Europe, and Germany against France.

While Marx's ideas were receding in the East, those of Dante, Kant, Monnet, and Schuman were advancing in the West. The year 1986 saw the signing in The Hague of the Single European Act, a modification of the Treaty of Rome. It brought the twelve member states of the European Economic Community into a unified market and thereby reinforced the basis for the European Union itself. In February 1992, the twelve leaders met in the Dutch city of Maastricht to sign the treaty creating the EU. They officially raised the union's flag—a circle of twelve gold stars on a blue field—alongside their national ones. Like some of the founders of the UN, they adopted Beethoven's *Ode to Joy* as their anthem.

More important than the stirring music were some prosaic words, none more so than *subsidiarity*. It referred to a form of federalism, anticipated by Dante, pushing governance downward, so that public policy is made and administered by the smallest (or lowest) competent authority, closest to the citizens it is meant to serve and to whom elected officials should be held accountable. Subsidiarity was intended to ensure that integration did not mean homogenization or suppression of distinct cultures and communities. It was meant to cultivate and institutionalize a pan-European equivalent of the attitudes and practices that had kept the Flemish and Walloons together in Belgium, the Castilians and Catalans in Spain, and the English and Scots in Britain.

The Maastricht Treaty also contained a provision that would be the basis for the European Economic and Monetary Union and the eventual creation of the euro, which would replace the national currencies of thirteen countries with populations totaling more than three hundred million people.* Otmar Issing, the first chief economist of the European Central Bank (and a former student of classics), would later note that the Eurozone re-created one of the key features that kept the Roman Empire together.[1] Jean-David Levitte, a French diplomat with whom I worked closely in the nineties and who subsequently served as ambassador to Washington, defined the essence of the European Project in terms pointedly intended to make clear how far ahead his region was from the rest of the world, and in particular North America: "For the Europeans, building on the lessons of two world wars, sovereignty is in a sense shared. We are building our European destiny together. A euro is shared sovereignty. Would you consider sharing the dollar with the Mexicans and the Canadians? Give them a say in the future of the dollar? Of course not. Sovereignty for you is paramount. For us it's the value which must be shared in the world of today and even more tomorrow."[2]

---

* Austria, Belgium, Finland, France, Germany, Greece, Ireland, Italy, Luxembourg, the Netherlands, Portugal, Spain and, as of 2006, Slovenia. Cyprus and Malta are set to join in 2008.

• • •

MEANWHILE, ANOTHER BIT OF EUROPEAN JARGON of recent derivation suddenly became a buzzword for the era and the world. As far back as 1961, *Webster's Third New International Dictionary of the English Language* had contained a new entry, *to globalize,* which meant "to make things global in scope and application." The "things" to which the verb applied were originally economic and commercial. Then, in the late 1970s, Eurocrats in Brussels, pondering the interdependencies of international trade and finance, started using a clunky noun, *globalization.* That it was a neologism implied that it described something new. In fact, humanity had been establishing interdependencies at great distances, including across oceans, for millennia. A word often used for that phenomenon is *globalism.* The difference between *globalism* and *globalization* is that the latter refers to the way in which distances have seemed to shrink and borders have seemed almost to disappear because of the speed and ease with which people—along with their ideas, money, culture, information, products, and any microbes along for the ride—can move around the globe.[3]

The acceleration that distinguishes *globalism* from *globalization* has occurred in a relatively short period of time—a matter of decades—and to a degree that has been transforming, sometimes for good, sometimes for ill, and often in ways that are ambiguous. It is still possible for immigration and customs officials to check passports and visas at airports and for border inspectors to conduct spot checks on containers coming off ships, but it is not possible to monitor or control the vast amount of data that is moving in and out of countries at the speed of light over the airwaves and, with the advent of the commercial Internet in 1993, through cyberspace. More than ever, international cooperation is essential to expedite the movement of people traveling for innocent, legal, and beneficial purposes; keep tabs on those traveling for dubious ones; regulate cross-border transactions and transfers of funds; and impede the spread of disease, thereby introducing an element of order into globalization. In short, globalization itself needs to be governed.

The form that governance should take has been a matter of negotiation. Therefore diplomacy became more important than ever with the end of the cold war and the growing awareness of globalization. In 1992, nearly four years after leaving office, Ronald Reagan said he believed that the UN had the potential to become "a humanitarian velvet glove backed by a steel fist of military force" to maintain international peace and end humanitarian outrages.

Initially, NATO would provide the armed might, but Reagan could foresee "a standing UN force—an army of conscience—that is fully equipped and prepared to carve out human sanctuaries through force if necessary." [4]

THOSE WERE HEADY TIMES, conducive to high hopes for multilateralism and the UN now that the Security Council had been liberated from the frequent deadlocks of the cold war. That was certainly my view. I did my best, which was never good enough, to defend it in a running debate with one fellow journalist in particular. Charles Krauthammer was already among the more formidable intellects focused on American foreign policy. In the eighties and early nineties, we both wrote for *Time* and were regulars on a weekly talking-heads television show, *Inside Washington.* We occasionally took in movies with our families, shared an attachment to border collies, met for brown-bag lunches at his office, which was a few blocks from mine, and sometimes played a quick game of chess—quick because it took him so few moves to demolish me.

As it became apparent that the Soviet Union was in deep trouble and might even come apart at the seams, Krauthammer and I discussed what the demise of the Great Other might mean for the international system. When I argued that we should make the most of global and regional organizations such as the UN, the incipient European Union, and NATO, Krauthammer countered that we must not let ourselves fall into the trap of "giddy Wilsonianism." A return to the delusions of Versailles in 1919 (or of San Francisco in 1945) would, he believed, guarantee that we would fritter away a chance to deal forcefully with new enemies—or newly armed old ones, especially radical forces in the Arab and Islamic worlds that were, he believed, bent on acquiring weapons of mass destruction. The best hope for a post–cold war peace, he believed, resided with an assertive United States that was prepared to throw its weight around, not with universal organizations like the UN (which he saw as a playground for mischief makers), or regional ones like NATO (which represented "pseudo-multilateralism," since it was only U.S. military might that counted), or an integrated Europe (which he believed was a mirage).

Krauthammer made his case in a lecture in September 1990, then turned it into an influential article in the annual "America and the World" special issue of *Foreign Affairs* that appeared at the beginning of 1991, the last year of the U.S.S.R.'s existence. The headline was "The Unipolar Moment," a phrase that referred to a period Krauthammer believed would last for several decades.

"No doubt multipolarity will come in time," he wrote, but not for a genera-tion or more, when Europe, China, Japan, and post-Soviet Russia finally got their acts together. In the meantime, the United States, as "the unchallenged superpower," would be "the center of world power," the principal maker and enforcer of rules for everyone else, and the metropole of a modern (or per-haps postmodern) global empire.*

From my reporting on nuclear arms control, I knew a smattering of physics. I told Krauthammer that my disagreement with his article began with its title: there was no such thing in physics as "unipolarity" (or, for that matter, "multipolarity"). I checked with a nuclear physicist and guru of mine on arms control, Sidney Drell, a professor at Stanford, and he confirmed that since polarity itself requires a positive and a negative, there is only bipolarity.[5] The cold war world was bipolar. The disappearance of the negative pole of the Evil Empire seemed to me an invitation to think in terms of other, non-polar concepts and phenomena from physics: complex molecules and com-pounds, perhaps, with the emphasis on the bonding power of common values and interests. In this revisionist variant of the metaphor from nuclear physics, I could see the outlines of a successor to the imperial and balance-of-power systems—the glimmer of what John Ikenberry, a political scientist at Princeton who specializes in international institutions, would term a "post-realist order of liberal hegemony."[6]

American might and leadership were more important than ever, but they would be most effective if applied through institutions that the United States had fostered at the beginning of the cold war and could now expand and strengthen with the end of that struggle. Just because we were, as the cliché had it, the sole remaining superpower did not mean we could count on being, in Krauthammer's term, "unchallenged." If we pushed others—in-cluding our friends and even our supposed allies—too hard, they would find ways to thwart us.

---

* In the years that followed, a number of authors developed Krauthammer's theme, ex-horting Americans to accept their country's imperial responsibility to spread liberal values and the rest of the world to accept the United States in that role. See, for example, Niall Fergu-son, *Empire: The Rise and Demise of the British World Order and the Lessons for Global Power* (New York: Basic Books, 2003) and *Colossus: The Price of America's Empire* (New York: Pen-guin, 2004); Deepak Lal, *In Defense of Empires* (Washington, D.C.: AEI Press, 2004); and Max Boot, "The Case for American Empire," *Weekly Standard*, October 15, 2001. The political sci-entist Michael Doyle, who served as an assistant secretary-general of the UN under Kofi Annan, has characterized this school of thought as "liberal imperialism" (as opposed to "lib-eral internationalism"), in the sense that it advocates the promotion of liberal values and ideals through imperialistic means.

Fortunately, what the United States and the world needed in the late eighties and early nineties was what it got: a president with a preference for diplomacy as the best means to advance America's interests in the world and a knack for making other countries feel that he was advancing, or at least respecting, theirs as well.

THE AMBASSADOR IN THE OVAL OFFICE

While I had reported on every chief executive since Richard Nixon, George H. W. Bush was the first with whom I had anything like a social relationship. We shared a connection with Yale and, during his eight years as vice president, a regimen that included jogging on the St. Albans School track, not far from where he lived on Massachusetts Avenue and from Brooke's and my home on Calvert Street. He and I were distantly related—a connection that brought us together occasionally at holiday receptions at the vice presidential mansion and sometimes for family events, including a visit to Walker's Point in Kennebunkport, Maine. The occasion was a memorial service in August 1990 for Bush's uncle, John Walker, whose wife, Louise, is my father's cousin and godmother to our son Adrian. After the ceremony at St. Ann's Episcopal Church, Brooke and our boys had the ritualistic honor of pitching horseshoes with the president of the United States. Among those gathered was George W. Bush, a classmate of mine at Yale, who was managing general partner of the Texas Rangers at the time. We had barely known each other at Yale and had seen nothing of each other since.

I was not on anything like close personal terms with the first President Bush, either. While always courteous and prepared from time to time to discuss issues I was writing about, he regarded me, correctly, as in the liberal camp of the not-always-friendly press corps. Far more than Reagan, he followed commentary on his performance closely and was easily stung by criticism, and I delivered my share in the pages of *Time*.

Nonetheless, I felt a certain affinity with where he was coming from politically—namely, the East Coast internationalist wing of the Republican Party. That was where my parents had positioned themselves since the forties and where I might have ended up if the party had not moved in a different direction about the time I was coming of age politically. In 1964, as an eighteen-year-old just out of Hotchkiss and on my way to Yale, I worked as a volunteer for Governor William Scranton of Pennsylvania in his quixotic campaign to prevent Barry Goldwater from getting that year's Republican nomination. From the bleachers at the Cow Palace in San Francisco, I witnessed the stri-

dency and savagery with which the Goldwater forces attacked Scranton and Nelson Rockefeller during the convention. The experience contributed to my defection from what I thought of as Bush's original political tribe.

Bush was a Connecticut Yankee, a graduate of prep school and Yale, who had tried, not altogether successfully, to make it in Texas politics (he won a seat in the House of Representatives but lost a bid for the Senate). When Richard Nixon made him the American permanent representative to the UN, Bush found the life of an ambassador better

George H. W. Bush

suited to his temperament and operating style than the rough-and-tumble of politics. He quickly established a reputation for being unusually collegial and solicitous. Almost every day he would make a point of calling on two or three other permanent representatives to gauge what was happening in their part of the world and ask them their reaction to U.S. policy.

Gerald Ford sent Bush to Beijing for fourteen months to head the U.S. liaison office, a precursor to a full embassy.* Once again Bush relished the assignment, this time to a remote part of the world. His approach to his next job, as director of Central Intelligence, was more pinstripe than cloak-and-dagger. To the admiration of some colleagues and the dismay of others, he tended to attach as much importance to what he heard on overseas trips and from visitors to Washington as to the intelligence gathered by American spies and satellites. More than any of his predecessors and most of his successors, Bush would send CIA assessments back to their authors for reappraisal on the basis of what he heard from foreigners whom he knew and trusted.

Well before moving to the Oval Office, Bush, by his own subsequent account, came to believe that "personal diplomacy and leadership went hand in hand," and that "there are actually commonsense reasons for an American

---

* Ford's successor, Jimmy Carter, would establish full diplomatic relations with the People's Republic of China, close the U.S. embassy in Taipei (leaving in its place the "American Institute in Taiwan"), and replace the liaison office in Beijing with an embassy.

president to build relationships with his opposites. If a foreign leader knows the character and the heartbeat of the president (and vice versa), there is apt to be far less miscalculation on either side."[7] When he began running for president, Bush resigned from the Trilateral Commission and the Council on Foreign Relations and denounced these bastions of the American foreign policy establishment as "too liberal," in order to make himself acceptable to conservatives. But once he succeeded Reagan, he steered American foreign policy along lines associated with the East Coast establishment: heavy reliance on consultation, diplomacy, alliances, international law, and multilateral institutions. He was a team player who found himself the captain of the ultimate team. Of all the managerial—or leadership—qualities he valued, the one that he spoke of most often, especially when dealing with danger and crisis, was prudence. While covering his presidency, I heard him use the word numerous times, and it was often attributed to him by his friends and aides as well. I also heard him use cautions, such as, "We've got to be careful not to screw this up," or—my personal favorite—"We can't make the wrong mistakes."[8]

THE ISSUE ON WHICH I found Bush most disappointing was one which I had been raised to believe was of paramount importance: the environment. My father, a lifelong birdwatcher and outdoorsman, had drummed into me since childhood an awareness that the human species was, as he put it, "fouling its own nest." He tracked the decline and disappearance of whole species of wildlife. When I returned to my parents' home for visits in the eighties and nineties, my father showed me how the frogs in a nearby pond were beginning to display bizarre deformities. I remember his saying that we should regard these amphibians as canaries in a mine shaft.

My father made sure that I paid attention to the occasional good news as well. He took heart from the Montreal Protocol—signed in 1987 and updated in the years that followed—which successfully limited the emission of chlorofluorocarbon compounds, commonly called Freons, and other substances that had opened a hole in the ozone layer of the atmosphere, depriving the earth and its inhabitants of protection from harmful ultraviolet rays. If we could close the ozone hole, he believed, we ought to be able to do something about global warming.

With regular prodding and a steady flow of scientific articles from my father, I criticized Bush in several *Time* columns for failing to deliver on a promise he had made as a candidate in 1988, the hottest year then on record, to address the buildup in carbon dioxide and other greenhouse gases, so called because they trap radiation from the sun. It was projected that if the trend continued, by the end of the twenty-first century the quantity of greenhouse gases in the atmosphere would have tripled, raising the average global temperatures by as much as 10 degrees Fahrenheit (more than the increase in temperature since the end of the last Ice Age, ten thousand years ago).

Bush had pledged to be an "environmental president" who would counteract "the greenhouse effect" with "the White House effect." The United States, with 5 percent of the earth's population, produced nearly a quarter of all the CO_2 from fossil fuels. Reducing those emissions by any meaningful degree would require tough new federal standards for automobile fuel economy; government-sponsored inducements to increase efficiency in the production of electricity by utilities—as well as in consumption by homes and businesses; and a major research-and-development program for alternative sources of energy. As president, Bush pushed for none of those measures, nor did he propose or support any legislation mandating cuts in CO_2 emissions. A year after his election I wrote a column under the headline "Why Bush Should Sweat."

If Bush had followed his personal instincts on the environment, his policies might have been different. I remember hearing that he and William Reilly, the head of the Environmental Protection Agency, led what was sometimes called the "green faction" in internal debates. But the majority of Bush's subordinates did not agree with him, and neither did the Republican base of big business and social conservatives. Bush was willing to yield to those interests, much as he did on a number of domestic issues, in part because he believed it gave him extra room to conduct a multilateralist foreign policy with heavy reliance on the UN, vigorous engagement with the Soviet Union, activism in the Middle East, and strong support for the unification of Europe.

In June 1992, the UN convened a two-week "Earth Summit" in Rio de Janeiro. With 117 heads of state or government in attendance, it was, at the time, the largest gathering of world leaders in history.* The U.S. delegation, led by Bush, stood against most—and, on some issues, all—of the other nations represented. The United States alone refused to sign a treaty to preserve forest biodiversity, and it was the only industrialized nation to oppose targets and deadlines for reducing greenhouse emissions contained in another treaty, the UN Framework Convention on Climate Change. While the ten thousand journalists covering the event raised public awareness around the world about the dangers facing the planet, the meeting resulted in only

* That record was broken by the Millennium Summit at the UN in 2000 (with 143 leaders) and the World Summit at the UN in 2005 (156).

rhetorical commitments and the most modest steps toward achieving its stated goal of finding worldwide, economically sustainable solutions. By playing the spoiler rather than the leader in Rio, the United States turned the summit into the environmental equivalent of the League of Nations—a worthy international effort hobbled by an abdication of American leadership.

BUSH'S INSTINCTS AND GUMPTION served him and the world much better when it came to the use of force in support of American foreign policy. His guiding principle was "together if possible, alone if necessary." The invasion of Panama in late 1989, Bush's first year in office, was the exception that proved the rule. He had come to the presidency with a grudge against General Manuel Noriega, who had been the corrupt, drug-trafficking, and brutal head of Panamanian military intelligence in the late 1970s when Bush was at the CIA. After Noriega canceled the results of a presidential election and had his thugs beat up his political opponents in the fall of 1989, Bush sent in troops from the 82nd Airborne Division along with infantry and ranger units and hauled Noriega off to Miami to face drug charges. The Pentagon called the invasion "Operation Just Cause." In a session with reporters that I attended, Bush's secretary of defense, Dick Cheney, called it "Operation Just Because," as in, "We did this *just because* we could— and we wanted the world to know it."

Cheney's we'll-show-you impulse did not strike a chord with Bush himself. No sooner did the troops move into Panama than the president was on the phone to more than a dozen foreign leaders, many of them in Latin America. He went to great lengths to explain what he saw as the exceptional nature of the episode and asking for their candid reactions. By and large, they were polite, in some cases even supportive, but in virtually all cases cautionary: here was Uncle Sam back to his old habit of occupying a small country to the south—and at a time when the Soviet Union finally seemed to be getting out of the business of invading neighboring states. Bush took these concerns to heart. He slapped down aides who publicly gloated over the ease with which the United States had dealt with Panama. As U.S. forces mopped up the remnants of the Noriega regime and made it possible for the winner of the earlier election to take office, the spin from the White House and the State Department was heavy on disclaimers: no, the invasion was not a precedent; no, it did not represent a "Bush Doctrine."

Much of the world was willing to give Bush a pass on Panama. His friend and national security adviser, Brent Scowcroft, who had strong reservations about the invasion, later acknowledged, "Traditionally, such action would have provoked a firestorm of outrage from Latin American leaders sensitive to foreign, especially Yankee, intervention. . . . [But] the fact that these leaders knew George Bush, and understood his goals and what kind of man he was, resulted in a very muted and quite inconsequential opposition."[9]

FOR THE REMAINDER of Bush's presidency, and on virtually all other foreign policy issues that arose, he took full advantage of Air Force One to consult face-to-face with his fellow leaders. While in Washington, he worked the telephone constantly. Scowcroft (who had served Nixon and Ford as well) ventured that Bush "spoke with more foreign leaders more often than his four or five predecessors combined."[10]

Bush also devoted considerable energy to strengthening existing institutions, including NATO and the UN, and helping to establish new ones. One was the Asia-Pacific Economic Cooperation forum (APEC), which held its first meeting in Canberra in 1989, with the foreign ministers of twelve Pacific Rim countries attending. In his desire to emphasize the multilateral dimension of his foreign policy, Bush quietly pulled back, even if he did not quite repudiate, unilateral projects, such as Star Wars, which he inherited from Reagan. In addition to crediting the view of most scientists that the anti-missile scheme would never work, Bush did not want to play up the danger of a predatory U.S.S.R., ready to hurl rockets at the United States—especially in the face of growing evidence that the Soviet empire was imploding.

As popular resistance mounted against the communist regime in East Germany in 1989, it was clear that Moscow would do nothing to save it. Bush set about systematically coaxing Gorbachev to accept not just the loss of a Warsaw Pact ally but the decision of a unified Germany to remain a member of NATO. This outcome was important in its own right, since it would have been difficult to sustain NATO if a united Germany had withdrawn. It also set an important precedent for other former Soviet satellites—and former Soviet republics—that would want to join a post–cold war NATO in the future.

The simultaneous achievement of German unification, the preservation of NATO, and the avoidance of a breach in relations between Washington and Moscow was, in Bush's view, "personal diplomacy in the finest sense of the term. Coalition-building, consensus, understanding, tolerance, and compromise had forged a new Europe, transformed and unified. There was no Versailles, no residual international bitterness."[11]

CONDOLEEZZA RICE, a political scientist on leave from Stanford who worked for Scowcroft on the staff of the National Security Council, played a significant role in helping Bush act on his mantra of the time: making Europe "whole and free." In particular, she was instrumental in designing and executing the policy of keeping Germany in NATO. I knew her better than I knew anyone else in the Bush White House, since she had devoted much of her career to studying the Soviet bloc. We had met frequently over the years at conferences and traveled together in the U.S.S.R. and China in the eighties. The presidential historian Michael Beschloss and I saw her frequently when we were writing a study of Bush's policy toward the U.S.S.R.[12] We viewed her as representative of the Bush administration's sure-footedness in dealing with its single biggest challenge: managing the end of the cold war.

SHOWDOWN WITH SADDAM

On August 2, 1990, Saddam Hussein—who had pretensions of being a successor to Hammurabi and Nebuchadnezzar and upholder of the legacy of Saladin—sent two Republican Guard divisions and other forces into Kuwait on the basis of a claim that Kuwait belonged to Iraq.[13] Slowly and deliberately, the U.S. administration began to consider how to reverse the Iraqi aggression. Three weeks into the crisis, Bush and Scowcroft went fishing off Kennebunkport. The blues weren't biting that day, so the two men had four nearly uninterrupted hours to talk about how they might embed the bad news of what had happened in the Gulf within the larger good news of a "world transformed" by the end of the cold war.* Bush and Scowcroft wanted a replacement for "containment," the motto of American foreign policy for forty years. One reason that "containment" had worked so well was that, packed into those three syllables, were five implications: recognition of a threat to the vital interests of the United States; a muscular American response to the threat; American leadership of a military alliance; steadiness of purpose and consistency of policy; and confidence that the United States and the free world would prevail without another world war.

In sifting through possibilities for a successor to "containment," Bush and Scowcroft had the United Nations and partnership with the Soviet Union very much in mind. Now that the superpower standoff was over, the United States and U.S.S.R. could act together in opposing aggression, much as the

---

* A World Transformed was the title that Bush and Scowcroft chose for the memoir they co-authored and published in 1998.

founders of the world body had intended before the cold war ruined any chance of that happening.

The phrase that Bush and Scowcroft settled on while they were bobbing on the water, a "new world order," was hardly original. Woodrow Wilson's contemporaries and subsequent historians applied the term to his Fourteen Points and his hopes for the League of Nations. More recently— and more sparingly (in part because it sounded uncomfortably similar to the Nazis' *Weltherrschaft*)—"new world order" had been used in connection with the United Nations and the Bretton Woods system. In its post–cold war context, Gorbachev himself had used the term in a speech at the UN in 1988.[14]

Bush made the phrase—the global analogue to "Europe whole and free"—his own in the autumn of 1990. He, too, floated it from the podium of the UN, using it as part of his rallying cry as an American-led coalition was positioning itself in the Saudi desert for the liberation of Kuwait. Addressing the General Assembly on October 1, he trumpeted the "collective strength of the world community expressed by the UN [and] an historic movement towards a new world order," a line he used frequently in the months that followed.

When the president was not working Capitol Hill (where support for use of force passed in the Senate, which was controlled by the Democrats, by a vote of only 52–47), he was using his famous Rolodex to reach out to foreign leaders who would decide how much support he got in the UN. Like Truman in the case of Korea, Bush had resolved that he would go forward with military action supported by as many other countries as possible even if the UN balked. But it wasn't even close. A series of twelve Security Council resolutions conferred legitimacy on the war that would begin in early 1991. The most important, Resolution 678, which passed on November 29, 1990, invoked Chapter VII of the Charter, which gives the international community the right "to restore or maintain international peace and security." The resolution authorized member states to use "all necessary means"—UN boilerplate for means that include armed force— against Iraq if it did not vacate Kuwait within six weeks. The vote was 12–2, with China abstaining (that is, not using its veto) and, more remarkably still, with the U.S.S.R. voting in favor.*

---

* The Chinese tended, in general, to use their veto sparingly. The two votes against the resolution were cast by Cuba and Yemen, which were rotating—i.e., non-veto-bearing— members of the Security Council.

• • •

THE U.S.-LED THIRTY-FOUR NATION COALITION began military operations in mid-January. After four weeks of bombing had devastated Iraqi air defenses, communications, roads, and oil facilities, the ground war began. It took a hundred hours to retake Kuwait and thrust over a hundred miles into Iraq.

Bush regarded the eviction of Saddam from Kuwait as one of the signature achievements of his administration for reasons that went well beyond the accomplishment of the goal at hand. "We were both struck with the thought," recalled Scowcroft, "that we were perhaps at a watershed of history. The Soviet Union was standing alongside us, not only in the United Nations, but also in condemning and taking action against Iraqi aggression. . . . If the attack on Kuwait marked the end of forty-odd years of superpower competition, what vistas might open up? The Security Council could then perform the role envisioned for it by the UN framers." [15]

Defending themselves from critics who believed the administration should have sent coalition forces all the way to Baghdad to topple Saddam's regime, Bush and Scowcroft wrote jointly:

> We [were] self-consciously trying to set a pattern for handling aggression in the post–Cold War world. Going in and occupying Iraq, thus unilaterally exceeding the United Nations' mandate, would have destroyed the precedent of international response to aggression that we hoped to establish. Had we gone the invasion route, the United States could conceivably still be an occupying power in a bitterly hostile land. It would have been a dramatically different—and perhaps barren—outcome. . . . Our prompt withdrawal helped cement our position with our Arab allies, who now trusted us far more than they ever had. . . . [The Gulf War's] magnitude and significance impelled us from the outset to extend our strategic vision beyond the crisis to the kind of precedent we should lay down for the future. . . . Building an international response led us immediately to the United Nations, which could provide a cloak of acceptability to our efforts and mobilize world opinion behind the principles we wished to project. . . . Unilaterally going significantly beyond [the Security Council mandate authorizing the operation], we might have undermined the confidence of the United Nations to make future grants of such deadly authority. [16]

BUSH'S VICTORY OVER SADDAM in Kuwait was the high point of his administration. Thanks in large measure to Bush's skillful management of

Gorbachev, the Soviet Union had made it much easier for America to exercise its muscle in concert with a newly empowered UN. For the first time, conservative Arab states in the Gulf were willing to establish security ties with the United States. The prospects for an Israeli-Palestinian peace seemed to brighten. Conventional wisdom that the United States was a declining economic power faded. The dollar gathered strength against foreign currencies, and America became more attractive to foreign investment. At home, Bush's approval ratings soared to nearly 90 percent, largely because of the robust and adroit way he dealt with Saddam.

Bush shared his moment of glory with the UN. On February 6, 1991, while U.S.-led air strikes were crippling the Iraqi forces in preparation for the ground campaign that would begin two weeks later, Bush proclaimed, in a speech before the Economic Club of New York, "My vision of a new world order foresees a United Nations with a revitalized peacekeeping function." A similar sentence in a speech Bush gave on March 6 drew applause from the assembled members of the U.S. Senate and House. In the months that followed, there were constant references from the administration to what presidential staffers shorthanded as the "NWO." *New world order* had the ring of a slogan for the era and also for Bush's upcoming campaign for reelection.

The phrase was also meant as an antidote to the criticism that Bush lacked what he called, with exasperation, "the vision thing." [17] He felt, with justification, that he deserved credit for taking advantage of the strategic opportunities that came with the end of the cold war. It frustrated him to be chided for failing to convey a bold and inspirational sense of purpose. Part of the problem was that he did not want to seem excessively idealistic. As a result, he tended to hedge his uplifting rhetoric with caveats. In another speech at the UNGA, in September 1991, he felt compelled to include, in a sentence hailing multilateral institutions and international rule of law, a subordinate clause noting the the new world order would be one "in which no nation must surrender one iota of its own sovereignty."

In that same speech, however, Bush made equally clear that he had no use for the imperial view of American power: "Let me assure you, the United States has no intention of striving for a Pax Americana. However, we will remain engaged. We will not retreat and pull back into isolationism. We will offer friendship and leadership. And in short, we seek a *Pax Universalis* built upon shared responsibilities and aspirations."

In trying to stay out of political trouble, Bush left it to others to debate whether it was possible to have effective international law or universal peace without some degree of pooling, if not sacrifice, of absolute national sovereignty.

But trouble came nonetheless. While Bush's rhetoric buttressing his adoption of "a new world order" as a slogan was reassuring to moderates, it drew fire from right-wing Republicans. One voice captured the complaint of a growing chorus. In October 1991, soon after Bush's UNGA speech, David Funderburk, a conservative congressman from North Carolina, achieved fleeting notoriety by denouncing Bush for "surrounding himself with people who believe in one-world government. They believe that the Soviet system and the American system are converging," presumably at the expense of American values, virtues, and interests. Moreover, warned Funderburk, despite Bush's pledges to protect American sovereignty, it was already being surrendered to the United Nations, "the majority of whose 166 member states are socialist, atheist, and anti-American." [18]

Around the time of these and similar fulminations—a year before the 1992 presidential election—the president, seeking to solidify his rather shaky base within his party, stopped talking about a new world order.

NOT WITH A BANG . . .

Bush had another reason for dropping the phrase: by 1992, when he had to face the voters in his bid for reelection, the new world was not looking very orderly, nor was it clear that Europe was indeed becoming whole and free. In the months after his triumph in Iraq, Bush had grown concerned about the extent to which his friend Gorbachev was losing control in the U.S.S.R. Like Gorbachev himself, Bush was slow in recognizing the logic and momentum of events. The state that Gorbachev was trying to reform had depended on intimidating and lying to its citizens and stoking their fear of external enemies. Gorbachev's repudiation of those long-standing features of Soviet power politics had the opposite effect from the one he intended: the entire edifice began to crumble. As a result, the policies that made Gorbachev so revered abroad made him doubly vulnerable at home. First, stalwarts of the Soviet system were increasingly worried that their leader was, as one of them put it to me on a visit in early 1991, "reforming it to death." Second, leaders of independence movements in the non-Russian republics were impatient to break free of Moscow as quickly as possible, lest the prospective disintegration of the U.S.S.R. provoke Gorbachev's comrades to overthrow him and re-instate the policies of the bad old days.

The danger of a coup by hard-liners was, I sometimes sensed, more on Bush's mind than Gorbachev's. The Soviet leader possessed a self-confidence that sometimes seemed almost delusional, while Bush could imagine the U.S.S.R. dissolving into chaos. I saw signs of that possibility myself during reporting trips to the Soviet hinterland, especially in the Caucasus and Central Asia. On a visit to Georgia in 1990, I had a chance to look the danger of post-Soviet nationalism in the face. For many ethnic Georgians, the man of the hour was Zviad Gamsakhurdia, a distinguished philologist and the son of a much-lionized literary figure. However, as a leader of the Georgian independence movement and later as president, the best that could be said of Gamsakhurdia was that he was a romantic patriot in the nineteenth-century tradition, the kind whom Heinrich Heine had seen, a century earlier, as the harbinger of "dark ferocious times." I saw something worse: a fanatic whose xenophobia extended to the nearly eighty non-Georgian ethnic groups who shared a country the size of West Virginia with those he considered "real" Georgians.

"We'll achieve freedom by fighting," said Gamsakhurdia during an interview at his villa in a suburb of Tbilisi in 1990. "I expect death for myself and civil war for my country." He uttered these words with neither resignation nor foreboding but ecstatic defiance. He denounced as traitors any of his own countrymen who dared to disagree with him on virtually any subject. "We cannot tolerate collaborationists" who were "nothing but tools of the [Soviet] state and will be dealt with as such," he said. The more he talked, the more inclusive that indictment seemed to become. When my colleagues and I left, it took nearly twenty minutes for four burly body-guards, using the butts of their automatic rifles, to force a pack of Dober-mans into a corner of the garden so that my colleagues and I could safely reach our car.[19]

The encounter was a reminder that empires, troublesome as they can be when they are strong and assertive, pose a whole different category of danger—to their own people, their neighbors, and the world—when they are in the throes of disintegration: the cruelties and artificialities that were used to weld diverse peoples together into a superstate give way to the equally cruel, equally artificial forces of "naked nationalism," the curse that John Keegan saw threatening Europe on the eve of World War I.

· · ·

IN MY VISITS TO MOSCOW during this period, I found Gorbachev taking the blame for the way in which the U.S.S.R. was like a glacier that had finally reached the sea and large chunks were dropping off its edge and floating out to sea. He was also being excoriated for the crisis in the economy. The Soviet apparatus for providing its citizens with the basics of life had always been a cruel mess. *Perestroika* was largely a matter of restructuring a ruin, a contradiction in terms that made for a sorry spectacle. Yet the world was, as never before, invited to watch. Scenes of empty shelves in Moscow grocery stores appeared on TV news programs almost every evening. At least some of the food so conspicuously missing in state outlets was on sale, off camera and a few blocks away, from private vendors at higher prices.

Glasnost led to a kind of reverse Potemkinism—a late-Soviet tendency to portray the situation as even worse than it was. As my closest Russian friend, Slava Luchkov, put it, "We have really only two words in our language: *ura* (hurrah) and *uvy* (alas)." After generations of being forced to cheer, 286 million people now seemed to be lamenting in unison, and they were booing the man who had permitted them to do so.

On one of my trips, I took with me Gabriel García Márquez's novel *The General in His Labyrinth*, about the last days of Simón Bolívar. It made for eerie reading in my room at the Berlin Hotel off Red Square. Having cast off the shackles of empire and earned the title of "The Liberator," Bolívar is facing up to his defeat. What he wants most is a single South American republic, reaching from Caracas to Quito. But the passions of the revolution he led have given way to those of separatism that he cannot control. His "golden dream of continental unity" becomes an embarrassing abstraction to his people, who begin following regional leaders instead. "Let's go," Bolívar tells his Sancho Panza–like aide. "No one loves us here." Terminally ill, fearful of assassination, mocked on the streets, Bolívar sets off on a mule into self-imposed exile. "It's destiny's joke," says one of his few remaining loyalists. "It seems we planted the ideal of independence so deep that now these countries are trying to win their independence from each other." [20]

When I got back to Washington, I told Condoleezza Rice at the NSC that I was struck by the analogy. She had a less melancholy—and, as I realized, more useful—one in mind: she saw Gorbachev as the late-twentieth-century equivalent of Kemal Ataturk. What Ataturk had done for the Anatolian core of the Ottoman homeland, Gorbachev was doing for Russia. However reviled he might be within the U.S.S.R., Gorbachev would someday get credit from his own people for beginning the process of unloading the dead weight of restive colonies and enabling Russia, like Turkey, to become fully part of Europe. Such, at least, was my hope—and Rice's.

IN DEALING WITH THE INCREASINGLY BELEAGUERED Soviet president, George H. W. Bush sought, as he and Scowcroft put it, to convince Gorbachev "that we were not trying to gain an advantage from the problems of the Soviet Union or its allies and that we sincerely wanted perestroika to succeed." [21] To that end, Bush did everything he could to build up Gorbachev in the estimation of the world—and of the Soviet people. Along with John Major, the prime minister of the United Kingdom, and the other leaders of the Group of Seven or G-7, Bush invited Gorbachev to be a guest in London for part of their annual summit in mid-July 1991.

The G-7, which grew out of small, lower-level consultations in the seventies, originally brought together the finance ministers of the world's leading economies to coordinate their response to the oil shock triggered by the 1973 Middle East war. The president of France, Valéry Giscard d'Estaing, elevated the group to heads of state and government in 1975. Since the G-7 represented more than half of the world's economic output at the time, the deliberations conducted at those summits and the statements released after each one influenced the decisions of the World Bank, the IMF, and the UN. An explicit purpose was to harmonize, as much as possible, the policies of the self-designated "major industrial democracies": Canada, France, Italy, Japan, the United Kingdom, the United States, and West Germany. Much like the Great Powers at the Congress of Vienna, the Council of the League of Nations, and the P-5 of the UN, the G-7 saw itself as a de facto governing board of the world.

At the London summit in 1991, the G-7 conspicuously broadened and elevated its agenda by releasing a political declaration titled "Strengthening the International Order" and praising the direction in which Gorbachev was taking the Soviet Union. [22] Soon afterward, Bush decided to take his message of personal support for Gorbachev to Kiev, the capital of Ukraine, a Soviet republic that was straining against its tether to Moscow. On arriving there at the beginning of August, Bush was unsettled to find the crowds that greeted him brandishing posters that read, "Moscow has 15 colonies!" "The Empire of Evil still lives!" "53 million Ukrainians demand independence!" and "If being part of an empire is so great, why did America get out of one?" Bush went into Dutch-uncle mode. He did some last-minute toughening up of a speech to the Ukrainian parliament. He accentuated the praise for Gorbachev, urged the Ukrainians to accept a Soviet version of American federalism, and denounced those calling for secession: "Americans will not support those who seek independence in order to replace a far-off tyranny with a local despotism. They will not aid those who promote a suicidal nationalism based on ethnic hatred."

The speech played badly with the locals and back home in the United States as well. In his eagerness to provide cover for Gorbachev's reforms, Bush had, in the view of his critics on both ends of the American political spectrum, managed to put himself at odds with America's traditional support for the right of peoples around the world to choose their form of government.

Nor did Bush's defense of Gorbachev do the Soviet president any good against his own domestic opponents. Three weeks after Bush's speech in Kiev, a group of die-hard communists seized power in Moscow and had Gorbachev put under house arrest at his dacha on the Black Sea. The coup quickly fizzled, partly because of the incompetence of its perpetrators but also because Boris Yeltsin, a protégé turned rival of Gorbachev, led a popular uprising against the usurpers.

Bush's son, George W., who was an adviser to the '92 reelection campaign, remarked to reporters that the incident should remind the American people that the world was still a dangerous place and they needed an experienced statesman in the White House: "Do you think the American people are going to turn to a Democrat *now*?"

Had the coup in Moscow succeeded, Bill Clinton, who was still two months away from announcing his candidacy for the Democratic nomination, would have agreed with the younger Bush. Before the outcome in Moscow was clear, Clinton told me that "the end of the end of the cold war" would make President Bush a shoo-in for reelection. A few days later, once it was clear that the coup had been the last gasp of the Soviet hard-liners, Clinton and I talked again. He was relieved for the world and had also regained his confidence about his chances of unseating an incumbent whose strong suit was foreign policy.

THE IMMEDIATE TARGET of the protests led by Yeltsin was the putschists, but Gorbachev's own political fate, along with that of the state he led, was now sealed. Within days, Estonia and Latvia declared independence, setting off a stampede, with Ukraine formally seceding in December.* I remember thinking that the young woman who had been my guide in Estonia a few years before no longer needed permission from Moscow to travel to Helsinki—or, for that matter, to the Dallas of her dreams—and that the grandchildren of the old woman I had met in Uzhgorod in 1969 would grow up as citizens of an independent Ukraine.

On December 25, 1991, Gorbachev turned the Kremlin over to Yeltsin, who had been democratically elected president of Russia while it was still a republic of the U.S.S.R. The red hammer-and-sickle flag of the U.S.S.R. was lowered for the last time; in its place was raised the Russian tricolor, originated by Peter the Great in the early eighteenth century. One of Gorbachev's last acts as president of the U.S.S.R. was to phone Bush, who was with his family for Christmas at Camp David. They exchanged official farewells and reminisced about the work they had done together. That evening, Bush went to the White House to deliver a televised address to the nation announcing diplomatic recognition of Russia, Ukraine, and the other former Soviet republics.

Bush had been less than clairvoyant about how hopeless Gorbachev's position was. The Soviet leader was savaged by critics, especially on the right, for failing to support the independence movements among the republics. Still, I believed then, and believe now, that his cautiousness (or "prudence"), along with his dogged support for Gorbachev, had a salutary effect at a dangerous moment and beneficial consequences during the period that followed. In the turbulent months after the failed coup, Bush had assumed the role of a sympathetic, attentive, highly competent air-traffic controller, guiding Gorbachev as he piloted the Soviet Union in for a soft landing on the ash heap of history.

BUSH WASTED NO TIME in establishing good relations with the new man in the Kremlin. In July 1992, when the G-7 gathered for its annual summit in Munich, Yeltsin received the same kind of honored-guest treatment that Gorbachev had enjoyed the previous year, along with $24 billion in economic aid commitments. The political declaration coming out of the summit stressed the opportunity for "former adversaries of East and West" to cooperate on a range of political, economic, and security issues. At a press conference, Bush called Yeltsin's reforms "a tribute to his leadership and vision in working to bring a great country firmly into the family of democratic, market-oriented countries," and welcomed Yeltsin's association with the

* Lithuania had been the first to pull out of the U.S.S.R., more than a year earlier, in March 1990.

G-7: "Now, we are working in concert with our allies. We've got a global economy. It's just not one country that solves a problem. I've believed since I've been president in working multilaterally when it's in our interest and when it can produce the most good, and I'm going to continue to do that."

THE HORROR BEGINS

The Munich G-7 also focused on the need for heightened diplomatic attention to hot spots from the South Caucasus and the Baltics in the former Soviet Union to Africa, Iraq, the Korean peninsula, and the Middle East. But one crisis was already so acute that it required a communiqué of its own: in marked contrast to the relatively peaceful dissolution of the Soviet Union, the disintegration of Yugoslavia was turning increasingly violent, especially in Bosnia. On the basis of a referendum supported by the Muslim majority of the population, the Bosnian government had declared its independence in early March. Croatia and Slovenia had seceded from Yugoslavia a year before. Weeks after the Bosnian move, ethnic Serb forces inside the republic, with support from Belgrade, began shelling Sarajevo and forcibly evicting Muslims from eastern Bosnia. The Muslim-dominated Bosnian government, in an alliance of convenience with ethnic Croats, fought back. But by summer, Serb forces controlled about two-thirds of Bosnian territory.

There were several strains of commentary at the time that I found to be nonsense. One was that there was something poisonous in the air or water—or in the history—of the Balkans that explained why Bosnian Muslims, whose ancestors had converted to Islam, were suddenly subjected to genocidal atrocities. As Brooke and I had seen twenty years earlier, the ethnic groups of the region were perfectly capable of living in harmony. They had spent far more of the past centuries getting along than they had slitting one another's throats. The term that entered the lexicon of the 1990s, *ethnic cleansing*, was technically inaccurate, since, in Bosnia, the victims, like their killers, were Slavs. The "cleansing" was not ethnic—it was cultural, communal, and religious.

Another canard was that Woodrow Wilson bore a large share of blame for the violent breakup of Yugoslavia and the peaceful one of Czechoslovakia (the "velvet divorce"), since both events proved how misguided self-determination was as the basis for a new world order after the Great War. Yet there was nothing in Wilson's strategy to preordain that Yugoslavia and

Czechoslovakia would succumb, first, to fascist occupation in the early forties, then to communist rule for more than four decades afterward. Rather, the double hit of totalitarianism—with its corrosive and stunting effect on political culture—doomed those states.

A related factor triggered the Wars of Yugoslav Secession: the federation suffered from exceedingly bad luck in its leadership during the eighties and nineties. Slobodan Milošević, the Serbian president, was the worst of a bad lot who fell out among themselves. In their free-for-all grab for power and territory, they substituted for the Wilsonian category of South Slavs the idea that Serbs, Croats, Macedonians, and Slovenes were distinct nations, each with their own grievances, their own entitlements to sovereignty, and their own irredentist claims against one another. The communal first person plural—"we Yugoslavs"—gave way to the sectarian "us versus them."

The contrast between Milošević and his ilk on the one hand and Yeltsin and his fellow post-Soviet leaders could not have been starker. While Milošević tried, through a policy of systematic forced expulsion of non-Serbs, to carve a "Greater Serbia" out of the flanks of Croatia and Bosnia, Yeltsin engaged in no such quest for a "Greater Russia" that would include the large numbers of ethnic Russians living outside of Russia. (Ethnic Russians made up 30 percent of the populations in both Latvia and Kazakhstan, 25 percent in Estonia, and 17 percent in Ukraine.) One of the most positive and important of Yeltsin's legacies was a presidential decree that the lines demarcating the republics of the old U.S.S.R. would remain unchanged now that they had become international borders within the Commonwealth of Independent States. If he had done otherwise—that is, if he had turned out to be a Russian Milošević—the result might have been a civil war across eleven time zones, with tens of thousands of nuclear weapons in the mix.

THE VIOLENCE IN YUGOSLAVIA, especially in Bosnia, escalated through the summer and into the fall of 1992. To Washington's relief, the Europeans took the position that they could handle the crisis. A colleague of mine at *Time*, Jef McAllister, got Bush's secretary of state, James Baker, to go on the record with what became the widely quoted judgment, "We don't have a dog in that fight." Baker's memoirs, published three years later, made the same point, though in less folksy terms: "It was time to make the Europeans step up to the plate and show that they could act as a unified power. Yugoslavia was as good a first step as any."[23]

Some critics of the administration's determination to stay on the sidelines recalled Bush's line a year earlier in Kiev about the destructive potential of postcommunist "suicidal nationalism." Bush had made the right point, but at the wrong time and in the wrong place.

Especially with a presidential election looming, Bush and Baker clung to the hope that they could play up the war in Iraq that they had won rather than letting themselves get drawn into an imbroglio in the Balkans where the outcome was far from certain. Bush's strategy of trying to protect his lead coming off his thumping victory in Iraq backfired. By the fall of 1992, Iraq was old news; bad news from Bosnia was in the headlines. Milošević was toying with the Europeans and the UN. His Bosnian Serb henchmen had laid siege to Sarajevo in the spring and killed many of its citizens with artillery shells and sniper fire. The international response was the creation and deployment of a woefully ill-prepared, underequipped entity called UNPRO-FOR, which stood for "United Nations Protection Force," a hodgepodge of units from dozens of countries. The soldiers had neither the weapons nor the authority to deal with well-armed Serbs who were driving women and children into the countryside while rounding up men and boys and putting them into concentration camps.

Clinton went on the political offensive, accusing Bush of being "reactive, rudderless and erratic" in precisely the area where he was supposed to be strongest—managing U.S. interests and defending American values abroad, including, when necessary, destroying faraway monsters.

AS PART OF A LAST-DITCH EFFORT to salvage his campaign in the face of discouraging polls, Bush went to the UNGA on September 21, 1992, and proposed a concerted international effort to strengthen the world body's capacity for peacekeeping and humanitarian operations. He urged that member states designate special military units and stockpile equipment and relief supplies that would be available on short notice at the request of the Security Council. He offered to make the U.S. military bases available for training multinational forces and proposed linking NATO and other regional security structures, including the one that Russia was trying to set up with its former Soviet neighbors, so that they could field peacekeeping troops in support of UN operations. In the peroration of his address, Bush looked out at four of the post-Soviet leaders in the room—Yeltsin, Leonid Kravchuk of Ukraine, Nursultan Nazarbayev of Kazakhstan, and Stanislav Shushkevich of Belarus—and said, "This is the first General Assembly to seat you as truly independent and free nations. And to you and the leaders of the other independent states, I say: welcome home. . . . With the cold war's end, I believe we have a unique opportunity to go beyond artificial divisions of a first, second, and third world to forge instead a genuine global community of free and sovereign nations. . . . Our peace is so interconnected, our security so intertwined, our prosperity so interdependent that to turn inward and retreat from the world is to invite disaster and defeat. . . . let us pledge ourselves to fulfill the promise of a truly United Nations."

The prolonged applause suggested that no one in the chamber that day believed that the forty-first president of the United States suffered from lack of "the vision thing." But for the audience Bush most wanted to impress and persuade—the American electorate—it was already too late.

13

SEIZING THE DAY

This moment of possibilities creates vast opportunities for all our
people. . . . But while progress spreads quickly in our global
neighborhood, problems can, too.
—BILL CLINTON, *June 30, 1997.*[1]

Ol' Boris—we were lucky to have him around for a while. On most
of the big stuff, he did the right thing, and it was almost never the
easy thing for him. I had it easy compared to that guy.
—CLINTON, *April 24, 2007, the day after Boris Yeltsin died.*[2]

RECUSING myself from writing about the 1992 presidential race in
Time was easy enough, since my column appeared in the "World" section of the magazine, and campaign coverage was confined to the
"Nation" section.* What was harder was seeing little of Brooke for nearly ten
months as she traveled around the country with Hillary Rodham Clinton,
who was appearing at rallies, fund-raisers, state fairs, colleges, high schools,
hospitals, and local television and radio stations. A week before the election,
the polls showed Bill Clinton the likely winner. The slogan, "It's the economy,
stupid!" was working: the electorate, like the candidate, was focused on domestic issues. I decided to send a message to the president-presumptive.
Using a friend who was part of his traveling entourage as an intermediary, I
wrote Clinton a memo urging that he surprise everyone by quickly demonstrating that he was as much of a foreign policy president as Bush, and that he

---

* The one exception to my recusal was a two-page column published in the issue of April 6,
1992, when Clinton was a presumed but still undeclared candidate for the presidency. Under
the headline "Clinton and the Draft: A Personal Testimony," I recounted what I remembered
of the facts behind the controversy over how he avoided being drafted, which was causing a
stir in the campaign. I tried to correct what I regarded as mistakes, distortions, and falsehoods
about an episode in Clinton's life that I had observed at close quarters, since we had been sharing a house in Oxford during much of that time.

make the most of new opportunities for multilateralism that came with the end of the cold war, thereby taking advantage of his natural penchant for big-tent politics.[3]

A day or so later, Clinton called from the hustings and left a message on my answering machine at home. His voice was raspy from giving his stump speech a dozen or more times a day, but he sounded chipper. "Got your message," he said. "Got the point too. Actually, already thought of it." Then he added: "Got a deal for you: we win this thing, you get Brooke back." She returned late in the afternoon on Election Day, in time to join me and our sons in front of the television set just as the networks were declaring Clinton the winner on the basis of the exit polls. She fell asleep on the carpet in front of the television long before Clinton gave his victory speech well past midnight.

CLINTON CAME INTO OFFICE eager to try his hand at diplomacy, particularly at the UN. During a meeting in Little Rock in November 1992, when he asked Madeleine Albright to be the U.S. permanent representative, he told her it was the job he had always dreamed of having, second only to the one to which he had just been elected.

The leaders' annual meeting at the UN General Assembly was one of the high points of the year for him. What those of us who worked for him regarded as a chore, he saw as a chance to star in a show he had been watching for years. Forty years after the Cuban missile crisis, Clinton vividly remembered being transfixed by television coverage of Adlai Stevenson presenting the American case to the Security Council. Dag Hammarskjöld was, like John F. Kennedy, one of Clinton's martyred heroes. Hammarskjöld's *Markings*—a mixture of poetry, aphorisms, and mystical musings on nature, religion, ethics, and mortality, published posthumously in a translation by W. H. Auden—made a deep impression on Clinton as an undergraduate at Georgetown. His favorite course in college had been a seminar on the institutions designed to keep the phrase "international law" from being an oxymoron. His political role model then and for years afterward was J. William Fulbright, the longtime chairman of the Senate Foreign Relations Committee. Fulbright instilled in Clinton an appreciation of the UN as an instrument for advancing American interests, leveraging American power, and subjecting American foreign policy to the court of international public opinion.[4]

The UNGA offered Clinton diplomatic one-stop shopping combined with the razzle-dazzle of a political convention. The whole scene suited his perspective and temperament. His tag line for globalization, "We're all in this thing together," could have been the UN's motto. The sheer multitude and diversity of participants in the General Assembly appealed to his curiosity and expansiveness. The near chaos suited his preference for improvisational events over scripted ones. The UN's culture of compromise, conciliation, and polite disagreement meshed with his political technique. Clinton liked to win an argument by pretending there was none. In the eight years I worked for him, there must have been a thousand times when I heard him say "I agree with that," even when he didn't. His way of luring an opponent over to his side was to make a battlefield look like common ground. Variations on that subterfuge—sometimes to keep negotiations from breaking down, sometimes to make sure they went nowhere—were standard UN stratagems. The only complaint I ever heard from Clinton about the UNGA was that the combination of the poor acoustics in the cavernous hall of the General Assembly and the need for simultaneous interpretation made it hard to tell a joke.

WHILE RELISHING THE WHIRL of multilateralism in Turtle Bay, Clinton was at his best in bilateral diplomacy, and in that respect he concentrated on Boris Yeltsin. Even as Clinton prepared to assume the presidency, the subject that interested him most was what was going on in Russia: a nasty political tug-of-war between the forces of reform and the still-powerful remnants of the old Soviet political establishment, which was deeply entrenched in the parliament. However primitive, real politics had come to Russia, and Clinton was champing at the bit to get involved in a way that would help Yeltsin prevail.

I was a beneficiary of the priority that Clinton gave to Russia policy throughout his administration, but starting even before he was inaugurated. In December 1992, at Clinton's suggestion, the secretary of state-designate, Warren Christopher offered me a newly created position in the State Department as Ambassador-at-Large and Special Adviser to the Secretary of State for the New Independent States of the Former Soviet Union. With that cumbersome title came the bureaucratic advantage of being responsible for an area of foreign policy where the president was known to be fully engaged. When domestic aides reminded him of his campaign promises to focus on the U.S. economy, Clinton blew them off, saying, often in so many words, that there was no point in reinvigorating American prosperity "if Russia goes to hell." While Clinton did not use the phrase "new world order," he knew there was one, and he, like Bush, knew it depended on the peaceful integration of the former evil empire into a U.S.-led international system. That gave me, as the administration's point man on Russia policy, an advantage when it came to competing for resources and presidential time.*

Bill Clinton and Boris Yeltsin

One of the first White House meetings I attended after Clinton's inauguration dealt with the upcoming G-7 meeting, which was to be held in Tokyo in July 1993. "We've got to bring Boris aboard this whole G-7 thing," said the president. "If we give him and Russia a seat at the table—make 'em feel that they're still big boys even though they're not big *bad* boys—they'll feel more like they're on our side of history and act accordingly."

Some skeptics, including within the G-7, worried that Yeltsin's bumptious presence would be disruptive and distracting. He did indeed hog the limelight and, in the closed sessions, gave long, booming speeches on multiple subjects. He loved the photo ops and trumpeted his success in getting the G-7 to give Russia a nearly $30 billion package of incentives to help with its transition. Still, the Tokyo summit was unusually productive. The leaders came to an unexpected agreement on how to give an impetus to global trade talks, an issue on which Yeltsin was on the sidelines; and Clinton used his private meeting with Yeltsin to achieve breakthroughs on two nonproliferation issues where Russia was front and center—and had, until then, been stalling. One was stopping the sale of Russian ballistic missile technology to India, which, having refused to join the Non-Proliferation Treaty, was known to be developing nuclear weapons. The other was ensuring that Russia, Ukraine, Belarus, and Kazakhstan—the four newly independent republics of the former U.S.S.R. that had Soviet ICBMs on their territory—agree that Russia alone would remain a nuclear-weapons state. The hardest part of that deal involved getting Ukraine to give up its nuclear arms while getting Yeltsin to guarantee Ukraine's territorial integrity—in effect, to protect Ukraine against Russian irredentists. In both cases, Yeltsin promised in Tokyo to

* I have recounted in *The Russia Hand: A Memoir of Presidential Diplomacy* (New York: Random House, 2002) my impressions of Clinton's political trajectory, as well as my experiences working for him on policy toward the former Soviet Union.

overrule those in his own government who were holding up the necessary agreements.

Six months later, in January 1994, when Clinton made his first trip to Moscow to meet Yeltsin, he pointed out that he was wearing a tie emblazoned with the words *Carpe Diem:* "It's a new day, Boris, and we've got to seize it together." By then I already suspected that, sooner or later, the G-7 would become the G-8. By the time that happened—in 1998, at a summit that Prime Minister Tony Blair hosted in Birmingham, England—the group had continued to broaden its agenda to include combating poverty, drugs, corruption, international crime, and the proliferation of dangerous technology. All those problems would be easier to deal with if Russia were prepared to be part of the solution.

EXPANDING THE MISSION AND MEMBERSHIP of the G-7 was one of several examples of Clinton's attempt to renovate the post–World War II international system. To that end, another major project of his first two years in the White House was preparing and then convening the Summit of the Americas. That event, in Miami in December 1994, brought together thirty-four leaders of the Western Hemisphere for the first time in nearly three decades to discuss cooperative measures on democracy-building, education, security of energy supplies, and efforts to control drug trafficking, strengthen the rights and political empowerment of women, lower trade barriers, and shore up the stability of currencies in the region.

Ten days after the closing ceremony in Miami, the Mexican peso went into free fall, threatening a depression that might spread to neighboring countries. The U.S. Treasury Department pushed through emergency American loan guarantees and a U.S.-brokered package of IMF/World Bank measures that made it possible for the Mexican economy to recover.

Clinton's critics often cited his tendency to let public-opinion polls influence his policies. The vigorous response to the Mexican crisis was a dramatic example of his willingness to push an unpopular but, in his view, vital cause. Surveys showed that Americans opposed the bailout by a margin of more than four to one.[5] The Summit of the Americas also provided an impetus for the North American Free Trade Agreement, which was bitterly opposed by most unions, including the AFL-CIO, and many pro-labor members of Clinton's own party. NAFTA passed in the House of Representatives in 1993 by a vote of 234–200, with a majority of Democrats voting against their president. (The margin in the Senate was safer: 61–38.)

• • •

THE END OF THE COLD WAR created an opportunity to convert the Conference on Security and Cooperation in Europe from a series of occasional meetings into a permanent institution with a wider mandate and greater effectiveness. The CSCE had helped inculcate the values and forms of governance traditionally associated with the West in the countries of the East that were emerging from Soviet communism. A highlight of that process, which had begun under Bush, was an agreement among CSCE member states in 1991 that responsibility to govern democratically and respect human rights "do[es] not belong exclusively to the internal affairs of the state concerned," and that violations of those principles were of legitimate interest to the transatlantic community as a whole.[6] That accord had moved Europe another step away from the old principle of absolute sovereignty, affirmed at Westphalia and in the Congress of Vienna, toward the new principle of "conditional sovereignty," implicit in Basket 3 of the Helsinki Accords sixteen years earlier: what happens inside a country is, if it violates certain basic norms of civilized behavior and governance, the business of outsiders.

In December 1994, Clinton joined fifty-one other heads of state and government in Budapest for a summit at which the CSCE changed its name to the Organization for Security and Cooperation in Europe. In the years that followed, the OSCE took on modest functions in arms control (for example: the removal of land mines and the recovery or destruction of light weaponry such as shoulder-fired rockets that could be used by terrorists to shoot down planes), the enforcement of prohibitions on arms smuggling and trafficking in women, counterterrorism, and measures aimed at building democratic institutions, strengthening the rule of law, and protecting the freedom of the media.

IN ADDITION TO THE GOOD IT DID IN EUROPE, the OSCE served as a model for other regions, especially East Asia. The Australian foreign minister at the time, Gareth Evans, had been promoting an "Asian OSCE" for several years.[7] This was an idea that appealed to Clinton from the day he entered office. During his first trip to Asia as president—the one that took him to Tokyo for the G-7 in July 1993—he gave two speeches promising that the United States would use its influence in the region to support new, more capable and expansive regional mechanisms based, to the extent possible, on existing ones.[8]

That year it was America's turn to host the annual meeting of the Asia-

Pacific Economic Cooperation (APEC) forum, which had grown from its original twelve members to seventeen. Clinton decided to attend himself, thereby establishing by precedent that the event would be elevated from the level of foreign ministers to top leaders. He used the summit—held on Blake Island near Seattle—to give a much needed high-level push to the global trade talks. Over the next five years, APEC would expand to twenty-one members, including Russia.

The other major organization in the Pacific region was the Association of Southeast Asian Nations (ASEAN). For much of the cold war, its original six members had been united by little more than a desire to contain Vietnam. By the nineties, however, Vietnam—though still under Communist rule—was knocking on the door of ASEAN.*

In addition to taking in what had been the pariahs of the neighborhood, ASEAN established an auxiliary grouping that brought together foreign ministers from other Asia-Pacific nations: Australia, China, Japan, New Zealand, South Korea, Russia, and the United States, with the European Union invited to send a representative as well. The ASEAN Regional Forum (ARF) eventually grew to include twenty-six countries. It is as close as the transpacific area has come to replicating the function that the OSCE has performed in the transatlantic region. In the nineties, the ARF focused on economic cooperation and generally steered clear of "interfering" in the internal affairs of its member-states (notably Burma, which has long been under a military dictatorship). Over time, however, the organization began cautiously to take on political and security issues as well and helped defuse several potentially dangerous disputes, such as the one between China and the Philippines over the Spratley Islands in the South China Sea.

After I became deputy secretary of state in early 1994, my job sometimes entailed representing the United States at gatherings of regional organizations, including ones in Africa and Latin America. I found the sessions educational and of some use diplomatically. Preparing for and participating in such a meeting was a crash course in the politics of a part of the world where I had a lot to learn and an opportunity to get to know leaders whom I rarely saw in other settings except for set-piece visits to Washington and in the roiling confusion of the UN General Assembly. But I quickly came to believe that the United States had, for decades, done nowhere near enough to encourage,

---

* ASEAN was founded in 1967 by Indonesia, Malaysia, the Philippines, Singapore, and Thailand. Brunei joined in 1984, Vietnam in 1995, Laos and Burma in 1997, and Cambodia in 1999.

strengthen, consult, and coordinate with these regional organizations on a consistent basis. It would have been in our interest to do so, since had they been more effective and more closely in touch with us, they would have been more helpful when crises broke out in their regions.

THE NEW NATO

While Clinton was always on the lookout for opportunities to buttress the regional components of global architecture, he continued to concentrate his own efforts on the integration of Russia into the principal structures. Over time, that became a harder task. Creating the G-8 and bringing Russia into APEC and the ASEAN Regional Forum was easy, since Yeltsin wanted Russia to join every club there was. Far more difficult was getting the Russian leader to live with an expanding NATO that was not going to include Russia any time in the foreseeable future. Yeltsin represented many of his countrymen in fearing that in consequence if not in intent, the expansion of NATO into central and Eastern Europe would turn former Soviet allies and republics into potential enemies of Russia. His objections struck a chord with the foreign policy establishments on both sides of the Atlantic, where many felt that NATO was a relic of the cold war and should either be retired with honor or frozen in its membership in order to avoid provoking a backlash from Russia. It pained Clinton no less than it did me that as esteemed a figure as George F. Kennan, then well into his nineties, hurled thunderbolts from his study in Princeton at the idea of NATO enlargement, calling it a "strategic blunder of potentially epic proportions" (although we took some solace in recalling that Kennan, in his regret over how containment had acquired what he regarded as an excessively military dimension, had opposed the formation of NATO in the first place—a judgment that had hardly withstood the test of time).[9]

Clinton saw the danger that enlarging NATO would alienate a reforming Russia, but he felt it was offset by several considerations. The states emerging from communism had suffered from Nazi and Soviet occupation in the twentieth century; it would be the worst sort of double jeopardy to leave them in limbo out of deference to Russian paranoia in the twenty-first. Moreover, the security that came with membership in NATO would make the states of central and Eastern Europe less likely to bicker among themselves and more likely to adopt the democratic values and institutions that were the norm within the alliance.

Furthermore, as Helmut Kohl, the chancellor of a now-unified Germany, stressed to Clinton, NATO expansion would prod the European Union to open its own doors to the East. The prospect of membership in the EU would exert a gravitational pull on former Warsaw Pact members similar to the one that the European Community had exerted on Greece, Spain, and Portugal in the 1970s and eighties. Kohl believed that the EU needed more "breadth" (expansion) and "depth" (strengthening of its internal cohesiveness and capacity for a degree of supranational governance).* Since Germany had the strongest economy in Europe, Kohl had a unique position from which to exercise leadership. It also helped that he had a personal bond with Clinton, who believed it was in the United States' interest for the EU to grow and prosper.

Over the course of four years and frequent one-on-one meetings with Yeltsin, Clinton chipped away at the Russian president's resistance to NATO expansion. In early 1997 Clinton finally got Yeltsin to acquiesce. Shortly afterward, the alliance announced its decision to admit the Czech Republic, Hungary, and Poland. Other applicants, including the three Baltic states, were next in line for a future round of expansion. In order to make this painful concession somewhat more palatable for Yeltsin, Clinton negotiated with him a NATO-Russia partnership that took the form of monthly meetings between NATO and Russian ambassadors and military officers, as well as semiannual meetings at the levels of defense and foreign ministers, on topics ranging from peacekeeping in the Balkans to military exchanges, arms control, and counterterrorism. Looking to the future, Clinton was careful not to rule out Russia's own eligibility for the alliance.

Since Russia was largely out of the superpower game, the military competition and the danger of confrontation that had been the backdrop of U.S.-Soviet relations for decades all but disappeared. When Clinton came into office, he was still shadowed by a military aide with the briefcase (known as "the football") containing the codes to launch a nuclear attack, and the Doomsday Plane, a specially outfitted 747, was still standing by at Andrews Air Force Base to serve as an airborne command center in the event of World War III. But containment of Soviet aggressiveness, which had been Job One

---

* There was then, and still is an active debate among European policy experts on whether Europe should emphasize supranational mechanisms (whereby states cede some of their authority to Europe-wide institutions to make decisions on their behalf) or intergovernmental ones (whereby states send representatives to meetings to reach an agreement). In practice, the EU tries to strike a balance between the two concepts rather than choosing one over the other, with security issues generally handled more through the intergovernmental approach and economic and regulatory issues more through the supranational one.

of American foreign policy since the fifties, had given way to the goal of integrating post-Soviet Russia into the community of democracies of which the United States was the leader. Clinton sought to marshal a combination of political influence and economic resources to keep the internal dynamics of Russia and the other former Soviet republics moving in the right direction. In Russia's case, NATO enlargement was an obstacle to that task, but Clinton felt confident he could manage Yeltsin's anxieties.

The challenge of handling Yeltsin suited Clinton's preferred way of dealing with people and problems. What was happening in Russia and its neighborhood, while immensely complex and fraught with uncertainty and difficulty, was still basically good news. As such, it appealed to Clinton as an optimist and a conciliator. He bent Yeltsin to his will by countering the volatile Russian's pugnacity with his own more amiable and subtle brand of stubbornness. Both men knew that Clinton held the high cards. Yeltsin could stamp his feet and turn blue, but there was nothing that he—or Russia—could actually do to stop NATO from taking in new members. In that sense, Clinton's position was a form of stonewalling, although he made it seem (to use one of his favorite metaphors) more like "bridge-building" between the old, failed East and the new, more expansive West.

When we finally sealed, with great difficulty, Russia's acceptance of the terms of its partnership with an expanding NATO, leaders from forty-three countries, including all the former republics of the U.S.S.R., inaugurated the Euro-Atlantic Partnership Council (EAPC), a forum designed to promote consultation and cooperation between NATO and its former adversaries of the Warsaw Pact.*

NATO brought the EAPC together for a giant summit in Madrid in July 1997. There was a sense of something-old, something-new in the occasion. In some respects, it was a late-twentieth-century replica of the grand parleys of the past—Westphalia, the Congress of Vienna, Versailles. But in Madrid, unlike those earlier assemblies, it was not just the great powers gathering to decide the fate of the not-so-powerful. Clinton told the assembled leaders of smaller countries that previously, "The big powers have had the habit of talking about you without you. We're getting away from that way of doing the world's business, and it's about time." As the president was leaving the hall, he commented to Sandy Berger (the national security adviser in the second

---

* The EAPC was the political arm of the Partnership for Peace, a mechanism for military coordination and cooperation that was largely conceived by General John Shalikashvili, who served both as Supreme Allied Commander in Europe and as chairman of the Joint Chiefs of Staff.

term) and me that he liked the idea of being seated at the giant table next to the president of Uzbekistan and across from the leaders of Albania, Armenia, and Azerbaijan.

That evening, Madeleine Albright, who was secretary of state in the second term, and I stopped by the Prado before going to a quiet dinner of tapas at a sidewalk cafe. After a quick look at the Velázquez collection, we moved to the basement, where Goya's "black paintings" were on display. We stood for a while before a picture of a giant, the specter of war, stalking a devastated landscape. We had the same thought: Goya was not just depicting the ravages that Napoleon had inflicted on Spain—he was providing a prophetic glimpse of what was in store for Europe as a whole a hundred years later. If we could build on the progress we were making in consolidating and expanding the transatlantic security community, that continent stood a decent chance of having a peaceful twenty-first century.[10]

WARLORDS

While diplomacy came easily to Clinton, he was far less comfortable with its often indispensable auxiliary, the credible threat of force, especially in the first two years of his presidency. That is one reason why he—and those of us who were advising him—failed to pay more attention, and take more action, with regard to the most conspicuous downside of the end of the cold war: the violent breakup of former communist states, especially Yugoslavia. Clinton had scored points against Bush during the 1992 campaign for "timidity," "turning [the American government's] back on violations of basic human rights" and "being slow on the uptake" in the Balkans. But once in office, Clinton was no more eager than Bush had been to involve the United States in a conflict that was going from bad to worse. By the early spring of 1993, the Bosnian Serbs, backed by Belgrade, controlled two-thirds of Bosnia, and Bosnian Croats and Muslims were fighting each other in the other third. By then, the "CNN effect" had kicked in: public opinion was outraged by broadcasts showing the carnage that the Serbs were inflicting on Sarajevo, Srebrenica, Tuzla, Zepa, Goražde, and Bihać. Despite the warnings of Boutros Boutros-Ghali, the Egyptian secretary-general of the UN, the Security Council had declared these six cities to be "safe areas" but had done nothing to reinforce the UN "protective" force's ability to make either designation anything but a cruel delusion.

In May—four months into his presidency—Clinton sent Secretary of State Christopher to Europe to "consult" with America's allies. This move struck even some of Clinton's own team as excessive multilateralism—or, as many outside the administration put it, a failure to provide the U.S. leadership necessary for multilateralism to be effective.[11]

WHILE DITHERING over whether to use force against the Bosnian Serbs, the United States stumbled into two traps in the fall of 1993—one deadly, the other merely humiliating—that raised questions about whether the new administration even knew *how* to use force.

The first was in Somalia, on the Horn of Africa, where warring clans vied for control over much of the country, including the capital, Mogadishu. By 1992, Somalia was no longer a state in any meaningful sense. It had become, in the phrase of James Traub, a writer for the *New York Times Magazine* and a chronicler of the UN, "a madhouse run by warlords."[12] The UN dispatched an undersized, ill-equipped Pakistani contingent to provide enough security for the delivery of food, medicine, and other forms of aid. In the final, lame-duck months of his presidency, Bush had agreed to join the UN in sending 37,000 troops from thirty-four nations—28,000 of them from the United States—in order to provide security and deliver aid to a population that was starving, largely because of the clan warfare. Unlike the Gulf War nearly two years earlier, which had been in response to aggression and in support of traditional U.S. geopolitical interests, this time—and for the first time—the United States was deploying combat troops in large numbers as part of a multinational force that was authorized under a UN flag to deal with the humanitarian consequences of a civil war.

Bush made this decision largely because of an appeal, with a heavy dose of guilt-tripping, from Boutros-Ghali. The secretary-general said there was growing resentment in the developing world that the United States and other rich, powerful countries were quick to use the UN to make sure that Saddam Hussein did not control Persian Gulf oil, but there was apparently no comparable political will in the West to come to the aid of poor, black Muslims in a country like Somalia. The argument struck a chord with Bush. He authorized what Brent Scowcroft called a "humanitarian-heavy, strategic-light" operation to keep the aid flowing. Scowcroft told Sandy Berger, who was working on the Clinton transition team, that he was hopeful U.S. forces would be out of Somalia by Inauguration Day.[13]

Several months into the new administration, American forces were still in

Somalia. Moreover, they were charged by a series of UN decisions, some of them in the form of Security Council resolutions, with disarming clan militias and laying the groundwork for the reestablishment of civil order. What had begun as a relief effort had morphed into an effort to impose order on chaos—that is, to change the way in which Somalia was governed. It was a textbook case of "mission creep" in a textbook example of a failed state. If the United States was going to take on that task, it would need far more troops of its own, supplemented by a far larger international force.

Rather than going down that road, for which there was neither stomach in the Clinton administration nor support in the Congress, Washington reduced its presence, leaving behind five thousand American troops as part of a UN force that was now all the more vulnerable. In June, the most notorious of the warlords, Mohammed Farah Aideed, killed twenty-six Pakistani peacekeepers in an ambush. The Security Council, prodded by the United States, authorized "all necessary precautions" against further outrages—the equivalent of the Chapter VII use-of-force resolution that had made the Gulf War a UN operation.

The trouble was, this time there was no buildup of overwhelming military might: instead, a 160-man unit of Army Rangers and Delta Force commandos suddenly had been converted into a posse on a manhunt. It was a make-my-day opportunity for Aideed, and his day was October 3, 1993. His private army shot down two U.S. Black Hawk helicopters over Mogadishu and killed eighteen Army Rangers in an extended firefight. Images of the mutilated body of one of the Rangers dominated the news, and a bipartisan congressional chorus demanded that America get out.

Clinton, like most presidents, had a mental map of the world with regions and countries color-coded according to whether they were primarily of humanitarian or geopolitical concern. The Horn of Africa was in the first category. Unlike Latin America, it was far away; unlike the Middle East, it was not a vital source of oil; unlike Europe, it was not covered by a U.S.-led alliance. Clinton, like Bush before him, believed that the U.S.-led international community had an obligation to prevent famine and human misery in Somalia. But once a relief mission had turned into a shootout with warlords, fatal to American soldiers, Clinton decided to cut America's losses. The president made a bad situation worse by saying—at the UN, no less—that the organization should learn to say "no" to operations of this kind. He was trying to shield himself from withering Republican criticism. But the effect was to make it look as though he was siding with UN-bashers in Congress in blaming the organization itself for what had happened rather than accepting responsibility for American—and presidential—decisions that had allowed the debacle to occur.

By April 1994, all U.S. troops had been withdrawn. Kofi Annan—the UN's undersecretary-general for peacekeeping—feared that the lesson the Aideeds of this world would draw from the incident was that "the easiest way to disrupt a peacekeeping operation is to kill Americans."[14]

Or, he might have added, humiliate them.

Eight days after the Black Hawks went down in Mogadishu, a long-simmering crisis in Haiti boiled over. Two years before, in 1991, a military junta had overthrown Jean-Bertrand Aristide, a former priest who was the first democratically elected president in Haiti's history, and driven him into exile. Bush had applied a combination of economic sanctions and political pressure. The Clinton administration was no more effective using essentially the same tactics. On October 11, 1993, an American warship, the USS *Harlan County,* tried to bring engineers to Haiti to help rebuild the infrastructure that had been destroyed in the violence that had occurred since the coup. This mission was to be the first step in a UN-brokered plan to increase international pressure on the military junta to give up power and allow the return of Aristide. The ship never made it to the pier in Port-au-Prince. It was turned away by a jeering, rock-throwing pro-junta mob. One of its chants was "We are going to turn this into another Somalia!"

By the spring of 1994, the deteriorating situation in Haiti was contributing to a domestic political crisis in the United States. As many as a thousand Haitians a day were fleeing the island in rickety boats, trying to make the nearly six-hundred-mile trip to Florida. Hundreds drowned or died of dehydration. The Congressional Black Caucus and human rights advocates were hammering the administration to do something. I was part of a team from Washington that dashed around the region trying to cajole governments into accepting refugees. We did our best to seem dignified, or at least not desperate. I doubt we succeeded. My only trip to Cuba as a government official was that spring, when my friend and counterpart at the Pentagon, Deputy Secretary of Defense John Deutch, arranged for the U.S. naval base at Guantánamo Bay to convert facilities into housing for ten thousand refugees. That number soon doubled, but the ability of the base to accommodate all those prisoners did not.*

---

* Guantánamo Bay had served as a landing point for U.S. Marines and Cuban forces fighting against the Spanish in 1898. After the war, the United States was given a lease over the area.

At one point when Clinton was coping simultaneously with Bosnia, Soma-lia, and Haiti, he remarked to me, with a wan smile, "Boy, do I ever miss the cold war." I reminded him that if the cold war had continued, he would never have become president. "Yeah, yeah, I know," he said. "I'm just saying we've traded in one big problem for a whole bunch of little ones. But they sure don't feel little when they're blowing up in your face."[15]

The world was rife with such explosive conflicts. The United States had neither the will nor the way to defuse all of them. Nor did the United Nations. A recurring challenge of the 1990s was identifying those that deserved prior-ity, by dint of the human cost if the international community did not act ef-fectively. Africa, in the first year of the Clinton administration, had been the scene of one such challenge. That continent provided us with another in our second year—this time, unlike in Mogadishu, with no loss of American lives but with vast loss of African ones.

GENOCIDE

Nearly every working day that I was in government began with an intelli-gence briefing on troubles brewing around the world. In theory, it was part of what was supposed to be an early-warning system, so that policymakers, in addition to being updated on ongoing challenges to American interests, could be alerted to ones that might be averted. In practice, the system often failed for a combination of two reasons: intelligence officials, who had the most sophisticated technical resources at their disposal but no crystal ball, failed to bring dangerous developments to the attention of policymakers, or policymakers failed to act on the information they received.

In the spring of 1994, Africa bore close watching for a number of reasons. One breaking story was welcome: in South Africa, preparations were under way for Nelson Mandela to be sworn in as president, marking his country's transformation from an outcast to a regional leader and, potentially, a major player in the world.

There was plenty of bad news as well. I dimly remember being briefed on ominous events in Rwanda, but I did not spend much time probing the roots of the conflict or asking for scenarios on how it might unfold. Like most offi-cials at my level and above, I was concentrating on Haiti and Bosnia. Insofar as my peripheral vision took in Africa, I was concerned about the harrowing, not to mention ignominious, withdrawal of the last American troops from

Somalia. On their way out, they were in danger of being attacked by Aideed and the other warlords.

Later, after the fact, when the magnitude of what had happened in Rwanda finally sunk in, it pained me to recall a line for which Neville Chamberlain, speaking in 1938 about the crisis precipitated by Nazi Germany's takeover of the Sudetenland in Czechoslovakia, will be forever remembered: "a quarrel in a faraway country between people of whom we know nothing."

The brief mention of European colonial and mandatory rule in Rwanda in Chapter 8 of this book—about the League of Nation's divvying up of imperial holdings in Africa—contains more than I knew on that subject when I entered the State Department after a twenty-year career in writing about international affairs. Only when it was too late did I learn something about Hutus, the Tutsis, and the uneasy, sometimes volcanically violent relations between them.

After the UN pressured Belgium to grant Rwanda independence in 1962, a Hutu nationalist government came to power in an election. With its protection, Hutu mobs killed some twenty thousand Tutsis and drove ten times that number out of the country. That gave the Tutsis a score of their own to settle. Starting in the mid-1980s, they began cross-border raids back into Rwanda. A full-fledged civil war flared in 1990. With help and encouragement from the United States and France, the Organization of African Unity—a regional body established in 1962 to eradicate colonialism and promote solidarity on the continent—brokered a fragile peace accord in 1993. But the principal consequence of the agreement was to provoke Hutu hard-liners to form militias and use government-run radio and television stations to urge the Hutu majority to take action before again being "enslaved" by the Tutsi "cockroaches."

In April 1994, unidentified extremists shot down a plane carrying the Hutu president of Rwanda, Juvénal Habyarimana, who was flying home from a conference in Tanzania that had been intended to conclude yet another agreement on Hutu-Tutsi reconciliation. Habyarimana was killed in the crash. So was the president of Burundi—Cyprien Ntaryamira, who was also a Hutu. A UN peacekeeping force of 2,500 that had trickled into Rwanda since the previous October had neither the manpower nor the authority to quell the Hutu-on-Tutsi violence that followed. The inadequacy of the UN presence was in part a result of American policy. The United States, with its hands full (and burned) in Somalia, resisted proposals by the UN's department of peacekeeping operations for a more robust force of up to eight thousand soldiers. Nigeria was willing to deploy a significant contingent if the United States had agreed to provide airlift and make armored personnel carriers available. The Clinton administration, in the midst of its post-Mogadishu trauma, refused.

During the eruption of violence that followed the downing of the Rwandan president's plane, a legacy of Belgian rule—compulsory identification cards for all Rwandans identifying them by tribe—helped Hutu militiamen manning checkpoints decide whom to shoot or hack to death with machetes. Fifteen UN troops, including ten Belgian, were sent to the home of the moderate Tutsi prime minister, Agathe Uwilingiyimana, to escort her to Radio Rwanda so that she could broadcast an appeal to the nation for calm. Outnumbered and operating under highly restrictive "rules of engagement," the blue helmets were captured by Hutus, who tortured and assassinated the prime minister, then murdered and mutilated the ten Belgians.

Just as Kofi Annan had feared, the Hutus had learned a lesson from Aideed: a Mogadishu-like incident would prompt Western troops to withdraw. Most of the participating states pulled out, leaving a unit of about five hundred that was supposed to symbolize the international community's concern but in fact symbolized its impotence.

I arrived in Brussels on NATO business just as the bodies of the murdered Belgian soldiers were coming home. "And they call this *peacekeeping!*" said one of my colleagues in the foreign ministry.

American officials who spoke to the press during the spring of 1994 avoided using the word *genocide* to describe what was happening in Central Africa. Even after Boutros-Ghali used the word himself in May, it remained virtually taboo in Washington. Administration lawyers warned that American official utterance of those three syllables might trigger an obligation on the part of the United States and all other signatories to enforce the 1948 UN Convention on the Prevention and Punishment of the Crime of Genocide. We were hesitant to make good on that piece of international law in a region that the United States had almost never considered of vital national interest. A brief and limited exception had been during the cold war, when the Soviets and their allies made inroads in Congo, Somalia, Ethiopia, and Angola. But even then, rather than intervening directly, the United States sought to undermine Moscow-backed regimes through proxies. We had no proxies, in Africa, Europe, or anywhere else, to stop the killing in Rwanda.

That was at least part of the explanation for what happened—and what did not happen—in Rwanda. But it was not an excuse. In less than six months, Africa had been the scene of two blights on the UN's record and on the Clinton administration's as well. The first, in Somalia, had been largely the result of the UN and the United States trying to do too much, but without sufficient force. The second, in Rwanda, was the result of all outside parties doing too little too late.

Over the course of a hundred days, more than eight hundred thousand Rwandans—mostly members of the Tutsi minority but also tens of thousands of moderate Hutus who opposed the extremists—were slaughtered. That toll constituted 11 percent of the population of the country and 84 percent of Rwanda's Tutsis. The militias raped a quarter of a million women and children, leaving many of them HIV-positive.

In June, the French intervened with UN Security Council backing and U.S. assent. They were supposed to create small "safe zones" (foreigners, mostly white, had already been evacuated). Many of the *genocidaires* were able to make it over the border into Zaire (formerly Congo), where they raised hell for years afterward.[16]

FOR KOFI ANNAN, who was still in the post of undersecretary-general for peacekeeping, the Rwanda catastrophe was a personal as well as an institutional trauma. A Ghanaian, Annan had, in his youth, been greatly influenced by the Congolese leader Patrice Lumumba as a champion of Africa's liberation from colonialism and as a believer in "progressive nation-building."[17] Once he began his career in the UN system, Annan became an equally ardent admirer of Dag Hammarskjöld, particularly for Hammarskjöld's willingness to intervene personally—and, as it turned out, at the cost of his life—in African civil strife. But by his own admission, Annan, like American policymakers, let the fresh memory of the humiliation in Mogadishu obliterate serious consideration of another humanitarian intervention in an even more remote region of Africa where the situation was even more inflamed than it had been in Somalia. An independent postmortem of the episode went further, faulting Annan's peacekeeping department for allowing bureaucratic, legalistic, and political considerations to stand in the way of pressing the Security Council to take action.[18]

For Bill Clinton, too, the episode was, and I believe always will be, a source of remorse. In March 1998, four years after the war, he visited Rwanda and told a group of survivors, "We in the United States and the world community did not do as much as we could have and should have done." He was slammed from the right for apologizing and from the left for not apologizing enough.

As late as 2007, six years after he had left office and thirteen years after the genocide, he still obsessed about what he had publicly called "the greatest regret" of his administration. On several occasions, I would be talking to him on some entirely unrelated subject—American politics, our shared concern about developments in Russia and Iraq, Hillary's chances for winning the nomination and the presidency, our children and their careers—and out of the blue, Clinton would suddenly say something like, "Explain to me again why we blew it in Rwanda." Fortunately, he did not give me a chance for a reply, since I had no good one. Instead, he would rattle off a series of rhetorical questions: "Couldn't we have gone in there and stopped the killing rather than dealing with it as a refugee crisis after the fact? Okay, so we didn't have our eye on the ball early enough. But once we knew what was going on, even if we came in late, couldn't we have saved a lot of those people? And couldn't we have shut down those damn radios that were stirring up all that hate and vengeance? And rather than just evacuating all the whites, couldn't we have protected the people we were leaving behind?"

There was no simple answer to any of Clinton's questions, to say nothing of the whole barrage. A plausible scenario for what we might have done to avoid or mitigate the disaster and the shame would have to be contingent on numerous other what-might-have-beens: we might have risen to the challenge if we had received better, more timely, more foresighted reporting from the region; if we had given prompt, high-level attention to the reports we received; if there had been readily available, experienced, well-equipped peacekeepers and the means to transport them to Africa from other continents; if there had been willing, capable African national governments and institutions on which to draw for political, diplomatic, and military support; and if the most powerful countries in the international community had treated Africa as fully part of that community and therefore treated its people, when they were slaughtering each other, as subject to protection for the victims and punishment for the perpetrators. All those prerequisites were missing, notably the last one.[19]

14

HARD POWER

The world in all doth but two nations bear—
The good, the bad, and these mixed everywhere.
—*ANDREW MARVELL*[1]

This was genocide in the heart of Europe—not in 1945, but in 1995.
Not in some grainy newsreel from our parents' and grandparents'
time, but in our own time, testing our humanity and our resolve.
—*BILL CLINTON*[2]

UNLIKE the crisis in Rwanda, the two others facing the Clinton administration in the spring of 1994 both fell within the traditional scope of American vital interests. Haiti was a hemispheric neighbor, and the remnants of Yugoslavia were "over there," in Europe, where the United States had spent much of the twentieth century trying to protect the locals from external enemies and, it often seemed, rescuing them from the demons of their history.

In the course of 1994, Clinton responded to the military regime in Haiti in a way reminiscent of the three-stage approach George H. W. Bush had used in liberating Kuwait from Iraq in 1991: the application of diplomatic pressure, combined with sanctions; the mobilization of political support from global and regional organizations; and the buildup of an international armed force, with the United States at its head, in case diplomacy and sanctions failed.

But in a key respect, the test that Clinton faced in the Caribbean was different from the one Bush had faced in the Gulf. Saddam's invasion of Kuwait had been a classic case of one state committing aggression against another. It was a clear-cut violation of the law of nations and the UN Charter. That made it relatively easy for Bush to elicit the support of the UN and America's

NATO allies, who contributed forces to Operations Desert Shield (the defense of Saudi Arabia) and Desert Storm (the eviction of Iraqi forces from Kuwait).

By contrast, the coup against Aristide and the ensuing violence against his supporters belonged in the realm of the internal affairs of a member state of the UN. That made the junta no less deserving of international protests and economic sanctions—comparable, say, to those imposed on the apartheid regime of South Africa in the 1970s and '80s. Yet the Bush administration had gone further. The coup, James Baker vowed, "will not stand"— a deliberate echo of Bush's public response to Saddam Hussein's invasion of Kuwait.

Throughout the summer of 1994, the Clinton administration worked to get an international consensus in favor of moving against the junta. We concentrated on the Organization of American States. Meanwhile, in New York, Madeleine Albright, then our permanent representative at the UN, worked for two months on a resolution authorizing a military operation led by the U.S. to restore the democratically elected leadership of Haiti. On July 31, 1994, the measure was approved by a vote of 12-0. China abstained, which was the best we could hope for. Even better, Russia actually voted with us.[3]

During one of my trips to New York shortly afterward, Albright and I went out to dinner at a Chinese restaurant near the UN and talked about the importance of Resolution 940. She and I both saw it against the backdrop of several watershed moments in history when international bodies had asserted the right to interfere in the domestic affairs of individual states. The one most on our minds was the Helsinki Final Act of 1975, which gave the West a mechanism for bringing pressure to bear on communist regimes that were violating the human rights of their citizens. The UN's resolution on Haiti, like those that authorized humanitarian relief missions in northern Iraq after the Gulf War and in Somalia, went much further—from finger-wagging to use of the fist. A condition of cruelty or chaos *inside* a country could now qualify, under Chapter VII of the Charter, as a legitimate reason for military intervention.

THOSE OF US RESPONSIBLE FOR HAITI POLICY were well aware that driving the military dictators out was going to be the easy part of the job. Restoring Aristide to the presidential palace in Port-au-Prince would leave Haiti with a dysfunctional governing apparatus and the danger of resistance and chaos. As a result, the United States, along with its international partners, would have to provide security and administration until Aristide could reestablish control. Therefore we went in "heavy," with 21,000 troops—more than enough to maintain security. As a result, we suffered no combat casualties. During the long run-up to what the Pentagon dubbed "Operation Restore Democracy," a large, well-integrated, highly collaborative interagency team spent many more hours planning for the enforcement of a security regime and the establishment of an interim administration—that is, an occupation authority—than for the invasion itself. Sandy Berger, who, as deputy national security adviser in the first term, often chaired these meetings, had a mantra: "Planning for the postwar is as important as planning for the war itself. If we lose the postwar, it doesn't matter if we win the war."

The first wave to sweep over Haiti was a multinational force (MNF), not a blue-helmeted UN Peacekeeping Operation (PKO). The difference is important, and it carries with it a major lesson about how to overcome the weakness of PKOs that are assigned the task of keeping the peace where conflict has either begun or is imminent. The answer is to combine the legitimizing and convening power of the UN with the military power of member states that are prepared to contribute battle-ready troops. An MNF is authorized by the Security Council but assembled and deployed outside the UN's decision-making structure. The units involved are under a system of command that is determined by the coalition's leading members, whereas the operational details of a PKO—what the rules of engagement are, how orders are approved and carried out, which states are supposed to contribute units of what kind, how to pay for the whole operation—have to be worked out within the UN itself, a process that tends to be cumbersome, time-consuming, and inefficient.

In Haiti, twenty-seven nations contributed small units totaling 2,000 troops to the American core of 21,000. The operation as a whole was under American command. Six months later, the majority of the MNF was gone, replaced by the blue helmets of a PKO, still led by an American general but consisting of only 6,000 troops. By then, the hard work in Haiti had fallen to the UN special envoy, Lakhdar Brahimi, an Algerian diplomat who was studiedly gentle in manner but dogged in working the problem at hand. Brahimi and his team of about four hundred UN specialists and locals worked with relentless patience to coax Aristide and the various Haitian factions into some semblance of normal politics and also to rebuild and supervise the police force, document human rights abuses, provide medical aid, and help displaced persons return to their homes.

On my fairly frequent trips to the troubled nation, my admiration for Brahimi was matched only by my exasperation with Aristide and his rivals, who seemed bent on destroying one another, at least politically, even at the risk of whatever chance there was of "restoring"—that is, establishing for the first time in Haiti's history—a functioning democracy. By then, the U.S. Congress was under the control of the Republicans, many of whom disdained this sort of high-minded but expensive, often risky interventionism and were eager either to cut or restrict appropriations for Haiti. In 1996, the United States turned over command of the peacekeeping force to Canada and withdrew all but a handful of American troops.

IN THE MONTHS AND YEARS that followed, the situation in Haiti slipped back into civil unrest and corrupt, incompetent, often violent politics. To borrow a phrase associated with a mistake our successors made in Iraq, we prematurely declared that our mission had been accomplished.

Part of the problem was that we underestimated the difficulty of establishing democracy in a country that had never really had such a thing. In this respect, we were neglecting a lesson of history: nations build themselves, and democracy emerges slowly and iteratively; outsiders can only encourage the process. Haiti never had any experience of stable, pluralistic political culture, and its experience of American intervention earlier in the twentieth century (under Woodrow Wilson, no less) was far from salutary.* Aristide had come to power in a free and fair election, but that neither made Haiti a democracy nor made him a democrat. Once we returned him to office, he proved too incompetent, stubborn, vindictive, and authoritarian to form a sustainable indigenous government with widespread support—and Haiti became an example of what Fareed Zakaria has called an "illiberal democracy."[4]

While marginally better off than it had been under the military dictatorship we had sent packing, Haiti, under Aristide and his successors, wallowed

* In 1915, after an outbreak of political violence in Haiti, the United States invaded and occupied the country for the next nineteen years. While the Americans tried to import an American-style liberal constitution, build educational and public-health facilities, and improve infrastructure, the occupation had many negative consequences: it disrupted society, enriched and empowered various unsavory figures and factions, and fed a nationalist insurgency, which in turn triggered brutal reprisals and repression by the U.S.-backed government.

in stagnation, then lapsed into violence, and remained a nagging problem for years to come.*

THE CLINTON ADMINISTRATION SHOULD NOT HAVE left Haiti to its own devices and its deeply flawed leadership, thereby allowing an initial success to turn into a failure. There are at least two explanations for why we made that mistake, and they both stood as a warning to us for the remainder of our time in office and should have done the same for those who came after us.

The first is that the United States suffers from what seems to be a chronic attention deficit disorder with regard to its own neighborhood. When thinking geopolitically, Americans tend to look east and west, but rarely south. Only when all hell breaks loose in Latin America or the Caribbean—when Castro takes power in Cuba, or a Marxist wins the presidency in Chile, or the Sandinistas take over in Nicaragua, or the Mexican economy is on the brink of collapse—does that region loom large on the American radar screen.

The second explanation is a lamentable but enduring reality of the world of policymaking: the tendency of the urgent to drive out the merely important. The reconstruction of Haiti was, for a while, recognized to be very important indeed. But the nearly simultaneous meltdown of Yugoslavia was truly urgent, not least because it was in Europe, where Americans are much more inclined to see vital interests at stake.

Nation-building might, more accurately though cumbersomely, be described as the intervention of a U.S.-led military coalition to take over a failed state or a nation misruled by a rogue regime until it can become, either once again or for the first time, a normal country, capable of fending for itself and governing itself decently. By whatever name, it is a long-term job, even for a superpower with adequate help from the rest of the world.[5]

Since I was involved in both Haiti and Balkan policy, I experienced firsthand the sense of being worn down by the demands that these two ongoing crises, 5,500 miles apart, made on our government. Long meetings on Haiti in the windowless Situation Room in the basement of the West Wing of the White House would, with the briefest of coffee and bathroom breaks, turn

---

* In 2004, an uprising, combined with pressure from the United States and France, forced Aristide back into exile. An interim government was replaced by an elected leadership, and the UN deployed a "stabilization force" to Haiti. But the country continued to suffer from chronic violence, principally between rival gangs and political groups, and the UN described the human-rights situation as "catastrophic."

into long meetings on Bosnia. The human factor—the limits of individual energy, the toll that exhaustion takes on the capacity for clear-headed decision-making—is often underestimated by diplomatic and military historians, but not by veterans of diplomacy and war.

In those seemingly interminable meetings, we had to switch gears from one "situation" to the other and think our way through multiple dimensions of what we had to do to get it right.

WITH BOSNIA, AS WITH HAITI, the Clinton administration had to make the case to the American public and to Congress that what was happening was not just a humanitarian catastrophe and an offense to American values, but also a threat to international peace and security and, as such, to American interests. The horrors under way in Bosnia amounted, after all, to a civil war, or at least could be depicted that way. Milošević was abetting the Bosnian Serbs in their massacres, but he was not committing aggression as flagrant as Saddam's in Kuwait.

As with Haiti, we relied heavily on the UN for support in Bosnia—too heavily, from the standpoint of many who were justifiably impatient with the pace and degree of international action. The French and the British were merely reluctant to threaten force, while the Russians were adamantly opposed to the idea. They regarded the Serbs, who were fellow Orthodox Slavs, as a kindred nationality, and were deeply suspicious of the Bosnian Muslims, not least because Russians worried about separatist tendencies among some of their own Muslim minorities. For all these reasons, they recoiled at the prospect of military action by NATO in the Balkans, especially now that NATO was moving toward admitting new members from the ranks of former Soviet allies in Central and Eastern Europe. The best we could hope for was to keep the Russians sullen but not mutinous. We devised a strategy to include them in the diplomacy as much as possible and dissuade them from vetoing UN authorization of the use of force. Clinton worked hard on Yeltsin in their frequent personal meetings and phone calls, while the State Department created an ad hoc mechanism, known as the "Contact Group," that included Russia along with the United States and key Western European countries in the application of diplomatic pressure on Milošević.

Diplomacy was accompanied by what the press and the Bosnians derided as "pinprick" NATO air strikes against Serb weapons depots and an airfield from which Serb planes were flying missions against UN safe areas (NATO pilots had instructions to bomb only the runway and not the warplanes nearby). The result was worse than nothing, since the Serbs concluded that if this was the most that the mightiest alliance in history could do, they had nothing to worry about. Rather than giving a UN peacekeeping operation the capability to become a peace-enforcing operation, NATO had allowed itself to be afflicted with the weakness that had, for decades, been the bane of so many UN peacekeeping activities, in Africa and elsewhere. Somehow, we had to find a way of combining what Joseph Nye, a Harvard political scientist who was working in the Clinton administration, had dubbed, in 1990, "hard power," the ability to force others to do what you want (through economic pressure and military means), with "soft power," the ability to induce them to want what you want (through reliance on diplomacy, an appeal to universal values, and a respect for the principles of international law).[6]

DURING THIS PERIOD, I felt like a punching bag in meetings I held with private citizens, many of them personal friends and former colleagues, whose exasperation with the inadequacy of the American response in Bosnia matched their indignation over outrages the Serbs were perpetrating. Among the most vociferous and eloquent of these visitors to my office were the financier and philanthropist George Soros, Mort Abramowitz (a Foreign Service officer who had gone on to be the president of the Carnegie Endowment for International Peace and a founder of the International Crisis Group, which monitors and advocates action to deal with conflicts around the world), and Paul Wolfowitz (a high-powered official in several Republican administrations who was, in the nineties, the dean of the Johns Hopkins School of Advanced International Studies). The diversity of that trio underscored how domestic pressure to move beyond pinpricks was rising across the political and ideological spectrum.

In late May 1995, Serb forces captured nearly four hundred UN peacekeepers and held them for weeks as human shields, thereby holding NATO in check; just to make sure that the message got out to the world, the Serbs handcuffed Spanish peacekeepers to a bridge for the benefit of a CNN camera crew. Emboldened by the success of such tactics, Serb troops overwhelmed Srebrenica in July. They took hostage some blue-helmeted Dutch troops and executed some seven thousand unarmed Muslim men and boys. The victims had been led to believe, right up to the point that they were rounded up for extermination, that they were under the protection of the United Nations and NATO.

As had been the case during the Rwanda bloodbath and for the same reason—to avoid triggering an obligation to intervene effectively—the U.S. government avoided calling the crime genocide.

MORE IMPORTANT THAN WORDS, however, was action, and finally there was some. I joined Warren Christopher, his undersecretary for political affairs, Peter Tarnoff, and his chief of staff, Tom Donilon, in convincing the White House that a problem as big as Bosnia required a problem-solver as experienced, energetic, and determined as Richard Holbrooke. Detractors and admirers alike compared him to a hurricane. God help anyone who got in his way. We wanted to put Milošević in the path of this particular storm.

Christopher brought Holbrooke, then ambassador to Germany, back to Washington as assistant secretary of state for Europe in 1994 and made him chief negotiator for Bosnia in 1995. In that capacity, Holbrooke was both the good cop and the bad cop. He synchronized a stepped-up effort to negotiate a peace with preparations to use NATO air power much more forcefully. In late August, just as Holbrooke was on his way to the region, the Bosnian Serbs fired a mortar into a market in downtown Sarajevo, killing at least thirty-five people. I took a call from Muhamed Sacirbey, the pugnacious, thoroughly Americanized foreign minister of Bosnia. "No more fucking around with the UN!" he shouted at me over the phone. "You people have to bring in NATO air strikes *now*!"

Two days later, we were ready to do so. By then we were heading into the Labor Day weekend, and the president and his Cabinet were all on vacation. That left the deputies in the various departments and agencies in charge. Fortunately, a deputy was in charge at the UN as well. Boutros-Ghali was traveling at the time, leaving the organization temporarily under the command of Kofi Annan. His searing experience in Rwanda had led him to understand better than Boutros-Ghali that the use of force was sometimes a necessary prelude to peacekeeping. Madeleine Albright asked me to make several calls to Annan to reinforce her efforts with him to ensure that NATO could launch air strikes without being second-guessed by UN officials back in New York.

Warplanes based in Italy and aboard the aircraft carrier *Theodore Roosevelt* in the Adriatic began Operation Deliberate Force. They pounded Serb artillery positions and ammunition depots for two days. Finally, the United Nations and the United States had agreed on the division of labor necessary to force Milošević to the negotiating table: the UN would keep up the diplomatic pressure while the U.S. armed forces, with allied help, applied the muscle. We were late in doing so, but not too late to establish a peace that the UN could then keep.

MILOŠEVIĆ JOINED THE PRESIDENTS of Croatia and Bosnia, Franjo Tudjman and Alija Izetbegović (accompanied by Sacirbey), along with representatives of the United States, the European Union, and Russia (i.e., the Contact Group), in peace talks that began on November 1, 1995. Holbrooke, who masterminded the negotiations, chose as a venue Wright-Patterson Air Force Base outside Dayton, Ohio. It was isolated enough from Washington to make it harder for the Balkan leaders to use press leaks to jockey for position, yet close enough to Washington for senior administration figures—in particular, Warren Christopher and Tony Lake, the president's national security adviser in the first term—to make appearances if they were needed to prod the process.

I made the trip only once, even though Holbrooke liked to tease me that he had picked Dayton as a way of getting me back to my birthplace, which I had not visited for some years. My principal activity in those days was bouncing back and forth across the Atlantic to consult with our European allies and persuade the Russians to warn the Serbs that they would face a resumption of bombing if they misbehaved in Dayton. The Russians could also help induce the Balkan parties to make peace by offering them the carrot of cheap oil and gas. Therefore Holbrooke asked me to come to Dayton in early November 1995 to demonstrate that the administration was coordinating its Russia policy with his orchestration of the talks. Brooke joined me for the trip. During a fancy dinner in the rooftop dining room at the Dayton Racquet Club, she found herself seated between Milošević and Izetbegović, whose fellow Muslims Milošević's minions were slaughtering. Izetbegović, dour under the best of circumstances, was practically catatonic, while Milošević turned on the charm. He reminisced to Brooke about his career as a "businessman and banker," explained in detail how hard he was working to maintain regular electricity supplies for his beleaguered citizens, and inquired solicitously about what specialties of Serbian cooking Brooke had most enjoyed when we lived in Belgrade.

When the Dayton talks were formally in session, the parties insisted on interpreter booths for simultaneous translation of the proceedings into Serbian, Croatian, and Bosnian, as though these were separate languages, mutually unintelligible to the participants. Serbo-Croatian, the common language of the old Yugoslavia had officially ceased to exist when the country broke up. It was diplomatic theater of the absurd, advertising to the world not the legitimacy but the speciousness of the delegations' claims to be representing separate nations.*

After three weeks of suspense, histrionics, threatened walkouts, and a combination of cajolery and jawboning by Holbrooke, the parties agreed to a deal that would keep the country whole as a federation but with autonomous governments for Serbs, who controlled 49 percent of the territory, and for the Muslims and Croats, who jointly controlled 51 percent. Nearly 60,000 NATO troops, including 20,000 Americans, replaced the UN peacekeepers to enforce the accords and maintain stability. A variety of international organizations divided up the other tasks: the UN High Commissioner for Refugees took the lead on humanitarian issues; a UN tribunal was established to try those accused of war crimes; the OSCE supervised disarmament and elections; the International Committee of the Red Cross took charge of prisoner-of-war and missing-persons issues; and the World Bank and European Union provided funds to rebuild destroyed infrastructure and institutions.

THE SITUATION FACING US in the Balkans was more complicated and dangerous than the one in Haiti. The Bosnian population was split into communal factions. Having been at war with one another for years, the combatants were heavily armed and supported by outsiders. After years of violence and virtually no experience of democracy, the people of Bosnia were unlikely to settle naturally or quickly into normal politics. With sufficient international support and monitoring, we hoped that the elections might qualify as "free and fair," but the governing structures that they produced were unlikely to meet that standard any time soon, since Bosnian warlords-turned-politicians would remain a thuggish lot.

As in Haiti, we had pursued diplomacy in Bosnia on one track, prepared for military action on another, and tried to imagine everything that could go wrong with an occupation and everything we could do to preempt or at least manage those difficulties. Unlike in Haiti—and in part because of the sobering experience we had had there—we recognized in advance of military ac-

---

* While there were minor regional differences in dialect and diction between the two components of Serbo-Croatian, the principal difference was that the language used in Serbia was written in the Cyrillic alphabet, and the one used in Croatia was written in the Latin alphabet.

tion that the United States and its international partners would have to maintain a significant presence in Bosnia for a long time. Those partners included the Russians, who agreed to provide troops as part of a U.S.-led NATO operation.

THE EXPERIENCE IN BOSNIA further solidified Clinton's already strong multilateralist instincts. It also highlighted how important it was that the key institutions with which we had the most influence, NATO and the UN, be led by individuals who shared our concept of "diplomacy backed by force." Over time, that phrase acquired a talismanic quality for the administration. With Haiti and Bosnia in mind, Clinton had foreshadowed the principle in his first Inaugural Address: "When our vital interests are challenged, or the will and conscience of the international community is defied, we will act; with peaceful diplomacy whenever possible, with force when necessary."[7] Diplomacy backed by force implied a de facto collaboration between the UN, as the body that could confer legitimacy on the use of force, and NATO as the best means of applying it.

Precisely because of the value that the UN and NATO had for the United States, we were not reticent about exerting our clout in Turtle Bay and Brussels, even though we knew that our handling of two key personnel appointments would cause our allies to complain that we were throwing our weight around to an obnoxious extent.

In 1995, the secretary general of NATO, Willy Claes, a low-key but hard-working and skillful Belgian, had to resign because of a domestic political scandal. Several European governments favored Ruud Lubbers, a former Dutch prime minister, to be Claes's successor. Lubbers flew to Washington for a job interview over a working lunch with Warren Christopher. He flunked. Christopher found that Lubbers was given to long theoretical musings. He did little to hide his distaste for the idea that NATO might ever be called upon to apply force. He made virtually no reference to the central role of the United States in NATO, suggesting that he regarded the alliance as an almost entirely European institution.

The U.S. government threw its weight behind Javier Solana, the foreign minister of Spain. He went on to be superb both at NATO and, after that, as secretary-general of the Council of the European Union and as the EU's High Representative for the Common Foreign and Security Policy—a post he held for years. The power that comes with titles is often inversely proportional to their length, and Solana's was no exception. He had to serve twenty-seven heads of state and government, share authority with various EU commissioners responsible for external affairs, enlargement, and trade, and respect the priorities and sensitivities of whichever country happened to hold the EU presidency, which rotated every six months—and all on a shoestring budget that he did not fully control. But by force of his political and diplomatic skills, he made the most of a complex and constraining mandate—and made himself the closest thing the EU has ever had to a foreign minister.

In 1996, when Boutros-Ghali sought a second term as secretary-general of the UN, he had the support of much of the General Assembly and all the permanent members of the Security Council except the United States. France was his leading proponent, largely because Boutros-Ghali was seen as willing to stand up to the United States (and, if the occasion required, do so in elegant French). Secretary Christopher, along with Albright and others, felt that Boutros-Ghali had to go. In the eyes of many conservatives in Congress, Boutros-Ghali had come to symbolize the inefficiency of the UN, while to liberals who favored humanitarian intervention, he seemed to be (like Lubbers) force-averse. Kofi Annan was the U.S. choice. Based on my own dealings with him—especially during the Labor Day crisis over Bosnia the year before—I welcomed the idea of his replacing Boutros-Ghali.

The Clinton administration's decision, in effect, to fire the secretary-general was far from popular in Turtle Bay or capitals around the world. A vote taken among the members of the Security Council—permanent and rotating—on November 19, 1996, came out 14–1 in Boutros-Ghali's favor, with the United States casting a veto. Over the weeks that followed, we made clear we would continue to block Boutros-Ghali. For all the Clinton administration's commitment to multilateralism, starting with the president himself, there were going to be times when we would have to act unilaterally. This was one of those times.

I remember a heated argument with a French colleague, Gérard Errera, then his country's ambassador to NATO. When I said that sometimes we had to stand up to our friends and allies in order to protect an institution that would allow us to act together effectively in the future, Errera replied that I sounded like the American major in Vietnam who had said he had to destroy a village in order to save it. I did not attempt a snappy comeback. Sometimes just sitting there and taking it from an angry representative of *La Grande Nation* came with jobs like mine. It occurred to me more than once that the chip on the French shoulder has something to do with sibling rivalry: the two countries are twins of the Enlightenment, with universalism and exception-

alism in our genes, but one of us grew up big and strong, with a whole continent to expand across, while the other has had it harder and has never gotten
over the sense of rivalry and resentment.

On December 12, an informal straw poll was 14–1 for Annan, this time
with France the only dissenter. President Jacques Chirac and his colleagues
no doubt thought that by
holding out against U.S. insistence, they were asserting
their prerogatives as a member of the P-5. In fact, they
were just reminding the
world that one of the five was
more equal than the others.
The French made the choice
of Annan unanimous a few
days later.*

Kofi Annan and Javier Solana

Solana and Annan, who
worked together frequently,
turned out to be a perfect
combination. For strong men, they had the mildest of manners. Each had
management and diplomatic styles that were almost, but not quite, deferential, thereby conveying respect and receptivity without seeming meek or uncertain. They were also very different in affect. Solana was stereotypically
Latin: he bantered, laughed, and joked; he was given to elaborate hand ges-
tures during a conversation and to abrazos before and after. With the exception of Bill Clinton, I don't think I've ever known a public figure who seemed
to be having more fun in his work. Yet beneath all the ebullience was a combination of determination and psychological acuity, as well as the discipline
of a trained physicist and political skills honed in the years he had spent rising to the top of the Socialist Party and serving in several ministries of the
Spanish government, including that of foreign affairs. I came to regard him
as the best of diplomatic partners as well as a good and lasting friend.

Annan's personality was almost the opposite. He was remote and reserved,
as cool as Solana was hot. But, in my eyes, he was no less admirable and

---

* After leaving office in 1997, Boutros-Ghali became secretary general of La Francophonie,
the international organization of French-speaking nations. In 1999 he wrote a bitter memoir,
Unvanquished: A U.S.-U.N. Saga, in which he calls the American action to remove him a "rejection of democracy."

no less effective. He struck me, in all our dealings, as tough-minded, straight-forward, and principled. Like Hammarskjöld, Annan understood that his "voice" counted for more than his office—and it was a voice he seemed never to raise.

Together, Solana and Annan managed to maintain the confidence of the United States while quickly establishing the respect of those (notably the French and the Russians) who worried they would be a pair of American puppets. They also worked together seamlessly.

Those attributes of Solana and Annan were indispensable in 1999, when NATO went to war for the first time in its history and in virtual collaboration with the UN.

THE PROTECTORATE

After Milošević's expansionist designs on Bosnia and Croatia had been thwarted, he turned his fury and racism inward, within Serbia, against the ethnic Albanian community in the province of Kosovo. This place name was barely more recognizable to most Americans in the early to mid-1990s than Rwanda or Srebrenica had been a few years earlier. For the Serbs, however, it was a battle cry. At Kosovo Polje ("the Field of the Blackbirds") in 1389 the Ottoman armies of Sultan Murad I overwhelmed an army of Christian forces—Bulgarians, Bosnians, Albanians, Poles, and Hungarians—under the Serbian Prince Lazar. Milošević exploited a lingering strain of aggrieved nationalism among many of his fellow Serbs who believed that they had to avenge an epic defeat their forefathers had suffered nearly seven centuries earlier, and once again defend the eastern battlements of Christendom against the Kosovo Albanians, who were depicted as remnants of the "Turkish yoke."

After depriving Kosovo of the autonomy it had been granted under Josip Broz Tito (who died in 1980), Milošević unleashed a campaign that would eventually leave some ten thousand Muslims dead and drive more than eight hundred thousand from their homes.

Since the Kosovo Albanians were culturally as well as religiously distinct from the Serbs, what started as brutal suppression of protests turned into real ethnic cleansing. Thousands of refugees poured across the border into Macedonia, a fragile post-Yugoslav state whose uneasy relationship between a Slavic majority and an ethnically Albanian minority made it prone to destabilization.

During 1998, the Security Council voted three times for resolutions that called the crisis in Kosovo a threat to international peace and security. However, the council stopped short of warning it would use "all necessary means" under Chapter VII of the Charter because Russia refused to approve language that would authorize military intervention in an internal conflict. The Russians were especially adamant since the attacking force would be NATO-led, the targets (or victims) would be Orthodox Slavs, and the beneficiaries would be Muslim secessionists who, in Russian eyes, were not unlike the Chechens, a Muslim people in the North Caucasus who were seeking independence from Moscow. Some Russians told me flatly they feared that UN approval for military action against Serbia would establish a precedent that NATO might someday use—perhaps with the pretext of turmoil in the Caucasus—to attack Russia itself.

KOFI ANNAN SAW THE NEED FOR ACTION IN KOSOVO, even if it meant bucking the opposition of Russia in the Security Council. In a speech in June 1998 at Ditchley Park, a conference center in a converted manor house outside of Oxford, Annan endorsed a robust corollary to the doctrine of conditional sovereignty: if the behavior of a regime toward its own people is egregious, it is not just outsiders' business to object but their responsibility to step in, stop the offenses, and even change the regime. "State frontiers," Annan said, "should no longer be seen as a watertight protection for war criminals or mass murderers. The fact that a conflict is 'internal' does not give the parties any right to disregard the most basic rules of human conduct." He acknowledged that "the Charter protects the sovereignty of peoples," and that it prohibits the UN from intervening "in matters which are essentially within the domestic jurisdiction of any State."[8] However, he added, that principle "was never meant as a license for governments to trample on human rights and human dignity. Sovereignty implies responsibility, not just power."

In this case, Annan was saying, the spirit of the Charter overrode the letter—and, in particular, it overrode the first part of Chapter I, Article 2, Paragraph 7 ("Nothing contained in the present Charter shall authorize the United Nations to intervene in matters which are essentially within the domestic jurisdiction of any state"), while relying heavily on the second part of that Article ("but this principle shall not prejudice the application of enforcement measures under Chapter VII").

Annan recognized that he was creating an "uncomfortable precedent" in his Ditchley Park speech: "Can we really afford to let each state be the judge of its own right, or duty, to intervene in another state's internal conflict?" Answering his rhetorical question, he went on to argue that only the Security Council "has the authority to decide that the internal situation in any state is so grave as to justify forceful intervention."

The speech did not receive much attention at the time. I only became aware of it because William Shawcross, a British journalist whom Brooke and I had known since living in the Balkans, sent it to me as an e-mail attachment with a note: "Kofi is breaking new ground here."*

A number of Annan's colleagues in the Secretariat and many delegates in the General Assembly were either apprehensive or appalled at where the logic of his position would lead: Milošević would step up his atrocities; the international community would, as before, cry out for the UN to take effective steps; the Russians would never approve; either the Security Council would be paralyzed by the Russian veto, or the three NATO members among the P-5—the United States, Britain, and France—would act without the legitimacy of a Chapter VII resolution. The dilemma for the UN, and for its secretary-general, would be whether to give primacy to what Annan depicted as a moral obligation to intervene or, as he and others had done in previous instances, to abide by a strict reading of the organization's rules—and do nothing.

Without specifying at Ditchley Park exactly how that dilemma should be resolved, Annan seemed to be signaling that if the Russians blocked a Security Council resolution, he might give U.S. and NATO use of force some sort of qualified approval on his own. The most soft-spoken public official I have ever known had come closer than any of his predecessors to acknowledging that the UN would sometimes need the big stick of American military power even without the blessing of the Security Council.

IN MARCH 1999, MILOŠEVIĆ gave the back of his hand to a last-ditch diplomatic effort by the Contact Group, and then to Holbrooke, who undertook a solo mission to Belgrade. On March 24, the United States, working with Solana and the NATO allies, launched a bombing campaign against Serbia.

That same day, after much personal anguish and intense, sometimes acri-

---

*Shawcross was at that time working on a book about Annan—*Deliver Us from Evil: Peacekeepers, Warlords and a World of Endless Conflict* (New York: Simon & Schuster, 2000).

monious debate within his own team, Annan issued a statement expressing his regret that war had broken out and that NATO had felt it had to
act without Security Council approval—but also blaming Milošević for
the breakdown of the negotiations: "The Yugoslav authorities have persisted
in their rejection of a political settlement, which would have halted the
bloodshed in Kosovo and secured an equitable peace for the population
there."

Then Annan echoed—this time with the entire world paying the closest
attention—what he had said at Ditchley Park the previous June: "It is indeed
tragic that diplomacy has failed, but there are times when the use of force
may be legitimate in the pursuit of peace." Even qualified with "may be," the
second half of that sentence was diplomatically innovative, politically courageous, and—for an American administration that earnestly wanted to support, and be supported by, the UN—invaluable. It was also, Annan said
privately at the time, the most difficult statement he felt he had to make since
he became secretary-general.[9]

In public, however, Annan held firm. Two weeks into the war, he said,
"What gives me hope—and should give every future ethnic cleanser and
every state-backed architect of mass murder pause—is that a universal sense
of outrage has been provoked. Emerging slowly, but I believe surely, is an international norm against the violent repression of minorities that will and
must take precedence over concerns of state sovereignty."[10]

As many delegates and some of his own staff pointed out, Annan had no
authority to bless NATO action in the absence of a Security Council resolution. He was, after all, the servant of the Council, not its chief executive. But
in giving priority to outcome over process and putting his personal prestige
on the line, he not only helped the Clinton administration manage its difficulties with Russia—he saved the organization from once again risking irrelevance.[11]

ALMOST SIMULTANEOUSLY WITH GIVING THE ORDER to start
the bombing, Clinton was back on the phone to Moscow, trying to limit the
damage to the U.S.-Russian relationship and, more immediately, enlist
Yeltsin in the effort to bring the war to a quick conclusion. I joined Clinton in
the Oval Office for several telephone conversations with a bombastic and
sometimes inebriated Russian president during those hair-raising days. Clinton did a lot of listening. He smiled ruefully and shook his head more in sympathy than annoyance as Yeltsin ranted about the hell he was catching at

home. When Clinton could get a word in edgewise, he did his best to play on their good chemistry in the past and their demonstrated ability to find solutions to tough problems. He promised Yeltsin that Russia would be—indeed, must be—as much involved in the diplomacy to end the war as it had been in the diplomacy to avert it.

Yeltsin, who was desperate to be in on everything important, responded positively. He knew that Milošević was counting on Russia to side with the Serbs and keep the Security Council split. To disabuse the Serbian leader of that hope, Yeltsin empowered his former prime minister, Viktor Chernomyrdin, to work with me and Martti Ahtisaari, the president of Finland, who had previously been a UN official with experience in Africa and the Balkans. The three of us were able to bring the concerted pressure of Russia, the European Union, and the United States on Milošević to capitulate to NATO's demands and pull his forces out of Kosovo.

Meanwhile Secretary Albright was talking to Annan constantly, and I met him frequently as well—in New York, Washington, Geneva, and London. His end of our conversations contained subtle reminders of how hard it had been for him to justify the war in the absence of a Security Council resolution, how eager he was for it to end, and how important it was for the UN to be centrally involved in the peace to come. We sometimes differed over how best to manage the strain between what he saw as the UN's prerogatives and what I saw as the United States' political and military requirements. When he felt that I was making his part of that job harder, he would narrow his eyes, and his voice, always soft, would become almost inaudible in a way that suggested he was exerting extra effort to control his annoyance.

While we sometimes disagreed on tactics, we managed to avoid public disputes so that neither Russia nor Milošević could play the UN and the United States against each other while NATO bombed government facilities in Belgrade and military, communications, and infrastructure installations throughout Yugoslavia. Much of the bombing was conducted at night, partly to make it harder for Serb antiaircraft units to hit allied planes and also to minimize civilian casualties. Despite precautions, a few of the thirty-eight thousand air sorties hit the wrong targets. In early May NATO pilots mistook a column of Kosovo Albanian refugees for a Serbian military convoy and killed at least fifty people. A few days later, a site that turned out to be the Chinese embassy was bombed because it was misidentified on an out-of-date CIA map. Three Chinese were killed, sparking riots in China.

Of the several trips I made to "the theater of operations," the one I remember best was to Skopje, the capital of Macedonia. While I was traveling in Western Europe, a violent mob of Macedonian Serbs scaled the walls of our embassy in Skopje and wrecked everything they could get their hands on. The American staff had to hole up in a basement vault. Meanwhile, local leaders needed much more help than they were getting from the outside world as they tried to cope with the sudden influx of refugees from Kosovo. Responding to an urgent request from our ambassador, Christopher Hill, my traveling team and I suspended the consultations we were holding in Rome with the Italian government and flew to Skopje. Shortly before landing, our small troop and cargo transport had to take evasive action when it was "painted" by Serbian antiaircraft radar. Once we had landed, I plunged into a day of trying to help Hill buck up embassy morale, visiting refugee camps, and assuring the Macedonian government that the end of the war was in sight (more of a hope than a conviction on my part). That night I was billeted in a government guest house and could not get to sleep because of what sounded like the world's longest freight train rumbling by all night long. It was the air forces of NATO sending constant sorties of bombers to pound targets in Serbia.

Throughout the war, Brooke and I received outraged and despairing e-mails from people who had been our friends in Belgrade nearly thirty years before. One, from Mirjana Komarecki, who had worked for me as well as for the New York Times, consisted of three questions: "What are you doing? Why are you doing this? Are we so responsible for this dreadful man Milošević who calls himself our president that we should be punished?" We had good, or at least adequate, answers to the first two questions, but not to the third. Decision-making in government often boils down to choosing the least bad option. Going to war so qualifies when the only other option is doing nothing and thereby abetting aggression or barbarism.

The seventy-eight-day bombardment degraded Milošević's military capability, and the combined diplomatic pressure from the United States, the EU, and Russia broke his political will. While the air campaign was critical, the war was won in Milošević's living room when Ahtisaari and Chernomyrdin—neither of whose countries were members of NATO—sat side-by-side and conveyed in unmistakable and unbending terms the EU's and Russia's endorsements of the alliance's nonnegotiable terms.

On June 3, Milošević unconditionally agreed to those terms. It was among the bigger payoffs we got from the relationship that Clinton had cultivated with Yeltsin from the beginning of the administration.*

I am not sure how much longer we could have sustained domestic and international support for the war. As pressure built on us to achieve victory quickly, the Pentagon prepared options for Clinton that would entail sending in ground troops. That prospect raised fears in Washington of high American casualties, but it scared Milošević as well. My guess is that the possibility of an invasion weighed at least as heavily as the bombing in his decision to give up.

MILOŠEVIĆ WITHDREW HIS FORCES from Kosovo and accepted the stationing of foreign troops in the war-torn province. After a week of technical negotiations, the bombing halted on June 10. That day, the United States went back to the Security Council, which passed Resolution 1244 authorizing the immediate deployment of an international security force and establishing a postwar administrative structure in Kosovo under Chapter VII of the UN Charter.

The reaction abroad to the United States' actions in the Balkans included a mixture of awe (sometimes tinged with anxiety) at U.S. military prowess, gratitude (sometimes grudging) for American leadership, and unease at the magnitude and reach of American power. In February 1999—shortly before the war—the French foreign minister Hubert Védrine had labeled the United States *l'hyperpuissance*, or the hyperpower. He meant it as neither a compliment nor a condemnation; rather, it was, as he saw it, an objective fact that France had to learn to live with. It was also his way of acknowledging what Charles Krauthammer called "the unipolar moment," with the difference that the French looked forward to the day when the world would be "multipolar," with Paris, of course, as one of the poles.

From our standpoint in Washington, we had managed, with difficulty, to use our hyperpower to good effect. A Security Council resolution, supported by the still grumpy Russians and the even grumpier Chinese, vested civil authority in Kosovo with the UN itself, while the EU and the OSCE were subordinated to a UN special representative designated by Kofi Annan. Part of my

---

* It was also a ragged, nerve-racking, and dangerous denouement. Chernomyrdin faced open insubordination from the Russian military, including its representative on his own negotiating team. A bizarre episode, in which the Russians "occupied" an airfield in Kosovo before NATO troops could get there, carried the risk of a confrontation between Russia and the alliance. I have recounted this story, and others about the war, in *The Russia Hand*.

job was to help cobble that arrangement together. It was one of the most sat-
isfying assignments I had in eight years, since it meant putting into practice
the ideas—and the ideals—that had informed so much of my thinking over
the years about the way the world as a whole ought to respond when countries or regions disintegrate into chaos. I remember, in particular, a working
dinner at Truman Hall, the Flemish mansion on a bucolic estate outside
Brussels that serves as the U.S. ambassadorial residence, with the envoys not
just of our NATO allies but neutral Finland (because of the Ahtisaari connection) and Russia as well.

It was fashionable at the time (and became more so later, during the next
administration) for some American officials and foreign policy experts to
roll their eyes and shake their heads at what was seen as a plethora of European and transatlantic organizations. Depending on what definition one
used, there were at least seventeen. Planning, not to mention attending all
their meetings, and keeping straight which organization was supposed to do
what demanded considerable time from government officials. My own view,
and that of my principal colleagues at the State Department (including both
secretaries I worked for, Warren Christopher and Madeleine Albright), was
that American support for this proliferation of institutions and groupings
was worth the trouble. Nearly every year, in the coldest, darkest days of winter, I would make my way to some small city north of the Arctic Circle for the
Barents Euro-Arctic Council and find myself admiring the way in which,
among other tasks, that little-known organization was helping the northern
regions of Russia to develop their economies and deal with radioactive waste,
venereal disease, and tuberculosis—in short, to learn the benefits of integration into the West. We called it our "Hanseatic strategy." *

I commissioned the CIA to come up with a Venn diagram showing these
organizations and how their memberships and missions overlapped and, in
key respects, reinforced each other. I dubbed it "the Euromess chart," but it
depicted good news. One way to look at it was as the wiring diagram for the
European Project, with the added dimensions of the longstanding transatlantic relationship and now the incorporation of former Soviet satellites
and republics as well. It could also be seen as a political galaxy, in which mul-

---

* The term was originated by Ronald Asmus, a former RAND Corporation analyst whom
I recruited to work on European integration and NATO enlargement. The evocation of a commercial arrangement five hundred years in the past had particular resonance since Novgorod,
in northwestern Russia, had been among the inland cities that thrived as a trading outpost of
the Hanseatic League.

tiple, intersecting solar systems generated a combined gravitational field that exerted a westward pull on the historical and political "East." Progress in institutionalizing the ability of postcommunist states to assimilate and collaborate with the West was directly proportional to the number of regional, subregional, and transregional organizations operating in Europe.

Kosovo was a test case of the ability of several of those organizations to work together to end both a threat to common interests and an offense to common values. It was no accident that charts for other parts of the world were not at all messy, and the most conflict-ridden of them—the Greater Middle East—was virtually a blank sheet of paper.[12]

IT WAS DURING THIS PERIOD that I also got my first look inside Le Palais des Nations in Geneva, once for a meeting with Kofi Annan on how to shift functions in Kosovo from NATO to the UN, and on another occasion to discuss with Sadako Ogata, the UN High Commissioner for Refugees, how to expedite the return to Kosovo of Albanian refugees from their camps in Macedonia. On both occasions, I found a little time to wander around the grounds, verify that there really were peacocks in residence, and wonder how Woodrow Wilson would have felt about the Balkan Wars of the 1990s and their aftermath that continued well into the next decade. His feelings, I suspect, would have been mixed. On the one hand, he would have seen, in the collaboration between the United States and the United Nations to end those wars, a realization of at least some of his hopes for the League. But he would also have seen several painful ironies. One was the destruction of Yugoslavia— a Wilsonian artifact—on whose territory the Wilsonian principle of national self-determination ran amok.

For this breakdown of regional peace and stability I have always felt that the European Union bears considerable responsibility. If the EU had been more advanced in its capacity to deal with failed states on its periphery, it might have been able to stop, or at least slow down and bring about peacefully the breakup of Yugoslavia and the subsequent breakup of Serbia. Independence for Kosovo was not, in my view, by any means the best outcome. While the rest of Europe was integrating nation-states into a multinational union, the Balkans was living up to its reputation by *dis*integrating into fragments of pseudo-states.

Kosovo was the latest example. The slogan "Kosovo for the Kosovars" (as members of the Albanian majority called themselves) would threaten and alienate the Serb minority living in the breakaway province, while it would

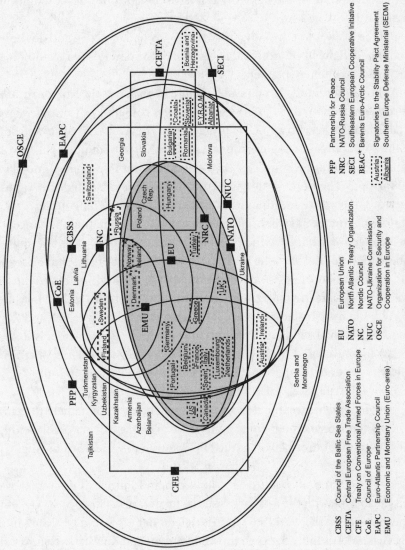

Euromess 2000

CBSS	Council of the Baltic Sea States	
CEFTA	Central European Free Trade Association	
CFE	Treaty on Conventional Armed Forces in Europe	
CoE	Council of Europe	
EAPC	Euro-Atlantic Partnership Council	
EMU	Economic and Monetary Union (Euro-area)	

EU	European Union
NATO	North Atlantic Treaty Organization
NC	Nordic Council
NUC	NATO-Ukraine Commission
OSCE	Organization for Security and Cooperation in Europe

PFP	Partnership for Peace
NRC	NATO-Russia Council
SECI	Southeastern European Cooperative Initiative
BEAC*	Barents Euro-Arctic Council
Austria; Albania	Signatories to the Stability Pact Agreement
	Southern Europe Defense Ministerial (SEDM)

appeal to the Albanian minority in Macedonia. Far better than independence would have been for the EU to take Kosovo under its wing, help it through the long process of political stabilization, communal reconciliation, and economic development, and defer for as long as possible the question of its ultimate status.

But the EU was not up to that task, so the UN had to step in and do the best it could, with the likelihood that at the end of the day, Kosovo would indeed be "graduated" to independence.

As I rushed around Europe and back and forth across the Atlantic in 1999, I occasionally referred in interviews and press conferences to what we were establishing in Kosovo as a UN "protectorate." Several journalists and some of my own colleagues in government told me the term sounded patronizing. Patronizing toward whom? I asked. The Serbs, whom we'd just bombed into submission? The Kosovo Albanians, whom we'd just liberated? I also raised eyebrows in private meetings with my European and UN counterparts by wondering out loud if we shouldn't think about resuscitating the concept of the Trusteeship Council, which was in a state of indefinite if not permanent hibernation, to deal with the realities we now faced in Bosnia and Kosovo—and, by the way, in Haiti as well. I was told that these words—*protectorate* and *trusteeship*—were freighted with invidious associations. Okay, I replied. Never mind that trusteeship was promoted by Franklin Roosevelt and Ralph Bunche, who had solid anti-imperialist credentials. Let's spend a little time with a thesaurus and find some synonyms, or perhaps even euphemisms. Since we're going to pretend that the Trusteeship Council no longer exists, then we'll have to invent one.

And that is what we did: Kosovo went from being a killing field to being a ward of the international community—an example of what Paul Kennedy calls "foundlings dropped off at the UN's door in the middle of the night." [13]

IN THE AUTUMN OF 2007, American and European diplomats were still squabbling with the Russians over the final status of Kosovo and whether a permrep from the world's would-be newest nation would be seated in the UN General Assembly between those of Kiribati and Kuwait. Even advocates of that outcome were saying that Kosovo's "independence" would have to be "supervised," an adjective that would seem to contradict the noun.

However the United States, Europe, and the UN nurture Kosovo through the years ahead, they had better get it right—for the sake of Kosovo and its neighbors, but also with an eye to lessons that can be applied elsewhere for a long time to come. History, modern as well as ancient, has seen a constant interplay between the integration and disintegration of states. That pattern will continue into even the best of futures, though the forces of integration had better be able to cope with those of disintegration (preferably without resort to bombing campaigns). That will happen only if there are more capable regional organizations in all parts of the world—each fitting sensibly, if not neatly, into a globomess chart that features a more capable UN.

15

A THEORY OF THE CASE

It is the gods' custom to bring low all things of surpassing greatness.
—*HERODOTUS*[1]

If the Lord Almighty had consulted me before embarking on
creation, I should have recommended something simpler.
—*ALFONSO X, King of Castile in the thirteenth century, known
as "The Wise" and "The Astrologer"*[2]

I N early June of 2000, as Bill Clinton was nearing the end of his presidency, he traveled to Moscow for a predictably unproductive meeting
with Vladimir Putin, who had been elected president of Russia three
months earlier. Putin was biding his time, waiting to see who would win the
U.S. presidential race that fall. En route to Russia, Clinton stopped in Aachen,
Germany, and, in recognition of his contribution to European integration,
became the first American president to receive the Charlemagne Prize. (Previous recipients included Winston Churchill, Jean Monnet, and Robert
Schuman; a subsequent one—in 2007—would be Javier Solana.) I had been
in Moscow preparing for the summit with Putin and flew to Aachen just in
time to hear Clinton accept the award in a ceremony at the local cathedral,
known as the *Kaiserdom*, since Charlemagne himself had overseen its original construction.

Clinton's speech had a valedictory quality, but in a minor key. He paid
homage to the ninth-century warrior-king in whose name he was being honored, but he did not gloss over how bloody the intervening twelve centuries
had been: "Here, Charlemagne's name summons something glimpsed for the
first time during his life, a sense that the disparate people of this earth's
smallest continent could actually live together as participants in a single civilization. In its quest for unity, even at the point of a sword, and in its devo-

tion to the new idea that there was actually something called Europe, the Carolingian idea surpassed what had come before, and to an extent, it guides us still. . . . Today, that shining light of European union is a matter of the utmost importance, not just to Europeans but to everyone on this planet, for Europe has shown the world humanity at its best and at its worst. Europe's most violent history was caused by men claiming the mantle of Charlemagne, men who sought to impose European union for their own ends without the consent of the people."

Talking to Clinton afterward on Air Force One during the short flight to his next stop, Berlin, I found him uncharacteristically melancholy and distracted. It was hard for him to focus on his upcoming meeting with Putin, partly, as he put it, because "ol' Putin's going to blow me off. He's interested in the next guy. He'll be polite, since he knows I'm on my victory lap. I just wish I had a few more victories."

I tried to cheer him up by complimenting him on the speech—and, more important, on what he had done to earn the prize. "Yeah," he said, "I've put a lot into this whole new-Europe, new-world thing. I really believe in it. But I'm running out of time, and it hasn't all come together—not by a long shot." He was brooding over his legacy. It was something that he had been doing even before he had one, at the beginning of his presidency. Part of the problem, and I suspected it was one reason he was not in a better mood after his speech in Aachen, was that he never felt that he had quite found the right words to explain what he was trying to do in his foreign policy and why it deserved the support of the American people.

That problem had bedeviled the administration as a whole from the beginning. When Warren Christopher settled into the State Department, he had a portrait of Dean Acheson, whom he admired greatly, moved from the gallery of former secretaries in the outer lobby on the seventh floor to his spacious, mahogany-paneled office. The painting became something of a conversation piece when Christopher would assemble his inner circle for strategy sessions. Acheson had helped Truman lay the foundations of the post–World War II international order, and Christopher hoped to play a similar role for Clinton now that the cold war was over. Acheson had titled a memoir of his years as secretary of state *Present at the Creation*.[3] Christopher, along with those of us who worked for him, sometimes remarked on how Acheson's aristocratic eyebrows, arched above a sharp gaze, made him look slightly sardonic, as though he were reserving judgment on whether his successors would be up to the tasks awaiting them. Peter Tarnoff captured the sense we shared of being both blessed and tested. "We're present at the *re-creation*," he said. "But the re-creation of *what*?"[4]

CLINTON HIMSELF HAD COME TO THE PRESIDENCY with what he called a "theory of the case" about how to manage the way the world was changing: the United States should lead in harnessing the benefits and combating the dangers of globalization. "Communications and commerce are global," he said in his first Inaugural Address. "Investment is mobile; technology is almost magical; and ambition for a better life is now universal. We earn our livelihood in peaceful competition with people all across the earth. Profound and powerful forces are shaking and remaking our world, and the urgent question of our time is whether we can make change be our friend and not our enemy."

Listening (and shivering—it was the coldest inauguration day on record) from a few rows behind him outside the Capitol, I felt it was a good rhetorical opening. Yet in the months and years that followed, Clinton struggled, rarely to his own satisfaction, for the right words to describe the essence of his foreign policy. This may seem like an odd deficiency, given his skills as a speaker. But his real ability was as a *talker*. He was a great communicator, but no one ever called him *the* Great Communicator, a title that had been retired with Ronald Reagan. It is hard to imagine that, if Clinton had been president a decade earlier, he would have used a trip to Berlin to challenge Mikhail Gorbachev to "tear down this wall"—or, a quarter century earlier, to proclaim, as Kennedy did, *"Ich bin ein Berliner!"* In both cases, Clinton would probably have tried not just to excite the audience in front of him but to engage the Soviet and East German leaders listening from the far side of the wall. When he had the microphone, he was more interested in using it for conversation than as a bullhorn. Partly as a result, "the lift of a driving dream"—the Holy Grail of speechwriters and those for whom they write—eluded him. He was less an orator than a Baptist preacher with highly responsive parishioners. His speeches were easy to listen to but hard to sum up in a few memorable phrases.[5]

When it came to foreign policy, there was one phrase that he could not seem to escape: "post–cold war era." He hated it when it appeared in texts prepared for him. "What kind of message does *that* send?" I remember him asking when one of us in his traveling team used the term in a briefing session aboard Air Force One. "It defines where we are in terms of where we've been rather than where we're going. I'm tomorrow's boy, and I don't like being seen as doing yesterday's business."

. . .

MORE THAN A YEAR AND A HALF into his first term, on September 22, 1994, Clinton convened his foreign policy advisers to discuss the address he was about to give at the UN General Assembly. His speechwriting shop had come up with a draft that sounded a call for a new generation of American leaders to consolidate the gains of the old one that had won World War II and established the policies and mechanisms for successfully conducting the cold war. Clinton hated it: "You're having me tell a generation that's already bored that their mission is going to be even more boring! We're supposed to get people charged up at the prospect of putting the icing on a cake that someone baked forty years ago?" He wanted to talk about building something new, not just renovating something old—and that went for the United Nations itself. "We've got a chance," he said, "to make the UN what FDR and Churchill intended it to be before their plans were interrupted and truncated by the cold war."

He had just finished Doris Kearns Goodwin's study of Franklin and Eleanor Roosevelt, *No Ordinary Time*, and David McCullough's biography of Truman.[6] While reading about those presidents did not diminish Clinton's admiration for them, it gave him some solace to be reminded that Roosevelt and Truman had frequently improvised and that subsequent analysis made their policies seem more coherent and prescient than they themselves would have claimed. "They were making it up as they went along too, just as we are," said Clinton. "But they still managed to convey a sense of direction and purpose. Harry Truman didn't say he was going to consolidate the gains of World War II. He said he was going to take the world in a whole new direction. The cold war helped because it provided an organizing principle. Our operative problem of the moment is that a bunch of smart people haven't been able to come up with a slogan for where we are and what we're doing and why and where it's going to take us that's better than where we've been. And saying there are no more slogans isn't a slogan, either. There's got to be a sense of direction to this history stuff: World War I gave way to the New Deal but also to World War II, which gave way to the cold war, which gave way to the new world order Bush talked about, but now everyone's afraid that's going to fall apart. So what's next, you guys?"

Vice President Al Gore took a stab at an answer. "What we were doing in the cold war had resonance in people's lives because it made sense in terms of the threat they could feel—the threat of nuclear war, the threat that the Russians were coming. People now feel in their bones that there's something fundamentally different about the world in which we live: palpably, ours is becoming a global civilization. There's a universal sense that democracy is humankind's chosen form of political organization and that the free market is humankind's chosen form of economic organization." As Gore built up momentum, he started citing the great figures of the past: "Jefferson argued with Hamilton that the principles of democracy were not limited to the United States. Hamilton disagreed, but Jefferson was right. We don't want to be triumphalist, but we do need to lead. Rousseau said the body politic is a moral being possessed of a will. He was thinking on the national level. We need to take it to the international one. We need to make the leap from nationhood to a sense of identity that is truly global, but that embodies Rousseau's point: the blueprint is there and Jefferson wrote it."

I had never seen Gore in quite this mode before. Neither, I suspect, had Clinton. He was listening attentively and appreciatively, a smile playing at the corner of his mouth. But when Gore finally wound down, Clinton was still looking for a tag-line. "That's great stuff, Al. What you're saying is that the end of the cold war isn't the end of threats, but it makes possible a whole set of new victories. Still, we can litanize and analyze all we want, but until I can say it in a single phrase, we're sunk. The perception out there now, right or wrong, is that there's no clear line from principle to action, and that previous administrations were clearer in that regard. When we make it up as we go along, they say that it's all adhockery, and that we are making it up solely on the basis of domestic politics."

I felt sorry for the president's speechwriting staff. As one of Clinton's aides, Bob Boorstin, gathered his papers and headed for the door, he grumbled about how "there are a lot of contradictions in all this great stuff." Clinton overheard him. "Never mind, Bob," he said with a grin. "You guys can do it. But we need some big think that gets us a headline!"

The speech that Clinton gave to the General Assembly four days later advocated multilateralism and new institutions for a new—though still nameless—age; it played on the challenge of globalization and used Gore's formulation about a conflict between hope and fear.[7] The front-page newspaper stories covered nothing but the passages in the speech about Haiti and Bosnia. The most indicative headline was deep inside the *New York Times*: "City Yawns, Roads Snarl as Clinton Visits U.N."—hardly what the president had wanted. His political antennae were attuned to the danger of being accused of suffering from his own deficit of the "vision thing."

By the second term he was beginning to take criticism on that score from some of the advisers who were already gathering around his would-be successor, George W. Bush. In September 1997, when I visited Stanford to give a foreign policy speech, I paid a visit on Condoleezza Rice, who was provost of the university. She was, as usual, generally friendly and polite, but she slipped in one dig: the namelessness of the nineties, she said, spoke volumes about the aimlessness of the administration. I mentioned this to Clinton on my return to Washington. "She's wrong about us not having a sense of direction," he said, "but she's right about our doing a lousy job of explaining it."

NOT UNTIL AFTER CLINTON was out of office did he give speeches and interviews that flowed and soared on the subject of American leadership in the age of globalization. One short, simple sentence in a speech he gave at Yale in October 2003 struck me with particular force: "We must build a global social system."[8] In 2006, while I was working on this book, I reminded Clinton of that sentence and asked him to elaborate on it. He did so in the context of his attitude toward international institutions. "When I became president," he said, "everybody thought we were the biggest dog in the hunt. But America had significant domestic problems. These social, budgetary, and economic problems would constrain our ability to act alone internationally. Second: even more importantly, I was heavily influenced by the success of the post–World War II and cold war multilateral organizations—the establishment of the UN, NATO, IMF, World Bank, the Marshall Plan, and the OECD.* I saw that they worked, and at the end of the cold war, I saw an opportunity for the first time in history to globalize them in a way that the East-West division had prevented. Third: I was always obsessed with the notion that sooner or later—since I believe intelligence and ability are evenly distributed throughout the world but opportunity and organization aren't—as the global economy continued to expand, eventually America would no longer be the sole economic, political, and military superpower. So I wanted to build a world for our grandchildren to live in where America was no longer the sole superpower, for a time when we would have to share the stage."[9]

The last part of his answer surprised me. Having known Clinton for nearly forty years and worked for him for eight, I thought I understood the funda-

---

* The Organisation for Economic Cooperation and Development is a grouping of countries with a proclaimed commitment to democratic governance and the market economy. The OECD's forerunner, the Organisation for European Economic Cooperation, was an offspring of the Marshall Plan.

mentals of his thinking about the world and America's role in it. But I had never heard him lay out this particular rationale for a multilateralist foreign policy, at least not this clearly. I recalled that occasionally, during his presidency, he would say, in private and in an offhand way, something to this effect: "We're not going to be cock of the roost forever, you know," or, "Other countries that didn't have our head start are going to catch up with us at some point." He had China particularly in mind.

Clinton's view was diametrically opposed to Charles Krauthammer's concept of the "unipolar moment," which held that the United States had a several-decade window of opportunity to get its way unilaterally—unencumbered by the need for consensus-building and compromise—before the world became multipolar. Clinton believed just the opposite: what we had in the wake of the cold war was a *multilateral* moment—an opportunity to shape the world through our active leadership of the institutions Clinton admired and Krauthammer disdained.

But Clinton kept that belief largely to himself while he was in office. In public, and even in meetings with administration insiders and political supporters, Clinton's political instincts told him it would be inviting trouble to suggest that the sun might someday set on American preeminence. Ronald Reagan's optimism about "morning in America" had helped him defeat Jimmy Carter, who had, in the eyes of many, inadvertently associated his presidency—and, therefore for some time to come, his party—with the word *malaise.**

It was one thing for Clinton to take advantage of a yearning in the United States to cash in a peace dividend that came with the end of the cold war, but it would have been folly for him to play into the hands of his opponents on the right by suggesting that the American victory was anything but permanent.

FOR MOST OF HIS TIME IN OFFICE, Clinton was equally careful not to broadcast his belief in a version of Darwinism in its most optimistic form: the notion that globalization was conducive to the emergence—or evolution—of an increasingly cooperative international system. In off-the-cuff public remarks, in prepared speeches, and in private conversation, I heard him field-test the idea that the spread of democracy, open society, mar-

---

* Carter did not use the word *malaise* in his politically disastrous televised speech of July 15, 1979. Instead, he referred to a "crisis of confidence." But his opponents—first Senator Edward Kennedy, who was challenging him for the Democratic nomination, and then Ronald Reagan—started calling it "the 'malaise' speech," and that label stuck.

ket economy, and individual empowerment was the wave of the future. An example came during a joint press conference in Beijing with President Jiang Zemin of China on June 27, 1998, when Clinton ad libbed, "[I]t is important that whatever our disagreements over past action, China and the United States must go forward on the right side of history for the future sake of the world. The forces of history have brought us to a new age of human possibility, but our dreams can only be recognized by nations whose citizens are both responsible and free."

He stopped well short of endorsing the idea that something like a self-governing world community was a desirable outcome, not to mention a predetermined one. Later, however, he moved in that direction. In 2000, his last year in office, Clinton read Robert Wright's *Nonzero: The Logic of Human Destiny*. Wright, then a visiting fellow at the University of Pennsylvania, argued that, despite all the ups and downs and zigs and zags, history evinces positive "directionality": humankind has been moving from a competitive and war-torn world of its own making to one that exhibits cooperation on a larger and larger scale and in which war is less and less in the interest of nations: "[in] history's basic trajectory . . . new technologies arise that permit or encourage new, richer forms of non-zero-sum interaction. . . . As a result, people become embedded in larger and richer webs of interdependence." [10]

Wright acknowledges the pitfalls of analogizing between biology and politics. Progress in history, like progress in evolution, can be fitful, often violently so. Long before we reach the safe and distant future toward which we may be gradually moving, we could blow ourselves up or make our environment unlivable. Still, Wright's thesis resonated profoundly with Clinton. I had seen him spout ideas he had picked up from books before, but rarely with the enthusiasm and persistence with which he cited *Nonzero*. Despite the danger that an embrace of views like Wright's would play into the hands of critics and political adversaries eager to portray him as a woolly-headed liberal internationalist, Clinton repeatedly talked about the book in public while he was still president and continued to do so for months afterward. [11]

Wright returned the compliment in an article he wrote for the *New York Times* that appeared four days before Clinton left office. He predicted that Clinton's legacy would be the "One Big Idea" of how to govern a globalizing world. [12] But it was a big idea that Clinton would not articulate until he was a private citizen. It was not his speechwriters' fault that he never quite found his presidential voice on "foreign policy big think"; it was because he was holding himself in check.

RUMBLINGS ON THE RIGHT

Despite Clinton's restraint, his conservative critics had long suspected he was a latter-day one-worlder. He had been vulnerable on that score from the moment he won the presidency. The shift to the right in the nation's political center of gravity was accompanied by an erosion of support for multi-lateralism.

The dramatic extent of the change was personified by the contrast between the two chairmen of the Senate Foreign Relations Committee during the first years of the Clinton administration, from Claiborne Pell of Rhode Island to Jesse Helms of North Carolina. When I paid a courtesy call on Pell in early 1993, just after I was nominated for my first job at the State Department as head of the bureau responsible for the former Soviet Union, he pulled out of his pocket a tattered copy of what he called "my little blue book" and quizzed me on my familiarity with its contents. It was the United Nations Charter, and it was the last time I would see that document, not to mention any sign of reverence for it, on my numerous trips to Capitol Hill over the next eight years.

When I appeared before Pell's committee again, early in 1994, to be considered for confirmation as deputy secretary of state, it was Helms, as the ranking Republican, I had to contend with. He grilled me on pieces I had written for *Time* that he believed exposed me as an apologist for America's enemies, possibly a dupe of the KGB, and certainly an apologist for "those people" at the UN. Needless to say, he had a field day with my 1992 "Birth of the Global Nation" column in *Time*.

WHEN THE REPUBLICANS LAUNCHED a political offensive to take control of both houses of Congress in the midterm elections of 1994, they put out a manifesto called the "Contract with America." It claimed that "the Clinton administration appears to salute the day when American men and women will fight, and die, 'in the service' of the United Nations." After the Republican victory, Helms replaced Pell as chairman of the Senate Foreign Relations Committee. He called the UN "the longtime nemesis of millions of Americans" who were "tired of pouring hard-earned money down rat holes." Robert Dole, the new Senate majority leader and likely standard-bearer for the party in the next presidential race, vowed, "When we recapture the White House, no American boys are going to be serving under the command of Field-Marshal Boutros Boutros-Ghali." [13]

Not only was UN-bashing on the rise, but some of it was directed at the former president, George H. W. Bush, as well as at Clinton. Typical of this sentiment was an op-ed piece in the conservative *Washington Times*, on December 12, 1994, by Lawrence Di Rita, a foreign policy expert at the Heritage Foundation: "In fairness, it wasn't President Clinton but his predecessor who tried to make us all believe the UN secretary-general was rather more general than secretary. When President Bush first requested UN permission to defend America's well-recognized and legitimate access to Persian Gulf oil prior to Desert Storm, he planted the seeds for the multinational tree under which the one-worlders in the Clinton administration eagerly seek their shade. . . . The administration should discard its faith in the United Nations for anything more significant than coordinating international postage rules."*

"Humanitarian intervention" was a phrase that administration officials would use in public at their peril, not just in congressional testimony or before conservative audiences but with the East Coast foreign policy elite as well. Michael Mandelbaum captured the growing skepticism in the title of a scathing article he wrote for *Foreign Affairs* about Somalia, Haiti, and Bosnia: "Foreign Policy as Social Work."[14] A professor of American foreign policy at the Johns Hopkins School of Advanced International Studies in Washington, Mandelbaum had been a close friend of mine from college days. In the seventies and eighties we collaborated on several projects, including a book on U.S.-Soviet relations. He helped the Clinton campaign in '92. Then, to my disappointment and puzzlement (and Clinton's), Mandelbaum turned down an offer to be director of policy planning in the State Department—the job that George F. Kennan had been the first to hold—and became a caustic critic of the administration for the next eight years. Even before I finished reading Mandelbaum's *Foreign Affairs* piece, I found myself arguing with the implication of the headline. If "community" means anything, surely it means that the members look out for one another's legitimate interests. They do so not just out of the goodness of their hearts but for reasons of self-interest as well. If one part of town is poverty-stricken, it is likely to be crime-ridden, too, and therefore pose a danger to the safety of neighboring areas. A community needs social services as much as it needs police and fire departments. So what, I asked myself, is *wrong* with the idea of foreign policy as social

* Di Rita would serve as Secretary of Defense Donald Rumsfeld's press spokesman in the George W. Bush administration.

work? Doing the humane thing—i.e., something good for the people of Haiti or Bosnia or Kosovo—could also be the smart and, to use the word commandeered by critics of such policies, the *realistic* thing, since it was good for the United States to avert instability in the Caribbean and the Balkans.

By the mid-nineties even some establishment commentators seemed to be holding their noses when using the phrase "international community," which had been in circulation for more than a century. I noticed the growing frequency with which the phrase was modified with a skeptical "so-called" on the op-ed pages of American newspapers.[15] In January 2000, Condoleezza Rice, as part of a critique of liberal internationalism, wrote that it was a mistake to let "the 'national interest' [be] replaced with 'humanitarian interests' or the interests of 'the international community.' " One can only imagine how she—not to mention Mandelbaum—would have reacted to the concept of a "global social system" that Clinton, as an ex-president, propounded at Yale three years later.

Rice's article, published in *Foreign Affairs,* was read widely and analyzed closely, since she was among the most influential of "the Vulcans" advising Governor George W. Bush.[16] For her, like other Republican critics of the Clinton administration, "nation-building" became a term of disparagement for what the United States was doing in Haiti and the Balkans. Later in the year, on the eve of the election, she suggested that Bush, if elected, would withdraw troops from the Balkans, leaving the Europeans and the UN in the lurch.

Fritz Stern, the Columbia historian who had helped Richard Holbrooke and me understand European history and politics, was sufficiently alarmed by Rice's piece to write an open letter about what he felt her views portended: "According to this scheme, humanitarian involvement apparently does not conform to national interest; potentially, this is a global death sentence. What should our allies make of this announcement, so clearly geared to this election campaign? They may as well take it as an early warning that a Bush administration would practice unilateralism in a way it has never been practiced before."[17]

When Bush emerged as the front-runner for the Republican nomination, he became his own spokesman for the view that American hard power should be reserved for use against America's enemies, not those, like Milošević or the junta in Haiti or the government-backed militias in Rwanda, who were committing atrocities against their own people. "We should not send our troops to stop ethnic cleansing and genocide in nations outside our strategic interest," he said. American armed force should be held in reserve to "fight and win war"—and, he added, "to overthrow the dictator when it's in our best interests."

Bush's use of the phrase "*the* dictator" echoed his father's frequent references to "the dictator Saddam."[18] The Iraqi tyrant, with his record of invading and bombing neighboring countries and his putative arsenal of weapons of mass destruction, was, in George W. Bush's view, a legitimate target of *Realpolitik*. Bush seemed to be laying down a marker to distinguish a hardheaded U.S. foreign policy he would conduct from softheaded diversions of American resources into nation-building and humanitarian intervention favored by liberal Democrats.

In the face of these attacks, key figures in the Clinton administration made rhetorical adjustments. Rather than expunge a word that had been crucial to her prior job at the UN and was just as important to her current one at the State Department, Madeleine Albright had already started referring to "*assertive* multilateralism," hoping that the adjective, with its implication of the United States providing the necessary ingredient of forcefulness, would keep the critics at bay.

IT WAS NOT JUST THE TERMINOLOGY of internationalism that was under fire but the substance, structure, and financial and political support for it as well. The increasingly powerful and confident conservative wing of the Republican Party went after the United Nations with a vengeance. Jesse Helms mounted a campaign to strangle the organization by refusing to pay American arrears that had accumulated in recent years and by drastically cutting future funding.

When, as the new secretary-general of the UN, Kofi Annan made his first trip outside of New York to Washington and to Capitol Hill, he argued that "the United Nations needs the United States to achieve our goals, and I believe the United States needs the United Nations no less." The amount of money involved—about a billion and a half dollars—was less than a thousandth of the U.S. federal budget of $1.7 trillion. But it was vitally important to the UN system, with its own budget of around $10 billion. Compounding the absurdity of the situation was the prospect that, even though the United States remained, with Japan not far behind, the largest contributor to the UN, it might lose its voting rights in the General Assembly because of its dereliction in paying its dues. The best the administration could do was work with the Foreign Relations Committee's ranking Democrat, Joseph Biden of Delaware, to reach a compromise with Helms on a Hobson's choice for the

UN: either you reform yourself and we'll reduce our dues, or you don't reform and we'll give you no money at all.

Richard Holbrooke, who had returned to private life soon after Dayton, was brought back into service as permanent representative to the UN. After a long fight over his confirmation by the Senate, primarily over payment of American dues, he threw himself once again into shuttle diplomacy, only this time between New York and Washington. At the UN, he browbeat his fellow permreps into lowering American dues and assessments for peacekeeping operations and agreeing to just enough in the way of reforms to satisfy Congress and to put in place some administrative innovations that were long overdue.

On Capitol Hill, Holbrooke's tactics were different: he praised the bipartisanship of firebrands of the far right and the statesmanship of members of Congress who in some cases had never had a passport before being elected and would have gotten an F in elementary-school geography. In dealing with skeptics, Holbrooke soft-pedaled to the point of inaudibility any talk of America's international obligations and waxed eloquent instead about how the UN helped the United States advance its own national interests. His stock line on the world body was "flawed but indispensable." (After hearing him say this for the umpteenth time, I asked him if the same couldn't be said of the role of the United States in the world, and in the UN itself. Richard grinned and replied, "Only if you reverse the word order and start with 'indispensable'—and even then, better just think it, not say it.")

For months, Holbrooke concentrated his powers of persuasion, blandishment, and showmanship on the skeptic in chief, Jesse Helms. In January 2000, when the United States held the rotating presidency of the Security Council, Holbrooke flabbergasted his colleagues in New York and Washington by inviting Helms to speak to the Council. Exuding courtesy and addressing the assembled foreign diplomats as "my friends," Helms excoriated the UN for undermining the "sanctity" of national sovereignty and trying to establish a "new international order of global laws and global governance. This is an international order the American people will not countenance." What the world would have to get used to was the principle that American interventions did not require the UN's seal of approval: any such action was "inherently legitimate."[19] Helms used the occasion to identify himself with Woodrow Wilson's nemesis, Henry Cabot Lodge, warning that the UN risked the same fate as the League—and for the same reason: UN-sanctioned multilateralism, especially if force was involved, violated the U.S. Constitution.

Yet implacable as Helms sounded, Holbrooke's gambit worked. Helms was just mollified enough by all the attention and the mostly feigned respect that he let sufficient funding go forward for the UN to escape a fiscal crisis. He even allowed himself to be photographed wearing a blue UN cap. When Helms retired from the Senate in 2003 and established a library in his name in Wingate, North Carolina, he included a replica of the Security Council, although he could not resist putting the Taiwanese rather than the communist flag in front of the Chinese seat.

"No Points for Trying"

While the Clinton administration managed to shield the United Nations from the worst of the conservative Republican onslaught of the nineties, the same cannot be said of its ability to protect the Non-Proliferation Treaty. The last two and a half years of Clinton's presidency were a forlorn chapter in the annals of nuclear diplomacy—and a prologue for worse to come. Adverse developments on the Korean peninsula and in South Asia conspired to put the NPT into what may turn out to be terminal jeopardy. In both cases, the U.S. Senate made a bad situation worse.

The North Koreans had for years been secretly trying to develop nuclear weapons. By means of an agreement reached in 1994, the Clinton administration halted North Korea's covert program to produce plutonium for nuclear bombs. The Republican-controlled Congress attacked that deal as insufficient and pressed for a system to defend against future North Korean ballistic missiles that could reach American territory. Under pressure, the administration proposed amending the Anti-Ballistic Missile Treaty in a way that would permit the development of a limited defensive system (a national missile defense, or NMD) as a hedge against the North Korean threat. That meant trying to persuade the Russians that their own retaliatory capability would not be affected if the system was ever deployed—a hard sell under any circumstances, particularly when the Russians could see that powerful Republicans in the Senate wanted to kill the ABM Treaty and resurrect Ronald Reagan's "Star Wars" program. As a result, for several months I conducted a bizarre sort of shuttle diplomacy of my own, between Moscow, where I was negotiating with Russians who wanted no change in the treaty, and Capitol Hill, where members of Congress demanded more change than the administration felt was necessary to deal with the North Korean problem.

During approximately the same period, we found ourselves in a similar bind between Congress and India. In May 1998, the Indians shocked the world by testing a cluster of nuclear devices in the Rajasthan desert. Since they had never signed the Non-Proliferation Treaty, they were not in violation of it. The Indian test prompted the Pakistanis (who were also non-signatories of the NPT) to conduct one of their own. This pair of developments raised the question of whether countries that were bound by the treaty might rethink their nuclear options and perhaps, in some cases, break out of the NPT. That danger would be especially acute if the Indians, having presented us with a fait accompli, were treated as de facto members of the nuclear club, entitled to international assistance with their civilian nuclear facilities and other benefits enjoyed by NPT-compliant countries. Rather than granting the Indians what would have looked to the world like a special exemption from the NPT, we tried to get them to accept some constraints on their building, testing, and deployment of nuclear weapons in exchange for easing the sanctions that were imposed on them because of their test.

The Russians stalled us on our ABM/NMD proposal, and the Indians did the same on our nonproliferation and arms control proposal, partly in hopes that they might get better deals from Clinton's successor. I was heavily involved in both these star-crossed efforts.*

For me, one of the worst days of the administration was October 13, 1999. I was in Helsinki as part of a tour of European capitals to muster support for the reconstruction of Kosovo. That night, as I returned to my hotel, I heard over a car radio that the U.S. Senate had just confronted the world with a surprise every bit as unpleasant and consequential as the Indian nuclear test: the Senate refused to ratify the Comprehensive Test Ban Treaty (CTBT)—a follow-on to the limited and threshold test bans of 1963 and 1974 respectively. The negotiation of the CTBT had been one of the signal achievements of the post–cold war period. Work on it had begun in earnest in 1993, the first year of the Clinton administration, as well as on treaties to forbid the development, production, stockpiling, and use of chemical and biological weapons. Clinton signed the CTBT in 1996 with the same pen Kennedy had used to sign the Limited Test Ban thirty-three years before.

Aside from being a stinging rebuke to the president, the Senate's rejection of the CTBT in 1999 deprived the administration of what little leverage it had with the Indians, since we were trying to get them to sign the treaty at just that time. The late R. W. ("Johnny") Apple, one of the most versatile and

---

* I have recounted the story of the ABM/NMD negotiations in *The Russia Hand,* and the nuclear-weapons dialogue with India in *Engaging India: Diplomacy, Democracy, and the Bomb* (Washington: Brookings Institution Press, 2004).

astute reporters of his time, captured the meaning and magnitude of the event on the front page of the next day's *New York Times*. He called it, "the most explicit American repudiation of a major international agreement in 80 years, and it further weakened the already shaky standing of the United States as a global moral leader. Not since the Versailles Treaty was voted down in November 1919, an action that was repeated in March 1920, has so far-reaching an accord been turned down. . . . By torpedoing a face-saving compromise that was in the works between the White House and the Republican leadership, conservative Republicans made a vote inevitable. And by denying the treaty not only the requisite two-thirds majority but even a simple majority, the conservatives and their allies made good on Senator Jesse Helms's promise to give the agreement a Capitol Hill 'funeral.' The control of nuclear weapons has been a central goal of American foreign policy since Dwight D. Eisenhower proposed a ban on all nuclear testing in 1958. All presidents in the four decades since, Republicans and Democrats, have sought to limit testing and weapons development." [20]

RIGHT-WING OPPOSITION also prevented the United States from accepting the jurisdiction of the International Criminal Court (ICC), a new permanent tribunal to prosecute those charged with genocide, crimes against humanity, war crimes, and crimes of aggression. This body was intended to replace and improve upon the ad hoc tribunals set up to deal with the perpetrators of the genocides and other war crimes in Bosnia in 1993 and Rwanda in 1994. American critics feared the ICC would expose the United States to politically motivated prosecutions. The administration insisted on safeguards against that danger. But by the time Clinton signed the treaty establishing the court, on December 31, 2000, it was clear it faced certain rejection, so Clinton decided not to send it to the Senate.*

In Clinton's mind, though, the most ominous setback was the one that

---

* In the late 1990s, some far-left groups in the United States and abroad called for senior U.S. officials to be indicted. In July 1998, outside an award ceremony in her honor, Madeleine Albright was heckled by protesters who accused her of being a war criminal because of continued U.S. support for sanctions against Iraq. In 1999, in the wake of the Kosovo War, similar groups made charges against Clinton and General Wesley Clark, the Supreme Allied Commander in Europe. The Serbian government also issued a complaint to the UN war crimes prosecutor charging that NATO's actions in Kosovo amounted to war crimes. The UN prosecutor found the charge completely unfounded. Safeguards against political ICC prosecutions included the following: defining more precisely the crimes under court jurisdiction to prevent misuse of the statutes; having some types of cases only appear before the ICC after prior

he—and, in his view, the world—suffered on the issue of climate change. Clinton had become seized of that subject largely because of the running tutorial he received from Gore. I sat in on a number of meetings when Gore went into a riff now familiar to millions around the world who have seen or read *An Inconvenient Truth*. He ticked off the evidence that climate change was already upon us: glaciers retreating, sea ice melting, permafrost buckling in Alaska and Siberia (threatening to release tens of billions of tons of another greenhouse gas, methane), record heat waves, the first signs of spring appearing nearly ten days earlier than three decades before. And all of that with an average temperature increase of only 1 degree Fahrenheit over the past century.

In the face of these inescapable facts, the world had done essentially nothing except promise to do something someday. The 1992 Earth Summit in Rio had set a goal for the international community of negotiating a climate change treaty by 1997. In July of that deadline year, as 160 nations gathered in Kyoto, Japan, to open talks, the Senate unanimously passed a resolution warning that it would not approve any agreement that failed to extract commitments from developing countries, including China. After the United States, China was the world's second-largest emitter of greenhouse gases. It was also already a powerhouse, threatening the United States not so much with the People's Liberation Army or with its Dong Feng missiles as with its manufacturing and marketing prowess. Giving China a pass in Kyoto, in the Senate's view, would result in "serious harm to the economy of the United States."

The Clinton administration agreed that China should be covered by Kyoto, since science showed that a climate change treaty required universal participation to be effective. But U.S. officials, including the president, also recognized that they were asking developing countries that had not had the economic benefit of two hundred years of industrialization to help bear the costs now that the bill was coming due. The United States therefore offered inducements, such as financial subsidies and access to clean technology, to developing countries. But developing countries continued to resist on the grounds that their economies should not be slowed down just as they were finally catching up with the rest of the world.

UN Security Council approval, where the United States had a veto; and ensuring that the ICC would only have jurisdiction over cases where the national government was unwilling or unable to investigate legitimate allegations against their citizens (which the United States has never failed to do). Clinton felt the safeguards were strong enough to sign the treaty while still working to improve it before sending it to the Senate for ratification.

Gore took the unusual step of making an appearance in Kyoto to prod the parties to compromise. Despite his efforts, the developing countries refused to budge, and the protocol, in its final form, exempted them from binding limits. The United States and the other developed countries faced a choice between a flawed agreement and none at all. Clinton decided to sign the treaty, calling the Kyoto Protocol a "good first step." He announced, however, that there would have to be meaningful participation by key developing countries before he would ask the Senate to ratify the accord. That was not good enough for a number of influential senators who vowed to kill any plausible version of a ratification bill on the grounds that significant measures to restrict greenhouse gas emissions would damage the American economy.

Seven years later, Clinton looked back on what amounted to the Senate's preemptive rejection of Kyoto as "particularly frightening to me because I thought the evidence was so compelling. It just broke my heart that we couldn't bind ourselves in any common effort to keep the planet from burning up."[21]

In 1998–99, Clinton labored under the additional burden of the Monica Lewinsky scandal, impeachment by the House, and the three-week trial in the Senate. That whole miserable episode coincided with a sudden awakening of the American people to a new species of international threat. In August 1998, agents of al-Qaeda bombed the U.S. embassies in Kenya and Tanzania, killing 220 people, including twelve Americans, and wounding over four thousand. In the weeks that followed, Madeleine Albright and I spent quite a bit of time presenting folded flags to the widows and widowers of Foreign Service officers who were among the victims.

While not yet household words, al-Qaeda and its leader, Osama bin Laden, were already very much on our minds and on the agenda of deliberations within the government. On February 26, 1993, a little more than a month after the administration had come into office, Islamist terrorists had detonated a car bomb in the garage beneath Tower One of the World Trade Center in New York, killing six people and injuring more than a thousand. One of the prime targets for follow-up attacks that had been planned to occur a few months later, along with the Lincoln Tunnel and the George Washington Bridge, was the United Nations.[22] Two years later, the mastermind of the attack, Sheik Omar Abdel-Rahman, who had preached in mosques in Brooklyn and Jersey City, was sentenced to life imprisonment. His Islamic Group was linked to al-Qaeda. One of his fellow conspirators,

Ramzi Yousef, was apprehended in Pakistan and flown back to the United States to stand trial. Passing over the twin towers, he remarked to the FBI agents with him that he regretted not having enough explosives to bring down the towers, adding the next time his "brothers" would succeed.

Ever since the first World Trade Center attack, in 1993, the U.S. government had been tracking bin Laden and members of al-Qaeda. After the bombing of our embassies in East Africa, Clinton ordered cruise-missile strikes against several of the organization's training camps in Afghanistan, apparently missing bin Laden by hours. The strikes came three days after Clinton's interrogation by a grand jury and his nationally televised address admitting he had made "misleading statements" about his relationship with Lewinsky. A president who had been pummeled by conservatives for being "soft" on national security was suddenly accused of manufacturing an excuse to use American military power in order to distract attention from his troubles at home—a charge that many of Clinton's congressional opponents rescinded after they were shown intelligence proving al-Qaeda's links to the embassy bombings.[23]

However close we came to killing bin Laden, the fact that we missed him assumed, in our minds, a metaphorical significance: *al-Qaeda* meant "the Base" in Arabic, but in fact it did not really have a base, any more than it had a capital, a flag, a seat in the General Assembly, or a return address to which we could reliably send cruise missiles in retaliation for its attacks against our people. Having originally operated out of Sudan, al-Qaeda had moved to Afghanistan, but that country was a virtual non-state actor itself, since it was a loose, fractious amalgam of tribes under the sway of the obscurantist Islamic cult known as the Taliban. Al-Qaeda also had spores in many other countries, and not just in the Arab or even the Islamic world. The United States and the international community had not just a new enemy but a new kind of enemy. Moreover, it was one that we had inadvertently helped bring into existence through our support of the anti-Soviet mujahideen during the U.S.S.R.'s folly of trying to occupy Afghanistan in the eighties. Having driven the Russian infidels from Afghanistan, the militants went global with their jihad, concentrating on American targets.

For the nearly two and a half years that remained of the Clinton administration, we were constantly trying to anticipate and thwart the sporadic, hit-and-run war that al-Qaeda was waging against America, primarily its citizens abroad. Ramzi Yousef's warning about another attack on U.S. soil was much on our minds as well. We undertook an array of offensive, defensive, and sometimes preemptive operations, many of them covert, often in concert with other governments. Successes, such as foiling a number of terrorist plots that were timed to occur on New Year's Day of 2000, were largely unnoted, and certainly unheralded. It is both difficult and imprudent to take credit for keeping bad things from happening, since we needed to protect our sources and methods and keep our operations quiet.[24]

No matter what other business we had to attend to, the senior staff meetings that began Secretary Albright's and my working days at the State Department always included an update on terrorist plots and what we were doing to foil them. At the White House, Sandy Berger set up a small group, dedicated to combating terrorism and consisting of senior officials from State, the Pentagon, the CIA, and, occasionally, the FBI. During periods when intelligence showed an increased level of threat, this group met every day to ensure that the issue got the highest level of attention and coordination from all relevant agencies. Virtually whenever I went to the Oval Office or to the Situation Room, no matter what the principal subject—Russia, the Balkans, Iraq, or South Asia—the meeting was also used to review where we stood in the hunt for bin Laden and the steps the United States was taking to head off new attacks.

DURING HIS LAST YEAR IN OFFICE, Clinton worked hard to build up the UN and concentrate as much as possible on Africa. In both respects, he relied heavily on Richard Holbrooke, who used America's turn in the presidency of the Security Council in January 2000 to declare "the month of Africa." The African Growth and Opportunity Act, passed in May 2000, offered incentives to African countries to develop their economies, create jobs, and build free markets. Clinton supported the UN's Millennium Declaration, which set a fifteen-year objective of cutting in half the number of people in extreme poverty, drastically reducing child and maternal mortality, combating HIV/AIDS and malaria, and ensuring universal primary education. The president also pressed Congress to increase foreign aid, which under the Republicans had fallen to one-tenth of 1 percent of the Gross Domestic Product, the lowest level since the end of World War II and a smaller percentage than in any other industrialized nation.

Finally, the last year of the administration saw, in East Timor, a trifecta of successful peacemaking, peacekeeping, and nation-building. Indonesia had seized this Portuguese colony in 1975 (with a wink and a nod from the Ford administration), occupied it in defiance of international law. The Indonesian military suppressed a stubborn and growing independence movement with a frenzy of murder, pillage, and arson. Kofi Annan worked tirelessly to persuade the Indonesian government to relinquish control in 1999 and "invite" an armed intervention (a feature that enabled China and Russia to support a Security Council resolution). Australia led the coalition with "boots on the ground," but the United States provided crucial diplomatic backup. Annan had help in New York from Holbrooke and in Washington from Clinton, who used the full weight of America's positions in the World Bank and IMF to apply economic pressure on Jakarta.

A hero of the story was Sergio Vieira de Mello, an elegant Brazilian UN veteran with a flare for tough, often dangerous assignments. Vieira de Mello had an affinity for the philosophy of Immanuel Kant.[25] He shared Kant's view of states and the international system as man-made structures, which good leaders could make better and bad ones could break or turn into monstrosities.[26] Vieira de Mello saw his own role as that of a reconstruction engineer specializing in disasters. In East Timor, he set up a highly effective "transitional administration"—yet another euphemism for *protectorate*—that shepherded the troubled region through exemplary elections to independence and a seat of its own in the UN for the Democratic Republic of Timor-Leste, the first newborn state of the twenty-first century.*

IT WAS IN PURSUIT OF PEACE in the Middle East that Clinton made his most sustained and determined effort and experienced his greatest frustration. At several earlier points, he had, with decisive and positive effect, thrown himself into peacemaking. He was the chief American mediator in the negotiations over Northern Ireland that produced the Good Friday Agreement in April 1998. In 1999, he personally defused a crisis between India and Pakistan that could have led to nuclear war.†

But his relentlessness with the Israelis and the Arabs was in a class by itself. He had been working on that dispute since the beginning of the administration. It was one issue on which Clinton felt that the UN should be kept at arm's length. The Israelis had long regarded the General Assembly, with its heavy representation of Islamic states, and the Security Council, with the U.S.S.R. occupying a permanent seat, as reflexively pro-Arab. Nonetheless,

---

* In a mistake comparable to the one the international community had made in Haiti, the UN pulled its peacekeepers out of East Timor too early. Renewed violence in 2006 required the introduction of another peacekeeping force, again led by Australia.

† This is an episode I recount in detail in *Engaging India*.

the Madrid process, a U.S.-Soviet diplomatic joint venture dating back to 1991 and George H. W. Bush's effort to build up Gorbachev, had continued under Clinton and Yeltsin. While the Israelis had little use for the exercise in its own right, it gave them cover to engage in direct negotiations with their Arab neighbors, including the recalcitrant Syrians, and it forced Yasser Arafat to represent the Palestinians under a Jordanian "umbrella." *

Because the Israelis so mistrusted the Russians, the real action was in Washington or wherever Clinton was prepared to go to advance the cause. This was not a task that he, or any other president, could delegate fully to envoys. It required a heavy investment of his time, energy, and political capital. In the Middle East, the question of peace requires leaders to make political, and sometimes literal, life-or-death decisions. They are unwilling to do so without the personal engagement of their American counterpart. Understanding this, Clinton was willing to host negotiations in or around Washington, receive Arafat at the White House more than any other foreign leader, fly to Geneva twice to meet with Syrian President Hafez Assad, hold two emergency summits with world leaders at Sharm el-Sheikh in Egypt, and make four trips to the Middle East.

In the summer of 2000, with the presidential election approaching, Clinton convened a marathon negotiation at Camp David aimed at reaching a final agreement. That effort continued until Clinton's last days in office. Three weeks before he left the White House, Clinton laid down the parameters for a final agreement that would have provided for a Palestinian state covering 95 percent of the West Bank and all of Gaza, as well as a capital in East Jerusalem and Palestinian sovereignty over most of the Old City, which is probably the most contested piece of land on earth. It is sacred both to Jews as the site of their original Temple and to Muslims because of the presence of the al-Aqsa Mosque and the Dome of the Rock, from which the Prophet is believed to have ascended to heaven.

---

* In October 1991, George H. W. Bush and Gorbachev had co-sponsored a Middle East peace conference in Madrid. Viewed in isolation from what was happening back in the U.S.S.R., the event was a breakthrough: never before had all the parties to the Arab-Israeli conflict come together for sustained direct negotiations; and never before had the American and Soviet governments been working so closely together. Yet in context, the Madrid conference was a charade, intended, without much success, to create the impression that Gorbachev was still in control of his own country at a time when the world could see that he was a spent force. The Israelis certainly saw that. Had it been otherwise, they would not have let the Soviets—or the Russians after the collapse of the U.S.S.R.—anywhere near the real action in the peace process, since they were convinced that any government in Moscow, no matter what its stripe, was pro-Arab.

Israeli Prime Minister Ehud Barak said yes, and Chairman Arafat said no.

On one of the last occasions when I saw Clinton in the Oval Office, he said, "You don't get points for trying in this game. You get points for delivering, and we came up short. This one goes down in the loss column: it's that simple." It was, he said—and would say again in the years that followed—the single most disappointing and frustrating experience of his presidency.

Clinton's frustration was compounded by the outcome of the Supreme Court's decision several days before to resolve the dispute over the Florida presidential election recount in George W. Bush's favor. In addition to being deprived of the chance to watch Al Gore build on the accomplishments and learn from the mistakes of their administration, Clinton feared that, with what amounted to a hostile takeover of the executive branch by the Republicans, the United States would lose whatever opportunity there might be for putting the Camp David process back on track. At a minimum, there was sure to be what he called "a hiatus" in U.S.-led diplomacy.

16

GOING IT ALONE

Don't bash the UN, Mr. President; you'll find you need us later.
—*KOFI ANNAN*[1]

Kofi, you've got to do what you've got to do, and I've got to do what
I've got to do.
—*GEORGE W. BUSH*[2]

O N December 19, 2000, the day after the Electoral College made
George W. Bush's victory official, Bill Clinton invited him to the
Oval Office for a private handoff meeting. The outgoing president
reviewed, in rank order, what he saw as the five major foreign policy challenges facing his successor: first, the terrorist threat posed by al-Qaeda and
Osama bin Laden; second, the breakdown in the Middle East peace process
and, in particular, the intransigence of Yasser Arafat; third, the continuing
tension between India and Pakistan; fourth, the nuclear menace posed by
North Korea; and, a distant fifth, the simmering crisis in Iraq.

After running through his list, Clinton added that he had followed carefully what Bush had said during the campaign about the security challenges
facing the nation. He had the impression that the two goals that mattered
most to the president-elect were dealing with Saddam Hussein and proceeding with plans to deploy a large-scale national missile defense system, presumably one that would require the United States to break free of the
Anti-Ballistic Missile (ABM) Treaty.

"That's absolutely right," Bush replied.

Clinton said he wished he had been more successful in dealing with Saddam himself: "One of my two or three greatest regrets is that I didn't get that
guy because he's going to cause you a world of problems."[3] In 1993, the Clinton administration had foiled an Iraqi plot to assassinate the senior Bush

during a visit to Kuwait and retaliated with cruise missile strikes against the headquarters of Saddam's Intelligence Service in Baghdad. In 1998 American bombers pounded Iraqi targets for four days to punish Saddam for obstructing UN inspections of facilities suspected of producing weapons of mass destruction. Still, Clinton felt that the Iraqi regime was a threat to be contained and did not rise to the same level of urgency as terrorism and the stalemate between the Israelis and Arabs, while Bush clearly had more in mind than the containment of Iraq.

IN HIS OPENING WEEKS IN OFFICE, Bush suspended American diplomatic engagement in the Middle East peace process, prompting outcries from European capitals. He also let it be known that he intended to withdraw U.S. peacekeepers from Bosnia and Kosovo, which raised concerns that a flagging American commitment would jeopardize the still-precarious process of stabilizing the Balkans. Without consulting Asian or other allies on the decision, he ruled out direct negotiations with Kim Jong Il of North Korea. Bush was acting largely on the advice of Vice President Dick Cheney, who was supported by Secretary of Defense Donald Rumsfeld. On the issue of Korea, Condoleezza Rice, the national security adviser, sided with Cheney and Rumsfeld against Secretary of State Colin Powell, who wanted to keep active diplomacy on track and felt it necessary to apologize publicly for leaning "too forward in my skis" with regard to North Korea.

During the months that followed, Bush pulled the United States out of multilateral negotiations on a small-arms treaty and made clear he would not seek ratification of the Comprehensive Test Ban Treaty. Political appointees in the Pentagon let it be known that they were flirting with the idea of developing new bunker-busting nuclear warheads that would require renewed American testing. Making good on what Bush had told Clinton, the administration notified the world of American intent to withdraw from the ABM Treaty (formal withdrawal came in December 2001), and it "unsigned"—that is, nullified Clinton's signature on—the treaty establishing the International Criminal Court.

At meetings in the White House Situation Room, Foreign Service officers and civil servants who had worked in the previous administration learned quickly to watch their language. Their new superiors derided *globalization* as a "Clinton word." When visitors to the White House used that word in Bush's presence and he felt he had to say something positive on the subject, he made comments like this one: "Oh, yes . . . globalization—that's free trade." The so-called Doha Round of the WTO was one of the few areas where the president supported multilateral negotiations.

References to global warming were considered lapses into "Gore talk" and therefore taboo. In mid-June 2001, Bush proclaimed the Kyoto Protocol "dead" and showed no interest in replacing it with something better. Denial of the extent, and even the fact, of human-induced climate change remained administration dogma for several years. Yet despite the hostility from on high, U.S. government agencies continued to generate evidence of how real and threatening climate change was, including in its economic and geopolitical ramifications. A Pentagon study commissioned in 2003 warned that changes in weather, temperatures, ocean currents, and sea levels would result in a "significant drop in the human carrying capacity of the Earth's environment."[4] Virtually none of these projections were reflected in what was said or done by the White House.

THE NEW ADMINISTRATION was distinctly standoffish toward Europe and the effort to integrate and ultimately unite the nations there. Some of the people around Bush claimed to be speaking for the president himself when they let it be known that they did not fully subscribe to the proposition— which had been part of the catechism of American foreign policy since the Truman administration—that European integration was very much in the U.S. interest. When Bush made his first trip as president across the Atlantic, in June 2001, Rice explained that he was concentrating on what she called "the new Europe"—she stressed his stops in Poland and Slovenia—with an eye toward developing a "new security framework."[5] Other officials, both on the road and back in Washington, were more explicit then and in the months that followed: the administration intended to downgrade the attention it gave to the European Union as such and deal more selectively with individual, "like-minded" (i.e., compliant) countries.

Administration officials began speaking of NATO as a "toolbox," from which the United States might draw a screwdriver for this project or a handful of nails for that one. It was hardly a figure of speech designed to reaffirm Harry Truman, George Marshall, and Dwight Eisenhower's vision of an alliance of democracies. Another instantly fashionable and no more flattering metaphor—"à la carte multilateralism"—suggested that NATO and other international institutions were dishes on a menu from which the United States could pick and choose.[6]

• • •

THE UNITED NATIONS, too, was treated with not-so-benign neglect. Bush did not give his first permanent representative to the UN, John Negroponte, the Cabinet rank that had often come with the post. The administration refused to support the Global Fund to Fight AIDS, Tuberculosis and Malaria unless it was physically and bureaucratically separated from UN headquarters by being based in Geneva. The chair of the fund was given to Tommy Thompson, the American secretary of health and human services, while Kofi Annan was designated "honorary president," a title intended by the United States to advertise his lack of authority over the effort.

The Norwegian Nobel Committee, celebrating its centenary in 2001, awarded that year's peace prize to Annan, who had just been appointed to a second five-year term, and to the United Nations itself. The honor, while couched in terms of praise for the man and the institution, was widely interpreted as an indirect rebuff to what was already seen as the least UN-friendly American administration in the fifty-six-year history of the organization.[7]

IN PUTTING HIS IMPRINT on U.S. foreign policy, Bush did not just distinguish himself from Clinton—he made clear that he was more skeptical about international institutions, international law, treaties, alliances, and diplomacy itself than any of his predecessors, notably including his father.

Governments around the world reacted with a mixture of confusion and apprehension. The United States was not just under new management but heading in an unwelcome direction. An editorial in the British newspaper, the *Guardian*, expressed the fear that Bush's foreign policy amounted to "trashing existing agreements without any clear idea of what to put in their place."[8] A poll showed that 65 percent of Germans disapproved of Bush's foreign policy and 79 percent of British respondents believed Bush was making decisions that took only U.S. interests into account.[9]

Bush aggravated foreign apprehensions by publicly reiterating his opposition to the Kyoto Protocol hours before leaving for Europe in June 2001.[10] At several stops, he encountered protesters holding posters calling him the "Toxic Texan" and depicting him with devil's horns. The leading German daily *Suddeutsche Zeitung* dubbed him "Bully Bush." Anti-Americanism was most virulent in the Middle East, largely because of the United States' disengagement from the Arab-Israeli peace process. In the spring and summer of 2001, Israeli military incursions into the Gaza Strip and West Bank intensified, and Palestinian suicide bombings were on the rise. During their visits to Washington in late March and early April 2001, the Egyptian president,

Hosni Mubarak, and Jordan's King Abdullah called for a more active U.S. role, but the Bush White House insisted that the parties themselves had to resolve the conflict. The French foreign minister, Hubert Védrine, as though nostalgic for *l'hyperpuissance*, compared Bush to Pontius Pilate.[11]

This was American unilateralism of a negative, almost sullen sort. The administration's message to the world seemed to be, "Here's what we're *not* going to do: we're not going to abide by old treaties; we don't intend to sign new ones; we're not going to do diplomacy; we're not going to do peacemaking or peacekeeping."

There was a lackluster, listless quality to the presidency as a whole. By August 2001, Bush's approval ratings were below 50 percent, a storm warning for a president so early in his first term. Conventional wisdom held that, like his father, this Bush might not be granted a second.

SEPTEMBER 11 HAD AN IMMEDIATE and transformative effect on the president and the nation alike. Three days after the attack, Bush, on a visit to the smoking wreckage of the Twin Towers, seized a bullhorn from a rescue worker. He seemed infused with a sense of purpose and resolve. Standing on a mound of debris, he declared, "The people who knocked these buildings down will hear from all of us soon." By then he had already declared the 9/11 attacks an "act of war." *Le Monde* captured a nearly worldwide sentiment with a banner headline: *Nous sommes tous Américains!* The Security Council passed a resolution requiring the Taliban regime in Afghanistan to close training camps for Osama bin Laden and all terrorists, freeze their financing, and deny them safe haven.[12] For the first time in its history, NATO invoked Article 5 of its treaty declaring an attack on one member state to be an attack on all, a provision intended in 1949 to deal with the contingency of Soviet tanks sweeping into central Europe.

In retrospect, 9/11 stands as one of the great missed opportunities of American history. The attack, while carried out on U.S. soil, was part of a threat to civilization itself. As the immediate victim, the United States could have combined retribution on its own behalf with the formation of a global alliance against the perpetrators of the terror everywhere and a comprehensive, sustained, sophisticated effort to address the root causes of the broader phenomenon, which included widespread alienation of the youth in countries such as Egypt and Saudi Arabia (the homelands of most of the 9/11 hijackers).

As a conservative Republican who had already demonstrated that he was no bleeding-heart one-worlder, Bush would have been especially well suited to the task of managing the domestic politics of a construction effort to build a "new world order." In that sense, he could have achieved a lasting break-through in an area where his father had made a promising start.

Instead, Bush chose, essentially, to go it alone. When the United States began its military campaign to drive the Taliban from power in Afghanistan, the administration largely bypassed NATO and rebuffed offers of allied sup-port. A number of Pentagon officials, mostly civilian political appointees who had come into office with Bush, cited the Clinton administration's expe-rience with Bosnia and Kosovo as an example of what they did *not* want to replicate: no more "war by committee," no more negotiating with pesky al-lied leaders in Paris and Berlin over targeting. This war would be run from Washington and nowhere else.

Running the war did not entail much in the way of planning for what to do after the Taliban was dispersed. That was work that could be handled by the UN. On October 11, four days after the operation began, Bush told a press conference, "It would be a useful function for the United Nations to take over the so-called nation-building," an activity Bush had disparaged during the campaign. After the Taliban was driven out of Kabul and al-Qaeda was holed up in the badlands along the Pakistani frontier, America handed off to the UN—and, increasingly, to European members of NATO—the task of trying to make a functioning state out of what had long been more of a buffer zone than a real country and had just been through two decades of constant war and occupation.

THE SPEED WITH WHICH THE AMERICAN MILITARY, acting almost entirely by itself, was able to bring down the regime in Kabul raised confidence in the upper reaches of the U.S. administration that it could ac-complish expeditiously—and unilaterally—the priority objective Bush had set himself before taking office: getting rid of Saddam Hussein. The president had devoted his first major National Security Council meeting, on January 30, 2001, to a discussion of restarting the flow of funds to Iraqi opposition groups. The main beneficiary was Ahmad Chalabi's Iraqi National Congress, whose funding the Clinton administration had cut off five years earlier be-cause Chalabi was seen as untrustworthy.

There were thirty-two more cabinet-level NSC meetings over the next eight months before there was finally one on terrorism.[13] After 9/11, of course, that subject was virtually always at the top of the agenda, but Bush saw it as intimately connected to his desire to use the administration's initial military success in Afghanistan to pivot toward Iraq.

From the White House's standpoint, the presumption that Saddam had a covert program to develop weapons of mass destruction fit neatly into the assertion that he was an enemy in the war on terror: the ultimate nightmare was an al-Qaeda-like organization armed not with box cutters to hijack airliners but with small, made-in-Iraq nuclear weapons that could be smuggled into American cities.

Saddam's WMD program was a virtual given—and not just in the view of the Bush administration. Along with most other officials of the previous administration, on the basis of what I had seen and heard when I was still at the State Department, I assumed Saddam was well on his way to developing a bomb. While the evidence I recall was far from conclusive, I believed that any president who took office in January 2001—whether it had been Al Gore or John McCain (Bush's principal rival for the Republican nomination)—would have had to deal with the danger of Saddam acquiring nuclear weapons. Doing so, however, would have—or should have—meant ratcheting up pressure on Saddam to open his country to UN inspections, rather than hyping the evidence at hand. In an effort to clinch the case, the Bush administration added the unsubstantiated and later discredited allegation that Saddam had operational contacts with al-Qaeda.

Bush spent much of the next year and a half laying the ground for intervention, while privately confiding to those he regarded as supportive and discreet that he had already made up his mind on what had to be done. In March 2002, a full year before the start of the Iraq war, Bush did a "drop-by" at a meeting that Condoleezza Rice was holding with a small group of friendly senators to discuss alternative strategies for dealing with the Iraqi dictator. In Bush's mind there were no alternatives to the course he had already chosen. "Fuck Saddam," he said, according to two people in the room. "We're taking him out."[14] On several occasions that year and later, he made clear in public how strongly he felt—and that it was personal. "After all," Bush later said, "this is the guy who tried to kill my dad." *

There were a few voices of caution from the sidelines, including from one of Bush 41's closest friends and confidants, Brent Scowcroft. In a *Wall Street Journal* op-ed article in August, Scowcroft warned that going after Saddam

---

* Bush was referring to the 1993 assassination plot against his father. He made the comment in Houston on September 27, 2002, when asked by the press why he was bearing down so hard on Saddam.

would distract energy and attention from the manhunt for Osama bin Laden. In September, the ninety-eight-year-old George F. Kennan gave an interview at a nursing home in Washington questioning whether the administration had any idea what it was in for in Iraq: "Today, if we went into Iraq, as the president would like us to do, you know where you begin; you never know where you're going to end." [15]

THAT SAME MONTH, the administration released with considerable fanfare what had, in the past, been a little-noticed, periodic in-house document known as the National Security Strategy. "[W]e will not hesitate to act alone, if necessary," it vowed, stressing the utility of "coalitions of the willing" as a way of "augmenting" permanent institutions like the UN and NATO.

National Security Strategies had been released generally every year since they were mandated by Congress in 1986. They were often used as much to summarize an administration's philosophy and strategic priorities as to address specific policy challenges. (The one that the Clinton White House put out in December 1999 opened with a quotation from Franklin Roosevelt that reflected Clinton's worldview: "We have learned that we cannot live alone at peace. We have learned that our own wellbeing is dependent on the wellbeing of other nations far away. We have learned to be citizens of the world, members of the human community.")

Presidents before George W. Bush had affirmed a long-held, often-asserted, and occasionally exercised right of the United States to act on its own—or, a preferred alternative, to assemble ad hoc alliances when formal ones were unable or unwilling to answer a call to arms from Washington. Those presidents, however, felt, and conveyed to the world, a clear desire to have the UN at America's side. Bush's predecessors looked to international alliances to strengthen their hand and worked to bring nations with differing viewpoints into the fold. They regarded unilateral action as an option of last resort. By contrast, many of the people working for George W. Bush—virtually all of them political appointees—saw Iraq as an opportunity for Uncle-Sam-as-Gulliver finally to free himself from the Lilliputians who dominated the "international community" and the UN.

The 2002 National Security Strategy made the case for what Bush and members of the administration referred to, almost interchangeably, as a "preemptive" or a "preventive" war. Preemptive and preventive wars are technically quite different: a preemptive one requires credible signs that the enemy is poised to attack immediately, while a preventive one is launched against a *potential* enemy. The former is arguably allowed under the UN Charter's recognition of the right of self-defense, while the latter is permissible only if authorized by the Security Council. Bush's team blurred the distinction in the National Security Strategy and in subsequent statements. Moving against Iraq would qualify as preventive war, but calling it preemptive sounded more robust in a post-9/11 world.

The United States had always maintained the right to strike first against an enemy, including with nuclear weapons, but it was an option that earlier presidents have regarded with apprehension and distaste.[16] At several key moments in its history, America had gone to war when it could claim that the enemy had struck first. The notable examples were the Confederacy's firing on Fort Sumter in 1861, the presumption that the Spanish had blown up the *Maine* in Havana Harbor in 1898, the sinking of U.S. merchant ships by German U-boats in 1917, and Pearl Harbor in 1941. The Korean conflict was precipitated by the North Korean invasion of the South in 1950; the American escalation in Vietnam stemmed from the Gulf of Tonkin incident in 1964; and the first major U.S. military engagement after the cold war was a result of Saddam Hussein's invasion and occupation of Kuwait in 1990.

Harry Truman spoke for predecessors and successors alike when he rejected preventive war as a weapon "of dictators, not of free democratic countries like the United States." The 1950 equivalent of the National Security Strategy, known as the United States Objectives and Programs for National Security (or, in shorthand, NSC-68), asserted, "It goes without saying that the idea of 'preventive war'—in the sense of a military attack not provoked by a military upon us or our allies—is generally unacceptable to Americans. . . . [It is] morally corrosive."[17] Dwight Eisenhower subscribed to the doctrine of "massive retaliation" in large measure because, as he said in an August 1954 news conference, "A preventive war, to my mind, is an impossibility today. . . . I don't believe there is such a thing, and frankly wouldn't even listen to anyone seriously that came in and talked about such a thing." Kennedy had much the same view. In the early days of the Cuban missile crisis, he slapped down a plan to destroy the missile installations in Cuba before they could be used to attack the United States on the grounds, as his brother Robert put it, that such an act "would be Pearl Harbor in reverse . . . [The United States was] fighting for something more than just survival . . . Our heritage and our ideals would be repugnant to such a sneak military attack. . . . For 175 years we have not been that kind of country." In 1981, Ronald Reagan's permanent representative to the UN, Jeane Kirkpatrick, criticized Israel for bombing an Iraqi nuclear reactor at Osirak since no one, not even the Israelis, claimed that Saddam Hussein was about to attack Israel. Reagan detested the strategy of nuclear deterrence, which held open the option of preemption. He embraced Star Wars precisely because it was, in theory at least, purely defensive. Had Star Wars worked, and had the United States shared the technology with the Soviets, as Reagan suggested, it would have taken the options of both preemptive and retaliatory nuclear war off the table.[18]

Yet with the National Security Strategy of 2002, George W. Bush, who considered himself an ideological successor to Reagan, made sure that precisely those options were very much on the table. In tone, content, and context—and, it is safe to speculate, in a way that his predecessors would have found repellent—the document made the case for unilateralism and preemption without apologies. As the international relations specialist John Ikenberry of Princeton put it at the time, the Bush administration, through its "wholesale depreciation of multilateral governance," had "render[ed] international norms of self-defense—enshrined by Article 51 of the UN Charter—almost meaningless."[19] Henry Kissinger voiced his own concern: "The new approach is revolutionary. . . . It is not in the American national interest to establish preemption as a universal principle available to every nation."[20]

The National Security Strategy made military doctrine out of a geopolitical precept that Bush's more conservative advisers had been advocating for more than a decade, when they had worked for his father: the United States should never allow another country to pose a challenge to U.S. forces either globally or regionally.* By adopting that posture, the president was, in effect, substituting a commitment to maintain American preeminence for the balance-of-power principle of the eighteenth and nineteenth centuries, not to mention the balance-of-superpower one of the cold war. Once again, Bush was not so much transfiguring the substance of American foreign and defense policy as he was enunciating it with an in-your-face bluntness that seemed to dare other countries to try to match U.S. power in their own regions and, without leaving much to the imagination, threatening any nation that tried to do so with defeat or, for that matter, with preemption.[21]

---

* Paul Wolfowitz and I. Lewis ("Scooter") Libby, who had both worked for Cheney when he was secretary of defense in the Bush 41 administration, featured this point in a 1992 Defense Department document that was leaked and later repudiated by the Bush 41 administration. Wolfowitz served as deputy secretary of defense in the first term of the Bush 43 administration, and Libby was Cheney's chief of staff until 2006, when he was indicted for perjury and obstruction of justice in the Valerie Wilson leak case.

During the summer and fall of 2002, I began to hear grumbling from traditional friends of the United States, as well as from those who were part of the old nonaligned movement or the communist camp, that the rest of the world needed to "contain" American power—not militarily, of course, but politically and diplomatically. Occasionally there were public statements, including from government officials, that a "unipolar" world—i.e., U.S.-dominated one—was uncomfortable for everyone else, and that one of many reasons to promote multilateralism was to counter American unilateralism.[22]

But these complaints were marked by a sense of resignation. There was little confidence abroad that an America roused to righteous fury by 9/11 could be stopped from doing whatever it wanted, and there was little concern in official Washington that the administration had much to worry about as it set about wreaking vengeance on its enemies and demanding obedience from everyone else.

IN THE SUMMER and early fall of 2002, around the time that the National Security Strategy became public, former colleagues who were Foreign Service professionals still in the executive branch told me about efforts they had made to get Secretary of State Colin Powell—the administration's increasingly lonely voice of moderation—to tell the president to his face how much he and his policies were disliked around the world. Powell replied that he was not going to "bell that cat" (confirming he knew there was a problem) unless and until he could make the argument that the United States would pay a meaningful price for Bush's unpopularity abroad. "What can they do to hurt us?" he asked. "What can they do to keep us from carrying out our policy objectives?" Unless he had an answer to that question, he was not going to confront the president. The Foreign Service officers replied that effective American leadership required a sense on the part of those being led that they were being respected and consulted, that they were part of a consensual process of setting goals and deciding how to achieve them. One veteran American diplomat in the meeting with Powell added that the United States was relying too much on hard power and neglecting the importance of its soft power. Powell found that argument "amorphous," and unlikely to elicit anything but disdain from the president. Besides, Bush was not going to be impressed by any bumper sticker with the word *soft* in it, especially since, according to the polls, he had considerable support where it really mattered—among the American people.

· · ·

EIGHT DAYS BEFORE THE RELEASE of the National Security Strategy and the day after the first anniversary of 9/11, Kofi Annan and George Bush gave back-to-back speeches at the General Assembly. It was a polite duel over American policy. Annan used the word *multilateral* nine times before mentioning Iraq. "Choosing to follow or reject the multilateral path must not be a simple matter of political convenience," said Annan as he opened the session. "When states decide to use force to deal with the broader threats to international peace and security, there is no substitute for the unique legitimacy provided by the United Nations." Annan was using a positive though hortatory formulation to issue a warning to the United States: if it acted alone, its actions would be illegitimate.

Hours later, just as obliquely and just as unmistakably, Bush countered with a warning of his own: "We created the United Nations Security Council, so that—unlike the League of Nations—our deliberations would be more than talk, and our resolutions would be more than wishes." He was saying that if the United Nations refused to back U.S. action, the organization would follow the League into oblivion—and deservedly so. "Saddam Hussein's regime is a grave and gathering danger," he continued. "Will the United Nations serve the purpose of its founding, or will it become irrelevant? . . . The Security Council resolutions will be enforced, or action will be unavoidable."

Bush, whose rhetoric tended to favor active-voice verbs, resorted in this instance to the passive voice; but his message was clear, and it accomplished its purpose, at least for the time being. The other members of the Security Council, notably including the French, feared irrelevance even more than they resented being bullied. Also, as long as they could maintain, through the Council, a degree of control over what happened in Iraq, they might have some influence over what the United States did there.

It was with these damned-if-we-do/damned-if-we-don't calculations in mind that the Council unanimously adopted Resolution 1441, which declared Iraq in breach of earlier resolutions and required new, invigorated inspections, including unscheduled visits to previously uninspected sites. The resolution put Iraq on notice that if it failed to comply, it would face "serious consequences." The United States alone took that phrase to be the equivalent of "all necessary means" in UN resolutions during the run-up to the first Gulf War—that is, code for authority to attack. Well before inspectors arrived in Iraq in the late fall, the Bush administration had begun its preparations for war.

The inspections found some scattered, undeclared warheads capable of delivering chemical weapons and three thousand pages of unreported documents at the home of an Iraqi scientist. Hans Blix, the Swede who headed the UN monitoring commission, criticized Saddam for playing cat-and-mouse with the inspectors, but the UN found no evidence of any Iraqi attempt to reactivate earlier nuclear-weapons programs. That did not stop Bush from repeatedly asserting that Saddam's regime "possesses and produces" chemical and biological weapons and had "reconstitut[ed] its nuclear weapons program." [23] The administration took the failure of the inspectors to find hard evidence of the program as proof of Saddam's success in hiding it.

On January 14, 2003, Bush said he was "sick and tired" of Iraq's "games and deceptions." In his State of the Union address on January 28, he implied he was losing patience with the UN as well: "We have called on the United Nations to fulfill its Charter and stand by its demand that Iraq disarm." Soon after, he added, "Now the Security Council will show whether its words have any meaning." It was "a moment of truth for the United Nations. The United Nations gets to decide, shortly, whether or not it is going to be relevant, in terms of keeping the peace, whether or not its words mean anything."

Lest anyone think that Colin Powell would serve as a counterbalance to the bellicosity elsewhere in the administration, he told the World Economic Forum in Davos, Switzerland, that "multilateralism cannot be an excuse for inaction" and that the United States "continues to reserve our sovereign right to take military action against Iraq alone or in a coalition of the willing." [24] I was in the audience, pondering the bizarre and tragic picture of Powell allowing himself to be cast in this role. Precisely because polls showed him to be the most admired and credible public figure in America—and precisely because he was known to be the administration's leading, if not sole, advocate of diplomacy—he was being used to prepare the way for unilateral action.

Weeks of wrangling in the Security Council pitted the United States against France. Russia and China, which both opposed use of force, could sit back and watch the sparks fly between Paris and Washington.

Britain was caught in the middle but tilting toward the United States. Prime Minister Tony Blair was a true believer in humanitarian intervention and the importance of marshaling international force against criminal regimes. He was also determined to protect Britain's "special relationship" with the United States, which meant not letting himself get crosswise with an American president who was hell-bent on invading Iraq. Blair thought that, by staying close to Bush, he might be able to guide American policy toward actions that would be less damaging to the international system. Yet because he kept private whatever efforts he made to moderate Bush, he got no credit for trying. And insofar as there were public hints that he was indeed privately trying, they called attention to his ineffectiveness. As a result, Blair prevented himself from having what might otherwise have been a stunningly successful prime ministership.

In the nineties, Blair had gone a long way toward establishing Britain's bona fides as a full part of the leadership of the European Union. Over Iraq, however, in the eyes of many continental Europeans, Britain seemed to be showing, once again, its true colors as an American aircraft carrier anchored off their coast.[25] That made it all the easier for President Jacques Chirac of France to play one of his favorite parts on the world stage: standing up to the hyperpower on behalf of Europe. On February 10, at a press conference in Paris with President Putin, Chirac said "nothing today justifies war" since "I have no proof that these weapons exist in Iraq."

Neither did anyone else, including those in the American intelligence community who had only circumstantial evidence on which to base their judgment. (Analysts assumed there were unaccounted-for stocks of chemical and biological weapons from the aftermath of the first Gulf War because they could not be certain that all of them had been destroyed.) France, Russia, and Germany (which held one of the rotating seats on the Security Council and chaired the Council that month) advocated a strengthened inspections regime rather than armed conflict. China took a similar position.

ON MARCH 17, Bush went on national television to issue an ultimatum: Saddam and his sons Uday and Qusay had forty-eight hours to surrender and leave Iraq. When the deadline expired, Bush went back on television to announce that Operation Iraqi Freedom had begun. Its purpose was "to disarm Iraq, to free its people and to defend the world from grave danger." The combination of the "shock-and-awe campaign"—a massive two-week bombing assault—and a lightning ground attack made quick work of Iraqi defenses. On April 9, crowds of cheering young men climbed atop the statue of Saddam Hussein in Firdos Square in central Baghdad and, with the help of a crane and some U.S. Marines, brought it crashing down, providing photographers with the first emblematic image of the war.

Three weeks later, a second photograph appeared on front pages around the world. Bush, who had been a pilot in the Texas Air National Guard during

the Vietnam War, briefly took the controls of a Navy S-3B Viking strike aircraft that landed on the USS *Abraham Lincoln* just off the coast of California.
He was wearing a flight suit, complete with parachute, water survival kit,
combat boots, and flight helmet. After saluting the sailors on the flight deck
and posing for the cameras, he declared, "Major combat operations in Iraq
have ended," adding, "We have removed an ally of al-Qaeda." (In fact, Sad-

The toppling of Saddam's statue

dam and Osama bin Laden were sworn enemies.) Behind the president, on the aircraft
carrier's tower, was a huge banner proclaiming "Mission Accomplished."

Ten days later, the American military
contingent in Iraq staged its first formal celebration of victory. The venue was one of
the fallen dictator's palaces in the provincial
capital of al-Hillah—a town sixty miles
from Baghdad built with some bricks and
stones that may have come from the Etemenanki ziggurat, which was possibly the
historic Tower of Babel. The ceremony featured an hourlong concert by the 3rd Ma-

rine Aircraft Wing Band, replete with patriotic songs plus one dedicated to
Saddam, "It's All Over Now."

The fall of Saddam was the high-water mark of American unilateralism—
and of what two colleagues at Brookings, Ivo Daalder and James Lindsay,
called, in a book they completed around that time, "the Bush revolution in
American foreign policy."[26]

ONE OF THE FEW MEMBER STATES to offer unambiguous support
for the American action was Israel, a successor state to the one that Nebuchadnezzar had tried to destroy. Virtually all Israelis welcomed the downfall
of one of their most implacable foes, and many hoped that the display of
power by their best friend in the world would have a restraining effect on
other hostile neighbors.

The effect on most Arabs was more one of humiliation. Even many of
those who loathed Saddam watched with a mixture of horror and shame as
the U.S. forces routed the notoriously fierce Republican Guard. As looting
and rioting spread across Iraq, several Arab leaders—including President
Mubarak of Egypt and the Saudi foreign minister, Prince Saud al-Faisal—

warned of chaos to come.[27] One of the most moderate, pro-American voices in the Arab world, the former Jordanian crown prince, Hassan bin Talal, expressed the anxiety in the region and around the world that the American juggernaut would keep rolling to Damascus and from there to Tehran.[28]

That prospect brought joy to enthusiasts for the Iraq war inside and outside the administration. Some could even imagine changing the regime in Pyongyang as well, thereby pulling off a hat trick against the "Axis of Evil" (Iraq, Iran, and North Korea) that Bush had denounced in his 2002 State of the Union address.

Europeans reacted angrily during the first weeks of the war, railing against Bush's ill-disguised contempt for the way they felt the world was supposed to work. The former foreign secretary of the United Kingdom, Robin Cook, an irascible but intellectually impressive and politically courageous figure with whom I had worked closely during the Kosovo crisis, had already quit as the Labour Party's leader in the House of Commons. In his resignation speech, three days before the war began, Cook lamented the impending American action, in which he saw his own government as already complicit. The invasion, said Cook, would be a major setback to the cause of a "world order governed by rules. . . . [T]he international partnerships most important to us are weakened: the European Union is divided; the Security Council is in stalemate. Those are heavy casualties of a war in which a shot has yet to be fired."

George W. Bush

Polls showed a precipitous decline in approval of the United States around the world.[29] In Beijing, Jakarta, Rabat, Madrid, and São Paulo protesters amassed in front of American embassies and consulates. Many of their placards called the war illegal. To the fury of the Bush administration, Annan endorsed that verdict in an interview with the BBC.[30] Just after letting this stark opinion be known publicly, Annan repeated a milder version of it in the General Assembly. In a speech on September 21, 2004, well aware of the irony, he invoked a Babylonian contribution to civilization. Hammurabi's code, he said, had been "a landmark in mankind's struggle to build an order where, instead of might making right, right would make might. Many nations represented in this chamber can proudly point to founding documents of their own that embody that simple concept. And this Organization, your United Nations, is founded on the same simple principle."

Annan had come a long way from his Ditchley Park Doctrine of 1998, when—preemptively, as it were—he endorsed the U.S.-led attack on Kosovo. But then, from Annan's perspective, the United States had come a long way, too, and very much in the wrong direction. The Clinton administration had done everything it could to wrap the Kosovo operation in the UN flag. The Russians had played the spoiler, although even they had ended up being recruited into the diplomacy that ended the war and the international force that imposed the ensuing peace.

In Iraq, by contrast, the U.S. administration, largely at the behest of Colin Powell, sought a UN blessing for the operation, but others in official Washington made no secret that they were relieved when Powell's effort failed. In the summer of 2003, when defenders of Operation Iraqi Freedom were still upbeat about its chances for success, I spoke privately with two members of the administration, both political appointees, one who worked in the White House, the other in the Pentagon. I recalled how the Clinton administration had agonized over how difficult it was to get a Security Council resolution to authorize the air war against Serbia in 1999. "That's the difference between you people and us, Strobe. Your type agonizes, ours seizes opportunities. You see our interests in Iraq and in the UN as in tension with each other; we see an opportunity to kill two birds with one stone"—that is, to bring down a dictator while further weakening an organization that, in their view, had outlived whatever usefulness it ever had and become an obstacle to America's getting its way in the world.

THE ADMINISTRATION'S TRIUMPHALISM was not shared by most American military leaders on the ground in Iraq nor by many of their fellow officers back in Washington. Just over a year after the invasion, I was invited to give a talk on the Bush administration's foreign policy to a group of Army generals who were holding an all-day conference at a hotel in Pentagon City. Virtually all had either already seen action in Iraq or were about to be sent there.

Not wanting to seem partisan or excessively critical of an enterprise in which they and their troops were risking their lives, I downplayed my opposition to Bush unilateralism and my concern about the extent to which the invasion had antagonized world opinion. I could see what I was saying was not going over very well—I assumed that, despite my restraint, the officers still felt I was bashing their commander in chief—so I cut short my remarks.

That was my one smart move because it gave them a chance to speak. I had it exactly backward: almost to a man, the generals felt I was much too forgiving of what they regarded as two colossal blunders by their civilian superiors: going in "light" (that is, without sufficient force to fill the security vacuum created by the fall of the Saddam regime) and dismantling the ruling Ba'ath party, the army, the police, and other sources of power (thereby creating a vast pool of unemployed, aggrieved, armed, and violence-prone recruits for militias and insurgent groups). I asked whether they would have preferred to have a UN mandate, complete with UN flags and blue helmets. The answer was a categorical and unanimous *yes*. With heads around him nodding, one general said, "The whole bugbear about the UN and black helicopters and our supposedly having an allergy to blue helmets is utter nonsense. Its right-wing talk radio crap. We prefer it when we've got others to help us in something like this, particularly when it comes to dealing with looters and police work and that kind of thing. All we care about is unity of command"—that is, American soldiers reporting to American officers all the way up the chain.

Toward the end of the session, another officer noted that he and his colleagues were too young to have served in Vietnam (a bit of a head snapper for me, since I realized I was older than they were), but many of them had been in military academies at the time. "We have spent pretty much all our careers putting Vietnam behind us," he said, "and hoping that we never got into that kind of quagmire again. Well, here we are: right back there in the soup."

Remembering vividly how unpopular Bill Clinton had been with many in the military, initially because of the controversy over his not having served in Vietnam and because of his gays-in-the-military policy in 1993, I was taken aback by the depth and openness of these soldiers' anger at the Bush administration, although they were careful not to mention the president himself.

I asked how the generals compared the invasion and occupation of Iraq to the interventions in the Balkans in the nineties. "Night and day," said one. As he and others elaborated, I realized I was in the midst of a bunch of multilateralists in olive-drab uniforms. They did not share the distaste for diplomacy that was so prevalent among their political bosses, not least because if diplomacy worked, it spared them having to watch their troops die. They regarded the cascade of bad decisions behind the invasion and occupation of Iraq as a case of staggering ineptitude.

·   ·   ·

WHAT HAD BEEN SO WORRYING the generals from the beginning of the operation was apparent to the world by the summer of 2003, when central Iraq was mired in a low-level but pervasive, growing insurgency. By the autumn, advocates of an "American empire" and self-described "liberal imperialists" watched their dream-come-true start turning into a nightmare.[31]

Meanwhile, impotent rage against the United States in Europe had turned to schadenfreude. On November 13, 2003, just over two years after its post-9/11 headline embracing America, *Le Monde* claimed that the chaos in Iraq vindicated Chirac's having stood up to Bush. Many at the UN, including on Kofi Annan's staff, argued that the United States should stew in its own juices. Perhaps it would learn a lesson from the experience and, duly chastened, return to its traditional role. Annan rejected this advice. He was determined to have the organization reengage in Iraq. In September 2002, Bush had said that the UN would render itself irrelevant if it failed to back the United States in enforcing the resolutions aimed at Saddam. Fearing precisely that perception, Annan jumped at the chance to prove Bush wrong and demonstrate that the UN was indispensable. For all Annan's opposition to the way the United States had gone to war in defiance of the UN, he felt the world organization had an obligation to the people of Iraq to try to halt the deterioration of the security situation in their country.

Overcoming resistance among the rank-and-file membership of the organization as well as in the Security Council and in the Secretariat itself, Annan pushed through a decision to send Sergio Vieira de Mello—the veteran peacekeeper who had performed so admirably in East Timor—to Baghdad to coordinate assistance. He and his team of some eight hundred workers from various UN agencies set up offices on three floors of the Canal Hotel on the far side of the Tigris River and three miles away from the "Green Zone," the heavily fortified headquarters of the U.S.-run Coalition Provisional Authority (CPA), which was eventually 3,700-strong yet considerably less capable than the UN contingent in its knowledge of the local language, culture, and politics.[32]

The administrator of the CPA, L. Paul (known as "Jerry") Bremer, a former diplomat and a longtime acolyte of Kissinger, gave Vieira de Mello little help. Bremer was only slightly less imperious toward his British deputies, John Sawers, who had formerly been Tony Blair's foreign policy adviser at No. 10 Downing Street, and Jeremy Greenstock, a professional diplomat of high renown who had previously been the United Kingdom's permanent representative to the UN and with whom I had worked closely during the Kosovo crisis.

• • •

ON AUGUST 19, 2003, a truck bomb detonated a ton of explosives beneath Vieira de Mello's office. The suicide bomber was later linked to an offshoot of al-Qaeda that had established itself in Iraq after the U.S. invasion. Vieira de Mello bled to death in the rubble, speaking to his would-be rescuers as they tried in vain to shift the masonry in which he was buried. Another twenty-one UN officials, local employees, and visitors were also killed. It was the worst day in the history of the organization since Dag Hammarskjöld's plane went down in Congo forty-two years before. Kofi Annan, nearly catatonic with grief, discouragement, and a sense of responsibility for sending his friend and colleague on what turned out to be a fatal mission, called Vieira de Mello's death "a bitter blow for the United Nations and for me personally." [33] The months afterward were, he said, a "depressed period" and a "nightmare" for him. [34]

Salim Lone, the Kenyan spokesman for the UN in Iraq who survived the bombing, said later, "It was clear to many of us in Baghdad that lots of ordinary Iraqis were unable to distinguish our UN operation from the overall U.S. presence in the country." [35] In the week following the bombing, Annan withdrew most of the UN entourage. After an attack on the local Red Cross headquarters in late October, Annan pulled out all non-Iraqi UN staff members. Oxfam (an international relief and development organization), the IMF, and the World Bank followed the UN out soon thereafter.

As 2003 drew to a close, Annan made clear that the UN had been a victim not just of the terrorists but of poor coordination with the Americans and ambiguity about what the organization was supposed to do: "Bad resolutions kill people." The UN would not return, said Annan, until there was "clarity" about its role. [36] In his annual end-of-year press conference, Annan, his penchant for understatement exaggerated by exhaustion, labeled 2003 "a rather hard year."

Yet within a month, Annan seemed to have overcome his personal discouragement enough to try again to find a renewed role for the UN. The Iraqis were pleading for him to do so, and the Bush administration had come, belatedly, to realize that the UN was better suited for the task ahead than Bremer and his team.

Annan met in New York with Bremer's hand-picked Iraqi Governing Council to discuss when elections could be held for a new Iraqi government. Annan followed up on the meeting by sending to Iraq a high-level personal envoy to assess how quickly elections could be arranged. His choice for that job was Lakhdar Brahimi, who had distinguished himself in the midst of adversity during the Haiti operation and gone on to do an excellent job in Afghanistan after the United States drove the Taliban from power there. Brahimi concluded that it would be at least a year before Iraq could hold elections. In addition to laying the ground for elections, Brahimi served as a "facilitator"—in effect, a buffer—between the Iraqis and the Americans. On June 8, 2004, the Security Council unanimously passed a resolution approving the transfer of sovereignty to a new Iraqi interim government that Brahimi made sure was more regionally, religiously, and ethnically representative than its predecessor, the Iraqi Governing Council. The resolution also established a timetable for the dissolution of this new interim government after the January 2005 national elections and reiterated authorization, under Chapter VII of the UN Charter, for the U.S.-led multinational force to maintain peace and stability in Iraq.

The long battle between Bush and Annan, which had seemed a thumping victory for Bush in the spring of 2003, now had the look of a draw. On the one hand, as Annan had predicted, the United States had come back to the UN for help and legitimacy. On the other hand, the war on which Bush had bet his presidency now had what he could claim was a UN imprimatur, even though it had been conferred reluctantly and nearly fifteen months after the invasion.

But it was a Pyrrhic draw, since the battle for the future of Iraq was far from over. If anything, it was heading toward a victory for forces inimical to both the United States and the United Nations. Coalition casualties—mostly American—at the hands of insurgents and militias, and also as a result of friendly fire, mounted steadily. The number of attacks on patrols escalated from sixteen a day in July 2003 to forty-five in July 2004 to seventy a day in July 2005 to one hundred and forty in July 2006 to one hundred and seventy-five in July 2007. By Christmas of 2006, the number of American armed service personnel killed in Iraq surpassed the number of victims of 9/11.

But it was Iraqi civilians who bore the brunt of the violence. Even by conservative estimates, an average of fifty Iraqis a day were being shot, blown up, beheaded, or tortured to death. Adjusted for population, that figure would be the equivalent of more than five hundred Americans a day.[37]

IN THE SPRING OF 2004, the bad news out of Iraq took on a whole new dimension. The United States, in the name of bringing to heel a rogue state, opened itself to the charge of being one itself. Not only had the United

States invaded Iraq in defiance of the UN and most of its allies; not only had it offered three rationales for the invasion that fell of their own weight (the presence of WMD, links to al-Qaeda, and the goal of democratizing Iraq and the Greater Middle East); not only was the United States botching the occupation—it was doing all this in open disdain for the very concept of international law, treaties, and institutions. The United States was holding hundreds of alleged terrorists in a detention camp at Guantánamo Bay, some of them in solitary confinement and many designated as "illegal enemy combatants," a term meant to exempt them from the rights and protections that were supposed to be accorded to prisoners of war.

The president and his subordinates believed they had acquired the right to resort to these extraordinary tactics as a result of their expansive reading of the president's constitutional powers as fortified by a series of Justice Department memos and laws passed in the wake of 9/11. The effect was to make the president virually the sole arbiter of what was permissible in waging "the global war on terror." According to this view, the commander in chief could disregard the rules set by the Geneva Conventions and the Uniform Code of Military Justice, and suspend the right of habeas corpus that had been a cornerstone of the law since the Middle Ages and affirmed in the U.S. Constitution. The president and those acting under his authority believed that they could decide what coercive techniques to use in extracting information from those held in custody. That claim effectively meant that the United States was no longer bound by the 1987 UN Convention against Torture and Other Cruel, Inhuman or Degrading Treatment or Punishment, even though that obligation had acquired force as U.S. law in 1994. Presidential decisions on these matters were now deemed to be inherently legitimate because the president made them. In addition to being tautological, this position was a reversal of John Adams's dictum—based on his respect for the thinking of Montesquieu, Kant, Hume, and others—that America should be established as "a government of laws and not of men."

Then came the revelation that American occupation personnel were torturing Iraqis in what had been one of Saddam's prisons at Abu Ghraib, west of Baghdad.

Seymour Hersh, the investigative reporter who had made his reputation thirty-five years before by breaking the story of the 1968 massacre of hundreds of Vietnamese villagers in My Lai by U.S. soldiers, published the details of what was happening at Abu Ghraib in the *New Yorker*.[38] The article was accompanied by photographs, taken by the perpetrators, of prisoners being subjected to sexual humiliation and physical torment. One picture in particular—of a hooded figure, his arms spread in an unintended and therefore all-the-more-grotesque parody of crucifixion, electrodes attached to his fingers—replaced the toppling of Saddam's statue as the defining image of the whole venture.

A CONSEQUENTIAL ABERRATION

Nothing is so fatal to a nation as an extreme of self-partiality, and the total want of consideration of what others will naturally hope or fear.
—*EDMUND BURKE*[1]

Americans should not fall in love with their own virtue, and should not expect non-Americans to take that virtue on faith.
—*REINHOLD NIEBUHR*[2]

SCORES of books and countless articles have chronicled and analyzed the American occupation of Iraq, but it is still not clear, to me at least, what drove George W. Bush to take the course he did. We have similar backgrounds, yet he and I grew up with—or somewhere along the way acquired—profoundly different views of the world and of America's role in it. Even though we were at Yale together and are distant relatives through a shared Walker connection, we saw virtually nothing of each other in New Haven in the mid to late sixties and met only twice during the next thirty-five years.*

During the 2000 presidential campaign, I found myself, for the second time in my life, in the small print of the news as a classmate of a presidential aspirant. A *Washington Post* story compared Bush, as the president of the jock fraternity at Yale, to the John Belushi character Bluto in *Animal House* and me to the guitar-playing wuss whom Bluto teases and bullies. I had to get my son Devin to explain the reference, thereby validating at least half the point of the story. Several newspaper and magazine profiles of Candidate Bush

---

* Other than being together for a family funeral in 1990, as mentioned in Chapter 12, I saw Bush in May 2003. We exchanged brief pleasantries in a receiving line at the White House when he invited members of our Yale class and their families to the East Wing for a reception on the occasion of our thirty-fifth reunion.

mentioned a grudge he bore against me as a bookish, hyperearnest under-graduate and a representative of the East Coast liberal foreign policy estab-lishment.[3] On December 9, 2000 (the day the Supreme Court stopped the Florida recount), Walter Isaacson, then the managing editor of *Time*, inter-viewed Bush at his ranch outside Crawford, Texas, for the magazine's annual "Person of the Year" issue. Learning that Isaacson and I were friends, Bush launched into a long, vituperative digression about how I stood for much of what he wanted to get away from after college. Given how little contact there had been between Bush and me, I suspected that whatever ancient animus he bore toward me had been freshened by my association with Bill Clinton, who, after all, had deprived his father of a second term.

Once Bush's assumption of the presidency was assured, I had little doubt that he and his team would go out of their way to distinguish themselves rhetorically from Clinton. But I also saw a chance that those who would ad-vise Bush 43 would nudge him toward a foreign policy not too different in substance from that of Bush 41. There was not much in the younger Bush's record to have led one to predict otherwise. He had traveled abroad rarely. As governor of Texas, he had cultivated cooperation with Mexico and focused on free trade and drug and immigration control.[4] Such signals as he sent from the campaign trail and during the debates with Al Gore stressed the need for clarity about U.S. interests and values, but with a caveat: American pride, hardheadedness, confidence, and "new realism" (presumably as dis-tinct from the dewy-eyed idealism of the Democrats) must be tempered by the need to be "humble in how we treat nations that are figuring out how to chart their own course."[5] In context, he was staking out his opposition to the use of American military force to change the ways, or the regimes, of brutal dictators. Specifically, he was against what the Clinton administration had done in Haiti, not to mention (and he did *not* mention) his father's humani-tarian intervention in Somalia. Bush also said that Clinton had been right not to intervene in Rwanda—an endorsement that Clinton hardly wel-comed, given his regret over having done nothing there.

Some commentators fretted that this theme of Bush's prefigured isola-tionism. I did not share that concern. I thought some combination of cir-cumstance and Bush's more experienced advisers would push him in the direction of a more activist foreign policy than the "humble" one he prom-ised the American people.

Other, more prescient observers worried that the incoming administra-tion would be too activist, or activist in the wrong way. They could imagine that some of "the Vulcans" might infect the candidate with their aversion to treaties, particularly arms control ones; given their attachment to the idea of using American hard power to export democracy, they might steer Bush into misguided and dangerous adventures.[6]

This concern struck a chord with me. In the eighties, I had written about the intramural struggles between Richard Perle and Paul Wolfowitz on the one hand and more moderate elements in the Reagan administration on the other. I knew that these two prominent hawks, now conspicuously on the Bush team (Perle as an adviser to the Pentagon, Wolfowitz as deputy secretary of defense), were intellectually and bureaucratically formidable, and they had the backing of Jesse Helms, chairman of the Senate Foreign Relations Committee, and like-minded members of Congress. But I also knew Colin Powell and Condoleezza Rice, who would outrank the neocons and, I thought, hold Perle and Wolfowitz in check.

Powell seemed particularly well suited to that role. I had covered him for *Time* when he was Ronald Reagan's national security adviser and, later, a key architect of the American-led victory in the first Gulf War. What I had seen of Powell in the Situation Room during the nine months we served together at the beginning of the Clinton administration, before he retired as chairman of the Joint Chiefs of Staff, led me to expect him to push back against the hawkish moralism of others around Bush 43. Powell did not much care for the Clinton team, partly because he saw us as too inclined to wield the big stick in Haiti and the Balkans.[7] I found it hard to imagine that any administration in which Powell was a major figure would use force recklessly. One thing I was fairly sure of: if the administration did throw its weight around, it would throw a *lot* of weight—that is, in any interventions it undertook, it would go in with plenty of force, more than the civilian leadership might think necessary, and with as much international political and military backing as possible. Powell would insist on that, and, given his popularity in the country and his standing as a soldier, he was sure to be uniquely influential.

Finally, I assumed that Bush would rely heavily on his father's advice, which in turn would be rooted in the elder Bush's own experience as a master multilateralist.

I WAS WRONG on every point, perhaps most so on this last one. Among the signs that I (along with many others) missed, or misunderstood, was Bush's determination to distinguish himself not just from Clinton but from

Bush 41 as well. Instead of considerable continuity among the two Bushes and Clinton, the world got an American president who had the double agenda of repudiating his immediate predecessor and proving himself tougher and more successful than his father. The two ambitions seemed to be closely linked in his mind: being more successful required being tougher.

In the ever-growing literature on the Bush 43 presidency, there is a subgenre of pop (and even some professional) psychologizing about what drove the son not to follow in his father's footsteps but to take the country in the opposite direction—away from the UN, alliances, diplomacy, and international law. I leave it to others to make the case in clinical terms. Some give extra weight to the prominence in the Bush 43 team of hard-liners from Bush 41 (Dick Cheney and Donald Rumsfeld) and the exclusion of moderate pragmatists (Brent Scowcroft and James Baker).[8] But that theory, while true up to a point, begs the question of *why* Bush chose to assemble the team he did. I find plausible an answer that focuses on what Bush seems to have had in common with Cheney and Rumsfeld: certitude to a fault, a belief in what might be called the higher stubbornness—a conviction that conviction itself is the ultimate virtue in politics and statesmanship alike. It was a quality that left little room for the one so cherished by Bush 41: prudence.

One manifestation of George W. Bush's refusal to bend was that it made him resistant to facts that did not support his predispositions or his decisions. Instead, it made him receptive to half-truths, over-simplifications, and falsehoods that *did* support what he believed or decided (e.g., "Saddam has WMD," or "Saddam is in cahoots with Osama bin Laden"). Bush had little interest in reexamining the assumptions underlying policy ("If we can just knock over Saddam's statue and regime, the Iraqis will greet us as liberators"). This preconception of what would happen helps explain why the administration was so quick to remove qualifications from intelligence reports ("we assess," "we estimate," "we judge"). From the president down, the administration wanted to convey absolute certainty about what it was doing.

The contrast with Clinton could not have been starker: Clinton sometimes exasperated his own advisers, me included, by challenging us to remake the case for a decision he had already taken, just to see if he still found the argument convincing. But it was a useful goad to subject the assumptions behind our policies to constant reassessment, and also to plan for the worst: that was one reason that we went into Haiti and the Balkans "heavy," while the Bush administration went into Iraq "light."

Bush was conspicuously impatient with views contrary to his own. On numerous occasions over the last several years I have heard from foreign ambassadors that Bush often interrupted them and visiting leaders when they tried to register differences. This quality was evident to Clinton during their handoff meeting in December 2000. Powell, who, like Clinton, prides himself on being a good listener, has remarked that Bush was nothing of the kind.[9]

Bush 41 had the opposite reputation: he clearly believed in the higher schmoozing as a crucial component of effective statecraft. People who have worked for both father and son have told me that when, early on, they suggested Bush 43 do what his father so often did—pick up the phone and call foreign counterparts to draw them into supporting an American position—Bush was not inclined to do so. On occasion he would say, in effect and sometimes in so many words, that he did not like "debating" or "negotiating" issues when he knew he was in the right.

Whatever else in the dynamics of their family may explain Bush's distancing of himself from his father, he has dropped hints, and others have discerned additional evidence, that he faulted Bush 41 for being too ready to compromise: with Congress and budgetary reality on the need to raise taxes, with Mikhail Gorbachev on when, where, and how to end the first Gulf War—and, for that matter, with Saddam Hussein.

Compromise, or at least a willingness to consider it, is at the heart of diplomacy. It is also at the heart of global governance, international law, and the workings of NATO and the United Nations. That is part of the reason why Bush 43 and the more influential members of his administration came into the office suspicious of all those enterprises. They were, quite simply, not in a compromising mood in their attitude toward those whom they regarded as flaccid allies, to say nothing of enemies.

Charles Krauthammer saw this trait in the president and his team early on, in an essay he wrote for *Time* at the end of February 2001, and he hailed it as just the sort of mettle that the country needed in order to take full advantage of the unipolar moment that Krauthammer had proclaimed a decade earlier: "America is no mere international citizen. It is the dominant power in the world, more dominant than any since Rome. Accordingly, America is in a position to reshape norms, alter expectations and create new realities. How? Through unapologetic and implacable demonstrations of will." The headline on Krauthammer's piece gave this view of America's role and responsibility in the world a name: "The Bush Doctrine."

It is usually the press that assigns presidents the doctrines that bear their names, but rarely does it happen only weeks into an administration.*

THE BUSH DOCTRINE CAME INTO ITS OWN when the American homeland itself was attacked. The national trauma of 9/11 was, by all accounts, including Bush's, a "defining moment," which transformed him and his presidency.[10] It simultaneously reinforced his concept of what it meant to be a "conviction politician" and the American people's willingness to go along, for a while at least, with his assertions that invading Iraq was the natural and necessary sequel to invading Afghanistan, and that the struggle against the insurgents in Iraq was "the central front in our war against terror."[11]

In Bush's mind, he and the nation now had a clear cause that eliminated the difficulty both his father and Clinton had faced in coming up with a tagline for the nineties. It was an indication of how out of touch Powell was with the president for whom he worked that, after 9/11, he mused that "the post-post-cold war era" had begun. In Bush's view, it was a new war; al-Qaeda had started it, and the United States would finish it. But not any time soon. The 2002 National Security Strategy acknowledged, even proclaimed with gusto, that the conflict would be "of uncertain duration." With the help of the American Enterprise Institute, a conservative think tank, Paul Wolfowitz assembled a group of informal advisers that produced a report predicting that the United States was "in for a two-generation battle with radical Islam."[12]

BUSH'S EVANGELISM UNDERGIRDED his certitude. It is commonplace to observe that nearly all American presidents have—to one degree or another, and with varying degrees of sincerity—made piety part of their public persona. Before Bush, there was probably no better example than Woodrow Wilson (who during a stressful moment at Versailles was overheard to say, "If I didn't feel that I was the personal instrument of God I couldn't carry on"). But while Bush is by no means the first president to invoke the Almighty on behalf of his foreign policy, he has gone further in this regard, and has been more explicit than any of his predecessors since Wilson in proclaiming his belief that his mission has been divinely inspired and guided and will, therefore, be victorious.

* In 1985, Krauthammer had been the most prominent commentator to dub as "the Reagan Doctrine" the practice of fighting the Soviets through proxies such as the Contras in Nicaragua and the mujahideen in Afghanistan.

In this respect, as in others, 9/11 had a clarifying, energizing, even liberating effect on Bush. "Today our nation saw evil," he said in a televised address to the nation from Barksdale Air Force Base in Louisiana about twelve hours after the attacks. In the days that followed, he referred several times to God's hand in world affairs—and in support of those who were on the side of "freedom." His constant identification of al-Qaeda "evildoers" was inspired by an echo of Proverbs 21:15, a passage he reread shortly after 9/11 ("When justice is done, it brings joy to the righteous but terror to evildoers").[13]

When Bob Woodward asked Bush if he had consulted with Bush 41 before sending American troops into Iraq, Bush replied, "He is the wrong father to appeal to in terms of strength. There's a higher Father that I appeal to."[14]

When running for reelection in 2004, Bush was reported to have told a group of Amish voters in Pennsylvania that God spoke not just to him but through him.[15] About six weeks later, in accepting his party's nomination for a second term, he adapted the most famous passage of Ecclesiastes to America's unilateral moment in a way that suggested it would last a very long time since it had a heavenly blessing: "To everything, we know, there is a season—a time for sadness, a time for struggle, a time for rebuilding. And now we have reached a time for hope. This young century will be liberty's century. By promoting liberty abroad, we will build a safer world. By encouraging liberty at home, we will build a more hopeful America. Like generations before us, we have a calling from beyond the stars to stand for freedom. This is the everlasting dream of America and tonight, in this place, that dream is renewed. Now we go forward grateful for our freedom, faithful to our cause, and confident in the future of the greatest nation on earth."[16]

In this flight of presidential rhetoric, particularly in the context of presidential action in Iraq and in the global "war on terror," Bush was compounding the ancient paradox of religion as a force that has been both unifying and divisive. Like the Jews when they worshipped "the God of Abraham, Isaac, and Jacob," Bush was claiming, for himself and his country, a unique and holy dispensation; he was proclaiming that Americans are a chosen people. But the Jews did so in a spirit of securing their own nation, while Bush was doing so in support of his claim to lead and defend *all* nations—or at least all good ones.

That was a relevant distinction, since Bush saw the world as a battleground between the forces of good and evil, and he believed the United States had a sacred entitlement to mete out justice by its own lights.

Perhaps the clearest statement of that mindset and its implications for diplomacy came not from Bush but from Cheney: "I have been charged by the president with making sure that none of the tyrannies in the world are negotiated with. We don't negotiate with evil; we defeat it." [17]

An extreme and grotesque consequence of this militant and absolutist view of American righteousness was revealed at Abu Ghraib: since America was not just a good country but the best country, it was not bound by the rules that applied to others; when dealing with the worst of evil-doers, the United States itself could behave like the worst of regimes—notably the one it had just brought down, and on the very premises where the deposed tyrant had tortured his own prisoners.

BY EXTENSION TO THE INTERNATIONAL SYSTEM more generally, Bush's Manichaean tendency meant that the United States could grant certifiably good countries leniency under international agreements, while bad ones could expect special stringency, including in the realm of arms control.

Previous administrations relied on treaties with the force of law. For Bush, the problem with law is that it is supposed to apply equally to everyone. Bush wanted more flexibility, especially for the United States but also for its friends.

At the outset of his administration, the president spiked efforts to ratify the Comprehensive Test Ban Treaty, withdrew from the Anti-Ballistic Missile Treaty, watered down the Strategic Arms Reduction process, and backed away from numerous other agreements. He did not attack or repudiate the Nuclear Non-Proliferation Treaty frontally, but he did little to improve its effectiveness and took a number of actions that harmed it.

After 9/11, the Bush administration established the "Proliferation Security Initiative" (PSI), which exhorted other countries to join the United States in ad hoc arrangements aimed at interdicting ships and taking other measures to bust networks that traffic in WMD-related materials. Any administration would have been smart to augment the NPT with something like the PSI, but this particular initiative has to be seen in the context of the Bush administration's skepticism toward treaties. Official spokesmen took pains to point out that the PSI was an "activity not an organization." It had neither a headquarters, an international secretariat, formal rules of procedure, nor even a budget. It was intended by its principal advocates more as a replacement for the NPT than as a reinforcement of it. PSI was to the nonproliferation effort what "coalitions of the willing" were to treaty-based alliances like NATO— another example of the Bush administration's preference for multilateralism à la carte.

The administration did more severe damage to the NPT with its policy toward India. As the world's largest democracy, a "strategic partner" of the United States, and an ally in the war on terror, India—in marked contrast to two other countries with nuclear ambitions, Iran and North Korea (the surviving members of the Axis of Evil)—earned treatment by the Bush administration as a certifiably good country. In 2006, Bush granted India what amounted to an exemption from the NPT: he pushed through Congress a law giving India virtually all the rights and privileges of membership in the nuclear-weapons-state club even though it did not qualify under the terms of the NPT and had tested a nuclear weapon. Iran, meanwhile, even though it was a signatory of the NPT and had not tested a nuclear weapon, was supposed to renounce its right—granted under the treaty—to become a producer of nuclear fuel.

The NPT is intended to be part of the bedrock of international security. As such, it can be effective only if it applied universally. Its provisions cannot be bent in favor of countries that the United States judges to be virtuous and responsible and against those it considers evil and reckless.

Yet that was exactly what Bush did: he made policy—and, as he saw it, a virtue—out of adopting and applying a double standard.

As a result of the Bush administration's virtual shutdown of American diplomacy early in its first term, Washington had already missed an opportunity in 2001 and 2002 to engage Pyongyang and Tehran in negotiations that might have kept Iran compliant with the NPT as a non-nuclear-weapons state and that might also have kept North Korea within the treaty.*

Seeing India get a break for being "good," those countries that knew they were considered evil were all the more likely to do what North Korea did in 2006: its regime set off a nuclear weapon of its own, largely to prove that it was not going to accept Washington's judgment of its virtue and abide by discriminatory rules. The North Koreans had an incentive to ensure their survival by going all out to acquire nuclear weapons before they were subject to American preemption. That was surely among the lessons the leaders in Tehran and Pyongyang drew from the way Bush chose to deal with Iraq as opposed to India: even though India was not a signatory to the NPT and had

---

* The Iranians made overtures to the administration in 2003, suggesting negotiations. They were motivated, apparently, by the ease and speed with which the United States had toppled the Iraqi regime, and they took seriously none-too-veiled hints out of Washington that they were next on the hit list. The administration blew the Iranians off.

developed weapons of mass destruction, the United States was allowing—indeed, helping—it to produce nuclear fuel. The result was a major setback for an already endangered global nonproliferation regime but for global governance more generally.

STAYING THE COURSE

Since neither the NPT nor global governance had much of a constituency in the United States, Bush's policies were subject to little effective criticism during most of his first term. All eyes were on Iraq, which Bush kept saying was the main battlefield in the global war on terror. Through most of 2003, he was able to convince a majority of Americans that the United States was winning that war.

In 2004, that changed, and Bush had reason to worry that, like his father, he might not be reelected. By the spring of that year, Iraq was beginning to look like a Hobbesian "war of all against all." Islamists, terrorists who had slipped across the border (an increasing number affiliated with al-Qaeda), Shiite and Sunni militias, former Ba'athists, and decommissioned Iraqi soldiers were killing one another, slaughtering civilians, targeting coalition forces, private contractors, NGO workers, and occasionally journalists. Explosions punctuated daily life. Single blasts sometimes claimed more than a hundred random victims. When a CIA report suggested the deteriorating situation could lead to civil war, American military officers scoffed at the future-conditional tense: they knew they were already in the middle of a civil war, with a mission quite different from the one their commander in chief had assigned them—and pronounced accomplished—a year earlier.

Iraq was falling into that exceptional category that Immanuel Kant had identified as obligating the international community to intervene: a failed state, dissolving into anarchy. Yet it was the U.S.-led intervention that had created the chaos.[18]

AS THE 2004 PRESIDENTIAL ELECTION approached, public opinion polls in the United States showed that less than half of the respondents thought Bush was doing a good job on Iraq, a drop of more than 30 percent since the heady days after the invasion. Surveys abroad showed approval of the United States at an all-time low, even in the eyes of some of its staunchest friends, a downward trend that would continue over the next several years.[19]

While Bush insisted that the United States had to "stay the course" in Iraq, he realized that some course correction was in order for American foreign policy as a whole. Before the election, he began to wrap himself rhetorically in the cloak of his internationalist (and Democratic) predecessors, particularly Franklin Roosevelt and Harry Truman, and he continued to do so after he was returned to office.[20] Condoleezza Rice and other administration officials buttressed the association in speeches of their own.[21] In Bush's second Inaugural Address, he emphasized "the quiet work of diplomacy" and noted that "across the generations we have proclaimed the imperative of self-government, because no one is fit to be a master, and no one deserves to be a slave." Parsing the speech, some commentators thought they heard echoes of Woodrow Wilson.[22]

By the second term, climate change was no longer treated as just "Gore talk." It had risen to a level of broad-based national concern that the administration could no longer brush off. At least twenty-nine states, in many cases with Republican governors (including California and New York), had begun to take action, passing legislation to limit carbon emissions and, in the case of Massachusetts, suing the federal government for its failure to regulate greenhouse gases as pollutants. In response to these developments, the administration began, grudgingly and belatedly, to acknowledge that climate change was not just a real problem but one of humankind's making.[23]

RICE'S ROLE IN MODERATING the tone and substance of policy was conspicuous but ironic. While still at the White House as national security adviser, she had done little to rein in the ultraconservatives, and she was largely indifferent and occasionally hostile to the UN. The only consistent high-level support the UN had in the administration during the first term came from Colin Powell.

In 2004, anti-UN members of Congress (especially Senator Norm Coleman, Republican of Minnesota) made a concerted effort to force Kofi Annan from office. The pretext was a raft of scandals, especially one emanating from the Oil-for-Food Program, a humanitarian mechanism for ameliorating the privations that the Iraqi people had suffered under Saddam. It came to light that the program had been riddled with mismanagement and outright corruption, including cases of UN officials and contractors receiving illegal payments. Kofi Annan, whose son was implicated, neither asked for nor received exoneration, and he accepted overall responsibility for the mess, which tarnished his reputation, hobbled his effectiveness, and made him all the more vulnerable to the UN's enemies in Congress.*

The most potent reason for the "get-Kofi campaign" on Capitol Hill was congressional anger over the secretary-general's effrontery in challenging the legality of the Iraq war. Except for Powell, who made clear he was speaking for himself, the administration let Annan hang out to dry for nearly a month. When Annan made a trip to Washington to give a speech, Bush snubbed him. Eventually, however, Rice concluded that the administration had enough trouble in Iraq; it did not need a fight in Turtle Bay over what most countries saw as a U.S.-orchestrated smear campaign.

AFTER HIS REELECTION, Bush dumped Powell and moved Rice to the State Department. From the day she moved into a transition office on the first floor of the department while awaiting Senate confirmation, she did her best to demonstrate that diplomacy was back, and so was bipartisanship. I was one of several people from the Clinton administration whom she invited to stop by for a private chat. She solicited advice and ticked off ways she and her team were going to reengage with America's allies and friends around the world. Soon after her confirmation, she traveled to Europe to pave the way for a trip by Bush, who, unlike in 2001, made a point of visiting EU headquarters in Brussels.

In its approach to NATO as well, the administration was not only more respectful than before—treating it like an alliance, not a toolbox—but more imaginative and ambitious. In July of 2005, my former executive assistant in

---

* As part of the sanctions the UN imposed on Iraq after its invasion of Kuwait in 1990 and that remained in effect after the Gulf War ended, Iraq was forbidden from selling its oil internationally. The Oil-for-Food Program allowed proceeds from specially permitted oil sales to pay for food, medical supplies, and other basic necessities. In designing and implementing the program, the U.S. and British governments made a tactical calculation: they knew that, given the nature and power within Iraq of the Saddam regime, there would inevitably be kickbacks to Saddam and other forms of corruption; that would have to be a price to be paid for keeping sanctions in place and containing Saddam. The operation lasted from 1997 until the U.S.-led invasion in March 2003. As a result of the subsequent investigation and reports, the director of the program, a Cypriot named Benon Sevan, came in for harsh criticism for failing to monitor the sanctions and for withholding evidence on kickbacks and illicit surcharges, and Kofi Annan's son, Kojo Annan, was alleged to have used his father's position to personal advantage. For a thorough assessment of the scandal and how it was used by the UN's critics, see Brian Urquhart, "The UN Oil-for-Food Program: Who Is Guilty?" *New York Review of Books*, February 9, 2006; and Jeffrey A. Meyer and Mark G. Califano, *Good Intentions Corrupted: The Oil-for-Food Scandal and the Threat to the U.N.* (New York: Public Affairs, 2006).

the State Department, Victoria Nuland, who had been working in Cheney's office, became U.S. ambassador to NATO. The expansion begun during the Clinton administration had continued: there were now representatives of twenty-six allies, including the three Baltic states, around the table at the North Atlantic Council. NATO had built up its cooperative relationship with Russia, Ukraine, and the other former Soviet republics. It was also developing ties with two traditionally nonaligned European countries, Sweden and Finland; with countries as far away as Australia, New Zealand, South Korea, Japan, and Argentina; and with Israel and six Arab states along the southern rim of the Mediterranean as well as four states in the Persian Gulf.*

These partnerships, while still at an early stage, had the potential of yielding concrete benefits in the future. They allowed the United States to enlist the help of the Australians, who were among the most militarily proficient of America's non-NATO allies and had peacekeeping experience in East Timor and elsewhere, in mentoring some of NATO's new, less capable members. Interaction between NATO and its Asian partners—Japan, South Korea, and New Zealand as well as Australia—helped put transatlantic security issues on the agenda of the ASEAN Regional Forum and bring Pacific security issues to the attention of the Europeans. Partnering with the states of the Greater Middle East was a means of inculcating them with a better understanding of how collective security might someday work in their region and getting them used to the idea of cooperation among national militaries and regional mechanisms in different parts of the world.

In short, NATO was taking the logic of the Euromess chart from my days at the State Department another step further and applying it globally. Such a program would have been unthinkable in the first Bush term. I said as much to Nuland when she visited Washington in 2006, adding that for someone who had warned me thirteen years before that "multilat is hell," she was sure doing a lot of it. She laughed, then borrowed a line from *The Godfather*: "This is the profession I have chosen."

It was a profession back in favor with the president of the United States, or so Bush told the world on a trip to Nova Scotia soon after his reelection. "A new term in office is an important opportunity to reach out to our friends," he said, adding that his "first great commitment is to defend our security and

---

* NATO's Mediterranean Dialogue partners were Algeria, Egypt, Mauritania, Tunisia, Jordan, Morocco, and Israel; its Istanbul Cooperation Initiative included Bahrain, Kuwait, Qatar, and the United Arab Emirates.

spread freedom by building effective multinational and multilateral institutions and supporting effective multilateral action."

BUSH'S AMBASSADOR TO THE UN AT THE TIME, John Danforth, a centrist former Republican senator from Missouri, would have been well suited to translate Bush's soothing tone into action in New York. But two days after Bush's speech in Nova Scotia, Danforth resigned, explaining that he wanted to return home to St. Louis and spend more time with his family.

As Danforth's replacement, Bush named John Bolton, who had long before made a name for himself as one of the most tenacious unilateralists ever to serve in the State Department. It was speculated at the time that the appointment could be explained by Bush's partiality to those he considered tough fighters and by his loyalty to those with whom he felt an ideological bond. But it also suggested presidential ambivalence about how new a foreign policy he really wanted, and it revealed a degree of incoherence in an administration that prided itself on its discipline and clarity of purpose. Everything Bolton had said and done under two Presidents Bush guaranteed that he would, in his handling of the UN assignment, make a mockery out of Bush and Rice's efforts to start the second term on a better footing with the rest of the world.

Bolton's mentor, Jesse Helms, had managed to place him in the Bush 41 administration as assistant secretary for international organizations. In that capacity Bolton saw it as his calling to keep the U.S. mission in New York in check. The first President Bush and his secretary of state, James Baker, put up with Bolton's obstreperousness in part because they saw him as a useful sop to the right wing.

Returning to the State Department eight years later, this time in an administration far more receptive to his views, he was given the higher-level job of undersecretary in charge of arms control, nonproliferation, and international security. To many of his American subordinates and foreign counterparts, Bolton seemed to oppose, almost on principle, the very activity for which he was responsible. He was the leading promoter of the Proliferation Security Initiative, which featured interdiction rather than negotiation, as a substitute for the Nonproliferation Treaty. With the active and visible help of the National Rifle Association, he derailed a UN effort to craft a ban on illicit trade in small arms and light weapons.

Early in the administration it fell to Bolton to "unsign" the treaty establishing the International Criminal Court. He did so with a three-sentence letter notifying Kofi Annan that "the United States does not intend to become a party to the treaty. Accordingly, the United States has no legal obligations arising from its [that is, President Clinton's] signature on December 31, 2000." Bolton would later call sending this letter "the happiest moment" in his public career. He also led the Bush administration's efforts to pressure, financially and otherwise, more than a hundred nations into signing bilateral agreements that exempted U.S. citizens from the court's jurisdiction.*

Bolton was remembered for a remark he had made in 1994 that the world would neither notice nor care if ten stories were lopped off the UN Secretariat Building. His assignment to one of the most important and prestigious diplomatic posts was all the more bizarre in that it came as a consolation prize for, in effect, being fired from the State Department, the seat of diplomacy itself. Rice did not want Bolton on her core team. However, his supporters in the administration and on Capitol Hill were adamant that he be kept on. The word in Foggy Bottom was that he was being "parked" at the UN. In fact, he got a promotion to a position where he was often able to thwart Rice's efforts to cultivate better relations with the UN.

BOLTON'S TENURE IN TURTLE BAY was foreshortened and his clout diminished by a shift in the political mood of the country. His reputation as an antidiplomat cast a cloud over his nomination in the Senate. Clinton had learned the hard way that multilateralism can come a cropper unless the process of negotiating treaties with other governments is synchronized with constituency-building in the United States and, in particular, through steady, effective engagement with Congress. In 2005, Bush discovered that unilateralism, too, must have a critical mass of domestic support. With his poll ratings falling and his authority on Capitol Hill eroding because of Iraq, the president—who nominated Bolton for the UN job in March—could not get him confirmed even by a Republican-controlled Senate. Yet instead of finding a politically acceptable alternative, Bush gave Bolton a so-called recess appointment, which allowed him to serve for the duration of the 109th Congress without benefit of Senate approval.

After Bolton finally arrived at his post in August 2005, he and Rice spent much of the next year and a half maneuvering against each other over a wide range of issues involving the direction and tenor of American

* The ICC became active in July 2002 after sixty nations ratified the treaty. Over the next five years, the Court agreed to take on cases relating to brutalities in three African countries— rejecting as lacking merit or outside its jurisdiction more than 1,500 other charges, including hundreds against the United States.

foreign policy. Perhaps his boldest move was an attempt to undo American acceptance of UN-sanctioned goals for increased assistance to developing countries as they sought to reduce hunger, child mortality, and disease, and to advance primary education and maternal health. Bolton took the position that meeting these goals would amount to "global taxes." In the same vein, he tried to delete "respect for nature" from the list of values the world leaders had endorsed, arguing it implied international environmental obligations that the United States did not accept. His own government eventually overruled him.*

Bolton also set about, with verve, ingenuity, and some success, to sabotage the most serious reform effort the UN had ever attempted. Annan launched the process with a speech in September 2003, followed by the establishment of an international blue-ribbon commission, formally known as the High-Level Panel on Threats, Challenges, and Change. The one American among the panel's sixteen members was Brent Scowcroft, a personification of the policies and worldview of Bush 41 and therefore, in the eyes of many, a brisk-walking, straight-talking counterweight to those of Bush 43.

In a wide-ranging and ambitious report, released in December 2004, the High-Level Panel made 101 recommendations. A number of them would, if implemented, have improved the effectiveness of the UN's specialized agencies where the real, often life-saving work is done. (For example, the panel wanted to increase the World Health Organization's capacity to spot and contain outbreaks of infectious disease before they become epidemics.)

The High-Level Panel also made a serious effort to address a conundrum that had stumped statesmen and kibitzers alike for decades: how to expand the membership of the Security Council to make it more representative while not diluting its effectiveness. The permanent membership of five members of the council had, in 1945, been considered a reflection of the geopolitical realities of the time. More than sixty years later, that inequity had become an anachronism. But since their veto power was divided five

---

* In September 2000, the leaders of the world, then including Clinton, had agreed to the Millennium Development Goals at the General Assembly Millennium Meeting. Bush, who took office the following January, finally endorsed the goals on March 14, 2002, in a speech to the Inter-American Development Bank in Washington—a week before he would travel to Monterrey, Mexico, to participate in a UN development conference. Bolton continued to wage a rearguard action against the Millennium Goals from his post at the State Department and then at the UN until Bush and Rice both made repeated public statements, including a presidential address at the UN in September 2005, affirming American commitment to the goals.

ways, there was no Alexander figure to cut the Gordian knot with a single whack of a sword: it would have to be untied strand by strand.

A reasonable solution would have been to give permanent membership to major powers in what used to be called the Third World. A logical accompanying step would have been to make room for newcomers by consolidating the representation of the old First World, giving the European Union one seat rather than the two that France and the United Kingdom had held from the beginning. But neither of those countries was about to give up its seat. In 2004, to make matters more complicated, Germany stepped up its push for a seat of its own (a problem that the Clinton administration abetted in the nineties by supporting the German aspiration). Italians wondered aloud why they should not be in the running. Japan wanted a seat, too, not least because it was unhappy about China's being the only East Asian state among the P-5, but also because Japan had the second-largest economy after the United States. The United States supported Japan, while China, predictably, objected.

As for the emerging powers, India, Brazil, and South Africa were often cited in Washington and Western capitals as obvious candidates for council membership. But they were not seen that way in Buenos Aires, Mexico City, Santiago, Islamabad, Seoul, and Lagos. Many governments objected to the very notion of permanent seats, and most of them objected to expanding the number of countries with a veto.

The High-Level Panel, unable to agree on a single plan for squaring all these circles, offered two. Both were crafted with an eye to redressing regional imbalances and taking into account contributions to the work of the UN, including peacekeeping, as a criterion for elevating states to the Council. The first variant was a simple expansion of the number of permanent—but not veto-bearing—members, and the second would create a new tier of rotating membership with longer, renewable terms. It was a heroic attempt to accomplish what, in the near term at least, was an impossible task. The issue was essentially shelved, at least for the time being, lest the attempt to solve it paralyze the Council and the UN as a whole.*

As a result, Bolton did not have to worry much about protecting the pri-

* Two other proposals are worth noting. The Turkish economist and statesman, Kemal Derviş, before he became head of the United Nations Development Program in 2005, proposed doing away with the veto and instituting instead a system of weighted voting that would give countries with large populations, economies, and contributions to peacekeeping or other global public goods more influence, thereby depriving any single state of the ability to paralyze the Council with its threat or use of a veto. The appeal of this plan—that it is more egalitarian—is, as Derviş has acknowledged, also its vulnerability: the five permanent mem-

macy of the P-5 or America's primacy within it. He concentrated instead on a number of the panel's other recommendations on which progress might have been possible. He mounted a dogged blocking action of the sort for which he was famous and even grudgingly admired by his critics. He had a genius for a form of nitpicking that served his larger purpose of keeping the UN in what he saw as its proper place, which was as far away as possible from real power and effective governance. When he felt it expedient, he allied himself, and therefore his country, with some of the most egregiously misgoverned states on earth, such as Zimbabwe and Belarus, who had their own reasons for protecting their sovereignty against meddling by the international community.

Bolton also continued the fight he had waged against arms control and nonproliferation treaties at the State Department by expunging any reaffirmation in any U.S.-approved UN document of existing arms control commitments, not to mention the possibility of a stricter, more comprehensive regime. Bolton was thereby clearing away any obstacle to the United States' proceeding with weapons programs that might allow it to build up its nuclear arsenal and test new weapons. He chipped away at efforts to reform the Human Rights Commission that Eleanor Roosevelt had been instrumental in founding. When a final proposal reached the floor of the General Assembly, 170 countries voted for it. The United States was one of four that voted against it.*

No one was more exasperated than Kofi Annan, who had been hoping that 2005 might see his own recovery and that of the UN as well from what he called the *annus horribilis* of 2004—especially since his term would expire at the end of 2006.

THE BELEAGUERED and increasingly lame-duck secretary-general had another reason for frustration in 2005: events in his native Africa cast a shadow over one of his more important achievements at the UN—his suc-

---

bers, which have to approve any reform, are not about to give up their veto. (See Derviş's *A Better Globalization: Legitimacy, Governance, and Reform* [Washington, DC: Center for Global Development, 2005].) Paul Kennedy has floated as a possible interim solution doubling the number of rotating members of the Security Council to around twenty and allowing some of them to serve multiple two-year terms, thereby giving them a chance to demonstrate leadership and the P-5 a chance to adjust to expansion. (See *The Parliament of Man: The Past, Present, and Future of the United Nations* [New York: Random House, 2006].)

* The other "no" votes were from the Marshall Islands, Palau, and Israel. Iran, Belarus, and Venezuela (under the control of Hugo Chavez) abstained, and several delegations were absent when the vote was taken.

cess in winning formal support for the international community's "responsibility to protect" populations from genocide, ethnic cleansing, war crimes, and crimes against humanity.

The UN's endorsement, by the General Assembly in September 2005, of the legal and ethical basis for humanitarian intervention represented a further dilution of state sovereignty. Throughout most of history, it had been a given that governments have the right to govern as they see fit, and that how they deal with their own populations is no one's business but their own. The Peace of Westphalia in 1648 gave that right to monarchs. Over time, that principle was challenged in theory and whittled away in practice. Rousseau argued that sovereignty extended to the citizenry, while Kant went a step further, asserting the sovereignty of the individual. Nearly two hundred years later, Basket 3 of the Helsinki Accords imposed on all its signatories—that is, on all the states of Europe, including the communist ones—an obligation to respect freedom of expression, religion, and travel.

In 2006, the UN went further still by warning governments that if they abused certain basic norms, notably the requirement to respect human life, the international community had not just the right but the responsibility to intervene and protect an abused community or citizenry over the objections of the offending regime and, if necessary, by use of force. In April, the Security Council affirmed that it was prepared to take decisive action if there were no peaceful means to stop atrocities and the national authorities failed or refused to do so.

Annan was finally obtaining the institution's endorsement of the lonely, controversial, and brave position he had taken at Ditchley Park in 1998, when he said, "State frontiers should no longer be seen as a watertight protection for war criminals or mass murderers." *

IF EVER THERE WAS A TEST CASE for the UN's responsibility to protect, it was in the Darfur region of Sudan, where a conflict had been roil-

---

* While Annan's initiative encountered resistance from within the UN and from individual governments, it had wide international support. In 2001, Gareth Evans, the former Australian foreign minister, who had become the president of the International Crisis Group, and Mohammed Sahnoun, an Algerian diplomat, led an international study group that endorsed the responsibility to protect. Newt Gingrich, a former Republican Speaker of the House, co-chaired, with George Mitchell, a former Democratic majority leader of the Senate, a congressionally mandated commission on UN reform that strongly supported the same concept in the summer of 2005. Several of my Brookings colleagues (Ann Florini, Ivo Daalder, and Michael O'Hanlon) served as experts to help the commission in its work.

ing for three years; it erupted into a full-scale massacre in the summer of 2005, when the government in Khartoum unleashed militias made up of Arab nomads who raped, murdered, and drove from their homes land-tilling African tribes. By the time the General Assembly convened in September, as many as four hundred thousand people had already died and two million more had been internally displaced—that is, they were refugees in their own country.

While most of the American media underplayed the story, the *New York Times* foreign affairs columnist Nicholas Kristof waged a one-man campaign to call attention to the crisis. African-American groups, evangelical Christian organizations, and celebrities such as Bono added their voices to a swelling chorus of outrage. Official protests started coming out of capitals around the world, and aid and emissaries began to flow into the region. There would be, in the months that followed, a few cease-fires, including one negotiated by Deputy Secretary of State Robert Zoellick, but they provided only brief and partial respites from the butchery.

Darfur was the latest evidence of the UN's difficulty in dealing effectively with warlordism, ethnic bloodletting, and other afflictions of failed states. The Security Council often defaults to paralysis, since at least one of its veto-bearing permanent members is likely to balk at applying force against a country that it regards as a customer, supplier, or protégé. In the case of Darfur, China was the principal obstructionist since it wanted to maintain good relations with Sudan as a source of oil for its economic boom. Moreover, the UN has roused itself to get tough with miscreant states only when the United States enables it to do so by getting tough itself. Since the UN's intervention in Korea to stop the North's invasion of the South in 1950, it has often taken relentless badgering by Washington—and even the threat that America might act unilaterally—to goad the UN into acting multilaterally.

In the face of these facts of life, UN-bashing is understandable but misdirected. When, in the nineties, the United States was vacillating over what to do about the Balkan crisis, Sergio Vieira de Mello remarked in exasperation, "The major powers will kick the UN, they'll scream at the UN, but at the end of the day they are getting the UN that they want and deserve. If the United States and Europe wanted a muscular peacekeeping operation here, they would insist on adding muscle. If they really wanted to stop the Serbs, they would have done so long ago."[24] Richard Holbrooke frequently made the same point more generically—and more colloquially: "Blaming the UN for inaction is like blaming Madison Square Garden when the Knicks lose."

Like Rwanda in 1994, Darfur in 2005 was not solely, or even mainly, a failure of the UN. In both cases, an American commander in chief was too preoccupied with a military debacle elsewhere—Clinton's retreat from an intervention gone horribly wrong in Somalia, and Bush's ever-deepening troubles in Iraq—to have the energy, the resources, or the political backing at home to get out in front of the Security Council. The contrasting cases were Kosovo in 1999, when Clinton led NATO to war without benefit of a UN resolution, and Iraq in 2003, when Bush invaded Iraq with only Tony Blair at his side. But by 2005, Iraq was going so badly that the U.S. administration, even though it was prepared to label as genocide what was happening in Darfur, had great difficulty translating that word into the basis for action.*

THE BACKLASH

When the Democrats won control of both houses of Congress in the midterm elections of 2006, Bush's advisers told him he had no choice but to sacrifice Bolton. The president procrastinated for a month, then held off announcing his decision until after December 5, when he and the First Lady, Laura Bush, were scheduled to give a farewell dinner at the White House for Kofi Annan, whose term was coming to an end. The guest list was drawn up mostly from Annan's friends and UN-boosters, making Bolton and to some extent Bush himself odd men out at an event marked by an air of strained cordiality. "Nobody sang 'Kumbaya,' " Bolton told a reporter covering the event.

The next morning the White House issued a statement in Bush's name pulling the plug on Bolton's nomination while congratulating him on a "job well done" and accusing a "handful" of senators of blocking him, "even though their tactics will disrupt our diplomatic work at a sensitive and important time."

A week later, Kofi Annan gave a farewell address at a venue of his own choosing—the Truman Library and Museum in Independence, Missouri. Senator Chuck Hagel of Nebraska—who had been more critical of the Bush administration than any of his Republican colleagues—gave Annan a glowing introduction. Annan was, by his standards, uncharacteristically blunt about American foreign policy under the current administration. "No state,"

---

* On August 31, 2007, after months of diplomatic wrangling, the UN Security Council finally authorized the deployment of up to 26,000 peacekeepers to Sudan.

he said, "can make its own actions legitimate in the eyes of others. When power, especially military force, is used, the world will consider it legitimate only when convinced that it is being used for the right purpose—for broadly shared aims—in accordance with broadly accepted norms. . . . The United States has given the world an example of a democracy in which everyone, including the most powerful, is subject to legal restraint. Its current moment of world supremacy gives it a priceless opportunity to entrench the same principles at the global level"—an opportunity, he strongly implied, the Bush administration had squandered.

On New Year's Day 2007, Annan turned over his post to Ban Ki-moon, the foreign minister of South Korea. Ban, the first secretary-general to come from a country allied to the United States, had been the American choice for the job for more than a year; but the administration had kept its support as quiet as possible lest it become a kiss of death at a time when the reputation of the United States was at its lowest point ever.[*]

IN THE MONTHS THAT FOLLOWED, Condoleezza Rice's efforts to jump-start diplomatic engagement with the North Koreans, the Iranians, and the parties in the stalled Middle East peace process bore a striking resemblance to initiatives of the prior administration. Bolton, now a private citizen, attacked the administration for going soft, especially on North Korea.

"Now I know we're doing something right," remarked Rice privately. Her under-secretary for political affairs, Nicholas Burns, the highest ranking of the professional diplomats on whom Rice relied and who had done constant battle with Bolton, gave a speech at his alma mater, Boston College, on April 11, in which he denounced "isolationism's twin evil—unilateralism."[†]

---

[*] According to Pew Research Center surveys conducted in 1999 and 2000, the last two years of the Clinton administration, more than 50 percent of foreign respondents held favorable views of the United States. In some countries it was as high as 83 percent. By June 2005, early in Bush's second term, another Pew project found that the United States had a 50 percent or higher favorability rating in only 37 percent of the countries surveyed. (By contrast, China had a favorable rating in 69 percent of the countries surveyed, and Japan, Germany, and France each received a favorable rating of 81 percent.) In January 2007, six years into Bush's presidency, a BBC World Service survey found that only 29 percent of the people polled in eighteen countries believed that the United States was playing a "mainly positive" role in the world—and that was a drop of 11 percent from two years earlier, at the end of Bush's first term.

[†] Burns had worked closely with Rice in the Bush 41 White House, then served in a series of important posts under Clinton. Another Foreign Service officer who had distinguished himself in the nineties and became part of Rice's inner circle was Christopher Hill, who was the lead negotiator in the talks with the North Koreans and whose role in the Balkan crisis I refer to in Chapter 14.

Those four words reverberated in the halls and in e-mail traffic at the State Department. A veteran of five administrations whom I knew from my time in government called to make sure I had seen Burns's speech. "We would have been nailed if we got caught even *thinking* such things a couple of years ago," he said. "Now it's part of the makeover. I just hope it's not too late."

Most of the large field of Republicans who were declared or presumed candidates for the '08 presidential nomination shied away from attacking Bush outright for his handling of foreign policy, but by and large they also tended to downplay mention of him. They paid constant homage to the party's iconic figure, Ronald Reagan. His name, they hoped, would remind voters of "morning in America," when the cold war was coming to an end on Western terms under a Republican president with a knack for turning optimism into successful policy. It was their way of changing the subject from the morass in Iraq.

Operation Iraqi Freedom already qualified, even in the assessment of some of its original advocates, as the most ill-conceived, poorly executed, and disastrous exertion of American power in the history of the republic. Early enthusiasts of the invasion and occupation, including a number who had been involved in the planning, rounded on the administration, arguing that the fault for the debacle lay not in the original policy but in the ineptitude of its execution.[25]

While this debate was interesting to its participants and to students of the ideological battles of the foreign-policy establishment, it did not seem to have much resonance with the citizenry as a whole.* Americans tend to care more about what works than what should have worked. Administration policy in Iraq had failed so massively that it discredited the concept of America's role in the world on which it was based. The Bush presidency had more than a year left in office. During that period, the "surge" of U.S. troops would reduce the violence in key parts of Iraq, increasing the possibility of a drawdown and eventual withdrawal under the next administration. Nonetheless, the Bush revolution in American foreign policy was over—an aberration in the unfolding history of American internationalism, but one with profound and potentially lasting consequences.

---

* One voice largely silent in this debate was that of Paul Wolfowitz, who had been moved from the Pentagon to the presidency of the World Bank, where his career ended in disgrace. The proximate cause was his involvement in arranging for his companion, a long-time employee of the bank, to get an extremely lucrative transfer to the State Department. The scandal sparked an explosion of resentment in the Bank's staff and on its board that had been building up against Wolfowitz's high-handedness, which many saw as yet another manifestation of the Bush team's penchant for unilateralism, applied, in this case, to the management of a multilateral institution.

Conclusion

YES, WE MUST

Some say the world will end in fire,
Some say in ice.
—*ROBERT FROST*[1]

I am doing it because it is right—I am doing it because it is
necessary to be done if we are going to survive ourselves.
—*HARRY TRUMAN, ON HIS MOTIVATION FOR
THE MARSHALL PLAN*[2]

As the seemingly interminable presidential campaign winnowed a field of eleven Republicans and eight Democrats down to the parties' nominees in the spring of 2008, I felt reasonably confident that, whichever candidate won, the next administration would repair the worst of the damage George W. Bush had done and put America in a stronger position to deal with the welter of troubles it faced around the world.

I had seen quite a bit of John McCain over the years—when I called on him in his senate office during my years at the State Department, when our paths crossed overseas after I left government (several times in Munich, at an annual international security conference, and in Tbilisi, Georgia, where we were part of an effort to promote free and fair elections, shortly before the Rose Revolution of 2003), and when he came to Brookings as a frequent and popular guest speaker. This was back in the days when he really was a straight-talking maverick.

When McCain launched his bid for the White House in April 2007, he was clearly the Republican candidate with the most experience in foreign policy. He was also the most moderate and independent (Chuck Hagel, another regular at Brookings events, contemplated running but decided not to). In my mind and many others', McCain's gung-ho defense of the Iraq war was offset by the way he separated himself from Bush with his sponsorship of legislation to address climate change and his advocacy of diplomacy to regulate nuclear weaponry.

On the basis of what I knew—or thought I knew—of McCain, I expected that, once he had feinted right and had the nomination locked up, he would move back to the center and take the high road as a unifier at home and an established statesman abroad. While I could hardly have been more wrong, McCain paid a huge price for proving me so. His divisive strategy in the general-election campaign backfired spectacularly.

As for Barack Obama, I had seen much less of him, since he was a newcomer to Washington; but I read his books, met him on a few occasions at the homes of friends, and watched how, in effect, he apprenticed himself on national-security issues to Richard Lugar of Indiana, a widely respected internationalist who had replaced Jesse Helms as the ranking Republican on the Senate Foreign Relations Committee.

It was an early cliché in the commentary on Obama that his biography was emblematic of the extent to which America was a product of globalization—and not just because he had a Kenyan father, but also because he had spent much of his childhood in Hawaii, the most heterogeneous of American states, and in Indonesia. Whether that feature of his life and identity would be a political asset was an open question, but he was forthright in trying to make it one. Soon after announcing his candidacy for the presidency, in February 2007, Obama began working into his speeches a riff on the practical implications of "a world more intertwined than at any time in human history." In such a world, the United States would have to find ways of simultaneously advancing its own interests, respecting those of others, protecting itself and its allies from the vulnerabilities that came with interdependence while taking advantage of opportunities for collaborative action. "Common security" and "common humanity" became part of his mantra. The phrases were often linked rhetorically as though they were two-thirds of a syllogism, the conclusion of which was that humanity as a whole had to *act* as a whole in order to ensure its safety and, for that matter, its survival.

On April 23, 2007, Obama gave a speech to the Chicago Council on Global Affairs providing a template for his foreign-policy views. He enumerated the principal problems that "can no longer be contained by borders and boundaries"—global warming, terrorism, pandemics, and the spread of weapons of mass destruction. "America," he said, "cannot meet the threats of this century alone, but the world cannot meet them without America. We must neither retreat from the world nor try to bully it into submission."

After losing the New Hampshire Democratic primary to Hillary Clinton on January 9, 2008, Obama sought to rally his disappointed supporters. In addition to summarizing his plans for the economy, he reprised the central point of his Chicago Council speech, vowing that as president, he would "unite America and the world against the common threats of the twenty-first century." He countered the self-styled realists who had targeted him as a naïve idealist: "We have been told we cannot do this [the full agenda, domestic and foreign] by a chorus of cynics who will only grow louder and more dissonant in the weeks to come. We've been asked to pause for a reality check. We've been warned against offering the people of this nation false hope. But in the unlikely story that is America, there has never been anything false about hope. For when we have faced down impossible odds; when we've been told that we're not ready, or that we shouldn't try, or that we can't, generations of Americans have responded with a simple creed that sums up the spirit of a people: Yes, we can."

Obama used those three words, with a cadence of defiant confidence, to punctuate each of the final five paragraphs. The crowd, catching on, became a chorus, and the device became a signature part of his rallies from then on.

Barnstorming through North Carolina on March 19, 2008, Obama added a line to the foreign-policy section of his stump speech: "While we strengthen our own capacity, we must strengthen the capacity of the international community." Throughout the campaign, he called for expanding partnerships, rebuilding alliances, and reforming institutions.

On no issue was Obama defining himself more starkly as the anti-Bush.

After sealing the nomination, Obama made his only trip abroad during the campaign—to Afghanistan, Iraq, Israel, Jordan, and Europe. The high point came on July 24, when he delivered an address to a huge crowd in the Tiergarten, an expansive park in the center of Berlin. "Tonight," he said, "I speak to you not as a candidate for president, but as a citizen—a proud citizen of the United States and a fellow citizen of the world."

The sentiment that had gotten Socrates into fatal trouble with the Athenian authorities thirty-four centuries ago was red meat for the conservative commentariat. In a column published on August 3, George F. Will chastised Obama for wanting "Berliners to know that he is proudly cosmopolitan. Cosmopolitanism is not, however, a political asset for American presidential candidates. Least of all is it an asset for Obama, one of whose urgent needs is to seem comfortable with America's vibrant and very un-European patriotism, which is grounded in a sense of virtuous exceptionalism." The far-right precincts of the blogosphere erupted in fulminations against Obama as a one-worlder. McCain did not explicitly join that pile-on, but his slogan

"Country First" offered American voters what Will believed they wanted: a brand of patriotism hostile to the very idea of being a citizen of the world.

Never mind that Obama was echoing not just Socrates but John F. Kennedy and Ronald Reagan. They, at least, waited until they had already attained the presidency before calling themselves citizens of the world (Kennedy did so in his inaugural address in 1961, while Reagan used the phrase from the podium of the United Nations General Assembly in 1982).

There were, however, limits to Obama's willingness to risk the political equivalent of sipping hemlock. He—like Reagan, George H. W. Bush, and Bill Clinton—believed in the concept and enterprise of global governance; but he, like they, assiduously avoided *that* phrase. His adversaries did not: "Obama's Drive for U.N. Global Governance" was a typical headline on blog postings by members of the black-helicopter crowd.

ONE OF OBAMA'S ROCKIER MOMENTS in an otherwise remarkably steady campaign came in August. Russia's invasion of Georgia played to McCain's advantage as a war hero, tested in the ways of a dangerous world, and a sharp critic of Russia's authoritarianism and its intimidation of its neighbors.

But that story quickly gave way to the Black September of the era of globalization. The stability of the world's financial system suffered a sudden, massive, and devastating setback. The epicenter of the crisis was the United States. A bubble in the housing market burst, and the revelation of excesses in the financing of mortgages exposed the inadequate supervision and regulation of financial institutions. As a result, confidence in the soundness of those institutions plummeted, with devastating effects on investment firms, insurance companies, banks, and automobile manufacturers, as well as on jobs, pensions, and savings plans. The turmoil mushroomed into an international calamity that many commentators found reminiscent of the Great Depression.

This new challenge to the international system had nothing to do with hard power and everything to do with the fragility of the global economy and the importance of diplomacy—themes that fit Obama's playbook, not McCain's. Thus, among the factors that contributed to Obama's victory was a breakdown in the governance of an interdependent world so spectacular that it served as a wakeup call on the need for a breakthrough.

As the crisis worsened, President Bush prepared to host the leaders of twenty nations for a summit intended to strengthen international financial regulation. On his way out the door, America's most unilateralist modern president found himself forced by circumstance to use his last days in office to set in motion a new multilateral process, the G-20, that he would bequeath to his successor. On October 12, while meeting with finance ministers gathered in Washington, the American leader who had made famous the line, "If you're not with us, you're against us," uttered a favorite Clintonism: "We're all in this together."

During the home stretch of the campaign, Obama came under attack from McCain and his running mate, Sarah Palin, for being a socialist. But that accusation had little bite at a time when a conservative Republican president and his secretary of the Treasury Henry Paulson—a former chief executive officer of Goldman Sachs—had the U.S. government buying shares in banks, thereby quasi-nationalizing them, and jawboning financial institutions to accept previously unimaginable degrees of regulation.

A new tagline came into fashion: the United States had entered "the post-Reagan era." I could picture Clinton, who so detested the phrase "post–cold-war," shaking his head ruefully at this latest resort to a backward-looking designation of a new era. Nonetheless, the phrase had, to my ear at least, a welcome forward spin: after decades of mistrusting "big" government and celebrating the virtues of the untrammeled—and, in some sectors, virtually unregulated—free market, elected officials and citizens alike had been shocked into recognizing the need for robust, activist national governance.

Whether that augured well for a higher degreee of receptivity in the United States for more robust, activist *transnational* governance was far from certain. Economic hardship tends to be conducive not to internationalism but to nationalism—and its economic manifestation: protectionism. Even in the absence of the financial panic, part of Obama's challenge, on entering the White House, would have been to make good on his pledge to protect existing American jobs and create new ones, while at the same time using U.S. influence to maintain an open system of global trade—a sine qua non for an orderly, governable world. Reconciling those responsibilities would be all the harder in what was sure to be a continuing, if not deepening, crisis.

As Election Day approached, Obama's growing confidence in victory was matched by his awareness of the multitude, magnitude, difficulty, complexity, and urgency of the troubles that would come to the job.

WHEN BARACK OBAMA MADE HIS FIRST APPEARANCE as president-elect—in Chicago's Grant Park, just before midnight on November 4—he included in his speech a passage that implicitly acknowledged the extent to which he was the choice of vast numbers of people around the world who had followed the election with an extraordinary level of interest, knowledge, and passion: "To all those watching tonight from beyond our shores, from parliaments and palaces, to those who are huddled around radios in the forgotten corners of the world, our stories are singular, but our destiny is shared, and a new dawn of American leadership is at hand."

Later in the speech, he turned briefly somber, then pivoted, in the peroration, back to a familiar upbeat note. "The challenges that tomorrow will bring," he said, "are the greatest of our lifetime—two wars, a planet in peril, the worst financial crisis in a century." It was, he continued, a test of "that American creed." The throng knew what was coming and responded seven times as he brought the speech to a close with the refrain: "Yes, we can."

As I PUT THE FINISHING TOUCHES on the paperback edition of this book in late December 2008, Obama is assembling his administration. He has been doing so with unusual secrecy. However as Thanksgiving approached, there were a few leaks—some that got ahead of the process itself. An early example came my way Saturday, November 8, four days after the election. The word was circulating in Democratic circles in Washington that Obama had asked Hillary Clinton to be secretary of state. I put in a call to Bill Clinton to let him know that the story was about to break. He called back on my cell phone while Brooke and I were walking our dogs in Battery-Kimball Park, just north of Georgetown. Clinton was intrigued by the rumor. He said Hillary had heard nothing from Obama that could be called a firm offer, but as he played out the idea, he quickly warmed to it. "Obama would be smart to offer her the job," said Clinton, "and she'd be great at it."

The following Thursday, Hillary called to tell me that the earlier tip seemed to be coming true and she was en route to Chicago. After another ten days of quiet deliberations and intense public speculation, she and Obama came to an agreement.

Now the merger between the two contending camps in one of the longest, toughest battles for a presidential nomination in U.S. history is underway. For Brooke and me—both of us having known Bill and Hillary since 1968 and 1971 respectively and having worked for Clinton from the first to the last day of his presidency—it is a hopeful ending to a suspenseful chapter, since it means that the best energies, talents, and experience of that earlier administration can be put to good use in the one that will take office in January 2009.

Presidential transitions always prompt an outpouring of advice from the sidelines of political power, including from Think Tank Row. That has been particularly the case in the fall of 2008—and appropriately so, given the contents of the inbox waiting for Barack Obama and Hillary Clinton on Inauguration Day. A number of my colleagues at Brookings have had a head start in this regard, since they have been advising Obama during the campaign and some are part of the transition team.* They and others who already have the ear of the president-elect, the secretary of state–designate or their advisers are assembling a list of concrete ways of refurbishing America's claim not just to leadership but to legitimacy. Some steps should be quick and easy, such as unambiguously obligating the United States to obey the Geneva Conventions on treatment of civilians and prisoners of war and the UN Convention Against Torture.

As a forceful statement of the importance Obama attaches to the UN, he has appointed Susan Rice to be the U.S. permanent representative there, with cabinet rank. Susan—a colleague of mine both in the Clinton administration and at Brookings—has been among Obama's closest foreign-policy advisors since early in his campaign. She has delved into some of the principal issues that constitute the new agenda of global politics, including the linkage between poverty and political instability and the extent to which weak states now constitute, in their own way, a threat to international peace and security as serious as the one that strong states posed in the past.

Introducing Rice at a press conference in Chicago on December 2, Obama said, "She knows the global challenges we face demand global institutions that work. She shares my belief that the UN is an indispensable and imperfect forum. She will carry the message that our commitment to multilateral action must be coupled with a commitment to reform. We need the United Nations to be more effective as a venue for collective action against terror and proliferation, climate change and genocide, poverty and disease."

OBAMA'S FAINT PRAISE FOR THE UN was not damning. Quite the contrary, it reflected the incoming administration's recognition that the challenge of strenthening a rule-based international order extends far beyond Turtle Bay—and beyond the UN system as a whole. The UN has the permanent advantage of combining universal membership, global scope,

* Brookings permits its scholars to advise candidates and campaigns on the condition that they do so on their own time and that they refrain from appearing publicly as representatives—or "surrogates"—for the candidate. If they do surrogate work, they are required to take an unpaid leave of absence.

and a comprehensive agenda. That makes the organization, as Obama said, indispensable as a convener of the governments of the world and as a legitimizer of decisions and actions taken in their name. If the UN had not existed since 1945, we would not be able to invent it now, especially with the United States the object of such widespread mistrust and resentment.

But the UN also has the permanent disadvantage of being spread too thin—of being too cumbersome and, ironically, too representative: the sheer size and diversity of its membership are often a drag on its utility. To offset that defect, the UN needs to be incorporated into an increasingly variegated network of structures and arrangements—some functional in focus, others geographic; some intergovernmental, others based on systematic collaboration with the private sector, civil society, and nongovernmental organizations. Only if this larger system has that kind of breadth and depth will it be able to supplement what the UN does well, compensate for what it does badly, and provide capabilities that it lacks.

One of the UN's prime deficiencies is the "policing" function that Franklin Roosevelt had in mind some sixty-five years ago. Someday the UN may have at its disposal on-call forces to deter, contain, and, if necessary, defeat and replace aggressive or dangerous regimes; intervene in and end civil wars; stop and punish genocide and ethnic cleansing; and provide security for peacemaking, peacekeeping, and nation-building. But that day is a long way off, and before then it will fall to the African Union, the Organization of American States, and various Asian groupings to provide dedicated, specially trained, and adequately equipped multinational units for rapid response to crises in their areas.

For that sort of decentralization to work, the United States will have to use its uniquely wide-ranging influence, enhanced by recovery of its legitimacy in the eyes of the world, to encourage regional organizations to develop their own capacities as well as habits of cooperation with one another and with the UN itself. When it comes to peacemaking and peacekeeping, the UN could provide—to an extent far beyond what it does today—coordination among regional and subregional bodies, clear criteria and timely authorization for the resort to force, rules for its application, help in maintaining civil and administrative order, and restoration and supervision of self-rule to countries or areas as they recover from conflict.

"Open regionalism" is more than just an antidote to the hostility of superregions that Orwell foresaw in *1984*; it is also a means of adapting to global politics the concept of federalism, which is one of history's best big ideas, since it allows nations to be both individually and collectively self-governing.

• • •

WHAT HAPPENS IN GLOBAL POLITICS will hinge largely on whether, when, and how the global economy recovers from the near-meltdown that it is experiencing as I conclude this book. Managing that dimension of the international system will depend, in the first instance, on stabilizing credit markets around the world. But over the longer run, the system will meet basic standards of equity and efficiency only if advanced industrial nations—along with the emerging major powers like China and India—trade freely, share more of their technology, and invest more in the eradication of poverty.

Moving in that direction is more than a humanitarian imperative—it is a security requirement. Ensuring a peaceful twenty-first century will depend in large measure on narrowing the divide between those who feel like winners and those who feel like losers in the process of globalization, and on shifting the ratio in favor of those who feel like winners. This is no longer a "North/South" divide—that is, between the "developed" and the "developing" worlds; it is now a divide within individual countries, including the United States, China, and India. Unless we bring more of humanity into the winners' column, and ameliorate the misery and address the grievances of the losers, globalization itself will become a loser for us all.

MEETING THESE GOALS will take decades of sustained, coordinated effort and a high degree of ingenuity and persistence in overcoming setbacks and working around obstacles.

It is humankind's self-inflicted misfortune not to have anything like that much time to come to grips with the financial crisis as well as two additional clear and present dangers. The Crash of 2008 came out of the blue, while a new wave of nuclear-weapons proliferation and a tipping point in the process of climate change have been looming on the horizon for some time.

Addressing these megathreats will be possible in the years immediately ahead only through multilateralism on a scale far beyond anything the world has achieved to date. That challenge puts a unique onus on the United States as the richest country on earth, the most formidably armed nuclear-weapons state, and for decades the largest producer of greenhouse gases. How long the United States maintains its leadership will depend to a significant degree on how quickly and successfully it addresses these three issues.

TO MAKE UP FOR LOST TIME in stanching proliferation, the United States needs to undertake a series of initiatives, starting with one directed to Moscow. Russia's nuclear-weapons stockpile is comparable in size to America's. Drastic reduction is important in its own right, as a model to other countries. It is also an obligation under international and U.S. law (the goal of eventually abolishing nuclear arsenals is written into the Nuclear Non-Proliferation Treaty, which the Senate ratified nearly forty years ago).

Until now, real disarmament has been treated as an object of lip service. That is beginning to change. Some prominent "realists"—including the most prominent of them all, Henry Kissinger—have publicly espoused the view that realism itself militates in favor of total, universal disarmament as a serious, though long-term, objective.* Obama has endorsed the ultimate goal of the NPT, which is, as he put it during the campaign, "a world without nuclear weapons." He plans to take steps toward that final goal by ending "the cold-war standoff that still characterizes the way we and the Russians deploy our forces and plan for their use" while negotiating deep, verifiable reductions in all U.S. and Russian nuclear weapons—deployed and nondeployed, intercontinental and shorter-range—and working with other nuclear powers to reduce global stockpiles dramatically by the end of his presidency.

By setting this example, Obama hopes to persuade the other members of the nuclear club to take similar steps and honor the tenets of the NPT. Coming into office with increased Democratic majorities in both houses of Congress, his administration will find that it has more political running room than its predecessors to negotiate with Moscow significantly lower levels of offensive nuclear weapons—and the closer to zero the better.

The United States should also resume negotiations with Russia on defensive systems, with an eye toward reinstating the premise of the Anti-Ballistic Missile Treaty. Over forty years ago, American statesmen persuaded their Soviet counterparts that the most dangerous, not to mention most expensive, kind of arms race is one in which each side tries to deflect the other's spears with an elaborate system of shields. An offense/defense competition has the perverse effect of leading to more spears. The Soviets reluctantly accepted that logic, but Ronald Reagan did not. Even though he left the ABM Treaty intact, he gave political respectability to the scientifically and strategically dubious notion that a massive national missile defense system can make offensive weapons impotent and obsolete.

George H. W. Bush saw Star Wars as a chimera and treated it with benign

* Kissinger, along with George Shultz, Bill Perry, and Sam Nunn published an article in January 2007 in the *Wall Street Journal*, urging abolition, and promoted the idea publicly over the following two years.

neglect, but his son tried to give strategic defenses a new lease on life. Bush 43 had support from the right wing of the Republican Party, where his goal is revered as a Reagan legacy. That is where the opposition will come from if the Obama administration seeks to revive the ABM Treaty. If the debate continues inconclusively or, worse, if it ends the wrong way, we are likely to see Russia and China respond by building up their offensive arsenals and taking a variety of countermeasures, including antisatellite capabilities, in order to overwhelm, penetrate, and blind a U.S. missile defense system. There could also be a contagion of interest in large-scale antimissile defenses on the part of India and Pakistan and among potential future nuclear-weapons states.

There is a growing number of countries in that category. Kennedy's prediction in 1963 that there could be as many as twenty-five nuclear-armed states by 1975 may have been essentially right, even if he was too pessimistic about how long it would take. Today there are nine such countries (the United States, Russia, China, the United Kingdom, France, India, Pakistan, North Korea, and, presumptively, Israel), with the possibility of a dozen or more blasting their way into the club over the next ten years or so.

The bilateral animosities that might trigger "small" nuclear wars already include India-Pakistan and North Korea-America. In the relatively near future that list could include Iran-Israel, Israel-Egypt, Iran-Saudi Arabia, China-Taiwan, China-Japan, China-America, Japan-North Korea, with others in play as well, including at least two U.S. allies. One is Turkey. The more worried that country is about its neighborhood and the less it feels part of the West and protected by NATO, the more likely it is to conclude it needs its own nuclear weapons. The other is Japan. During a visit there in May 2007, I heard senior members of the government, ruling party, and foreign policy elite suggest that the time may have come for a national debate over whether their country should acquire nuclear weapons.

So we are looking at the specter of multipolarity of the most unstable kind. The unraveling of the NPT would pose a danger that is less spectacular than a single, spasmodic "exchange" of ICBMs between the United States and the USSR; but that danger would be more plausible, since it is harder to regulate a deadly game with multiple players than with two.

To make matters worse, the more nations that are nuclear-armed, the greater the danger that some of their weapons will fall into the hands of nonstate actors. Terrorists with a few relatively primitive nuclear devices are, in their own way, scarier than a superpower with thousands of sophisticated ones. By definition, a suicide bomber is attracted, not deterred, by the prospect of mutual assured destruction. Therefore the NPT needs to be supplemented by new agreements and enforcement agencies that will keep tight control over lethal technologies.

The United States should work with the four other NPT-approved nuclear-weapons states to accept a moratorium on the production of fissile material for military purposes. That would be a step toward achieving another goal Obama has set for his administration: a verifiable ban that would extend to the non-NPT nuclear-weapons states as well.

It will help that Obama committed himself during the campaign to abstaining from the development of new nuclear weapons, thereby, in effect, promising to repudiate hints that have come from the Bush administration that America needs to preserve the option of testing a new generation of "bunker-busting" bombs—a notion that is likely to have some diehard proponents in the years ahead.

Obama has also vowed to seek ratification of the Comprehensive Test Ban Treaty, then to launch a diplomatic initiative to secure its entry into force. The fate of the CTBT is explicitly tied to that of the NPT, since the prospect of the CTBT's eventual entry into force was necessary for the signatories of the NPT to agree, back in 1995, to that treaty's indefinite extension. Without U.S. ratification of the CTBT, there will be a growing danger that the other nuclear "haves" will resume testing and that aspirants will test for the first time, and, inevitably, the prospects for rescuing the nonproliferation regime will diminish.*

HARD AS PREVENTING A SPIRAL OF NUCLEAR proliferation will be, it is easy compared to stabilizing climate change. Aside from the technological difficulties, there are daunting financial and political costs associated with the measures necessary for reducing the emission of greenhouse gases. (Arms control and nonproliferation, by contrast, actually save money.)

Furthermore, we have been living with the danger of blowing ourselves up for over sixty years, and we got just enough of a glimpse of what it might be like as a result of photographs from Hiroshima and Nagasaki, film clips of A-

---

* Bush's second secretary of defense, Robert Gates—whom Obama has asked to stay on at the Pentagon—publicly endorsed CTBT ratification in a talk at the Carnegie Endowment for International Peace a week before Election Day. It was a straw in the wind that there would be enough Republican support for ratification in 2009 for the senate to make up for its colossal blunder ten years before. An esoteric but important issue that would await debate and decision after Obama's inauguration was what do about the widely perceived need for a "reliable replacement warhead" (RRW) for aging warheads of declining reliability. During the campaign, Obama was careful not to rule out RRWs, on the grounds that they are not, strictly speaking, "new" weapons but replacements for old ones.

bombs exploding in the American desert and H-bombs obliterating atolls in the South Pacific, and the Cuban missile crisis.

By contrast, the danger that we will disastrously overheat the earth—or, depending on the vicissitudes of climate change, drown, starve, or, in some parts of the world, choke or freeze ourselves to death—is a new nightmare. The prospect of its coming true lies beyond the horizon of many of us alive today, and perhaps of our children, too.

The generation after theirs, however, may not be so lucky. Brooke and I are among the millions for whom that reckoning is not an abstraction. Our first grandchild, Lola, was born at the end of April 2007, while I was writing this book. She is the personification of our personal stake in a future Brooke and I will not live to see. Lola is one of approximately two billion children on the planet today. We—and now I mean the big "we," all 6.6 billion of us—do not want our offspring or their offspring to discover whether the optimists or the pessimists are right about climate change, especially since even the optimists—at least the scientifically respectable ones—are, with nearly every new report, less reassuring. Dick Cheney famously warned in the context of terrorism that if there is even a 1 percent chance of something very bad happening, we should act as though it were a certainty. Since the odds are approaching 100 percent that if humankind continues to pump greenhouse gases into the atmosphere, it will alter the planet in ruinous ways, Cheney's rule should make him, on the subject of climate change, Al Gore's soul mate.

In order to slow down the rate at which the earth is warming, the United States, China, the European Union, Russia, and eight other countries—the so-called "dirty dozen" that account for 80 percent of the problem—must radically cut their emission of greenhouse gases. Under the Kyoto Protocol, half are considered developing countries, which currently get a pass on binding reductions. The biggest increases in greenhouse gas emissions now come from India and China with their giant populations and economies that have surged over the past decade, while Brazil has become the leading source of greenhouse gases produced by tropical deforestation. Climate change cannot be solved without these countries as part of the effort.

The Kyoto Protocol will expire in 2012. Negotiations for a successor agreement are already underway, and much of the international community wants to conclude them at a conference scheduled to take place in Copenhagen in December 2009. Therefore President Obama will, early in his first term, have to play a decisive role in the design of a strong successor regime.

More important than the diplomatic deadline is the one imposed by the pace of global warming itself. Reflecting a consensus of hundreds of scientists around the world, the Intergovernmental Panel on Climate Change (IPCC) affirms that greenhouse gas emissions have put the planet on a trajectory to warm by more than 4.5 degrees Fahrenheit within the next four or five decades. Exceeding that threshold could trigger a series of mutually exacerbating catastrophes: arable land will turn into desert, higher sea levels will flood coastal areas, and changes in the convection of the oceans will alter currents, such as the Gulf Stream, that determine regional weather patterns. Manhattan and Florida might be under water, while Nevada could have no water at all. Russian acquaintances of mine have quipped that they would welcome a more temperate climate, but they would probably be sorry to lose St. Petersburg. Countries such as Bangladesh and Mali do not have the resources to mitigate or even to adapt to the impact of climate change; millions would flee coastal flooding and the desertification of farmlands, creating "climate refugees" and turning weak states into failed ones.

When my colleague from Brookings Carlos Pascual and I visited India in early 2008, the head of the IPCC, R. K. Pachauri, told us: "The cities, power plants, and factories we build in the next seven years will shape our climate in midcentury. We have to act now to create incentives to change the way we use energy and spread technology—and thereby avert nothing less than an existential threat to civilization."*

Pachauri's prognosis, based on the input of hundreds of scientists contributing to the IPCC, gives the world until 2015—half-way through a second Obama term, if there is one—to begin actually reducing emissions and thereby keeping the eventual increase in the earth's temperature below the 4.5 degree threshold.

The United States will have to lead by both diplomacy and example. Americans produce more than four times as much carbon per capita as the Chinese; twelve times as much as Indians; and more than twice as much as

* Carlos, a former Foreign Service officer with whom I had worked closely in the 1990s, is the vice president of Brookings in charge of our foreign policy program. Along with Stephen Stedman of Stanford University and Bruce Jones of New York University, Carlos has completed a two-year study called "Managing Global Insecurity" (MGI) addressing urgent transnational threats that demand global solutions. MGI provides recommendations to the new administration on how, working in partnership with other countries, to build an international security system for the twenty-first century. The project's *Plan for Action Report* was released in September 2008, and a book, *Power and Responsibility: International Order in an Era of Transnational Threat*, will be published January 2009 by the Brookings Institution Press. It includes a detailed chapter on climate change, as well as chapters on nuclear proliferation, financial instability, biotechnology and disease, transnational terrorism, and civil strife.

citizens of Germany, France, Britain, and Japan. Only if America passes legislation to impose stringent limits on itself and offers other countries, especially developing ones, substantial incentives to be part of a global effort will Kyoto be replaced by an accord that achieves universal reductions.

As a senator, Obama supported the creation of a cap-and-trade system that would limit national emissions (as did McCain). Trading among firms would put a price on carbon—an essential step toward changing industry behavior, encouraging energy conservation, and providing an incentive for new technologies. As the most powerful national economy, the United States can set a standard for the world in harnessing wind and solar power, "sequestering" (or capturing) carbon from coal plants, and developing cellulosic ethanol and safe civilian nuclear power as alternatives to fossil fuels.

The domestic obstacles to these and other measures are formidable. While some industries will prosper, other sectors of the economy, especially those that produce or rely on coal, steel, and cement, will contract. Electricity prices will increase in the near and middle terms. Many workers and households will need help with the costs of transition. Coping with the resulting economic and political hardships would be onerous even if Obama were inheriting a forward-looking climate-change policy rather than Bush's combination of denial, procrastination, and backsliding.

The task is greatly complicated by an American and global recession that will make politicians all the more loath to impose constraints on carbon that could hinder economic growth. Obama will need a policy that combines long-term vision and short-term sensitivity to the costs of what must be done. He will have to make investing in America's economic recovery consistent with a green future.

Obama will, therefore, need help from the private sector, NGOs, academia, and a network of grass-roots movements made up of citizens who understand the stakes and therefore will support, and indeed push, policies that involve sacrifices and changes in lifestyle.

Obama saw this need clearly a week before the election. In an interview on October 29 with Jon Stewart on *The Daily Show* (a program that both he and McCain used to reach younger voters), Obama said, "I hope, after the election, however it turns out, that we can work together because some of the problems we're talking about are ones that we're not going to be able to solve with one party just trying to dictate a solution to the problems. You look at something like global warming—that's really an all-hands-on-deck kind of situation [with the need to get] everybody on board—you know, conservative hawks who are worried about us buying oil from the Middle East, tree-huggers or environmentalists who are worried about the polar bears. Bringing all those folks together and saying, 'Everybody's got a legitimate point of view; let's figure out how to solve the problem'—I think that's the kind of attitude we're going to need going forward."

Especially, he might have added, given how far and how fast the world needs to move on other fronts at the same time.

IT IS ASKING A LOT OF AMERICA, ITS NEW PRESIDENT, and its citizens to grapple simultaneously with the financial crisis, nuclear proliferation, and climate change, but it is not asking too much, given the stakes. Public recognition of the way in which these and other challenges are connected might help galvanize support for the necessary remedies, sacrifices, and tradeoffs.

For example, policymakers and publics alike need to recognize that climate change could exacerbate the perils—themselves connected—of pandemics and the political dissolution of whole countries and even regions. The warming of the earth is almost certain to have a cascading effect. Some experts fear that as the permafrost melts, long-dormant microbes, perhaps including virulent pathogens, will be released into the environment. So will methane, a greenhouse gas twenty times more powerful in trapping heat in the atmosphere than carbon dioxide.

As farmlands turn to dust belts or deserts, and as heavily populated coastal areas are inundated, whole nations will be thrown into economic and political chaos, with all the potential that portends for internal and cross-border violence.

Projections indicate that the more onerous effects of climate change will be in poorer parts of the world, where soaring temperatures, encroaching sands, and rising sea levels are likely to cause or hasten the failure of fragile states. In failing, these countries will give us a hard lesson in the linkage between their misery and our insecurity: failed states are often outlaw states, sources of regional instability, incubators of terrorism, and bazaars for lethal technology.

There is also a connection between climate change and proliferation on the solution side of the equation: peaceful nuclear energy is coming back into fashion because it relies on available technology and produces no greenhouse gases. As the world increases its reliance on nuclear-generated energy, emerging nations will need assistance from advanced ones to build and fuel hundreds of new nuclear-power plants. In exchange for that help, they may accept tighter controls on the material and know-how that otherwise can be used for bombs and forgo efforts to acquire fuel-production technology, which can also be applied to making weapons. The result could be a twenty-first-century version of the Atoms for Peace plan of 1953 and a much-needed shot in the arm for the NPT.

Dwight Eisenhower chose to put his idea before the world from the podium of the General Assembly, and in the decades that followed, the UN system provided his successors with a mechanism for pursuing global arms control and nonproliferation. In a similar way, the UN can, in the years to come, serve as a forum for the diplomacy—in the first instance among the big powers, but involving the smaller ones as well—to strike the crosscutting deals that will be necessary to slow down climate change and stop nuclear proliferation.

This sort of systematic, coordinated multitasking is the essence of global governance. Designing and executing solutions in ways that take account—and make a virtue—of the interrelationship among seemingly disparate problems helps minimize the extent to which the various attempts to solve those problems compete with one another.

The same logic and strategy must be applied to international efforts on the financial front as well. Otherwise we will give in to the temptation of letting the priority given to solving the credit crisis force the downgrading or deferring of the no-less-urgent challenges of proliferation and climate change.

More robust regulation of financial transactions and credit flows could establish useful precedents, innovative methods, and fresh infusions of political will for jumpstarting the regulation of greenhouse gas emissions, rescuing the NPT, and resuscitating the World Trade Organization. Moreover, an effective international financial system is a precondition for the revival of a trading system that will enable the world better to deal with transactions in carbon credits with an eye to reducing emissions by 2015.

The ominous converse of these linkages is also true. Since the international system depends on the free, reliable, and orderly flow of financial resources, failure to solve the mess that boiled over in 2008 will stymie forward movement in those other areas—climate, proliferation, and trade—for decades to come. The whole system could go into a combination of paralysis and chaos just when we most need it to work well. By the same token, if we are unable to curb global warming, it will not matter, over the long run, whether we are brilliant in fixing other parts of the human enterprise that are broken.

THE STORY TOLD IN THIS BOOK is less than reassuring about whether humankind is capable of responding adequately—that is quickly, boldly, and simultaneously—to the financial crisis, proliferation, and climate change. Yes, we can does not mean yes, we will.

By and large, progress in nations' learning to work together has been reactive, coming in the wake of explosions in the laboratory of the Great Experiment: it took the bloody stalemate of the Battle of Kadesh for Pharaoh Ramses II to parley with the Hittite king Hattušili; it took the Thirty Years War to bring about the Treaty of Westphalia; it took the Napoleonic wars to inspire the Concert of Europe; it took World War I to achieve what turned out to be the false start of the League of Nations; only after World War II did the surviving leaders try again, more successfully, with the United Nations.

The most pertinent and encouraging exception to this woeful pattern was the maintenance of the nuclear peace during the cold war: it did not take World War III to spur the international regulation of national arsenals; the menace was enough to inspire proactive advances in diplomacy and rule-making.

With that precedent in mind, we can do more than hope: we can act on the hope that the threats posed by proliferation and climate change will similarly concentrate our minds and political will on what we must do.

Furthemore, if we take the steps necessary to fend off specific, imminent, and potentially cataclysmic threats, we will be giving ourselves time and useful experience for lifting global governance in general to a higher level. By solving problems that are truly urgent, we can increase the chances that eventually—perhaps by the time Lola has grandchildren of her own—the world will be able to ameliorate or even solve other problems that are merely very important.

Whether future generations make the most of such a world, and whether they think of it as a global nation or just as a well-governed community of nations, is up to them. Whether they have the choice is up to us.

Acknowledgments

BECAUSE of the amount of ground I have tried to cover in this book, I have been especially reliant on—and am therefore especially grateful for—the help of friends, colleagues, and those who are expert in areas where I am anything but. A number of them found time in their busy lives—and, in quite a few cases, while writing books of their own—to read my manuscript at various stages and offer valuable comments and advice: Hakan Altinay, Ken Bacon, Erik Berglof, Stephen Breyer, Nayan Chanda, Derek Chollet, Inis Claude, Frans van Daele, Thérèse Delpech, Kemal Derviş, Michael Doyle, Bob Einhorn, Gareth Evans, Gregory Freidin, Jim Goldgeier, Stanley Greenspan, Jeremy Greenstock, Richard Holbrooke, Letitia Holt, John Ikenberry, Walter Isaacson, Wolfgang Ischinger, Bob Kagan, Daryl Kimball, Michael Krepon, Walter LaFeber, Bill Luers, Bruce Jones, Ed Luck, Gunnar Lund, Mark Malloch Brown, Catherine Manning, Edward Mortimer, Moisés Naím, John Newhouse, John Norris, Patricia O'Toole, Anthony Pagden, Chris Patten, George Perkovich, Samantha Power, Itamar Rabinovich, Dennis Ross, John Ruggie, Mary Rusinow, Steve Schlesinger, Ian Shapiro, George Soros, Steve Stedman, Fritz Stern, Shashi Tharoor, Brian Urquhart, Jukka Valtasaari, Jim Wertsch, Harris Wofford, and Bob Wright.

Many members of the Brookings community helped me with the book in multiple ways and also made me feel that I had the support (and the indulgence) of the Institution. My particular thanks to Antoine van Agtmael, M. J. Akbar, Liaquat and Meena Ahamed, Bill Antholis, Steve Bennett, Ralph Bryant, Richard Bush, Roberta Cohen, Ivo Daalder, David de Ferranti, Ann Florini, Bart Friedman, Phil Gordon, Harold Koh, Martin Indyk, Mike O'Hanlon, Carlos Pascual, Jonathan Rauch, Susan Rice, David Sandalow, Jeremy Shapiro, Omer Taspinar, John Thornton, and Ezra Zilkha.

My research assistant, Andreas Xenachis, who came with me to Brookings from Yale in 2002, made this venture as much a part of his life as it has been of mine. Without his intelligence, breadth of knowledge, diligence, ingenuity, patience, good humor, and good sense, I never would have managed.

Andreas joins me in expressing appreciation to David Bair, Cy Behroozi, Sarah Chilton, John Grunwell, and Laura Mooney of the Brookings Library, as well as to Ray Geselbrach and Randy Sowell of the Truman Presidential Library and Museum in Independence, Missouri.

Thanks also to Karen Fahlgren, Carole Hall, Munish Puri, and Katie Short of the Executive Office at Brookings for all that they did to enable me to balance the demands of the book with my day job.

Others who provided encouragement and substantive advice along the way were: Madeleine Albright, Gerald Aronson, Timothy Garton Ash, Karen Barkey, Sandy Berger, Kathy Bushkin, Ellen Chesler, Warren Christopher, Chris Chyba, Jayati and Gautam Datta, David Detweiler, Jim Dobbins, Sidney Drell, Lee Feinstein, Jean-Marie Guéhenno, Morton Halperin, Jeffrey Herf, Dafna Hochman, Paul Kennedy, James Kugel, Tanvi Madan, Tony Marx, Bruce Mazlish, Berrien Moore, Eric Nonacs, Michael Northrup, Symmie Newhouse, Sherwin Nuland, Gary Samore, Gordon Smith, Brent Scowcroft, Elisabeth Sifton, Steve Sestanovich, Jaswant Singh, Tony Smith, Javier Solana, Jim Steinberg, and Peter Tarnoff. Thanks, also, to Bill Clinton for helping me better to understand several aspects of his view of the world and America's role in it.

Over the years, I have had a number of occasions to appreciate Esther Newberg's qualities as a friend and literary agent. I am grateful to her for putting this project in the hands of Alice Mayhew at Simon & Schuster. I have known and admired Alice for years, watching her skillfully shepherd the books of authors I have known from idea to print. Therefore I have long wanted to have her edit one of my books. I'm glad that happened with this one. I have benefited in myriad ways from her instincts, judgment, and ability to combine empathy and hardheadedness—to look at a piece of writing from the vantage of both the author and the reader, and in so doing to serve both parties well. I am also indebted to her team: Roger Labrie and Serena Jones, and the Copyediting team: Gypsy da Silva, Tom Pitoniak, Bill Molesky, Anthony Newfield, and Chris Carruth. They were, like Alice herself, always there for me.

Every book I've done has derived both inspiration and support from my family, but none more than this one. My siblings, Page, Marjo, and Kirk, and my in-laws, especially Marva, Derek, Sue, and Cody Shearer, and Lou

Scherer, have found ways of encouraging me along the way, and Mark Versh-bow provided vital help in getting me across the finish line.

Most of all, I am grateful to the seven people whose names appear on the dedication page: my parents, Jo and Bud; my wife, Brooke; our sons, Devin and Adrian. All five have proved themselves natural editors. Their abilities in that regard have been frequently and sometimes sorely tested, especially this time around. Devin's wife, Lauren, has contributed uniquely by bringing into this world Loretta Josephine, or Lola, who arrived just in time for all of us to have yet another reason for wanting the story I have tried to tell here to turn out well.

S.T.
October 7, 2007
Washington, D.C.

Illustration Credits

AP/Wide World Photos: 143, 231, 311, 361, 362

George H. W. Bush Presidential Library: 261

William J. Clinton Presidential Library: 283

Getty Images: 25, 73, 84

Hulton Archive/Getty Images: 60

Kunsthistorisches Museum, Vienna: 82

Library of Congress: 44, 89, 96, 107, 114, 115, 120, 130, 136, 144, 165, 169, 178, 181, 183, 195, 211, 216

Medway Archives and Local Studies Centre, London: front endpaper

Museo Nacional del Prado, Madrid: 108

Courtesy Ronald Reagan Presidential Library: 251

Keren Su/Getty Images: 61

Strobe Talbott: 321

Time/Life Pictures/Getty Images: 62, 64

Visions of America/Getty Images: back endpaper

Notes

INTRODUCTION: A GATHERING OF TRIBES

1. Lucretius, *De Rerum Natura*.

2. Gottfried von Strassburg's epic poem, *Tristan* (ca. 1210), ll. 8429–32, translated by A. T. Hatto, *Tristan* (New York: Penguin, 1960).

3. Eisenhower was speaking to a group of American supporters of the UN in the White House Rose Garden on September 23, 1953.

4. See G. John Ikenberry, *After Victory: Institutions, Strategic Restraint, and the Rebuilding of Order After Major Wars* (Princeton: Princeton University Press, 2001).

CHAPTER 1: CARAVANS AT REST

1. Patrick Leigh Fermor, *Mani: Travels in the Southern Peloponnese* (London: John Murray, 1958), p. 4.

2. Gabriel D. Rosenfeld, *The World Hitler Never Made: Alternate History and the Memory of Nazism* (New York: Cambridge University Press, 2005).

3. Carlyle's *On Heroes, Hero-Worship, & the Heroic in History* (London, 1841) features, among others, religious figures such as the Prophet Mohammed and Martin Luther; writers such as Dante, Shakespeare, Rousseau, and Samuel Johnson; and political and military leaders such as Napoleon and Cromwell.

4. Patrick Gardiner, ed., *Theories of History* (New York: Free Press, 1959).

5. See Gerhard L. Weinberg, *Visions of Victory: The Hopes of Eight World War II Leaders* (Cambridge, U.K.: Cambridge University Press, 2005), pp. 16–17 and 20.

6. Isabel Fonseca uses *Bury Me Standing* as the title for her study of the Gypsies (New York: Vintage, 1996).

7. I have used throughout the online version of the OED, http://www.oed.com.

8. See Jon Lee Anderson's *New Yorker* profile of Karzai, June 6, 2005, p. 66.

9. Adams in a letter to John Jay, August 10, 1785, in Charles Francis Adams, ed., *The Works of John Adams* (Boston: Little, Brown, 1850–56), vol. 8, pp. 298–99.

10. Oliver Wendell Holmes, "The Soldier's Faith," delivered May 30, 1895.

11. William Butler Yeats, "Letter to the Rev. J. K. Fielding," August 1901, in John Kelly and Ronald Schuchard, eds., *The Collected Letters of W. B. Yeats: 1901–1904* (New York: Oxford University Press, 1994), p. 108. The lines quoted are from Yeats's "On Being Asked for a War Poem."

12. Vishakha Desai made these comments at a conference on India and China in an age of globalization, inaugurating the Lee Kwan Yew School of Public Policy in Singapore on April 2–4, 2005.

13. See, as representative of the primordialists, Edward Shils, "Primordial, Personal, Sacred and Civil Ties," *British Journal of Sociology*, vol. 8, no. 2 (1957): 130–45 and Clifford Geertz,

The Interpretation of Cultures (New York: Basic Books, 1973); as a perennialist, Anthony D. Smith, *The Ethnic Origins of Nations* (New York: Oxford University Press, 1986); and as a modernist, Ernest Gellner, *Nations and Nationalism* (Ithaca: Cornell University Press, 1983).

14. Ernest Renan's essay is reprinted in "Qu'est-ce qu'une Nation?" in John Hutchinson and Anthony D. Smith, eds., *Nationalism* (New York: Oxford University Press, 1995), pp. 17–18.

15. Hugh Seton-Watson, *Nations and States: An Inquiry into the Origins of Nations and the Politics of Nationalism* (Boulder, Colo.: Westview, 1977), p. 5.

16. Julian Huxley and A. C. Haddon, writing in *We Europeans: A Survey of "Racial" Problems* (New York: Harper, 1936). Karl Deutsch made much the same observation, calling a nation "a group of people united by a common dislike of their neighbors and a shared misconception about their historical origins," in his *Nationalism and Its Alternatives* (New York: Knopf, 1969). See also Charles Glass, *Tribes with Flags: A Dangerous Passage Through the Chaos of the Middle East* (New York: Atlantic Monthly Press, 1990) and Yuri Selzkine, *The Jewish Century* (Princeton: Princeton University Press, 2004), p. 1.

17. Benedict Anderson, *Imagined Communities*, rev. ed. (London: Verso, 1991), p. 7.

18. See Plutarch, *Moralia*, vol. 3, "Of Banishment": "But Socrates expressed it better, when he said he was not an Athenian or a Greek, but a citizen of the world (just as a man calls himself a citizen of Rhodes or Corinth), because he did not enclose himself within the limits of Sunium, Taenarum, or the Ceraunian mountains."

CHAPTER 2: A LIGHT UNTO THE NATIONS

1. The phrase "refusal [or refusing] to accept the gods of the state"—which is sometimes translated as "not believing in the gods the state believes in"—appears in accounts of the trial by Plato, Xenophon, and Diogenes Laertius. I. F. Stone, in *The Trial of Socrates* (New York: Little, Brown, 1988), uses yet another translation, and explains it this way: the indictment against Socrates charged him with "disbelief in 'the gods of the city.' This was in the ancient Greek sense a *political* crime, a crime against the gods of the Athenian *polis*" (p. 201).

2. Many historians and other scholars have seen the Adam and Eve story as a parable about the birth of society, economies, and political systems. For example, more than sixty years ago, Arnold Toynbee wrote, "The sexual intercourse between Adam and Eve . . . is an act of social creation. It bears fruit in the birth of two sons who impersonate two nascent civilizations: Abel the keeper of sheep, and Cain the tiller of the ground." See Toynbee, *A Study of History: Abridgment of Volumes I–VI*, by D. C. Somervell (New York: Oxford University Press, 1947), p. 66.

3. Henri Frankfort, *Kingship and the Gods: A Study of Ancient Near Eastern Religion as the Integration of Society and Nature* (Chicago: University of Chicago Press, 1948), p. 3.

4. The Cyrus quote is from Amélie Kuhrt, "The Cyrus Cylinder and Achaemenid Imperial Policy," in *Journal for the Study of the Old Testament* 25 (1983): 83–94; and the Darius and Xerxes inscriptions can be found in Pierre Lecoq, ed., *Inscriptions de la Perse achéménide* (Paris: Gallimard, 1997), pp. 219–21 and 256–57. Both sources are cited in Chapter 1 of Anthony Pagden, *Worlds at War* (New York: Random House, 2008). Pagden also makes reference to two biblical passages in connection with Cyrus: Isaiah 45:1, which refers to Cyrus as the Lord's "anointed" ("Thus saith the Lord to his anointed, to Cyrus, whose right hand I have holden, to subdue nations before him; and I will loose the loins of kings, to open before him the two leaved gates; and the gates shall not be shut"), and Ezra 1:1–2, in which Cyrus claims God has given him dominion over the entire earth ("the Lord stirred up the spirit of Cyrus king of Persia, that he made a proclamation throughout all his kingdom, and put it also in writing, saying . . . The Lord God of heaven hath given me all the kingdoms of the earth; and he hath charged me to build him a house at Jerusalem"). Cyrus is treated with reverence

throughout the Bible for his military defeat of the Babylonians, who had enslaved the Hebrews, and for his tolerant rule, which allowed the Hebrews to return to the Holy Land to rebuild their society and religion.

5. The story of Noah and the flood is in Genesis 7; chapter 10 records Noah's lineage. One of his sons, Ham, had a son, Cush, who was the father of Nimrod. The New American Bible refers to "Nimrod, who was the first potentate on earth." In the King James Version of Genesis 10:8–9, Nimrod "began to be a mighty one in the earth." Other versions identify him as a "heroic warrior."

6. Genesis 10:10–13: "The beginning of [Nimrod's] kingdom was Babel, Erech, and Accad, all of them in the land of Shinar. From that land he went into Assyria, and built Nineveh, Rehoboth-ir, Calah, and Resen between Nineveh and Calah; that is the great city."

7. See Genesis 9:4–6: "Only you shall not eat flesh with its life, that is, its blood, for your lifeblood I will surely require a reckoning; of every beast I will require it and of man; of every man's brother I will require the life of man. Whoever sheds the blood of man, by man shall his blood be shed; for God made man in His own image."

8. According to the *Oxford Annotated Bible,* "The Lord is described [in the Tower of Babel story] as fearing the human power that might result from ethnic and linguistic unity . . . The Lord's scattering of humanity and confusing of language is the final step in creation of civilized humanity, with its multiple territorial and linguistic groups." See Michael Coogan, ed., *The New Oxford Annotated Bible,* 3rd ed. (New York: Oxford University Press, 2001), pp. 25–26, notes.

9. Some scholars say that Abraham himself came from the line of Eber, and that this word is the root of *Hebrew.* I have relied on Karen Armstrong's *A History of God: The 4,000-Year Quest of Judaism, Christianity and Islam* (New York: Ballantine, 1993), p. 11.

10. Genesis 12:1–3.

11. *Oxford Annotated Bible,* p. 27. See Genesis 12:16; 13:2, 5, 16; Job 42:12–13; 2 Samuel 7:9; 1 Kings 1:47.

12. What the King James Version translates as "the congregation of the mighty" is, in Hebrew, "the council (or assembly) of El"—an expression, derived from Ugaritic, that refers to the "divine council" or "council of the gods." Modern biblical scholars have been struck by the similarity between remnants of Ugaritic religious inscriptions and parts of the Bible.

13. The Scripture and biblical scholars are somewhat ambiguous on whether Jacob wrestled with God himself or with an angel representing God. Perhaps the best explanation comes from James Kugel: the "prophet Hosea says of Jacob, 'In his strength he fought with God, he struggled with an angel and overcame him'—Hos. 12:3–4. . . . [However] the distinction between God and angels does not seem to be consistently maintained, at least not in the oldest parts of the Bible. . . . [F]or many of these biblical narratives, the 'angel' never really ceases being God; the human form is a formality . . . the human form in one text turns out to be God in another. . . . [The angel in these passages] is not so much an emissary, or messenger, of God as God Himself in human form . . . but God unrecognized, God intruding into ordinary reality. . . . So call him a man, call him an angel; it really does not matter, since this is only a temporary, and altogether illusory, state of being." See Kugel, *The God of Old: Inside the Lost World of the Bible* (New York: Free Press, 2003), pp. 27–35.

14. Armstrong is worth citing in this connection: "Israelite religion was pragmatic and less concerned with the kind of speculative detail that would worry us. Yet we should not assume that neither Abraham nor Moses believed in their God as we do today. We are so familiar with the Bible story and the subsequent history of Israel that we tend to project our knowledge of later Jewish religion onto these early historical personages. Accordingly, we assume that the three patriarchs of Israel—Abraham, his son Isaac and his grandson Jacob—were monotheists, that they believed in only one God. This does not seem to have been the case. Indeed, it is

probably more accurate to call these early Hebrews pagans who shared many of the religious beliefs of their neighbors in Canaan. They would certainly have believed in the existence of such deities as Marduk [and] Baal. . . . They may not all have worshipped the same deity: it is possible that the God of Abraham, the 'Fear' or 'Kinsman' of Isaac and the 'Mighty One' of Jacob were three different gods. We can go further. It is highly likely that Abraham's God was El, the High God of Canaan." See Armstrong, *A History of God*, p. 14.

15. There is speculation that what the Bible records as the Israelites' escape from captivity was actually an instance of rebellion and migration by an Egyptian tribe, led by a renegade Egyptian nobleman. Exodus 2:1–10 tells the story of how Moses was abandoned by his own mother because she feared for his life (Pharaoh had ordered every Hebrew boy to be killed), so she left him on a riverbank, where he was found and adopted by Pharaoh's daughter, who gave him an Egyptian name and raised him in the royal household. As the *Oxford Annotated Bible* notes, the name *Moses* comes from "an Egyptian word meaning 'to beget a child' and perhaps was once joined with the name of an Egyptian deity" (p. 86). The pharaonic name *Ramses* literally means "The God Ra is Born," so perhaps *Moses* is a version of the end of a longer name of this type.

16. Here, too, Karen Armstrong puts the point forcefully: "The Israelites did not believe that Yahweh, the God of Sinai, was the only God but promised, in their covenant, that they would ignore all the other deities and worship him alone." See Armstrong, *A History of God*, p. 23.

17. Jaroslav Pelikan, *Whose Bible Is It?* (New York: Viking, 2005), p. 83, quoting Amos 9:7.

18. I have used, for this passage from Isaiah, the *Oxford Annotated Bible*, which is based on the New Revised Standard Version translation. The King James Version translates the key phrase as "a light to the Gentiles," meaning all nations other than Israel. There are repetitions of it in the New Testament as well (e.g., Luke 2:28–32; Acts 13:47). According to a commentary on the original phrase (p. 1035 of the *Oxford Annotated Bible*), "The Lord, creator of the world and source of all life, called Israel for a mission to alleviate ignorance and suffering among the peoples of the world."

19. Deuteronomy 7:1–5 has been the object of intense, sometimes anguished commentary largely because of its depiction of God as a ruthless warrior. According to the *Oxford Annotated Bible*'s summary of religious scholarship regarding this section of Deuteronomy, the passage was likely a stylized version written some five hundred years after the events it describes, and many of those are retold in a way to resolve controversies among the Hebrews at the time the book was being written. The passage's "polemic is directed at internal issues of religious purity in sixth-century Judah. Often the authors of Deuteronomy stigmatize as 'Canaanite' older forms of Israelite religion that they no longer accept." There are a number of inaccuracies in the passage of Deuteronomy if it were read as direct history rather than a stylized version meant for then-contemporary domestic consumption. For example, the Hittites are identified as a Canaanite tribe, whereas in fact they were centered in Anatolia (pp. 255–56).

20. Leviticus 19:34.

21. Numbers 15:15.

CHAPTER 3: THE ECUMENICAL STATE

1. Aristotle, *Metaphysics*, book 3, chapter 9.

2. Chris Patten, the last British governor of Hong Kong, in a review of Edward Luce's *In Spite of the Gods: The Strange Rise of Modern India* (London: Little, Brown, 2006).

3. See Pagden, *Worlds at War* (New York: Random House, forthcoming), and Peter Green, *Alexander of Macedon: A Historical Biography* (Berkeley: University of California Press, 1992), p. 428.

4. Pagden, *Worlds at War*. The translation of *oikumene* is from Pagden, "Europe: Concep-

tualizing a Continent," in Pagden, ed., *The Idea of Europe: From Antiquity to the European Union* (Washington, D.C.: Woodrow Wilson Center Press and Cambridge University Press, 2002), p. 39.

5. Plutarch, "The first oration of Plutarch concerning the fortune or virtue of Alexander the Great," *Moralia*, in William W. Goodwin, ed., *Plutarch's Morals* (Boston: Little, Brown, 1878), vol. 1, p. 481.

6. Plutarch produced two studies of Alexander, the biography in his *Lives* and the essay "On the Fortune or Virtue of Alexander" in *Moralia*. The quote about the intermarriage ceremony at Susa comes from "On the Fortune or Virtue of Alexander," I:7.

7. Apuleius' quote appears in chapter 7, "On Alexander and False Philosophers," in his *Florida (Blooms)*, a collection of orations delivered in Carthage during the 160s CE. See Lucius Apuleius, *Florida*, in H. E. Butler, trans., *The Apologia and Florida of Apuleius of Madaura* (Oxford: Clarendon Press, 1909), pp. 167–69, cited in chapter 2 of Anthony Pagden, *Worlds at War*. For W. W. Tarn, see his "Alexander the Great and the Unity of Humankind," *Proceedings of the British Academy* 19 (1933): 123–66; and *Alexander the Great* (Cambridge, U.K.: Cambridge University Press, 1948), especially vol. 2, "Chapter 25: Brotherhood and Unity," pp. 399–450. That work, which drew from and expanded upon Plutarch, continues to be the most widely read of the many twentieth-century works on Alexander. It laid out the thesis on integration: "When [at an intermarriage ceremony in the wake of his victory over the Persians, Alexander] prayed for a union of hearts and a joint commonwealth of Macedonians and Persians, he proclaimed for the first time, through a brotherhood of peoples, the brotherhood of man.... Alexander inspired [the] vision of a world in which all men should be ... citizens of one State without distinction of race or institutions, subject only to and in harmony with the Common Law immanent in the Universe, and united in one social life not by compulsion but only by their own willing consent or [as he put it] by Love."

8. I am grateful to Yale classicist Donald Kagan for calling my attention to this passage from Virgil's *The Aeneid*, trans. John Dryden (New York: Penguin, 1997), book 6, ll. 1168–77:

> Let others better mold the running mass
> Of metals, and inform the breathing brass,
> And soften into flesh a marble face;
> Plead better at the bar; describe the skies,
> And when the stars descend, and when they rise.
> But, Rome, 't is thine alone, with awful sway,
> To rule humankind, and make the world obey,
> Disposing peace and war by thy own majestic way;
> To tame the proud, the fetter'd slave to free:
> These are imperial arts, and worthy thee.

9. The first quotation from Cicero is from *De Republica*, the second from *De Officiis*, both cited in Pagden (who also uses the term "imperial republic"), *Worlds at War*.

10. Pagden, *Worlds at War*.

11. Ibid.

12. Ibid.

13. Edward Gibbon, *The History of the Decline and Fall of the Roman Empire* (New York: Harper Brothers, 1879), p. 34.

14. Matthew 22:17–21.

15. Matthew 27:11, Mark 15:2, Luke 23:3, and John 18:33–36.

16. Acts 22:25–28 relates an incident when Paul was detained by the local authorities after speaking in front of a crowd and then released when they found out he was a Roman citizen.

17. Galatians 3:28.

18. See Arthur C. Aufderheide and Conrado Rodriguez-Martin, *The Cambridge Encyclopedia of Human Paleopathology* (Cambridge, U.K.: Cambridge University Press, 1998), p. 318; J. O. Nriagu, "Saturnine gout among Roman aristocrats: Did lead poisoning contribute to the fall of the empire?" *New England Journal of Medicine* 308 (1983): 660–63; and A. Aufderheide et al., "Lead Exposure in Italy: 800 BC–700 AD," *International Journal of Anthropology* 7 (1992): 9–15.

19. Armstrong, *A History of God*, p. 105.

20. Armstrong, *Islam: A Short History*, rev. ed. (New York: Modern Library, 2002), p. 3.

21. See Abdullahi Ahmed An-Na'im, trans., *Mahmoud Mohamed Taha: The Second Message of Islam* (Syracuse: Syracuse University Press, 1987), cited in George Packer, "The Moderate Martyr; Letter From Sudan," *New Yorker*, September 11, 2006.

22. Koran 9.5.

23. Koran 7.157.

24. See especially chapter 5 ("The Coming of Islam") in Pagden, *Worlds at War*.

25. Armstrong writes, "When the Christian Waraqa ibn Nawfal had acknowledged [Mohammed] as a true prophet, neither he nor [Mohammed] expected him to convert to Islam. [Mohammed] never asked Jews or Christians to convert to his religion of al-Lah unless they particularly wished to do so, because they had received authentic revelations of their own. The Koran did not seek revelation as canceling out the messages and insights of previous prophets." *A History of God*, p. 152.

26. See in particular Maria Rosa Menocal, *The Ornament of the World: How Muslims, Jews and Christians Created a Culture of Tolerance in Medieval Spain* (New York: Little, Brown, 2002).

27. Armstrong, *A History of God*, p. 143.

28. Sherwin Nuland, *Maimonides* (New York: Schocken, 2005).

29. Pelikan, *Whose Bible Is It?*, p. 55.

30. Maimonides, *Iggert Teman (Letter to Yemen)*, also known as *Petah Tikvah (Gate of Hope)*, cited in Nuland, *Maimonides*, p. 85.

31. Jason Goodwin, *Lords of the Horizons* (New York: Henry Holt, 1998), p. 130.

32. The twelfth-century Sunni missionary Fakhr ad-Din ar-Razi wrote, "The order of the world is impossible without the existence of a king-emperor. From this, it is clear that the king is the Deputy of God. . . . The king is the shadow of God and the representative of the prophet." Antony Black, *The History of Islamic Political Thought: From the Prophet to the Present* (New York: Routledge, 2001), pp. 125–26.

33. See especially Linda T. Darling, *Revenue-Raising and Legitimacy: Tax Collection and Finance Administration in the Ottoman Empire* (New York: Brill Academic Publishers, 1996), pp. 283–99.

34. Goodwin, *Lords of the Horizons*, p. 193.

35. Ibid., p. 198.

36. Plutarch's biography of Alexander notes that, in the wake of a victory against King Porus in eastern Punjab, Alexander's army refused to go on: "But this last combat with Porus took off the edge of the Macedonians' courage, and stayed their further progress into India. For having found it hard enough to defeat an enemy who brought but twenty thousand foot and two thousand horse into the field, they thought they had reason to oppose Alexander's design of leading them on to pass the Ganges too . . . the banks on the further side covered with multitudes of enemies. . . . [of] eighty thousand horse, two hundred thousand foot,

eight thousand armed chariots, and six thousand fighting elephants." Alexander eventually relented and boated his troops down the Indus River, then they marched across the desert back to Persia.

37. Amartya Sen, *The Argumentative Indian: Writings on Indian History, Culture and Identity* (London: Allen Lane, 2005), pp. 15–21 and 81–83.

38. Ronald Findlay, "Globalization and the European Economy: Medieval Origins to the Industrial Revolution," in Henryk Kierzkowski, ed., *Europe and Globalization* (Basingstoke, U.K.: Palgrave Macmillan, 2002), p. 44.

39. In the Mongol language the phrase is *Yeke Mongghol Ulus*, and the last word has the connotations of "tribe," "dominion," "vassal kingdom," or "clannish commonwealth." The word *ulus* is still occasionally seen in the last two centuries in the languages of Afghanistan and the tribal areas of Pakistan.

40. The exhortation is attributed to Ch'u-ts'ai, a nobleman who served in the Chinese court of Genghis Khan's successor, Ögödei. Cited in Pagden, *Worlds at War*.

41. Jack Weatherford, *Genghis Khan and the Making of the Modern World* (New York: Random House, 2004), p. xxiii.

42. Ibid., p. 111.

43. Ibid., pp. 135 and 150.

44. The genetic research, conducted jointly by Chris Tyler-Smith of Oxford University and a number of Asian collaborators, appeared in a genetics journal in 2003. See Tatiana Zerjal et al., "The Genetic Legacy of the Mongols," *American Journal of Human Genetics* 72 (2003):717–21. This work was then cited in Ian Frazier, "Invaders: Destroying Baghdad," *New Yorker*, April 25, 2005.

45. See "China claims Genghis Khan as one of its own," *Financial Times* (U.S. ed.), December 29, 2006, p. 6.

46. See B. Gascoigne, *The Great Moghuls* (New York: Harper & Row, 1972), p. 15; Sir Wolseley Haig and Sir Richard Burn, *The Cambridge History of India*, vol. 4, *Mughal India* (Delhi: S. Chang, 1963), pp. 71–73; Michael Prawdin, *The Builders of the Mogul Empire* (New York: Barnes & Noble, 1965), pp. 127–28. See also Ashirbadi Lal Srivastava, *Akbar the Great*, vol. 1, *Political History, 1542–1605* (Agra: Shiva Lal Agarwala, 1962) and vol. 2, *Evolution of Administration, 1556–1605* (Agra: Shiva Lal Agarwala, 1967); Muni Lal, *Akbar* (New Delhi: Vikas, 1980); and Vincent A. Smith, *Akbar the Great Mogul, 1542–1605*, 2nd ed. (Oxford: Clarendon, 1919).

47. Amartya Sen confers upon Akbar a secular sainthood similar to Ashoka's, calling them both "articulate and ardent advocates of tolerance and mutual respect" who helped lay "the formal foundations of a secular legal structure and of religious neutrality of the state." Sen, *The Argumentative Indian*, pp. 18 and 46–47.

CHAPTER 4: THE POET AND "THE PRINCE"

1. Karel Čapek, *Amerikanismus* (Prague, 1926), originally published as a letter to the *New York Times* on Sunday, April 29, 1926. See also Kevin Wilson and Jan van der Dussen, eds., *The History of the Idea of Europe* (London: Routledge, 1995), p. 124.

2. Herbert Albert Laurens Fisher, *A History of Europe* (London: Eyre & Spottiswoode, 1935), p. 14.

3. Fernand Braudel, *A History of Civilizations*, trans., Richard Mayne (New York: Penguin, 1995), p. 304.

4. Pagden, *Worlds at War*.

5. Huntington's article "The Clash of Civilizations?," which appeared in *Foreign Affairs* in the summer of 1993, warned that cultural and religious identity were becoming the principal source of conflict in the post–cold war world, although Bernard Lewis had used the term in

"The Roots of Muslim Rage" in the *Atlantic Monthly* in September 1990. Huntington elaborated in *The Clash of Civilizations and the Remaking of the World Order* (New York: Simon & Schuster, 1996).

6. Yuri Slezkine translates *barbarian* as "babbler," itself derived from Babel. See *The Jewish Century*, p. 16.

7. These epithets were conferred on Charlemagne by, among others, Angilbert, his son-in-law and court poet. See Denis de Rougemont, *The Idea of Europe* (Cleveland: Meridian, 1968), p. 46.

8. See especially Braudel, *A History of Civilizations*, pp. 312–15. For his discussion of feudal civilization, Braudel drew upon the work of two of his mentors, Marc Bloch and Lucien Febvre. Bloch's opus was titled *Feudal Society* (*La Société féodale*) 2 vols. (Paris: A. Michel, 1939–1940), and Febvre's work appeared in the journal he and Bloch founded, *Annales d'histoire économique et sociale* as well as several standalone volumes such as *A Geographical Introduction to History* (*La Terre et l'évolution humaine, introduction géographique à l'histoire*) (Paris: Renaissance du Livre, 1922; English translation, New York: Knopf, 1932).

9. See Braudel, *A History of Civilizations*, pp. 3–4 and 312–15. For more detailed scholarship on which Braudel relied, see Bloch, *La Société féodale*; for the English translation see L. A. Manyon, trans., *Feudal Society* (Chicago: University of Chicago Press, 1961).

10. For a recent, authoritative, and riveting account of this episode, see Stephen O'Shea, *The Perfect Heresy: The Revolutionary Life and Death of the Medieval Cathars* (New York: Walker, 2000).

11. Weatherford, *Genghis Khan*, pp. 155–57.

12. Robert Hollander, *Dante: A Life in Works* (New Haven: Yale University Press, 2001), pp. xi–xiii.

13. In "On Literature in the Vernacular," Dante wrote that language "was created by God along with the first soul . . . and this form of language would have continued to be used by all speakers, had it not been shattered through the fault of human presumption. . . . In this form of language Adam spoke; in this form of language spoke all his descendants until the building of the Tower of Babel . . . [T]his is the form of language inherited by the Hebrews. . . . To these alone it remained after the confusion, so that our redeemer, who was to descend from them (in so far as He was human), should not speak the language of confusion, but that of grace." Steven Botterill, ed., *Dante: De vulgari eloquentia* (Cambridge, U.K.: Cambridge University Press, 1996), pp. 13–19. In suggesting that Europeans share "the same idiom," Dante was intuiting what linguists would conclude six hundred years later: virtually all European languages, with the exception of those spoken in Finland, Estonia, and Hungary, come from the same linguistic family, known as Indo-European.

14. *De Monarchia*, book 1, chapter 4, in *Monarchy and Three Political Letters*, trans. Donald Nicholl (New York: Noonday Press, 1954), cited in de Rougemont, *The Idea of Europe*, pp. 55–59. The relevant passage from *De vulgari eloquentia* (which Dante wrote in Latin), is from a translation by A. J. Ferrers Howell (London: J. M. Dent, 1934): "On account of the Confusion of Tongues . . . we have no slight reason for thinking that men were at that time first scattered through all the climes of the world and the habitable regions and corners of those climes. And as the original root of the human race was planted in the regions of the East, and our race also spread out from there on both sides by a manifold diffusion of shoots, and finally reached the boundaries of the West, it was then perhaps that rational throats first drank of the rivers of the whole of Europe. . . . But whether these men then first arrived as strangers, or whether they came back to Europe as natives, they brought a threefold language with them, and of those who brought it some allotted to themselves the southern, others the northern part of Europe, while the third body, whom we now call Greeks, seized partly on Europe and partly on Asia. . . . Afterwards, from one and the same idiom received at the avenging confusion, various ver-

naculars drew their origin. . . . For one idiom alone prevailed in all the country which from the mouths of the Danube, or marches of Maeotia [along the northern shore of the Black Sea, near today's border between Russia and Ukraine, which was the northernmost extent ever of the Roman Empire], to the western boundary of England, is bounded by the frontiers of Italy and France and by the ocean; though afterwards through the Slavonians, Hungarians, Teutons, Saxons, English, and many other nations it was drawn off into various vernaculars, thus alone remaining to almost all of them as a sign of their common origin. . . . Starting from this idiom, that is to say eastward from the Hungarian frontier, another language prevailed all over the territory in that direction comprised in Europe, and even extended beyond. . . . [T]he vernacular of these nations proceed from one and the same idiom."

15. Hollander, *Dante*, p. 151.

16. The Harvard Classics *Divine Comedy, Inferno*, Henry F. Cary, trans. (New York: Collier, 1909–14), canto 4, ll. 117–29:

> Electra there I saw accompanied
> By many, among whom Hector I knew,
> Anchises' pious son, and with hawk's eye
> Caesar all arm'd, and by Camilla there
> Penthesilea. On the other side,
> Old King Latinus seated by his child
> Lavinia, and that Brutus I beheld
> Whom Tarquin chased, Lucretia, Cato's wife
> Marcia, with Julia and Cornelia there;
> And sole apart retired, the Soldan [Saladin] fierce.
> Then, when a little more I raised my brow,
> I spied the master of the sapient throng [Aristotle],
> Seated amid the philosophic train.

17. Jaroslav Pelikan, *Whose Bible Is It?*, p. 17. Erasmus' 1522 colloquy, *The Godly Feast*, includes a dialogue between two characters. One says: "I think I've never read anything in pagan writers more proper to a true Christian than what Socrates spoke to Crito shortly before drinking the hemlock: 'Whether God will approve of my works,' he said, 'I know not; certainly I have tried hard to please him. Yet I have good hope that he will accept my efforts.' Diffident as he was about his own deeds, yet, by reason of his earnest desire to obey the divine will, he conceived a strong hope that God in his goodness would accept them, because he had endeavored to live righteously." The second character responds: "An admirable spirit, surely, in one who had not known Christ and the Holy Scriptures. And so, when I read such things of such men, I can hardly help exclaiming, 'Saint Socrates, pray for us!' "

18. Erasmus used the Latin phrase *omnium horarum*.

19. Peter Ackroyd, *The Life of Thomas More* (New York: Anchor, 1999).

20. Paul Kennedy's *The Rise and Fall of the Great Powers* (New York: Random House, 1987) calls the century and a half from 1519 to 1659 the era of the "Hapsburg Bid for Mastery" (pp. 31–72).

21. Antony Black, *Political Thought in Europe, 1250–1450* (Cambridge, U.K.: Cambridge University Press, 1993), pp. 87–91.

22. In one respect, Bruegel's Tower of Babel is like many of his other paintings: it transposes a scene from the distant or mythic past to an idealized and panoramic version of a Flemish landscape. But in another respect it is different. Often in the foreground of his work are peasants, wagon drivers, villagers, stonemasons, all going about their quotidian lives—merrymaking, feasting, squabbling, and laboring in the fields—unimpressed by the tragic, world-historical significance of what is happening in the background. The event or the fixture on the

landscape that occasions the painting but so little concerns the witnesses—the fall of Icarus, for example, or the place of execution on a distant hill in *The Procession to Calvary*—is just another detail, while the Tower of Babel totally dominated Bruegel's treatment of that subject. See Bob Claessens and Jeanne Rousseau's *Bruegel* (Antwerp: Mercatorfonds, 1984), a collection of prints with extensive annotations on the paintings and a compendium of what is known of Bruegel's life and much that is pertinent about his times. In the Kunsthistorisches Museum, the painting is accompanied by a text noting that Bruegel "makes the extensive undertaking seem feasible but demonstrates its fundamental impossibility. . . . The tower is deliberately portrayed as impossible and therefore incompletable, but only reveals its secrets gradually. The spectator is at first deceived by the many rational details of the construction based on classical Roman models and thus invested with their authority. Besides depicting a symbol of human pride, Bruegel's painting achieves a deeper significance as a parable of the ultimate failure of mere rationality." Bruegel painted a smaller version of the same scene, the so-called "Little" Tower of Babel, now in the Museum Boijmans Van Beuningen in Rotterdam.

23. Braudel, *A History of Civilizations*, p. 323.

24. See, for example, Robert Black, "Machiavelli, Servant of the Florentine Republic," in Gisela Bock, Quentin Skinner, and Maurizio Viroli, eds., *Machiavelli and Republicanism* (Cambridge, U.K.: Cambridge University Press, 1990), p. 75: "In his education, in his literary interests, in his technical command of language and style, Machiavelli was a fully-fledged humanist" by the time he began his government service in 1498. For Machiavelli on democracy, see Ian Shapiro, *Containment: Rebuilding a Strategy against Global Terror* (Princeton: Princeton University Press, 2007), p. 36, citing Machiavelli's *The Discourses*.

25. Machiavelli, chapters 12 and 17, in *The Prince*, trans. William K. Marriott (New York: E. P. Dutton, 1908).

CHAPTER 5: PERPETUAL WAR AND "PERPETUAL PEACE"

1. Heraclitus, Fragment 53, in Saint Hippolytus of Rome, *Refutation of all Heresies*, IX.9.4. The original Greek referred to war as a father rather than a mother: "War is father of all." The full quote runs, "War is father of all, and king of all. He renders some gods, others men; he makes some slaves, others free." See T. M. Robinson, ed., *Heraclitus: Fragments* (Toronto: University of Toronto Press, 1987), pp. 36–37 and 117–18.

2. No. 3101 of Erasmus' *Adages* (1515), in William Barker, ed., *The Adages of Erasmus* (Toronto: University of Toronto Press, 2001).

3. Geoffrey Parker, ed., *The Thirty Years War*, 2nd ed. (New York: Routledge, 1997), pp. 159–68; C. V. Wedgwood, *The Thirty Years War* (London: Jonathan Cape, 1938), pp. 450–80.

4. Pagden, *Worlds at War*, p. 14.

5. Thomas Hobbes, *Leviathan, or The Matter, Forme, & Power of a Common-Wealth Ecclesiasticall and Civill* (London, 1651). The first Hobbes quotation comes from chapter 22 ("Systems [of Commonwealth]—Subject, Political, and Private"); the second, from chapter 13 ("Of the Natural Condition of Mankind as Concerned their Felicity and Misery").

6. According to de Vitoria, "No war is legitimate if it is evident that it is waged to the detriment of the Commonwealth, rather than for its profit and advantage. . . . And since a State is only a part of the whole world, and since, a fortiori, a Christian province is only a part of the whole Commonwealth, it is my opinion that even if a war is useful to a province or a State, but detrimental to the world or to Christendom, then that war is unjust for this very reason." De Vitoria's work was called *Reflectiones theologicae tredecim* (1626), cited in de Rougemont, *The Idea of Europe*, pp. 77–78.

7. The Huguenot Maximilien de Béthune, the Duc de Sully, was a counselor to King Henry IV. For more on his "Grand Design," see de Rougemont, *The Idea of Europe*, pp. 98–103.

Crucé's work not only had a long title—"The New Cyneas or Political Discourse Expounding the Opportunities and Means for Establishing General Peace and Freedom for Trade Throughout the World, [addressed] to the Monarchs and Sovereign Princes of Our Time"—it ran for 249 pages consisting of two paragraphs. (See de Rougemont, *The Idea of Europe*, pp. 92–98.) Burgersdijk was best known for his compendium of Aristotelian philosophy. See Hans W. Blom, "The Republican Mirror," in Pagden, ed., *The Idea of Europe*, p. 99.

8. See Francisco Suárez, *Tractus de legibus ac de Deo legislatores* (1694), trans. James Brown Scott, in *The Catholic Conception of International Law* (Washington, D.C.: Georgetown University Press, 1934), cited in de Rougemont, *The Idea of Europe*, pp. 79–80: "The human race, howsoever many the various peoples and kingdoms into which it may be divided, always preserves a certain unity, not only as a species, but also, as it were, [as] a moral and political unity. . . . Therefore, although a given sovereign state, commonwealth or kingdom, may constitute a perfect community in itself, consisting of its own members, nevertheless, each one of these states is also, in a certain sense, as viewed in relation to the human race, a member of that universal society . . . [S]uch communities have need of some system of law."

9. In 1625, Grotius saw it as "advantageous, indeed in a degree necessary, to hold certain conferences of Christian powers, where those who have no interest at stake may settle the disputes of others, and where, in fact, steps may be taken to compel parties to accept peace on fair terms." Cited in H. Lauterpacht, *The Function of Law in the International Community* (Oxford: Clarendon, 1933), p. 7.

10. The *Project for Perpetual Peace* (Cologne, 1712), cited in de Rougemont, *The Idea of Europe*, pp. 112–20.

11. See definition 1.b of *federal*, in the *Oxford English Dictionary*, available online at http://www.oed.com.

12. See Leibniz's *Caesarinus Furstenerius (De Suprematu Principum Germaniae)* (1677) in Patrick Riley, ed., *Leibniz: Political Writings* (Cambridge, U.K.: Cambridge University Press, 1988), pp. 111–20; and Heinz H. F. Eulau, "Theories of Federalism under the Holy Roman Empire," *American Political Science Review* 35, no. 4 (August 1941), pp. 643–64; and Patrick Riley, "The Origins of Federal Theory in International Relations Ideas," *Polity* 6, no. 1 (Autumn 1973), pp. 87–121.

13. "It is wisely ordained by nature that private connections should commonly prevail over universal views and considerations; otherwise our affections and actions would be dissipated and lost. . . . Thus a small benefit done to ourselves, and our near friends, excites more lively sentiments of love and approbation than a great benefit done by a distant commonwealth." David Hume, *An Enquiry Concerning the Principles of Morals*, ed. J. B. Schneewind (Indianapolis: Hackett, 1983), p. 49.

14. Small republics, according to Hume, are "frail and uncertain," whereas "in a large government, which is modeled with masterly skill, there is compass and room enough to refine the democracy, from the lower people . . . to the higher magistrates, who direct all the movements. At the same time, the parts are so distant and remote, that it is very difficult, either by intrigue, prejudice, or passion, to hurry them into any measures against the public interest." Hume, "The Idea of a Perfect Commonwealth," in *David Hume: Selected Essays* (Oxford: Oxford University Press, 1996), p. 314.

15. Montesquieu, *Spirit of the Laws*, book 11 and (with respect to peace and trade) book 20.

16. This citation, which anticipates the European Union, comes from Rousseau's *Considérations sur le Gouvernement de Pologne et sur sa réformation projetée en 1772*, an essay he wrote in 1771 to help the Poles with their constitution. See de Rougemont, *The Idea of Europe*, pp. 149–55.

17. Voltaire, Letter 6 of his *Philosophical Letters*, trans. Ernest N. Dilworth (New York: Macmillan, 1961).

18. Voltaire, *De la Paix perpétuelle, par le Dr. Goodheart* (1769), cited in de Rougemont, *The Idea of Europe,* pp. 144–45.

19. Manfred Kuehn, *Kant: A Biography* (Cambridge, U.K.: Cambridge University Press, 2001), p. 387.

20. Kuehn, *Kant,* p. 97.

21. Ibid., p. 385.

22. Ibid., pp. 319 and 355.

23. Kant's "First Definitive Article for Perpetual Peace" asserts that "The Civil Constitution of Every State Should Be Republican." A republican constitution, he writes, "is established, firstly, by principles of the freedom of the members of a society (as men); secondly, by principles of dependence of all upon a single common legislation (as subjects); and, thirdly, by the law of their equality (as citizens). . . . The republican constitution, besides the purity of its origin (having sprung from the pure source of the concept of law), also gives a favorable prospect for the desired consequence, i.e., perpetual peace. The reason is this: if the consent of the citizens is required in order to decide that war should be declared (and in this constitution it cannot but be the case), nothing is more natural than that they would be very cautious in commencing such a poor game, decreeing for themselves all the calamities of war."

24. Inis L. Claude, Jr., *Swords into Plowshares: The Problems and Progress of International Organizations,* 3rd ed. (New York: Random House, 1964), p. 19.

25. Rousseau, *The Social Contract* (1762), trans. G. D. H. Cole (London: Everyman's Library, 1982), book 1, chapter 7.

26. "The inhospitable conduct of civilized states of our continent, especially the commercial states, the injustice which they display in visiting foreign countries and peoples (which in their case is the same as conquering them) seems appallingly great. America, the negro countries, the Spice Islands, the Cape, etc. were looked upon at the time of their discovery as ownerless territories; for the native inhabitants were counted as nothing." From "An Idea for a Universal History with a Cosmopolitan Purpose" and "Perpetual Peace: A Philosophical Sketch," in H. S. Reiss, ed., and H. R. Nisbet, trans., *Kant: Political Writings* (Cambridge, U.K.: Cambridge University Press, 1991), pp. 41–53 and 93–130.

27. I have been helped in this section by my Brookings colleague Bill Antholis's unpublished Ph.D. dissertation, "Liberal Democratic Theory and the Transformation of Sovereignty" (Yale University, 1993).

28. My understanding of Kant's contribution to the theory—and his anticipation of the practice—of liberal internationalism owes much to Michael Doyle, in particular to his "Kant, Liberal Legacies, and Foreign Affairs," *Philosophy and Public Affairs* 12, no. 3 (Summer, 1983): 205–35.

29. Kant, "An Idea for a Universal History with a Cosmopolitan Purpose," pp. 41–53, from which the title and epigraph are taken for Isaiah Berlin's *The Crooked Timber of Humanity: Chapters in the History of Ideas,* ed. Henry Hardy (New York: Knopf, 1991). Here is the full context of the famous quotation, which, in italics added below, is in the Reiss and Nisbet translation as opposed to the one Berlin preferred: "[I]f he lives among others of his own species, man is an animal who needs a master. For he certainly abuses his freedom in relation to others of his own kind. And even although, as a rational creature, he desires a law to impose limits on the freedom of all, he is still misled by his self-seeking animal inclinations into exempting himself from the law where he can. He thus requires a master to break his self-will and force him to obey a universally valid will under which everyone can be free. But where is he to find such a master? Nowhere else but in the human species. But this master will also be an animal who needs a master. Thus while man may try as he will, it is hard to see how he can obtain for public justice a supreme authority which would itself be just, whether he seeks this authority in a single person or in a group of many persons selected for this purpose. For each one of

them will always misuse his freedom if he does not have anyone above him to apply force to him as laws should require it. Yet the highest authority has to be just in itself and yet also a man. This is therefore the most difficult of all tasks, and a perfect solution is impossible. *Nothing straight can be constructed from such a warped wood as that which man is made of.* Nature only requires of us that we should approximate to this idea. A further reason why this task must be the last to be accomplished is that man needs for it a correct conception of the nature of a possible constitution, great experience tested in many affairs of the world, and above all else a good will prepared to accept the findings of this experience. But three factors such as these will not easily be found in conjunction, and if they are, it will happen only at a late stage and after many unsuccessful attempts."

30. For all of the quotations in the previous three paragraphs, see Kant's essay "Perpetual Peace: A Philosophical Sketch," in Reiss, ed., *Kant: Political Writings,* pp. 93–130. See especially the subsection ("Second Definitive Article") titled "The Law of Nations shall be Founded on a Federation of Free States."

31. More fully, Kant puts the exception this way: "But it would be quite different if a state, by internal rebellion, should fall into two parts, each of which pretended to be a separate state making claim to the whole. To lend assistance to one of these cannot be considered an interference in the constitution of the other state (for it is then in a state of anarchy). But so long as the internal dissension has not come to this critical point, such interference by foreign powers would infringe on the rights of an independent people struggling with its internal disease; hence it would itself be an offense and would render the autonomy of all states insecure." Kant, *Perpetual Peace* (1795), section 1, no. 5.

32. See Kant's 1793 essay "On the Relationship of Theory to Practice in Political Right (Against Hobbes)": "I maintain that the people too have inalienable rights against the head of state, even if these cannot be rights of coercion. Hobbes is of the opposite opinion. According to him, the head of state has no contractual obligations towards the people; he can do no injustice to a citizen, but may act towards him as he pleases." See also the introduction to Reiss, ed., *Kant: Political Writings*: "Kant assimilated or criticized the political ideas of many great thinkers. . . . [But of] these, only Hobbes was singled out for attack (in *Theory and Practice*), a fact which calls perhaps for comment. . . . Kant rejected Hobbes' authoritarian view of sovereignty, his rationalism, his attempt to apply the methods of geometry to human and social affairs and his explanation of society based on a psychological assumption, that of the fear of sudden death" (p. 10).

CHAPTER 6: BLOOD AND LEATHER

1. Beethoven in a letter to Archduke Rudolph, in connection with the composer's commission to write what became the *Missa Solemnis* for the archduke's installation as archbishop of Olmütz. Quoted in Edmund Morris, *Beethoven: The Universal Composer* (New York: HarperCollins, 2005), pp. 195–96.

2. Stendhal, *Scarlet and Black,* trans. Margaret R. B. Shaw, (London: Penguin, 1953), p. 500.

3. Maximilien Robespierre, "Declaration of Rights," presented to the National Convention on April 24, 1793 (also known as the Jacobin Constitution of 1793); and "Speech before the National Assembly," May 15, 1790. See de Rougemont, *The Idea of Europe,* pp. 179–80.

4. Kuehn, *Kant,* p. 342.

5. Edmund Burke, *Two Letters Addressed to A Member of the Present Parliament, on the Proposals for Peace with the Regicide Directory of France,* 2nd ed. (London, 1796). See also Pagden, *Worlds at War,* pp. 15 and 43.

6. C. A. Bayly, *The Birth of the Modern World 1780–1914* (Malden, Mass.: Blackwell, 2004), p. 108; cited in chapter 8 of Pagden, *Worlds at War.*

7. Paul D. Rémusat, ed., *Mémoires de Madame de Rémusat* (Paris, 1880), p. 274; cited in chapter 8 of Pagden, *Worlds at War*.

8. See Hugo's poem of 1828 "Lui" in the collection *Les Orientales:* "Toujours lui! lui partout!—ou brûlante ou glacée, / Son image sans cesse ébranle ma pensée. / . . . Vainqueur, enthousiaste, éclatant de prestiges, / Prodige, il étonna la terre des prodiges. / . . . Sublime, il apparut aux tribus éblouies / Comme un Mahomet d'occident."

9. Hegel made these observations in a letter to his friend, the philosopher and theologian Immanuel Niethammer, on October 13, 1806, the day before the decisive Battle of Jena: "I saw the Emperor—this world-soul—riding out of the city on reconnaissance. It is indeed a wonderful sensation to see such an individual, who, concentrated here at a single point, astride a horse, reaches out over the world and masters it . . . this extraordinary man, who it is impossible not to admire." Johannes Hoffmeister, ed., *Briefe von und an Hegel (Letters of and by Hegel),* Band 1, #74 (Hamburg: Felix Meiner, 1952), p. 114. See also Terry Pinkard, *Hegel: A Biography* (Cambridge, U.K.: Cambridge University Press, 2000), p. 228.

10. Morris, *Beethoven,* pp. 106–8.

11. Marquis de Laplace, *Exposition du suprème monde* (Paris, 1813), I, 142, cited in de Rougemont, *The Idea of Europe,* p. 213.

12. The Additional Act to the Empire's Constitutions (Acte additionnel aux Constitutions de l'Empire), written by Constant, was the new French constitution promulgated on April 22, 1815, and approved by plebiscite on June 1, 1815, only weeks before Napoleon's defeat at Waterloo. For more on the Additional Act, see also August Fournier, *Napoleon the First: A Biography* (New York: Henry Holt, 1903), ed. Edward Gaylord Bourne, trans. Margaret Bacon Corwin and Arthur Dart Bissell, pp. 702–7.

13. See Julia Blackburn, *The Emperor's Last Island: A Journey to St. Helena* (New York: Vintage, 1993).

14. These quotations from Napoleon come from his secretary, Emmanuel de Las Cases, who published them in *Le Mémorial de Sainte-Hélène* (London, 1823), cited in de Rougemont, *The Idea of Europe,* pp. 215–16.

15. De Rougemont, *The Idea of Europe,* p. 215.

16. Goethe, *Gespräche, zu Mickiewicz* (1829), and *Conversations with Eckermann* (Washington, D.C.: Walter Dienne, 1901), July 15, 1827; cited in de Rougemont, *The Idea of Europe,* p. 228.

17. Morris, *Beethoven,* p. 163.

18. The first quotation is from the record of the Congress of Châtillon, February 1814, the second from the Vichy Declaration from March 1814. Cited in de Rougemont, *The Idea of Europe,* p. 217.

19. Dean Acheson, *Present at the Creation: My Years in the State Department* (New York: Norton, 1969), p. 7.

20. Henry Kissinger, *Diplomacy* (New York: Simon & Schuster, 1994), p. 79. Kissinger's doctoral thesis on the Congress of Vienna was published as *A World Restored: Metternich, Castlereagh, and the Problems of Peace, 1812–22* (Boston: Houghton Mifflin, 1973).

21. Paul Kennedy, *The Parliament of Man: The Past, Present, and Future of the United Nations* (New York: Random House, 2006), p. 15.

22. Charles Darwin, *The Descent of Man, and Selection in Relation to Sex* (Princeton: Princeton University Press, 1981), pp. 100–1.

23. Paul Lafargue, *The Evolution of Property* (London: Allen & Unwin, 1890), cited in Ronald Cohen and Elman Service, eds., *Origins of the State: The Anthropology of Political Evolution* (Philadelphia: Institute for the Study of Human Issues, 1978), p. 216.

24. Marx's famous formulation—"The philosophers have only *interpreted* the world in various ways; the point is to change it"—appears in the eleventh of the *Theses on Feuerbach*.

25. Karl Marx and Friedrich Engels, ed., Garth Stedman Jones, *The Communist Manifesto* (New York: Penguin, 2002).

26. De Rougemont, *The Idea of Europe*, p. 261.

27. Heine, "Lutetia; or, Paris." In the *Augsberg Gazette* (1842), cited in de Rougemont, *The Idea of Europe*, p. 258.

28. As Kissinger notes in *Diplomacy*, "Bismarck achieved political prominence as the arch-conservative opponent of the liberal Revolution of 1848. [But] he was also the first leader to introduce universal male suffrage to Europe, along with the most comprehensive system of social welfare the world would see for sixty years. . . . The statesman who extolled *Realpolitik* possessed an extraordinary sense of proportion which turned power into an instrument of self-restraint. . . . He built so well that the Germany he created survived defeat in two world wars, two foreign occupations, and two generations as a divided country" (pp. 120–36).

29. According to Donald Cameron Watt's *Fontana Dictionary of Modern Thought* (London: Fontana, 1988), *Realpolitik* came into use with the publication of Ludwig von Rochau's 1853 *Grundsätze der Realpolitik (Fundamentals of Power Politics)*, which was intended largely as an attack on German liberals.

30. In the final years of his life, Marx became disillusioned at the prospects for the success of the movement he had helped create. In his last decade, he often complained of a "chronic mental depression" afflicting him when considering the state of the world, and he denounced what he saw as former revolutionaries making compromises with national governments throughout Europe. See *Encyclopædia Britannica Online*, s.v. "Marx, Karl," http://eb.com (2007), and Karl Marx, *Critique of the Gotha Programme* (London: Lawrence, 1933).

31. See Martin Meredith, *The Fate of Africa* (New York: Public Affairs, 2005), p. 2.

32. For a searing indictment of Belgium as the perpetrator of the worst human rights abuses in Africa during the nineteenth century, see Adam Hochschild, *King Leopold's Ghost: A Story of Greed, Terror, and Heroism in Colonial Africa* (New York: Houghton Mifflin, 1998). Hochschild identifies (pp. 111–12) the first person to use the phrase "crime against humanity" as George Washington Williams, a black American journalist and political activist who traveled through Congo and in 1890 published an "Open Letter" detailing some of the horrors he had seen. For a more general history of American policy—and often inattention—toward a number of genocides through the years, see Samantha Power's *A Problem from Hell: America and the Age of Genocide* (New York: Basic Books, 2002). For a thorough history of European colonialism in Africa, with a detailed account of Belgium's activities in Congo, see Thomas Pakenham, *The Scramble for Africa: White Man's Conquest of the Dark Continent From 1876 to 1912* (New York: Random House, 1991), pp. 239–56, 316–35, 434–51, and 585–601.

33. For more on the last three centuries of the Ottomans, their struggles with centralization, and their transition from empire to nation-state, see two works by Karen Barkey: *Bandits and Bureaucrats: The Ottoman Route to State Centralization* (Ithaca: Cornell University Press, 1994) and *Empire of Difference* (forthcoming).

34. See Taner Akçam, *A Shameful Act: The Armenian Genocide and the Question of Turkish Responsibility* (New York: Metropolitan, 2006).

35. Harry Magdoff, *Imperialism: From the Colonial Age to the Present* (New York: Monthly Review Press, 1978), pp. 29 and 35.

36. Joseph Chamberlain, Speech in Birmingham, England, May 12, 1904. Quoted in *Times* of London, May 13, 1904. Chamberlain's son, Neville, would become Prime Minister in 1937 and be notorious for the appeasement of Germany.

CHAPTER 7: MONSTERS TO DESTROY

1. Benjamin Franklin, "Letter to the Chevalier de Chastellux," April 6, 1782, in Jared Sparks, ed., *The Works of Benjamin Franklin*, vol. 9 (Chicago, 1882), pp. 198–99.

2. Theodore Roosevelt's inaugural address, March 4, 1905.

3. General Shalikashvili, in an interview with Phil Ponce on PBS's *NewsHour with Jim Lehrer,* September 25, 1997, was asked about the principal threat to American interests. His answer: "I think it's the instabilities. It's the ethnic tensions that exist now. It's the failed states that you see, all of those, posing the danger of undermining our interest. We're a global nation, global interest. And instability to us is very counter to our interest, and so whenever conditions arise, whether they're in Bosnia, or whether such instabilities were to arise on the Korean Peninsula or in the Middle East, they are uncountered, our interests, and it isn't then in our interest to ensure that we do those prudent things to stabilize the situation, to keep it from escalating into a conflict that we might have to intervene in." Bush used the phrase in an interview with Andy Hiller, the political correspondent for WHDH-TV, in Boston, November 4, 1999. As an example of Rumsfeld's fondness for the phrase, see his testimony before the House Armed Services Committee on June 21, 2001: "What the United States needs to do as a global nation is to reflect that in our force sizing and in our capabilities." I heard and read Holbrooke using the phrase often, including in an interview with Taimur Ahmad of *Global Agenda,* the magazine for the 2005 World Economic Forum at Davos, Switzerland: "How do you reverse the decline in American prestige, popularity and support in many parts of the world? How do you deal with the breakdown in the dialogue between the United States and the Islamic world? How do we win the war against AIDS? We're fighting it, but we're not winning it. We're losing it because the numbers are increasing. How do we get US-Chinese relations right? What do we do about Africa, beyond HIV/AIDS? The US is a global nation, it has global interests and it's involved globally. We need to do better."

4. Thomas Paine, *Common Sense* (Philadelphia, 1776); and *The Rights of Man* (London, 1791 and 1792). See also John Keane, *Tom Paine: A Political Life* (New York: Grove, 2003), p. 231: "Picturing himself as a sower of liberty's seeds, Paine was among the first modern political thinkers to universalize a single revolution. He set the compass for later revolutionaries who considered their own revolutions as important for the whole world by portraying the American Revolution as the harbinger of world citizenship and peace on earth. For example, in conversations with Benjamin Franklin and Oliver Goldsmith, Paine had often toyed with the idea of the 'universal citizen' and sometimes even described himself as 'a citizen of the world.' "

5. Keane, *Tom Paine,* p. xiii. Others have ascribed this Franklin quote to a letter, now lost to history, that he wrote to Benjamin Vaughan, March 14, 1783. See H. L. Mencken, *A New Dictionary of Quotations* (New York: Knopf, 1942), p. 682.

6. James Madison, *Letters and Other Writings* (J. B. Lippincott, 1865), p. 341; Hamilton from Ron Chernow, *Alexander Hamilton* (New York: Penguin, 2006), p. 60.

7. Stanley Elkins and Eric McKitrick, *The Age of Federalism: The Early American Republic, 1788–1800* (Oxford: Oxford University Press, 1993), p. 86.

8. Henry Cabot Lodge, ed., *Works of Alexander Hamilton* (New York: G. P. Putnam's Sons, 1904), vol. 5, pp. 105 and 206.

9. "Circular to the States," June 8, 1783, in *The Writings of George Washington from the Original Manuscript Sources, 1745–1799,* ed. John C. Fitzpatrick (Washington, D.C.: U.S. Government Printing Office, 1931–44), vol. 26, pp. 484–86, cited in Lloyd Gardner, Walter LaFeber, and Thomas McCormick, *Creation of the American Empire,* vol. 1, *U.S. Diplomatic History to 1901* (Chicago: Rand McNally, 1976), p. 31.

10. On Jefferson, see Robert W. Tucker and David C. Hendrickson, *Empire of Liberty* (New York: Oxford University Press, 1990).

11. As Madison wrote in *The Federalist Papers,* "It is evident that no other form [of government than that of a republic] would be reconcilable with the genius of the people of America; with the fundamental principles of the revolution; or with that honorable determi-

nation, which animates every votary of freedom, to rest all our political experiments on the capacity of mankind for self-government." *Federalist* No. 39, on "the Conformity of the Plan [for the Constitution] to Republican Principles," addressed to the people of the state of New York.

12. Kant expressed his admiration for what was happening in America primarily in his theoretical treatment of what he regarded as the best form of national government. For example, *The Philosophy of Law*, published in 1796, contains this passage: "It is by the cooperation of these three Powers—the Legislative, the Executive, and the Judicial—the State realizes its Autonomy. This Autonomy consists in its organizing, forming, and maintaining itself in accordance with the Laws of Freedom. In their union the Welfare of the State is realized. . . . But the Welfare of the State as its own Highest Good, signifies that condition in which the greatest harmony is attained between its Constitution and the Principles of Right—a condition of the State which Reason by a Categorical Imperative makes it obligatory upon us to strive after." (For an English translation of this work see W. Hastie, trans., *The Philosophy of Law: An Exposition of the Fundamental Principles of Jurisprudence as the Science of Right* (Edinburgh, 1887). For a scholarly interpretation of Kant's views on America, see the postscript of Reiss, ed., *Kant: Political Writings*, which notes, "Kant's views were broadly in agreement with the aims of the founding fathers of the American constitution. . . . Parliamentary democracy as practiced, for instance, in Britain or Canada would not, according to Kant's conception, be as close an approximation to his ideal of the separation of powers as is provided by the constitution and political practice of the United States of America" (p. 261).

13. Washington never actually delivered his farewell address—rather, he arranged for it to be published in newspapers throughout the country, starting on September 19, 1796, in the *American Daily Advertiser* of Philadelphia.

14. Adams gave his "monsters to destroy" speech on the floor of the House of Representatives on July 4, 1821, during Independence Day celebrations.

15. For Seward's statements, see Robert Kagan, *Dangerous Nation* (New York: Knopf, 2006), pp. 246–300.

16. Bradford Perkins, *The Cambridge History of American Foreign Relations*, vol. 1, *The Creation of a Republican Empire, 1776–1865* (Cambridge, U.K.: Cambridge University Press, 1993), p. 48, cited in Kagan, *Dangerous Nation*, p. 4.

17. J. A. Roebuck in the House of Commons, June 30, 1863, cited in Kagan, *Dangerous Nation*, p. 301.

18. Richard Pipes, *Russia Under the Old Regime* (New York: Scribner, 1975), p. 83. The Catherine the Great quotation is cited in Robert Cooper, *The Breaking of Nations* (London: Atlantic, 2003), p. 78.

19. Napoleon discussed the potentials of these different political systems with his secretary, Emmanuel de Las Cases, while exiled on Saint Helena. In April 1816, as he contemplated the chances that European monarchs, in a time of need, might choose to bring him out of exile, he noted: "I may be wanted to check the power of the Russians; for in less than ten years, all Europe may perhaps be overrun with Cossacks, or subject to republican government." See Count de Las Cases, *Memorial de Sainte Hélène* (London, 1823), vol. 2, part 3, p. 61. For Heine's reaction, see de Rougemont, *The Idea of Europe*, pp. 258–59.

20. Alexis de Tocqueville, *Democracy in America* (New York: Knopf, 1945), vol. 1, p. 434.

21. Thomas Andrew Bailey, *America Faces Russia: Russian-American Relations from Early Times to Our Day* (Ithaca: Cornell University Press, 1950), p. 124; and Kagan, *Dangerous Nation*, pp. 286–89.

22. Cathal J. Nolan, "The United States and Tsarist Anti-Semitism, 1865–1914," *Diplomacy and Statecraft* 3 (November 1992): 443, cited in Kagan, *Dangerous Nation*, pp. 287–88.

23. Harrison's comment was from his 1891 annual message to Congress. Twain's can be

found in Nolan, "The United States and Tsarist Anti-Semitism," cited in Kagan, *Dangerous Nation,* pp. 288-89.

24. Edmund Morris, *The Rise of Theodore Roosevelt* (New York: Coward, McCann & Geoghegan, 1979), p. 607.

25. Roosevelt could never identify exactly where or from whom he had picked up this saying, nor could his good friend Rudyard Kipling help him. The first known use of the phrase was in a Roosevelt letter to Henry L. Sprague, January 26, 1900. See also Patricia O'Toole, *When Trumpets Call: Theodore Roosevelt After the White House* (New York: Simon & Schuster, 2005); and Nathan Miller, *Theodore Roosevelt: A Life* (New York: HarperCollins, 1992), p. 337.

26. See Miller, *Theodore Roosevelt,* p. 251; and Morris, *The Rise of Theodore Roosevelt,* pp. 598 and 634.

27. Twain's pieces on this subject are collected in Jim Zwick, ed., *Mark Twain's Weapons of Satire: Anti-Imperialist Writings on the Philippine-American War* (Syracuse: Syracuse University Press, 1992).

28. Edmund Morris, in *Theodore Rex* (New York: Random House, 2001), believes that McKinley, even though he was commander in chief during the war, was less enthusiastic than younger members of his administration, notably Roosevelt. "A gulf, not merely of years but of ideology, separated [Roosevelt] from these heroes of the past. . . . The old soldiers had cheered when the young soldiers liberated Cuba, but they fell silent when similar 'freedoms' were imposed on Puerto Rico, Guam, and the Philippines. . . . Was their beloved republic, they asked, taking on the trappings of an imperial power? . . . The old soldiers remained fiercely opposed to expansionism. They asked how a nation that had won its independence in a colonial war could force dependence upon others" (pp. 23-24).

29. Henry Adams, *The Education of Henry Adams: An Autobiography* (Boston: Houghton & Mifflin, 1918).

30. Theodore Roosevelt, *The Strenuous Life* (New York: Century, 1900), pp. 31 and 34.

31. Morris, *Theodore Rex,* pp. 24-25.

32. Ibid., pp. 386-414.

33. Howard K. Beale, *Theodore Roosevelt and the Rise of American World Power* (Baltimore: Johns Hopkins University Press, 1956), pp. 267-68. Which ancestors, and of which nationality, Roosevelt had in mind can only be guessed. In *The Rise of Theodore Roosevelt,* Edmund Morris notes that the press corps called TR "Old 57 Varieties" because, no matter whom he met, he would ask about lineage and keep probing until he could claim a common ethnic bond. He was a Knickerbocker on his father's side but a rich mixture on his mother's. According to Patricia O'Toole, another of his biographers (with whom I corresponded on this point), TR knew Norse mythology and Viking history well—he identified strongly with the virility of it all—so it is quite possible that he saw a link between his Teutonic and Dutch strains and whatever ancient links they might have to Scandinavia. In any event, according to O'Toole, there is probably at least a grain of truth or high probability in his assertion. He had an astonishing knowledge of the whole scope of human history and felt himself connected to all of it.

34. Morris, *Theodore Rex,* pp. 386-87.

35. Angell's thesis as summarized in the preface to the book: "It is assumed that a nation's relative prosperity is broadly determined by its political power; that nations being competing units, advantage in the last resort goes to the possessor of preponderant military force, the weaker goes to the wall, as in the other forms of the struggle for life. The author challenges this whole doctrine. He attempts to show that it belongs to a stage of development out of which we have passed that the commerce and industry of a people no longer depend upon the expansion of its political frontiers; that a nation's political and economic frontiers do not now necessarily coincide; that military power is socially and economically futile, and can have no relation to the prosperity of the people exercising it; that it is impossible for one nation to seize

by force the wealth or trade of another—to enrich itself by subjugating, or imposing its will by force on another." See Norman Angell, *The Great Illusion: A Study of the Relation of Military Power in Nations to Their Economic and Social Advantage* (London: Heinemann, 1910).

36. Doyle, "Kant, Liberal Legacies, and Foreign Affairs," p. 222.

37. John Keegan, *The First World War* (New York: Knopf, 1999), pp. 10–23.

38. See Jean Variot, *Propos de Georges Sorel* (1935), cited in de Rougemont, *The Idea of Europe*, pp. 334–35.

39. Morris, *Beethoven,* p. 227.

40. For example, Clinton's first national security adviser, Anthony Lake, frequently described himself and the administration as "pragmatic neo-Wilsonian."

41. Henry Kissinger, *Diplomacy* (New York: Simon & Schuster, 1994), pp. 43–44.

42. For example, Roosevelt wrote, "To substitute internationalism for nationalism means to do away with patriotism and is as vicious and as profoundly demoralizing as to put promiscuous devotion to all other persons in the place of steadfast devotion to a man's own family. Either effort means the atrophy of robust morality. The man who loves other countries as much as his own stands on a level with the man who loves other women as much as he loves his own wife. One is as worthless a creature as the other. . . . The professional internationalist is a man who, under a pretense of diffuse attachment for everybody hides the fact that in reality he is incapable of doing his duty by anybody." Theodore Roosevelt, *The Great Adventure*, in *Collected Works*, vol. 19 (New York: Scribner, 1926), p. 372.

43. Woodrow Wilson, "The Study of Administration," *Political Science Quarterly* 2, no. 2 (June 1887): 197–222.

44. Roosevelt wrote these words in a long article for the magazine the *Outlook* in September 1914, about two months after World War I began. Cited in Harold Howland, *Theodore Roosevelt and His Times* (New Haven: Yale University Press, 1921), pp. 255–60.

45. During the 1916 election, Wilson's slogan was "He kept us out of war." But, by April 2, 1917, he had called Congress into special session to issue a declaration of war in response to German aggressions against American shipping. Wilson said to Congress: "The world must be made safe for democracy. . . . It is a fearful thing to lead this great peaceful people into war, into the most terrible and disastrous of all wars, civilization itself seeming to be in the balance. But the right is more precious than peace, and we shall fight for the things which we have always carried nearest our hearts—for democracy, for the right of those who submit to authority to have a voice in their own governments, for the rights and liberties of small nations, for a universal dominion of right by such a concert of free peoples as shall bring peace and safety to all nations and make the world itself at last free."

46. John M. Barry, *The Great Influenza: The Epic Story of the Deadliest Plague In History* (New York: Penguin, 2004).

47. Tony Judt, "Is the UN Doomed?" *New York Review of Books,* February 15, 2007.

CHAPTER 8: EMPTY CHAIRS

1. Georges Clemenceau, cited in Margaret MacMillan, *Paris 1919: Six Months That Changed the World* (New York: Random House, 2001), p. 460.

2. K. Anthony Appiah, *Cosmopolitanism: Ethics in a World of Strangers* (New York: Norton, 2006), p. 140.

3. Theodore Roosevelt, "The World War: Its Tragedies and Its Lessons," *Outlook*, September 23, 1914.

4. Henry F. Pringle, *Life and Times of William Howard Taft: A Biography*, vol. 2 (Hamden, Conn.: Archon, 1964), pp. 928–30.

5. According to historian Ronald Powaski, Wilson "regarded the Bolshevik regime as a demonic conspiracy that had destroyed the democratic promise [of post-czarist Russia]. . . .

And he found particularly offensive its doctrine of class warfare, the dictatorship of the proletariat, its suppression of civil liberties, and its hostility toward private property." Powaski, *The Cold War: The United States and the Soviet Union, 1917–1991* (Oxford: Oxford University Press, 1997), p. 8.

6. Herbert Hoover's memo to Wilson, March 28, 1919, excerpted in Thomas Paterson, ed., *Major Problems in American Foreign Policy* (Lexington, Mass.: D. C. Heath, 1978), p. 95.

7. Wilson, July 4, 1918, address at Mount Vernon, Virginia.

8. H. W. V. Temperley, ed., *A History of the Peace Conference of Paris*, 6 vols. (London: H. Frowde, and Hodder & Stoughton, 1920–24), vol. 1, p. 439.

9. Thomas J. Knock, *To End All Wars: Woodrow Wilson and the Quest for a New World Order* (New York: Oxford University Press, 1992), pp. 194–95.

10. Inis Claude writes: "Sitting at the conference table, [Wilson] had more than American power behind him; he was backed by the enthusiasm of masses of people in Western Europe who were newly conscious of international relations and conspicuously insistent that the lamb of peace not be devoured by the wolves of cynical diplomacy." Claude, *Swords into Plowshares*, p. 46.

11. MacMillan, *Paris 1919*, p. 11.

12. Robert Lansing, *The Peace Negotiation: A Personal Narrative* (Boston: Houghton Mifflin, 1921), pp. 97–98.

13. Wilson's speech to the joint houses of Congress on February 11, 1918, in which he replied to the Central Powers' reply to the terms he had set forth for peace.

14. Wilson, February 11, 1918, speech.

15. Zara Steiner, *The Lights That Failed: European International History 1919–1933* (Oxford: Oxford University Press, 2005), p. 36.

16. Hamilton Foley, *Woodrow Wilson's Case for the League of Nations* (Princeton: Princeton University Press, 1923), p. 64.

17. The first quotation is from Henry Cabot Lodge's speech in Washington, D.C., against the League of Nations, on August 12, 1919, the second from a speech he gave in the Senate on September 19.

18. Viscount Cecil [Lord Robert Cecil], *A Great Experiment: An Autobiography* (London: Jonathan Cape, 1941), p. 351.

19. See Hamilton Holt, "The League to Enforce Peace," *American Historical Review* 50, no. 2 (January 1945): 361–63: "Taft saw the proper path intellectually, but he put a faction of the Republican party above the world. . . . Had Taft and Lowell [Lawrence Lowell, Harvard president and another leader of the organization] not crumbled and had they supported the League with the fighting spirit shown by [Senator William E.] Borah, [Senator Hiram W.] Johnson, and Lodge in opposing it, the United States might have joined the League."

20. Inis Claude, Jr., "War and the United Nations," unpublished manuscript.

21. Claude, *Swords into Plowshares*, p. 87.

22. See Claude, *National Minorities: An International Problem* (Cambridge, Mass.: Harvard University Press, 1955).

23. Steiner, *The Lights That Failed*, pp. 358–63.

24. David Fromkin, *A Peace to End All Peace: The Fall of the Ottoman Empire and the Creation of the Modern Middle East* (New York: Henry Holt, 1989), pp. 449–55.

25. See Keyserling, *Europe*, trans. Maurice Samuel (New York: Harcourt, Brace & Co., 1928), pp. 371, 377, 379–81, 391. He used the German word for *supranationality* in the same work. See also de Rougemont, *The Idea of Europe*, pp. 414–16 and 425–29.

26. "Communist-party state" is a phrase that has been used by Sovietologists such as Leonard Shapiro and, more recently, by Timothy Garton Ash.

27. Dennis Mack Smith, *Mussolini* (New York: Knopf, 1982), p. 3.

28. The first Churchill quotation is from R. A. C. Parker, *Churchill and Appeasement* (London: Macmillan, 2000), p. 76; the second is from a minute by Sir A. Chamberlain, November 5, 1926, quoted in P. G. Edward, "The Foreign Office and Fascism, 1924–1929," *Journal of Contemporary History* 5: 2 (1970): 157. Both are cited in Steiner, *The Lights That Failed*, pp. 331–32.

29. See MacMillan, *Paris 1919:* "In the final reckoning, Germany may have paid about 22 billion gold marks (£1.1 billion, $4.5 billion) in the whole period between 1918 and 1932. That is probably slightly less than what France, with a much smaller economy, paid Germany after the Franco-Prussian War of 1870–71" (p. 496). See also Steiner, *The Lights That Failed,* esp. pp. 66 and 194–95, for a rebuttal of John Maynard Keynes's thesis, which he put forward in *The Economic Consequences of the Peace* (1919), that Wilson's fecklessness at Versailles, combined with the vindictiveness of the British and French toward the Germans, was responsible for the failures of the League and the return of German militarism in the thirties. Gerhard Weinberg notes the widespread failure of World War II–era statesmen to "attribute [Germany's renewed aggressiveness] to the strong, not weak, position that Germany had been left in by the peace settlement of 1919." Weinberg, *Visions of Victory*, p. 124.

30. The two books by Fritz Stern that most influenced me are *The Politics of Cultural Despair: A Study in the Rise of the Germanic Ideology* (Berkeley: University of California Press, 1961), and *Dreams and Delusions: The Drama of German History,* cited above.

31. Fonseca, *Bury Me Standing*, p. 88. The curse is taken from Genesis 4:12.

32. Historian Henry Friedlander estimates that between September 1939 and August 1941, the Nazi regime murdered about seventy-thousand physically or mentally handicapped patients, and an even larger number between 1942 and 1945. Friedlander, *The Origins of Nazi Genocide: From Euthanasia to the Final Solution* (Chapel Hill: University of North Carolina Press, 1995), pp. 85 and 112.

33. I am indebted to Jeffrey Herf for his help with this section. See his *The Jewish Enemy* (Cambridge, Mass.: Harvard University Press, 2006). Also, Weinberg, *Visions of Victory*, pp. 5–38; Weinberg, *Hitler, Germany and World War II*, new ed. (New York: Cambridge University Press, 2004); and Norman Goda, *Tomorrow the World: Hitler, Northwest Africa, and the Path Toward America* (College Station: Texas A & M Press, 1998).

34. According to Alan Bullock, "Stalin was as much aware as Hitler of the importance, and possibilities, of manipulating public opinion, and his regime employed many of the same techniques as well as some of his own. The unmasking of traitors and wreckers provided the urban population, ill fed, ill housed, and short of everything with a focus for the hatred and anger that might otherwise have been directed against the party leadership." Bullock, *Hitler and Stalin: Parallel Lives* (New York: Knopf, 1992), p. 287.

35. John Keegan, *The First World War* (New York, Knopf, 1999), p. 9.

36. Kennedy, *The Parliament of Man*, p. 21.

37. As John Lukacs has written, "The fact that the moribund League of Nations in December expelled the Soviet Union from its membership mattered little to Stalin," who was much more focused on the weak military showing the Red Army had been putting on. Lukacs, *The Last European War: September 1939–December 1941* (New Haven: Yale University Press, 2001), p. 66. Stalin would later tell Churchill and Roosevelt that he had been "annoyed" by the expulsion.

38. Steiner, *The Lights That Failed,* p. 349.

CHAPTER 9: THE MASTER BUILDER

1. I heard this quotation of Marshall from James R. Shepley, who was president of Time Inc. when I worked there and who, as a captain in the army, served on Marshall's staff during the war.

2. George Marshall, *Biennial Report of the Chief of Staff of the United States Army to Congress*, September 1, 1945, p. 6.

3. Franklin Roosevelt, *Whither Bound?* (Boston: Houghton Mifflin, 1926), p. 28.

4. David McCullough, *Truman* (New York: Simon & Schuster, 1992), pp. 347–48.

5. Most of Pasvolsky's views won out, and some of those that didn't, such as an attempt to dilute the veto power of the permanent members of the Security Council, would have done so if not for unified opposition from two American allies, the Soviet Union and Britain. Stephen Schlesinger writes: "For the seven years between 1939 and 1945—under two presidents, three secretaries of state, and three undersecretaries of state—[Pasvolsky] directed most of the department's committees preparing an international charter, immersed himself in every facet of the review process inside and outside of government, assisted in resolving disputes over the organization, and continuously briefed U.S. and foreign officials about the progress on the assembly's construction. . . . He nurtured the organization's first seeds in Washington and, by 1945, presided over its flowering in San Francisco." At the end of the war, Pasvolsky returned to Brookings, where he began a seven-volume analysis of the nascent UN, as well as writing on the Marshall Plan and other critical postwar instruments that he had helped to design. From 1946 to his death in 1953, he was the founding director of the International Studies Group, the Brookings Institution's first foray away from domestic and economic policy, which later would be renamed the Foreign Policy Studies Program. Schlesinger, *Act of Creation: The Founding of the United Nations* (New York: Westview, 2003), pp. 33–51, and Pasvolsky Files, Brookings Institution Library.

6. Doris Kearns Goodwin has reconstructed the story of Roosevelt's settling on the name "United Nations" as follows: "During the last week of December [1941], twenty-six nations at war with the Axis had negotiated a declaration of unity and purpose. The document, entitled 'A Declaration by the United Nations,' pledged the full resources of each signing nation to fight against the Axis, reiterated adherence to the principles of the Atlantic Charter, and pledged each country not to make a separate peace. It was Roosevelt who had come up with the phrase 'United Nations' to express the common purpose that united the Allies. Accounts vary as to how the president communicated his suggested title to the prime minister. By far the best story was told by Harry Hopkins, who claimed that the president was so excited by his inspiration that he had himself wheeled into Churchill's bedroom early one morning, just as the prime minister was emerging from his bath, stark naked and gleaming pink. . . . The president apologized and said he would come back at a better time. No need to go, Churchill said: 'The Prime Minister of Great Britain has nothing to conceal from the President of the United States.' " Goodwin, *No Ordinary Time* (New York: Simon & Schuster, 1994), p. 312.

7. Charles Peters, *Five Days in Philadelphia: The Amazing "We Want Willkie!" Convention of 1940 and How It Freed FDR to Save the Western World* (New York: Public Affairs, 2005).

8. FDR, cited in Claude, *Swords into Plowshares*, p. 63.

9. Robert Skidelsky, "Hot, Cold & Imperial," review essay, *New York Review of Books*, July 13, 2006.

10. Robert C. Hildebrand, *Dumbarton Oaks: The Origins of the United Nations and the Search for Postwar Security* (Chapel Hill: University of North Carolina Press, 1990), pp. 15–16 and 60–61.

11. Gerhard L. Weinberg writes in *Visions of Victory*, "[As early as 1940] Stalin ordered the annexation of *all* of Lithuania, including the small portion that was to have become German [as a result of earlier Soviet-German negotiations]. . . . Stalin's insistence that all three of the Baltic States were to be permanently incorporated entirely into the Soviet Union was a very high priority in his vision of the postwar world. . . . Stalin also pushed for additions to Soviet territory on the border with Romania. As in the partition of Poland, he had taken territory well beyond the borders of pre-1914 Russia. . . . [Stalin's] ambitions may have included fur-

ther steps against Finland; they certainly involved bases of some type in and control over Bulgaria . . . and control of the Straits [connecting the Black and Mediterranean seas and part of Turkish territory]. . . . Similarly, there were to be arrangements for the Soviet Union to have some yet to be defined access through Danish waters into the North Sea from the Baltic Sea. . . . Stalin wanted all Ukrainians to be under the rule of Moscow, a policy that . . . influenced his insistence on a major cession of territory by Czechoslovakia. . . . Stalin [also] developed additional territorial ambitions that were for the most part not realized, but they do provide significant insights into the sort of postwar world he would have preferred to see. These expansionist hopes focused on Greece, Turkey, Iran, and Japan" (pp. 99–121).

12. Roosevelt had written in opposition to quasi-imperial American adventures in Nicaragua and Haiti in *Foreign Affairs* in 1928, "The time has come when we must accept . . . a newer and better standard in international relations. . . . [If a Western Hemisphere country were to fall upon evil days,] it is rather the duty of the United States to associate with itself other American Republics, to give intelligent joint study to the problem, and, if the conditions warrant, to offer the helping hand or hands in the name of the Americas. Single-handed intervention by us in the affairs of other nations must end; with the cooperation of others we shall have more order in this hemisphere and less dislike." See Robert Dallek, *Franklin Roosevelt and American Foreign Policy, 1932–1945* (New York: Oxford University Press, 1979), p. 18.

13. Brian Urquhart, "Disaster: From Suez to Iraq," *New York Review of Books,* March 29, 2007, p. 33.

14. Shashi Tharoor, *India: From Midnight to the Millennium* (New York: Arcade, 1997), p. 7.

15. Niall Ferguson quotes Roosevelt saying to Churchill in 1943, "You have four hundred years of acquisitive instinct in your blood." Later that year, when Roosevelt brought up the India question, "Churchill erupted, retorting that an international team of inspection should be sent to the American South." In a 1944 address, "Hands Off the British Empire," Churchill noted angrily that the empire "must not be weakened or smirched to please sobstuff merchants at home or foreigners of any hue." *Empire* (New York: Basic Books, 2003), pp. 343–45.

16. Meredith, *The Fate of Africa*, p. 9. As Gerhard Weinberg notes in *Visions of Victory*, "De Gaulle was absolutely insistent that all French colonial possessions were to be returned in full sovereignty to France. . . . This fixation on the imperial past is also evident in de Gaulle's rejection of the Atlantic Charter of August 1941, with its renunciation of territorial expansion on the part of the signatories" (pp. 165–66).

17. Walter Isaacson, *Einstein: His Life and Universe* (New York: Simon & Schuster, 2007), pp. 474–75, 550.

18. Einstein's letter of July 30, 1932 is quoted in Isaacson, *Einstein*, p. 476.

19. Ibid., p. 478.

20. McCullough, *Truman*, p. 234.

21. Tennyson's poem is primarily a reflection on how the father of his fiancée "Amy" thwarted their engagement. Another couplet (ll. 141–42) expresses a similar hope for global harmony: "Knowledge comes, but wisdom lingers, and I linger on the shore, / And the individual withers, and the world is more and more." Near the end of his long life, in 1886, Tennyson repudiated his youthful optimism by writing a deeply gloomy poem titled "Locksley Hall Sixty Years After." The intervening decades, which had seen so much carnage in Crimea, Italy, Germany, and elsewhere, led him to despair: "Chaos, Cosmos! Cosmos, Chaos! Who can tell how all will end? . . . When was age so crammed with menace? madness? written, spoken lies?" This lament elicited a rebuttal from William Ewart Gladstone, four times prime minister of Britain, who urged that setbacks not discourage belief in progress. For more on the impor-

tance of the poem to Truman, see Schlesinger, *Act of Creation,* pp. 4–5; McCullough, *Truman,* pp. 64, 253, 393, and 508; and Kennedy, *The Parliament of Man,* pp. xi–xii, 4–5, and 281–84.

22. Henry L. Stimson and McGeorge Bundy, *On Active Service in Peace and War* (New York: Harper, 1948), pp. 635–36.

23. For more on MacLeish, see Stanley Meisler, *Kofi Annan: A Man of Peace in a World of War* (Hoboken, N.J.: Wiley, 2007), p. 5. Others involved in drafting the preamble were Jan Christiaan Smuts of South Africa, who provided a text that others felt was bland, clumsy, and prolix. One of the American delegates, Virginia Gildersleeve, with help from another delegate, Congressman Sol Bloom, attempted a rewrite. MacLeish worked quietly with them. Eventually some of Gildersleeve's phraseology made it into the final document, although Smuts fought back and reinstated some of his own language. I am grateful to Stephen Schlesinger for help on this point.

24. John Ruggie, "American Exceptionalism, Exemptionalism, and Global Governance," in Michael Ignatieff, ed., *American Exceptionalism and Human Rights* (Princeton: Princeton University Press, 2005).

25. Vandenberg's caveat: "To cooperate is not to lose our sovereignty. It is to use our sovereignty in quest of the dearest boon which the prayers of humankind pursue." Cited in Claude, *Swords into Plowshares,* p. 63, and in James Traub, *The Best Intentions: Kofi Annan and the UN in the Era of American World Power* (New York: Farrar Straus Giroux, 2006), p. 6. Dulles, quoted in the *New York Times,* June 15, 1945; cited in Traub, *The Best Intentions,* p. 6, and Schlesinger, *Act of Creation,* p. 260.

26. Truman, June 28, 1945, "Remarks Upon Receiving an Honorary Degree From the University of Kansas City," *Public Papers of the Presidents, Harry Truman,* http://www.presidency.ucsb.edu/ws/?pid=12190. (The University of Kansas City would change its name to the University of Missouri at Kansas City in 1963.) Truman returned to this theme almost verbatim three years later, at a war memorial dedication ceremony in Omaha, Nebraska, on June 5, 1948: "When Kansas and Colorado fall out over the waters in the Arkansas River, they don't go to war over it, they go to the Supreme Court of the United States, and the matter is settled in a just and honorable way. There is not a difficulty in the whole world that cannot be settled in exactly the same way in a world court."

27. R. Byron Bird, "Charles Allen Thomas," in National Academy of Sciences of the United States of America, *Biographical Memoirs,* vol. 65 (Washington: National Academy Press, 1994), pp. 338–53.

28. McCullough, *Truman,* pp. 424–25.

29. Richard Rhodes, *The Making of the Atomic Bomb* (New York: Simon & Schuster, 1986), pp. 690–91.

30. Tad Szulc, "The Untold Story of How Russia 'Got the Bomb,' " *Los Angeles Times,* August 26, 1984, p. D1.

31. See Brian Urquhart, "Looking for the Sheriff," *New York Review of Books,* July 16, 1998.

32. James Chace, *Acheson: The Secretary of State Who Created the American World* (New York: Simon & Schuster, 1998), p. 107.

33. Robert Beisner, *Dean Acheson: A Life in the Cold War* (New York: Oxford University Press, 2006), pp. 532, 625–26.

34. Ezequiel Padilla, cited in Claude, *Swords into Plowshares,* p. 61.

35. Bunche made this statement in December 1942 when representing the United States at a conference on postwar institution-building in Canada. See Brian Urquhart, *Ralph Bunche: An American Life* (New York: Norton, 1993), p. 106.

36. Claude, *Swords into Plowshares,* p. 330.

37. See Jaswant Singh, "Pakistan, By Definition," *Outlook* (India), February 21, 2005, a re-

view essay of a book by Stephen P. Cohen, *The Idea of Pakistan* (Washington, D.C.: Brookings Institution Press, 2004).

38. Hannah Arendt, *The Jewish Writings*, Jerome Kohn and Ron H. Feldman, eds. (New York: Schocken, 2007), p. 196. Isaiah Berlin, *Letters, 1928–1946*, Henry Hardy, ed. (Cambridge, U.K.: Cambridge University Press, 2004), p. 691.

39. See Urquhart, *Ralph Bunche*; Urquhart, *Decolonization and World Peace* (Austin: University of Texas Press, 1989); and (UN decolonization) *History*, http://www.un.org/Depts/dpi/decolonization/history.htm.

40. Claude, *Swords into Plowshares*, p. 66.

41. Michael Specter, "At the Museums: Know Einstein," *New Yorker*, November 25, 2002, p. 37.

42. The quotation is from Truman's radio address to the nation on August 5. On July 25, he had written in his diary, "The target will be a purely military one."

43. Truman's message to Congress on atomic energy, October 3, 1945.

44. Truman's remark, made on July 21, 1948, is quoted in *The Journals of David E. Lilienthal: The Atomic Energy Years, 1945–1950* (New York: Harper & Row, 1964), p. 391.

45. The citations in the text are from White's unsigned contributions to *Notes and Comments*, "The Talk of the Town," *New Yorker*, May 19, 1945, and August 18, 1945, and "Letter from the East," in the issue of December 15, 1956.

46. This Einstein-Oppenheimer exchange, in letters dated September 29 and October 10, 1945, is in the Einstein archive and was brought to my attention by Walter Isaacson in the course of his research for *Einstein: His Life and Universe* (New York: Simon & Schuster, 2007).

47. United Press interview, September 14, 1945, reprinted in *New York Times*, September 15, 1945, and cited in Isaacson, *Einstein*, pp. 487–88.

48. Einstein took up this theme in a number of interviews during this period. See, for example, his comments to Michael Amrine, "The Real Problem Is in the Hearts of Man," *New York Times Magazine*, June 23, 1946: "In the light of new knowledge a world authority and an eventual world state are not just desirable in the name of brotherhood, they are necessary for survival. In previous ages a nation's life and culture could be protected to some extent by the growth of armies in national competition. Today we must abandon competition and secure cooperation. This must be the central fact in all our considerations of international affairs; otherwise we face certain disaster. Past thinking and methods did not prevent world wars. Future thinking must prevent wars. . . . Reasonable men with these new facts to consider refuse to contemplate a future in which our culture would attempt to survive in ribbons or in underground tombs. Neither is there reassurance in proposals to keep a hundred thousand men alert along the coasts scanning the sky with radar. There is no radar defense against the V-2, and should a 'defense' be developed after years of research, it is not humanly possible for any defense to be perfect. Should one rocket with an atomic warhead strike Minneapolis, that city would look almost like Nagasaki. Rifle bullets kill men, but atomic bombs kill cities. A tank is a defense against a bullet but there is no defense in science against the weapon which can destroy civilization. Our defense is not in armaments, nor in science, nor in going underground. Our defense is in law and order. Henceforth, every nation's foreign policy must be judged at every point by one consideration: Does it lead us to a world of law and order or does it lead us back toward anarchy and death? I do not believe that we can prepare for a war and at the same time prepare for a world community."

49. Edward Teller, "Dispersal of Cities and Industries," *Bulletin of Atomic Scientists*, April 1946, p. 13.

50. Wesley T. Wooley, *Alternatives to Anarchy: American Supranationalism Since World War II* (Bloomington: University of Indiana Press, 1988), p. 42.

51. For more on Rice's high regard for Morgenthau, see Nicholas Lemann's profile of her in the *New Yorker*, October 14, 2004.

52. See Hans Morgenthau, *Politics Among Nations* (New York: Knopf, 1948), p. 480. See also Hidemi Suganami, *The Domestic Analogy and World Order Proposals* (Cambridge, U.K.: Cambridge University Press, 1989), pp. 99–100.

53. Raymond Aron, *The Dawn of Universal History*, trans. Dorothy Pickles (New York: Praeger, 1961): "Has the universal empire come into being already in the form of the Atlantic alliance, a military force under American command, or is the alliance only a first step toward the abolition of national sovereignties? In any case, Western civilization, assuming it constitutes a definite reality, ultimately is entering into an unprecedented situation marked by the creation of a genuinely worldwide politics. . . . [T]oday's nations, forged in the crucible of ages, are searching for an organization that will both outstrip them and respect them. . . . But it is not the juxtaposition of different kinds of states, some very large (several hundred million souls) and others very small (Iceland has only a few hundred thousand inhabitants), that is new. The unprecedented factor is that this diversity is now accompanied by closer relations than ever before, and by verbal support for a unique view of political organization. The diversity stands out because the human race is on its way to unity, and everywhere people use the same words. . . . In economics, politics, and ideology alike there is the same contradiction between closeness and distance. People everywhere are moving toward the same economic system, but the gap between the average income of a South American, an Asian, a European, a North American has grown wider. . . . Political unity and diversity, however, are complementary rather than contrasting features of the world today" (pp. 60–64). Aron concluded this series of essays about the new world order with this observation: "The diplomatic field has unified itself via the tragedy of two world wars. Industry has spread through a series of revolutions—French, Russian, and Chinese. . . . The wiles of reason invoked by the followers of Bossuet, Hegel, and Marx have not been sparing of man's suffering and blood. We have no proof that things have changed, or that from now on the rational process will reign in peace. But it is possible that, in this respect, universal history will be different from the provincial histories of past ages. It is just a hope, supported by faith. . . . Never had men had so many reasons to cease killing one another. Never had they had so many reasons to feel they are joined together in one great enterprise. I do not conclude that the age of universal history will be peaceful. We know that man is a reasonable being. But men?" (pp. 485–86).

54. See, for example, Cohen and Service, eds., *Origins of the State*, pp. 212–19, which makes the case on the basis of mathematical extrapolation. Over the millennia, as the population of the planet had grown, the number of self-governing communities had decreased. Anthropologists have estimated that in the second millennium BCE, there were roughly 40 million people on earth living in more than half a million autonomous and isolated communities. Over the subsequent 3,500 years—that is, down to the present day—the population of the planet multiplied about 150-fold, to 6.5 billion while the number of sovereign political entities declined by a factor of 2,500, to the nearly 200 member states of the United Nations. If more and more people are governed by fewer and fewer governments, then perhaps sooner or later there would be just one government. That brand of utopianism, which came into fashion in the wake of Hiroshima and Nagasaki, persisted for another thirty years, even though it overlooked the inconvenient fact that, thanks to decolonization, the number of self-governing member states in the UN nearly quadrupled. As recently as 1966, a respected anthropologist, Raoul Naroll, calculated a 95 percent chance that by the year 2750 there will be a unitary world state, a classic example of how you can prove—or predict—anything with statistics. See Naroll, "Imperial Cycles and World Order," *Peace Research Society Papers* 7 (1967): 83–101, cited in Robert L. Carneiro, "Political Expansion as an Expression of the Principle of Competitive Exclusion,"

in *Origins of the State*, p. 218. The Boas quotation in the footnote is from *Race and Democratic Society* (New York: J. J. Augustin, 1945), p. 100.

55. Eliot included the text of those radio broadcasts as an appendix in his *Notes Towards the Definition of Culture* (New York: Harcourt, Brace, 1949).

56. Wooley, *Alternatives to Anarchy*, pp. 52–53.

57. See Gilbert Jonas, *One Shining Moment: The Untold Story of the American Student World Federalist Movement, 1942–1953* (Lincoln: I-Village, 2000), pp. 41–47; Joseph Baratta, *The Politics of World Federation* (Westport, Conn.: Praeger, 2004), pp. 215–34.

58. Oppenheimer's letter to Einstein, October 10, 1945, in Isaacson, *Einstein*, p. 631. The Einstein letter to Cord Meyer was provided to me by Isaacson from his research in the Einstein archives.

59. Declaration on atomic energy by Truman and Prime Ministers Clement Attlee of Britain and W. L. Mackenzie King of Canada, November 15, 1945.

CHAPTER 10: A TRUSTEESHIP OF THE POWERFUL

1. Khrushchev made this comment, which was covered widely in the press at the time, to a group of foreign ambassadors and journalists at a reception at the Polish embassy in Moscow on November 17, 1956, shortly after returning from Warsaw, where he had worked out a compromise with the Polish leader Władysław Gomułka on how to keep Poland firmly in the Soviet camp.

2. Dwight Eisenhower, April 18, 1955, in a statement released on the occasion of Albert Einstein's death.

3. The origin of the phrase "the cold war" is in some dispute. In an October 19, 1945, article in the *Tribune*, George Orwell wrote, "A State which was . . . in a permanent state of 'cold war' with its neighbours." The journalist Herbert Bayard Swope put the term into a draft speech for Bernard Baruch in 1946. Baruch did not use it until the following year, when he said, "Let us not be deceived—today we are in the midst of a cold war." Lippmann's book *The Cold War* appeared that year. He downplayed his debt to Swope, saying that he had in mind a French phrase from the thirties, *la guerre froide*.

4. Kennan cites this lecture in his *Memoirs: 1925–1950* (Boston: Little, Brown, 1967), p. 319.

5. See, for example, Brian Urquhart's autobiography, *A Life in Peace and War* (New York: Harper & Row, 1987), pp. 110–11. See also Schlesinger, *Act of Creation*, pp. 271–73.

6. See Acheson, *Present at the Creation*, pp. 161–62.

7. Wooley, *Alternatives to Anarchy*, p. 50.

8. Cord Meyer, *Facing Reality: From World Federalism to the CIA* (New York: Harper & Row, 1980), p. 50.

9. Ibid., pp. 45–46.

10. *Time*, June 20, 1949, cited in Martin Walker, *The Cold War: A History* (New York: Henry Holt, 1993), pp. 66–67.

11. In a note to Senator Francis Myers of Pennsylvania, when Philadelphia was one of several cities vying strongly to be the UN's home, Truman wrote that he would stay neutral on the choice of which American city would be home to the UN: "The only thing I am interested in is to keep them in the United States." Letter to Francis Myers, December 9, 1946, *Papers of Harry Truman*, Truman Library.

12. See Leland M. Roth, *Understanding Architecture: Its Elements, History, and Meaning* (Boulder, Colo.: Westview, 1993), p. 10.

13. Maarten Doorman, *Art in Progress* (Amsterdam: Amsterdam University Press, 2003), p. 83. The Dutch-born art movement that he was describing influenced the development of the International Style. The same themes of universality would also be repeated by Interna-

tional Style architects in the following decades. See also Hugh Morrison, *Louis Sullivan: Prophet of Modern Architecture* (New York: Norton, 2001).

14. John Hersey, "Mr. President," *New Yorker*, April 7, 1951, pp. 49–50.

15. Meyer, *Facing Reality*, p. 56.

16. John Lewis Gaddis, *The Cold War: A New History* (New York: Penguin, 2005), pp. 48–49.

17. Nuclear Weapon Archive online, http://nuclearweaponarchive.org/Russia/Tsar Bomba.html; Viktor Adamsky and Yuri Smirnov, "Moscow's Biggest Bomb: The 50-Megaton Test of October 1961," *Cold War International History Project Bulletin*, issue 4 (Fall 1994): pp. 3 and 19–21; Steven J. Zaloga, *Target America: The Soviet Union and the Strategic Arms Race 1945–1964* (Novato, Calif.: Presidio Press, 1993); Thomas Reed and Arnold Kramish, "Trinity at Dubna," *Physics Today*, November 1996, pp. 30–35.

18. David Holloway, *Stalin and the Bomb: The Soviet Union and Atomic Energy, 1939–1956* (New Haven: Yale University Press, 1994), pp. 336–37.

19. Nikolai Leonov, chief of the KGB's Department of Cuban Affairs for thirty years, took part in a conference in Havana in October 2002, on the fortieth anniversary of the missile crisis. This quotation comes from a transcript of that conference, published in *Arms Control Today*, November 2002.

20. I reported these interviews in three pieces in *Time*: "A Call for 'Hardheaded Détente': Nixon urges Reagan to meet Andropov at the summit" (December 27, 1982, p. 18); "An Interview with Richard Nixon: The zero option, he says, can be a step toward a 'comprehensive compromise' " (May 4, 1987, p. 23, written with John F. Stacks); "Paying the Price: Richard Nixon believes he will always be known as the 'Watergate man,' the President who resigned the office, and expects little charity from history" (April 2, 1990, p. 46, also written with Stacks).

21. Truman in the joint statement he made with the British and Canadian prime ministers on November 15, 1945.

22. Kennedy's first prediction was during a presidential debate, October 13, 1960; the second, during a press conference on March 21, 1963, *Public Papers of the President of the United States: John F. Kennedy, 1963* (Washington, D.C.: Government Printing Office, 1964), p. 280.

23. Urquhart, "Looking for the Sheriff."

24. Article 100 of the Charter states: "In the performance of their duties the Secretary-General and the staff shall not seek or receive instructions from any government or from any other authority external to the Organization. They shall refrain from any action which might reflect on their position as international officials responsible only to the Organization."

25. Shirley Hazzard, *Defeat of an Ideal* (New York: Little, Brown, 1973), pp. i, xiv, 247, and 249.

26. For more on the international financial system, see Ralph C. Bryant, *Turbulent Waters: Cross-Border Finance and International Governance* (Washington, D.C.: Brookings Institution Press, 2003).

27. See Michael Oldstone, *Viruses, Plagues, and History* (New York: Oxford University Press, 1998), p. 27; Richard Preston, "Demon in the Freezer," *New Yorker*, July 12, 1999, pp. 44–61. I am indebted to Ernest May and Erez Manela of Harvard for assistance on this subject.

28. See David Koplow, *Smallpox: The Fight to Eradicate a Global Scourge* (Berkeley: University of California Press, 2003); F. Fenner et al., *Smallpox and Its Eradication* (Geneva: World Health Organization, 1988).

29. See Kennedy, *The Parliament of Man*, pp. 206–8, 238, and 285–88.

30. Urquhart, *A Life in Peace and War*, cited in Traub, *The Best Intentions*, p. 12.

31. United Nations Security Council Official Records, Eleventh Year, 751st Meeting, October 31, 1956, pp. 1–2.

32. E. B. White, in his *New Yorker* piece of December 15, 1956, cites an article in the *New York Times Magazine*, in which Lodge wrote: "As for the future, a world government which free men would accept is as far off as a worldwide common sense of justice—without which world government would be world tyranny."

33. As Bunche wrote in his journal, "[T]here has been this incredible lack of preparation; in a population of over 14 million people, there were, on independence day last June 30, only 17 men who had university education. There was not a doctor, or a dentist, or a lawyer, or a professional man of any kind. There was not a church; there was not anyone who could qualify to be a professor. No engineers in the entire population on the Congolese side. There was a complete lack of political and administrative experience amongst the Congolese. They had not been permitted to develop any." The Bunche journal entry can be seen in the 2001 PBS film, *Ralph Bunche: An American Odyssey*, based on Urquhart's biography of the same name. See also the film's accompanying Web site: http://www.pbs.org/ralphbunche/decol_congo .html.

34. The scholar who referred to "instant decolonization" was René Lemarchand; see *Encyclopædia Britannica Online*, s.v. "Congo," http://eb.com (2006).

35. See James Dobbins et al., *The UN's Role in Nation-Building: From the Congo to Iraq* (Santa Monica, Calif.: Rand, 2005).

CHAPTER 11: AN END AND A BEGINNING

1. Ortega y Gasset cited in Robert Bideleux, *European Integration and Disintegration: East and West* (New York: Routledge, 1996), p. 146.

2. Jean Monnet, *Mémoires* (Paris: Fayard, 1976).

3. See Pascaline Winand, *Eisenhower, Kennedy, and the United States of Europe* (New York: St. Martin's, 1993): "A united Europe came to be seen by top-echelon members of the American administration as a key element in the American blueprint for a peace settlement that would result in economic prosperity, political stability, and the dedication of western nations to common values and principles, such as democracy and the expansion of international trade" (p. x).

4. Baratta, *The Politics of World Federation*, pp. 73–93.

5. Churchill spoke at the University of Zurich on September 19, 1946, in Albert Hall in May 1947, and in Parliament in 1950. See also Vernon Bogdanor, "Great Britain, and other stories: A continuation of Churchill's master-work seems more about flag-waving than facts," *Financial Times Weekend Magazine*, October 28, 2006, p. 26.

6. Winand, *Eisenhower, Kennedy, and the United States of Europe*, p. 16.

7. Nicolson's quotation appears in Chris Patten, *Cousins and Strangers: America, Britain, and Europe in a New Century* (New York: Times Books, 2005), p. 5.

8. Cited in John Lewis Gaddis, *The United States and the End of the Cold War* (New York: Oxford University Press, 1992), p. 28.

9. George F. Kennan, "America and the Russian Future," *Foreign Affairs* 29, no. 4 (April 1951): 351–70.

10. I wrote some notes based on my trip to Uzhgorod, but the article never ran in *Time*. A year later, the movie *Waterloo*, which at an estimated cost of $100 million was then one of the most expensive films ever made, opened to mixed reviews (some admired the film's historical accuracy, while others, such as the *New York Times*' Roger Greenspun, criticized the "dullness of Bondarchuk's attempt to translate history into cinema [which] makes 'Waterloo' a very bad movie") and was a flop at the box office.

11. Years later, while writing this book, I asked Eliot Cohen, of the Johns Hopkins School of Advanced International Studies, about the theory that Napoleon's hemorrhoids changed the course of history. He dismissed it: in his view, Napoleon at Waterloo was already a spent force, not just physically but politically. Therefore, no matter how his showdown with Wellington

ended, Napoleon probably would have seen his ambitions crumble soon. As for Steiger's joke about Slavs speaking French, the Grande Armée already had tried conquering Russia, and, from a purely military standpoint, that had been an even bigger debacle than Waterloo.

12. The piece I wrote ("The Specter and the Struggle: Marx's theory, in Soviet practice, is both dangerous and in danger") ran in *Time* on January 4, 1982.

13. By the beginning of the 1980s, GNP growth had fallen from 5.2 to 2.2 percent, industrial growth from 6.3 to 2.6 percent, agricultural growth from 3.7 to 0.8 percent, and investment from 6 to 4.3 percent. As Leon Aron has noted, "In 1990, Gorbachev disclosed that, alongside oil exports, the vodka trade sustained the Soviet Union between 1970 and 1985." By the end of the Brezhnev era, while the Soviet Union certainly was not on the verge of complete economic collapse, it was nonetheless deeply stagnant. See Aron, "The 'Mystery' of the Soviet Collapse," *Journal of Democracy* (April 2006); Anders Aslund, *How Russia Became a Market Economy* (Washington, D.C.: Brookings Institution Press, 1995).

14. Brzezinski's speech was delivered on October 25, 1977, at the Eighth Meeting of the Trilateral Commission in Bonn, West Germany.

15. See Robert Gates: "[T]he most important continuity of all was between Carter and Reagan as, from 1977 on, the United States steadily increased the pressure on a weakening Soviet Union. . . . Reagan's strategic programs, covert confrontation with the Soviets in the Third World, economic pressures, eventual engagement on arms control, and attacks on the legitimacy of the Soviet government itself built on Carter's efforts in each arena—even though partisans of both Presidents would rather have their tongues turn black and fall out than admit to this." Robert M. Gates, *From the Shadows: The Ultimate Insider's Story of Five Presidents and How They Won the Cold War* (New York: Simon & Schuster, 1996), pp. 557–58.

16. George Orwell, *1984: A Novel* (Boston: G. K. Hall, 2001).

17. A number of these interviews, conducted with colleagues from the magazine, appeared in *Time*, including one that accompanied a special issue on January 1, 1990, designating Gorbachev "The Man of the Decade." I also interviewed the Soviet leader with Michael Beschloss for the book we wrote on the policy of the George H. W. Bush administration toward the Soviet Union, *At the Highest Levels: The Inside Story of the End of the Cold War* (New York: Little, Brown, 1993).

18. As Richard Reeves, a chronicler of the Reagan presidency, has noted, "Ironically, the scientist who had the most influence in the Soviet debate was Andrei Sakharov, the man called the father of the Soviet H-bomb, who had become the country's most famous dissident. Sakharov, winner of the Nobel Peace Prize in 1975, had been exiled to the city of Gorky in 1980 for publicly criticizing the Soviet invasion of Afghanistan. Allowed to return to teaching and research in Moscow on Gorbachev's personal orders, he persuaded other scientists and the General Secretary himself that SDI was more dream than threat. It almost certainly would not work, he told Gorbachev, and if it actually did, it could be easily breached for 10 percent of what it would cost the Americans to develop it, much less deploy it. . . . [A]n SDI system . . . could be easily and relatively cheaply defeated by building faster rockets and releasing warheads earlier. . . . [On the eve of the December 1987 Washington Summit] deputy foreign minister Alexander Bessmertnykh privately told his American counterparts. . . . 'It looked frightening initially, but it wouldn't work. It could . . . never [produce] a system covering the whole nation. . . . Gorbachev is not nervous about it now.' " Reeves, *President Reagan: The Triumph of Imagination* (New York: Simon & Schuster, 2005), pp. 440–41. Sakharov summarizes his views on missile defense in his *Memoirs* (New York: Knopf, 1990) as follows: "[Starting in 1965–67,] we tackled an investigation of antiballistic missile (ABM) systems and ways to counter them. In the course of many heated discussions, I, along with the majority of my colleagues, reached two conclusions which, in my view, remain valid today: 1) An effective ABM defense is not possible if the potential adversary can mobilize comparable technical and economic resources for military purposes. A way can always be found to neutralize an ABM de-

fense system—and at considerably less expense than the cost of deploying it. 2) Over and above the burdensome cost, deployment of an ABM system is dangerous since it can upset the strategic balance. If both sides were to possess powerful ABM defenses, the main result would be to raise the threshold of strategic stability, or in somewhat simplified terms, increase the minimum number of nuclear weapons needed for mutual assured destruction" (pp. 267–68).

19. For a balanced, authoritative treatment of this whole subject, see Jack F. Matlock, Jr., *Reagan and Gorbachev: How the Cold War Ended* (New York: Random House, 2004).

CHAPTER 12: THE NEW WORLD ORDER

1. Otmar Issing, interviewed by Ralph Atkins in *Financial Times*, October 28–29, 2006, p. W3.

2. Philip Gourevitch, "The Optimist," *New Yorker*, March 3, 2003, p. 72.

3. For the etymology of the word and the history of the phenomenon, see Nayan Chanda, *Bound Together: How Traders, Preachers, Adventurers, and Warriors Shaped Globalization* (New Haven: Yale University Press, 2007), esp. pp. 245–54. On *globalism* versus *globalization*, see Robert O. Keohane and Joseph S. Nye, *Power and Interdependence*, 3rd ed. (New York: Addison-Wesley, 2000), chapter 10.

4. Ronald Reagan, "The Work of Freedom . . . an Unending Challenge," *Washington Times*, December 14, 1992, based on an address he gave before the Oxford Union Society on December 4.

5. When writing this passage of the book, I checked with Sidney Drell by e-mail to make sure I was on solid ground here. Here is his reply: "When you think of magnets, which is what one usually thinks about when talking about poles, such as the earth's North Pole and South Pole, there are, as far as we know, no isolated, single poles. For every north pole there is a companion south pole with which it is paired. If you split a magnet in half, you don't end up with two separated north and south unipoles, but with two smaller magnets, each with both a north and a south pole. There are some speculative theories about the origin of the universe that insist that magnetic monopoles, or unipoles, were created at the time of the Big Bang some 13.5 billion years ago. However it is speculated that they have since decayed away to the point that none are left—or at best they are so rare now that none have been observed, although experiments have tried hard to find them. So you can rightly say that for magnetic poles, which is the context for most uses of the word 'pole' in physics, we know of no isolated 'poles,' or unipoles. Every pole is paired with its opposite unless it happens to be an ancient relic of the Big Bang at the moment of creation of our physical universe. Evidently a unipolar theory is only half the story, and is incomplete, or else it is a 'neandratholic' relic."

6. G. John Ikenberry, *After Victory: Institutions, Strategic Restraint, and the Rebuilding of Order after Major Wars* (Princeton: Princeton University Press, 2001), pp. 270–74, and amplified in a January 2007 e-mail exchange with the author.

7. George Bush and Brent Scowcroft, *A World Transformed* (New York: Knopf, 1998), p. 60.

8. Michael Beschloss and I chose the Bushism "I don't want to make the wrong mistakes" as the title for chapter 9 of our *At the Highest Levels*. Ryan J. Barilleaux and Mary E. Stuckey titled their 1992 book on Bush, *Leadership and the Bush Presidency: Prudence or Drift in an Era of Change* (New York: Praeger). In Bush's State of the Union message of February 9, 1989, he said, "And it's a time of great change in the world, and especially in the Soviet Union. Prudence and common sense dictate that we try to understand the full meaning of the change going on there, review our policies, and then proceed with caution."

9. Scowcroft and Bush, *A World Transformed*, p. 62. I took much the same tone of willing suspension of disapproval in a column that appeared in *Time*, under the headline "Operation Mismatch," on January 22, 1990.

10. Scowcroft and Bush, *A World Transformed*, pp. 60–61.

11. Ibid., p. 300.

12. Rice tells much of the story herself, with her own co-author and colleague, Philip Zelikow, in *Germany Unified and Europe Transformed: A Study in Statecraft* (Cambridge, Mass.: Harvard University Press, 1995).

13. On Saddam's pretensions, see, for example, the 2004 report by Charles A. Duelfer on Iraqi weapons of mass destruction, which in its introduction noted, "Saddam sees himself as the most recent of the great Iraqi leaders like Hammurabi, Nebuchadnezzar, and Saladin. In Babylon, where Iraq was reconstructing the historical city, the bricks were molded with the phrase, 'Made in the era of Saddam Hussein'—mimicking the ancient bricks forged in ancient Babylon and demonstrating his assumption that he will be similarly remembered over the millennia." Charles A. Duelfer, "Comprehensive Report of the Special Advisor to the DCI on Iraq's WMD," Central Intelligence Agency, September 30, 2004. Saddam also named his most elite military units after these men whose successor he claimed to be. The Hammurabi Republican Guard division was the first unit to move to Iraq's southern border in preparation for Saddam's August 1990 invasion of Kuwait. Saddam also noted that he especially esteemed Nebuchadnezzar and Saladin because they had captured Jerusalem.

14. On December 7, 1988, Bush, as vice president and president-elect, was in the audience when Gorbachev, then at the height of his international celebrity, said to the UN, "World progress is only possible through a search for universal human consensus as we move forward to a new world order." Three years later, on October 30, 1991, standing next to Bush in Madrid at the opening round of negotiations on peace in Middle East jointly sponsored by the United States and the U.S.S.R., Gorbachev said, "We see both in our country and elsewhere . . . ghosts of the old thinking. . . . When we rid ourselves of their presence, we will be better able to move toward a new world order . . . relying on the relevant mechanisms of the United Nations." Bush picked up on most of the phrase in May 1989, four months into his administration, when he told the graduating class at Texas A&M University that the United States was ready to welcome the Soviet Union "back into the world order." When Gorbachev's foreign minister, Eduard Shevardnadze, made his own appearance at the UN on September 25, 1990, he aligned his government with the United States on Iraq by describing Saddam Hussein's invasion of Kuwait as "an act of terrorism [that] has been perpetrated against the emerging new world order."

15. Scowcroft and Bush, *A World Transformed*, pp. 354–55.

16. *A World Transformed* is written in three voices: two solos, Bush's and Scowcroft's; and a duet, with the two writing together in the first-person plural; pp. 489–92.

17. The origin of that phrase, which stuck indelibly, was Robert Ajemian's *Time* profile on Bush during the 1988 presidential campaign: "Recently [George H. W. Bush] asked a friend to help him identify some cutting issues for next year's campaign. Instead, the friend suggested that Bush go alone to Camp David for a few days to figure out where he wanted to take the country. 'Oh,' said Bush in clear exasperation, 'the vision thing.' The friend's advice did not impress him."

18. Funderburk made the comment on October 29, 1991, during a speech in North Carolina.

19. I was part of a delegation that included Pamela Harriman, Robert Legvold of Columbia, and Ed Hewett of Brookings. The column on Gamsakhurdia was titled "Growls in the Garden" and appeared in the June 10, 1991, issue of *Time*.

20. I wrote a column along these lines under the headline, "The General Secretary in His Labyrinth," which appeared in *Time* on December 10, 1990.

21. Bush and Scowcroft, *A World Transformed*, pp. 564–65.

22. The key passage from the London G-7 Political Declaration: "Our support for the process of fundamental reform in the Soviet Union remains as strong as ever. We believe that

new thinking in Soviet foreign policy, which has done so much to reduce East/West tension and strengthen the multilateral peace and security system, should be applied on a global basis. We hope that this new spirit of international cooperation will be as fully reflected in Asia as in Europe. We welcome efforts to create a new union, based on consent not coercion, which genuinely responds to the wishes of the peoples of the Soviet Union. The scale of this undertaking is enormous: an open and democratic Soviet Union able to play its full part in building stability and trust in the world. We reiterate our commitment to working with the Soviet Union to support their efforts to create an open society, a pluralistic democracy and a market economy. We hope the negotiations between the USSR and the elected governments of the Baltic countries will resolve their future democratically and in accordance with the legitimate aspirations of the people."

23. See J. F. O. McAllister, "Atrocity and Outrage," *Time*, August 17, 1992, p. 20. See also James Baker, with Thomas DeFrank, *The Politics of Diplomacy* (New York: Putnam, 1995), p. 637.

CHAPTER 13: SEIZING THE DAY

1. Clinton, in a weekly presidential radio address, June 30, 1997.

2. Clinton made this comment in a phone call to me just before he joined former president George H. W. Bush for the flight to Moscow, where the two of them would represent the United States at Yeltsin's funeral.

3. The main passage in my memo to Clinton: "Your foreign policy should be multilateral. That may sound banal and obvious. But it's not. Maintaining and enhancing America's position as the senior partner if not the CEO of the G-7, UN, NATO, CSCE and other bodies is going to require powerful use of the bully pulpit and occasionally of Air Force One. Those four bodies don't have much of a constituency in the U.S.: the G-7 looks to many people like little more than a fancy men's club (now that Maggie's gone [Margaret Thatcher had been forced out of the leadership of the Conservative Party in November 1990; John Major had taken her place as prime minister]) which meets once a year and issues platitudes; the UN isn't wildly popular; NATO doesn't seem wildly relevant any more; and CSCE is a set of initials not many Americans recognize, much less understand, even less support. Moreover, there's a more general problem: multilateralism is still a suspect concept in the U.S. It smacks of goo-goo one-worldism, naïveté, even dubious patriotism. Americans are all for having the Japanese and West Europeans pony up to help pay for the Gulf War, but they are mighty chary about any arrangement that smacks of pooled national sovereignty or authority. The way to counter this resistance, of course, is to sell multilateralism as not just an economic imperative but as a means of preserving and enhancing American political leadership in the world, since the various multilateral outfits will be effective only if the U.S. does lead them. Quite simply, with the old order in shambles and with only one surviving superpower, the world isn't going to leave you alone to devote all your energies to the home front."

4. From my interview with Clinton in his office in Harlem on May 3, 2006. Others present were Sandy Berger, Eric Nonacs of Clinton's staff, and my research assistant, Andreas Xenachis.

5. *Los Angeles Times*, "The Times Poll; Americans Ambivalent on GOP's 'Contract,'" January 24, 1995, p. A1; R. W. Apple, Jr., "Mexican Rescue Plan: Risky Course for Clinton," *New York Times*, February 1, 1995, p. A1. See also Bill Clinton, *My Life* (New York: Knopf, 2004), pp. 641–45.

6. See "Document of the Moscow Meeting of the Conference on the Human Dimension of the CSCE," released in Moscow, October 3, 1991; and Paragraphs 8 and 12 of the "Concluding Document of 'Helsinki—The Challenge of Change,' the Fourth Follow-Up Meeting," Helsinki, July 10, 1992, which noted: "We emphasize that the commitments undertaken in the

field of the human dimension of the CSCE are matters of direct and legitimate concern to all participating states and do not belong exclusively to the internal affairs of the state concerned. The protection and promotion of human rights and fundamental freedoms and the strengthening of democratic institutions continue to be a vital basis for our comprehensive security. . . . Gross violations of CSCE commitments in the field of human rights and fundamental freedoms, including those related to national minorities, pose a special threat to the peaceful development of society, in particular in new democracies." These and other CSCE/OSCE documents are available at the Department of State's International Information Programs Web site: http://usinfo.state.gov/products/pubs/archive/humrts/osce.htm.

7. Since 1989, Australia had been pushing for APEC as a mechanism to increase regional free trade and economic cooperation on the EU and NAFTA models. As chairman of the first APEC foreign ministers' meeting, Evans talked up the need for a security organization as well. In "What Asia Needs Is a Europe-Style CSCA," his July 27, 1990, op-ed article in the *International Herald Tribune*, Evans wrote: "We should now be looking ahead to the kind of wholly new institutional processes that might be capable of evolving, in Asia just as in Europe, as a framework for addressing and resolving security problems. In Europe, wildly implausible as this would have occurred even just a year ago, the central institutional framework for pursuing common security has become a Conference on Security and Cooperation in Europe." He picked up this theme in a speech before the Trilateral Commission in Tokyo the following April, in 1991: "The central idea of 'common security' is that lasting security does not lie in an upwards spiral of arms development, fuelled by mutual suspicion, but in a commitment to joint survival, to taking into account the legitimate security anxieties of others, to building step-by-step military confidence between nations, and to working to maximize the degree of interdependence between nations—in other words, to achieving security with others, not against them." He also noted that these new structures must supplement, not replace, the old alliance structures in the region: "Traditional alliance relationships serve as a fail-safe support system in the event that security fails."

8. Clinton delivered these speeches at Waseda University in Japan and in the South Korean parliament. He laid out the economic and security logic for a "new Pacific Community built on shared strength, shared prosperity, and a shared commitment to democratic values." Clinton noted that America would not pull back from Asia, as some had suggested at the end of the Cold War, but rather work to reenergize its regional alliances and preserve our deterrent by maintaining military troops in the region. He signaled strong support for lowering trade barriers and praised APEC as a mechanism of regional economic cooperation. Clinton noted the importance of creating interconnected institutions to deal with problems in the region: "Since the Asian Pacific nations don't face a unitary threat, there is no need for us to create one single alliance. The challenge for the Asian Pacific . . . instead, is to develop multiple new arrangements to meet multiple threats and opportunities. These arrangements can function like overlapping plates of armor, individually providing protection and together covering the full body of our common security concerns."

9. For more on Kennan's opposition to NATO expansion and Clinton's and my reaction to it, see *The Russia Hand*, pp. 220, 231–32.

10. I recounted this experience in *The Russia Hand*, p. 250.

11. Richard Holbrooke, who was then ambassador in Bonn, later wrote of the episode in his book, *To End a War* (New York: Random House, 1998): "The Administration began to reel, destabilized by this rebuff and troubled by the deteriorating situation on the ground. As the chances of American involvement visibly declined, the Serbs became bolder. Croat attacks on Muslims also increased. . . . Meanwhile, the press was flaying the Administration for its weakness" (pp. 54–55). Ivo Daalder, a colleague of mine at Brookings, put it as follows in his own book on Bosnia, *Getting to Dayton: The Making of America's Bosnia Policy* (Washington:

Brookings Institution Press, 2000). "Christopher's presentation was hardly convincing. . . . Christopher's self-described 'conciliatory approach'—consisting of talking points that, at least in Whitehall, started with the phrase, 'I am here in listening mode'—differed so completely from the prevailing norm that the allies could not believe that the administration was serious. Indeed, London and Paris were as distraught over the fact that the Clinton administration was not really willing to take the promised lead of the West's Bosnia policy as they were over Washington's decision to propose a course of action that they had explicitly and repeatedly rejected (pp. 15–16).

12. Traub, *The Best Intentions*, p. 36.

13. Interviews with Scowcroft and Berger, August 7, 2006.

14. Gourevitch, "The Optimist," p. 65.

15. Clinton made this remark on October 6, 1993, three days after the killing of the U.S. soldiers in Mogadishu.

16. For a thorough and searing treatment of the Rwanda outrage, see Samantha Power's *A Problem from Hell*.

17. This recollection of Annan's early career come from Georges Abi-Saaba, an Egyptian who studied with Annan in Geneva, who is quoted by Gourevitch in "The Optimist," p. 62.

18. Traub, *The Best Intentions*, p. 53. For another informed account, very tough on Annan, the UN, and the Clinton administration, see Philip Gourevitch, "The Genocide Fax," *New Yorker*, May 11, 1998, pp. 42–46.

19. Power, in *A Problem from Hell*, pp. 329–89, reaches the following verdict—and, by implication, offers this answer to the questions Clinton posed: "The Clinton Administration did not actively consider U.S. military intervention, it blocked the deployment of UN peacekeepers, and it refrained from undertaking softer forms of intervention. . . . [American officials] believed that the UN and humanitarianism could not afford another Somalia. Many internalized the belief that the UN had more to lose by sending reinforcements and failing than by allowing the killings to proceed. Their chief priority, after the evacuation of the Americans, was looking after the UN peacekeepers, and they justified the withdrawal of the peacekeepers on the grounds that it would ensure a future for humanitarian intervention."

CHAPTER 14: HARD POWER

1. Andrew Marvell, *The Loyal Scott* (1650–52).

2. Clinton, in a televised address to the nation from the Oval Office on March 24, 1999, announcing the beginning of NATO air strikes against Serbia.

3. The operative language in Resolution 940: "The situation in Haiti continues to constitute a threat to peace and security in the region." See Madeleine Albright, *Madam Secretary* (New York: Miramax, 2003), pp. 195–203. As she recounts the episode, "The Russians didn't much care about what we did in Haiti, but they were determined to play a little diplomatic poker. Moscow's ambassador, Yuli Vorontsov, presented me with a series of questions about our mission, hinting that Russia's backing on Haiti would depend on U.S. support for Russian proposals in Georgia. . . . Russia had sent peacekeepers to Georgia and now wanted the council to designate them as an official UN force, thus relieving Moscow of 90 percent of the costs."

4. Fareed Zakaria, *The Future of Freedom: Illiberal Democracy at Home and Abroad* (New York: Norton, 2003).

5. During the cold war, the term *nation-building* was primarily used by the leaders in the developing world to describe their task of building independent nations out of those emerging from colonialism. Not until the mid-1990s did the term come to be used, sometimes disparagingly, to describe the idea of outsiders such as the United States trying to stabilize and rebuild a foreign nation. James Dobbins, an expert on the subject at the RAND Corporation, and who, as a Foreign Service officer, worked on Haiti, the Balkans, and Afghanistan, defines

nation-building as "the use of armed force in the aftermath of a conflict to underpin an enduring transition to democracy," but notes that others call the same activity "occupation," "stabilization," "peacekeeping," "reconstruction," and "peace enforcement." See his *America's Role in
Nation-Building: From Germany to Iraq* (Santa Monica, Calif.: RAND, 2003).

6. Nye first put forward the concept of soft power in book form in *Bound to Lead: The
Changing Nature of American Power* (New York: Basic Books, 1990), pp. 31–32. Nye served in
the Clinton administration during its first term as chairman of the National Intelligence
Council and as an assistant secretary of defense, working largely on U.S.-Japan relations.

7. See, for example, Wesley Clark, *Waging Modern War* (New York: Public Affairs, 2001),
p. 457: "Events proceed from diplomacy backed by discussions of threat, to diplomacy backed
by threat, to diplomacy backed by force, and finally to force backed by diplomacy." Clinton
used the phrase on numerous occasions, particularly in 1999, during the Kosovo crisis. So did
Richard Holbrooke in speeches, press conferences, and his book, *To End a War;* and Thomas R.
Pickering, undersecretary of state for political affairs, gave it prominence in his speeches (e.g.,
in an address at Supreme Allied Commander Atlantic, "The Transatlantic Partnership: A History of Defending Freedom; A Future for Extending It," Old Dominion University Sympo-
sium, Norfolk, Va. October 30, 1998).

8. Article II, Part 7 of the Charter.

9. Edward Mortimer, Annan's director of communications, recalled this remark in an
e-mail exchange I had with him in August 2006.

10. Annan made this second statement to the UN Human Rights Commission on April 8,
1999.

11. For a detailed reconstruction of this episode, see Traub, *The Best Intentions*, pp. 92–102.

12. I elaborated on this view of the virtues of the "Euromess" in "From Prague to Baghdad:
NATO at Risk," *Foreign Affairs* 81, no. 6 (November/December 2002). A version of the Euromess chart was used to illustrate that piece.

13. Kennedy, *Parliament of Man*, p. 108. See a book on the Kosovo war by two Brookings
colleagues, Michael O'Hanlon and Ivo Daalder, *Winning Ugly: NATO's War to Save Kosovo*
(Washington: Brookings Institution Press, 2000): "[E]ven though NATO eventually used force
without explicit UN backing, the allies returned to the UN system as part of the diplomatic effort to end the war. A UN administration was given political control of Kosovo and was
charged with managing and coordinating the mammoth task of building a stable, peaceful,
and, one hopes, a democratic Kosovo. The UN's administration of Kosovo is open-ended, thus
granting the Security Council the decisive role in determining the territory's political future.
On the whole, NATO's intervention in Kosovo did not weaken the UN's role in such situations; indeed, in some ways it strengthened that role" (pp. 218–19).

CHAPTER 15: A THEORY OF THE CASE

1. *The Histories of Herodotus,* book 7, chapter 10.

2. Attributed to King Alfonso X of Leon and Castile upon learning of Ptolemy's descrip-
tion of the solar system in the middle of the thirteenth century. See Owen Gingerich, *The
Great Copernicus Chase and Other Adventures in Astronomical History* (New York: Cambridge
University Press, 1992), pp. 57–62.

3. Acheson, *Present at the Creation*. Acheson used as an epigraph and inspiration for
the title of that book the same quotation of King Alfonso's that I have used as an epigraph for
this chapter.

As Christopher explained in an e-mail responding to my inquiry about his choice of the
Acheson portrait: "The book *The Wise Men* [by Walter Isaacson and Evan Thomas] had a
major influence on me, years before I had any idea that I might be Secretary of State. I read his
speeches, saw Acheson as a principal architect of the post war security structure, and admired
him for his ability to conceive and design, as well as execute. I felt that with the collapse of the

Soviet Union, we were at another watershed. In our years, we improved some of the structures in Europe and in the economic sphere, and we helped invent some new structures in Asia."

4. The phrase was in the air at the time. See, for example, a Policy Analysis paper produced by the Cato Institute on March 31, 1993, "Present at the Re-Creation: The Need for a Rebirth of American Foreign Policy," by Jonathan Clarke, a retired British Foreign Service officer.

5. John Harris, the author of an astute study of the Clinton presidency, makes a similar point: "Lyricism was simply not [Clinton's] natural voice. He soared when he threw away the text and spoke improvisationally, as at a late-night rally or from a pulpit." Harris, *The Survivor* (New York: Random House, 2005), pp. 10–11.

6. Doris Kearns Goodwin, *No Ordinary Time* (New York: Simon & Schuster, 1994), and David McCullough, *Truman* (New York: Simon & Schuster 1992).

7. Among the passages in which Boorstin and the presidential speechwriters tried to capture what had come out of the brainstorming session in the Cabinet Room: "It falls to us to avoid the complacency that followed World War I without the spur of the imminent threat to our security that followed World War II. . . . The dangers we face are less stark and more diffuse than those of the cold war, but they are still formidable: the ethnic conflicts that drive millions from their homes; the despots ready to repress their own people or conquer their neighbors; the proliferation of weapons of mass destruction; the terrorists wielding their deadly arms; the criminal syndicates selling those arms or drugs or infiltrating the very institutions of fragile democracy; a global economy that offers great promise but also deep insecurity and, in many places, declining opportunity; diseases like AIDS that threaten to decimate nations; the combined dangers of population explosion and economic decline . . . ; global and local environmental threats that demand that sustainable development becomes a part of the lives of people all around the world; and finally, within many of our nations, high rates of drug abuse and crime and family breakdown with all their terrible consequences. . . . The United States recognizes that we also have a special responsibility in these common endeavors that we are taking, the responsibility that goes along with great power and also with our long history of democracy and freedom. But we seek to fulfill that responsibility in cooperation with other nations. Working together increases the impact and the legitimacy of each of our actions, and sharing the burdens lessens everyone's load. We have no desire to be the world's policemen, but we will do what we can to help civil societies emerge from the ashes of repression, to sustain fragile democracies and to add more free markets to the world and, of course, to restrain the destructive forces that threaten us all. . . . It is time that we think anew about the structure of this global economy as well, tearing down walls that separate nations instead of hiding behind them . . . Here, at the United Nations, we must develop a concrete plan to meet the challenges of the next 50 years, even as we celebrate the last 50 years. . . . And let us not lose sight of the special role that development and democracy can play in preventing conflicts once peace has been established. . . . History has given us a very rare opportunity, the chance to build on the greatest legacy of this century without reliving its darkest moments."

8. From Nayan Chanda's interview with Clinton, October 31, 2003, for *YaleGlobal Online*. That day at Yale, Clinton gave a speech on global challenges that was among the most powerful he has ever made. It is available at http://yaleglobal.yale.edu/display.article?id=2840. See also Clinton's remarks before the Third International Early Warning Conference, Bonn, Germany, March 27, 2006; and before the Dutch Postcode Lottery, Amsterdam, December 6, 2006.

9. My interview with Clinton, May 3, 2006.

10. See Wright's *Nonzero: The Logic of Human Destiny* (New York: Vintage, 2001), pp. 5–6. Wright uses as an epigraph for *Nonzero* the Darwin quotation from *The Descent of Man*. Martin Wolf of the *Financial Times* makes similar use of the same Darwin passage in *Why Globalization Works* (New Haven: Yale University Press, 2004).

11. In the six months between reading *Nonzero*, in the summer of 2000 and leaving office

in January 2001, Clinton spoke about it at some length in at least twelve public appearances, from events connected with Hillary Clinton's campaign for the Senate to the annual White House Prayer Breakfast to speeches in front of the Democratic National Committee to an event on youth violence to remarks at a Princeton conference about the progressive tradition to an interview with *Wired* magazine. After leaving office, Clinton said at the Hay-on-Wye Literary Festival in May 2001, "Last year I read a book which influenced me greatly by a man named Robert Wright. It's called *Nonzero*, and, did you ever read a book where somebody says what you've been thinking, and you immediately decide the author is a genius? We've all done it. Because this person puts something, that you've been thinking and feeling but could never quite say in the way you wish you could have said it." At the anniversary of the Dayton Peace Accords, November 2001, on C-SPAN: "Last year I read a book that described the way the world works in ways better than I can, but I completely agree with it." At the Mayflower Hotel, Washington, D.C., September 2000: "There is an astonishing new book out, been out a few months, by a man named Robert Wright, called *Nonzero*—kind of a weird title unless you're familiar with game theory. But in game theory, a zero-sum game is one where, in order for one person to win, somebody has to lose. A non-zero-sum game is a game in which you can win and the person you're playing with can win, as well. And the argument of the book is that, notwithstanding all the terrible things that happened in the 20th century—the abuses of science by the Nazis, the abuses of organization by the communists, all the things that continue to be done in the name of religious or political purity—essentially, as societies grow more and more connected, and we become more interdependent, one with the other, we are forced to find more and more non-zero-sum solutions. That is, ways in which we can all win. And that's basically the message I've been trying to preach for eight years here . . . We have to have an expanding idea of who is in our family. And we in the United States, because we're so blessed, have particular responsibilities to people not only within our borders who have been left behind, but beyond our borders who otherwise will never catch up if we don't do our part. Because we are all part of the same human family, and because, actually, life is more and more a non-zero-sum game, so that the better they do, the better we'll do." In an interview with *Wired*, December 2000: "I basically buy the argument of Robert Wright's new book, *Nonzero*. . . . [It's] sort of a reverse social Darwinism: the more complex societies get and the more complex the networks of interdependence within and beyond community and national borders get, the more people are forced in their own interests to find non-zero-sum solutions. That is, win-win solutions instead of win-lose solutions." At the Hay-Adams Hotel, Washington, D.C., September 2000: "I think the idea that we are moving toward a world where more and more, we will find our own victories in other people's victories, because our interdependence forces us to seek non-zero-sum solutions—is a very helpful way to think about dealing with most social problems; and frankly, some economic challenges, like global debt relief and things like that."

12. Wright's article, in the January 16, 2001, *New York Times*, was titled "Clinton's One Big Idea" and included this judgment: "I think that future historians will have no trouble finding a unifying theme in the Clinton years, and that its importance will become only clearer as the decades pass. . . . I'm talking about the party's choice between economic nationalism and global economic engagement. Here Mr. Clinton has put Democrats on a course that will be hard to abandon and that could ultimately serve their constituents in ways many prominent Democrats still don't appreciate. . . . By ushering in the W.T.O., he has laid the rudiments of a system of global governance that, if wisely nurtured, will decades from now protect America's low-wage workers and its natural environment. Before the World Trade Organization, the regime that 'governed' global trade—the General Agreement on Tariffs and Trade—had no teeth. Today the W.T.O., by adjudicating trade disputes and authorizing sanctions against violators, arguably constitutes the most effective body of world governance in the history of the planet. . . . Free trade, left ungoverned, can yield the infamous 'race to the bottom,' dragging

down environmental standards and wages in affluent nations. The way to blunt this effect is to append labor and environmental standards to trade agreements. But unless those agreements have teeth in the first place—as in the judicial machinery of the W.T.O.—there is no point in appending anything to them."

13. Helms made his "nemesis" comment at a November 9, 1994, news conference in Raleigh, North Carolina, and Dole spoke at a presidential campaign rally in Manchester, New Hampshire, on February 21, 1996. See John M. Goshko and Daniel Williams, "U.S. Policy Faces Review by Helms," *Washington Post*, November 13, 1994, p. A1; and Martin Walker, "A New American Isolationism?" *International Journal* 52, no. 3 (Summer 1997): 391–410.

14. Michael Mandelbaum, "Foreign Policy as Social Work," *Foreign Affairs* (January/February 1996), pp. 16–32. In 1999 he followed up with "A Perfect Failure: NATO's War Against Yugoslavia," *Foreign Affairs* (September/October 1999), pp. 107–14.

15. For a balanced sample and analysis of the debate on the phrase, see "What is the International Community?" an assembly of essays by nine scholars and public personages, including Kofi Annan, in *Foreign Policy*, September/October 2002. Charles Krauthammer was especially scathing on this subject. See, for example, his column "What 'International Community'?" *Washington Post*, December 26, 1997, p. A29 (in which he disparaged "the theme running through five years of Clinton foreign policy: the attempt in almost every endeavor—Bosnia, Haiti, Somalia, the Persian Gulf, trade, treaties, conventions, wartime coalitions—to subsume America in some larger international construct"); and "A World Imagined," *New Republic*, March 15, 1999, pp. 22–26 (in which he writes, "the international community is a fiction," and criticizes liberal internationalism because it "seeks to establish an international order based not on power but on interdependence").

16. Condoleezza Rice, "Promoting the National Interest," *Foreign Affairs* (January/February 2000), pp. 45–62.

17. See Michael R. Gordon, "Bush Would Stop U.S. Peacekeeping in Balkan Fights," *New York Times*, October 21, 2000, p. A1, and Stern's letter to the editor, "Bush's Road Out of the Balkans," October 25, 2000.

18. These quotations are from an interview Bush gave Sam Donaldson of ABC News on January 23, 2000, and from the second presidential debate with Al Gore at Wake Forest University in Winston-Salem, North Carolina, on October 11, 2000.

19. Helms's speech elaborated on his argument that while national sovereignty was not, in theory, an absolute, it was so in the American case: "The sovereignty of nations must be respected. But nations derive their sovereignty—their legitimacy—from the consent of the governed. Thus, it follows, that nations can lose their legitimacy when they rule without the consent of the governed; they deservedly discard their sovereignty by brutally oppressing their people. Slobodan Milošević cannot claim sovereignty over Kosovo when he has murdered Kosovars and piled their bodies into mass graves. Neither can Fidel Castro claim that it is his sovereign right to oppress his people. Nor can Saddam Hussein defend his oppression of the Iraqi people by hiding behind phony claims of sovereignty. And when the oppressed peoples of the world cry out for help, the free peoples of the world have a fundamental right to respond." However, he disagreed that the UN was the way to legitimate such actions against tyrants who hid behind sovereignty: "It is a fanciful notion that free peoples need to seek the approval of an international body (some of whose members are totalitarian dictatorships) to lend support to nations struggling to break the chains of tyranny and claim their inalienable, God-given rights. The United Nations has no power to grant or decline legitimacy to such actions. They are inherently legitimate. What the United Nations can do is help. The Security Council can, where appropriate, be an instrument to facilitate action by 'coalitions of the willing,' implement sanctions regimes, and provide logistical support to states undertaking collective action. . . . [T]he American people will never accept the claims of the United Nations to

be the 'sole source of legitimacy on the use of force' in the world. . . . No UN institution—not the Security Council, not the Yugoslav tribunal, not a future ICC—is competent to judge the foreign policy and national security decisions of the United States."

20. R. W. Apple, "Defeat of a Treaty," *New York Times*, October 14, 1999, p. A1.

21. My interview with Clinton, May 3, 2006.

22. See especially Daniel Benjamin and Steven Simon, *The Age of Sacred Terror* (New York: Random House, 2002), pp. 16–18; and Steve Coll, *Ghost Wars: The Secret History of the CIA, Afghanistan, and Bin Laden, from the Soviet Invasion to September 10, 2001* (New York: Penguin, 2004), pp. 250–58.

23. One of Clinton's most persistent critics, Senator Dan Coats of Indiana, issued a statement saying, "There does appear to be credible evidence to suggest that targeting an Osama bin Laden terrorist training site was necessary." Coats canceled plans to appear on weekend talk shows to attack Clinton after being given a White House briefing on August 21, 1998.

24. Clinton did refer broadly to having thwarted the terror attacks. On May 17, 2000, in front of more than five thousand people at his commencement address to the U.S. Coast Guard Academy, New London, Connecticut, Clinton mentioned that during the millennium we had stopped major plots in Seattle and in Jordan that were linked to bin Laden, and announced new counterterrorism funding. The story was barely picked up by the press. As Benjamin and Simon note about the successful response to the Millennium Plots: "[T]he results were spectacular: it was the most successful operation against jihadists to date, with cells broken up in more than a dozen countries . . . [But] Ironically, the *foiling* of terrorist attacks did not help the administration persuade people outside the executive branch of the reality of the threat." Benjamin and Simon continue to show that the public and most elected representatives did not really feel the urgency even after the Administration laid out the threat: "Concerned that al-Qaeda was still laundering its money in places such as the Bahamas, Liechtenstein, and other well-known havens that offer no-questions banking, the administration introduced legislation in March 2000 that would have expanded its authority to ban U.S. residents and companies from doing business with banks in countries that refused to clean up their laws. The bill . . . was derailed in the Senate because of the opposition of Senate Banking Committee chairman Phil Gramm. The Texas Republican declared that he did not believe that 'bureaucrats should have the authority to close down banks.' . . . The world's greatest deliberative body was not seized by the issue of terrorism" (*The Age of Sacred Terror*, pp. 312–14).

25. Vieira de Mello wrote a thesis on Kant and Saint Augustine in the 1970s. It was titled *Civitas Maxima: origins, fondements et portee philosophique et pratique du concept de supranationalite*, and it argued that the "City of God" could be created on earth. In July 1991, he delivered a lecture at the Geneva International Peace Research Institute on "Philosophical History and Real History: The Relevance of Kant's Political Thought in Current Times." I am grateful to Samantha Power for this information, which I learned in reading the manuscript of her forthcoming *Chasing the Flame: Sergio Vieira de Mello and the Fight to Save the World* (New York: Penguin, 2008).

26. Vieira de Mello sparked in Kofi Annan an interest in Kant. For example, in the Cyril Foster Lecture that he delivered at Oxford on June 19, 2001, Annan cited *Perpetual Peace:* "Kant argued that 'republics'—by which he meant essentially what today we call liberal or pluralistic democracies—were less likely than other forms of State to go to war with one another. Broadly speaking, the history of the last 200 years has proved him right." Another influence on Annan in this regard was Michael Doyle, then an assistant secretary-general of the UN and special adviser to Annan and now a professor of political science at Columbia. Doyle has written about Kant's relevance to twentieth- and twenty-first-century international relations.

CHAPTER 16: GOING IT ALONE

1. Annan's comment to George W. Bush came after Bush had addressed the UN General Assembly on September 12, 2002; Traub, *The Best Intentions*, p. 175.

2. Bush quoted by Traub, *The Best Intentions*, p. 183.

3. Clinton interview, May 3, 2006, supplemented by follow-up discussion with him on December 23, 2006, as well as interviews with members of his staff to whom he reported on the conversation with Bush within hours after it occurred. Clinton also recounts a short version of this episode in his memoir, *My Life* (New York: Knopf, 2004), p. 935.

4. Peter Schwartz and Doug Randall, "Imagining the Unthinkable: An Abrupt Climate Change Scenario and Its Implications for United States National Security," October 2003, available at http://www.grist.org/pdf/AbruptClimateChange2003.pdf. See also Bill McKibben, "Crossing the Red Line," *New York Review of Books*, June 10, 2004.

5. Rice told the press during a briefing in Warsaw on June 15, 2001, "If you take all of this together, what you're talking about is a new security framework that recognizes how much the world has changed; that recognizes that starting in Spain, says something about the new Europe; that having your first state visit in Poland says something about the new Europe; that going to Ljubljana with the President of Russia says something about the new Europe. This is not the average, normal American President's first tour to Europe. There are messages in the locations that he's chosen, there are messages in the way that he's talking about this Europe. And I think he's moved the ball very far forward in a very short period of time."

6. The phrase was coined by one of the administration's prominent moderates, Richard Haass, the director of the State Department's policy planning staff. In 2002, Haass, who had worked for Bush 41 on the Middle East and had been director of foreign policy studies at the Brookings Institution in the nineties, explained the concept of "Imperial America," then fashionable within the administration and among its advocates on the right, as requiring caution: "Great as our advantages are, there are limits. We have to have allies. We can't impose our ideas on everyone. We don't want to be fighting wars alone, so we need others to join us. American leadership, yes; but not American unilateralism. It has to be multilateral. We can't win the war against terror alone. We can't send forces everywhere. It really does have to be a collaborative endeavor. Is there a successor to the idea of containment? I think there is. It is the idea of integration. . . . Integration is about locking [other countries] into these policies and then building institutions to lock them in even more." See Nicholas Lemann, "The Next World Order," *New Yorker*, April 1, 2002, p. 46. Haass left the administration after two and a half years to become president of the Council on Foreign Relations.

7. See, for example, the *New York Times* report from Oslo the day after the Nobel Peace Prize award ceremony: "Adolfo Perez Esquivel, an Argentinian campaigner for human rights who won the 1980 peace prize, attacked the United States because, he said, it failed to grasp the nuances of the present conflict. 'That kind of black-and-white thinking, where good is set against evil, reminds me of cowboy films,' he said." See Sarah Lyall, "In Nobel Talk, Annan Sees Each Human Life as the Prize," *New York Times*, December 11, 2001, p. 3. In the *Washington Post*, columnist Jim Hoagland called Annan's speech in Oslo "subtly subversive" in challenging the notion of absolute sovereignty. See his "Kofi Annan's Challenge," December 13, 2001, p. A37. Meanwhile, conservative stalwarts attacked Annan for operating on principles different from Bush. In a column titled "Black and White are Back," *Washington Times* columnist Diana West criticized Annan, along with "blurry bastions of moral equivalence as the State Department and the European Union," for not displaying "the consistent clarity George W. Bush has projected" (December 14, 2001, p. A23). Another *Washington Times* columnist wrote that "Kofi Annan . . . has just been (incomprehensibly) nominated for the Nobel Peace Prize," and voiced a worry among the right wing of the Republican Party that "the unilateralist they helped elect, the man who would look out for America's interests and not apologize for it, has

turned multilateralist on them [in the wake of September 11]." See Helle Bering Dale, "Which President Bush?" *Washington Times*, December 12, 2001, p. A21.

8. "Proliferator in Chief: Bush Blocks Treaty . . . Again," *Guardian*, July 26, 2001.

9. Pew Global Attitudes Project, "Bush Unpopular in Europe, Seen As Unilateralist," August 15, 2001, Pew Research Center report.

10. In a Rose Garden ceremony on June 11, 2001, Bush said that ten weeks of high-level review led him to conclude that "the Kyoto Protocol was fatally flawed in fundamental ways." My colleagues at Brookings, Philip Gordon and Jeremy Shapiro, have contrasted Bush's handling of Kyoto and Ronald Reagan's rejection, nineteen years before, of the UN Convention on the Law of the Sea: "In that case, the Reagan administration also decided to reject a treaty that its predecessors had supported, but before doing so it sent a special envoy—ironically, Donald Rumsfeld—to consult with allied governments and to convince them not to sign or not to ratify the treaty. While that position hardly endeared him to European publics, Reagan's willingness to conform to established practices of consultation meant that criticism focused on the U.S. objections to the treaty rather than on its potential to cause a breakdown in the alliance." Gordon and Shapiro, *Allies at War: America, Europe, and the Crisis Over Iraq* (New York: McGraw-Hill, 2004) p. 54.

11. Joseph Fitchett, "Europeans Take Lead in Mideast from U.S.: Leaders Complain About Washington's Hands-Off Approach," *International Herald Tribune*, August 31, 2001.

12. Security Council Resolution 1373, passed on September 28, seventeen days after the attack, was a reiteration of an earlier one (1333, from December 19, 2000).

13. *The 9/11 Commission Report: Final Report of the National Commission on Terrorist Attacks Upon the United States* (New York: Norton, 2004), pp. 201 and notes 172–74 on p. 509.

14. This story was reported by Michael Elliott and James Carney in "First Stop, Iraq," *Time*, March 31, 2003, issue (posted March 23, 2003). The senators were in the White House to report to Rice on the annual Wehrkunde security conference in Munich, which they had just attended. The White House never denied the story.

15. Brent Scowcroft, "Don't Attack Saddam," *Wall Street Journal*, August 15, 2002. Albert Eisele, "George Kennan Speaks Out About Iraq," *The Hill*, September 26, 2002.

16. Article 2(4) of the UN Charter states: "All members shall refrain . . . from the threat or use of force against the territorial integrity or political independence of any state, or in any other manner inconsistent with the purposes of the United Nations." The only exception to this prohibition on the use of force is the Article 51 clause, which allows for the possibility of self-defense if a nation *has been* the target of an "armed attack."

17. Part IX of NSC-68, April 7, 1950, made the case why a preventive war would ultimately not be successful in achieving America's larger goals: "Many would doubt that [a preventive war] was a 'just war' and that all reasonable possibilities for a peaceful settlement had been explored in good faith. . . . It would, therefore, be difficult after such a war to create a satisfactory international order among nations. Victory in such a war would have brought us little if at all closer to victory in the fundamental ideological conflict." See also Scott A. Silverstone, "The Ethical Limits to Preventive War," Carnegie Council, May 2004, cited in Ian Shapiro, *Containment: Rebuilding a Strategy against Global Terror* (Princeton: Princeton University Press, 2007).

18. Eisenhower press conference, August 11, 1954, *Public Papers of the Presidents of the United States: Dwight D. Eisenhower*, vol. 2 (Washington, D.C.: U.S. Government Printing Office, 1960). The Robert Kennedy quotation is from Arthur M. Schlesinger, Jr., *A Thousand Days: John F. Kennedy in the White House* (Boston: Houghton Mifflin, 1965), pp. 806–7. For Jeane Kirkpatrick, see her speech in the Security Council, June 19, 1981 ("we were shocked by the Israeli air strike on the Iraqi nuclear facility and promptly condemned this action. . . . we

believe the means Israel chose to quiet its fears about the purposes of Iraq's nuclear program have hurt, and not helped, the peace and security of the area"), and "Mrs. Kirkpatrick's Speech Before Vote," *New York Times,* June 20, 1981, p. 5. Kirkpatrick and the Reagan administration also pushed for a temporary suspension of F-16 shipments to Israel and helped push through Security Council Resolution 487, passed unanimously on June 19, 1981, to condemn Israel for the Osirak attack.

19. John Ikenberry, (first quotation) "The Security Trap," *Democracy* (Fall 2006): 13, and (second quotation) "America's Imperial Ambition," *Foreign Affairs* (September/October 2002): 44–60.

20. Henry Kissinger, "Our Intervention In Iraq," *Washington Post,* August 12, 2002.

21. The most forthright presidential assertion of this principle was in a speech Bush gave at West Point on June 2, 2002, partly to prepare the way for the National Security Strategy, which was then very much in progress: "America has, and intends to keep, military strengths beyond challenge—thereby making the destabilizing arms races of other eras pointless, and limiting rivalries to trade and other pursuits of peace." Analysts zeroed in on this passage as saying that the United States would prevent a "peer competitor" (in the language of international relations) from arising anywhere in the world. The September 2002 National Security Strategy similarly states, "Our forces will be strong enough to dissuade potential adversaries from pursuing a military build-up in hopes of surpassing, or equaling, the power of the United States" (p. 30).

22. For example the Brazilian ambassador to UN, Gelson Fonseca, said in 2003, "We're committed to multilateralism because the rules of international law protect us from the powerful." Traub, *The Best of Intentions,* p. 175.

23. Bush, speech in Cincinnati, October 7, 2002.

24. "Powell: U.S. Prepared to Act Alone," CNN.com, January 26, 2003.

25. For more on Blair in the run-up to the Iraq war, see Christopher Meyer, *DC Confidential: The Controversial Memoirs of Britain's Ambassador at the Time of 9/11 and the Iraq War* (London: Weidenfeld & Nicolson, 2005); Peter Stothard, *Thirty Days: Tony Blair and the Test of History* (New York: HarperCollins, 2003); and Geoffrey Wheatcroft, "The Tragedy of Tony Blair," *Atlantic Monthly,* June 2004.

26. Ivo Daalder and James Lindsay, *America Unbound: The Bush Revolution in American Foreign Policy* (Washington, D.C.: Brookings Institution Press, 2003). They turned in the manuscript in June of that year, three months after the coalition's capture of Baghdad. Jim Lindsay subsequently went to the Council on Foreign Relations as director of studies, and then to the Lyndon B. Johnson School of Public Affairs at the University of Texas.

27. Mubarak asked the U.S. forces to "ensure that the stabilization of the conditions in Iraq . . . goes as quickly as possibly to a transitional government . . . and prevents a chaotic situation." Reacting to the images of looting and rioting throughout Iraq, al-Faisal called for "an end to this lawlessness, which could lead, God forbid, to a total security collapse."

28. Hassan made this statement on the PBS program, *NewsHour with Jim Lehrer,* April 10, 2003.

29. See, for example, the Pew Global Attitudes Project, "Views of a Changing World 2003: War With Iraq Further Divides Global Publics," June 3, 2003, Report by the Pew Research Center for the People and the Press. According to a study from WorldPublicOpinion.org and the Chicago Council on Global Affairs ("Groundbreaking Study Probes Global Opinion on Key International Issues," June 21, 2007, pp. 29–30), "In 10 out of 15 countries, the most common view is that the United States cannot be trusted to 'act responsibly in the world.' " The study also finds that "[m]ajorities in 13 out of 15 publics polled say the United States is 'playing the role of world policeman more than it should be.' " The countries surveyed were China, India, the United States, Russia, Indonesia, France, Thailand, Ukraine, Poland, Iran, Mexico,

South Korea, the Philippines, Australia, Argentina, Peru, Armenia, Israel, and the Palestinian territories.

30. On September 16, 2004, Annan had given an interview to the BBC. The most quoted part was: "Q: I wanted to ask you that—do you think that the resolution that was passed on Iraq before the war did actually give legal authority to do what was done? A: Well, I'm one of those who believe that there should have been a second resolution because the Security Council indicated that if Iraq did not comply there will be consequences. But then it was up to the Security Council to approve or determine what those consequences should be. Q: It was illegal? A: Yes, I have indicated it is not in conformity with the UN Charter, from our point of view and from the Charter point of view it was illegal."

31. See, for example, Max Boot, "Reconstructing Iraq," *Weekly Standard*, September 15, 2003, p. 25; Niall Ferguson, "An Empire in Denial: The Limits of US Imperialism," *Harvard International Review* 25, no. 3 (Fall 2003): 64; and Robert Kagan and William Kristol, "Do What It Takes in Iraq," *Weekly Standard*, September 1, 2003, p. 7.

32. See George Packer, *The Assassin's Gate: America in Iraq* (New York: Farrar, Straus & Giroux, 2005), pp. 213–16.

33. See Kofi Annan, public statement issued August 20, 2003. Two days later he told the Security Council, "Wherever the United Nations goes in to help and whatever measures are taken for staff security it is sustained by the perception among the local population that the United Nations is there to help them. . . . The blue flag has never been so viciously assaulted as it was yesterday. The terror attack ripped away the cloak of neutrality that had been the UN's principal protection in hotspots around the world."

34. Kofi Annan interview on BBC News On-Line, October 2, 2006.

35. Felicity Barringer, "U.N. Senses It Must Change, Fast, or Fade Away," *New York Times*, September 19, 2003.

36. Warren Hoge, "Annan Resists Calls to Send U.N. Staff Back to Baghdad," *New York Times*, December 28, 2003. A small mission of thirty-five internationals led by a Pakistani diplomat, Ashraf Jehangir Qazi, did indeed return a year after the attack.

37. There are several databases and studies that attempt to track the number of Iraqi casualties as of March 2003, including the Iraq Index, published by my colleague at the Brookings Institution, Mike O'Hanlon (http://www.brookings.edu/fp/saban/iraq/index.pdf), which estimates approximately 1,400 civilian deaths per month. Another is Iraq Body Count, a private British Web site (http://www.iraqbodycount.org), which tallies reported casualties from roughly 40 media sources, thus recording only a portion of the actual deaths. As of mid-2007, the estimate is between 68,973 and 75,423, or approximately 1,500 per month. In October 2006, the Johns Hopkins School of Public Health released a controversial and methodologically questionable study (see Paul Reynolds, "Huge gaps between Iraq death estimates," BBC News, October 20, 2006), reporting an estimated 655,000 Iraqi deaths, or 16,000 per month. (Gilbert Burnham, Riyadh Lafta, Shannon Doocy, and Les Roberts, "Mortality after the 2003 invasion of Iraq: a cross-sectional cluster sample survey," *The Lancet*, October 21, 2006, vol. 368, issue 9545.) In November 2006, the Iraqi Health Minister extrapolated from morgue statistics that about 150,000 Iraqis had been killed, at a rate of roughly 3,000 per month. See "Iraqi health minister estimates as many as 150,000 Iraqis killed by insurgents," Associated Press, November 9, 2006. In addition to the Iraq Index, the Iraq Coalition Casualty Count (http://icasualties.org/oif) tracks closely with the Department of Defense's reports (http//:www .defenselink.mil/news/casualty.pdf). Iraqi population estimates range from 26 to 29 million, especially given the flux of refugees (estimated at 4 million) and the approximately 2 million internally displaced persons (IDPs)—with nearly 50,000 additional IDPs each month. (See also UN High Commissioner for Refugees Report, "Humanitarian Needs of Persons Displaced Within Iraq and Across the Country's Borders," March 30, 2007, p. 4; Mark Oliver, "Mi-

gration body urges more aid for displaced Iraqis," *Guardian Unlimited,* July 17, 2007.) The calculation of fifty Iraqi deaths a day assumes a conservative estimate of 75,000 Iraqi casualties since March 2003, with a population of 27.5 million. For a compendium of estimates and a critique of the war, see Mark Danner, "Iraq: The War of the Imagination," *New York Review of Books,* December 21, 2006, pp. 81–97.

38. That Abu Ghraib story was first broken on April 28 by *60 Minutes II;* the Hersh piece, "Torture at Abu Ghraib," appeared in the *New Yorker,* on May 10, 2004. For more on the basis of administration policy on treatment of prisoners, see James Bovard, "Sins of Commission," *The American Conservative,* December 18, 2006; Nat Hentoff, "Protect the Constitution; Terror Suspects Deserve Habeas Corpus Right," *Washington Times,* October 16, 2006; Jane Mayer, "The Hidden Power," *New Yorker,* July 3, 2006, and "The Memo: Annals of the Pentagon," *New Yorker,* Feb. 27, 2006.

CHAPTER 17: A CONSEQUENTIAL ABERRATION

1. Edmund Burke, "Remarks on the Policy of the Allies with Respect to France," *Works of the Honourable Edmund Burke,* vol. 4, cited by Anatol Lieven and John Hulsman, *Ethical Realism: A Vision for America's Role in the World* (New York: Pantheon, 2006), p. xvii.

2. Reinhold Niebuhr, *The Irony of American History* (New York: Scribner's, 1952).

3. See, for example, Hanna Rosin, "Bush's Resentment of 'Elites' Informs Bid," *Washington Post,* July 23, 2000: A01, which leads with this paragraph: "The Yale class of '68 bred a social type George W. Bush and his friends called The Grind. He was a tireless striver, more sober than his teachers, who split his time between the library and admirable social causes. Back then, King of the Grinds was Strobe Talbott, now deputy secretary of state, then president [the actual title was chairman] of the *Yale Daily News,* Rhodes scholar and anti-war activist in a most responsible way" (p. A1).

4. David E. Sanger, "The 2000 Campaign World Views: Rivals Differ On U.S. Role in the World," *New York Times,* October 30, 2000.

5. Bush's full comment during the second presidential debate on October 11, 2000: "I think the United States must be humble and must be proud and confident of our values, but humble in how we treat nations that are figuring out how to chart their own course."

6. See James Mann, *Rise of the Vulcans: The History of Bush's War Cabinet* (New York: Penguin, 2004).

7. For example, see Powell's description of his first National Security Council meeting in the Clinton administration: "This meeting was my introduction to the new administration's decision-making style. Tony Lake, the new National Security Advisor, sat in the chairman's seat, but did not drive the meeting. . . . As President Reagan's National Security Advisor I had run structured meetings where the objectives were laid out, options were argued, and decisions were made. I had managed to adjust to the looser Bush-era approach, and I would somehow adapt to the Clinton style. But it was not going to be easy. At subsequent meetings, the discussions continued to meander like graduate-student bull sessions or the think-tank seminars in which many of my new colleagues had spent the last twelve years while their party was out of power. . . . [Clinton] was not well served by the wandering deliberations he permitted." Colin Powell with Joseph E. Persico, *My American Journey* (New York: Random House, 1995), pp. 560–62.

8. See Peter and Rochelle Schweizer, *The Bushes: Portrait of a Dynasty* (New York: Doubleday, 2004); Kevin Phillips, *American Dynasty: Aristocracy, Fortune, and the Politics of Deceit in the House of Bush* (New York: Viking, 2004); and Craig Unger, *House of Bush, House of Saud: The Secret Relationship Between the World's Two Most Powerful Dynasties* (New York: Scribner, 2004), and David Greenberg, "Fathers and Sons," *New Yorker,* July 12, 2004, pp. 92–98.

9. See Karen DeYoung's *Soldier: The Life of Colin Powell* (New York: Knopf, 2006), p. 334. DeYoung notes: "Powell found Bush better-spoken and more thoughtful in private than his public posturing as a rough-hewn, plain-spoken Texan would indicate, although he found Bush's fidgety impatience irritating, along with his tendency to interrupt everyone, from his Cabinet officers to visiting heads of state. . . . Powell insisted to disbelieving aides that Bush listened to, and even acted on, his advice. 'The president has good instincts . . . an instinctual grasp' of issues, he often told them. But he usually followed with an acknowledgment that Bush 'has got these rough edges—his cowboy, Texan rough edges—and when he gets them exposed, there are other people who know how to use them' to their advantage. Time and time again during the administration's bumpy first year, Powell had seen Rumsfeld and Vice President Cheney intervene to nudge a willing Bush away from moderation and diplomacy, and toward a hard line on foreign policy issues from North Korea to the Middle East."

10. Bush interview with Matt Lauer, *Today*, NBC, September 2, 2004.

11. Bush address to American Legion National Convention, Salt Lake City, Utah, August 31, 2006.

12. The existence of the group (known as "Bletchley II") and the report, drafted by Christopher DeMuth, the president of AEI, is revealed in Bob Woodward, *State of Denial* (New York: Simon & Schuster, 2006), pp. 83–85.

13. David Greenberg, "Fathers and Sons," *op. cit.* p. 96.

14. Bob Woodward, *Plan of Attack* (New York: Simon & Schuster, 2004), p. 421. Woodward also quotes Bush looking back to when he gave the final Iraq go-ahead on March 19, 2003: "Going into this period I was praying for the strength to do the Lord's will. . . . I'm surely not going to justify the war based on God. . . . Nevertheless, in my case I pray that I be as good a messenger of his will as possible" (p. 379).

15. Bush's comments first appeared as a direct quotation in a July 16, 2004, column by Jack Brubaker of the local paper, the *Lancaster New Era*, ("Bush quietly meets with Amish here; they offer their prayers," p. A-8). As the story began to resonate in the national media—including the late-night comedian Jay Leno—the White House insisted that it was a misquote. "The president did not say that," says Jim Morrell, a White House spokesman, "but I am confident that the president likely talked about his own faith as he has on many occasions. The president has said that his faith helps him in his service to people and that his faith sustains him." The *Lancaster New Era* wrote a clarification a week later saying that they no longer stood by that exact wording in the president's remarks but that the tenor of the comments had been accurately reported.

16. One of many examples of Bush speaking at length about the intersection of his religious beliefs and his sense of political mission is in Peter Baker, "Bush Tells Group He Sees a 'Third Awakening,' " *Washington Post*, September 13, 2006, p. A5. The article reports a ninety-minute meeting in the White House with a group of conservative journalists. The headline refers to Bush's anticipation of a third in a series of "awakenings" of religious devotion in the United States (the first occurred in the American colonies in the mid-eighteenth century, and the second in the late eighteenth and nineteenth). "A lot of people in America see [the war on terror] as a confrontation between good and evil, including me," said Bush.

17. Warren P. Strobel, "Vice President's Objections Blocked Planned North Korean Nuclear Talks," Knight Ridder Washington Bureau, December 20, 2003.

18. A colleague at Brookings, Kenneth Pollack, put this point succinctly in a talk he gave to a visiting group of Japanese and Chinese policy analysts in November 2006: "In April 2003 the United States created a security vacuum and a failed state in Iraq. Because we have never properly filled that security vacuum or rebuilt a functional state, these remain the foundational problems plaguing Iraq today. All of Iraq's other challenges—from the insurgency, to organized crime, to corruption, to sectarianism—stem from these two core problems and until they are dealt with, the situation will only continue to deteriorate."

19. According to the Pew Global Attitudes Project, between 2002 and 2006 the percentage of people with a "favorable opinion" of the United States fell from 75 down to 56 percent in the United Kingdom, 63 to 39 percent in France, 61 to 37 percent in Germany, 61 to 43 percent in Russia, 61 to 30 percent in Indonesia, 25 to 15 percent in Jordan, and 30 to 12 percent in Turkey. Also according to Pew, the percentage of those who believed that the United States took their country's interests into account was 38 percent in Germany, 32 percent in the United Kingdom, 21 percent in Russia, 20 percent in the Netherlands, 19 percent in Spain, 19 percent in Canada, 18 percent in France, 17 percent in Jordan, 14 percent in Turkey, and 13 percent in Poland. By 2007, an average of only 29 percent of people polled in eighteen different countries from all over the world had a "mainly positive" view of the United States, a level that had fallen from 36 percent in 2006 and 40 percent in 2005. Cited by Phil Gordon, *Winning the Right War: The Path to Security for America and the World* (New York: Times Books, 2007), p. 31.

20. For invocations of Truman, see Bush speech on enlargement of NATO, at White House, March 29, 2004; on Iraqi elections, at Woodrow Wilson Center, December 14, 2005; and commencement address at the United States Military Academy at West Point, New York, May 27, 2006.

21. Condoleezza Rice, speech at Princeton University's Celebration of the 75th Anniversary of the Woodrow Wilson School of Public and International Affairs, September 30, 2005. Philip Zelikow, "Practical Idealism: Present Policy in Historical Perspective," speech before the Stanford Institute of International Studies, May 6, 2005.

22. See, for example, Ronald Brownstein, "Bush Forges Weak Links to Legacies of Democratic Predecessors," January 31, 2005, *Los Angeles Times.* The closest Bush publicly came to identifying with Wilson was during his 2003 state visit to the United Kingdom: "The last President to stay at Buckingham Palace was an idealist, without question. At a dinner hosted by King George V, in 1918, Woodrow Wilson made a pledge; with typical American understatement, he vowed that right and justice would become the predominant and controlling force in the world." Royal Banqueting House, Whitehall Palace, London, England, November 19, 2003.

23. In a news conference in Denmark in July 2005, Bush said, "Listen, I recognize that the surface of the earth is warmer and that an increase in greenhouse gases caused by humans is contributing to the problem." But when the Environmental Protection Agency, in May 2002, endorsed the view of almost all respectable scientists that the problem was of humankind's making, Bush had said only, "I've read the report put out by the bureaucracy." Not until January 2007 did a White House–approved public document—a statement from the National Oceanic and Atmospheric Administration, a federal agency within the Department of Commerce that provides independent scientific data on the conditions of the oceans and the atmosphere—unequivocally assert that a buildup of greenhouse gases was heating up the planet.

24. Samantha Power, "Introduction," *A Man for Dark Times.* See also Samantha Power, "United It Wobbles," *Washington Post,* January 7, 2007: "To gauge the relative responsibility of the organization, it might be helpful for U.N. bashers to ask, 'But for Kofi Annan or the presence of U.N. peacekeepers, would the response of the countries on the Security Council have been any different in Bosnia, Rwanda or Darfur?' The answer, sadly, is no. . . . Annan's office has spoken out more about Darfur than almost any government."

25. See Nigel Parry, "Neo Culpa," in *Vanity Fair,* January 2007, in which such Reaganite hard-liners as Richard Perle and Frank Gaffney, along with David Frum (the proud author of Bush's "Axis of Evil" line), Michael Rubin (a former political adviser to the Coalition Provisional Authority in Iraq), James Woolsey (a Democratic neocon who briefly served as Clinton's director of Central Intelligence), Danielle Pletka (a former Senate staffer on Middle East issues and now the vice president of foreign and defense policy studies at the American Enterprise Institute in Washington, a think tank which also counts Perle, Rubin, and Frum among its scholars), Eliot Cohen (a historian at the Johns Hopkins School of Advanced Inter-

national Studies) defend the righteousness of the cause in Iraq while venting their spleen at what a number call the "incompetence" of the administration in its prosecution of the war. Charles Krauthammer took a different tack. While acknowledging "serious mistakes" in American conduct of the occupation, he blamed the failure in Iraq on the Iraqis themselves and on their "particular political culture, raped and ruined by thirty years of [Saddam] Hussein's totalitarianism." Charles Krauthammer, "Why Iraq Is Crumbling," *Washington Post,* November 17, 2006.

CONCLUSION: YES, WE MUST

1. Robert Frost, "Fire and Ice," *Collected Poems, Prose, and Plays,* Richard Poirier and Mark Richardson (eds.), p. 204.

2. David McCullough, *Truman,* p. 583.

INDEX

Page numbers in *italics* refer to illustrations.

Abdel-Rahman, Sheik Omar, 341–42

Abdullah, King of Jordan, 351

Abraham, 34–35, 36, 48, 53, 54, 75, 93

Abramowitz, Mort, 305

Acheson, Dean, 112–13, 186, 190, 221, 325

Ackroyd, Peter, 78

Adam and Eve, story of, 27–28, 29, 31, 33, 68, 72, 93

Adams, Henry, 137

Adams, John, 22, 368

Adams, John Quincy, 132

Aeneid (Virgil), 102

Afghanistan, 45, 248, 375*n*, 395
    al-Qaeda training camps in, 342, 351
    as artificial construct, 21–22, 342
    Soviet invasion of, 219, 235, 247, 342
    Taliban and, 342, 351, 352
    U.S. invasion of, 352, 353, 375

Africa, 28, 30, 46, 91, 99, 142, 232–36, 247, 276, 286, 294–98, 343, 384*n*, 387–90
    colonialism in, 120–21, 160–61, 169, 232–35
    U.S. embassy bombings in, 341, 342

African Growth and Opportunity Act (2000), 343

African Union, 400

Against the Murdering, Thieving Hordes of Peasants (Luther), 79

Ahtisaari, Martti, 316, 317–18, 319

Aideed, Mohammed Farah, 292, 293, 295, 296

Akbar, Emperor, 7, 64–65, *64*

Albright, Madeleine, 2, 281, 290, 300, 306, 310, 319, 335, 339*n*, 341, 342

Alexander I, Czar of Russia, 109, 111

Alexander III, Czar of Russia, 134, 135

Alexander the Great, 7, 44–46, *44*, 61, 80, 317
    ecumenical ideal of, 45–46, 52, 57, 90, 107
    India and, 59
    intermarriage promoted by, 45–46, 65

koinonia concept of, 45, 60

Alexandria, 56–57, 68

al-Faisal, Saud, 361–62

Almohads, 56

al-Qaeda, 341–43, 347, 353, 361, 368, 375, 376
    Afghan training camps of, 342, 351
    in Iraq war aftermath, 366, 379
    1993 World Trade Center bombing by, 341–42
    U.S. embassies in Africa bombed by, 341, 342

America First Committee, 176

American Anti-Imperialist League, 136–37

American colonies, 8–9, 92

American Communist Party, 205

American Revolution, 98, 99, 107, 127, 128

Amos, book of, 37

Amphictyonic League, 100, 117, 154

Anderson, Benedict, 24

Andropov, Yuri, 249

Angell, Norman, 140

Annan, Kofi, 3, 259*n*, 293, 296, 316, 318, 320, 325, 347, 358, 383–84, 385
    conditional sovereignty doctrine invoked by, 313–14, 315, 387–88
    East Timor and, 344
    farewell address of, 390–91
    Iraq war aftermath and, 365, 366–67, 381
    Iraq war deplored by, 262–63
    Nobel Peace Prize of, 350
    Oil-for-Food Program scandal and, 380–81
    personality of, 311–12
    Rwanda genocide and, 297
    U.S.-backed selection of, 310–12, *311*
    use of force approved by, 306

Anti-Ballistic Missile (AMB) Treaty (1972), 218, 219, 402
   National Missile Defense (NMD) and, 337, 338
   U.S. withdrawal from, 347, 348, 377
anti-Semitism, 89, 117
   in medieval Europe, 72
   Nazi, 18, 167–68
   in Russia, 134–35
Antoninus Pius, Emperor of Rome, 47, 48
Appiah, K. Anthony, 148
Apple, R. W. "Johnny," 338
Apuleius, 46
Arab-Israeli wars, 192–93, 230, 273
Arabs, 40, 53–57, 190, 258, 268, 361–62
   in Darfur, 388–90
   Palestinian, see Palestine, Palestinians
   pre-Islamic, 53
   see also Islam
Arafat, Yasser, 345, 346, 347
Arendt, Hannah, 193
Aristide, Jean-Bertrand, 293, 300–303
Aristides, Aelius, 47
Aristotle, 41, 45, 75
arms control, 215–20, 227, 277–79, 283, 285, 287, 372
Armstrong, Karen, 53
Aron, Raymond, 198–99
ASEAN Regional Forum (ARF), 286, 287, 382
Ashoka, Emperor, 7, 59–60, 60, 61, 64, 66
Asia-Pacific Economic Cooperation (APEC) forum, 265, 285–86, 287
Asmus, Ronald, 319n
Assad, Hafez, 345
Association of Southeast Asian Nations (ASEAN), 286
Assyrians, 30, 38, 39
Ataturk, Mustafa Kemal, 151–52, 272–73
Atlantic Charter, 180
atomic bomb, 181–83, 185, 188–89, 194–99, 202, 203, 206, 404–5
   dropped on Japan, 189, 194, 195–96, 195, 214, 404
   human survival threatened by, 196, 213, 214, 218, 221–22
   Soviet acquisition of, 183, 189, 206, 207, 211, 213
   see also cold war
Attila the Hun, 67, 142
Attlee, Clement, 192
Augustus Caesar, Emperor of Rome, 73
Australia, 18, 180, 208, 285, 286, 344
Austria, 92, 99, 108, 109, 111, 112, 116, 159, 172
Austro-Hungarian Empire, 23, 141, 150

Averroes, 75
Avicenna, 75

Babylonian Captivity, 39–40, 43, 72
Babylonians, 30, 31–34, 35, 39–40, 74, 362
   Gilgamesh epic of, 31
   language of, 34
   ziggurats of, 31–32, 43, 361; see also Tower of Babel
Baker, James, 277, 278, 300, 373, 383
balance of power, 11, 140, 190, 198, 218, 259
   European system of, 8, 11, 92, 112–13, 120, 128, 153, 154, 356
   Napoleon's disruption of, 113
Balfour Declaration, 161
Balkans, 3, 18, 43, 58, 126, 152, 276, 290, 303, 304, 320, 364
Bangladesh, 406
Ban Ki-moon, 391
Barak, Ehud, 346
barbarians, 18, 67–68, 137, 139
Barbary pirates, 132
Barents Euro-Arctic Council, 319, 321
Baruch, Bernard, 221
Basques, 19, 167
Beethoven, Karl Julius Maria van, 143
Beethoven, Ludwig van, 104, 107, 108, 112, 113, 225, 256
Belarus, 278–79, 283
Belgium, 110, 141, 151, 162, 172, 208, 240, 241, 256
   African mandates of, 160–61, 295, 296
   colonial empire of, 121, 179, 232, 237
Bell, Gertrude, 161
Beowulf, 88
Berger, Sandy, 289–90, 291, 301, 318, 342
Berlin, Isaiah, 100, 193
Bernadotte, Count Folke, 193
Beschloss, Michael, 266
Bhagavad-Gita, 188
Biden, Joseph, 335–36
Bierce, Ambrose, 136
bin Laden, Osama, 341–42, 343, 347, 351, 353–54, 361, 373
biotechnology, 406n
"Birth of the Global Nation, The" (Talbott), 125–26, 332
Bismarck, Otto von, 118–19, 166, 218
Black, Antony, 80
Black Sea, 31n, 66, 274
Blaine, James, 134–35
Blair, Tony, 284, 359–60, 365, 390
Blix, Hans, 359
Boas, Franz, 199n
Bolívar, Simón, 131, 272
Bolsheviks, 149–50, 165–66, 171

Bolton, John, 383–87, 390, 391
Bondarchuk, Sergei, 244
Boniface III, Pope, 68
Boorstin, Bob, 328
Boot, Max, 259*n*
Bosnia, 3, 42, 141, 276–78, 290–91, 294, 303–9, 322, 328, 333, 339, 348, 352, 364
    establishing democracy in, 308–9
    Muslims in, 276, 277, 304, 305, 307
    NATO in, 304–5, 306–7, 308, 309
    peace negotiations in, 306–8
    Serb outrages in, 276, 278, 290, 304, 305–6, 307
    UN peacekeeping mission in, 278, 290, 304–9, 313
Bourbons, 92, 112, 116, 118
Bourgeois, Léon, 157
Boutros-Ghali, Boutros, 290, 291, 296, 306, 310–11, 332
Brahimi, Lakhdar, 301–2, 366–67
Braudel, Fernand, 66, 69, 70, 83
Brazil, 208, 223, 386, 405
Bremer, L. Paul "Jerry," 365, 366
Brewster, Kingman, 201
Brezhnev, Leonid, 219, 242, 246, 249
Briand, Aristide, 163
Brookings, Robert S., 175
"brotherhood of man," 28, 144
Brown, Harold, 219
Bruegel, Pieter (the Elder), 81–83, 121, 225
Brussels Treaty (1948), 240
Brzezinski, Zbigniew, 247–48
Buddhism, 59–60, 64, 66
Bunche, Ralph, 191, 193, 227, 230, 231*n*, 232, 332
Burgersdijk, Franco Petri, 90–91
Burke, Edmund, 105–6, 113, 129, 238, 370
Burns, Nicholas, 391–92
Bush, George H. W., 5, 6, 220*n*, 228*n*, 255, 260–79, *261*, 280, 285, 353, 372–73, 391*n*, 402–3
    as CIA director, 261
    environmental policy of, 262–64
    EU supported by, 263, 265–66
    Gorbachev and, 265, 268–69, 273–74, 275, 345, 374
    at G-7 summits, 273, 275–76
    Gulf War and, 266–70, 278, 299–300
    G. W. Bush and, 350, 352, 356, 371, 372–73, 374, 376, 383, 385
    Haiti crisis and, 293–300
    Iraqi assassination plot against, 347–48, 353
    Kiev speech of, 273–74, 277–78
    NATO and, 265, 266, 278

"new world order" slogan of, 255, 266–67, 269, 270, 327
    Panama invasion ordered by, 264–65
    personal diplomacy of, 261–62, 264–65, 267, 374
    political style of, 262
    reelection campaign of, 269, 270, 274, 278, 279, 290
    Somalia conflict and, 291, 292, 371
    Soviet Union and, 263, 265, 266–67, 270
    UN and, 2, 261, 263, 265, 266–67, 269–70, 333
    UNGA addressed by, 267, 269–70, 278–79
    Wars of Yugoslav Secession and, 276–78
Bush, George W., 126, 228*n*, 260, 274, 329, 346, 347–69, 370–92, 393
    anti-Americanism provoked by, 350–51, 357, 379–80
    approval ratings of, 351, 357, 362, 379, 384, 391
    author's relationship with, 370–71
    "Axis of Evil" and, 362, 378
    certitude of, 373–75
    Clinton's handoff meeting with, 347–48, 374
    contrary views rejected by, 373–74
    evangelism of, 375–77
    foreign policy of, 11, 350, 354–57, 361, 363–64, 371–72, 375, 380, 383, 384–85, 390–92
    G. H. W. Bush and, 350, 352, 356, 371, 372–73, 374, 376, 383, 385
    G20 summit hosted by, 396–397
    humanitarian intervention criticized by, 334–35
    Hussein, vendetta against, 335, 352–54, 358
    Israeli-Palestinian peace process suspended by, 348, 350–51
    Kyoto Protocol rejected by, 349, 350
    multilateralism professed by, 382–83
    9/11 terrorist attacks and, 351–52, 355, 358, 367, 368, 375, 376
    reelection of, 376, 379–81
    UN challenged by, 358–59, 365
    unilateralism of, 5–6, 334, 348, 349, 351, 352, 354–57, 361, 376, 383, 384, 391, 392*n*
    war on terror of, 353, 368, 375, 376, 379
    see also Iraq war
Bush (G. W.) administration, 333*n*, 348–69, 373, 374
    Afghanistan invasion organized by, 352, 353, 375
    arms control policy of, 377–79, 383, 387
    climate change acknowledged by, 380
    climate change denied by, 349

Bush (G. W.) administration (*cont.*)
  European Union downgraded by, 349
  ICC treaty nullified by, 348, 383–84
  India policy of, 378–79
  multilateralism resisted by, 356, 359
  NATO's relationship with, 349, 352,
    381–82
  Proliferation Security Initiative (PSI) of,
    377, 383
  treaties mistrusted by, 371–72, 377
  2002 National Security strategy of,
    354–57, 375
  UN downgraded by, 350, 363, 380, 383–87
"Bush Doctrine, The" (Krauthammer),
    374–75
Byzantine Empire, 40, 52–53, 57, 70

Caesar, Julius, 63
Cain and Abel, story of, 28, 33, 167
Caligula, Emperor of Rome, 48, 52
Canaan, Canaanites, 30, 34–35, 37–38
Canada, 5*n*, 129, 180, 208, 240, 273, 302
Capek, Karel, 66
Carlyle, Thomas, 16, 80
Carnegie, Andrew, 136
Carter, Jimmy, 219, 247–48, 261*n*, 330
Cathars, extermination of, 71
Catherine II "the Great," Empress of Russia,
    99, 133, 203
Cecil, Lord Robert, 154, 157, 162, 173, 181,
    320
Central Intelligence Agency (CIA), 32, 191,
    211, 212*n*, 233, 261, 319–20, 342, 379
Central Treaty Organization (CENTO), 240*n*
Chagall, Marc, 225
Chalabi, Ahmad, 352
Chamberlain, Joseph, 122
Chamberlain, Neville, 295
Chandragupta, 59
Charlemagne, 69–70, 74, 79, 80, 324–25
Charlemagne Prize, 324–25
Charles I, King of England, 89
Charles V, Holy Roman Emperor, 80–81, 83
Cheney, Dick, 264, 348, 356*n*, 373, 376–77,
    382, 405
Chernenko, Konstantin, 249, 250
Chernomyrdin, Viktor, 316, 317–18
Chiang Kai-shek, 171, 177, 206–7, 210
China, 24, 67, 137, 142, 162, 163
  as civilizational state, 65
  Japanese invasion of, 170–71, 178
  Mongol rulers of, 64
  Qin Emperor of, 7, 60–61, 61, 64, 66
  Qing dynasty of, 120, 170, 171
China, Nationalist, 171, 177–78, 206–7, 210,
    212*n*, 223, 337

China, People's Republic of, 206–7, 217, 228*n*,
    255, 259, 261, 286, 330, 331, 401, 405
  Korean War and, 210
  Kosovo bombing and, 316–17
  Kyoto Protocol and, 340
  as nuclear power, 222, 397, 403
  in UN Security Council, 267, 300, 337,
    344, 359, 360, 386, 389
  U.S. rapprochement with, 218
Chirac, Jacques, 311, 360, 365
Christendom, 68, 69, 70–71, 73, 90, 312
Christianity, 35, 48–53, 56, 63, 67, 77, 117
  heterodoxy banned by, 50–51
  iconography of, 68, 69
  Mongol sympathy for, 63*n*
  Nicene Creed of, 51, 52
  Ottoman Empire and, 58
  proactive inclusiveness of, 48, 49–51,
    54–55
  see also Jesus
Christopher, Warren, 2, 282, 291, 306, 307,
    309, 310, 319, 325
Churchill, Winston, 3, *178*, 179, 188, 191*n*,
    192, 324, 327
  Chinese as viewed by, 178
  European union proposed by, 239
  "Franco-British nation" proposed by,
    238–39
  imperialism of, 179–80
  "iron curtain" speech of, 203–4
  Mussolini and, 166
  at Potsdam conference, 188, 189
Church of England, 17, 77–78
Cicero, 47–48
city-states, 47, 177
  Greek, 45
  Hanseatic, 96
  Italian, 73–74
  Medina as, 54
civilizational state, 65, 66
civil vicinity, 105–6
Civil War, American, 16, 22, 132–33, 208
Civil War, British, 89
civitas, 47
Claes, Willy, 309
Clark, Wesley, 339*n*
Claude, Inis, 158, 171, 192, 194
Clausewitz, Carl von, 119, 159
Clemenceau, Georges, 148, 151, 157
Clement VIII, Pope, 77, 78
Cleveland, Grover, 136
climate change, 11–12, 393, 401
  Gore and, 340, 341, 349
  government agencies' projections of, 349
  G. W. Bush administration's approach to,
    349, 380

Kyoto Protocol on, 340–41, 349, 350
Obama and, 394, 399
stabilizing measures for, 398–401, 404–8
Clinton, Bill, 1–2, 11, 143, 274, 278, 280–98,
    299–323, 324–46, 347–48, 354, 371,
    374, 385n, 398
  APEC forum attended by, 285–86
  Asian regional organizations supported
      by, 285–87
  Charlemagne Prize awarded to, 324–25
  climate change issue and, 340–41
  diplomacy backed by force and, 309–12
  at EAPC summit, 289–90
  first Inaugural Address of, 309, 326
  foreign policy of, 280–81, 282–84, 287–90,
      325–30, 331, 333–34
  globalization issue and, 281–82, 326,
      327–28, 329–31, 334, 348
  at G-7 summit, 283–84, 285
  ICC treaty signed by, 339, 348, 383–84
  legacy of, 325, 331
  loss of U.S. preeminence envisioned by,
      329–30
  Middle East peace pursued by, 344–46
  military leaders' relationship with, 364
  multilateralism of, 5, 281, 282, 291, 309,
      310, 328, 329–30, 332, 335, 384
  negotiating technique of, 282, 289
  in 1992 election, 280–81, 290, 333
  at OSCE summit, 285
  at Oxford, 17, 280n
  political evolution as belief of, 330–31
  "post-cold war era" and, 326, 327–28, 330
  post-presidency good-works projects of, 6
  Putin's meeting with, 324, 325
  Rwanda genocide regretted by, 297–98,
      371
  Saddam Hussein and, 347–48
  Somalia debacle and, 292–93
  Summit of the Americas project of, 284
  underlying assumptions reexamined by,
      373
  at UNGA, 281–82, 327, 328
  unpopular causes supported by, 284
  use of force, reluctance for, 290–94
  Yeltsin and, 280, 282–84, 283, 287–89,
      315–16, 318, 345
Clinton, Hillary Rodham, 280, 394, 398
Clinton administration, 281–90, 299–323,
    325–29, 332–43, 352, 353, 363, 386,
    391n, 399
  anti-terrorist efforts of, 341–43
  intelligence briefings of, 294
  Iraqi assassination plot thwarted by,
      347–48, 353
  NATO expanded by, 287–90, 382

1999 National Security Strategy of, 354
  nuclear diplomacy of, 337–39
  peacekeeping missions supported by, see
      Bosnia; Haiti; Kosovo; Rwanda;
      Somalia
  postwar planning of, 300–301
  right-wing opposition to, 302, 330,
      332–41, 342
  unilateral actions of, 310–12
"Clinton and the Draft: A Personal
    Testimony" (Talbott), 280n
"CNN effect," 290, 305
cold war, 11, 203–36, 238, 240, 247, 250, 258,
    259, 265, 266–67, 274, 279, 285, 286,
    288–89, 294, 296, 326, 327–28
  arms control in, 215–20
  deterrence in, 213, 214–15
  Gorbachev's peace overtures in, 250–52
  Korean War in, 209–13, 267, 355, 389
  limiting nuclear proliferation in, 220–24
  Soviet "Czar Bomb" in, 213
  spies in, 211–12
  strategic defense systems in, 218, 220
  U.S. containment policy in, 204, 211, 214,
      242, 266, 287, 289
Coleman, Norm, 380
collective security, 93, 149, 153–54, 157, 163,
    176, 382
colonialism, 90, 91–92, 99, 119–22, 129, 208,
    232–35
  Belgian, 121, 179, 232, 237
  British, 7, 21, 22, 40, 91, 109, 120, 121, 122,
      141, 142, 151, 179–80, 192, 237
  decolonization vs., 40, 122, 179, 191,
      232–33
  Dutch, 7, 91, 120, 151, 179, 231
  French, 91, 106, 120, 121, 141, 151, 179,
      180, 237
  German, 120, 121, 160–61, 169, 191, 235
  Japanese, 151, 170, 179, 194
  Portuguese, 91, 120, 151, 343
  Spanish, 7, 91, 120, 121, 131, 133, 135–36
  UN and, 191–94
commerce, 8, 83, 96, 113, 116, 119, 120
  in empires, 42, 46, 62–63, 64
  of Hanseatic League, 95–97, 319
  international, 93–94
Common Sense (Paine), 128
communism, 9, 149–50, 164–65, 167, 177,
    205, 211–12, 247, 255, 287, 300
  fascism vs., 169–70
Communist Manifesto, The (Marx and
    Engels), 116–17
Comprehensive Test Ban Treaty (CTBT),
    338–39, 348, 377, 398, 404
Comte, Auguste, 115–16

Concert of Europe, 112, 113, 118, 140, 410

Conference on Security and Cooperation in Europe (CSCE), 247, 285

Congo, 121, 208, 232–35, 296, 297

Congress, U.S., 126, 146, 149, 152, 156, 164, 175, 190, 200, 205, 293, 310, 343, 354, 378, 384

   see also House of Representatives, U.S.; Senate, U.S.

Congress of Vienna, 10, 109–10, 111–13, 117, 119, 179, 247, 285

Congress System, 112, 113

Conrad, Joseph, 121

Constant, Benjamin, 110

Constantine the Great, Emperor of Rome, 51–53, 55, 57, 110

Constantinople, 52–53, 68

Constitution, U.S., 9–10, 23, 130, 133*n*, 155, 186, 336, 368

constitutional democracies, 9, 99, 152

constitutionalism, 11, 170

"Contact Group" (United States, European Union, Russia), 304, 307, 314

Cook, Robin, 362

Coolidge, Calvin, 162

Copernicus, Nicolaus, 76

Cosby, Bill, 15

cosmopolis, 45

cosmopolitanism, 97, 111, 116

counterfactuals, 212–13, 250

   of Napoleon at Waterloo, 244–45

crimes against humanity, 121, 339, 388

Critique of Pure Reason, The (Kant), 97, 98

Cromwell, Oliver, 89

Crucé, Emeric, 90

Crusades, 17, 40, 57, 70–71, 75, 91

Cuba, 135–36, 208, 235, 267*n*, 293, 303

Cuban missile crisis, 158*n*, 216, 281, 355, 405

Cyrus the Great, King of Persia, 32

Czechoslovakia, 153, 155, 159, 172, 204, 208, 242, 276–77, 288, 295

Daalder, Ivo, 361

Danforth, John, 383

Dangerous Nation (Kagan), 132*n*–33*n*

Dante Alighieri, 10, 11, 73–76, *73*, 81, 84, 85, 101, 113, 199, 238, 255, 256

   federalism advocated by, 75, 93, 110, 200

   global governance envisioned by, 73, 74–75, 84, 115, 117, 149

   humanism of, 75–76, 84

   universal peace envisioned by, 74–75, 85, 93

Darfur, 388–90

Darius the Great, King of Persia, 32, 44

Darwin, Charles, 113–15, *114,* 116, 332

   on political evolution, 114–15, 145, 175, 199

David, King of Israel, 39, 75

Declaration of Independence, 9, 129

Defeat of an Ideal (Hazzard), 226

de Gaulle, Charles, 180

de Laurentiis, Dino, 244

democracy, 59, 70, 75, 102, 103, 115, 129, 146, 177, 232, 273, 287, 328, 330–31, 391

   constitutional, 9, 99, 152

   countries resistant to, 302–3, 308–9

   EC as community of, 241

   historical emergence of, 302

   illiberal, 302–3

   Kant's view of, 98

   League of Nations and, 150, 151, 155

   liberal, 78, 169

   minority rights in, 155

   pluralistic, 10, 128

   weak, 166

Democratic Party, 157, 206, 261, 267, 274, 284, 330*n,* 335, 380, 390

Deng Xiaoping, 255

de Rougemont, Denis, 111

Derviş, Kemal, 386*n*–87*n*

Desai, Vishakha, 23

determinism, 115–16, 167

Deutch, John, 293

diaspora, 28

Din-i-Ilahi, 65

Diocletian, Emperor of Rome, 52

Diplomacy (Kissinger), 144

Di Rita, Lawrence, 333

"Disasters of War, the" (Goya), *108,* 109

Divine Comedy, The (Dante), 73, 75, 85

Dole, Robert, 332

Donilon, Tom, 306

Doyle, Michael, 259*n*

Drell, Sidney, 259

Dryden, John, 102

Dubček, Alexander, 242

Dulles, John Foster, 187, 214–15, 242

Earth Summit (1992), 203–4, 340

East Timor, 21, 343–44, 365

   as Democratic Republic of Timor-Leste, 344

Ecclesiastes, book of, 376

ecumenical state, 58, 87, 90–91, 121, 164

   Alexander the Great's concept of, 45–46, 52, 57, 90, 107

   empires as, *see* empires

   medieval Europe as, 74

Egypt, 18, 32, 55, 56–57, 142, 350–51, 361–62
  ancient, 30, 33, 36, 38–39, 43–44, 66
  in British empire, 121, 193
  Mamluk, 40
  1956 Suez Canal incident in, 230–32
Einstein, Albert, 181–82, *181*, 195, 197–98, 201–2, 213
Eisenhower, Dwight D., 3, 203, 210–12, *211*, 214–15, 216, 230, 240, 242, 349
  "Atoms for Peace" speech of, 221–22, 409
  Korean War and, 210–11
  "massive retaliation" doctrine of, 215, 221, 355
  1956 Suez Canal incident protested by, 230–32
  nuclear test ban proposed by, 216, 339
  preventive war rejected by, 355
  UN peacekeeping missions supported by, 233
Eliot, T. S., 199–200
Emerson, Ralph Waldo, 180–81
empires, 34, 36, 38–40, 41–65, 69–70, 129, 171, 232, 237, 269
  commerce in, 42, 46, 62–63, 64
  independence movements within, 27, 39, 40, 42, 106, 117, 133
  institutionalized tolerance in, 8, 42, 57, 58, 59–60, 62, 63, 64–65
  intermarriage encouraged in, 45–46, 63–64, 65
  internal peace of, 42, 46, 58, 62–63
  legal codes of, 43, 46–47, 61
  mobility within, 46, 50, 62
  provincial autonomy of, 8, 47, 48, 58, 64
  religious freedom in, 47–48, 58, 60, 63, 65
  turmoil at dissolution of, 60, 61, 64, 69, 271
  vulnerability of, 38–39, 42
  see also colonialism
Engaging India: Diplomacy, Democracy, and the Bomb (Talbott), 338*n*
Engels, Friedrich, 116, 117, 119, 164
Enlightenment, 10, 93–103, 107, 128, 154–55, 170, 310
  French Revolution and, 104–6
environmental issues, 262–64, 331, 385
  see also climate change
Erasmus, Desiderius, 76–77, 81, 86
Errera, Gérard, 310
Etemenanki ziggurat, 43, 361
Ethiopia, 38, 120, 171–72, 247, 296
ethnic cleansing, 3, 276, 312, 334, 388, 400
euro, 256
Euro-Atlantic Partnership Council (EAPC), 289–90

Euromess chart, 319–20, *321,* 382
Europa, myth of, 67
Europe, 8–10, 16, 27, 43, 62, 65, 66–85, 86–103, 104–22, 303, 324–25
  balance-of-power system in, 8, 11, 92, 112–13, 120, 128, 153, 154, 356
  as civilizational state, 66
  colonial powers of, *see* colonialism
  confraternity of trade in, 95–96
  1848 uprisings in, 116–18
  grand vicinage of, 105–6
  Great Power peace of, 111–13, 118, 119, 137
  national flags of, 68
  nineteenth-century web of alliances in, 140–42
  Ottoman invasions of, 80, 90, 91, 121
  as "peninsula of Asia," 66–67
  Russian expansionism feared by, 133–34
  U.S. as federal model for, 130
  U.S. disputes with, 127–28
  U.S. hegemony feared in, 133–34
  in Venus/Mars dichotomy, 128, 133*n*
  Wars of Religion in, 86–87
  xenophobia in, 164, 168
Europe, medieval, 67–68
  anti-Semitism in, 72
  barbarian invasions of, 67, 68
  "Black Death" in, 63
  as Christendom, 68, 69, 70–71, 73, 90, 312
  Crusades of, 17, 40, 57, 70–71, 75, 91
  as ecumenical state, 74
  feudal system of, 69, 71
  humanism in, 73–78
  Islam in, 70–71, 73
  Mongol invasions of, 71–72
  non-Christian minorities in, 72, 73
  scholasticism in, 76
European Atomic Energy Community, 241
European Coal and Steel Community, 241
European Common Market, 97
European Community (EC), 241, 288
European Economic and Monetary Union, 256
European Economic Community (EEC), 241, 255–56
European Parliament, 79*n*
European Union (EU), 3, 4, 9, 68, 74, 97, 121, 237–41, 258, 286, 307, 308, 324–25, 349, 360, 381, 405
  American postwar assistance and, 238
  flag of, 256
  G. H. W. Bush's support of, 263, 265–66
  intergovernmental vs. supranational mechanisms of, 288*n*

European Union (EU) (*cont.*)
  Kosovo War and, 316, 317, 318, 319, 320–22
  Maastricht Treaty of, 256
  NATO expansion and, 288
  on Security Council, 386
  Solana and, 309–10
  Yugoslav dissolution and, 277–78
Evans, Gareth, 285, 388n
evolution, human, 28–29
  Darwinian, 113–15, 199
  political, 114–15, 145, 199, 330–31
Exodus, book of, 36–38

Facing Reality (Meyer), 212n
family of man, concept of, 31
fascism, 9, 165–70, 277
  communism vs., 169–70
federalism, 8–9, 47, 93–95, 128, 130, 163, 274
  Bolívar's vision of, 131, 272
  Dante's advocacy of, 75, 93, 110, 200
  definitions of, 93
  derivation of term, 93
  of Gioberti, 117
  of Kant, 98–99, 100, 110, 131, 154–55, 200
  of Napoleon I, 106–7, 110–11
  subsidiarity in, 256
  as theological term, 93
  world, 145, 182, 184, 200–202, 206, 209, 212n
Federal Reserve, U.S., 164
Federation of American Scientists, 197–98
Ferdinand I, Holy Roman Emperor, 80
Ferdinand II, King of Castile, 72, 80
Ferguson, Niall, 259n
Fermor, Patrick Leigh, 15
feudal system, 69, 71
financial crisis of 2008–2009, 396–97, 398, 401, 406n, 408, 409
Finland, 159, 172, 223, 249, 316, 319
Fisher, Herbert Albert Laurens, 66
Flavius Phocas Augustus, Eastern Emperor of Rome, 68
Flood, myth of, 31–32, 33
Ford, Gerald, 206, 217, 219, 247, 261, 343
Foreign Affairs, 204, 242, 258, 333, 334
"Foreign Policy as Social Work" (Mandelbaum), 333–34
France, 67, 80, 93–94, 99, 104–11, 122, 131, 132, 134, 137, 158, 162, 171, 172, 176, 241, 293, 407
  colonial empire of, 91, 106, 120, 121, 141, 151, 179, 180, 237
  1848 uprising in, 116, 118
  "Franco-British nation" proposal rejected by, 238–39
  in G-7, 273
  monarchy of, 83, 92, 108, 112, 116, 118
  as nation-state, 88
  in 1956 Suez Canal campaign, 230–32
  as NPT signatory, 378
  as nuclear power, 222, 397, 403
  Rwanda genocide and, 295, 296
  in Thirty Years War, 86
  in UN Security Council, 179, 223, 304, 310–11, 359, 386
  U.S. relationship with, 128, 240, 310–11, 318, 351, 360
  Vichy government of, 239
  war debts of, 164
  in World War I, 140–43
Francisco de Vitoria, 90
Francis Ferdinand, Archduke, 141, 155
Francis II, Holy Roman Emperor, 108
Franco, Francisco, 241
Francophonie, La, 311n
Franco-Prussian War, 118, 141
Frankfort, Henri, 32
Franklin, Benjamin, 125, 128, 130
Franks, 67, 69, 74
Frederick I "Barbarossa," Holy Roman Emperor, 69n
Frederick II "the Great," King of Prussia, 89
Freedom of the Seas (Grotius), 91
free-trade agreements, 96, 401
French Revolution, 104–6, 107, 128, 135
  as international enterprise, 104–5
  Reign of Terror in, 105, 131
Freud, Sigmund, 182
Fulbright, J. William, 200n, 281
Funderburk, David, 270

Gaddis, John Lewis, 212–13, 250
Galileo Galilei, 76
Gamsakhurdia, Zviad, 271
Gandhi, Mohandas, 142, 192
García Márquez, Gabriel, 272
Garden of Eden, 27–28
Gardiner, Patrick, 16
Gates, Robert, 404n
Gellner, Ernest, 24
Genesis, book of, 27–28, 30–36, 39
Geneva Conventions, 163, 368, 399
Genghis Khan, 7, 61–65, 62, 71–72
  direct descendants of, 63–65
  Great Mongol Nation of, 61–62
  religious freedom granted by, 63
genocide, 276, 299, 339, 388, 394, 399
  in Rwanda, 294–98, 305, 334, 371
  as term to be avoided, 296, 305–6
geopolitics, 29–30, 39, 134, 138–39, 159, 247, 291, 292, 303, 349, 356, 385

George III, King of England, 99
George Washington, 150, 171*n*
Georgia, 68, 165, 271, 396
German Confederation, 118
Germanic peoples, 67, 68, 70, 74
German states, 72, 79, 80, 87, 92, 108, 109, 124
   nationalist movement among, 117–18
Germany, Federal Republic of, 241, 288, 324,
   360, 386, 407
Germany, Imperial, 118–19, 120, 137, 166,
   171, 355
   colonial empire of, 120, 121, 160–61, 169,
     191, 235
   pre-World War I buildup of, 138–39
   war reparations of, 164
   in World War I, 140–43, 145–47, 150, 158,
     169, 170
Germany, Nazi, 9, 18, 166–70, 171, 176, 179,
   181, 199, 238–39, 267, 287, 295
   anti-Semitism in, 167–68
   Aryans and, 168
   euthanasia in, 169
   expansionism of, 167, 169
   racism of, 18, 167–69
   Soviet "Nonaggression" Pact with, 172,
     177, 178
   swastika emblem of, 168
Germany, Weimar Republic of, 166–67, 171,
   208
Gibbon, Edward, 48
Gilgamesh, epic of, 31
Gingrich, Newt, 388*n*
Gioberti, Vincenzo, 117
Giscard d'Estaing, Valéry, 273
glasnost, 250, 255, 272
Glass, Charles, 24
global citizenship, 25, 26, 32, 97, 225*n*, 397
global common, 91
Global Fund to Fight AIDS, Tuberculosis,
   and Malaria, 350
global governance, 1–12, 65, 113–18, 125–26,
   197, 214, 218, 237, 336, 374, 379
   "American system" of, 11
   atomic bomb and, 196–99
   Cicero's vision of, 47
   Dante's view of, 73, 74–75, 84, 115, 117,
     149
   Darwin and, 114–15
   of ecumenical state, 45–46
   Einstein's advocacy of, 197–98
   FDR's vision of, 181
   Kant's plan for, 100–103, 104, 117
   Marxist, 115–17
   More's concept of, 77
   "scaling up" to, 7
   in U.S. foreign policy, 5–6

globalism, 257
globalization, 8, 83, 140, 257–58, 394, 396, 401
   Bush administration's derision of, 348
   Clinton and, 281–82, 326, 327–28,
     329–31, 348
   Mongol, 62–63
global nation, 125–35
global trade talks, 283
global warming, *see* climate change
Goebbels, Josef, 168
Goethe, Johann Wolfgang von, 111
Goldwater, Barry, 261
Gompers, Samuel, 136
Good Friday Agreement (1998), 344
Goodwin, Doris Kearns, 327
Goodwin, Jason, 57, 58
Gorbachev, Mikhail, 220*n*, 249–52, *251,* 255,
   267, 270–75
   coup against, 270–71, 274, 275
   domestic protests against, 270–74
   George H. W. Bush and, 265, 268–69,
     273–74, 275, 345, 374
   glasnost of, 250, 255, 272
   at G-7 summit, 273, 275
   perestroika of, 250, 255, 272, 273
   Reagan and, 251–52, *251,* 326
Gore, Al, 327–28, 340, 341, 346, 349, 353,
   371, 380, 405
Goya, Francisco, *108,* 109, 113, 290
Great Britain, 17, 47*n,* 68, 99, 113, 137, 158,
   171, 240, 241, 256, 407
   appeasement policy of, 172
   Civil War of, 89
   colonial empire of, 7, 21, 22, 40, 91, 109,
     120, 121, 122, 141, 142, 151, 179–80,
     192, 237
   1848 upheaval avoided by, 117
   in G-7, 273
   Gypsies in, 17–20
   Hitler's racist view of, 168
   Mideast mandates of, 161–62, 192–93
   monarchy of, 83
   Napoleonic wars of, 109–10, 112
   in 1965 Suez Canal campaign, 230–32
   as nuclear power, 221, 397, 403
   Parliament of, 18, 133, 158
   slavery abolished by, 130
   "Ten-Year Rule" of, 159, 170
   in UN Security Council, 177, 178, 223,
     304, 359–60, 386
   U.S.'s "special relationship" with, 359–60
   war debts of, 164
   in War of 1812, 132
   in World War I, 140–43
   World War I casualties of, 143, 147
Great Depression, 396

Great Illusion, The (Angell), 140
Great Man theory of history, 16, 80, 116, 141, 250
Great Power peace, 111–13, 118, 119, 137
Great Seal of the United States, motto on, 130
Great Wall of China, 61, 66, 227
Greece, 68, 117, 159, 208, 241, 288
Greek language, 28, 44, 45, 57, 60, 67, 77
Greeks, ancient, 9, 25, 39, 40, 44–46, 50, 52, 59, 67, 107
    Amphictyonic League of, 100, 117, 154
    city-states of, 45
    cosmopolitanism as ideal of, 97
    mythology of, 67
    treason as defined by, 26
greenhouse gases, 262–63, 340–41, 380, 405, 406–7
Greenstock, Jeremy, 365
Grey, Edward, 158
Grishin, Victor, 250
Gromyko, Andrei, 250
Grotius, Hugo, 91, 101
Group of Seven (G-7), 273, 275–76, 283–84, 285
    as G-8, 284, 287
Guantánamo Bay naval base, 293, 368
Gulf Stream, 406
Gulf War, 266–70, 278, 291, 299–300, 355, 358, 360, 372
Guntram the Rich, 79
Gypsies, 17–20, 27, 167, 168
    history of, 18
    Romani language of, 18, 19, 67
    UN and, 19

Habyarimana, Juvénal, 295
Hagel, Chuck, 390, 393
Hague Conventions, 137, 138, 142
Haile Selassie I, Emperor of Ethiopia, 171
Haiti, 47, 106, 322, 328, 333, 334, 373
    as illiberal democracy, 302–3
    military coup in, 293–94, 299–304, 313, 334, 371
    Wilson's administration of, 302
Hamilton, Alexander, 128, 129
Hammarskjöld, Dag, 230–34, *231*, 281, 297, 312, 366
Hammurabi, King of Babylon, 43, 59, 66, 266, 362–63
Hanseatic League, 95–97, 319
Hapsburgs, 7, 79–83, 90, 92, 108, 110, 117, 141, 151
Harding, Warren, 162
Harriman, Averell, 203
Harrison, Benjamin, 135

Harrison, George, 188–89
Harrison, Wallace K., 208
Hassan bin Talal, 362
Hattušili, King of the Hittites, 44, 410
Hay, John, 137
Hayward, Max, 242–43
Hazzard, Shirley, 226
Hebrew language, 34, 35
Hegel, Georg Wilhelm Friedrich, 16, 107
Heine, Heinrich, 117–18, 134, 271
Helena, Saint, 53, 110
Helms, Jesse, 332, 335–36, 339, 372, 383, 394
Helsinki Final Act (1975), 247, 285, 300, 388
Henry IV, King of France, 90, 130
Henry VII, Holy Roman Emperor, 74
Henry VIII, King of England, 77–78
Heraclitus, 86
Herod, King, 81
Herodotus, 324
Hersh, Seymour, 368
Heuaktion, 168–69
High-Level Panel on Threats, Challenges, and Change, 385–87
Hill, Christopher, 317, 391*n*
Himmler, Heinrich, 168
Hinduism, 59, 64, 65, 188
history, 16–17
    deterministic, 115–16
    as directional, 331
    emerging democracies in, 302
    Great Man theory of, 16, 80, 116, 141, 250
History of Civilizations (Braudel), 66
Hitler, Adolf, 16, 166–69, *169*, 171, 175, 176, 182, 189, 199, 204
    Catholic clergy and, 78
    long-term campaign plan of, 169, 172
Hittites, 38, 39, 44, 410
Hobbes, Thomas, 10, 89–90, *89*, 101, 103, 106, 113, 150, 159, 379
Hohenzollerns, 118, 151, 166
Holbrooke, Richard, 126–27, 167, 306, 307, 308, 314, 334, 336, 343, 344, 389
Holmes, Oliver Wendell, Jr., 22
Holy Roman Empire, 69–70, 73, 74, 171
    decline of, 83
    Hapsburg dynasty of, 7, 79–83, 90, 92, 108, 110, 117, 141, 151
    Napoleon's dissolution of, 108
    in Thirty Years' War, 86–87
Hoover, Herbert, 150, 164
Hoover, J. Edgar, 182
House of Representatives, U.S., 146*n*, 206, 269, 284
housing bubble, 396
Hugo, Victor, 107
Hull, Cordell, 175, 178

humanism, 10, 73–78, 106, 107, 121
  church persecutions of, 76, 78
  of Dante, 75–76, 84
  definition of, 76
  of Erasmus, 76–77
  of Galileo, 76
  of Kant, 97–99
  of Machiavelli, 84
  of More, 77–78
  religious dogma vs., 76
  resolving interfaith disputes in, 81
  sovereignty of individual in, 98–99
humanitarian intervention, 359–60, 371,
  387–90
  G. W. Bush's scepticism of, 334–35
  right-wing rejection of, 333–35
humanitarianism, 136, 140, 162, 170, 292,
  304
humanitarian missions, UN, 291, 297, 300,
  310, 333–34, 380–81
human rights, 9, 115, 227, 247, 285, 290, 300,
  302, 303*n*, 313, 387
Hume, David, 93, 129, 154
Hungary, 18, 62, 71, 80, 108, 117, 153, 155,
  159, 204, 288
Huns, 67, 71
hunter-gatherers, 28–30
Huntington, Samuel, 67
Hussein, Saddam, 39, 304, 355–56, 374, 381*n*
  Clinton and, 347–48
  in Gulf War, 266–70, 299–300, 355
  G. W. Bush's vendetta against, 335,
  352–54, 358
  WMD program of, 348, 353, 359, 360,
  368, 373
  see also Iraq war
Hutchins, Robert Maynard, 198
Hutus, 161, 295–97
Huxley, Julian, 24
hydrogen bomb, 198, 207, 213, 214–15

"Idea for a Universal History with a
  Cosmopolitan Purpose, An" (Kant), 99
Ikenberry, John, 259, 356
Imagined Communities (Anderson) 24
imperator, 46, 47, 51
imperialism, 7–8, 9, 11, 27, 32–33, 37, 69, 99,
  135–37, 170, 237, 259
  of Churchill, 179–80
  decline of, 40, 151–52, 191–94
  stages of, 39
  see also empires
Inconvenient Truth, An (film), 340
India, 7, 18, 23, 24, 61, 62, 66, 91, 99, 142,
  223, 231*n*, 347, 401
  Alexander the Great and, 59
  anticolonial movement in, 142
  in British colonial empire, 21, 22, 120,
  180, 192
  as civilizational state, 65
  greenhouse gasses emitted by, 405,
  406
  G. W. Bush administration policy on,
  378–79
  independence of, 192
  Mauryan dynasty of, 59–60
  Mogul emperors of, 64–65, 120
  as nuclear power, 283, 337–38, 344,
  378–79, 397, 403
Indo-European languages, 21
indulgences, 79
Industrial Revolution, 13, 119
Inferno (Dante), 75
influenza epidemic of 1918–20, 147
Intergovernmental Panel on Climate
  Change (IPCC), 406
International Atomic Energy Agency
  (IAEA), 222, 227
International Conference on Naval
  Limitation, 162
International Criminal Court (ICC), 339,
  348, 383–84
internationalism, 6–7, 102–3, 106–7, 109,
  126, 128, 164, 167, 170, 173, 176,
  183–84, 335, 380, 392
  see also liberal internationalism
international law, 43, 63, 90–95, 111, 165–66,
  269, 281, 366, 374, 377
  Kant and, 100, 102
  maritime and commercial, 96, 136
  UN and, 178, 186, 187–88, 296, 299,
  305
International Monetary Fund (IMF), 228,
  273, 284, 329, 344, 366
International Pan-European Union, 79*n*
International Romani Union, 19
International Style, 208–9
Iran, 19, 62, 223, 235, 240*n*, 391
  in Axis of Evil, 362, 378
  as nuclear power, 378, 397, 398
  Shah of, 32
Iraq, 19, 62, 127, 193, 223, 235, 240*n*, 276,
  300, 339*n*, 347, 395
  as British Mandate, 161–62
  Israeli air strike on, 355–56
  Jews in, 39
  monarchy of, 162
  UN inspection teams in, 348, 353, 358,
  359, 360
  U.S. retaliatory air strikes on, 347–48
  see also Gulf War; Hussein, Saddam
Iraqi National Congress, 352

Iraq war, 5, 11, 39, 302, 353–69, 361–69, 370, 376, 379–80, 381, 384, 390, 392, 393
  Abu Ghraib scandal in, 268–69, 377
  al-Qaeda in, 366, 379
  Arab reactions in, 361–62
  bad decisions in, 364, 392
  G. W. Bush's "Mission Accomplished" flight and, 360–61, 362
  casualties in, 366, 367
  elections in, 366–67
  Hussein's toppled statue in, 360, 361, 369
  insurgency in, 365, 366, 367, 375, 379
  as Operation Iraqi Freedom, 360, 392
  as preemptive or preventive, 354–56
  UN and, 365, 366–67
  U.S. invasion in, 360–61, 363, 373, 375, 378n, 381n, 392
  U.S. military leaders in, 363–64, 379
  world opinion antagonized by, 362–63, 365, 379–80, 391
Ireland, 23, 222–23, 241
irredentism, 117, 141, 277, 283
Isaacson, Walter, 182, 371
Isabella I, Queen of Castile, 72, 80
Isaiah, book of, 26, 37, 46
Islam, 9, 35, 53–58, 107
  in Bosnia, 276, 277, 304, 305, 307
  forced conversion to, 55–56
  meaning of term, 54, 58
  militant dogmatism of, 56
  Mogul emperors in, 64–65
  in Moorish Spain, 55–56, 69, 72, 80
  political and religious authority combined in, 54–55
  radical, 258, 341–43; see also terrorism
  relative tolerance of, 55
  Renaissance of, 75
  Shiite vs. Sunni, 161–62
  spread of, 55, 59, 70–71, 73
  as unbounded, 54–55
  see also Ottoman Empire
isolationism, 156, 176, 187, 189n, 269, 371, 391
Israel (ancient), 26–40
  Babylonian Captivity of, 39–40, 43, 72
  children of, 36
  derivation of term, 35–36
  enemies of, 37–38
  as God's chosen people, 34–38, 376
  God's covenant with, 36, 68, 93
  as Hebrews, 34–38, 40, 45–46, 75
  intermarriage forbidden in, 45–46
  Jerusalem Temple of, 48
  kings of, 39
  as "light unto the nations," 37, 161
  as nation, 7, 35, 37–38

  patriarchs of, 34–36, 48, 53, 54, 75
  pluralism and, 38
Israel (modern), 7, 19, 26–27, 39, 54, 127, 223, 395, 403
  Arab wars with, 192–93, 230, 273
  in Balfour Declaration, 161
  Iraqi nuclear reactor bombed by, 355–56
  in 1956 Suez Canal campaign, 230–34
  Iraq war supported by, 361
  post-Soviet Russia distrusted by, 344–45
  UN creation of, 40, 192–93
  UN viewed as pro-Arab by, 344
Israeli-Palestinian peace process, 269, 344–46, 347, 348, 391
  Clinton's involvement in, 344–46
  G. W. Bush's suspension of, 348, 350–51
Issing, Otmar, 256
Italy, 107, 117, 121, 151, 158, 162, 208, 241, 273
  fascist, 165–66, 169
  Jews of, 106
  medieval, 73–76
Izetbegović, Alija, 307

Jacob, 35–36, 48
Jacobins, 104–5, 106
James, William, 136
Japan, 158, 159, 160, 162, 259, 286, 335, 397
  atomic bombing of, 189, 194, 195–96, 195, 214, 404
  as Axis power, 169, 174, 178
  colonial empire of, 151, 170, 179, 194
  expansionism of, 170–71, 178
  in G-7, 273
  in Russo-Japanese War, 138–40
  Security Council seat sought by, 386
Jefferson, Thomas, 129, 130, 228–29, 328
Jeremiah, 39
Jerusalem, 48, 53, 54, 57, 75, 192–93, 345
Jesus, 49, 50, 54, 55, 72, 93, 117
  Mongolian language and, 63n
Jewish Revolts, 48
Jews, 18, 19, 24, 40, 48, 53, 75, 81, 107, 159, 161
  in Alexandria, 56–57
  diaspora of, 39, 57
  as distinct community, 27, 72
  Iraqi, 39
  in medieval Europe, 72
  in Moorish Spain, 55–56
  Napoleon's liberation of, 106
  Nazi persecution of, 167–68
  in Ottoman Empire, 58
  Polish, 89
  Russian immigrant, 134, 175
  Saladin and, 57
  as scapegoats for Mongol invasions, 72
  see also Israel (ancient); Israel (modern)

Jiang Zemin, 331
John, Gospel According to, 49
Johnson, Andrew, 132
Johnson, Lyndon, 217–18
Johnson, Samuel, 144
Jones, Bruce, 406n
Jordan, 395
Judah, kingdom of, 39
Judaism, 55–57
   Christianity's origin in, 48–50
   Mosaic Law of, 49
   polytheistic derivation of, 35–37
Judea, 40
   in Roman Empire, 48, 49, 81
just war, theory of, 91

Kadesh, Battle of, 44, 410
Kagan, Robert, 132n–33n
Kahn, Herman, 215
Kant, Immanuel, 10, 95–103, 96, 108, 113,
   131, 154, 159, 166, 238, 241, 255, 269,
   344, 379
   on Barbary pirates, 132
   federalism of, 98–99, 100, 110, 131,
   154–55, 200
   French Revolution welcomed by, 104–5
   global governance plan of, 100–103, 104,
   117
   Hobbes vs. 103
   humanism of, 97–99
   imperfect human nature noted by, 11,
   100–101
   interventionist idea of, 102–3, 105–6
   Königsberg home of, 95–97, 99, 204
   lifestyle of, 95
   monarchies as viewed by, 98, 99, 104
   "Perpetual Peace" treatise of, 99–103, 106,
   132, 149
   personality of, 98
   political theory of, 98–103
   realism of, 100–102, 103
   sovereignty as viewed by, 98–99, 388
Kara Mustafa Pasha, Grand Vizier, 90
Karl I, Emperor of Austria, 79
Karmal, Babrak, 248
Karzai, Hamid, 22
Kasavubu, Joseph, 234
Kazakhstan, 277, 278–79, 283
Keegan, John, 140–41, 170, 271
Kellogg, Frank B., 163
Kellogg-Briand Pact, 163, 170
Kennan, George, 135
Kennan, George F., 11, 203, 204–5, 333,
   354
   containment policy proposed by, 204
   expanded NATO opposed by, 287

   "Long Telegram" of, 203
   Soviet "mellowing" predicted by, 242–43,
   246, 247
Kennedy, Edward, 330n
Kennedy, John F., 200, 206, 216–17, 216, 326,
   338, 396, 403
   in Cuban missile crisis, 158n, 216, 281,
   355
   on nuclear proliferation, 222, 224, 397
   preventive war rejected by, 355
Kennedy, Paul, 113, 171, 229, 322, 387n
Keyserling, Count Hermann von, 164
Khomeini, Ayatollah, 32
Khrushchev, Nikita, 203, 216, 234
Kim Jong Il, 348
"king of kings," as title, 32–33, 44
kings, kingship, 31–33, 35, 70, 89–90, 129
   conqueror-, 32–33
   divine right of, 32, 115
   god-, 30, 43
   Gypsy, 18–19
   of Israel, 39
   philosopher, 60
   warrior-, 31–32, 51, 68, 69
   see also monarchies
Kingship and the Gods (Frankfort), 32
Kirkpatrick, Jeane, 355–56
Kissinger, Henry, 59, 61, 402
   Bismarck admired by, 119
   on Congress of Vienna, 113
   diplomatic accomplishments of, 218–19
   "flexible response" advocated by, 215
   on idealism vs. realism, 144
   preemption and, 356
   realism of, 85
Kohl, Helmut, 288
koinonia, 45, 60
Komarecki, Mirjana, 317
Königsberg, 95–97, 99, 204
Koran, 55
   Meccan vs. Medinan verses of, 54
Korean War, 209–13, 267, 355, 389
Kosovo, 3, 6, 312–23, 339n, 348, 352, 363,
   364
   civilian casualties in, 316–17
   ethnic Albanians in, 312, 316, 320, 322
   NATO in, 312, 313, 314–15, 316–17, 318,
   339n, 390
   war aftermath in, 318–23
Kosygin, Aleksei, 217
Krauthammer, Charles, 258–59, 318, 330,
   374–75
Kravchuk, Leonid, 278–79
Kristof, Nicholas, 389
Kublai Khan, 64, 65
Kuehn, Manfred, 97, 100

Kurds, 19, 167
  of Iraq, 161–62
Kuwait, 266, 267, 268, 299, 304, 348, 355
Kwiek, Luminitsa, 19
Kyoto Protocol (1997), 340–41, 349, 350, 405

Lafargue, Paul, 115
Lake, Tony, 307
Lal, Deepak, 259n
Langer, William, 189n
Lansing, Robert, 152
Laplace, Marquis de, 109
Latin, 20, 46, 47, 51, 75, 269
law of nations, see international law
Lazar, Prince, 312
League of Nations, 10, 148–73, 181, 194, 198,
  204, 264, 267, 410
  achievements of, 159–60
  Article 10 of, 153–54, 157, 159, 176
  Covenant of, 154–55, 157, 176
  demise of, 170–73, 358
  democratic governance within, 150, 151,
  155
  enforcement lacked by, 157, 176
  Geneva headquarters of, 158, 172, 224,
  320
  mandate system of, 160–62, 191, 192–93,
  235, 295
  Permanent Court of International Justice
  of, 160
  as supranational, 162, 173
  U.S. rejection of, 155–58, 162, 175, 176,
  183, 187
  in World War II, 172
League to Enforce Peace, 149, 153, 157
Le Corbusier, 208
Lehi Group (Stern Gang), 193n
Leibniz, Baron Gottfried Wilhelm von, 93,
  95, 113, 154–55
Lend-Lease Act, 176
Lenin, Vladimir, 149, 165, 166, 246, 250
Leonov, Nikolai, 216
Leopold II, King of Belgium, 121
Levitte, Jean-David, 256
Lewinsky, Monica, 341, 342
Libby, I. Lewis "Scooter," 356n
liberal imperialism, 259n
liberal internationalism, 10, 103, 211, 259n,
  331, 334
  realism vs. 84–85
Lie, Trygve, 207, 210
Lieberman, Joseph, 251
Lilienthal, David, 221
Limited Test Ban Treaty (1963), 217, 338
Lincoln, Abraham, 16, 132
Lindsay, James, 361

Lippmann, Walter, 198, 204
Lithuania, 90, 159, 172, 275n
  Treaty of Westphalia and, 88–89
Livy, 47
Lloyd George, David, 161
Locke, John, 129
"Locksley Hall" (Tennyson), 184, 209, 210
Lodge, Henry Cabot, 156, 157, 187, 336
Lodge, Henry Cabot, Jr., 231–32
London Stock Exchange, 94
Lone, Salim, 366
Longfellow, Henry Wadsworth, 75n
Lords of the Horizons (Goodwin), 57
Lord's Prayer, 50
Los Alamos Laboratory, 182–83, 185,
  188
Louis XVI, King of France, 105
Louis XVIII, King of France, 112
Lowell, Lawrence, 157
Lubbers, Ruud, 309, 310
Luce, Henry, 127
Luchkov, Slava, 272
Lugar, Richard, 394
Luke, Gospel According to, 49
Lumumba, Patrice, 233, 234, 297
Lusitania, sinking of, 146
Luther, Martin, 79, 80
Lutheranism, 83

Maastricht Treaty (1992), 256
McAllister, Jef, 27
MacArthur, Douglas, 210, 212–13
Maccabees, 40
McCain, John, 251, 353, 393–94, 395–96,
  397, 407
McCarthy, Joseph, 205
McCullough, David, 327
Macedonia, 44, 277, 312, 317, 322
Machiavelli, Niccolò, 10, 84–85, 84, 106, 150,
  218
McKinley, William, 135, 137, 174
MacLeish, Archibald, 186
McNamara, Robert, 217–18
Madison, James, 128, 130, 328
Mahan, Alfred Thayer, 135–36
Mahler, Halfdan, 229
Maimonides, Moses, 55–57
Maine, USS, 136, 146, 355
Mali, 406
Major, John, 273
Malenkov, Georgi, 213, 214
Malik, Jacob, 210
Mandela, Nelson, 235, 294
Mandelbaum, Michael, 333–34
Manhattan Project, 182–83, 206
manifest destiny, doctrine of, 29–30

Mao Zedong, 61, 64, 171, 177, 206, 210, 212–13
Marduk, 31, 43
Mark, Gospel According to, 49
Markings (Hammarskjöld), 281
Marlborough, John Churchill, First Duke of, 92
Marshall, George, 174, 206, 239–40, 349
Marshall Plan, 239–40, 329, 393
Martel, Charles, 69
Marvell, Andrew, 299
Marx, Karl, 115–17, *115*, 119, 164, 255
Massacre of the Innocents, The (Bruegel), 81
Masters, Edgar Lee, 136
Matthew, Gospel According to, 49, 50
Mayakovsky, Vladimir, 242
Mehmed VI, Sultan, 151
meritocracy, 61, 62, 70
Mesopotamia, 30, 31–34, 46, 161
Metternich, Prince Klemens von, 110, 111, 112, 113, 116, 119, 133, 218, 238
Mexican-American War, 146
Mexico, 138, 146, 191, 284, 303, 371, 385n
Meyer, Cord, 201, 202, 206, 211–12
Michelangelo, 81
Milošević, Slobodan, 277, 278, 304, 306–8, 312, 334
    Kosovo war of, 312–13, 314, 315, 316, 317–18
Minoans, 30, 38
minority groups, 153, 155, 159, 304, 315
    medieval non-Christian, 72, 73
    privileged, 161
    Soviet, 165, 271, 277
Mobutu, Joseph, 233, 234
Mogul emperors, 64–65, 120
Mohammad Reza Pahlavi, Shah of Iran, 32
Mohammed, Prophet, 53–55, 59, 80, 345
    in *Inferno*, 75n
monarchies, 87, 128, 129, 162, 170, 230, 388
    French, 83, 92, 108, 112, 116, 118
    Hobbes's view of, 89–90
    Kant's view of, 98, 99, 104
    modern, 83
    sovereignty of, 98
Mongols, 21, 61–65
    capital cities of, 63, 64, 72
    Europe invaded by, 71–72
    globalization by, 62–63
    Great Mongol Peace of, 62–63
    language of, 63n, 71
    new technologies encouraged by, 62
    see also Genghis Khan
Monnet, Jean, 237, 239, 241, 255, 324
Monroe, James, 132

Monroe Doctrine, 132
Montesquieu, Baron de la Brède et de, 93–94, 95, 129, 131
Montreal Convention (1987), 262
Moralpolitik, 146
More, Saint Thomas, 77–78, 81
"Moretum" (Virgil), 130n
Morgenthau, Hans, 198
Morocco, Sultan of, 180
Morris, Edmund, 112
Moses, 36–37, 44, 48, 54, 93
Mubarak, Hosni, 350–51, 361–62
Müller, Johannes von, 133–34
multilateralism, 1–6, 10, 87, 112, 126, 220, 258, 263, 269, 276, 336, 349, 356, 358, 359, 372, 382, 392n
    of Clinton, 5, 281, 282, 291, 309, 310, 328, 329–30, 332, 335, 384
    G. W. Bush's profession, 382–83
    of U.S. military, 363–64
Mussolini, Benito, 165–66, 169, 179
    Churchill's view of, 166
    Ethiopian campaign of, 120, 171–72
mutual assured destruction (MAD), 218, 403–4
My Country (Smetana), 23

Namibia, 235–36
Napoleon I, Emperor of France, 106–11, *107*, 118, 119, 131, 238, 290, 410
    on American and Russian Expansionism, 134
    balance of power upset by, 113
    Beethoven symphony dedicated to, 107, 108
    dynastic ambitions of, 108
    exiles of, 109–11, 112
    expansionism of, 109, 113
    federalism of, 106–7, 110–11
    internationalism of, 106–7, 109, 110–11
    legal code of, 106, 109
    movie about, 244–45
    Peninsular Campaign of, 109
    personal power pursued by, 107–11
    reforms instituted by, 106
    religion and, 107, 109
    Russia invaded by, 109, 110
    Waterloo defeat of, 110, 112, 244–45
Napoleon III, Emperor of France, 118
Nasser, Gamal Abdel, 230
national identity, 17, 20, 23, 39, 54, 88n, 116, 167
    religion in, 27, 107
    self-invention of, 35
    of Socrates, 25
    vulnerability of, 39

nationalism, 24, 42, 54, 101, 126, 141, 150,
    164, 165, 170, 173, 182
  American exceptionalism as, 5
  German, 117–18, 167
  post-Soviet, 270–75
  romantic, 167
  in Yugoslav dissolution, 276–78
national pride, 22, 120
national purity, 63
National Security Strategies, 354
nation-building, 70, 133n, 193, 297, 303,
    334, 335, 343–44, 352
nations, 15–25, 26–27, 33, 36, 46–47, 74, 115,
    117, 130
  academic theories of, 16–17, 23–24
  Central Asian stans, 21–22
  as coterminous with mankind, 24–25
  definitions of, 20–25
  derivation of term, 20
  flags of, 17, 68, 275
  global, 125–35
  Gypsies as, 17–20
  Israel as, 35, 37–38
  on maps, 15–16
  self-sacrifice in defense of, 22
  twentieth-century emergence of, 20
  unifying forces of, 6–7, 40
nation-states, 8, 24, 87–88, 92, 129–30, 141,
    153, 320
Native Americans, 130
naval treaties, 162
Navy, U.S., 150, 176, 216
  Guantánamo Bay base of, 293, 368
Navy Department, U.S., 135–36, 174
Nazarbayev, Nursultan, 278–79
Nebuchadnezzar II, King of Babylon, 39,
    266, 361
Negroponte, John, 350
neoconservatives, 127
Neolithic Revolution, 30
Nero, Emperor of Rome, 50
Netherlands, 80, 83, 87, 240, 241
  colonial empire of, 7, 91, 120, 151, 179,
    231
"new world order," 266–67, 269, 270, 274,
    276, 282, 327, 352
New Yorker, 83, 196, 368–69
Nicaragua, 235, 247, 248–49, 303, 375n
Nicene Creed, 51, 52
Nicholas II, Czar of Russia, 138, 139
Nicolson, Harold, 240
Nimrod, 31–32, 33
1984 (Orwell), 204, 249, 400
1929 stock market crash, 163–64
Nixon, Richard, 200, 216, 217, 218–19, 222,
    247, 261

Noah, 31, 33, 36, 75
Nobel Peace Prize, 139, 140, 157–58, 163,
    193, 234, 350
Non-Proliferation Treaty (NPT) (1968),
    222–24, 337–39, 402–3
  G. W. Bush administration's undermining
    of, 377–79, 383
  India's rejection of, 283, 337–38, 378–79
Nonzero: The Logic of Human Destiny
    (Wright), 331
No Ordinary Time (Goodwin), 327
Noriega, Manuel, 264
North American Free Trade Agreement
    (NAFTA), 284
North Atlantic Treaty Organization
    (NATO), 3, 4, 6, 68, 133n, 240, 242, 247,
    258, 329, 349, 352, 374, 403
  Afghanistan occupied by, 352
  in Bosnia, 304–5, 306–7, 308, 309
  expansion of, 287–90, 304, 382
  G. H. W. Bush and, 265, 266, 278
  in Gulf War, 299–300
  G. W. Bush administration's relationship
    with, 349, 352, 381–82
  in Kosovo, 312, 313, 314–15, 316–17, 319,
    339n, 390
  reaction to 9/11 of, 351
  Solana as U.S.-backed secretary-general
    of, 309–10, 311–12, 311
Northern Ireland, 344
North Korea, 209–13, 223, 348, 355, 389, 391
  nuclear program of, 337, 347, 378, 397,
    398, 403
Ntaryamira, Cyprien, 295
nuclear energy, peaceful, 221–22, 227, 241,
    378–79
nuclear proliferation, 12, 220–24, 227,
    283–84, 387, 399, 401, 403–5, 406n,
    408, 409
  see also Non-Proliferation Treaty
nuclear weapons, 11, 277, 283, 337–38, 348,
    355, 359, 393, 402
  see also atomic bomb; cold war
Nuclear Weapons and Foreign Policy
    (Kissinger), 215
Nuland, Victoria, 1, 3, 6, 133n, 381–82
Nunn, Sam, 402n
Nye, Joseph, 305

Obama, Barack, 11, 394–95, 397–98, 399
  climate change and, 406, 407–8
Obama administration, 403, 404
"Ode to Joy" (Schiller), 225, 256
Office of Strategic Services (OSS), 191
Ogata, Sadako, 320
Ögödei, 71–72

oikumene, 45
Oil-for-Food Program scandal, 380–81
olive branch, symbol of, 31
One World (Willkie), 176, 197–98
one-world movement, 11, 209, 211
One World or None (Federation of American
    Scientists), 197–98
On Monarchy (Dante), 74–75, 84, 85, 93
On the Law of War and Peace (Grotius), 91
open regionalism, 400
Oppenheimer, J. Robert, 188, 197, 202
Organization for Economic Cooperation
    and Development (OECD), 329
Organization for Security and Cooperation in
    Europe (OSCE), 3, 4, 285, 286, 308, 318
Organization of African Unity, 295
Organization of American States (OAS),
    300, 400
Ortega, Daniel, 248–49
Ortega y Gasset, José, 237
Orwell, George, 204, 249, 400
Ottoman Empire, 7, 40, 41–42, 57–58, 160,
    161, 191, 272
    decline of, 121–22
    demise of, 151–52
    Europe invaded by, 80, 90, 91, 121
    Greek war of independence from, 117
    Jews welcomed by, 72
    Lazar's defeat by, 312
    provincial autonomy of, 58, 72
    Sublime Porte of, 58, 121, 132
Oxford University, 16–20, 97, 242–43, 280*n*
ozone layer, 262

Pachauri, R. K., 406
Padilla, Ezequiel, 191, 227
Pagden, Anthony, 47, 67, 87
Paine, Thomas, 128
Pakistan, 59, 223, 231*n*, 338, 347, 344, 397
    derivation of term, 21
    in Somalia peacekeeping mission, 291,
    292
Paleolithic age, 28–29
Palestine, Palestinians, 19, 39, 167
    as British Mandate, 161, 192
    state of, 192–93, 345
    see also Israeli-Palestinian peace process
Palin, Sarah, 397
Panama, U.S. invasion of, 264–65
pandemics, 394
Panuch, Joseph, 205
Paris Peace Conference, 10, 151–56, 175, 179
Partnership for Peace, 289*n*
Pascual, Carlos, 406
Pasvolsky, Leo, 175, 190
Patriote français, 105

Patten, Chris, 41
Paul, Saint, 50–51
Paulson, Henry, 397
Pax Romana, 46, 137
Pax Universalis, 269
Peace of Augsburg (1555), 83
Peace of Westphalia, *see* Westphalia, Treaties
    of
Peasant's Revolt, 79
Pelikan, Jaroslav, 37
Pell, Claiborne, 332
perestroika, 250, 255, 272, 273
Perle, Richard, 372
Permanent Court of Arbitration, 137, 138
Perry, Bill, 402*n*
Persia, 18, 32, 38, 39, 40, 44, 62, 64
Pétain, Marshall Henri, 239
Peter, Saint, 50
Peter I "the Great," Czar of Russia, 275
Philip II, King of Spain, 80
Philippines, 99, 136–37, 179, 208, 240*n*, 286
Philistines, 37, 38
Pilate, Pontius, 49, 351
Plato, 75
pluralism, 84, 199–200
Plutarch, 25, 45, 59
Poland, 62, 90, 159, 204, 288, 349
    Congress of Vienna partitioning of, 111
    Nazi invasion of, 172
    Solidarity movement in, 248
    Treaty of Westphalia and, 88–89
Politics Among Nations (Morgenthau), 198
Pope, Alexander, 92, 199
popes, 68, 69*n*, 71, 73, 75, 75*n*, 77, 78, 79, 80,
    83, 107
Portugal, 92, 162, 237, 241, 288
    colonial empire of, 91, 120, 151, 343
    Napoleon's invasion of, 109
Potsdam conference, 188, 189, 204, 209, 247
Powell, Colin, 348, 357, 359, 363, 372, 374,
    375, 380, 381
preemptive defense, 29–30, 91, 100, 217, 342,
    354–56, 378
Present at the Creation (Acheson), 325
preventive war, 354–56
Prince, The (Machiavelli), 84
Princip, Gavrilo, 141, 143, 155
Project for a New American Century, 127
"Project for Perpetual Peace" (Saint-Pierre),
    92, 94, 95, 98
Protestantism, 79, 80, 83, 86, 87, 90
Proverbs, book of, 376
Prussia, 89, 98, 99, 107, 109, 110, 111, 112,
    116, 117, 119, 204
    Franco-Prussian War won by, 118
    Hohenzollern dynasty of, 118, 151, 166

Psalms, book of, 20, 35
public intellectuals, 106
Putin, Vladimir, 324, 325, 360

Qin Emperor, 7, 60–61, *61*, 64, 66
Qing dynasty, 120, 170, 171

racism, 18, 134, 160, 167–69
raison d'État, 101, 118, 144
Ramses II, Pharaoh of Egypt, 43–44, 410
Reagan, Ronald, 200, 214, 219–20, 228*n*, 248,
    262, 330, 372, 396, 397
    Gorbachev and, 251–52, *251*, 326
    preventive war rejected by, 355–56
    SDI program of, 220, 251, 265, 337, 356,
        402–3
    UN military force advocated by,
        257–58
Reagan Doctrine, 248, 375*n*
realism, 10, 94, 190, 198, 211, 214
    idealism vs., 144
    of Kant, 100–102, 103
    of Machiavelli, 84–85
Realpolitik, 118–19, 144, 146, 150, 162, 218,
    335
Reformation, 79, 80, 87, 89
refugees, 160, 228
    from Haiti, 293
    from Kosovo, 312, 316, 317, 320
regional organizations, 258, 278, 299, 323,
    400
    Asian, 285–87
    Euromess chart of, 319–20, *321,* 382
Reilly, William, 263
religion:
    civil, 100
    determinism in, 116
    dogma of, 76
    London Stock Exchange and, 94
    monotheistic vs. polytheistic, 35–36, 37,
        51, 55
    in national identity, 27, 107
    origin of, 28–30
    politics and, 26–27
    in service of national sovereign, 77–78
    as unifying force, 26, 50, 68
    in Westphalia treaties, 87
religious freedom, 38, 81, 84, 135
    within empires, 47–48, 58, 60, 63, 65
Renaissance, 10, 65, 73, 75, 76, 77
Renan, Ernest, 24
Republican Party, 7, 156, 176, 187, 206,
    260–61, 343, 346, 392
    1994 "Contract with America" of, 332
    right-wing, 270, 292, 332, 335–41, 364
Republica totius orbis, 47–48

Rice, Condoleezza, 198, 265–66, 329, 334,
    348, 349, 353, 372, 380
    on Gorbachev, 272–73
    as secretary of state, 381, 383, 384–85,
        391
Rice, Susan, 399
Richard I "Lion Heart," King of England,
    75
Ridgway, Matthew, 240
Rights of Man, The (Paine), 128
Robespierre, Maximilien François Marie
    Isidore de, 104–5
Rockefeller, Nelson, 261
Roebuck, J. A., 133
Roman Catholic Church, 42, 72, 77–78, 86
    Cathar campaign of, 71
    cosmology of, 85
    declining moral authority of, 78–79, 84
    dogma and, 76
    Hitler and, 78
    Inquisition and, 76, 78
    as international society, 80
    non-Christians assigned to hell by, 75
    scholasticism and, 76
Roman Coliseum, 82
Roman Empire, 40, 46–53, 57, 61, 68, 69*n*,
    73, 79, 165, 256
    citizenship in, 46, 50
    extent of, 46
    Germanic invaders of, 68, 70
    Hun invasion of, 67
    Jewish Revolts against, 48
    Judea in, 48, 49, 81
    legal system of, 46–47, 69
    madness in emperors of, 52
    mobility within, 46, 50, 69
    monotheism in, 51
    provincial autonomy of, 47, 48
    religious freedom in, 47–48
Romanov, Grigory, 250
Romanovs, 23, 135, 138, 142, 151
Rome, ancient, 7, 9, 46, 47, 53, 67
    fasces of, 165
    lead water pipes of, 52
    polytheism of, 48, 51
    population of, 68
Romulus Augustulus, Emperor of Rome, 68
Roosevelt, Franklin D., 5, 10, 174–83, *178,*
    207, 224, 322, 354, 380, 400
    anti-imperialism of, 179–80
    atomic bomb and, 181–82
    Four Freedoms speech of, 175
    global governance system envisioned by,
        181
    UN planned by, 174–81, 183, 186, 187,
        191, 192, 226, 229, 235, 327

Roosevelt, Theodore, 125, 135–40, *136*, 174
  anti-Russian sentiments of, 135, 138–39
  League of Nations advocated by, 148
  muscular idealism of, 144
  Nobel Peace Prize of, 139
  as peacemaker, 137–40
  in Spanish-American War, 135–37
  U.S. intervention in World War I
    advocated by, 145–46, 148
Rosenberg, Alfred, 168
Rose Revolution, 393
Rousseau, Jean-Jacques, 93, 94, 95, 98, 101,
  113, 129, 131, 328, 388
Ruggie, John, 187
Rumsfeld, Donald, 126, 333*n*, 348, 373
Rusk, Dean, 217
Russia, 47, 62, 63, 88–89, 96
  anti-Semitism in, 134–35
  czarist, 22, 99, 111, 112, 117, 118, 120,
    133–35, 142, 165, 203, 246
  expansionism of, 133–35
  Napoleon's invasion of, 109, 110
  in World War I, 141–43
Russia, post-Soviet, 3, 5, 259, 274–75, 277,
  278–79, 324–25, 396
  in Asian regional organizations, 286, 287
  Bosnia and, 304, 307, 309
  Chechen Muslims of, 313
  Clinton's policy on, 282–84, 287–90
  flag of, 275
  as G-8 member, 284, 287
  Israel's distrust of, 344–45
  Kosovo and, 313, 314, 315–16, 317,
    318–19, 322
  Muslim minorities of, 304
  NATO and, 265, 287–90
  as nuclear power, 283–84, 337, 338, 402,
    403
  old republic borders retained by, 277
  in UN Security Council, 300, 304, 313,
    314, 343, 344, 359, 360
  see also Yeltsin, Boris
*Russia Hand, The: A Memoir of Presidential
  Diplomacy* (Talbott), 283*n*, 318*n*, 338*n*
Russian language, 20, 272
Russian Revolution, 139, 149–50, 151,
  164–66, 171, 242
Russo-Japanese War, 138–40
Rwanda, 160–61, 339, 390
  genocide in, 294–98, 305, 313, 334, 371

Sachs, Alexander, 181–82
Sacirbey, Muhamed, 306, 307
Sahnoun, Mohammed, 388*n*
Saint-Pierre, Abbé de, 92, 94, 95, 98
Sakharov, Andrei, 251

Saladin, 56–57, 266
  in *Inferno*, 75
Salazar, António de Oliveira, 241
San Francisco Conference, 184–85, 187, 191,
  223
Saul, King of Israel, 39
Sawers, John, 365
Schiller, Friedrich von, 225
Schmedeman, Albert, 157–58
scholasticism, 76
Schuman, Robert, 255, 324
Scowcroft, Brent, 264–65, 266–67, 268, 273,
  291, 353–54, 373, 385
Scranton, William, 260–61
Scriptures, Christian, 49, 50, 54
Scriptures, Hebrew, 27–28, 30–38, 39, 43–44,
  45–46, 54, 376
sedentism, 30
self-determination, 83, 148, 152–53, 155,
  160, 170, 177, 180, 190, 274, 276–77
Seljuk Turks, 57, 58
Semitic languages, 30*n*
Sen, Amartya, 60
Senate, U.S., 10, 146*n*, 162–63, 219, 267, 269,
  284, 394
  Comprehensive Test Ban Treaty unratified
    by, 338–39
  confirmation hearings of, 332, 336, 384
  International Criminal Court opposed by,
    339
  Kyoto Protocol opposed by, 340–41
  right-wing members of, 205, 332, 335–41,
    380–81, 383
  UN funding opposed by, 335–37
  UN membership ratification of, 179,
    186–87, 189
  Versailles Treaty unratified by, 155–58,
    176, 183, 187
separation of church and state, 9, 49, 129,
  131
September 11, 2001, terrorist attacks of, 355,
  358, 367, 368, 375, 376
  worldwide sentiment of solidarity with
    U.S. after, 351–52, 365
Seton-Watson, Hugh, 24
Seven Years War, 99
Seward, William Henry, 132–33, 134
Shalikashvili, John, 126, 289*n*
shamans, 29
Shamir, Yitzhak, 193*n*
Shawcross, William, 314
Shipstead, Henrik, 189*n*
Shultz, George, 402*n*
Shushkevich, Stanislav, 278–79
Sibelius, Jean, 23
Silk Road, 62–63

Single European Act (1986), 255–56
Skidelsky, Robert, 177
Slezkine, Yuri, 24
smallpox, eradication of, 228–29
Smetana, Bedřich, 23
Smoot-Hawley Tariff Act (1930), 164
social contract, 70, 98, 115, 129, 154
Socrates, 25, *25*, 26, 75, 77, 128, 188, 395, 396
Sodom and Gomorrah, 33
Sol (Roman sun god), 51
Solana, Javier, 309–10, 311–12, *311*, 314, 324
Solomon, King of Israel, 39
Somalia, 247, 291–93, 294–95, 296, 300, 313, 333, 371
Somoza, Anastasio, 248*n*
Sorel, Georges, 141, 142
Soros, George, 305
South Africa, 47, 142, 223, 235, 294, 300, 386
South Korea, 209–13, 223, 286, 355, 389, 399*n*
Southeast Asia Treaty Organization (SEATO), 240*n*
sovereignty, 39, 83, 98–99, 115, 136, 152, 197, 256
sovereignty, national, 92–93, 158, 163, 173, 182, 190, 197, 201, 227*n*, 269–70, 277, 279, 336, 359
    conditional, 270, 285, 300, 313–14, 315, 388
"sovereignty hawk," 102–3
Soviet Union, 9, 11, 20, 62, 97, 149–50, 163, 164–65, 167, 169, 176, 196*n*, 277, 282, 287, 289, 332, 356, 375*n*
    Afghanistan invaded by, 219, 235, 247, 342
    atomic bomb secrets acquired by, 183, 189, 206, 207, 211, 213
    expansionism of, 203, 204, 247–48, 296
    G. H. W. Bush and, 263, 265, 266–67, 270
    movie about Napoleon filmed in, 244–46
    national minorities of, 165, 271, 277
    Nazi Nonaggression Pact with, 172, 177, 178
    in UN Security Council, 177, 178, 204, 210, 212, 221, 223, 233, 234, 267, 268
    U.S. détente with, 218–19
    see also Cold War
Soviet Union, dissolution of, 235, 236, 237–38, 241–52, 255, 258, 265, 266, 270–76
    economic crisis in, 246, 250, 272
    information revolution and, 246, 249
    Kennan's prediction of, 242–43, 246, 247
    lack of internal cohesion in, 241–46
    nationalist independence movements in, 270–75, 278–79

U.S. indirect opposition to, 247–49, 296, 342
Western pressure on, 246–47
see also Gorbachev, Mikhail
Spain, 83, 108, 241, 256, 288, 309, 311
    colonial empire of, 7, 91, 120, 121, 131, 133, 135–36
    EAPC summit in, 289–90
    Moorish, 55–56, 69, 72, 80
    Napoleonic Wars in, 109
Spanish-American War, 135–37, 293*n*, 355
Stalin, Joseph, 164–65, *165*, 167, 169, 172, 178, *178*, 183, 190–91, 203, 204, 241, 242, 243, 246
    Korean War and, 210
    Mao's treaty with, 212–13
    nationalism of, 165
    at Potsdam conference, 188, 189
    on unusability of atomic weapons, 213, 214
Stanley, H. M., 121
Stassen, Harold, 201
State Department, U.S., 2, 4, 5*n*, 11, 70, 126, 133*n*, 162–63, 203, 205, 295, 319, 325–26, 332, 333, 335, 343, 381–82, 383, 384, 392
states, 6–7, 19, 35, 36, 98, 101, 105, 116, 126, 173, 182, 190, 197
    civilizational, 65, 66
    communist party-, 164
    derivation of term, 20
    failed, 103, 292, 303, 320, 379, 389
    family in, 27
    fascist, 169–70
    gods of, in Athens, 26
    Hebrew nation as, 35, 39
    minority groups of, 153, 155, 159
    noninterference in internal affairs of, 113, 119–20, 134–35, 186–87, 285, 300, 388
    parental, 27, 28
    privileged minorities in, 161
    sovereign, *see* sovereignty, national
    territorial, 83, 84
Stedman, Stephen, 406*n*
Steiger, Rod, 244–45, 250
Steinberg, Saul, 83
Steiner, Zara, 154, 172–73
Stern, Fritz, 167, 334
Stevenson, Adlai, 281
Stewart, Jon, 407
Stimson, Henry, 183, 185, 188–89
Stoicism, 45
Strassburg, Gottfried von, 1
Strategic Arms Limitation Talks (SALT), 217–20

Strategic Arms Reduction Talks (START), 219–20
Strategic Defense Initiative (SDI) "Star Wars," 220, 251, 265, 337, 356, 396, 402–3
Suárez, Francisco, 91
subsidiarity, 256
Suez Canal, 193, 230–32
Suleiman "the Magnificent," Sultan, 80
Sully, Duc de, "Grand Design" of, 90, 130
Summit of the Americas, 284
Sumner, William Graham, 136
supranationalism, 9, 162, 164, 173, 176, 182, 198, 201, 205, 212n, 237–38, 288
Sweden, 99, 109, 208, 231
  in Åland Islands dispute, 159
  as nation-state, 88
  in Thirty Years War, 86
Swords into Plowshares (Claude), 171n

Taft, William Howard, 149, 153, 157
Talleyrand, Charles-Maurice de, 112, 218
Tamerlane, 64
Tarbell, Edmund, 175
Tarn, W. W., 46
Tarnoff, Peter, 306, 325–26
technological development, 52, 113, 119, 198–99, 331
  communications, 246, 249, 257
  military, 62, 137, 140, 142
  Mongol encouragement of, 62
  Tennyson's visions of, 184
Teller, Edward, 198
Temperance (Bruegel), 81
Ten Commandments, 36–37
Tennyson, Alfred, Lord, 184, 209
terrorism, 285, 348, 351–53, 394, 399, 403–4, 405, 406n
  G. W. Bush's war on, 353, 368, 375, 376, 379
  of 9/11, 351–52, 355, 358, 367, 368, 375, 376
  of 1993 World Trade Center bombing, 341–42
  nuclear, 397–98
  see also al-Qaeda
Teutonic Knights, 89
Thatcher, Margaret, 251
Thirty Years War, 86–89
Thomas, Charles A., 182, 188, 189
Thompson, Tommy, 350
Threshold Test Ban Treaty (1974), 224, 338
Tiberius Caesar, Emperor of Rome, 49
Tiergarten, 395
Tilly, Charles, 24
Tito (Josip Broz) 312
Tocqueville, Alexis de, 134
Tolstoy, Leo, 16–17

totalitarianism, 9, 167, 169–70, 204–5, 238, 241, 249, 277
"Toward Perpetual Peace" (Kant), 99–103, 106, 132, 149
Tower of Babel, 33–34, 35, 38, 39, 43, 204, 361
  Bruegel's painting of, 81–83, 82, 225
  in Dante's writing, 74, 81
  UN as, 225–26
Traub, James, 291
Treasury Department, U.S., 164, 284
Treaty for the Renunciation of War, 162–63
Treaty of Friendship and Alliance, 212–13
Treaty of Rome (1957), 241, 255
Treaty of Utrecht (1713), 92
Treaty of Versailles, 10, 151–58, 166–67, 170, 172, 179, 339
  Article 10 of, 153–54, 157, 159
  disarmament provisions of, 154, 159
  international boundaries redrawn by, 150–51, 152, 153, 155
  racial equality clause omitted from, 160
tribes, 6, 12, 24, 27, 31, 45, 69, 145
  of Afghanistan, 21–22, 342
  African, 160–61
  Germanic, 67, 68, 70, 74
  Hebrew, 34–38, 40, 68
  Iraqi, 161–62
  Native American, 130
  Nordic, 66, 88, 139
Triumph of Death, The (Bruegel), 81
Trotsky, Leon, 149, 164–65
Truman, Harry S., 10, 183–89, 183, 203, 205, 206–7, 239, 240, 325, 327, 349, 393, 390
  atomic bomb and, 185, 188–89, 195–96, 202
  internationalism of, 183–84, 380
  Korean War and, 210, 212–13, 267
  "Locksley Hall" and, 184, 209, 210
  peaceful nuclear energy proposal of, 221
  preventive war rejected by, 355
  at San Francisco conference, 184–85, 187
  UN established by, 183–85, 186, 187–88, 189, 207, 209, 226
Tshombe, Moise, 234
Tuchman, Barbara, 158n
Tudjman, Franjo, 307
Türkenangst, 90
Turkey, 19, 52, 57, 99, 150, 151–52, 159, 240n, 272–73, 397
Turtle Bay, origin of term, 208
Tutsis, 161, 295–97
Twain, Mark, 135, 136–37
Two Treatises on Government (Locke), 129

Ukraine, 273–75, 277, 278–79, 283–84
Union of Utrecht, 83

"Unipolar Moment, The" (Krauthammer), 258–59, 318, 330, 374
United Nations, 1–4, 6, 10–11, 21, 25, 28, 112, 173, 174–202, 203–12, 222–36, 256, 273, 329, 339n–40n, 344, 354, 374, 399–400
  achievements of, 227–29
  Afghanistan aftermath handed off to, 352
  architects of, 207–8
  atomic bombs and, 196–99
  Atomic Energy Commission of, 221
  budget of, 335
  bureaucratic system of, 224–25, 226–28, 385
  Chagall window in, 225
  Charter of, 186–87, 189, 191–92, 194, 197, 207, 225, 230, 267, 292, 299, 300, 313, 318, 332, 355, 367
  colonialism and, 191–94
  Conference on Disarmament of, 224
  construction materials of, 208
  Convention against Torture of, 368, 399
  Convention on the Prevention and Punishment of the Crime of Genocide of, 296
  critics of, 225–26
  Earth Summit convened by, 203–4
  on Euromess chart, 320
  as extraterritorial, 224–25
  FDR's planning of, 174–81, 183, 186, 187, 191, 192, 226, 229, 235, 327
  flag of, 31
  G. H. W. Bush and, 2, 261, 263, 265, 266–67, 269–70, 333
  G. W. Bush administration's relationship with, 350, 363, 380, 383–87
  G. W. Bush's challenge to, 358–59, 365
  Gypsies and, 19
  Hammurabi's Law monolith replicated at, 43
  High Commissioner for Refugees of, 228, 308, 320
  humanitarian missions of, 291, 297, 300, 310, 333–34, 380–81, 400
  IAEA and, 222, 227
  International Style of architecture at, 208–9
  Iraq inspected by, 348, 353, 358, 359, 360
  in Iraq war aftermath, 365, 366–67
  Kant's anticipation of, 100
  Korean War and, 209–11, 389
  Kosovo and, 312–23
  Millennium Development Goals Declaration of, 343, 385
  mission of, 2–4, 25, 191, 207
  New York headquarters of, 207, 208–9, 225, 243

  Nobel Peace Prize of, 350
  Non-Proliferation Treaty and, 222–24
  as planned al-Qaeda target, 341
  right of self-defense recognized by, 187, 197, 355, 356
  right-wing attacks on, 205–6, 234–35, 270, 292–93, 332–37, 380–81
  San Francisco Conference on, 184–85, 187, 191, 223
  Secretariat Building of, 209, 230, 384
  secretary-general of, 230–31
  spies at, 225
  state of Israel created by, 40, 192–93
  Truman's establishment of, 183–85, 186, 187–88, 189, 207, 209, 226
  Trusteeship Council of, 191–94, 232, 235–36, 322
  U.S. dues owed to, 335–37
  U.S. military leaders' approval of, 364
United Nations, peacekeeping function of, 3–4, 105–6, 176–77, 204, 208n, 229–36, 257–58, 292–93, 296, 336, 389
  in Bosnia, 278, 290, 304–9, 313
  in Congo, 232–35
  in East Timor, 343–44, 365
  frequent weakness of, 305
  Gulf War and, 266–70, 299–300
  in Haiti, 293, 299–304, 313
  multinational force (MNF) vs. Peacekeeping Operation (PKO) of, 301
  peacekeepers' endangerment in, 292, 296, 305, 366
  as rightful intervention in states' internal affairs, 300
  in Rwanda, 294–98, 313
  in Somalia, 291–93, 294, 295, 296, 300, 313
United Nations General Assembly (UNGA), 1–2, 19, 192–93, 234, 267, 333, 344, 388, 396, 409
  Clinton at, 281–82, 327, 328
  G. H. W. Bush's addresses to, 267, 269–70, 278–79
  G. W. Bush's address to, 358–59
United Nations Security Council, 3, 186–87, 190–91, 229, 230, 235, 258, 279, 297, 355
  anti-terrorism resolution of, 351
  Bosnia and, 290
  conditional sovereignty principle affirmed by, 388
  Congo resolution of, 233
  Cuban missile crisis and, 281
  Darfur resolution of, 389–90
  East Timor resolution of, 344
  France in, 179, 223, 304, 310–11, 359, 386
  Great Britain in, 177, 178, 223, 304, 359–60, 386

Gulf War authorized by, 267, 268, 299–300
Haiti resolution of, 300
Helms's address to, 336–37
Iraq war and, 358, 359–60, 367
Kosovo resolutions of, 313, 314, 315, 316,
    318–19, 363
membership restructuring of, 385–87
MNF authorized by, 301
Nationalist China in, 177–78, 206–7, 210,
    212n, 223, 337
People's Republic of China in, 267, 300,
    337, 344, 359, 360, 386, 389
permanent members of, 177–79, 194,
    223–24, 310–11
rotating presidency of, 336, 343
Russia in, 300, 304, 313, 314, 343, 344,
    359, 360
Somalia resolutions of, 292
"sovereign equality" and, 178–79, 186–87
Soviet Union in, 177, 178, 204, 210, 212,
    221, 223, 233, 234, 267, 268
veto power in, 179, 187, 194, 210, 212, 221,
    234, 236, 267, 304, 310, 314, 385–86, 389
United States:
anti-imperialist sentiment in, 136–37
anti-Russian sentiment in, 134–35
as constitutional democracy, 9
exceptionalism of, 5, 9, 126–27, 310
"exemptionalism" of, 186–87
as federation, 101, 128, 130, 131, 201–2
Founders of, 9, 25, 128–32, 156, 186
geopolitics and, 291, 292, 303
as global nation, 126–35
gold reserves of, 164
Great Seal of, motto on, 130
greenhouse gases emitted by, 406–7
in G-7, 273, 275–76, 283–84, 285
Gypsies in, 18
hemispheric neighbors of, 299, 303
humanitarian values of, 136, 140, 304
as "hyperpower," 318
naval engagements of, 132
"permanent" European alliances avoided
    by, 132, 156
presidential rejections of preventive war
    in, 355–56
protective tariffs of, 164
Roman law and, 47
Russian expansionism and, 133–35
slavery in, 130, 132–33
in Venus/Mars dichotomy, 128, 133n
westward expansion of, 129
United States Objectives and Programs for
    National Security (NSC-68), 355
United World Federalists, 200–201, 205, 211,
    212

UN Population Fund, 228
Unvanquished: A U.S.-U.N. Saga (Boutros-
    Ghali), 311n
Urquhart, Brian, 179, 230, 381n
Utopia (More), 77
Uwilingiyimana, Agathe, 296

Valdemar IV, King of Denmark, 96
Vandenberg, Arthur, 187, 190
Vatican, 71, 78
Védrine, Hubert, 318, 351
Versailles, 118, 151, 157, 158
    see also Treaty of Versailles
Vespucci, Amerigo, 80
Victor Emmanuel III, King of Italy, 171
Victoria, Queen of England, 120, 120, 122
Vienna, 81–82
    Congress of, 10, 109–10, 111–13, 117, 119,
        179, 247, 285
    Ottoman siege of, 90, 121
Vienna, Battle of (1683), 90, 121
Vieira de Mello, Sergio, 344, 365, 389
    death of, 366
Vietnam War, 217, 218, 310, 355, 360–61,
    364, 368
Virgil, 46, 130
    Aeneid of, 102
    in Divine Comedy, 73
Voltaire, 69, 94–95, 131

Wallace, Henry, 183
War of 1812, 132
War of Spanish Succession, 92
Warsaw Pact, 237, 241, 242, 244, 247, 265,
    288, 289
Wars of Religion, 86–87
Wars of Yugoslav Secession, 276–79
Washington, George, 129, 132, 156
Watt, James, 113
"Waves of Darkness" (Meyer), 201
weapons of mass destruction (WMD), 258,
    335, 348, 353, 360, 368, 373, 377, 379
Weatherford, Jack, 62–63
Weber, Max, 24
Wellington, Arthur Wellesley, Duke of, 110
Westerfield, H. Bradford, 97
Westphalia, Treaties of (1648), 10, 86–89,
        108, 119, 285, 388, 401
    aftermath of, 87–89, 91–92, 117, 118
    nation-states created by, 87–88, 92,
        129–30, 141, 153
White, E. B., 196–97, 200n
Wilhelm I, Kaiser of Germany, 118, 151
Wilhelm II, Kaiser of Germany, 138–39, 166,
    171
Will, George, F., 395–96

Willkie, Wendell, 176, 197–98
Wilson, Arnold, 161
Wilson, Woodrow, 10, 143–47, *144*, 148–58,
    159, 162, 166, 176, 181, 194, 198, 320,
    336, 380
  Bolsheviks and, 149–50
  covenant as concept of, 154–55
  Fourteen Points of, 149–50, 154, 267
  Haiti administered by, 302
  Nobel Peace Prize of, 157–58
  at Paris Peace Conference, 151–56
  piety of, 375
  self-determination concept of, 148,
    152–53, 155, 160, 177, 190, 276–77
  stroke suffered by, 157
  Theodore Roosevelt vs., 144
  and U.S. entry into World War I, 145–46,
    148, 149, 155
  U.S.-led world federation imagined by,
    145, 174–75
Wilsonians, 143–44, 258, 277
Wolfowitz, Paul, 305, 356n, 372, 375, 392n
Woodward, Bob, 376
World Bank, 4, 228, 273, 284, 308, 329, 344,
    366, 392n
world federalism, 145, 182, 184, 200–202,
    206, 209, 212n
World Federalist Movement, 200–202
world government, 4, 196–202, 205–6, 209,
    232, 269, 270
World Health Organization (WHO), 4,
    228–29, 385
World Heritage Sites, 227
World Trade Organization, 409
World Transformed, A (Bush and Scowcroft),
    266n
World War I, 9, 10, 16, 23, 42, 109, 122, 138,
    140–43, *143*, 148–51, 154, 169, 174,
    179, 183, 196, 271, 355, 410
  as "accidental," 158–59, 171
  author's grandfather in, 147

  casualties of, 142–43, 147
  Central Powers of, 150, 170
  European web of alliances in, 140–42
  1918 influenza epidemic and, 147
  refugees of, 160
  U.S. entry into, 145–47, 148, 149, 155
World War II, 9, 10, 16, 20, 127, 152, 169,
    172, 174–77, 178, 179, 180, 184,
    194–96, 201, 203, 238–39, 327, 329,
    355, 410
Wright, Robert, 331

Xanadu, 64
Xerxes, King of Persia, 32
Xian, tomb complex of, 60

Yalta conference, 179, 247
Ybarnegaray, Jean, 239
Yeats, William Butler, 23
Yeltsin, Boris, 274, 277, 278, 280, 282–84,
    283, 304, 345
  at G-7 summit, 275–76, 283–84
  Kosovo War and, 315–16, 318
  NATO expansion resisted by, 287–89
Yesugai, 63n
Yousef, Ramzi, 341–42
Yugoslavia, 41–42, 153, 155, 159, 299
  dissolution of, 276–78, 290–94, 303, 320
  Serbo-Croatian language of, 307–8

Zakaria, Fareed, 302
Zealots, 48
Zeno of Citium, 45
Zeno of Elea, 45n
Zhdanov, Andrei, 205
ziggurats, 31–32, 43, 361
  see also Tower of Babel
Zimmerman Telegram, 146
Zionism, 37, 161, 193
Zoellick, Robert, 389
Zoroastrians, 55

About the Author

Strobe Talbott is president of the Brookings Institution. He was the founding director of the Yale Center for the Study of Globalization in 2001–2002, deputy secretary of state from 1994 to 2001, and ambassador-at-large with responsibility for policy toward the former Soviet Union in 1993. Before joining government, he was Washington bureau chief and foreign policy columnist for *Time*, and a regular panelist on *Inside Washington*. He is the author of nine books and the translator-editor of Nikita Khrushchev's two volumes of memoirs. He has also written for the *New York Times*, *Financial Times*, the *Washington Post*, *Foreign Affairs*, *Foreign Policy*, the *New York Review of Books*, and the *New Yorker*.